ENCYCLOPEDIA OF
UNITED STATES
NATIONAL SECURITY

ENCYCLOPEDIA OF
UNITED STATES
NATIONAL SECURITY

RICHARD J. SAMUELS EDITOR
MASSACHUSETTS INSTITUTE OF TECHNOLOGY

2

A DWJ BOOKS Reference Work

A SAGE Reference Publication

SAGE Publications
Thousand Oaks ▪ London ▪ New Delhi

Developed by DWJ BOOKS LLC

For information:

Sage Publications, Inc.
2455 Teller Road
Thousand Oaks, California 91320
E-mail: order@sagepub.com

Sage Publications Ltd.
1 Oliver's Yard
55 City Road
London EC1Y 1SP
United Kingdom

Sage Publications India Pvt. Ltd.
B-42, Panchsheel Enclave
Post Box 4109
New Delhi 110 017 India

Printed in the United States of America

Library of Congress Cataloging-in-Publication data

Encyclopedia of United States national security / Richard J. Samuels, general editor.
   p. cm.
"A Sage reference publication."
Includes bibliographical references and index.
ISBN 0-7619-2927-4 (cloth : alk. paper)
  1. National security—United States—Encyclopedias. 2. Military art and science—United States—Encyclopedias. 3. United States—Military policy—Encyclopedias. 4. United States—Armed Forces—Weapons systems—Encyclopedias. I. Samuels, Richard J.
UA23.E571274 2006
355′.033073—dc22   2005015550

Acquiring Editor:	Rolf Janke
Editorial Assistant:	Sara Tauber
Project Editor:	Kristen Gibson
Proofreaders:	Taryn Bigelow and Teresa Herlinger
Typesetter:	C&M Digitals (P) Ltd.
Indexer:	Teri Greenberg
Cover Designer:	Ravi Balasuriya

Contents

Editorial Board

List of Entries

Reader's Guide

This list is provided to assist readers in locating articles on related topics. It classifies articles into 15 general topical categories: Armed Forces and Other Defenders; Alliances, Pacts, and Treaties; Armaments and Weapons Systems; Concepts and Theories; Decision Makers and Others; Key Events; Movements; Military Hardware; Military and Nonmilitary Strategy; Organizations, Institutions, and Groups; Places; Politics and Policy; Special Populations; Technology; and Wars and Warfare. Some article titles appear in more than one category.

ARMED FORCES AND OTHER DEFENDERS

Air Cavalry
All-Volunteer Force
Base Closure
Civil Air Patrol
Coast Guard, The, and National Security
Codetalkers
Conscription/Volunteer Force
Conventional Forces in Europe
    Treaty (1990)
Enlisted Personnel
Green Berets
Military Draft
Militia
National Guard
Noncommissioned Officer
Protective Gear
Rapid Deployment Force (RDF)
Reserve Forces
Reserve Officers' Training Corps (ROTC)
Rules of Engagement
Signals Intelligence (SIGINT)
Special Forces
Strategic Forces
U.S. Air Force
U.S. Army
U.S. Coast Guard
U.S. Marine Corps
U.S. Navy

U.S. Northern Command
U.S. Pacific Command
U.S. Southern Command

ALLIANCES, PACTS, AND TREATIES

Alliance for Progress
Alliances
Antiballistic Missile (ABM) Treaty (1972)
ANZUS Security Treaty (1951)
ASEAN
Atlantic Alliance
Atlantic Charter
Australia Group
Biological Weapons Convention
Bretton Woods Conference
Chemical Weapons Convention
Comprehensive Test Ban Treaty (1996–)
Dayton Accords
European Union
General Agreement on Tariffs and Trade (GATT)
Geneva Conventions
Hague Convention (1907)
Holy Alliance
Limited Test Ban Treaty
MERCOSUR
North American Free Trade Agreement (NAFTA)
North Atlantic Treaty Organization (NATO)
Nuclear Non-Proliferation Treaty (NPT)
OPEC (Organization of Petroleum
    Exporting Countries)

DECISION MAKERS AND OTHERS

Bundy, McGeorge (1919–1996)
Bush, George H. W., and National Policy
Bush, George W., and National Policy
Carter, Jimmy, and National Policy
Cheney, Richard (1941–)
Church, Frank (1924–1984)
Clinton, Bill (William Jefferson), and National Policy
De Gaulle, Charles (1890–1970)
Doolittle, Jimmy (1896–1993)
Eisenhower, Dwight D., and National Policy
Ford, Gerald R., and National Policy
Gorbachev, Mikhail (1931–)
Hiss, Alger (1904–1996)
Hoover, J. Edgar (1895–1972)
Huntington, Samuel P. (1927–)
Iklé, Fred (1924–)
Jackson, Henry (1912–1983)
Johnson v. Eisentrager (1950)
Kahn, Herman (1922–1983)
Kennan, George (1904–2005)
Kennedy, John F., and National Policy
Khrushchev, Nikita (1894–1971)
Kissinger, Henry (1923–)
LeMay, Curtis (1906–1990)
Lindh, John Walker (1981–)
Lugar, Richard (1932–)
MacArthur, Douglas (c. 1880–1964)
Machiavelli, Niccolò (1469–1527)
Mao Zedong (1893–1976)
McNamara, Robert (1916–)
Mihn, Ho Chi (1890–1969)
Morgenthau, Hans (1904–1980)
Moussaoui, Zacarias (1968–)
Nitze, Paul H. (1907–2004)
Nixon, Richard, and National Policy
Nunn, Sam (1938–)
Oppenheimer, J. Robert (1904–1967)
Patton, George (1885–1945)
Powell, Colin (1937–)
Putin, Vladimir (1952–)
Reagan, Ronald, and National Policy
Roosevelt, Franklin D., and National Policy
Roosevelt, Theodore (1858–1919)
Rumsfeld, Donald (1938–)
Saddam Hussein (1937–)
Schelling, Thomas (1921–)
Sherman, William Tecumseh (1820–1891)
Stalin, Joseph (1878–1953)
Sun-Tzu (300s BCE)
Teller, Edward (1908–2003)

Thucydides (c. 460–400 BCE)
Truman, Harry S., and National Policy
Unabomber (Theodore J. Kaczynski, 1942–)
Von Braun, Werner (1912–1977)
Von Clausewitz, Karl (1780–1831)
Westmoreland, William (1914–)
Yeltsin, Boris (1931–)

KEY EVENTS

Afghan Wars
Afghanistan, War in
Al-Khobar, Attack on U.S. Troops at (1996)
Arab Oil Embargo
Arab Americans
Arab-Israeli Conflict
Arms Race
Bali, Terrorist Bombing in
Bay of Pigs
Berlin Airlift
Berlin Crises
Berlin Wall
Blitzkrieg
Bosnia Intervention
Bretton Woods Conference
Bulge, Battle of the
Camp David Accords
Cold War
Comprehensive Test Ban Treaty
Cuban Missile Crisis
Dayton Accords
D-Day
Dien Bien Phu
Dresden, Bombing of
Ex Parte Quirin
Freedom of Information Act (1967)
Fulda Gap
Gas Protocol of 1925
Grenada Intervention
Guadalcanal, Battle of (1943)
Gulf of Tonkin Resolution
Hague Convention (1907)
Hiroshima
House Un-American Activities Committee (HUAC)
In re Territo (1946)
Inchon Landing
INF Treaty
Iran-Contra Affair
Iranian Hostage Crisis
Iraq War of 2003

Blitzkrieg
Bomber Gap
Bottom-Up Review
Brinkmanship
Bush Doctrine
Carpet Bombing
Central Front in Europe
Coalition Building
Coercive Diplomacy
Collective Security
Combat Effectiveness
Containment
Containment and the Truman Doctrine
Counter-Force doctrine
Counterterrorism
Covert Action
Covert Operations
Cryptology
Defense Budgeting
Demilitarized Zone (DMZ) in Korea
Détente
Deterrence
Disarmament
Distant Early Warning (DEW) Line
Dual-Use Technology
Duck and Cover
Electronic Warfare (EW)
Emergency Preparedness and Response
First Strike
Forward Basing
Germ Warfare
Homeland Security Advisory System
   (Color-Coded Alerts)
International Peacekeeping and Overseas
   Deployment
Joint Chiefs of Staff
Joint Defense Planning
Joint Operations
Limited Nuclear Option
Major Theater Wars
Manhattan Project
Mutually Assured Destruction (MAD)
National Missile Defense
National Security Strategy of the United States
Nuclear Deterrence
Offensive Biological Weapons Program
Offshore Balancing
Preemption
Preemptive Force
Preemptive War Doctrine

Preventive Defense Strategy
Quadrennial Defense Review (QDR)
Satellite Reconnaissance
Sealift
Secure Second Strike
Single Integrated Operational Plan (SIOP)
Space Race
Strategic Bombing
Suicide Bombing
Tactics, Military
Theater Missile Defense
Threat Assessment
Two-Theater War
War Games
War Planning

ORGANIZATIONS, INSTITUTIONS, AND GROUPS

Armed Services Committees
Arms Control and Disarmament Agency
Ba'ath Party
Branch Davidians
Bureau of Alcohol, Tobacco and Firearms
CENTCOM
Central Intelligence Agency (CIA)
Council on Foreign Relations
Defense Contractors
Defense Information System Agency (DISA)
Defense Intelligence Agency (DIA)
Defense Threat Reduction Agency
Department of Defense, U.S. (DoD)
Department of Energy, U.S.
Department of State, U.S.
European Union
Federal Bureau of Investigation (FBI)
Federal Emergency Management
   Agency (FEMA)
Food and Agriculture Organization (FAO)
Halliburton Corporation
Homeland Security Council
Homeland Security, Department of
House Un-American Activities
   Committee (HUAC)
International Atomic Energy Agency
International Criminal Court
International Monetary Fund
INTERPOL
Irish Republican Army (IRA)
Jackson Committee

Johnson, Lyndon B., and National Policy
Justice, Department of
League of Nations
MERCOSUR
Military Sealift Command (MSC)
Military Traffic Management
   Command (MTMC)
Missile Technology Control Regime (MTCR)
National Counterintelligence Center (NACIC)
National Defense Panel (NDP)
National Defense University
National Security Agency (NSA)
National Security Committee
National Security Council (NSC)
National Security, U.S. Commission on (USCNS)
North Atlantic Treaty Organization (NATO)
Office of Domestic Preparedness
Office of Naval Research (ONR)
Office of Net Assessment
Office of Strategic Services (OSS)
   (*see also* Central Intelligence Agency [CIA])
Office of the Secretary of Defense (OSD)
OPEC (Organization of Petroleum
   Exporting Countries)
Organization for Security and
   Co-Operation in Europe (OSCE)
Organization of American States
Peace Corps
Pentagon
RAND Corporation
Secret Service
Selective Service
Signal Corps
Southeast Asia Treaty Organization (SEATO)
Strategic Air Command
Strategic Command, U.S.
Supreme Court, Role of U.S.
Think Tanks
Transportation Security Administration
United Nations
United Nations Monitoring, Verification, and
   Inspection Commission (UNMOVIC)
United Nations Special Commission (UNSCOM)
UN Security Council
UNOSOM
U.S. Agency for International Development (USAID)
U.S. Air Force Academy
U.S. Central Command (USCENTCOM)
U.S. Military Academy (West Point)
U.S. Naval Academy (Annapolis)

U.S. Northern Command (USNORTHCOM)
U.S. Pacific Command (USPACOM)
U.S. Southern Command (USSOUTHCOM)
Veterans Administration
Voice of America
War Colleges
World Bank
World Customs Organization (WCO)
World Trade Organization (WTO)

PLACES

Bay of Pigs
Berlin Airlift
Berlin Wall
Bikini Atoll
China and U.S. Policy
Commonwealth of Independent
   States (CIS)
Cuban Missile Crisis
Democratic People's Republic of
   Korea (North Korea)
Dien Bien Phu
Early Warning
Federally Funded Research and
   Development Centers (FFRDCs)
Guam
Guantánamo
Hiroshima
Korea, North and South
Latin America and U.S. Policy
Los Alamos
Middle East and U.S. Policy
Nagasaki (*see also* Hiroshima)
Okinawa
Oklahoma City Bombing
Pearl Harbor
Pentagon
Pusan Perimeter
Republic of China on Taiwan
Reykjavik
Rogue State
Ruby Ridge
Somalia Intervention (1992)
Soviet Union, Former (Russia), and
   U.S. Policy
Union of Soviet Socialist Republics (USSR)
U.S. Air Force Academy
U.S. Military Academy (West Point)
U.S. Naval Academy (Annapolis)

POLITICS AND POLICY

SPECIAL POPULATIONS

TECHNOLOGY

Land Mines
Missiles
Mortar
Multiple Independently Targetable
  Reentry Vehicles (MIRVs)
Nanotechnology
Neutron Bomb
NORAD
Patriot Missile
Penetrating Munitions
Radar
Radiological Dispersion Device
  (RDD) or Dirty Bomb
Science, Technology, and Security
Sea-Launched Ballistic Missiles (SLBMs)
Smart Bomb
Space-Based Weapons
Sputnik
Spy Satellites
Stealth Technologies
Stinger Missiles
Submarines
Surface to Air Missile (SAM)
Tactical Nuclear Weapons
Tanks
Tomahawk Cruise Missiles
Unmanned Aerial Vehicles (UAVs)
V-22A Osprey

WARS AND WARFARE

Afghan Wars
Afghanistan, War in
Air Warfare
Air-Land Battles
Amphibious Warfare
Antisubmarine Warfare
Arab-Israeli Conflict

Arms Race
Asymmetric Warfare
Bulge, Battle of the
Carpet Bombing
Cold War
D-Day
Dresden, Bombing of
Fulda Gap
Grenada Intervention
Guadalcanal, Battle of (1943)
Guerrilla Warfare
Gulf War
Inadvertent War
Inchon Landing
Information Warfare
Iraq War of 2003
Kamikaze
Korean War (*see also* Korea,
  North and South)
Kosovo Intervention (1999)
Leyte Gulf, Battle of (1944)
Middle East Conflicts (1956, 1967, 1973)
Midway, Battle of (1942)
Narcotics, War on
Normandy Invasion
Operation Desert Storm (1991)
Preventive War
Psychological Warfare (PSYOPS)
Spanish-American War (1898)
Submarine Warfare
Suez Canal Crisis (1956)
Terrorism, War on International
Tet Offensive
Trade Wars
Two-Theater War
Vietnam War
World War I (1914–1918)
World War II (1939–1945)

N

NAGASAKI

Japanese city that was the target (on August 9, 1945) of the second U.S. atomic bomb dropped in World War II. The bombing effectively ended the war because Japan surrendered within days.

Three days before the bombing of Nagasaki, the United States dropped the world's first atomic bomb on the city of Hiroshima. Most U.S. military and government leaders felt that a single bomb would be sufficient to convince Japan to surrender. However, when the bombing of Hiroshima did not produce an immediate Japanese response, the decision was made to drop a second bomb. In addition, the Los Alamos scientists who developed the bomb wanted to determine whether a uranium- or plutonium-based bomb worked better. The Little Boy bomb dropped on Hiroshima used uranium; the Fat Man bomb destined for Nagasaki used plutonium.

Nagasaki was not the first choice of targets for Fat Man. Although it had major shipbuilding facilities and a military port, it was bombed five times in the preceding year, so the impact of the atomic bomb would be obscured by the already damaged condition of the city. Also, Nagasaki was spread over hills and valleys and broken by waterways. The three primary targets for the second bomb were Kokura, Kyoto, and Nigata. Kyoto dropped off the list because it was a sacred city to many Japanese, and the United States feared that bombing it would only stiffen Japanese resistance. After Nigata was eliminated because it was too far away, the choice came down to Kokura. However, on the day of the raid, the weather over Kokura was too cloudy to

sight the target properly. *Bock's Car*, the B-29 bomber carrying Fat Man, then headed for Nagasaki, which was also clouded-over. A last-minute break in the clouds allowed the bomb to be dropped.

The devastation at Nagasaki was almost as terrible as that at Hiroshima. Fat Man obliterated an area 2.3 by 1.9 miles square. Reports of deaths varied according to different sources. The 1953 U.S. Strategic Bombing Survey estimated 35,000 dead, 60,000 wounded, and 5,000 missing because of the bomb. The Japanese in 1960 cited a figure of 20,000 dead and 50,000 wounded. A later report by the Nagasaki Prefectural Office claimed that the bombing resulted in 87,000 deaths and the destruction of 70% of the industrial zone. Because Nagasaki was a frequent target of American bombers, the residents became somewhat casual in their response to air raid warnings. As a result, people did not seek shelter as early or as urgently as they might otherwise have, and many more lives were lost than necessary. On the other hand, Nagasaki's hilly and broken topography helped limit the amount of damage and the spread of fires.

The bombings of Hiroshima and Nagasaki remain controversial. Defenders of the bombings cite the massive casualties—some estimates predicted a million lives—that an invasion of Japan would have cost. Critics claim that the weapons were too horrific and that nothing justified their use on civilians. They argue that the United States should have targeted military facilities or an unoccupied site as a demonstration of the bomb's power. Many opponents are especially critical of the decision to drop a second bomb after the destruction of Hiroshima. Proponents respond by pointing out that the bombing of Hiroshima did not force Japan to surrender, which necessitated dropping another bomb. Although the controversy is unlikely to be settled, the bombing of Nagasaki remains the last time nuclear weapons were used in combat.

See also Atomic Bomb; Hiroshima; Nuclear Weapons; World War II (1939–1945)

NANOTECHNOLOGY

The science of constructing devices at the molecular level. Taking its name from a nanometer (one-billionth of a meter), nanotechnology is poised to change numerous aspects of industrial technology; it also promises potentially wide-ranging social ramifications.

Everything in the physical world is composed of atoms, and the properties of any material depend on how its atoms are arranged. Arranging carbon atoms one way produces coal; arranging them in a different way produces diamonds. With modern technology, scientists can rearrange the atoms in sand, add in other elements, and produce computer chips. However, current manufacturing methods at this low level are very crude.

Today's computer chips are produced by etching electrical circuits onto a silicon wafer in a process known as lithography. Using this technique, chip designers can manipulate bits of silicon approximately as small as a micron (1,000 nanometers). With nanotechnology, however, designers could manipulate pieces of silicon thousands of times smaller, thus dramatically reducing the size of computer chips. Nanotechnology has been heralded as the next major leap in the evolution of computing.

Research in nanotechnology began in the late 1950s, when the famed physicist Richard Feynman (who worked on the Manhattan Project that developed the atomic bomb) gave a talk titled "There's Plenty of Room at the Bottom." Feynman envisioned the ability to manipulate atoms and molecules directly by developing machine tools at one-tenth scale. These tools would then be used to help develop one-hundredth scale machine tools, and so on until a truly microscopic scale was reached. As the tools get smaller, however, the relative strength of various forces, such as gravity and surface tension, would change. This would require redesigning some tools to account for these changes.

In the late 1980s, development of the scanning tunneling microscope (STM) by Gerd Binnig and Heinrich Rohrer made true nanotechnology research and development possible. The STM allows the imaging of solid surfaces with unprecedented resolution, down to the nanometer level. This process gives researchers the opportunity to move molecules and fabricate new, never-before-seen particles and devices. Since that time, the U.S. government has become increasingly involved in nanotechnology research. Government-sponsored spending on nanotechnology has risen from $116 million in 1997 to nearly $1 billion in 2004. Meanwhile, private industry is investing billions more in nanotechnology research and development. The National Science Foundation has predicted that the nanotechnology goods and services market could reach $1 trillion by 2015.

The U.S. military is especially interested in nanotechnology. Among the current military research related to nanotechnology are efforts to reduce the weight and increase the strength of armor, produce advanced protective materials for soldiers, develop sensors for biological and chemical agents and land mines, and make ever-smarter weapons. The development of smaller thermonuclear devices with decreased radioactive fallout also appears possible. Many other countries are also at work on military applications of nanotechnology.

Besides studying its possible beneficial uses, the U.S. government is also concerned about possible negative effects of nanotechnology, which could compromise national security. One of these concerns is the possibility of creating *grey goo*—out-of-control, self-replicating nanomachines. One of the principles of nanotechnology is that the devices created with it would be capable of making copies of them without human direction. Opponents of nanotechnology worry that science will be unable to control the nanodevices it creates. A similar fear is *green goo*—the creation of artificial molecules that could displace or destroy vital natural elements, leading to ecological catastrophe.

Some critics also fear widespread economic disruption from nanotechnology. Because nanotechnology could be used to produce an infinite variety of products cheaply and quickly, those who control the technology would be able to force competitors out of business. Because few people would be needed to run nanotechnology enterprises, this could lead to massive unemployment and social breakdown. The owners of nanotechnology would wield immense power disproportionate to their numbers and would not be answerable to the public for their actions. The possibility of such wide-ranging societal effects represents new challenges to national security in the 21st century.

NARCOTICS, WAR ON

Enforcement of laws prohibiting the sale and distribution of controlled substances, such as marijuana, cocaine, heroin, MDMA ("ecstasy"), LSD, and a number of others. Under U.S. law, the term *narcotic* refers specifically to opium and opium derivatives. Although coca and cocaine are technically not narcotics, they are classified as such under the Controlled Substances Act. The phrase *war on narcotics* is often used interchangeably with the phrase *war on drugs*.

Although narcotics can be consumed in a variety of ways, most commonly they are smoked, sniffed, or injected. Effects depend upon dosage, previous drug history, and the mood of the user. In the short term, narcotic use generally results in a sense of euphoria, happiness, or general well-being. Long-term effects include loss of energy, sleeplessness, nausea, dilation of blood vessels, constipation, diarrhea, and vomiting.

Health risks associated with drug use are infection, overdose, and diseases. The use of needles for intravenous injection can result in AIDS or hepatitis, and the fact that drug use is primarily a subculture makes nonsterile practice common. In addition, the supply of illegal street drugs is by nature unregulated; therefore, the purity of a substance is often impossible to determine.

Repeated narcotic use leads to increased tolerance and addiction. The development of tolerance creates the need to administer progressively larger doses to achieve the same effect. Physical, emotional, and psychological dependence occur as the user's body comes to require the substance to avoid feelings of withdrawal. Narcotics users move from using the drug for recreational purposes to requiring the drug to function normally. Withdrawal symptoms include depression, watery eyes, runny nose, sneezing, anxiety, loss of appetite, tremors, nausea, and vomiting. Withdrawal also involves bone and muscle ache, excessive sweating, and spasms. Psychological dependency tends to result in relapse even after the physical withdrawal is complete. The amount required to induce a fatal dose increases proportionally over time with tolerance; although there is always a point that will constitute an overdose.

Although abuse of narcotics can be initiated by exposure through medical treatment, most people begin drug use because of social interaction. The social acceptance of drugs and their influence upon and reflection in popular culture makes the war on narcotics increasingly complex.

HISTORY OF NARCOTICS INTERDICTION

The first law specifically targeting the use of narcotics was an ordinance passed in San Francisco in 1875, which prohibited the smoking of opium in opium dens. At the time, construction of the west-east portion of the transcontinental railroad was dependent upon Chinese labor; this legislation against opium is often associated with general fears about Chinese immigrants and the corrupting influence of Asian culture. Federal laws followed, prohibiting Chinese from trafficking in opium; however, laudanum, a drug containing opium and popular in the wider culture, remained legal. During the same period, cocaine was used in the manufacture of Coca-Cola.

The Harrison Narcotics Tax Act, passed in 1914, was the first comprehensive federal drug law that regulated the manufacture, importation, and distribution of narcotics. The proximate cause for the Harrison Act was the U.S. occupation of the Philippines following the Spanish-American War (1898), after which the U.S. government was confronted with the question of how to deal with the regulation of opium use for the first time. At the time, opium use was legal in the Philippines under a licensing system. A commission was established to study alternatives to this system, resulting in a recommendation that narcotics be subject to international control.

A series of international opium conferences followed, which also dealt with concerns over the so-called *opium wars* between Great Britain and China. The outcome was the Hague Convention of 1912, which has the distinction of being the first international narcotics agreement. Meanwhile, in the United States, Secretary of State William Jennings Bryan urged the passage of the Harrison Act as a gesture of compliance with the desires of the international community.

The purpose of the Harrison Act was simply to regulate narcotics; however, it was interpreted more broadly and had the effect of tightly curtailing the availability of opiates in the United States. In 1924, the importation of heroin was banned outright. Other drug laws followed, including the Marijuana Tax Act of 1937, which is often associated with prejudice against Mexicans crossing the border to find work during the Great Depression.

WAR ON NARCOTICS

The current war on narcotics began in 1972, when President Richard Nixon used the term *war on drugs* to refer to U.S. domestic drug policy. The phrase echoed President Lyndon Johnson's War on Poverty, which established the Social Security Act of 1965, implementing Medicare and Medicaid. The phrase has since become popular as a way of indicating a high level of intent toward dealing with a specific problem or situation. However, like other metaphorical wars, the war on narcotics is highly controversial.

Sailors off load more than 3,000 pounds of cocaine.

Source: Corbis

Attempts to deal with domestic drug problems in the 1970s came to focus on elimination of drug production. The vast majority of cocaine was produced in Colombia, South America, so the U.S. government began pressuring the Colombian government to participate in helping end the drug trade. Drug smuggling grew from small-scale operators flying into the United States on commercial airliners to a highly profitable, organized business that brought in hundreds of millions of dollars. Attempts by the Colombian government to interfere with large-scale operators like the Medellín cartel and the Cali cartel nearly drove the country of Colombia into civil war. Thus, the domestic war on narcotics had the unintended consequence of nearly setting off an actual war outside of the United States.

Domestic efforts have focused on education and mandatory minimum sentencing. A policy of zero tolerance for narcotics distribution and possession was declared, and the phrase *zero tolerance*, like *war on . . .* , has also been repeatedly invoked with reference to a wide variety of other topics. However, zero tolerance policies, with regard to controlled narcotics, have come under increasing criticism for resulting in the incarceration of large numbers of individuals in an already overcrowded prison system. The fact that minorities constitute the vast majority of those thrown in jail under minimum sentencing for narcotic use, distribution, and possession adds to the controversy.

Antinarcotic education programs have focused on adolescents. Those best known are the Just Say No campaign, begun during the Reagan administration, and the Drug Abuse Resistance Education (DARE) program. The success of these campaigns has been difficult to measure. Criticism has centered on the fact that all drugs—from so-called soft drugs such as marijuana to more serious narcotics such as cocaine—are all treated similarly. In addition, drug campaigns are forced to contend with the complexities of peer pressure and the content of popular culture.

PAST EXPERIENCE AND FOREIGN EXAMPLES

The failure of Prohibition in the early 20th century is regarded by many as indicative of the problems currently faced by agencies waging the war on narcotics. By contrast, Europeans, who historically have taken a far more liberal approach toward drug use, today demonstrate lower rates of crime associated with drug use than is found in the United States. Explanations range from the value of demystification to the constructive treatment of drug addiction as a health problem.

—*William de Jong-Lambert*

See also Drug Cartels; Narcotrafficking

Further Reading

Alexander, Ann, and Mark S. Roberts, eds. *High Culture: Reflections on Addiction and Modernity*. Albany: State University of New York Press, 2003.

Cherry, Andrew, Mary E. Dillon, and Douglas Rugh. *Substance Abuse: A Global View*. Westport, CT: Greenwood, 2002.

NARCOTRAFFICKING

International transfer and sale of illegal narcotics. Narcotrafficking is a feature of the so-called war on narcotics or war on drugs. In regard to the United States, narcotrafficking refers to the production of drugs such as cocaine, heroin, marijuana, hashish, or other controlled substances in a foreign country and their subsequent illicit importation to this country. Although the term *narcotic* defines only opium or opium derivatives, the term is generally applied to all illegal drugs.

The negative impact of opium brought into the United States by foreign nationals was first formally recognized by the passage of the first drug law in the United States—in San Francisco at the end of the 19th century. Aimed at the Chinese immigrant population, the law prohibited the smoking of opium. Throughout the 20th century, the United States passed a series of laws banning the production, sale, and possession of a variety of drugs, including alcohol during the 1920s. The ineffectiveness and unpopularity of Prohibition led to its repeal in the 1930s, but other drugs have remained illegal.

During the administration of President Richard Nixon, a public antidrug campaign was launched called the War on Drugs. The program was the product of a number of factors, including research linking different kinds of drugs with rising crime rates, the growing social acceptance of drugs such as marijuana among young people, and reports about the use of more serious drugs, such as heroin, by U.S. troops in Vietnam. The increased government focus on drugs led to prescriptions for interdiction at the level of importation and production. South America and the country of Colombia in particular became the focus of these efforts.

The trafficking of illegal drugs into the United States changed dramatically in method and scale during the 1970s. As demand for cocaine grew, drug cartels developed, which functioned as organized crime networks handling every stage of the process. Drugs were produced in jungle laboratories and then transported in large shipments north to the United States. The method of transporting these drugs across the border and into the major cities changed from being dependent upon individual smugglers to involving the use of private aircraft. The volume thus transformed as well, from the amount that one smuggler could carry, to the amount that could be transported by a small plane.

As profits grew, so did competition. The Medellín drug cartel in Colombia dominated the cocaine trade until the 1980s, when the group was supplanted by the Cali cartel. The Cali cartel worked in conjunction with the Colombian government and the U.S. Drug Enforcement Agency (DEA) to destroy the Medellín cartel. As a result, the Cali cartel grew more successful. Although the Cali cartel itself was finally liquidated in the 1990s, its leaders are said to be operating the cartel from behind bars.

Since becoming the focus of the international antidrug effort by the United States, Colombia has ceded its central role in production to Mexico, so the primary point of entry into the United States has shifted from Florida to California.

Meanwhile, the focus on the production and illegal importation of drugs into the United States has shifted to a focus on the role of the illegal drug trade in terrorism. The terms *narcoterrorism* and *narcoterrorist* have emerged to describe the use of profits from the sale of illicit substances to fund terrorist activities. By associating drug use with support for terrorism, the new strategy focuses on cutting the demand for drugs in the United States.

See also Drug Cartels; Terrorism, War on International

Further Reading

Baum, Dan. *Smoke and Mirrors: The War On Drugs and the Politics of Failure*. Boston: Back Bay Books, 1997.

Scott, Peter Dale, and Jonathan Marshall. *Cocaine Politics: Drugs, Armies and the CIA in Central America*. Berkeley: University of California Press, 1998.

NATIONAL COUNTERINTELLIGENCE CENTER (NACIC)

Early post–Cold War effort to improve the use and coordination of U.S. counterintelligence information. The National Counterintelligence Center (NACIC) was created through a 1994 presidential directive by President Bill Clinton. President Clinton signed the directive after a review of U.S. counterintelligence, which was shaken by the revelation that senior U.S. operative Aldrich Ames was a longtime Soviet spy. The directive defined counterintelligence as "information gathered and activities conducted to protect against espionage, other intelligence activities, sabotage, or assassinations conducted by or on behalf of foreign governments, foreign organizations, foreign persons, or international terrorist activities."

The Ames investigation made clear that various federal agencies needed to increase their cooperation, accountability, and integration of crucial counterintelligence information. It found a particularly worrisome communications failure between the intelligence community and law enforcement communities. In response to these shortfalls, the NACIC was meant to serve as an interagency forum for reviewing complementary national-level intelligence activities and promoting interagency cohesiveness and information sharing. The directive established the NACIC as an independent federal entity, initially headed by a senior executive of the Federal Bureau of Investigation (FBI), which employed representatives from a wide range of government agencies, including the armed forces, Central Intelligence Agency (CIA), FBI, National Security Agency, Defense Intelligence Agency, Department of State, and Defense Security Service.

Based at the CIA, NACIC reported to the National Security Council (NSC) through the National Counterintelligence Policy Board. The board, also created through the 1994 directive, was the principal mechanism for reviewing and proposing legislative initiatives and executive orders related to U.S. counterintelligence to NSC staff. The center also worked toward creating a better understanding between the federal counterintelligence community and private industry, as well as raising public awareness of threats such as economic espionage. Along those lines, the NACIC produced many publications, including the classified *Counterintelligence Digest*, which summarizes current concerns by country and subject matter. The center also distributes an unclassified annual report to Congress on foreign economic information collection and industrial espionage.

In 2001, President George W. Bush signed a presidential decision directive that replaced the NACIC and the National Counterintelligence Policy Board with the National Counterintelligence Executive (NCIX) and the National Counterintelligence Board of Directors. The NCIX, under the provisions of the Counterintelligence Enhancement Act of 2002, serves as the head of national counterintelligence for the U.S. government, subject to the direction and control of the president.

See also Clinton, Bill (William Jefferson), and National Policy; Economic Espionage; Espionage

NATIONAL DEFENSE EDUCATION ACT (NDEA)

Federal legislation passed in 1958 providing aid to education in the United States at all levels, both public and private. Instituted primarily to stimulate the advancement of science, mathematics, and modern world languages, the National Defense Education Act (NDEA) has also provided assistance in other areas, including technical education, geography, English as a second language, counseling and guidance, school libraries, and educational media centers. The act also provided for low-interest loans to college students. The NDEA is considered the most important federal law concerning higher education since the 1862 Morrill Act.

Cold War rivalries between the United States and the Soviet Union led to the passage of the National Defense Education Act of 1958. The successful Soviet launch of Sputnik, the first satellite to orbit the earth, and well-publicized American space failures induced a climate of national crisis. Critics pointed to the educational deficiencies of American students, especially in mathematics and science.

Thus, Congress passed the NDEA to help ensure that highly trained individuals would be available to help the United States compete with the Soviet Union in scientific and technical fields. President Dwight D. Eisenhower signed the NDEA on September 2, 1958. Because of the NDEA, federal expenditures for education more than doubled in the years that followed. For higher education, this included funding for federal student loan programs, graduate fellowships in the sciences and engineering, aid for teacher education, and increased funds for curriculum development.

In the United States, education was (and remains) primarily a state and local governmental responsibility. States and communities—as well as public and private organizations—establish schools and colleges, develop curricula, and determine the requirements for enrollment and graduation. The NDEA recognizes this local control of education; the act prohibits federal direction, supervision, or control over the curriculum, program of instruction, administration, or personnel of any educational institution.

The NDEA laid the foundation for further federal legislation concerning education. These acts include the Elementary and Secondary Education Act (1965), Higher Education Act (1965), Education for All Handicapped Children Act (1975), Goals 2000: Educate America Act (2000), and No Child Left Behind Act (2001).

See also Cold War; Eisenhower, Dwight D., and National Policy

NATIONAL DEFENSE PANEL (NDP)

Independent congressional body formed in 1996 to conduct a major review of U.S. military security policy and structure. The nine-member National Defense Panel (NDP) was chaired by Philip Odeen, chief executive officer of the private information technology firm BDM International.

In 1997, the NDP released its final report, titled "Transforming Defense—National Security in the Twenty-First Century." The NDP recommended that the "United States must take a broad transformation of its military and national security structures, operational concepts and equipment, and the Defense Department's key business processes" and accelerate changes already under way. Four years before the September 11, 2001, terrorist attacks on New York and Washington, DC, the report identified the threats posed by terrorist groups and rogue states. It warned of their potential acquisition of weapons of mass destruction, and called for improved homeland defense.

The authors of the report also advised spending between $5 and $10 billion to ward off these threats while continuing to reduce the U.S. nuclear stockpile. In his introductory letter to Secretary of Defense William Cohen, NDP Chairman Odeen stated that "We are convinced that the challenges of the 21st century will be quantitatively and qualitatively different from those of the Cold War and require fundamental change to our national security institutions, military strategy, and defense posture by 2020." He wrote that the NDP report expanded on the latest Quadrennial Defense Review (QDR), which was also conducted in 1997, but looked farther into the future and offered a more developed transformation strategy. Mandated only to produce the report, the NDP disbanded after its release.

See also Homeland Security; Rogue State; Terrorism, War on International

NATIONAL DEFENSE UNIVERSITY

A graduate-level institution for military officers and civilians from the United States and allied nations, consisting of four colleges, five strategic research centers, and one leadership training program. The National Defense University grants master's of science degrees in National Resource Strategy and National Security Strategy. University facilities are located in Washington, DC, and Norfolk, Virginia. More than 1,000 students are enrolled, and more than 500 master's degrees are awarded each year.

HISTORY

Before World War II, needs for advanced scholarship in military strategy were met separately by each service branch on an ad hoc basis. The bloodiest war of the 20th century, however, brought to light the need for closer ties between the military, the defense industry, and the diplomatic community. The founding of the National War College (NWC) and the Industrial College of the Armed Forces (ICAF) in the immediate aftermath of the war addressed this need.

In 1976, the NWC and ICAF joined to form the National Defense University, which expanded with the addition of the Joint Forces Staff College in 1981 and the Information Resources Management College the following year. In 1993, another key milestone in the history of the National Defense University was passed when President Bill Clinton signed legislation granting the school authority to award master's degrees. This was in response to the Goldwater-Nichols Act of 1986, which reemphasized the importance of joint services experience for the nation's military officers. The first master's degrees were awarded on June 15, 1994.

RESEARCH CENTERS

The National Defense University administers five research centers to broaden understanding of strategic areas of the world and one program to develop civilian leadership skills. The Center for Hemispheric Studies, founded in 1997, educates civilians from Western Hemisphere nations in military affairs. The Defense Leadership and Management Program was inaugurated the same year to develop leadership skills among civilians working in the defense field.

In addition, the year 2000 saw the establishment of the Africa Center for Strategic Studies, the Near

East-South Asia Center for Strategic Studies, and the Center for the Study of Chinese Military Affairs. Of these, the Africa Center for Strategic Studies is particularly notable for its role in fostering democratic governance in Africa through courses geared to civilian and military leaders from the continent. The Center for Technology and National Security opened its doors in 2001 to study the relationship between technological development and defense planning.

A member of the Texas National Guard (Lieutenant General Wayne D. Marty) saluting the American flag during the 49th Armored Division formation as Apache helicopters fly over in July 2004. The oldest military force in the United States, the National Guard consists of citizens trained as soldiers and aviators. Service in the guard has often been viewed as a part-time job, but approximately 40% of the U.S. troops stationed and fighting in Iraq since 2003 have come from either the guard or the Army reserves. As of September 2004, more than 90,000 members of the Army Guard were deployed to Afghanistan and other countries in the front lines of the war on terrorism.

Source: U.S. Army.

PRESENT AND FUTURE

In the present global security environment, the role of joint operations, regional knowledge, and personal diplomacy is paramount. To meet these needs, which will play a vital role in global security, the National Defense University prepares military and civilian leaders from around the globe to face present and emerging security threats through education in military strategy and application of the latest technology, as well as foreign culture and strategic thinking.

See also War Colleges

NATIONAL GUARD

Reserve component of the U.S. military that is organized on a state-by-state basis and is under state, rather than federal, control. An outgrowth of the early state militias of the American colonial period, the U.S. National Guard is the oldest organized military structure in the United States. It also has the unique distinction of providing an armed force that serves both a federal and state mission.

The first state militia was established in Massachusetts in 1636 by the General Court of the Massachusetts Bay Colony. By the time of the American Revolution, every state had its own militia. During the Revolutionary War, the militia played a significant role in defeating British forces and actually fought in greater numbers than the Continental Army. In 1787, the U.S. Constitution mandated the maintenance of a militia as well as a regular army. The state militia system existed side by side with the U.S. Army until 1903, when Congress reorganized the state militias into the National Guard system.

The National Guard plays a unique dual role among U.S. military units. It has both a federal and a state mission, and both federal and individual state governments dictate the size, structure, and implementation of national guard units. U.S. National Guard servicemen and servicewomen hold the joint position as a U.S. soldier and a soldier from their respective state. There are 54 national guard organizations for the United States: one for each of the 50 states, and one each for Guam, Puerto Rico, the Virgin Islands, and Washington, DC.

The National Guard is administered by the National Guard Bureau, a joint bureau of the Army and Air Force. The National Guard Bureau administers the federal regulations and missions of the Army and Air National

Guard. The federal mission of the National Guard is to maintain well-trained and well-equipped forces, whose size is mandated at the federal level, for fast mobilization in times of war or national emergency. The National Guard's state mission includes providing peace, order, and public safety, and responding to emergencies such as natural disasters. The state mission requires National Guard personnel to report to their state's governor.

The National Guard is divided into two branches, the Army National Guard and the Air National Guard. Although both fulfill the dual state and federal mission, each is charged with specific reserve roles to reinforce active duty U.S. military personnel. The Army National Guard's mission is to train, equip, and maintain forces to assume crucial combat, combat support, and combat service support roles. The Air National Guard similarly plays a unique role in accordance with its federal mission. The Air National Guard provides almost half of the tactical airlift support, combat communications functions, and aeromedical evacuation capability for the entire Air Force. It is charged with maintaining well-trained and equipped forces in support of the broader Air Force.

Both the Army National Guard and the Air National Guard also figure prominently in U.S. homeland security policy. The Army National Guard has become a central component of homeland security policy because the National Guard's state-by-state organization allows it to respond quickly to emergencies and crises at home. The Air National Guard holds responsibility for U.S. domestic air defense.

The National Guard was called upon to play a major role in both the Gulf War of 1991 and the Iraq War of 2003. The latter war placed severe strains on the National Guard because troop shortages required many Guard troops to serve past their discharge dates. This practice, called *stop loss*, along with quick rotations that put units back into action after only a brief time at home, had a negative impact on recruiting and retention rates. This has become a subject of concern among military planners. With its expanded role as both a military reserve and homeland defense force, the National Guard is perhaps more important now than it has been since the American Revolution.

See also Gulf War (1990–1991); Homeland Security; Iraq War of 2003; Militia; Reserve Forces

Further Reading

Doubler, Michael D. *Civilian in Peace, Soldier in War: The Army National Guard, 1636–2000*. Lawrence: University Press of Kansas, 2003.

Goldstein, Donald M. *The National Guard: An Illustrated History of America's Citizen-Soldier.* Dulles, VA: Potomac Books, 2003.

NATIONAL INTERESTS

See NATIONAL SECURITY STRATEGY OF THE UNITED STATES

NATIONAL MISSILE DEFENSE

System for which planning began in the United States in the 1960s to guard against a nuclear attack. The concept of missile defense is a product of the Cold War, a time in which the international framework was determined by competition between the two global superpowers: the United States and the Soviet Union.

During the Cold War, both superpowers possessed overwhelming arsenals of nuclear weapons, so the prospect of nuclear war played a central role in diplomatic relations between them. The purpose of a National Missile Defense system would be to intercept nuclear missiles before they could strike the United States. Thus, the initiative was conceived as purely defensive. However, the fact that an impermeable defense umbrella would also undermine the concept of mutually assured destruction (MAD)—the idea that neither side would start a nuclear war because the consequences of retaliation were too severe—put the development of a National Missile Defense system at the center of arms negotiations in the early 1970s.

EARLY PROJECTS

The Nike-Zeus Program, initiated in the late 1950s, introduced the ultimately unpalatable prospect of nuclear missiles being used to intercept nuclear missiles. The Nike warhead would detonate in the vicinity of the incoming Soviet intercontinental ballistic missile (ICBM), thus destroying the enemy missile. The risks to the project were obvious, and the potential countermeasures (such as decoys) were easily imaginable. The Nike-Zeus project was therefore abandoned in 1961.

U.S. Defense Secretary Robert McNamara announced the Sentinel program in 1967, in the midst of the Vietnam War. Rather than attempting to account for a general nuclear attack against the United States, the Sentinel was envisioned specifically to safeguard against a nuclear attack from China. (It was assumed that China would be capable of launching an intercontinental ballistic missile by 1970.) A secondary advantage of developing the Sentinel system is that it allowed the United States to continue arms-reduction talks with the Soviet Union because the program was not directed against it. Opposition to the Sentinel program became part of the more general protest movement at the time against the Vietnam War. The Sentinel system was ultimately abandoned and replaced with a program called Safeguard to defend ballistic missile sites in North Dakota.

The development of the Sentinel raised the problem of MAD. The possibility that a nation might feel forced to initiate a preemptive strike—realizing that after the system was in place it would have no retaliatory capability—led to the signing of the Antiballistic Missile Treaty in 1974. It also left open the question of how a defense system could be developed that would not be perceived as offensive.

The Strategic Defense Initiative (SDI), better known as Star Wars, was initiated during the administration of President Ronald Reagan as a system that would provide a space-based defense umbrella for the United States. Reagan's stated goal was to share the technology with the Soviet Union, thus negating the question of MAD. Funding for SDI began in 1984, but the fall of the Berlin Wall and subsequent collapse of the Soviet Union in the early 1990s removed motivation for the project. Star Wars has been reinvented to serve in the war on terrorism with President George W. Bush's National Missile Defense program.

CONTEMPORARY ISSUES

Work on a missile defense program continued under President Bill Clinton, but with little momentum. The terrorist attacks of September 11, 2001, provided a new rationale and a new approach to the concept of missile defense. President George W. Bush announced the National Missile Defense program in 2002, soon renamed the Ground-Based Missile Defense system because the idea of ground-based interceptors seemed, at least in the short run, to be more technologically feasible. In recognition of the U.S. role as the sole remaining global superpower, the purpose of the system is projected to guard against acts of nuclear terrorism. However, the question of whether any kind of missile defense system—deployed against terrorists or another nation—could ever be effective remains controversial.

See also Strategic Defense Initiative (SDI)

Further Reading

Causewell, Erin V. *National Missile Defense: Issues and Developments*. Hauppauge, NY: Nova Publishers, 2002.

Cordsman, Anthony H. *Strategic Threats and National Missile Defenses: Defending the U.S. Homeland*. Westport, CT: Praeger, 2001.

Wirtz, James J., and Jeffrey A. Larsen, eds. *Rocket's Red Glare: Missile Defenses and the Future of World Politics*. Boulder, CO: Westview Press, 2001.

NATIONAL POWER, DETERMINANTS OF

Factors that dictate a state's strengths and weaknesses in its relations with other nations.

A state's national power determines whether it can obtain what it wants and whether it can influence others to do what it wants them to do.

States draw national power from several sources, including the size of their populations, their natural resources, and their geographic position. A state's national power also depends upon how effectively it exploits, organizes, and uses these different resources. In their relations with other states—including hard power, soft power, and economic power—states possess and use various types of national power.

HARD POWER

The threat of force or the actual use of force to compel another state to do something or refrain from doing something is called hard power. For example, in September 2001, the United States threatened to invade and forcibly remove the Taliban regime in Afghanistan if it did not hand over international terrorist Osama bin Laden. When the Taliban refused, the U.S.-led coalition invaded Afghanistan the following month and quickly ousted the Taliban regime. Both the U.S. threat of force and its actual use of force constituted hard power.

To increase hard power, a state can build up its military capabilities. If a state is strong militarily, it can coerce other states effectively and resist coercion itself. Currently, the United States is the strongest military power in the world and thus exhibits immense hard power. Its military spending in 2002 and 2003 was greater than the military spending of the next nine spenders combined. The U.S. possesses the world's most advanced military technologies, including its sophisticated nuclear arsenal and vast space technologies. These assets set the United States apart from any other state in the world.

Other factors also contribute to a state's hard power. Surrounded by two oceans, the United States' geographic position protects it from land-based threats. Meanwhile, the fact that it lies on two oceans allows it to project its sea power worldwide. The United States can also draw from its huge population and extraordinarily abundant natural resources. The legitimacy of the U.S. government and the public support that the government receives also contribute to the United States' military effectiveness and thus its hard power.

States have accumulated and used hard power in different ways throughout history. During the 19th century, Britain used its naval prowess to create an empire. It used the natural resources drawn from its empire to further strengthen its navy. In contrast with the United States, the small island nation came to dominate the globe despite its lack of natural resources and a small population at home.

SOFT POWER

In contrast with hard power, a state can use soft power to influence a targeted state by persuading it, rather than coercing it, to alter its behavior. If the targeted state can be convinced that the change is beneficial to its condition, it does not have to be coerced. Positive national image, persuasive leadership, strong cultural affinities, economic trade, and international prestige all contribute to a state's soft power. A state can use its soft power to co-opt other states and build relations of *complex interdependence*, in which states become linked through mutually beneficial economic and social exchange.

Throughout the Cold War, the soft power of the Western states was exhibited in their ability to persuade the members of the Soviet bloc of the benefits of liberal democracy and capitalism. Such persuasion was consciously conducted through cultural exchanges between East and West and through the projection of media programs, such as Radio Free Europe, into the East.

Perhaps more importantly, the Western states set an example for the East with the prosperity that they attained with their liberal economic and political policies. The allure of the West's economic and political success gave it an advantage over the Soviet Union in winning the allegiance of the states of Eastern Europe. This contributed to the momentum that brought down the Berlin Wall in November 1989. With the collapse of the Soviet Union two years later, the countries of Eastern Europe aligned their political and economic policies with those of the West.

ECONOMIC POWER

A third way in which a state can affect the behavior of other states is by using economic power. Economic power is determined by the degree to which a state can affect the flow of goods or the level of prices in the international economic system. Economic power can be wielded by offering positive incentives or by imposing economic sanctions. Because of the degree to which most states rely on international trade, economic power is an important factor in determining relations in the international system.

A state can offer positive incentives to induce another state to change its behavior. The United States, for example, might offer most-favored-nation (MFN) status to another country, which lowers trade barriers and allows the other country access to lucrative U.S. markets. In the 1980s, the United States granted China MFN status, but this status would have to be renewed every year. The United States was content to renew China's MFN status until the Chinese crackdown on prodemocracy demonstrators in Tiananmen Square in 1989. Since then, the U.S. has used renewal as a way to pressure China to modify its human rights policies.

Sanctions are another way in which a state can wield its economic power. Sanctions can include the imposition of embargoes or the freezing of the overseas assets of a targeted state. In the midst of the Iranian revolution in 1979, student protesters overtook the U.S. embassy in Tehran and held dozens of Americans hostage. To force the Iranian revolutionary leadership to free the hostages, U.S. President Jimmy Carter froze $8 billion of Iranian assets in the United States and imposed a complete economic embargo on Iran. On January 20, 1981, the Iranian leadership agreed to release the hostages in exchange for having the assets unfrozen and the embargo lifted.

States can form cartels as a way of concentrating economic power. The most prominent example is the Organization of Petroleum Exporting Countries (OPEC). OPEC is a cartel in which 11 major suppliers of oil collude to control prices and supplies. The clearest demonstration of OPEC's power came during the oil crisis of 1973. On October 17, 1973, the OPEC countries declared that they would refuse shipment of oil to states that supported Israel in the 1973 Yom Kippur War against Egypt. The shock of this embargo had wide-ranging international effects. Western European and Japanese foreign policies shifted toward favoring Arab countries, and the United States transferred fuller control of oil production in Saudi Arabia to the Saudi government.

Statecraft involves the use and interaction of all three types of national power. Hard power is often referred to as the stick that is coupled with the carrot of positive economic incentives to induce a target state into changing its behavior. Proponents of soft power do not question the significance of a state's hard power or economic power. They simply propose that states have other national means, such as persuasion, through which they can influence the behavior of other states. The most powerful states in history have relied on all three types of national power.

See also Economic Sanctions; Interdependence

Further Reading

Keohane, Robert O., and Joseph S. Nye. *Power and Interdependence*. 2nd. ed. Boston: Little, Brown and Co., 1989.

Morgenthau, Hans J. *Politics Among Nations: The Struggle for Power and Peace*. New York: McGraw-Hill, 1993.

Nye, Joseph S. *Soft Power: The Means to Success in World Politics*. New York: Public Affairs, 2004.

Waltz, Kenneth. *Theory of International Politics*. New York: McGraw-Hill, 1979.

NATIONAL SECURITY ACT (1947)

Congressional act that reorganized the structure of the U.S. armed forces following World War II. The National Security Act created the office of secretary of defense to oversee the nation's military establishment, as well as separate departments for each branch of the armed forces. It also provided for the coordination of the military with other departments and agencies of the government concerned with national security.

The stated goal of the National Security Act was "to provide a comprehensive program for the future security of the United States" and "to provide for the establishment of integrated policies and procedures for the departments, agencies, and functions of the Government relating to national security." To accomplish these goals, the act made several organizational changes. It replaced the former Department of War with a Department of Defense (DoD), and included the departments of the Army, Air Force, and Navy (which also included the U.S. Marine Corps) under the DoD.

The reorganization was intended to create a clear and direct line of command for all military services, to eliminate the duplication of effort in the DoD (particularly in the fields of research and engineering), to provide more efficient and economical administration in the defense establishment, to provide unified strategic direction for the armed forces, and to facilitate the operation of the military under unified command—but not to establish a single chief of staff over the armed forces nor an overall armed forces general staff. However, the act did establish the Joint Chiefs of Staff (JCS) to advise the president on military strategy and planning.

The National Security Act placed a tremendous amount of emphasis on the coordination of national security with the intelligence community and its many capabilities. Most notably, the legislation created the Central Intelligence Agency (CIA) and established the position of director of central intelligence, which was charged with managing the CIA as well as overseeing the entire intelligence community. As specified in the National Security Act, the intelligence community included not only the CIA but also the National Security Agency (NSA), the Defense Intelligence Agency (DIA), and the National Reconnaissance Office, along with other intelligence and reconnaissance-related offices within the DoD and the individual services.

The National Security Act also established the National Security Council (NSC) to assist in the coordination of the nation's security assets. The NSC includes the president, vice-president, the president's national security advisor, the secretary of state, the secretary of defense, and other presidential appointees approved by the Senate. The NSC also manages smaller subcommittees to address threats to national security.

See also Department of Defense, U.S. (DoD); Joint Chiefs of Staff; National Security Agency (NSA); National Security Council (NSC)

NATIONAL SECURITY AGENCY (NSA)

A cryptological agency of the U.S. government, which is responsible for the security of government communications as well as the collection and analysis of foreign communications through the Internet, radio, and other means. Part of the Department of Defense, the National Security Agency (NSA) is headquartered at Fort Meade, Maryland, and employs an estimated 35,000 staff members.

The roots of the NSA can be traced at least as far back as its predecessor, the short-lived Armed Forces

Security Agency, founded in 1949. Although the goal of that agency was to coordinate all cryptological analysts under one organization, the agency failed in its mission because of a lack of centralization.

The United States thus entered the Cold War without a truly effective cryptology service. With the outbreak of the Korean War in 1950, which took the United States by surprise, the country needed to unite its civilian and military code specialists under one roof. This led to the creation of the NSA.

The NSA was created by a classified executive order from President Harry S. Truman in June 1952. It went to work immediately, providing intelligence to the military in Korea under its first director, Army Lieutenant General Ralph Canine. In 1957, amid mounting Cold War tensions, the NSA moved to its current headquarters in Fort Meade to place it out of harm's way in case of a possible nuclear attack on the nation's capital. With the world on the brink of war in the 1961 Cuban Missile Crisis, the agency closely followed Soviet naval communications and helped avert tragedy by informing President John F. Kennedy that Moscow had turned its ships around in the face of the U.S. blockade of Cuba.

The NSA faced its next big challenge in Vietnam, where specialists were dispatched four years before the first U.S. Marines landed at Da Nang in 1965. Cryptologists were sometimes forward deployed during the 10-year U.S. campaign in Southeast Asia, risking and sometimes losing their lives to intercept enemy communications. After the last combat troops pulled out of South Vietnam in 1972, NSA specialists stayed to the end at the U.S. embassy in Hanoi to provide secure communications and intelligence on the communist North.

During the Cold War, research conducted by the NSA had considerable spillover effect into everyday civilian life. The agency's research contributed to the development of the supercomputer, cassette tapes, the microchip, semiconductors, nanotechnology, and data encryption. In 1993, the highly secretive organization offered the public a glimpse into its activities with the opening of the National Cryptologic Museum at NSA headquarters, in which memorabilia such as the World War II German Enigma machine and the recently declassified Cray computer can be viewed.

With the end of the Cold War and the September 11, 2001, terrorist attacks on New York and Washington, DC, the NSA is gearing up to adapt its human and material resources to a far more agile, shadowy threat

than the Soviet Union. Twenty-first century telecommunications have enabled anyone with sufficient know-how to intercept and encode communications. Not only can terrorist organizations and insurgents in countries such as Iraq and Afghanistan fully exploit this modern technology to call others to arms, but they have also demonstrated the ability to communicate effectively by low-tech means not vulnerable to NSA eavesdropping.

In the new century, the NSA thus faces the challenge of adapting to new technologies and new equally versatile adversaries who unfortunately have demonstrated the threat they present to the security of the United States.

See also Department of Defense, U.S. (DoD); Intelligence and Counterintelligence

NATIONAL SECURITY COMMITTEE

Committee in the U.S. House of Representatives, formerly the House Committee on Armed Services, which is a standing committee of Congress concerned with national security issues. The National Security Committee is responsible for supervising the activities of and making appropriations to support the military forces of the United States.

Composed of approximately 55 members of Congress and a staff more than twice as large, the National Security Committee includes five subcommittees with responsibility for military installations and facilities, military personnel, military procurement, military readiness, and military research and development. The committee was established on January 2, 1947, as a part of the Legislative Reorganization Act of 1946, by merging the Committee on Military Affairs and the Committee on Naval Affairs. The committee has jurisdiction over military and naval activities and appropriations, as well as oversight jurisdiction to review and study on a continuing basis all laws, programs, and government activities dealing with or involving international arms control and disarmament and the education of military dependents in schools.

The committee also has jurisdiction over ammunition depots; forts; arsenals; Army, Navy, and Air Force reservations and establishments; the common defense in general; conservation, development, and use of naval petroleum and oil shale reserves; and general aspects of the Department of Defense (DoD). The

House of Representatives granted the committee additional legislative and supervisory authority over merchant marine academies, national security aspects of the merchant marine policy and programs, and interoceanic canals. The enabling legislation for the committee codified the existing jurisdiction of the committee over tactical intelligence matters and the intelligence-related activities of the DoD.

In practice, the committee has interests that range far and wide. In 1997, for example, topics considered by the committee included ballistic missile defense, base realignment and consolidation, and the People's Republic of China (PRC). The committee also covers lesser concerns, such as the shooting down of two army helicopters in Iraq before the Iraq War of 2003, prisoners of war and troops missing in action from the Vietnam War and the Korean War, and extremism within the ranks of the military. Working in conjunction with the U.S. Senate and the executive branch, the committee is a key actor in the national security process.

See also National Security Act (1947)

NATIONAL SECURITY COUNCIL (NSC)

Agency established by the National Security Act of 1947 to coordinate foreign and defense policy and harmonize diplomatic and military policies and engagements. The National Security Council (NSC) is the principal forum in which the president of the United States discusses and shapes national security and foreign policy issues. The function of the NSC is to advise the president in these areas and coordinate policy among government agencies. The importance and role of the NSC has varied with the managerial style of each president and his personal relationships with the principal members.

The NSC is chaired by the president. Although the National Security Act established the secretaries of defense and state as key members, the vice president, secretary of the treasury, and national security advisor are also regular NSC attendees. In addition, the chairman of the Joint Chiefs of Staff (JCS) serves as military adviser, and the director of central intelligence holds the title of intelligence adviser to the NSC. The president's chief of staff, the counsel to the president, and the assistant to the president for economic policy

can also attend NSC meetings. The attorney general and the director of the Office of Management and Budget attend meetings when the subject matter falls under their jurisdiction. Other senior officials attend meetings when necessary.

Although the NSC was established by the National Security Act of 1947 to coordinate foreign policy and defense issues, in reality this stipulation gave way to the understanding that the NSC would directly serve the president in an advisory role. The NSC is, in fact, often a forum for the president to control and encourage cooperation among competing departments.

During the administration of President Harry S. Truman, the secretary of state was the dominant player on the NSC. The military experience of President Dwight D. Eisenhower, however, reshaped the NSC into an elaborate staff structure to monitor implementation of key foreign policy decisions closely.

In the 1960s, President John F. Kennedy initially relied on Secretary of State Dean Rusk to handle diplomacy, but he soon turned to the national security advisor and other ad hoc groupings of experts and associates when it became apparent that the state department lacked sufficient authority over other departments. Kennedy also dismantled Eisenhower's NSC staff structure, which blurred the distinction between policy making and implementation that had been clear under his predecessor. President Lyndon B. Johnson often relied on informal groups of experts and friends for advice on diplomatic issues. The elaborate NSC machinery established during the Eisenhower administration continued to shrink in the Johnson years.

During the administrations of presidents Richard Nixon and Gerald Ford, the NSC staff, under the direction of Secretary of State Henry Kissinger, provided intelligence to the national security advisor who, in turn, presented the president with a range of decisions on foreign policy issues. This arrangement reflected the executive style of President Nixon, who preferred detailed written evaluations to informal advisory groups. Although Kissinger attempted to restore the distinction between policy formulation and its execution, as secretary of state he frequently found himself performing both, such as the negotiation of the 1973 Paris peace accords to end the Vietnam War.

President Jimmy Carter continued to rely on his national security advisor as a primary source of foreign affairs consultation. National security staff members were recruited and managed to fit this arrangement.

However, the national security advisor's proximity to the president created tensions among other NSC members, which were often noted in the press.

In the 1980s, President Ronald Reagan returned to a collegial style of policy making, with his chief of staff coordinating between and among cabinet members. This arrangement, however, eventually collapsed amid highly publicized conflicts between department heads. NSC staff emerged as a separate entity vying for power during this time.

Reagan's successor, President George H. W. Bush, brought considerable foreign policy experience to the presidency and successfully restored a collegial approach to foreign policy issues in the NSC. President Bush reorganized the NSC to include a principal's committee, deputies committee, and eight policy-coordinating committees. The NSC guided U.S. diplomacy during such crucial events as the fall of the Soviet Union, German reunification, and Operation Desert Storm.

President Bill Clinton continued to emphasize an informal, collegial approach within the NSC during his two terms in office. Clinton also expanded NSC membership to its present form by officially including the secretary of the treasury, the ambassador to the United Nations, the assistant for economic policy, the president's chief of staff, and the national security advisor.

Entering into the 21st century, President George W. Bush molded the NSC into a close circle of advisers to direct the global war on terrorism following the terrorist attacks of September 11, 2001, and the Iraq War of 2003. Because President Bush particularly valued loyalty among his advisers and associates, those with dissenting views resigned or found their influence diminished. Among NSC members in the Bush administration, the vice-president, secretary of defense, and national security advisor are among those who have wielded the most influence in shaping foreign policy and military deployments.

Since the National Security Act of 1947, the NSC has played a central role in shaping and implementing U.S. foreign policy. Although the membership of the council and the influence it wields have changed significantly over nearly 60 years and nine presidents, National Security Council members are a steady hand guiding American diplomacy through turbulent times.

See also National Security Act (1947); National Security Agency (NSA)

NATIONAL SECURITY DECISION DIRECTIVE (NSDD)

Highest-level documents issued by modern U.S. presidents pertaining to all elements of U.S. national security policy: foreign policy, defense policy, intelligence, and international economic policy, as well as organizational structure and initiatives. These directives are signed or authorized by the president and issued by the National Security Council (NSC). Many recent directives are classified as top secret or higher and have been given different names by different presidential administrations.

Documents from the Truman and Eisenhower administrations, called NSC policy papers, combined a study of a particular subject with policy recommendations. These papers were accepted in their original form and became the basis for policy or were sent back by the NSC for revision. A less formal system was introduced in the Kennedy administration, which instituted the National Security Action Memorandum (NSAM), a series of study directives and decision directives. Study directives are commissioned by the NSC or other government agencies to perform studies and serve as aids to decision making. Decision directives announce policy decisions, but might also ask for studies and reports. Sources for the studies and implementing documents include a wide range of government agencies, including the departments of state, defense, and justice, the Central Intelligence Agency (CIA), and the Joint Chiefs of Staff (JCS).

Each administration assigned new names for the directives. Thus, study memoranda and decision directives became presidential review memoranda (PRMs) and presidential directives (PDs) in the Clinton administration. The practice of separating decision and study directives ended when President George W. Bush signed National Security Presidential Directive (NSPD) 1 in February 2001. That directive abolished both the presidential decision directives (PDDs) and presidential review directives (PRDs) of the Clinton administration and replaced both with the NSPD series.

A recent variation of security directives came in the wake of the September 11, 2001, terrorist attacks on New York and Washington, DC. President Bush designated special presidential directives called homeland security presidential directives (HSPDs) to be issued by the president of the United States with the advice and consent of the Homeland Security Council. The first such directive created the Homeland Security Council, whereas the second changed immigration policies to combat terrorism.

—John D. Becker

See also National Security Act (1947); National Security Council (NSC); National Security Strategy of the United States; National Security Strategy Reports

NATIONAL SECURITY EDUCATION ACT OF 1991

The brainchild of U.S. Senator David Boren of Oklahoma, federal legislation that created the National Security Education Board, the National Security Education Program, and a trust fund in the U.S. Treasury to provide resources for scholarships, fellowships, and grants.

In December 1991, President George H.W. Bush signed the National Security Education Act, which has a three-part mission. The act leads in developing the national capacity to educate U.S. citizens to: (1) understand foreign cultures, (2) strengthen U.S. economic competitiveness, and (3) enhance international cooperation and security.

The National Security Education Board is composed of 13 members, 7 of whom are senior federal officials, and 6 of whom are senior nonfederal officials appointed by the president of the United States. The board provides program policies and direction, as well as determining the criteria for the awards and recommending critical areas that the program should address. Supporting the board is a broadly-based group of advisers composed of distinguished Americans in the field of higher education—people who have international expertise.

The overall objectives of the National Security Education Program include equipping Americans with an understanding of less commonly taught languages and cultures that will enable the nation to remain integrally involved in global issues related to U.S. national security. The act also aims to build a critical base of future leaders, both in government service and in higher education, who have cultivated international relationships with, worked with, and studied alongside experts of other countries.

Another objective of the National Security Education program is to develop a cadre of professionals who have more than the traditional knowledge of language and culture and can use this ability to help the United States make sound decisions about and deal effectively with global issues related to U.S. national security. Finally, the legislation aims to enhance institutional capacity and increase the number of faculty who can educate U.S. citizens toward achieving these goals.

Scholarships, fellowships, and grants are made to both undergraduate and graduate students enrolled in educational institutions. They can include domestic as well as international components of language and training in regions deemed critical to the United States. One unique condition of the awards for this program is the requirement that within five years of earning their degrees, recipients must serve in the federal government, working in the general area of national security.

See also National Defense Education Act (NDEA)

NATIONAL SECURITY STRATEGY OF THE UNITED STATES

Plan that dictates the overall political and military goals of the United States and the methods used to accomplish those goals. A nation's security strategy is driven by its perceived national interests—those objectives the nation sees as vital to its survival.

EVOLUTION OF NATIONAL SECURITY STRATEGY

Throughout most of its early history, the U.S. national interests focused on laying claim to all of North America, with its vast natural resources. This goal was summed up in the phrase *Manifest Destiny*. The United States, according to this belief, was destined to expand across North America.

In his farewell address, the nation's first president, George Washington, warned his colleagues in government against becoming involved in "foreign entanglements." Washington's advice and the notion of Manifest Destiny led the United States to adopt an isolationist foreign policy. Avoiding international politics as much as possible, the government's main security concerns were internal challenges such as the regional dispute over slavery and conflicts with Native Americans.

The Spanish-American War of 1898 ushered in a major change in U.S. national security strategy. With its victory, the United States gained possession over Spanish colonies in Cuba, Puerto Rico, and the Philippines. Suddenly, the United States had several foreign possessions; this made avoiding international politics extremely difficult. Even so, the United States made significant efforts to remain apart from foreign political disputes. When World War I started in 1914, the United States remained neutral. Only a series of extreme German provocations finally brought the United States into the conflict in 1917.

The United States reverted to an isolationist stance soon after the war's end, declining to the join the post-war League of Nations. By this time, the United States possessed the world's largest economy and was the most rapidly growing new global power. Nevertheless, it chose to absent itself from world affairs. This decision undermined the authority of the League of Nations and emboldened countries such as Germany and Japan to ignore the League's efforts to maintain peace in Europe and Asia.

When World War II began in 1939, the United States again chose to remain neutral, although the U.S. government provided significant nonmilitary assistance to Great Britain. The Japanese attack on Pearl Harbor in December 1941 ended U.S. isolationism, both in World War II and after. At the end of the war, the United States was one of two superpower nations left standing, along with the Soviet Union. The two nations, although allied to defeat Nazi Germany, were ideological enemies.

After the war, Soviet attempts to spread communism by force led the United States to abandon its historical isolationism. For the next half-century, the national security strategy of the United States would be defined by Cold War politics. The Soviet Union was the nation's primary enemy, and stopping the expansion of Soviet influence and the spread of communism were the main goals of U.S. strategy during this time.

The collapse of the Soviet Union in 1991 marked a sea change in U.S. national security strategy. That event not only eliminated the object of U.S. strategic planning for the past 45 years but also produced a host of new issues that shaped U.S. national security strategy for the 21st century. Many former Soviet-dominated nations erupted in civil war or attacked one another as long-suppressed ethnic and religious hatreds burst to the surface. Dealing with failed states and the resulting ethnic and civil conflict were important security issues of the 1990s.

The September 11, 2001, terrorist attacks on New York and Washington, DC, introduced a new element into U.S. national security policy. Although international terrorism had been a problem for years, the direct and devastating attack on U.S. soil gave the issue a new immediacy. Combating international terrorism and rogue states that supported it became the centerpiece of U.S. national security strategy.

CURRENT STRATEGY

In September 2002, President George W. Bush unveiled a comprehensive new national security strategy for the United States. Key components included combating terrorism, promoting democracy and free trade, support for offensive actions to protect America, and qualified support for multilateral security operations.

Fighting Terrorism

Terrorism, the premeditated and politically motivated attack of innocent civilians, was identified as the number one security threat for America and the world. The current plan to challenge terrorism is a three-pronged strategy: targeting terrorists and those who support them, bolstering homeland defense, and contributing to development in impoverished countries that are likely to be breeding grounds for terrorists.

U.S. operations in Afghanistan can be understood as a direct challenge to terrorist organizations and the states that support them. The Iraq War of 2003 was justified by the Bush administration's claim that President Saddam Hussein was a supporter of terrorism and had the potential to provide weapons of mass destruction (WMD) to terrorists. Current diplomatic pressures on Libya and Iran are further evidence of the Bush administration's commitment to targeting terrorist-friendly states. A policy of regime change, adopted by President Ronald Reagan during the 1980s, has again found favor as an integral component of U.S. national security. Whereas regime change under Reagan was characterized by covert attempts to overthrow unfriendly regimes, the current administration favors regime change that is carried out overtly and with significant military backing.

The current national security strategy also aims to combat terrorism by increasing resources for homeland defense. Policies regarding airport security and immigration have been particularly targeted to combat terrorism, with more federal oversight of airline security and significantly stricter immigration policies in the post–September 11 era. In addition, the administration created a new department devoted entirely to issues of domestic security: the Department of Homeland Security.

In an attempt to decrease the number of terrorists in the future, the U.S. national security strategy also recognizes the importance of development assistance. In societies in which poverty is rampant and opportunities are few, terrorists often have little difficulty recruiting members. As such, the current security strategy calls for increasing the reach of democracy and economic aid to impoverished countries that have historically been the birthplace of terrorists.

Free Trade and Democracy as a Security Strategy

Since September 11, the promotion of free trade and democracy has been articulated as critical to the security interests of the United States. Establishing democracy has been a central goal of the Bush administration, particularly in states that formerly harbored terrorists. In Afghanistan and Iraq, democracy is seen as the antidote to the emergence of extremist regimes and terrorism. China has also been targeted as a key state to undergo a democratic transformation, with many in the Bush administration believing that a democratic China would be less threatening than a communist China.

Free trade has been suggested as a powerful weapon in the fight against terrorism because it might help improve the economies of severely impoverished nations. This is seen as critical in decreasing the number of recruits for terrorist activities. Further, some observers have argued that the anti-American sentiment behind the terrorist attacks of September 11 was economically motivated. They suggest that other nations are not content with the increasing wealth of the United States and the continued impoverishment of much of the rest of the world. To the extent that free trade can address this disparity, it might be helpful for decreasing future terrorist attacks.

OFFENSIVE SECURITY POSTURE

The current national security strategy can be characterized as offensive in nature. The Bush administration has adopted a proactive strategy for instigating regime change, preventing the potential spread of WMD, and dismantling terrorist cells before they attack. This has been a point of significant controversy, with some suggesting that the United States, in its desire to fight terrorism, is actually being unjustly aggressive. Such a criticism can be heard from key U.S. allies in Europe, as well as domestically. Thus far, however, the United States has remained committed to this offensive security posture, choosing to act unilaterally and without United Nations approval in the war in Iraq.

THE UNITED STATES AND ITS ALLIES

Despite a penchant for offensive security measures that have not always received support from American allies, the current national security strategy does emphasize the importance of global cooperation in the war on terrorism and the preservation of peace. Current security policy calls for the strengthening of NATO as well as its expansion eastward across Europe. Further, increased and improved information sharing among governments is seen as critical in the war on terrorism, and the United States has been quite successful in opening information channels among European allies; the sharing of information has had more limited success among African, Middle Eastern, and Asian allies.

The United States has also recognized the importance of multilateral assistance in nation building, with the United Nations and several foreign governments providing financial aid, military support, and technical assistance in the rebuilding of Afghanistan and Iraq. This multilateral approach has clear limits, though, with current national security policy stating that when necessary, the United States will not hesitate to act unilaterally to protect its security.

NATIONAL SECURITY IN THE 21ST CENTURY

U.S. national security strategy in the 21st century is likely to continue to focus on nonstate actors and the proliferation of chemical, biological, and nuclear weapons of mass destruction. The threats of rogue states, as well as the difficulties of failed states, are likely to remain strong challengers to the security of the United States. It is too early to assess whether long-term development strategies will prove to be effective insurance against threats to American security, but certainly such programs will be closely monitored for their efficacy. Finally, U.S. national security strategy currently contains strands of unilateralism and multilaterism, and the balance between these two principles will likely be a critical question in the coming century.

—Erica Bouris

See also Border Policy; Bush Doctrine; Bush, George W., and National Policy; Cold War; Communism and National Security; Containment and the Truman Doctrine; Democracy, Promotion of, and Terrorism; Development, Third-World; Globalization and National Security; Grand Strategy; Homeland Security; Immigration and National Security; Interventionism; Isolationism; Manifest Destiny; Multilateralism; New World Order; Preemptive War Doctrine; Terrorism, War on International; Trade and Foreign Aid; Unilateralism

Further Reading

Columbus, Frank, ed. *The National Security Strategy of the United States of America.* New York: Nova Science Publications, 2003.

Korb, Lawrence J. *A New National Security Strategy in an Age of Terrorists, Tyrants, and Weapons of Mass Destruction: Three Options Presented as Presidential Speeches.* Washington, DC: Council on Foreign Relations Press, 2004.

NATIONAL SECURITY STRATEGY REPORTS

Annual reports to Congress that describe the national security goals of the United States and the strategies used to accomplish those goals. The reports, which are prepared by the National Security Council (NSC), examine various issues that shape national security goals, including U.S. foreign policy, military and security commitments overseas, and current national defense capabilities. They also feature proposals for the short-term and long-term use of political, economic, and military power to promote U.S. interests, and they evaluate the effectiveness of these elements of national power in supporting national security strategy.

Section 108 of the National Security Act of 1947 calls for the president to submit a comprehensive report on the national security strategy of the United States to Congress every year. A sitting president must present both the national security strategy report and the following year's federal budget to Congress on the same date. A newly elected president must submit the report within 150 days of taking office. The report is submitted in two forms: a classified version for officials with high security clearances and an unclassified version available to the public.

The first national security strategy report was NSC-68, presented to Congress by President Harry S. Truman in 1950. Truman's report focused on the growing rivalry between the United States and the Soviet Union since the end of World War II. It outlined the doctrine of containment—the worldwide use of American political and military power to resist the spread of communism—that dominated U.S. foreign policy during the Cold War era. Each president since that time has submitted reports that have reflected the most pressing national security issues of the day and indicated the direction of national security policy.

The national security strategy report submitted by President George W. Bush in September 2002 signaled a major change in U.S. security policy. Since the 1950s, the United States pursued a policy of deterrence—the threat of massive retaliation to prevent attacks against it or its allies. The report of September 2002 called for a new policy of preemption, in which the United States announced its intention to strike at enemies it perceived as threats before they actually attacked.

This change came about largely because of the September 11, 2001, terrorist attacks against the United States. The Bush administration maintained that the United States could no longer afford to wait until it was attacked by terrorist groups or states that support terrorists to respond to the threat they posed. In addition to changes in military policy, the report also proposed changes in the structure and organization of the U.S. military to enable it to meet these new security challenges.

Despite its focus on armed threats, the national security strategy report considers more than military policies and strategies. For example, the September 2002 report outlined diplomatic and economic policies to work with other nations and international organizations to defuse conflicts around the world. It also presented plans to promote the spread of free market economic principles and to reduce the toll of HIV and AIDS and other infectious diseases. These aspects of the report reflected the belief that providing effective national security depends as much on addressing economic and social challenges as it does on meeting military threats.

—John Haley

See also National Security Agency; National Security Council (NSC); NSC-68 (National Security Report); September 11/WTC and Pentagon Attacks; Terrorism, War on International

NATIONAL SECURITY, U.S. COMMISSION ON (USCNS)

A federal advisory commission, more commonly known as the Rudman-Hart Commission, formed under President Bill Clinton and funded by the secretary of defense, established to look comprehensively at how the United States provided for its own security since the National Security Act of 1947.

Cochaired by Senator Warren Rudman and Senator Gary Hart, the U.S. Commission on National Security (USCNS) included 12 other prominent Americans chosen by the secretary of defense, the secretary of state, and the national security advisor. The commission released three reports over three years (1999–2001) that warned of the potential for terrorist attacks at home, and offered a long list of short- and longer-term reforms.

The report, whose final volume was released shortly before the September 11, 2001, attacks, warned that "attacks against American citizens on American soil causing heavy casualties are likely over the next quarter century." It added, "These attacks may involve weapons of mass destruction and weapons of mass disruption," and that "The United States is today very poorly organized to design and implement any comprehensive strategy to protect the homeland."

Chartered in 1998, the USCNS's project was intended as a study that would last two and a half years, and was divided into three phases of research. The first report, completed on September 15, 1999, entitled, "New World Coming: American Security in the 21st Century," endeavored to describe the world as it would emerge in the first quarter of the 21st century. Among its conclusions, the report stated that "America will become increasingly vulnerable to hostile attack on our homeland, and our military superiority will not entirely protect us," and "Foreign crises will be replete with atrocities and the deliberate terrorizing of civilian populations."

The second phase of the report, completed on April 15, 2000, entitled, "Seeking a National Strategy: A Concert for Preserving Security and Promoting Freedom," attempted to devise a U.S. national security strategy to deal with the world in 2025. The report defined an American strategy based on U.S. interests and key objectives. It outlined a "strategy for America to reap the benefits of a more integrated world to expand freedom, security, and prosperity and to dampen the forces of instability."

The third and final report, "Roadmap for National Security: Imperative for Change," was completed on February 15, 2001. That report recommended "significant and comprehensive institutional and procedural changes throughout the Executive and Legislative Branches in order to meet the challenges of 2025." The report suggested major changes to many of the executive branch departments and recommended the creation of a department of homeland security.

The USCNS consisted of Gary Hart and Warren Bruce Rudman as cochairs, with 12 additional commissioners: Anne Armstrong, Norm R. Augustine, John Dancy, John R. Galvin, Leslie H. Gelb, Newt Gingrich, Lee H. Hamilton, Lionel H. Olmer, Donald B. Rice, James R. Schlesinger, Harry D. Train II, and Andrew Jackson Young, Jr.

—*Eric Watnik*

See also Homeland Security, Department of; National Security Act (1947)

Further Reading

Hart, Gary. *America—Still Unprepared, Still in Danger*, http://www.cfr.org/pdf/Homeland_TF.pdf, Council on Foreign Relations, October 17, 2002.
"New World Coming: American Security in the 21st Century." http://www.cfr.org/pdf/Hart-Rudman1.pdf, Council on Foreign Relations website.
"Roadmap for National Security: Imperative for Change." http://www.cfr.org/pdf/Hart-Rudman3.pdf, Council on Foreign Relations website.
"Seeking a National Strategy: A Concert for Preserving Security and Promoting Freedom." http://www.cfr.org/pdf/Hart-Rudman2.pdf, Council on Foreign Relations website.

NATIONALISM

Political concept in which a group of people living in the same area derives a common identity from shared governance. Nationalism is what causes the people of a territory to recognize one another as sharing the same general goals and encourages them to work together toward those goals honoring that nation above all others. It is also what gives the government legitimacy and allows it to make decisions in the name of the citizenry.

CHARACTERISTICS OF NATIONALISM

Nationalism stands in contrast to group identity based on race, ethnicity, language, or religion. However, any or all of these elements can be associated with the nationalism of a particular country. For example, most modern European countries arose from related linguistic and ethnic groups. Thus, shared language and ethnicity play a role in the nationalism of those states. By contrast, the borders of most modern African states were drawn by European colonial powers in the 1800s, ignoring the local distribution of ethnic and linguistic groups. As a result, many of these nations contain several distinct—and often historically hostile—groups that compete for power and resources. This has been the source of much of modern Africa's instability.

Nationalism in the United States stemmed largely from the shared economic and political sentiments of British colonists in 18th century North America. American merchants and manufacturers were opposed to British laws that restricted what kinds of goods the colonies could produce and with whom they could trade. The practice of billeting British soldiers in colonial homes and forcing the colonies to pay for the soldiers' expenses also rankled many Americans. These grievances united colonists who disagreed over other issues such as slavery or religious practice.

Factors other than economics and politics also played a unifying role in colonial America. Americans were mostly white and European, and many of those who were not were slaves. In addition, although the religious affiliations of Americans included a wide variety of sects, most of them shared basic Christian beliefs. No other major religion competed for Americans' faith. These additional factors provided a broad base of common support for U.S. nationalism.

Nationalism has psychological as well as physical dimensions. It can include love of one's state or nation, but can also extend to a feeling of superiority over other states or nations. Nationalism can reflect the sentiment of different peoples sharing a common identity within a state or peoples with different identities seeking to found a new state of their own. It can lead to calls to unite against an outside enemy that threatens the common identity or calls to rid the state of perceived enemies within. Although nationalism has often led to great sacrifice and patriotism, it has also been used to justify repression, ethnic violence, and genocide.

FORMS OF NATIONALISM

Two major forms of nationalism include large group identity and inclusion, and small group identity and separation. The first brings disparate peoples together into a common state; the second exists when a group or groups of people within a state seek to separate from it. Both forms of nationalism have had positive and negative effects, historically, and both have the potential to reduce or inflame security concerns.

Large Group Identity and Inclusion

The formation of large group identity can be thought of as the nationalism of unity because it involves creating a single people out of separate groups. In Europe, the ancient Roman Republic (and later Roman Empire) created a nationalism based on shared Roman citizenship that united peoples from Spain to the Middle East. After the fall of the Roman Empire, Europe splintered into hundreds of separate ethnic and linguistic groups with no powerful central authority.

Beginning around 750 CE, kings arose in Europe to unify local groups who shared similar cultural and ethnic ties. By the year 1100, stable kingdoms arose in England, France, and Spain that would stand for hundreds of years. These lands eventually shed their kings, but their people retained a shared identity based on hundreds of years of common political leadership.

Drawing peoples together, however, can have significant negative consequences as well. States and empires seeking to create a single culture sometimes repress minority cultures in the interest of unity, and they can mask diversity by presenting a unified front. This was particularly evident in the case of Russia, and later the Soviet Union and the countries that fell under its domination during World War II.

During the 17th century, Russia began a dramatic expansion of its empire that eventually led to Russian control over one-sixth of the world's land surface. Included in this territory were thousands of different ethnic and linguistic groups practicing hundreds of separate religions. As in Africa, many were longtime and bitter adversaries. To control these tensions and maintain order, Russian czars brutally repressed ethnic and religious minorities and imposed Russian culture on its conquered territories.

This practice continued after communists overthrew the Russian government in 1917. The Soviet Union that arose from the former Russian Empire extended it by resettling large numbers of people as a way to destroy troublesome groups. Following World War II, these same methods were used in other communist countries, particularly in multiethnic Yugoslavia. As the Soviet system collapsed between 1989 and 1991, ethnic and religious tensions erupted in Yugoslavia and in several Soviet republics. Conflicts in Bosnia, Kosovo, Chechnya, Azerbaijan, and Georgia are some of the legacies of forced Russian inclusion.

Small Group Identity and Separatism

In contrast with inclusion, small group identity is the nationalism of separatism, in which groups within an existing nation break away from the state. This typically occurs when a minority population feels marginalized on religious, ethnic, linguistic, cultural, or economic grounds. The minority feels that the government of the state in which they are living is hostile to their interests, and they seek a separate autonomous territory or outright independence.

History is filled with examples of smaller subgroups seeking independence from the larger nations. The Kurdish people in the Middle East have been seeking to create their own state for hundreds of years. During that time, they have fought Mongol khans, Ottoman sultans, British kings and queens, and modern Middle Eastern democrats and dictators. In Europe, Basques of the border region between Spain and France have long sought independence from both of those nations. Like many separatist movements, both the Basques and the Kurds have often resorted to violence to advance their causes. By contrast, the French-speaking people of Quebec have tried unsuccessfully several times to vote to secede from Canada. They have not engaged in organized violence to gain their independence, however.

The record of separatist movements in established nations is checkered at best. Most disaffected minority groups in any country are too small or too divided to achieve independence. However, there have been a few recent exceptions. The nation of Eritrea successfully separated from Ethiopia in 1993, and the province of East Timor won independence from Indonesia in 2002.

NEGATIVE EFFECTS OF NATIONALISM

Nationalism frequently has been misused to justify the marginalization or oppression of certain groups, including such extreme measures as forced expulsion, mass detention, ethnic cleansing, and genocide. Governments that practice such policies justify them as necessary to "purify" the nation by removing the so-called undesirables.

Historically, nation building often has included the expulsion of minority ethnic or religious groups that were not part of the dominant culture. In medieval Europe, for example, Jews were expelled from England, Spain, and other places by Christian communities seeking a monocultural society. The United States' principle of Manifest Destiny, which entailed nationalist expansionism across the continent, led the government to remove Native Americans from their lands so that white settlers could appropriate those lands.

Nationalism in the past and present has included a strong expansionist element. Attempts to bring similar peoples under the umbrella of a single empire or nation, to glorify one nation through acquisition of others' territory, or to conquer peoples considered inferior to serve the needs of the nation often have encroached on the rights of other groups. All these elements were part of the nationalist expansion of Germany under Adolf Hitler in the 1930s and 1940s.

Hitler deliberately reinforced nationalistic tendencies by trying to create a strong German identity and a deep love of the German fatherland. This shared identity brought hope to a people devastated by World War I and the humiliating terms of the Treaty of Versailles that ended the war. However, Hitler's Nazi Party also manipulated public opinion to make the country's Jews the scapegoat for its ills and to convince Germans of the superiority of their culture to those of other peoples. Ideas of "Aryan" superiority were used to justify Germany's right to seize lands from "inferior" peoples and exploit those people for the benefit of the German nation. This attitude led to World War II and the subsequent Holocaust, in which millions of innocent people were slaughtered.

Nationalism can be used to justify atrocities on both sides if two separate groups lay claim to the same lands. Both the Israelis and the Palestinians have put forth historic claims for their nations in the region known as the Holy Land. For both groups, the city of Jerusalem is a sacred site. Both Israelis and Arabs have attempted to establish exclusive rights in Palestine, and they have resorted to land appropriation and war to consolidate their claims.

NATIONALISM AND SECURITY

Nationalism can be used to strengthen a state, and internal stability can promote external stability. Crafting a common identity, affirming a common history, drawing on similar mythologies, and ensuring equality for disparate groups can prevent separatist movements and foster support for the country in which different groups live. The common identity that supports, but does not supplant, ethnic or religious or other small group identities is often the most successful form of nationalism.

Although nationalism can strengthen a state, nationalistic factions can also destroy states or peoples from the inside. Repression of groups based on language, ethnicity, religion, or culture often leads to separatist movements because the repressed groups perceive that the state opposes their interests. If the separatist movements succeed, the result can be partition and a total loss of resources to the newly independent territory, diminishing the economic base of the original state.

Nationalism can also foster outside opposition that undermines a state's security. Secession movements by peoples seeking greater autonomy can weaken a state and make it more susceptible to external threats such as invasion. Importantly, nationalism taken to extremes (as in the case of Hitler's Germany) can also spur other states to intervene on behalf of the repressed groups. More recently, the ethnic and religious conflict between Serbs, Croats, and Muslims in Bosnia led to intervention by both the United Nations and the North Atlantic Treaty Organization (NATO), both of which intervened to restore order and stability to the region.

The increasing technological and cultural interconnectedness of the modern world presents a threat to nationalism. Multinational corporations, for example, operate in many different countries and seek private gain above the interests of the state. The loyalty of shareholders and employees of such corporations are therefore often divided between what is good for the company and what is good for the nation.

The growth of international terrorism also threatens to undermine nationalism by challenging the legitimacy of governments that oppose terrorist goals. Al-Qaeda and other Islamic terror groups, for example, call for an overthrow of all western-influenced governments in the Islamic world and war against those who support them. In many Middle Eastern countries, these groups seek to drive a wedge between the government and the people. They hope to replace the current governments with regimes based on Islamic law and shared Muslim culture, and ultimately with a state that encompasses all Islamic lands. Islamic terrorism thus represents a rejection of modern nationalism in favor of a return to empire based on common religion.

See also Colonialism; Decolonization; Ethnic Cleansing; Genocide; Globalization and National Security; Hegemony; Manifest Destiny; McCarthyism; Nation-State; New World Order; Propaganda; Regionalism; Sovereignty; Terrorists, Islamic

Further Reading

Hastings, Adrian. *The Construction of Nationhood: Ethnicity, Religion and Nationalism.* Cambridge, UK: Cambridge University Press, 1997.
Moaddel, Mansoor. *Islamic Modernism, Nationalism, and Fundamentalism: Episode and Discourse.* Chicago: University of Chicago Press, 2005.
Puri, Jyoti. *Encountering Nationalism.* Oxford, UK: Blackwell, 2003.

REFLECTIONS

Notes on Nationalism

In 1945, the internationally known British author and political philosopher George Orwell published a brief essay titled "Notes on Nationalism." In the piece, he outlined what he believed were the basic features, strengths, and drawbacks of nationalism. He also drew a distinction between patriotism and nationalism, which he summed up as follows:

Nationalism is not to be confused with patriotism. Both words are normally used in so vague a way that any definition is liable to be challenged, but one must draw a distinction between them, since two different and even opposing ideas are involved. By "patriotism" I mean devotion to a particular place and a particular way of life, which one believes to be the best in the world but has no wish to force on other people. Patriotism is of its nature defensive, both militarily and culturally. Nationalism, on the other hand, is inseparable from the desire for power. The abiding purpose of every nationalist is to secure more power and more prestige, not for himself but for the nation or other unit in which he has chosen to sink his own individuality . . .

A nationalist is one who thinks solely, or mainly, in terms of competitive prestige. . . . He sees history, especially contemporary history, as the endless rise and decline of great power units, and every event that happens seems to him a demonstration that his own side is on the upgrade and some hated rival is on the downgrade. But finally, it is important not to confuse nationalism with mere worship of success. The nationalist does not go on the principle of simply ganging up with the strongest side. On the contrary, having picked his side, he persuades himself that it *is* the strongest, and is able to stick to his belief even when the facts are overwhelmingly against him. Nationalism is power-hunger tempered by self-deception. Every nationalist is capable of the most flagrant dishonesty, but he is also—since he is conscious of serving something bigger than himself—unshakably certain of being in the right.

NATION BUILDING

The process of rebuilding infrastructure, government, and industry in postconflict or failed states. One of the largest projects of nation building during the 20th century was the reconstruction of Germany and Japan after World War II. Since the end of the Cold War, the United States has again been drawn into the arduous task of helping nations rebuild after years of conflict and violence.

The two most recent attempts at nation building can be seen in Afghanistan and Iraq. Following the U.S.-led interventions in each of these nations, the United States, supported by members of the international community, has worked to help these nations develop their governments, rebuild vital infrastructures (including roads, power systems and schools), and lay the groundwork for functioning and productive industry.

Nation building is a process filled with challenge—it is expensive, time-consuming, and often only marginally successful. Some of the many challenges include the introduction of a democratic form of government in a state that may have been ruled by tyranny for many years. There might be a shortage of qualified, educated leaders to fill government positions, corruption might be rampant, and the norms of democracy, including voting and civilly managing conflict, might not be well-established among the population of the country.

Particularly in protracted conflicts (such as in the Balkans during the 1990s), the possibility of significant devastation to basic infrastructure is high. Although the rebuilding of infrastructure is a high priority in nation building, garnering the necessary resources and protecting these projects from postconflict flares of violence is often challenging. Particularly in rural areas, it often takes many years to rebuild roads, install power lines and water purification systems, and rebuild and staff schools.

Ideally, rebuilding the infrastructure and establishing a functioning government provides the basis for the return of industry. Here, too, there are significant challenges, including the lack of an educated workforce, the decimation or nonexistence of natural resources, and sometimes the control of economic resources by a small group of elites unwilling to contribute to the overall economic health of the populace. In addition, nations that for years have been mired in conflict might find it particularly difficult to compete on the global market.

One final challenge in the process of nation building is the ever-present threat that violent conflict might return. As the process of nation building in Iraq has demonstrated, members of the deposed regime can and often do violently disrupt the process of nation building.

Despite obstacles, nation building remains an important task for the international community. It serves to promote national stability, spreads a doctrine of human rights and democracy, and, if successful, can significantly improve the quality of life for those who live in postconflict societies. The international community's continued experience with nation building has led to the adoption of certain best practices.

First, it is clearly critical to involve all ethnic, religious, and minority groups within the state in the process. Doing so ensures that the democratic goals of representative government can be met, and further decreases the likelihood of marginalized groups challenging the legitimacy of the new government. Second, adequate resources, are important; as the United States quickly learned in Iraq, rebuilding a nation takes significant financial resources—resources that few single nations can afford to commit. Soliciting aid from the

United Nations, other foreign nations, and nongovernmental organizations is clearly critical if nation building is to be successful.

The international community has learned about the importance of carefully timing and managing the inaugural elections. The first elections are a time of excitement but also fear—fear that if a particular group or political party wins or loses, a return to violence might follow. The election processes in the transition from an interim government to an elected government are carefully monitored by the international community.

Finally, nation building is a long process and requires a long-term commitment—not only of resources but in terms of a military presence. Bosnia, Kosovo, Afghanistan, and Iraq continue to require the presence of foreign troops to maintain peace, and there is little indication of a withdrawal of troops in the near future.

See also Afghanistan, War in; Bosnia Intervention; Iraq War of 2003; Kosovo Intervention; Peacekeeping Operations

NATION-STATE

Autonomous area inhabited by a people sharing a common culture, history, and/or language. The term *nation-state* (or *nation-state*), although often used interchangeably with the terms *unitary state* and *independent state*, refers to recognized authorities, or states, in which a single nation is dominant. Spain, Ireland, and France are examples of nation-states. A nation-state can be a federal state at the same time (for example, the Federal Republic of Germany, the United States of America, and, previously, the Union of Soviet Socialist Republics).

The origins of the modern nation-state are traced to the Treaty of Westphalia, which most historians believe shaped subsequent relations between countries. The Treaty of Westphalia is a collective name given to the two treaties concluded on October 24, 1648, which ended the Thirty Years War, one of the most destructive conflicts in European history. The war initially pitted Protestant Germany against Catholic France and Spain, but it eventually drew in Swedes, Danes, Poles, Russians, Dutch, and Swiss. Commercial interests and rivalries played a part, as did religion and power politics.

The Peace of Westphalia established the principle of national sovereignty—the notion that states should have control of their own internal affairs without outside interference. One of the factors that sparked the war was the Holy Roman Emperor's attempt to impose Protestantism on the various kingdoms and duchies in Germany. The Peace of Westphalia recognized each state's right to choose its own religion. The German states also won the right to exercise independent foreign policies, but not to declare war on the emperor. Before the Peace of Westphalia, most European wars were sparked at least partly by religious matters. Afterward, wars became rooted in state self-interest rather than on purely religious grounds. From this point on, European powers instigated conflict in accordance with their perceived political and commercial interests.

The nation-state remains the main organizing principle in international relations, but its status has weakened in recent years. The formation of nongovernmental organizations such as the United Nations and of supra-national bodies such as the European Union (EU) have raised challenges to the ultimate authority of the nation-state. Multinational corporations have become so large and influential that they also rival state governments as sources of power and influence. In today's era of globalization, porous borders, and powerful nonstate participants, there is some debate about whether the concept of the nation-state will soon become obsolete.

See also Globalization and National Security; Nationalism

Further Reading

Rosenau, James N. *Distant Proximities: Dynamics Beyond Globalization*. Princeton, NJ: Princeton University Press, 2003.

NATO *See* NORTH ATLANTIC TREATY ORGANIZATION (NATO)

NATURAL RESOURCES AND NATIONAL SECURITY

The contribution of a nation's natural wealth to its security. Natural resources can influence security in a variety of ways. A nation that is rich in natural resources such as oil or minerals is more able to afford a strong military to defend its borders than a resource-poor nation. In addition, a nation possessing a rich variety of natural resources is likely to enjoy greater economic security because it is not dependent upon foreign sources of vital commodities. On the other hand, poor government in a wealthy country can cause significant instability as competing interests struggle for control of the nation's wealth. Many resource-rich African nations have been plagued by unrest and civil war caused by weak or corrupt central governments.

World War II provides an excellent example of a direct relationship between natural resources and the security of a nation. The Axis Powers, Germany and Japan, being neither as large nor as rich in natural resources as the United States, had to conquer and subdue vast overseas empires to fuel and supply their respective militaries. The United States, on the other hand, was able to shift its own massive domestic industrial base quickly from consumer to wartime production. U.S. factories easily out-produced those of Germany and Japan combined, becoming the driving engine of the final Allied victory.

The reality of U.S. industrial superiority was recognized by its foes. Japanese Admiral Isoroku Yamamoto, who planned the attack on Pearl Harbor, is alleged to have remarked that the attack had awakened a "sleeping giant." A German soldier captured by the Americans in Europe recalled feeling that his country was foolish to declare war on a nation that could fill the horizon with tanks and planes. In this case, both Germany and Japan were defeated in a prolonged conventional war with a resource-rich nation dubbed by its own leader an "arsenal of democracy."

The post–World War II world, by contrast, offers several examples of resource-poor nations increasing national security by achieving economic success. After its defeat in World War II, Japan was occupied and rebuilt by U.S. forces under a program called *centrally planned capitalism*. Under this plan, the Japanese government promoted and protected industries that imported raw materials to create goods for export. The result was a boom in the Japanese export trade, which brought in large sums of money that fueled Japan's economy. Between 1945 and 2000, Japan went from a broke and war-devastated country to the world's second largest economy. Besides enriching the country, Japan's economic might made it a valuable asset to the United States and other capitalist

nations. Because the United States forbade the Japanese from maintaining large armed forces after the war, U.S. forces have provided security guarantees to Japan since 1945.

In a similar manner, resource-poor South Korea was devastated by the Korean War (1950–1953) and faced a hostile North Korea across the 38th parallel. South Korea developed close ties between government and industry to create industrial conglomerates known as *chaebols*. Like Japan, this government-business partnership led to export success; by 2000, South Korea was the 12th-largest economy in the world. The Korean success also had a complex relation with the U.S. military protection of South Korea. Following the Korean War, the reasons for U.S. security guarantees to South Korea were mainly ideological—South Korea was a symbol of western refusal to accept the forcible expansion of communism. After the South Korean economy blossomed, however, defending the country's large capitalist economy became an added reason for U.S. protection.

Recent history shows that many factors must be taken into account when considering the relationship between natural resources and national security. Nations blessed with a rich variety of natural resources might see their national security threatened by incompetent governance at home and military might from abroad. Resource-poor nations might ensure a strong economy as well as their national security through close alliance with a foreign power that provides an export market along with its military might.

The appearance of asymmetrical threats such as terrorism, however, threatens to challenge the relationship between natural resources and security. Natural resources contribute to the formal state-organized capacity for defense and military action, whereas terrorists tend to concentrate on civilian targets. As demonstrated by the September 11, 2001, terrorist attacks on New York and Washington, DC, a handful of determined individuals using relatively crude weapons can slip past the defenses of even the most sophisticated military forces. In such an environment, nontangible resources such as international cooperation, communication, and information sharing might prove more valuable than traditional natural resources in ensuring national security.

See also Asymmetric Warfare; Korea, North and South; U.S.-Japan Alliance destroy one another. The nuclear arms race was underpinned by the notion of mutually assured destruction (MAD), requiring the maintenance of a state of affairs in which the prospect of launching a nuclear offensive would always be deterred by the likelihood of a devastating counterstrike. An oft-cited contributing cause for the collapse of the Soviet Union was the inability to afford competition with the United States in building and maintaining a large nuclear arsenal.

The development of nuclear weapons required extensive testing and also resulted in a large number of accidents because of radioactive contamination. The problem of nuclear proliferation (i.e., the development of nuclear weapons by nations other than the United States, the Soviet Union (Russia), Great Britain, and China) was recognized even during the Cold War. Because they are so powerful, the development of nuclear weapons by countries previously not possessing them consistently provokes controversy in the international community. In recent years, concern has shifted to the possibility of a nuclear attack by terrorists.

DEVELOPMENT OF NUCLEAR WEAPONS

The potential power of the atom was understood before the outbreak of World War II, a conflict ultimately ended by nuclear weapons. Developments in theoretical physics during the early 20th century laid the foundations of knowledge for nuclear weapons. In 1905, Albert Einstein published his theory of general relativity, in which he showed that mass and energy are basically the same thing and that mass can be turned into energy. Einstein and other physicists realized that if enough mass could be turned into energy at once, the power generated by the reaction would be tremendous. This raised the happy possibility of creating a nearly perpetual source of energy, but also the dark shadow of a terrible source of destructive power.

THE MANHATTAN PROJECT

In 1938, German chemists Otto Hahn and Fritz Strassman were the first scientists to split an atom successfully. The following year, the publication of the process of nuclear fission by Lise Meitner and Otto Robert Frisch made the development of atomic weapons seem increasingly feasible. Chillingly, both of these advances occurred in Nazi Germany, a totalitarian country seemingly bent on dominating Europe by force.

In 1939, Einstein and several colleagues wrote a letter to U.S. President Franklin D. Roosevelt, alerting him to the dangerous possibilities resulting from recent discoveries in nuclear physics. Roosevelt decided that it was imperative for the United States and Great Britain to develop nuclear weapons before the Germans did. That year, the U.S. government initiated the Manhattan Project to research the creation and construction of a nuclear weapon. Research was directed by Robert J. Oppenheimer, an eccentric genius who received his Ph.D. in theoretical physics from Harvard University at the age of 22.

The Manhattan Project was based at New York City's Columbia University, but most of the research and development work was carried out at Los Alamos, New Mexico, the University of Chicago, the Oak Ridge National Laboratory in Oak Ridge, Tennessee, and the Hanford site in Washington state. These last two (designated Site X and Site W, respectively) were charged with producing uranium and plutonium, the nuclear fuel used to power the weapon.

The Germans and the Japanese were also conducting research to develop an atomic bomb during World War II. The Japanese were still many years away from success by the time the war ended, but the status of the project under the Nazis is more controversial. The German atomic weapons program was led by Werner Heisenberg, a close friend and coworker of Niels Bohr, who later contributed to the Manhattan Project. The question of where Heisenberg's loyalties lay with regard to the Nazis and the reasons for his personal fallout with Bohr inspired wide speculation. Some suggest that Heisenberg had moral qualms about developing a Nazi atomic bomb, but others contend he had no such reservations. In any event, the Germans were unsuccessful in producing a nuclear weapon before the end of the war.

USING THE BOMB

By the summer of 1945, the Manhattan Project had produced two working atomic bombs. One was a uranium-based bomb called Little Boy; the other was a plutonium-based weapon dubbed Fat Man. With Japan still unwilling to surrender, and facing the possibility of an invasion that could cost as many as a million lives, U.S. President Harry S. Truman ordered the dropping of the world's first nuclear weapon on Japan. On August 6, 1945, Little Boy obliterated the Japanese city of Hiroshima. Three days later, with no

Naval Aviation 513

Further Reading

Blank, Steven. *Natural Resources and National Security Policy: Sources of Conflict and the U.S. Interest.* Carlisle, PA: Strategic Studies Institute, U.S. Army War College, 2001.

Klare, Michael T. *Resource Wars: The New Landscape of Global Conflict.* New York: Owl Books, 2002.

NAVAL AVIATION

Planes and pilots in service to the U.S. Navy. Naval aviators operate from aircraft carriers—warships designed for the launching and landing of aircraft at sea. These carriers facilitate the mobility of U.S. air power and reduce reliance on permanent air bases overseas in foreign territory.

The Navy's interest in aviation began as early as 1898, when naval officers were appointed to an inter-service board that considered the military potential of the airplane. Naval observers subsequently attended air meets in the United States and overseas, as well as public demonstrations by Oliver and Wilbur Wright. In 1910, the Navy designated an officer to be in charge of aviation matters. The following year the first naval officer reported for flight training and the Navy purchased its first plane.

An American pilot, Eugene Ely, was the first person to take off successfully from a stationary ship. In 1910, Ely took off from a temporary platform built on the deck of the cruiser USS *Birmingham*. The following year, he became the first person to land on a stationary ship—the battleship USS *Pennsylvania*. In these early days of naval aviation, existing ships were modified to accommodate aircraft. However, in 1922, Japan built the first ship specifically designed to launch and retrieve aircraft. At the same time, the United States tested small air detachments in exercises with ocean fleets. The United States also began building aircraft carriers in the 1920s, and three carriers were in service with the Navy by the end of the decade.

The Great Depression of the 1930s had a stifling impact on the development of U.S. naval aviation. America's economic problems and isolationist attitude toward international affairs meant less funding for the military. However, the growing threat of an aggressive and expansionist Japan, with its powerful carrier-based navy, led to increased training of U.S. Navy pilots in the late 1930s.

On December 7, 1941, Japan demonstrated the power of naval aviation with a surprise attack on the U.S. fleet at Pearl Harbor, Hawaii. Four Japanese carriers, lying some 250 miles northwest of Pearl Harbor, launched more than 400 dive-bombers, torpedo bombers, and escorting fighters against the unsuspecting Americans. Tactically, the raid was a complete success: The Japanese sank or seriously damaged 12 large U.S. warships, destroyed or damaged more than 300 aircraft, and killed 2,403 U.S. troops and civilians on the base. However, the primary targets of the attack, the U.S. carriers, were not in port that day and so escaped damage. The following summer at the Battle of Midway, those U.S. carriers would inflict a crippling defeat against Japan, sinking four Japanese carriers and their experienced and irreplaceable aircrews.

Naval aviation played a key role in land warfare during World War II in the Pacific. To overcome Japan, the United States first had to defeat dozens of fortified island outposts located hundreds of miles from the nearest U.S. airbases. Naval aircraft were invaluable to amphibious invasions of these islands, softening up Japanese defenses before U.S. troops landed, and providing support for the actual attacks. By the end of the war, it was clear that the day of the battleship as king of the ocean was over. The aircraft carrier had proven itself the most powerful weapon in the U.S. Navy's arsenal.

Naval aviation underwent a major revolution in the 1950s, when the Navy replaced most of its propeller-driven planes with jet aircraft (even today, the Navy retains propeller-driven planes for some weather, radar, and intelligence-gathering functions). The faster speeds at which jets travel required modifications to existing carriers and spurred the evolution of carrier design. For example, jets need a longer runway than propeller-driven planes, but there are practical limits to the size of carrier decks. The solution was to mount steam-powered catapults on the flight deck to help launch planes more quickly. Carriers also became larger to accommodate more planes and the many different types of weapons modern combat aircraft can carry.

The Korean War and Vietnam War reaffirmed the combat value of naval aviation. In Korea, Navy pilots attacked North Korean troops, supplies, and infrastructure in support of United Nations land operations. Naval aviators also performed some of the most extensive bombing campaigns in history during the Vietnam War. In both conflicts, naval aircraft operating off carriers gave the United States a powerful weapon that was almost invulnerable to its opponent. Throughout the Cold War, U.S. carrier groups served as a symbol of America's military might and commitment to defend its allies throughout the world. They also allowed the United States to respond quickly to any perceived Soviet threat in Asia or Africa.

At the end of the Cold War, navy pilots were among the first U.S. forces to participate in the invasion of Iraq in the Gulf War of 1991. Operating from carrier groups in the Indian Ocean and Persian Gulf, U.S. Navy planes flew thousands of sorties in the four days of combat. After the war, navy pilots took part in enforcing the no-fly zones for Iraqi aircraft in northern and southern Iraq. The importance of naval aviation again was demonstrated in the Iraq War in 2003. Despite the inability to base large numbers of aircraft on allied territory in the region, the United States was able to maintain substantial air power by using carrier-based aircraft.

Naval aviation's flexibility—both in mobility and in the range of duties it can perform—makes it well-suited to modern military missions. It can be as equally effective at striking terrorist bases, enemy facilities, and hostile troops. With the potential for hostilities in faraway places, including the Middle East and North Korea, naval aviation will likely continue to be a central element of U.S. military might.

See also Air Warfare; Aircraft Carrier; U.S. Navy

Further Reading

Kaplan, Philip. *Fly Navy: Naval Aviators and Carrier Aviation, A History.* New York: Metrobooks, 2001.

U.S. Museum of Naval Aviation. *U.S. Naval Aviation.* Westport, CT: Hugh Lauter Levin, 2001.

NEOCONSERVATISM

A uniquely right-wing U.S. political philosophy that seeks to promote American values across the globe, is sympathetic to traditional moral values, is highly suspicious of various forms of world government, and is overtly supportive of both the sovereign state of Israel and the broader need to maintain a democratic foothold in the Middle East. Neoconservatives believe strongly that liberal democracy is the political and economic model toward which all societies should strive. In comparison with traditional conservatives,

neoconservatives are more comfortable with the presence of the welfare state, tend to be less isolationist in philosophy, and view the People's Republic of China (PRC) as a serious and growing threat to the United States.

Neoconservatism began as an offshoot of left-wing, New York intellectualism of the 1960s and early 1970s. These intellectuals were highly supportive of U.S. social progress (particularly as it pertained to equal rights), but were troubled by what they perceived as the social excesses and weakening anticommunist stances of the political left.

Modern neoconservatives opted to leave the Democratic party in favor of the right-wing politics of conservatives Richard Nixon, Barry Goldwater, and Ronald Reagan. Although they eventually found an intellectual home within the Republican party, their mission continues to revolve around its transformation. As Irving Kristol, the so-called godfather of neoconservatives, noted in a 2003 issue of *The Weekly Standard* (a popular neoconservative magazine), the project of neoconservatism is "to convert the Republican party, and American conservatism in general, against their respective wills, into a kind of conservative politics suitable to governing a modern democracy."

During the 1980s, neoconservatism was most closely aligned with (and defined by) the staunch anticommunism of the Reagan administration. However, with the crumbling of Soviet hegemony in the 1990s, support for the neoconservative movement—and for the large military budgets that typically accompanied it—began to wane. The United States found itself in the midst of a new multilateralism, as evidenced by the formation of the Operation Desert Storm coalition during the Persian Gulf War of 1991, the passage of the North American Free Trade Agreement (NAFTA) in 1993, and the establishment of the World Trade Organization (WTO) in 1995.

Neoconservatism experienced a major setback in 1991 when President George H.W. Bush, largely on the advice of General Colin Powell, refused to remove Iraqi dictator Saddam Hussein from power and liberate the Iraqi Kurds at the conclusion of the Gulf War. However, with the election of President George W. Bush in 2000 and the introduction of a massive U.S. effort to curtail international terrorism after the terrorist attacks of September 11, 2001, neoconservatism has experienced a rebirth.

Sustained military operations in Iraq, Afghanistan, and other parts of the world reflect the neoconservative belief that the United States can ill afford simply to contain threats to the American way of life—it must prevent them altogether. More broadly, such efforts are in line with the neoconservative belief that the United States should actively flex its political, economic, and military might around the globe, and that such actions, even if they appear imperialistic, represent the best hope for bringing about a new era of peace.

The establishment of the so-called Bush Doctrine, giving the United States the moral authority to take preemptive, unilateral action abroad for the purpose of fighting international terrorism, represents a new high-water mark for the neoconservative movement. Although there is much speculation as to whether or not President George W. Bush is himself a true neoconservative, few would argue that his administration included many prominent neoconservative figures (such as Deputy Secretary of State Paul Wolfowitz), as well as others who are highly supportive of neoconservatism's stance on U.S. foreign policy (such as Vice President Richard Cheney and Defense Secretary Donald Rumsfeld).

Those most worried about the neoconservative movement and its imperial tendencies often cite as evidence a draft of the 1992 Defense Planning Guidance, written secretly by Paul Wolfowitz and Dick Cheney and leaked to the *Washington Post* shortly after it was prepared. The report argues that the top priority for U.S. interests abroad should be "to prevent the re-emergence of a new rival." The harshest critics of the foreign policy of the Bush administration insist that the ongoing war on terrorism is a thinly veiled attempt to do exactly that.

See also Bush Doctrine; Bush, George H. W., and National Policy; Bush, George W., and National Policy; Cheney, Richard (1941–); Powell, Colin (1937–); Rumsfeld, Donald (1932–)

NEUTRON BOMB

A small thermonuclear weapon that produces a minimal blast and heat while releasing large amounts of lethal radiation. Sometimes called enhanced radiation warheads, neutron bombs are designed to kill troops—especially those protected by armor. The bomb's blast and heat can be confined to a relatively small area, perhaps a few hundred feet in radius, but the bomb throws off a massive wave of neutron and gamma radiation that can penetrate armor and is extremely pernicious to humans.

The weapon can be delivered to the battlefield via missile or aircraft, or it can be launched from an 8-inch howitzer, making it effective against tanks and infantry formations. A neutron bomb disables tank crews in minutes, and troops exposed to the radiation wave die within days.

The alloys used to protect tanks can absorb the radiation and become radioactive themselves. Some types of tank armor, such as the M-1 tank, employ depleted uranium, which can undergo fast fission after being exposed to the radiation wave generated by a neutron bomb blast. These tanks remain toxic to crews for some time. The United States suspended production of neutron bombs in 1978, but production was resumed in 1981.

See also Nuclear Weapons

NEW WORLD ORDER

New era in international relations and global economics following the end of the Cold War. The phrase *new world order* came from a speech in which President George H. W. Bush described the beginnings of the Gulf War. The expression was apt for both the time and the global situation. In early 1991, the world was poised to enter a new era in international relations—the communist governments of Eastern Europe (including the Soviet Union) had collapsed, leaving the United States as the sole surviving world superpower.

The end of the intense Cold War ideological competition created a partial ideological vacuum. Part of the world, having seen the collapse of its previous framework, was ready for a new system of thought. The United States was in an ideal position to bring its ideas forward. It could also encourage other nations to embrace reforms it saw as desirable—reforms leading countries politically toward liberal democracy and neoliberal economic principles. Some regard the emerging new world order as Euro-American imperialism or as an order based on—and maintained by—U.S. power and influence. Others regard it as opening the door to a fair and just international civil society.

The plan to create such a world culture is complex and implies new priorities in international politics. First and foremost, it signifies a break from the previous competitive world order and a transformation of the international system. The new world order relies upon cooperation among nations, rather than the sometimes-precarious balance of power that existed during the Cold War. Great powers especially need to take leadership roles in creating international order.

The new world order also encourages international institution of the rule of law. Ideally, the rule of law will bring an end to impunity and to government abuses in nations around the world. President George H. W. Bush's speech also focused particularly on an expanded role for the United Nations and the UN Security Council in world affairs. These organizations could do more to help maintain international peace and security, as they were designed to do; peacekeeping operations would be especially encouraged. In addition, the new world order foresaw increased participation of international organization in world affairs. These organizations could help smooth the progress of nations toward liberal development.

Domestically, the new world order stresses the development of multiparty democracies in countries previously living under dictatorships or other forms of authoritarian rule. The creation of liberal democracies means creating governments that protect the ability of citizens to participate meaningfully in the political process, to dissent, to form opposition parties, and so on. The international community can put pressure on developing countries to form such governments; loans and other forms of assistance are often tied to the establishment of *good governance*.

The new world order also encourages different economic and social priorities. In the economic realm, liberalization of economies and increased economic interdependence are favored. By transitioning to market economies, countries around the world would be able to enjoy the fruits of capitalism. Consumers would have more choice and producers more opportunity than ever before because of the virtues of the market. Greater economic freedom would prevail. Liberalization includes the creation of laws that structure enforceable contracts and enforce rights to private property. It also includes lowering trade barriers and privatizing public industry. Trade and foreign investment are encouraged. The economic integration implied by these moves would not only produce positive economic results but would also raise the costs of warfare substantially, in the hope of promoting peace and harmony.

The new world order supports economic globalization. It also tacitly advances philosophical and social globalization. It encourages the spread of western rationalist, secularist principles around the world. These principles are intended to be the hallmarks of a world without war, a world of freedom, a world without persecution or discrimination. In some countries (such as in the former communist states of Eastern Europe), these ideas have been accepted more eagerly and have advanced social equality. In other places, however, these principles have been rejected (such as in China and Iran).

The ideas of the new world order are utopian to some extent, which leave them open to criticism. There are two principal kinds of critics of the new world order: those who want to reform it and those who reject it. The reformers believe that the move toward liberalism in politics and economics will be a long-lasting or permanent global change. Thus, they do not challenge the system itself; they criticize the vastly uneven distribution of society's benefits in a liberal market economy—poor individuals and poor countries not only receive little but also tend to get poorer. As a result, the reformers support social liberalism—a market economy that tries to correct market failures and create social safety nets.

Those rejecting the new world order want to replace it with another system entirely. Many tend to subscribe to various forms of Marxism. Some argue that the liberal system is inherently exploitative and they want to replace it with a more egalitarian order. Others who want to replace the new world order altogether loathe its insistence on secularism. Some Islamist groups, for example, oppose it on these grounds and want to replace the existing order with an Islamic society. Extremist groups around the world (including religious extremists and right-wing paramilitary groups) see the new world order as an international conspiracy of shadow governments that lies at the root of political evils. It is an idea and a system these groups want to see destroyed.

For better or worse, the idea of a new world order retains ideological dominance in international politics and economics. It continues to influence policymakers at the UN, the World Bank, the International Monetary Fund (IMF), and other multilateral institutions.

See also Multilateralism

NITZE, PAUL H. (1907–2004)

Leading strategist, arms control expert, and eminent public figure of the U.S. strategic and foreign policy establishment during the years spanning the Cold War. Born on January 16, 1907, in Amherst, Massachusetts, Paul H. Nitze was German by descent; his grandfather immigrated to the United States from Germany after the Civil War.

After graduation from Harvard University and a decade working as an investment banker, Nitze joined the U.S. government in 1940 and advised every president from Franklin Roosevelt to Ronald Reagan (with the exception of Jimmy Carter). In 1950, while at the state department, Nitze was responsible for the formulation of NSC-68—the document that provided the framework for the Cold War between the United States and the former Soviet Union. Nitze also served as director of the department of state policy planning staff, as deputy secretary of defense, and as a member of the U.S. delegation to the Strategic Arms Limitation Talks (SALT) from 1969 to 1974. In 1962, he was a member of the group of top officials who met daily with President John F. Kennedy to advise him during the Cuban Missile Crisis.

As head of the U.S. negotiating team at the arms control talks in Geneva from 1981 to 1984, Nitze took a now famous walk in the woods with Soviet negotiator Yuli Kvitsinsky in an effort to break the deadlock between the superpowers on the issue of missiles in Europe. From 1984 to 1989, he was ambassador-at-large and special adviser to the president and secretary of state on arms control matters, playing a crucial role in negotiating the Immediate-Range Nuclear Force (INF) and strategic arms treaties. President Reagan awarded Nitze the Presidential Medal of Freedom in 1985 for his contributions to the freedom and security of the United States.

Nitze founded the School of Advanced International Relations (SAIS) in 1943, along with Christian Herter and other leading statesmen. In 1989, the school, which became a division of the Johns Hopkins University in 1950, was renamed in his honor to recognize his distinguished private and public career and exceptional service to SAIS and the university for five decades.

See also Arms Control; NSC-68 (National Security Report)

REFLECTIONS
Wise Counselor

The guided missile destroyer USS *Nitze* was completed in 2004 by Bath Iron Works in Bath, Maine, and officially commissioned by the U.S. Navy on March 5,

2005. In awarding him the Medal of Freedom in 1985, President Reagan called Paul Nitze,

> the wisest of counselors, exemplifying the powers of mind, commitment and character needed to fulfill America's world responsibilities. And I think to put his name on this ship which will sail the world will be a great symbol to the world itself, to the men and women who are serving us in the Navy, in the military. And it will remind people, I think, of Paul's passionate commitment to avoid war by being prepared to fight it.

NIXON DOCTRINE (1969)

Policy announcing the U.S. intention to support its threatened allies with economic and military aid rather than ground troops. During the Vietnam War, at the beginning of a 1969 global tour, President Richard Nixon spoke with reporters on the island of Guam. In this informal discussion, Nixon stated that the United States could no longer afford to defend its allies fully. He added that although the United States would continue to uphold all of its treaty responsibilities, it would expect its allies to contribute significantly to their own defense.

Nixon also indicated that the United States would continue to extend economic and military assistance (arms), especially in cases where it was in the national interest of the United States. At the same time, he reassured U.S. allies by promising that the United States would continue to use its nuclear arsenal to shield its friends from nuclear threats.

The Nixon Doctrine was not intended to influence U.S. actions in its engagement in the Vietnam War, in which ground troops were already committed. It was, in fact, because of the tremendous drain of the Vietnam War on U.S. resources that Nixon created the doctrine. Even so, from 1969 onward, although the Nixon Doctrine was a firm message to U.S. allies, the Nixon administration did not adhere absolutely to the doctrine. The U.S. invasions into Cambodia in 1970 and Laos in 1971 employed the use of U.S. ground troops, contradicting the intentions of the doctrine.

Historians and foreign policy experts emphasize that with the Nixon Doctrine, Nixon and his national security advisor, Henry Kissinger, were intent on shifting U.S. foreign policy away from a bilateral view of international relations—that is, away from a sole focus on the U.S.-Soviet struggle for power. Nixon and

Kissinger also envisioned a world in which the United States would share power with a number of its allies.

According to this multilateral view, the United States would not be the sole rescuer of the free world but would share that responsibility with its most powerful allies. Nixon hoped that one day the United States, the Soviet Union, Western Europe, the People's Republic of China (PRC), and Japan would coexist peacefully and trade together to their mutual benefit.

The Nixon Doctrine influenced the United States in its decision to sell arms to Iran and to Israel in the early to mid-1970s. In Iran, the United States agreed to a request by Mohammad Reza Shah Pahlavi (the shah of Iran) to purchase conventional weapons. The shah purchased a total of $15 billion in U.S. arms, buying weapons that were technologically superior to most of those in the U.S. arsenal. Nixon and Kissinger believed that strengthening Iran's weapons program would stabilize the Middle East, thereby not only protecting Iran's oil supply but also the oil reserves in all nations bordering the Persian Gulf.

An unintended negative consequence of the decision to sell arms to Iran was its impact on the U.S. economy. To pay for the weapons, the shah raised oil prices, creating a situation that contributed to the already heavily inflated Organization of Petroleum Exporting Countries (OPEC) oil prices, which hurt U.S. oil consumers.

Although the sale of arms to Israel improved U.S. relations with that country, the use of the Nixon Doctrine in this case may have inadvertently supported Israel in its development of nuclear weapons. Although the United States intended to stabilize the Middle East by selling arms to Israel, its entry into the nuclear community destabilized the region and raised the specter that Israel might resort to using nuclear weapons if attacked by Arab nations.

During the administration of President Jimmy Carter, continuing violence in the Middle East and the overthrow of the shah of Iran by Ayatollah Ruhollah Khomeini in 1979 so destabilized the region that the guidelines of the Nixon Doctrine no longer met the U.S. national interests. In the Carter Doctrine of 1980, Carter declared that if any power attempted to control any nation within the Persian Gulf region, the United States would retaliate, and, if necessary, resort to military force, including the use of ground troops.

See also Carter Doctrine; Kissinger, Henry (1923–); Nixon, Richard, and National Policy; Vietnam War (1954–1975)

Further Reading

Genovese, Michael A. *The Nixon Presidency: Power and Politics in Turbulent Times.* Westport, CT: Greenwood, 1990.

Hoff, Joan. *Nixon Reconsidered.* New York: Basic Books, 1994.

Litwak, Robert S. *Détente and the Nixon Doctrine: American Foreign Policy and the Pursuit of Stability, 1969–1976.* New York: Cambridge University Press, 1984.

NIXON, RICHARD, AND NATIONAL POLICY

Thirty-seventh president of the United States (1969–1974), who sought to maintain U.S. military strength, contain communism throughout the world, and end the Vietnam War with "peace and honor" while advocating global peace and security through improved relations with the Soviet Union and the People's Republic of China (PRC). Richard Nixon (1913–1994) also became the first president to resign from office—a result of the notorious Watergate scandal.

KISSINGER AND VIETNAM

In December 1968, shortly after being elected president, Nixon selected Harvard political scientist Henry Kissinger as his national security advisor. Once in office, Nixon emphasized the role of the National Security Council (NSC) in the formulation of his foreign policy. He rarely depended on the advice of either his secretary of state, William Rogers, or his secretary of defense, Melvin Laird. Nixon primarily consulted Kissinger and the large staff of analysts in the NSC, a significant departure from the policy making of previous presidents.

From the moment Nixon became president, he was embroiled in the ongoing crisis of the Vietnam War. He was determined to uphold his campaign promise to withdraw U.S. troops from Vietnam and end the war, but he insisted that he must accomplish this goal with the nation's honor intact. Nixon and Kissinger believed that from a national security standpoint, the United States could not afford to lose prestige or its standing in the court of world opinion. When Nixon urged communist North Vietnam to begin peace negotiations, the North Vietnamese were adamant that they would not stop fighting until the United States had withdrawn from Vietnam and discontinued its support of the government of South Vietnam led by Nguyen Van Thieu. Because Nixon refused to abandon the South Vietnamese regime, the talks did not progress.

Nixon tried to force the peace negotiations forward by bombing North Vietnam into compliance. Despite intense bombing raids, the North Vietnamese did not waver. Moreover, the U.S. bombings and invasions of Cambodia from 1969 to 1970 and of Laos in 1971—designed to eliminate North Vietnamese strongholds in these countries—did not persuade the North to alter its demands. Late in 1972, Nixon promised South Vietnam one billion dollars in military assistance and informed Thieu that he must accept the peace terms the United States (through Kissinger) had negotiated with the North or the United States would strike a separate agreement with the North Vietnamese. Although the terms Nixon was forcing on Thieu were certain to result in the fall of South Vietnam to the North Vietnamese, Thieu reluctantly agreed. The peace talks proceeded, leading to a signed agreement on January 23, 1973.

Nixon's decision making in Vietnam ran counter to his stated national security policies. Although he advocated decreased military spending and declared in his Nixon Doctrine that U.S. ground troops would no longer be deployed to fight the battles of U.S. allies, he discovered that he could not conclude the war while adhering to these objectives.

Nixon and Kissinger perceived the powerful antiwar movement in the United States as a threat to national security. Nixon believed that some peace groups were funded by foreign sources and sought to undermine traditional U.S. values. He ordered the Central Intelligence Agency (CIA) to step up its infiltration of antiwar groups as part of Operation CHAOS, an illegal project that had its beginnings in 1967 during the administration of President Lyndon B. Johnson. (Operation CHAOS was illegal because the CIA charter prohibits domestic intelligence gathering.)

THE SOVIET UNION AND COMMUNIST CHINA

Nixon and Kissinger were far more successful in their dealings with the Soviet Union and the PRC. Nixon favored a policy that aimed to foster improved relations with the Soviets, limit the U.S.-Soviet arms race, and sustain a balance of power between the two nations.

In the early 1970s, Soviet leaders indicated that they were amenable to pursuing nuclear arms reductions.

During the Moscow summit of May 1972, Nixon and Soviet leader Leonid Brezhnev made agreements that instituted a brief era of détente, or a relaxation of hostilities, between the two superpowers. The two leaders agreed to sign two treaties that emerged from the Strategic Arms Limitation Talks (SALT I) of 1969–1972. The Antiballistic Missile (ABM) Treaty limited antiballistic missile systems, whereas the other agreement called for a freeze (until 1977) on the production of intercontinental ballistic missiles (ICBMs), submarine-launched ballistic missiles (SLBMs), and submarines carrying SLBMs.

While détente with the Soviet Union was developing, China indicated that it would be open to communication with the United States. Nixon grasped this opportunity in the hopes that better relations with China might encourage its leaders to persuade the North Vietnamese to end the war. The president traveled to Beijing to meet with Chinese leaders, particularly Premier Zhou Enlai, in late February 1972. The trip was especially noteworthy because it initiated an era of rapprochement, or cordial relations, between China and the United States, although not much else was accomplished.

POLICY TOWARD THE MIDDLE EAST

In the troubled Middle East, Nixon was determined to contain communism and ward off Soviet incursions. According to the Nixon Doctrine, pronounced in February 1970, the United States declared that it would supply its Middle East allies with economic and military assistance (instead of ground troops) in the event of a crisis, thus ruling out a large-scale military engagement such as Vietnam.

As Israel clashed with the Arab states of Syria and Egypt, the United States supplied weapons to Israel and Iran to counterbalance the arms the Soviet Union provided to Syria and Egypt. During the Yom Kippur War of 1973, the Arab states protested U.S. arms assistance to Israel by initiating an embargo on oil destined for the United States through the Organization of Petroleum Exporting Countries (OPEC). Spiraling oil prices and the resulting U.S. oil crisis of 1973–1974 forced Nixon and Kissinger to take action. Kissinger's so-called shuttle diplomacy, in which he flew from one meeting with Mideast leaders to another, may have kept the conflict from escalating into a larger war and influenced OPEC to discontinue the oil embargo in March 1974.

LATIN AMERICA

Even before the procommunist Salvador Allende was elected the president of Chile in 1970, CIA operatives, on orders from President Nixon, covertly discouraged his election. President Lyndon Johnson had stated in his Johnson Doctrine that the United States would stop a communist government from gaining control of any nation in the Western Hemisphere. Nixon, according to the Johnson and Nixon Doctrines, ordered the CIA to undermine the Allende government and force him from power. A military coup in 1973 overthrew Allende, resulting in his assassination. The CIA acknowledged its support of the coup, but denied any involvement in the assassination.

The Watergate scandal, which came fully to U.S. public attention in 1973, distracted President Nixon from foreign affairs and diminished his overall effectiveness. During this crisis, Kissinger assumed a greater involvement in foreign policy making, becoming Nixon's secretary of state in 1973. This scandal and Nixon's resignation in August 1974 ended his foreign policy initiatives, most of which were not carried forth by subsequent administrations. This outcome was primarily the result of Nixon's and Kissinger's private, behind closed doors method of policy making, which blocked the state department, Cabinet members, and other advisers from building on the successes of the Nixon administration.

See also Antiballistic Missile (ABM) Treaty (1972); Central Intelligence Agency (CIA); Détente; Johnson, Lyndon B., and National Policy; Kissinger, Henry (1923–); Nixon Doctrine (1969); OPEC (Organization of Petroleum Exporting Countries); Strategic Arms Limitation Talks (SALT)

Further Reading

Genovese, Michael A. *The Nixon Presidency: Power and Politics in Turbulent Times.* Westport, CT: Greenwood, 1990.
Hoff, Joan. *Nixon Reconsidered.* New York: Basic Books, 1994.
Litwak, Robert S. *Détente and the Nixon Doctrine: American Foreign Policy and the Pursuit of Stability, 1969–1976.* New York: Cambridge University Press, 1984.

NIXON SHOCKS

Policies initiated by the administration of U.S. President Richard Nixon that challenged the prevailing strategic and economic relationship between the United States and Japan. This account traces events leading up to and culminating in the Nixon Shocks. Although not all of these events directly impacted the decisions that produced the Nixon Shocks, they offer a context for understanding the political atmosphere that shaped important international policies of the Nixon administration.

U.S.-JAPANESE RELATIONS

Following its victory over Japan in World War II, the United States forged a security relationship with Japan based on containment of Chinese communism in Asia. In 1951, the two nations signed the U.S.-Japan Security Treaty, which allowed the United States to maintain armed forces in and about Japan to deter any armed attack against that nation. The treaty was signed in the expectation that Japan would increasingly assume responsibility for its own defense against direct and indirect aggression by outside powers. In addition to this security arrangement, a strong dollar and open American market served as engines driving Japan's economic growth.

STRATEGIC ISSUES AND THE OKINAWA QUESTION

By the time Nixon took office in 1969, the Soviet Union was approaching strategic military parity with the United States, and economic policies pursued by Western Europe and Japan threatened American prosperity. By 1971, ballooning trade and balance of payments deficits eroded faith in the dollar and reduced Washington's global influence. By the spring of 1971, foreign pressure to redeem dollars for gold reached a climax. For the first time since World War II, American global economic interests collided with those of the European allies and Japan. Facing an economic crisis unprecedented since 1945, Nixon was forced to introduce the New Economic Policy, which economically and strategically hurt its chief Asian ally at the time, Japan.

In March 1969, Japanese Prime Minister Eisaku Sato told the Japanese Diet (parliament) that he intended to make the return of a nuclear weapons-free Okinawa the first issue of business with President Nixon. The American government considered the Okinawa bases to be of inestimable value, not just for the ongoing U.S. operations in Vietnam but also for the U.S. strategic position in the Pacific. Japanese-American negotiations over Okinawa began in earnest in June 1969 and continued through the Nixon-Sato summit that November.

The two sides tacitly agreed on several points that, although not legally binding, went beyond previous commitments. The United States agreed to withdraw its nuclear weapons from Okinawa and return the island to Japanese control. In return, Japan would allow the United States to use existing military Okinawa bases for a wider variety of combat operations against Vietnam than other bases in Japan. The Japanese also agreed to adopt a "positive attitude" toward the use of U.S. bases in Japan to defend South Korea and Taiwan.

THE NIXON DOCTRINE

As the diplomats worked on the details of the Okinawa deal, Nixon took a lengthy trip though Asia. On July 25, at a press briefing in Guam, the president issued a statement on future security policy that his aides soon dubbed the Nixon Doctrine. In his speech, Nixon pledged to honor existing security pacts with Asian nations and promised to provide material support to resist aggression. However, he also stressed that Asian nations must take primary responsibility for their own defense.

The call for a new security structure in Asia reflected both political and economic realities. At the time, the emergence of dynamic export economies among America's European and Asian allies were hurting American manufacturers and creating an unfavorable trade balance. Complaints by American textile companies (who had contributed generously to Nixon's 1968 campaign) made the president especially anxious to get Japan to agree to reduce the export of synthetics to the United States.

In Sato's eagerness to assure the rapid return of Okinawa under acceptable terms, he accepted the American export restraint formula without consulting Japanese manufacturers and ministries, whose approval and cooperation was required under Japanese law. Japan ultimately failed to implement the export restrictions, causing Nixon to complain about Japanese "betrayal" of the United States.

THE NIXON-SATO SUMMIT

Efforts to broker a deal on Okinawa appeared comparatively simpler. Because of diplomatic negotiations in late 1969 led by Secretary of State Henry Kissinger, both sides agreed to several concessions, and Nixon agreed to return Okinawa to Japan by 1972. After the formal talks concluded, however, a private meeting supposedly took place between Nixon and Sato, with

Kissinger present. In the meeting, Nixon explained that the U.S. military, Congress, and other interest groups in the United States objected to the nuclear-free return of Okinawa as a "give-away." As payback, the president wanted Sato to implement the synthetic textile restraint deal. Kissinger and Nixon were certain that Sato agreed to implement export controls and that "he committed his sincerity and all his efforts" to carry out the export restraint agreement.

In December 1969, Sato parlayed the results of the Okinawa agreement into an electoral victory, but the stalemate over textiles continued. Despite months of additional negotiations during 1970 and another visit by Sato in October 1970, the Japanese prime minister failed to implement the export restraint agreement that Nixon and Kissinger believed he had agreed to at the earlier summit meeting. On March 8, 1971, representatives of the Japanese textile industry announced that they and U.S. Congressman Wilbur Mills concluded a voluntary three-year export restraint program that precluded the need for a government-to-government agreement. Nixon was furious; not only had Sato failed to deliver on his promise, but he appeared to be colluding with one of Nixon's Democratic rivals.

THE TWIN JOLTS

On March 11, 1971, Nixon denounced the Japanese industry plan as too lenient and refused to approve the agreement. Sato, hoping he could still deal with Nixon, reshuffled his cabinet and named two political allies as ministers for trade and foreign affairs. Just as these officials were assuming their new posts, Nixon administered the first jolt to Japan—his July 15 announcement of a planned visit to China.

By the summer of 1971, the festering textile dispute blended into the larger economic problems dividing the United States from its trading partners. Nixon feared that European nations holding dollars would demand that the U.S. redeem those dollars in gold. This would be a major shock to the U.S. economy. He hurriedly assembled his political and economic advisers and on August 15 announced that the United States would no longer exchange dollars for gold.

In addition to removing the U.S. from the so-called gold standard, Nixon also announced a 10% surcharge on imports, imposed a temporary freeze on all wages and prices in the United States, provided investment incentives to industry, and reduced federal spending. In September, Nixon threatened to impose quotas on

Japan's textile exports under the terms of the Trading With the Enemy Act. These initiatives had a disproportionate impact on Japan, given its dependence on the American market and the fact that more than 90% of its exports were subject to the new surcharge. Delinking the dollar from a gold standard also caused a decline in the value of the dollar and a corresponding rise in the value of the Japanese yen. This further hurt Japanese exports to the United States by making them more expensive to U.S. consumers.

Just as the opening to China overturned the political ground rules of the postoccupation Pacific alliance, Nixon's New Economic Policy undermined the basis of the postwar economic relationship between the United States and Japan. Although the China shock had primarily injured Japan's pride, the economic shock was designed (as Nixon put it) to really "stick it to Japan."

TRIANGULAR DIPLOMACY

Nixon and Kissinger's interest in opening a dialogue with China reflected deeper changes in the Cold War. Upon taking office, both men recognized that the Soviet Union had achieved a rough nuclear parity with the United States. However, even as Washington realized that a more cooperative relationship with Moscow was needed, the political and economic policies pursued by Europe and Japan had begun to clash frequently with American interests. Tensions within the western alliance were matched by fragmentation of the Sino-Soviet bloc. At the same time, Japan's growing wealth and assertiveness—including Sato's pledge to support the defense of South Korea and Taiwan—raised for China the specter of a rearmed, expansionist Japan.

It was in America's best strategic interests to keep China, Japan, and the Soviet Union concerned with one another to maintain the balance of power in Asia and restrict the rise of any one single power. This calculation on the part of the United States required it to engage in *triangular diplomacy* among Japan, China, and the Soviet Union. It also required Nixon to play the "China card" first.

Nixon's calculated announcement of his visit to China stunned most Japanese, particularly Sato. The timing was particularly brutal because while Washington and Beijing moved toward cooperation from 1970 to 1971, Sino-Japanese relations were simultaneously deteriorating. Chinese leaders expressed alarm over Japan's expanding economic power and

rising military budget. Chinese Premier Zhou Enlai issued strict new guidelines governing Sino-Japanese trade. These new rules prohibited Chinese trade with Japanese companies assisting or investing in Taiwan and South Korea, manufacturing arms for the American war effort in Southeast Asia, or engaging in joint ventures with American firms.

Sato urged Japanese business leaders to resist Chinese pressure. Nevertheless, business groups were anxious to enter China, which was (and still is) the largest market in Asia. Many political observers in Japan argued that strategic and economic cooperation with China seemed imperative to ensure Japanese prosperity in the post-Nixon shock environment. Although Sato probably agreed with much of this assessment, his desire to retain American goodwill constrained his actions.

On September 21, at roughly the same time as he threatened to invoke the Trading With the Enemy Act against Japan, Nixon finally sent the Okinawa reversion treaty to the U.S. Senate. The treaty won easy passage on November 10, 1971, and Okinawa returned to Japan on May 15, 1972. On September 26, in a sign that he desired to resume a dialogue with Tokyo, President Nixon flew to Alaska to greet Japanese Emperor Hirohito.

AFTERSHOCKS

The effects of the Nixon Shocks were not limited to the United States and Japan; they produced worldwide economic and political changes. On December 17, 1971, the so-called Group of Ten (the major Western European powers plus Canada, Japan, and the United States) reached an agreement to revalue the world currencies. The member states agreed to a devaluation of the dollar by approximately 9%. The yen-dollar exchange rate fell from 360 to 1 to approximately 308 to 1, and Washington dropped the import surcharge.

Following the Group of Ten conference, Nixon embarked on his trip to China. During his week there, he stressed the point that America's alliance with Japan was in China's interest. However, Nixon's effort to sell Beijing on the U.S-Japan security treaty fell short. In the joint Shanghai Communiqué issued by Nixon and Zhou at the end of the visit, the Chinese declared their opposition to "the revival and outward expansion of Japanese militarism." By allowing himself to be associated with this assertion, Nixon came close to endorsing Beijing's basic views. Even without knowing the details of the Nixon-Kissinger-Mao-Zhou discussions, the Shanghai Communiqué shocked Sato. Although leaders of Sato's Liberal Democratic Party varied in their responses to the Nixon shocks, nearly all now recognized that Sato's days as prime minister were numbered.

China's view of Japan changed and evolved rapidly after the Nixon visit. During the summer of 1972, Zhou announced that China no longer objected to the U.S-Japan security treaty. That fall, a new Japanese Prime Minister, Tanaka Kakuei, normalized relations with the People's Republic of China (PRC). The Chinese not only ceased complaining about resurgent militarism in Japan but also praised Tokyo as an incipient ally.

By the twilight of the Nixon years, American views of both China and Japan altered radically from those prevailing in 1969. A new realism about the necessity for the United States and China to coexist peacefully replaced the ideological hostility toward Beijing and sympathy toward Tokyo. The logic that underlay the post–World War II system of favoring Japan because of its anticommunist orientation was rapidly giving way to a multipolar world in which Japan was both ally of and competitor with the United States.

See also China and U.S. Policy; Cold War; Communism and National Security; Nixon Doctrine; Nixon, Richard, and National Policy; Okinawa; U.S.-Japan Alliance.

Further Reading

Angel, Robert C. *Explaining Economic Policy Failure: Japan in the 1969–71 International Monetary Crisis.* New York: Columbia University Press, 1991.

Kutano, Atsushi. *Two Nixon Shocks and Japan-U.S. Relations.* Princeton, NJ: Princeton University Center of International Studies, 1987.

Mann, James. *About Face: A History of America's Curious Relationship with China, from Nixon to Clinton.* New York: Knopf, 1988.

NON- AND COUNTERPROLIFERATION

Efforts to slow or prevent the spread of weapons of mass destruction (WMD) to decrease the risk of such weapons being used in an armed conflict. Nonproliferation and counterproliferation policies are based on the assumption that the proliferation of these types of weapons increases the threat of war, amplifies the destructiveness of war, and raises the costs of preparing for war.

Nonproliferation regimes include treaties, sets of international organizations, and the states that subscribe to them. For example, the nuclear nonproliferation regime consists of the Treaty on the Non-Proliferation of Nuclear Weapons (NPT), the International Atomic Energy Agency (IAEA), parts of the United Nations, and the states that subscribe to the NPT. Nonproliferation regimes also exist for chemical and biological weapons and for their delivery systems, notably missiles.

By contrast, counterproliferation policies, such as those advanced by the United States, are intended to convince or compel states to discontinue weapons programs, by force if necessary. Counterproliferation policies can take various forms, including war (as in the case of the U.S.-led invasion of Iraq in 2003) or even negotiated aid packages (as in the case of the Agreed Framework negotiated with North Korea in 1994).

Despite these varied approaches for slowing proliferation, nonproliferation regimes and counterproliferation policies often work in tandem to achieve the common goal of halting the spread of WMD. This was the case from 1991 to 1999 with the United Nations Special Commission (UNSCOM), which combined both approaches in preventing Iraq from continued development of WMD.

NONPROLIFERATION AND THE COLD WAR

During the Cold War, efforts by individual states and the UN to slow the spread of WMD focused primarily on the nonproliferation of the nuclear weapons through multilateral and bilateral agreements. Many countries believed that proliferation would end if the nuclear states agreed not to share nuclear weapons technology with nonnuclear states. Despite this widespread belief, the creation of an international nonproliferation treaty regime actually was quite complicated and required extensive international bargaining.

The creation of the IAEA in 1957 was the first cooperative response to controlling the proliferation of nuclear technology for weapons use. Six years later, the Limited Test Ban Treaty was signed, prohibiting nuclear weapons tests in the atmosphere, in outer space, and under water. The NPT, which entered into force in 1970, marked the most significant international cooperative prohibition on the proliferation of nuclear weapons.

The treaty forbids nonnuclear weapons member-states from manufacturing, controlling, or receiving the transfer of nuclear weapons. It also prohibits nuclear weapons member-states from assisting them in developing nuclear technology for weapons purposes. Article VI of the NPT requires the five certified nuclear weapons member-states—the United States, Great Britain, France, Russia (the former Soviet Union), and China—"to pursue negotiations in good faith on effective measures relating to cessation of the nuclear arms race at an early date and to nuclear disarmament."

Bilateral U.S.-Soviet talks during the Cold War showed that both parties wanted to slow nuclear proliferation. These talks led to negotiation of the Antiballistic Missile (ABM) Treaty and the Strategic Arms Limitation Talks (SALT I and SALT II) in the 1970s. However, the independent development of nuclear weapons by France and China in the 1960s demonstrated the possibility that states could acquire nuclear weapons without the assistance of others. The later development of nuclear weapons by non-NPT signatories India, Pakistan, and Israel revealed that the uncontrolled spread of nuclear weapons would likely continue, despite the best efforts of international regimes to prevent it. Moreover, the use of chemical weapons in the Iran-Iraq war (1980–1989) highlighted the fact that international nonproliferation regimes could no longer focus solely on nuclear weapons.

NONPROLIFERATION AFTER THE COLD WAR

The discovery of Iraq's extensive clandestine weapons program following the 1991 Gulf War was a turning point for the international regimes. The scope of Iraq's WMD program was revealed in international inspections by UNSCOM. These discoveries generated wide debate about whether the nonproliferation regimes were effective, and whether the United States should limit its counterproliferation policies to efforts within the framework of the regimes.

Many of the assumptions from the Cold War era are no longer appropriate for non- and counterproliferation. Advancements and diffusion of technology have made WMD more accessible. The dual-use nature of nuclear, biological, and chemical technologies, combined with their spread, has made it difficult to track programs and judge their intent.

Some efforts to strengthen nonproliferation regimes in the post–Cold War era have been successful. Unilateral decisions by states (e.g., South Africa and Libya) to dismantle WMD programs have demonstrated that nations can change course and choose to renounce programs within the regimes' frameworks.

Moreover, additional NPT signatories, the indefinite extension NPT (1995), and the development of the IAEA Additional Protocol have strengthened the nuclear nonproliferation regime. The Chemical Weapons Convention of 1997 and the negotiation of measures to strengthen the Biological Weapons Convention reveal other positive trends in nonproliferation.

The spread of international terrorism since the 1990s has broadened the objectives of nonproliferation regimes and U.S. counterproliferation policies. For example, the 1995 sarin gas attacks by Aum Shinrikyo in Tokyo suggested that the use of WMD by terrorists was already a threat. The stated determination of terrorist groups such as al-Qaeda to acquire WMD has raised the specter of their use in future terrorist attacks. Furthermore, the discovery of an illicit trading network in nuclear material operated by the Pakastani nuclear scientist AQ Khan reveals the ease with which terrorists may be able to acquire WMD.

Nonproliferation and counterproliferation efforts are no longer limited to slowing the spread of WMD to states. Efforts such as the revived Nuclear Suppliers Group (NSG) and UN Security Council Resolution 1540 seek to prevent terrorists and rogue states from acquiring WMD. The United States has also implemented the Cooperative Threat Reduction program to assist Russia in protecting poorly guarded weapons from being stolen or illegally sold.

See also Antiballistic Missile (ABM) Treaty (1972); Arms Control; Arms Race; Biological Weapons and Warfare; Biological Weapons Convention; Chemical Weapons; Chemical Weapons Convention; Comprehensive Test Ban Treaty (1996–); Limited Test Ban Treaty (1963); Nuclear Proliferation; Nuclear Test-Ban Treaty; Nuclear Weapons; Verification

Further Reading

Mueller, Harald, David Fischer, and Wolfgang Koetter. *Nuclear Non-proliferation and Global Order*. Oxford, UK: Oxford University Press, 1994.
Sagan, Scott, and Kenneth Waltz. *The Spread of Nuclear Weapons*. New York: Norton, 2003.

NONCOMMISSIONED OFFICER

Officer appointed by a commissioned officer in the military hierarchy. The noncommissioned officer corps is the administrative apparatus of the U.S. military. A noncommissioned officer (NCO) usually supervises enlisted men and serves as adviser to the officer corps. NCOs receive their authority from commissioned officers, who in turn receive their authority from a sovereign power, such as the United States government.

The laws of war require the existence of an officer class in the military, although there are commissioned officers who are not members of the military. These individuals work in the uniformed services such as the National Oceanic and Atmospheric Administration (NOAA) and the Public Health Service (PHS) commissioned corps. The distinction between civilians and combatants is crucial to the laws of war. The motivation for commissioning officers is so they cannot be legally tried as spies if captured on the battlefield.

NCOs are considered vital to the day-to-day management of military operations. They typically function at the rank of sergeant, but they can also serve as corporals and petty officers. NCOs can receive advanced military training.

The position of tactical NCO exists at the level of the military academy. Tactical NCOs are responsible for training leaders for companies of cadets at the U.S. Military Academy. Their responsibilities range from teaching and supervising drill and ceremony procedures to military training.

See also U.S. Air Force; U.S. Army; U.S. Marine Corps; U.S. Navy

Further Reading

Fisher, Ernst F. *Guardians of the Republic: A History of the Noncommissioned Officer Corps of the US Army.* New York: Fawcett Books, 1994.

Winkler, John D. *Future Leader Development of Army Noncommissioned Officers: Workshop Results.* Arlington, VA: RAND, 1998.

NONPROLIFERATION

See NON- AND COUNTERPROLIFERATION

NORAD (NORTH AMERICAN AEROSPACE DEFENSE COMMAND)

Military headquarters established by the United States and Canada to monitor and defend North American airspace. The agreement that created the North American Aerospace Defense Command (NORAD) was signed on May 12, 1958. It was a Cold War deterrent to airborne threats to North America from outside the region. The agreement has been renewed eight times since 1958.

NORAD uses data from satellites and ground-based radar installations to monitor, validate, and warn of attacks against North America by aircraft, missiles, or space vehicles. NORAD also provides surveillance and control of U.S. and Canadian airspace and operates fighter aircraft. Before the September 11, 2001, terrorist attacks on New York and Washington, DC, NORAD was focused on airborne threats to the Canadian and U.S. borders. After the terrorist attacks, NORAD's mission has broadened to include threats from domestic airspace.

NORAD is integrated into the command and intelligence structures of both the U.S. and Canadian armed forces. The commander in chief of NORAD is appointed by the president of the United States and the prime minister of Canada and reports to both leaders. NORAD is headquartered at Peterson Air Force Base in Colorado, but the command and control center for its worldwide system of sensors designed to detect aerospace threats is located at Cheyenne Mountain in Colorado.

NORAD's area of responsibility stretches from Clear, Alaska, to the Florida Keys and from St. John's, Newfoundland, to San Diego, California. It operates three regional sectors to perform its dual mission of aerospace warning and aerospace control: the Alaskan NORAD Region (ANR), headquartered near Anchorage; Canadian NORAD Region (CANR) in Winnipeg, Manitoba; and the Continental United States NORAD Region (CONR). The CONR is broken into three sectors: Western Air Defense Sector at McChord Air Force Base in the state of Washington; Northeast Air Defense Sector at Rome, New York; and Southeast Air Defense Sector at Tyndall Air Force Base, Florida. Tyndall Air Force Base is the CONR headquarters.

See also Deterrence; Nuclear Deterrence

NORMANDY INVASION

The Allied endeavor to open a second front on the French coast of Normandy in the European theater of operations during World War II. The Battle of

Normandy (code-named Operation Overlord) activated a second front with amphibious Allied landings on the morning of June 6, 1944.

Although often and famously referred to simply as D-day, the fighting in Normandy lasted for months, with the bulk of the German resistance finally eliminated by late August. The objectives of the operation were to establish a beachhead from which to liberate occupied regions and eventually drive back the German Reich.

Although ultimately successful, the early assault at Normandy was extremely costly in terms of men and materiel. The landings on the coast of Normandy involved a massive joint operation of mostly U.S., British, and Canadian forces—with naval, aerial, and paratroop elements supporting the main amphibious assault. In their path, the Germans placed three *Panzer* divisions under the command of Field Marshal Erwin Rommel, which were reinforced by only minimal air and armor support. As part of their Atlantic Wall defenses, the Germans had extensively fortified the foreshore area, but they manned it with only a haphazard collection of troops, including non-German nationalities (mainly Russians) who agreed to fight for the Germans rather than endure prisoner of war camps.

Following the initial landing phase of the Normandy invasion, many more Allied troops and equipment continued to come ashore after D-day. By the end of July, more than one million Allied troops were entrenched along the Normandy coast. In the end, Operation Overlord succeeded in its objective by sheer force of numbers in both men and materiel.

Although the footing the Allies gained at Normandy was crucial to the efforts and success of the western front, it may not have affected the ultimate outcome of the war. By the time of D-day, the Red Army of the Soviet Union was irreversibly advancing toward Germany from the east. In 1942–1943, the incursion into Stalingrad had been the Third Reich's high-water mark, but by the time of the Normandy invasion, Hitler's army was in retreat.

Despite the fact that four-fifths of the German forces were in the east, the Soviets had the capacity to defeat Germany by itself. With its repulse of the German Army, the Soviet Union laid claim over Eastern European states left in the wake of its drive toward Berlin. A complete occupation of Europe by communist forces, therefore, was within the realm of possibility.

To ensure the survival of democracy in Europe, a U.S. and British presence may have been needed to counter the extent that communism would spread in Western Europe. Accordingly, the Battle of Normandy not only has historical relevance in regard to the events of World War II but is also significant within the context of the postwar period. With the cessation of hostilities between the Axis and the Allies, a new arena of conflict was to emerge immediately: the era of Cold War rivalries and power alignments. The Normandy invasion signaled the eventual end of one global struggle and the harbinger of another.

See also D-Day; World War II (1939–1945)

NORTH AMERICAN FREE TRADE AGREEMENT (NAFTA)

A trilateral agreement among the United States, Canada, and Mexico that eliminated tariffs and other barriers to trade. The North American Free Trade Agreement (NAFTA) both succeeds and expands upon the Canada-U.S. Free Trade Agreement of 1989. Trade barriers were to be eliminated within 10 years for most products and sectors, and within 15 years for others. Exceptions to the program include the trade of some agricultural products between the United States and Canada, cultural industries, and petroleum production.

NAFTA took effect on January 1, 1994. Beyond just reducing tariffs, the NAFTA nations also pledged in the agreement to eliminate nonbarriers to trade such as labeling requirements and import quotas); facilitate the cross-border movement of goods and services between the nations by investing in transportation and technology improvements; promote conditions of fair competition within the free trade area; substantially increase investment opportunities by giving potential investors access to a shared market; provide adequate and effective protection and enforcement of intellectual property rights; create effective procedures for the joint administration of the agreement and for the resolution of disputes; and establish a framework for further trilateral, regional, and multilateral cooperation to expand and enhance the benefits of the agreement.

Following a lengthy series of trilateral negotiations among the United States, Canada, and Mexico, NAFTA was ratified by the Canadian Parliament in June 2003 and by the United States and Mexican senates in November 2003. Proponents in the United States and Canada hoped that the opening of the

Mexican market would translate into thousands of new, high wage, export-producing jobs, and afford domestic businesses access to a free trade area on par with those developing in Europe, Asia, and various other parts of the globe. NAFTA supporters in Mexico presumed that the agreement would trigger an infusion of American and Canadian capital, stabilize economic growth, and create countless jobs in emerging industries.

Critics of NAFTA in the United States, both on the left and right, cite the widening trade deficits with Canada and Mexico as indications of the agreement's failure. Between 1993 and 2002, the U.S. export deficit with the NAFTA nations increased by 281% to $85 billion. Although U.S. exports to its NAFTA partners increased considerably over that time (95% to Mexico and 41% to Canada), imports from those nations grew faster still (195% from Mexico and 61% from Canada). Moreover, opponents claim that the United States lost nearly 900,000 net jobs during the first 10 years that NAFTA has been in effect. Over the same period, the total share of U.S. exports to Mexico represented by Maquiladora imports (U.S. parts and components that are shipped to Mexico and assembled into final products for sale in the United States) rose from 39% to 61%.

The extent to which NAFTA can be seen as either a success or failure is largely a matter of perspective. Large transnational firms have been helped considerably by the ability to site production facilities in whatever geography within the free trade area is most advantageous. More-skilled and higher-paying segments of the production process (for example, research and development) have gravitated toward the United States and Canada, whereas less-skilled and lower-paying segments (for example, simple assembly) have become more common in Mexico.

See also Free Trade; Multilateralism

NORTH ATLANTIC TREATY ORGANIZATION (NATO)

The quintessential example of a collective defense system, an alliance that extended over the 40 years of the Cold War and evolved in its aftermath into a collective security system. The altered threat posed by changing world conditions after the Cold War has changed the alliance system. The North Atlantic Treaty Organization (NATO) originally opposed the expansion of the Soviet Union into Western Europe, but today many threats remain unnamed and might call for operations outside of the region of the NATO members. The United States has dominated NATO since its inception in 1949, but the growing strength and independence of its member states have proven frustrating to U.S. leadership, especially in recent years.

BACKGROUND

As the Allied coalition of World War II deteriorated in the wake of Germany's defeat, and as Cold War discords emerged, Western Europe teetered on the brink of economic collapse. The renewed strength of communist parties in the region seemed to argue for an impending breakdown of the entire social and political system. As an initial step toward European recovery and strengthening the democratic political parties of Western Europe, the United States developed the European Recovery Program, or Marshall Plan. Because the Marshall Plan tended to escalate competition with the Soviet Union, and incidents such as the Berlin crisis of 1948 demonstrated the intractable nature of Soviet hegemony in Eastern Europe, a military component of the Western alliance seemed even more necessary.

Europe was not under threat of immediate Soviet attack in the early Cold War years, but the introduction of a U.S. military deterrent would provide security for the economic and political recovery in the west. The participation of the United States in a collective defense of Europe would not only deter aggression against it but also provide the essential assurance to West Europeans that the disunity and weakness of previous attempts to achieve collective defense would not happen again.

Under these circumstances, 12 countries inaugurated NATO in Washington, DC, on April 4, 1949: Belgium, Canada, Denmark, France, Iceland, Italy, Luxembourg, the Netherlands, Norway, Portugal, the United Kingdom, and the United States. Greece and Turkey joined NATO in 1952, completing the alliance plans for the Mediterranean—but leading critics to question how these two countries had been "moved" into the North Atlantic as if by magic. West Germany joined the NATO alliance in 1955 after a debate over how the Germans could be rearmed, settling upon a special command arrangement for West German forces under NATO. Spain was the last to join, in 1982 before the Cold War ended, and the *NATO 16* considered the future of the alliance.

NATO AND U.S. POLICY

The United States entered an alliance system reluctantly and relatively recently. The long-term tradition, lasting until 1941, was that the United States would enter no permanent alliance. Alliances were considered the source of incipient warfare among European nations, and would be best avoided by the United States, which saw itself as a trader nation.

However, the twin political shocks of World War I and World War II, culminating in the Cold War of permanent opposition and enduring readiness, led the United States to reconsider its opposition to permanent alliance. Thus, the United States and its West European allies founded the NATO pact and created a doctrine of containment versus the Soviet Union and other communist states.

After a century and a half of avoiding permanent entanglements, the United States launched into a "pact-o-mania" of alliances. In addition to NATO, the United States joined alliances in Southeast Asia (SEATO), with east Asian nations (bilaterals with Japan and Korea), with Australia and New Zealand (ANZUS), and the Baghdad Pact (CENTO), which became its most glaring major failure. Bilateral defense agreements also blossomed in the years since NATO was established.

The United States served as the major member in all these alliances, and it distributed military and financial aid to the others, relying at the time upon its extensive stores of World War II materiel. With such military aid frequently came requests for base rights, and the United States built a large number of bases, principally for its strategic bomber force, to add teeth to the doctrine of containment.

Thus, from the beginning, the United States entered into alliance politics as the dominant partner. Although the politics of democracy emphasized that this was not an imperial concept and was a true partnership for peace and freedom, the conduct of foreign policy and military relations remained indistinguishable from any other doctrine of imperial defense.

In fact, the NATO alliance worked successfully only because the lesser members acceded to the leadership of the major members and, in effect, deferred their control of defense and foreign policy in part to

the alliance. However, NATO then evolved from a collective defense agreement of mostly weakened and war-ravaged nations to a dominant alliance system composed of some of the wealthiest and prosperous world nations.

In time, the other NATO nations began to chafe at the continuing dominion of the United States and its interests. The recovery of Western Europe also restored the economic balance and renewed the rivalry of that bloc with the United States (and later, Japan). When U.S. leadership frustrated British and French designs on the Suez Canal in 1956 and brought NATO close to war over Berlin in 1961 (and again over Cuba in 1962), European leaders, especially the French under President Charles De Gaulle, began to edge away from loyalty to the United States. U.S. leaders had taken European subordination for granted for decades and reacted spitefully to any signs of wavering, especially as the U.S. presence in Vietnam took form in the mid-1960s and European criticism grew against U.S. cultural and economic imperialism.

U.S. leaders, for their part, remained ever suspicious of Europeans. First were the usual suspicions that they remained as quarrelsome and warlike as in the days when the United States sought no alliances. Also, the Western Europeans allowed real socialists into their governments, and this flirting with Marxism seemed a real and present danger to the security of the American world.

When the treachery of renewed economic rivalry became noticeable, and the larger European nations demanded more of a partnership in NATO affairs, the lines were drawn. France departed from the operational participation in NATO in 1965, forcing the alliance to give up facilities (and U.S. bases) on its territory. French President De Gaulle announced an independent French defense policy and strategic deterrent force.

Since then, the major powers have continued cordial relations, and the French have even returned to full NATO status. However, the period of interdependency has disappeared from the foreign affairs of the United States and its European allies. For the latter, this is a refreshing dose of reality and does not mean that they will refuse most U.S. requests for coordination or joint actions. However, the United States has not adjusted well to increasing independence among its erstwhile allies in the few alliances remaining from the 1950s.

Nuclear weapons proved a particular dilemma for NATO, stemming from the 1950s period of true military dependence of Europe upon the United States.

Most Europeans lived on the potential battlefield and believed in absolute nuclear deterrence. Unwilling to trust to a conventional defense, the Europeans considered early resort to strategic U.S. nuclear weapons as the only way to deter Soviet moves toward any type of warfare in Europe.

In effect, there was no distinctive conventional defense of Europe. U.S. policy sought to conserve its central strategic arsenal, and if a conventional defense could be mounted, so much the better. Even a tactical nuclear defense of Europe (that is, not including strategic weapons fired from U.S. soil against the Soviet Union) was preferable for the American leadership.

The United States introduced tactical nuclear weapons to counter the numerically superior forces of the Soviets and their Warsaw Pact allies. These weapons took the form of smaller-sized and smaller-yield devices designed for use in artillery projectiles, short-range rockets, and aerial bombs. However, the continuing improvements in warhead design and miniaturization began to blur the distinction in these weapons between tactical and strategic arms by the late 1960s.

The ultimate nuclear dilemma was the introduction of short-range nuclear ballistic missiles by the United States to offset perceived Soviet superiority in that class of weapons. The Pershing II ballistic missile and the land-based cruise missiles based in several European countries provoked much anguish among political factions. Many of them questioned whether these were credible balances to the opposing armaments and whether they represented disengagement of NATO regional defense from the strategic nuclear umbrella that had traditionally provided the ultimate deterrence to a NATO–Warsaw Pact conflict—a strategic exchange between the superpowers on each side.

NATO DEFENSES

Early in NATO planning, the members hoped to raise a combined force in the region of some 60 ground divisions and a balanced air component. It soon became clear, however, that the defense budgets of the participating countries could not provide them. Moreover, the population base of a Europe experiencing the so-called economic miracle of 1954–1966 was also limited in military components. The addition of West Germany to the alliance allowed a high-quality ground force to be established on the NATO central front, backed by a superior tactical air force.

The northern front of NATO consisted of the Norwegian Sea, the Icelandic Straits, the common Norwegian border with the Soviet Union, and the Baltic approaches. With regional manpower at a premium, the defense of these sectors depended on air and sea superiority and the use of highly mobile ground reinforcements from other member states. In the south, NATO defenses hinged on the land defense of Turkey, the other member-state sharing a common border with the Soviet Union, and the defense of the Mediterranean by air and sea forces to shore up the land defenses of Italy and Greece—which would face second-echelon attacks in a NATO–Warsaw Pact conflict.

Although hopes continued for a common approach to defense procurement, national sentiments required healthy defense industries for the major powers. Initially, U.S. surplus weaponry from World War II provided a great deal of commonality to NATO forces. However, in the mature alliance, what counted most were interoperability standards that established common fuels and lubricants, munitions, command, control, and communications, and the compatible infrastructure of bases, pipelines, cargo handling, and other myriad features of the most successful peacetime permanent alliance.

Operationally, NATO never had to enter a conflict until it was called upon for peacemaking and peacekeeping duties in the Balkans in the 1990s. A brief air campaign to subjugate Serbia as a final measure of Balkan security activities came in 1999. By that time, the NATO alliance had begun to change into a collective security arrangement, adding members from the former Warsaw Pact and extending cooperative links to eastern neighbors not technically qualified for membership.

After a difficult period of persuasion, even Russia began to actively cooperate and participate in NATO exercises. As of 2004, NATO has expanded to include 26 nations, with the addition of Bulgaria, the Czech Republic, Estonia, Hungary, Latvia, Lithuania, Poland, Romania, Slovakia, and Slovenia. A new set of joint forces commands and headquarters charged with preparing missions in and out of the NATO areas have replaced the old Atlantic northern, central, and southern commands.

—Kenneth W. Estes

See also Alliances; Atlantic Alliance; Berlin Crises (1958–1961); Bosnia Intervention; Burdensharing; Central Front in Europe; Cold War; Collective Security; Containment; Conventional Forces in Europe Treaty (1990); Cooperative Security; Cruise Missile; De Gaulle, Charles (1890–1970); Deterrence; European Union (EU); Mutual and Balanced Force Reductions (MBFR); Nuclear Weapons; Prepositioned Equipment; Soviet Union, Former (Russia), and U.S. Policy; Tactical Nuclear Weapons; Treaties; War Planning; Warsaw Pact; World War II (1939–1945)

Further Reading

Faringdon, Hugh. *Confrontation: The Strategic Geography of NATO and the Warsaw Pact.* London: Routledge and Kegan Paul, 1986.

Treverton, Gregory F. *Making the Alliance Work: The United States and Western Europe.* London: Macmillan, 1985.

NORTH KOREA CRISES (1994–)

Series of diplomatic and military incidents since the mid-1990s, which have strained the tense political relationship between the United States and North Korea. The end of the Cold War brought a decade marred by several bouts of crisis between North Korea and what it views as its primary foe—the United States. The fall of the Soviet Union in 1991 left North Korea without its most important political ally and trading partner, drastically damaging it politically, militarily, and economically. It also gave North Korea renewed impetus to continue pursuing the nascent nuclear program it began nurturing in the previous few decades.

Citing security concerns each time, North Korea tried to use its growing nuclear capabilities repeatedly in the early 1990s to gain economic, diplomatic, and military concessions from the United States. Each time, diplomatic agreements were reached, but they were broken, or deemed so, by one or both parties. The latest such agreement was the 1994 Agreed Framework, which is a nonbinding document signed by North Korean leader Kim Jong Il and former U.S. President Bill Clinton. Under the Agreed Framework, the United States offered North Korea some measure of security guarantees and fuel aid, and promised to construct two light-water nuclear reactors for North Korea. In turn, North Korea promised to freeze nuclear activities, renew its membership to the Nonproliferation Treaty, and reinstate International Atomic Energy Agency (IAEA) inspections.

The Agreed Framework brought about some positive results, including the successful freezing of operations at North Korea's main nuclear facility in Yongbyon for eight years, verified by inspections at the end of 2002. Also, since 1994, North Korea created no new plutonium nor extracted plutonium from existing fuel rods—a main point of contention during the negotiations. However, North Korea made little progress toward freezing nuclear activities, and construction of the two light-water reactors was never completed.

In August 1998, North Korea test-launched a ballistic missile over Japan into the Pacific Ocean, causing the United States to consider withdrawing from the Agreed Framework. Rather than take such drastic action, President Clinton determined that the best strategy was for the United States to coordinate a message and strategy with China, South Korea, and Japan. In May 1999, the four nations approached North Korea together with the goal of attaining "verifiable elimination of the nuclear and missile programs." They promised that they would not attack North Korea to change its behavior, but that such a promise was binding only if North Korea gave up its nuclear ambitions. Deterrence must be limited to conventional weapons, and a road would be paved for nuclear dismantlement and for North Korea's reintegration into the international community. North Korea agreed to a moratorium on tests of long-range missiles, to continue the freeze at Yongbyon, and to conduct a series of talks with South Korea. This resulted in the 2000 summit meeting of the leaders of the two countries.

In contrast with the efforts of the Clinton administration to work with North Korea, President George W. Bush turned a relatively cold shoulder to North Korea from his first day in office. Some observers cite this as one of the factors motivating North Korea to renew its nuclear posturing. In November 2002, the United States confronted North Korea with intelligence that showed North Korea's likely possession of two nuclear bombs and its operation of a uranium enrichment plant. North Korea subsequently admitted that it had indeed restarted its nuclear program, and it withdrew from the Nonproliferation Treaty on New Year's Eve 2002. At the beginning of 2003, North Korea ejected IAEA inspectors, capped IAEA surveillance cameras, and rejected the Agreed Framework.

In the midst of the 2002 crisis, North Korea called for direct negotiations with the United States. The U.S. policy demanded that any negotiations be held on a multilateral level and must include other prominent regional powers, such as China, Russia, South Korea, and Japan. Two rounds of talks have been held since 2002, but the general consensus is that these negotiations have not led to any concrete shifts in the situation. The fact that each of the regional parties involved in the negotiations has very different objectives and positions toward North Korea has further complicated efforts to reach an agreement.

President George W. Bush listens as Chinese Premier Wen Jiabao makes a point during a press conference in the Oval Office of the White House on December 9, 2003. During meetings at the White House, President Bush encouraged Wen to help resolve the year-old North Korean nuclear crisis. The continued development of nuclear weapons by North Korea has been a vital concern of the United States, which wants to limit the proliferation of nuclear weapons. Such weapons in the hands of a rogue state such as North Korea is especially worrisome.

Source: Corbis.

See also Agreed Framework; Bush, George W., and National Policy; Clinton, Bill (William Jefferson), and National Policy; International Atomic Energy Agency; Korea, North and South; Non- and Counterproliferation; Nuclear Non-Proliferation Treaty (NPT); Nuclear Proliferation

NSC-68 (NATIONAL SECURITY REPORT)

Official report written in 1950 that was one of the critical U.S. government documents defining the Cold War and establishing the U.S. strategy for winning that war.

Paul H. Nitze of the state department wrote the National Security Council Report 68 (NSC-68) at the behest of Secretary of State Dean Acheson. The report forecast a Soviet capability to attack the United States with nuclear weapons by 1954. It called for increased U.S. arms spending to destroy the Soviet Union and give the United States unmatched military capabilities.

Specifically, NSC-68 was a top secret internal document designed to convince President Harry S. Truman to increase military spending well above the low limits he had set in the downsizing after World War II. Initially, Truman refused to increase spending, but the outbreak of the Korean War convinced him to spend more on defense. The defense budget soon doubled and then tripled.

NSC-68 remilitarized the United States and set up a permanent war economy and national security structure. It used national security to justify the right of the United States to claim scarce resources anywhere in the world.

The report said that "Soviet domination of the potential power of Eurasia, whether achieved by armed aggression or by political and subversive means, would be strategically and politically unacceptable to the United States."

NSC-68 revealed the mindset of U.S. cold warriors. It begins by explaining that World War II had ended the German and Japanese empires and the exhaustion of the French and British ones. The report noted that two great powers remained standing and in competition for world dominance and leadership—the United States and the Soviet Union. One of these two powers, the United States, stood for good, whereas the other, the Soviet Union, was evil.

NSC-68 assumed that the Soviet Union wanted to expand until it controlled the Eurasian landmass, and that its eventual goal was world domination. The threat was of such magnitude that it might destroy the United States, if not civilization itself. Thus, however unwillingly, the United States faced a mortal challenge from the Soviets. To counter the threat, the United States had to dominate the world and create an environment amenable to its survival and prosperity.

Realistically, the United States would have pursued this course whether or not the Soviet threat existed. But because the threat existed, the United States had to contain it while protecting the free world. The containment of communism and the protection of freedom would require a strong military deterrent. Soviet aggression or sponsorship of aggression by others might well require the military to defeat aggression, whether limited or total.

According to NSC-68, the United States and the Soviet Union were at war as leaders of a bipolar world. Only one would survive. U.S. policy would use the Soviet threat as justification for establishing political, economic, and military dominance of the free world. Given that the war was real and not just one of words, the United States had to be aggressive politically and militarily. It should use psychological warfare to create defections from the Soviet bloc and otherwise hamper Soviet efforts. Covert economic, political, and psychological techniques would encourage and abet revolts and unrest in satellites. At home, meanwhile, the United States needed to implement internal security and civil defense programs so that the American people would accept the need to fight and win nuclear war, even on a global scale.

NSC-68 was a basic U.S. foreign policy document for the Cold War and after. Since the release of NSC-68, every U.S. administration has established hardline policies consistent with the basic assumptions of the report. The report's assumptions that the United States should seek hegemony, with the right to control global resources, continued past the Cold War.

With the demise of the Soviet Union in 1991, a new world enemy was needed. The new rationale became a so-called clash of civilizations. As late as 2004, the legacy of Nitze and NSC-68 was apparent as Nitze's intellectual disciples—which included such advisers to the administration of President George W. Bush as Paul Wolfowitz, Richard Perle, and James Woolsey—dominated the voices that pushed for war with Iraq after the terrorist attacks of September 11, 2001.

See also National Security Act (1947); National Security Agency (NSA); Nitze, Paul H. (1907–2004)

NUCLEAR DETERRENCE

Strategy aimed at preventing war by maintaining a sufficient nuclear arsenal to dissuade a similarly armed adversary from initiating an attack for fear of a destructive retaliation. Nuclear deterrence is a strategic policy implemented to make the cost of going to war too high for a country to instigate conflict because the potential response would be devastating. The necessary component in deterrence strategy is to maintain a credible capability to balance the adversaries' own resources.

In early August 1945, the Little Boy and Fat Man atomic bombs were dropped on Hiroshima and Nagasaki in Japan, thereby introducing the nuclear weapon into modern warfare. The advent of this new technology coincided with the beginning of the Cold War between the United States and the Soviet Union. As nuclear weapon proliferation by these two superpowers increased, strategic policies likewise began to incorporate the nuclear component.

Traditionally, strategic policy focused on conventional deterrence. This included bolstering the size and capability of the armed forces, developing new weapons technology, and augmenting defense capabilities to deter opponents' aggression. During the Cold War, however, strategic policy began to integrate a nuclear deterrent to reinforce the conventional military capability.

Beginning in 1950, this change was reflected in U.S. strategic policy with the National Security Council Report 68 (NSC-68), which recognized the threat of a nuclear-armed Soviet Union. In 1954, in response to the potential Soviet threat, the United States formulated its nuclear deterrence policy in terms of massive retaliation. This policy asserted the United States' right to respond to aggression with massive retaliatory force.

During the 1960s and 1970s, however, the United States clearly possessed a superior strategic nuclear capability, and massive retaliation was replaced by assured destruction, a policy that reflected the U.S. advantage. Assured destruction became the guiding deterrent policy. It was predicated on the ability to absorb a first strike from the Soviets and have a subsequent capability to retaliate with unacceptable damage on the Soviets. Unacceptable damage was defined as destroying more than one-third of the population, two-thirds of Soviet industry, and more than 200 Soviet cities.

Two key elements of the assured destruction capability included survivability and flexible response. The survivability aspect describes a nuclear weapons system capable of absorbing a nuclear strike and still being able to function at sufficient strength to retaliate. Flexible response includes possessing a triad of nuclear delivery options—by land, air, and sea. This versatility bolstered the nuclear deterrent, enabling the dispersal of attack options.

During the 1970s, the Soviets significantly increased their nuclear arsenal, and U.S. strategic nuclear superiority diminished. The United States therefore modified its deterrent policy to reflect this reality in the way of mutually assured destruction (MAD). MAD was based on both countries possessing a significant second-strike capability to retaliate and inflict unacceptable damage on the adversary following a first strike.

Currently, advances in technology have significantly improved the precision of nuclear warhead delivery methods and subsequently altered some elements of nuclear deterrence. Whereas with massive retaliation, assured destruction, and MAD, targeting was aimed at countervalue elements—including enemy population centers, industries, and resources. Modern technology has facilitated a transition to counterforce targeting, which is directed at destroying enemy military infrastructure and capabilities.

During the Cold War and continuing through to this day, several additional countries have acquired a nuclear capability: China, France, Great Britain, India, Israel, and Pakistan. However, their deterrent capability in relation to the United States or Russia is minimal because of the overwhelming numeric and technological advantage held by these two countries.

Beginning in the late 1940s, U.S. and Russian nuclear stockpiles grew significantly, and this increase lasted through several decades as both countries entered into a nuclear arms race. From 1945 through the 1990s, the combined total of nuclear warheads for the United States and the Soviet Union was more than 100,000. Through arms limitation and reduction talks, and following the dissolution of the Soviet Union in 1991, the nuclear stockpiles of both countries have been significantly reduced. It is estimated that the United States now possesses 10,455, and Russia has 8,400.

See also Counter-Force Doctrine; Countervalue; Deterrence; Mutually Assured Destruction (MAD); Nuclear Proliferation; Nuclear Weapons

NUCLEAR NON-PROLIFERATION TREATY (NPT)

Treaty intended to halt the spread of nuclear weapons that obliges nonnuclear weapons member-states to agree not to manufacture, control, or receive the transfer of nuclear weapons. Nonnuclear weapons states also agree to accept certain safeguards to verify that nuclear materials are not being diverted from peaceful uses to nuclear weapons. In exchange, nuclear weapons state signatories with advanced nuclear technology pledge to assist them in developing nuclear energy for peaceful purposes. The Nuclear Non-Proliferation Treaty (NPT) entered into force on March 5, 1970, and as of 2005, it has been signed and ratified by 189 countries.

The testing of nuclear weapons by France in 1960 and China four years later gave impetus to the formation of a nuclear nonproliferation treaty regime. Both countries had independently developed their nuclear weapons, which raised concerns that other industrial countries might also attempt to develop nuclear weapons. Reasoning that nuclear proliferation increases the risk of nuclear war, a treaty regime intended to prevent the further spread of nuclear weapons was proposed at the United Nations. After a decade of intense negotiations, primarily between the Soviet Union and the United States, the UN endorsed the treaty and opened it for signature in 1968.

The most significant feature of the NPT is the separation of all potential parties into two groups—states that manufactured and detonated a nuclear weapon prior to January 1, 1967, and those that had not. Under the terms of the treaty, nuclear weapons states—namely the United States, the Russian Federation, the United Kingdom, France, and China—are permitted to keep their nuclear arsenals, provided that they do not transfer nuclear weapons to nonnuclear weapons states or assist them in developing nuclear weapons.

In addition, under Article VI of the treaty, the nuclear weapons states pledge to pursue negotiations in good faith to end the nuclear arms race and achieve complete nuclear disarmament. However, little progress has been made toward reducing nuclear arsenals, prompting controversy that the nuclear-weapons states are not meeting their obligations under Article VI. Nonnuclear weapons states argue that failure to meet these obligations is discriminatory because they bear the majority of the costs and responsibilities under the treaty, whereas the nuclear weapons states maintain a monopoly over the transfer and control of nuclear weapons.

A key element of honoring the NPT is the verification of compliance with its terms through the implementation of safeguards. The international organization responsible for verifying compliance is the International Atomic Energy Agency (IAEA). Founded in 1957 and headquartered in Vienna, Austria, the IAEA is an independent organization, not a UN agency. It conducts audits of declared nuclear materials and on-site inspections in nonnuclear weapons states. The IAEA cannot conduct inspections on undeclared or indigenously developed nuclear facilities, however.

The discovery of clandestine nuclear activities during the 1980s and 1990s in Iraq and North Korea revealed the ineffectiveness of the verification system. It demonstrated the IAEA's inability to provide credible assurances against prohibited nuclear activity occurring within a member-state. To resolve these shortcomings, the Additional Protocols, which would allow for more intrusive inspections of nuclear facilities, were proposed in 1997. However, NPT member-states remain reluctant to ratify the Additional Protocols, mainly because of concerns for the security of sensitive nuclear technology and increased discrimination against nonnuclear weapons states.

Article X of the NPT gives member-states the right to withdrawal from the treaty provided a state gives three months notice. North Korea is the only member-state to have exercised this right. It announced its intentions to withdraw immediately from the treaty on January 10, 2003, stating that its previous announcement to withdraw in 1993 was never suspended, so it was not required to give three months' advanced notice to the security council and other NPT parties. Although issues remain as to whether North Korea's withdrawal should be recognized, it no longer considers itself bound by the treaty.

North Korea's withdrawal from the NPT further damages the treaty's effectiveness in stopping the spread of nuclear weapons. Its refusal to comply with IAEA safeguards and eventual expulsion of IAEA inspectors implies that North Korea had an advanced nuclear program prior to its withdrawal from the treaty. Although the IAEA Board of Governors referred the North Korea issue to the UN Security Council, it has yet to decide on the matter. North Korea's withdrawal without consequences reveals the limited capability of the regime to respond to those who breach the treaty, lending further uncertainty to the legitimacy of the NPT.

The NPT's lack of universality and its inability to control nuclear weapons outside of the treaty are its most serious challenges. The ambiguous status of North Korea and the three de facto nuclear weapons states—Israel, India, and Pakistan—pose an uncontrolled threat to the international community. It is unlikely that these nations will be persuaded to join the NPT as nonnuclear states, citing the discriminatory features of the treaty and prevailing security concerns. Granting these states any special status within the NPT, however, might assign value to the possession of nuclear weapons.

Because of gaps in the NPT, many member-states have called for strong reforms of the treaty and the IAEA verification system. Without reforms, they argue, the legitimacy of the NPT regime will continue to be jeopardized and never achieve its original objective of stopping the spread of nuclear weapons. Despite its weaknesses, though, the NPT continues to have a prominent role in maintaining the security of its member-states and the international community.

See also Arms Control; Arms Race; Comprehensive Test Ban Treaty (1996–); International Atomic Energy Agency; Limited Test Ban Treaty (1963); Non- and Counterproliferation; Nuclear Test-Ban Treaty; Nuclear Weapons; Verification

Further Reading

Dunn, L. *Controlling the Bomb*. New Haven, CT: Yale University Press, 1982.

Muller, Harald, David Fischer, and Wolfgang Kotter. *Nuclear Non-Proliferation and Global Order.* New York: Oxford University Press, 1994.

Spector, L. *Going Nuclear.* Cambridge, MA: Ballinger, 1987.

NUCLEAR PROLIFERATION

International spread of nuclear technology. The term *nuclear proliferation* may refer to nuclear energy, but it is more often used in reference to nuclear weapons.

In 1945, the United States was the only country that possessed nuclear weapons technology. Despite extensive efforts to protect the nuclear secret, the Soviet Union exploded its own atomic bomb in 1949. Over the next decade, the pace of nuclear weapons development would accelerate dramatically. By 1955, both nations had developed powerful thermonuclear weapons and were designing more-sophisticated systems to deliver them.

By the late 1950s, other nations had caught up to the United States and Soviet Union in nuclear technology. France and Great Britain both exploded thermonuclear devices in the 1950s; China followed in 1968. Fears about the uncontrolled spread of nuclear weapons led to the creation of the Nuclear Non-Proliferation Treaty (NPT) in 1968. The purpose of the treaty was to limit the possession of nuclear weapons to the five countries that possessed them at the time: the United States, Great Britain, the People's Republic of China (PRC), France, and the Soviet Union. The treaty was subsequently signed by the vast majority of the world's nations. However, since that time a number of other countries have acquired nuclear weapons, and others are close to doing so.

India, Israel, Pakistan, and South Africa refused to sign the treaty. All four countries have admitted to (or have been suspected of) possessing nuclear weapons. South Africa did finally sign the treaty in the 1990s after dismantling its nuclear weapons program. North Korea was an original signatory to the treaty, but revoked its signature after a conflict with nuclear inspectors over the question of secret nuclear facilities. Iran is also believed to be in the process of developing nuclear weapons capability.

Throughout the Cold War, the problem of nuclear weapons was framed by the conflict between the United States and the Soviet Union. Proliferation at this time was mainly concerned with slowing and eventually stopping *vertical proliferation*—the growth of the nuclear arsenals of the world's two superpowers. The spread of nuclear technology to China (1968) and India (1974), and the suspicion that Israel possessed nuclear weapons made *horizontal proliferation* to formerly nonnuclear states a pressing issue.

The collapse of the Soviet Union in 1991 created a new set of proliferation concerns that centered around the fate of the former Soviet nuclear arsenal. Although thousands of weapons that had been placed in former Soviet Republics such as Belarus and the Ukraine were destroyed, the entire Soviet arsenal never has been comprehensively accounted for. Investigators in the former Soviet Union uncovered several cases of cash-strapped scientists trying to sell nuclear technology to foreign nations.

In 1990, the possibility of increased special inspections and expansion of routine safeguards under the NPT was proposed. The necessity of increased vigilance was more apparent in the wake of the Gulf War of 1991, when inspections in Iraq revealed an extensive secret program to develop nuclear weapons. Iraq had been attempting to acquire nuclear weapons since the 1960s, and Israeli bombers destroyed a production plant in 1981.

After years of elusiveness about its nuclear intentions, North Korea announced in 2003 that it did indeed possess nuclear weapons. North Korean dictator Kim Jong Il has used the threat of these weapons to prevent the international community from pressing for regime change in North Korea. In 2002, U.S. President George W. Bush named North Korea as part of an "Axis of Evil," along with Iraq and Iran. The latter nation's potential development of nuclear weapons has recently become a focus of concern in the international community, particularly given the continued political instability in the Middle East.

See also Arms Control; Arms Race; Cold War; Loose Nukes; Non- and Counterproliferation; Nuclear Non-Proliferation Treaty (NPT).

Further Reading

Allison, Graham. *Nuclear Terrorism: The Ultimate Preventable Tragedy.* New York: Times Books, 2004.

Reiss, Mitchell, and Robert S. Litwak. *Nuclear Proliferation After the Cold War.* Washington, DC: Woodrow Wilson Center Press, 1994.

NUCLEAR TEST-BAN TREATY

International agreement that aims to ban all types of nuclear explosions under any conditions in any location. The treaty was opened for signing on September 24, 1996, and by 2005 had been signed by a total of 71 nations.

Signatories to the Comprehensive Nuclear Test-Ban Treaty (CTBT) agree not to undertake any type of nuclear weapons test explosion or any other type of nuclear explosion, as well as to prohibit such explosions from taking place on any territory under their jurisdiction. Moreover, signing parties agree to refrain from causing, encouraging, provoking, or in any way taking part in or having anything to do with any type of nuclear testing involving an explosion for any purpose, including weapons development.

The CTBT was preceded by the 1963 Partial Test-Ban Treaty, which prohibited nuclear tests in the atmosphere, under water, and in outer space. However, neither China nor France, both of whom possessed nuclear weapons, signed the Partial Test-Ban Treaty. By contrast, both joined the three other nuclear powers (the United States, Great Britain, and Russia) in signing the CTBT.

The desire to ban nuclear weapons was expressed from the start of the arms race in the late 1940s and early 1950s. This reflected fears concerning not only nuclear war but also the potential environmental damage caused by repeated nuclear tests. The issue was first raised by Indian Prime Minister Jawaharlal Nehru in 1954, but mutual U.S.-Soviet paranoia during the Cold War made the problem of verification insurmountable.

The policy of the United States with regard to nuclear warfare in the 1950s was massive retaliation, also known as Nuclear Utilization Theory (NUT). This meant the United States was prepared to fight a nuclear war and considered the use of nuclear weapons a legitimate response to threats to national security. The primary site for nuclear testing by the United States at this time was the Marshall Islands. These South Pacific islands were the location of 67 U.S. atmospheric nuclear tests between 1946 and 1958.

It was only in the 1960s that the policy of mutually assured destruction (MAD) became the centerpiece of U.S. nuclear policy. MAD was based upon the recognition that both the United States and the Soviet Union already possessed more than enough weapons to destroy one another many times over. During this time, the question of proliferation attracted international attention, resulting in the Nuclear Non-Proliferation Treaty (NPT) of 1968. However, weapons development continued, and the issue of testing remained unresolved.

During the 1970s, the United States and the Soviet Union held repeated talks meant to defuse the arms race by lowering the number of nuclear weapons possessed by both sides. These included Strategic Arms Limitation Talks (SALT), Strategic Arms Reduction Talks (START), the Antiballistic Missile (ABM) treaty, Strategic Offensive Reduction Treaty (SORT), and others. Agreements such as the Hotline Agreements and Treaty at Sea Agreements were intended to reduce the risk of accidental nuclear war by improving emergency communication on both sides.

An important precursor to the CTBT was the Threshold Test-Ban Treaty, also known as the Treaty on the Limitation of Underground Nuclear Weapon Tests, which opened for signing in July 1974. The treaty established a threshold of 150 kilotons for nuclear test explosions. Neither the United States nor the Soviet Union signed the treaty immediately, but in 1976 both announced their intentions to abide by it. Additional provisions and protocols were added, and the agreement entered into force in December 1990.

Even so, problems of mistrust and verification remain, even after the Cold War. In 1997, the United States accused Russia of having violated the treaty based upon seismographic data received from a location near a Russian test site. The earth tremors, however, turned out to have been the result of a small earthquake. The United States Senate rejected the CTBT in 1999, adding it to the list of nuclear powers that have refused to sign: India, Pakistan, and North Korea. China has signed the CTBT but has yet to ratify it. The nonparticipation of so many nuclear states seriously compromises the effectiveness of the CTBT.

See also Arms Control; Disarmament; International Atomic Energy Agency; Non- and Counterproliferation; North Korea Crises (1994–); Nuclear Non-Proliferation Treaty (NPT); Nuclear Proliferation; Treaties

Further Reading

Oliver, Kendrick. *Kennedy, Macmillan, and the Nuclear Test-Ban Debate, 1961–63.* New York: St. Martin's, 1997.
Renaker, John. *Dr. Strangelove and the Hideous Epoch: Deterrence in the Nuclear Age.* Claremont, CA: Regina Books, 2000.

NUCLEAR UTILIZATION THEORY (NUT)

United States military doctrine in the late 1950s and early 1960s, underpinned by the belief that nuclear war was winnable. First associated with the nuclear policy of U.S. President Dwight D. Eisenhower, nuclear utilization theory (NUT) was intended to intimidate the Soviet Union and lead it to believe the United States considered the use of nuclear weapons a viable military option.

After the Cuban Missile Crisis in 1962, U.S. policy shifted to mutually assured destruction (MAD), which held that nuclear war was unwinnable and could result only in the destruction of both sides. Belief in MAD maintained the balance of power in the latter half of the Cold War and motivated arms limitation talks in the 1970s to prevent one side from acquiring the ability to strike securely. In the 1980s, this policy was transformed as U.S. president Ronald Reagan once again adopted the stance that nuclear war was winnable.

It has been argued that one of the motivations for dropping the atomic bombs on Hiroshima and Nagasaki was to intimidate the Soviet Union with a massive display of U.S. military power. However, just four years later, the Soviets successfully tested their own nuclear weapon and quickly worked to achieve parity with the United States. Both sides also worked to develop viable means of actually delivering the weapons to make their threats more credible. The advent of long-range bombers in the late 1940s and early 1950s made this possible. Recognizing the numerical superiority of Soviet troops in Europe, Eisenhower articulated an official nuclear policy of massive retaliation.

The policy of nuclear utilization received further impetus from events in the Middle East, coupled with the desire to prevent the spread of communism. The Soviets hoped to use the 1956 Suez Crisis as a pretext to increase their influence in the Middle East. The crisis began when Egyptian President Gamal Nasser nationalized the Suez Canal and closed it to Israeli shipping. This alarmed Great Britain and France, who were not only allied with Israel but also did not want the pro-Soviet Nasser to have control over the canal. French, British, and Israeli troops subsequently invaded Egypt to prevent Egypt from seizing the canal. However, the United States opposed the invasion and pressured the invading nations to withdraw their troops from Egypt.

The Soviet Union kept its distance in this dispute, glad to let the United States humiliate its allies and reduce the European presence in the Middle East. In the longer term, the Soviets attempted to use the Suez war as a pretext to forge closer political and military ties with Egypt. For his part, Nasser adopted a stance of "positive neutrality," which allowed him to manipulate both the United States and the Soviet Union for Egypt's benefit. Announcing its intention to use nuclear weapons in case of war was a way for the United States to compensate for having effectively undermined western influence in the region.

The notion that nuclear weapons represented any kind of viable military option soon became outmoded by advances in military technology. The development of ballistic missile submarines at the end of the 1950s created the possibility of a nuclear force that could survive a first strike to retaliate successfully. Even if the United States struck first, there was no guarantee that using nuclear weapons would ensure victory. This realization led U.S. Defense Secretary Robert McNamara to adopt the doctrine of MAD in the early 1960s.

Despite the prevalence of MAD, arguments for the limited use of nuclear weapons, and for the idea that the United States should be prepared to fight a nuclear war remain current. Under the administration of President George W. Bush, the United States announced its intention to continue research and development of tactical nuclear weapons for use on the battlefield. This signals a continued willingness on the part of military and civilian leaders to consider use of nuclear arms in a combat situation.

See also Doctrine; Eisenhower, Dwight D., and National Policy; McNamara, Robert S. (1916–); Mutually Assured Destruction (MAD); Nuclear Deterrence; Nuclear Weapons; Suez Canal Crisis (1956)

Further Reading

Oakes, Guy. *The Imaginary War: Civil Defense and American Cold War Culture.* New York: Oxford University Press, 1994.

NUCLEAR WASTE DISPOSAL

Storage and elimination of radioactive by-products of nuclear weapons production, nuclear power generation,

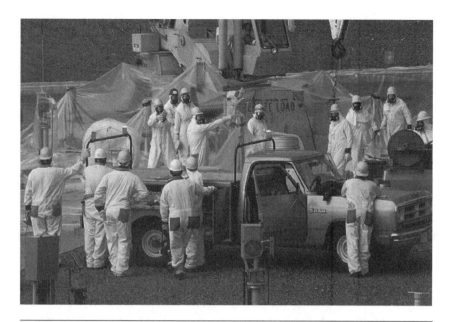

Workers in radiation suits standing by trucks at a nuclear waste site, waiting to pump one million gallons of high-level radioactive waste at the Hanford Nuclear Reservation in Washington state. The safe disposal of nuclear waste has been a growing concern of many since the 1970s. Because such waste can remain dangerous for hundreds of thousands of years, it can pose a continuing threat to many generations of people in the future unless it is disposed of safely.

Source: Corbis.

and other uses of nuclear materials. The management of nuclear waste of any sort received little attention from government policymakers in the three decades after the atomic bomb's development in 1945. Although the nation spent billions of dollars to produce nuclear weapons and commercialize nuclear power in the 1950s and 1960s, only a few hundred million dollars were spent researching storage and disposal processes. Starting in the 1970s, however, considerable public and government attention and resources have focused on nuclear waste as a serious national problem.

Radioactive materials from nuclear waste must be kept from entering the atmosphere, the ground, and the water supply. This is usually possible only by storing the waste securely beyond reach—what is known as *shielding*. Storage facilities must provide maximum protection against the escape of radioactivity, sometimes for thousands of years. There are two main types of nuclear waste: defense-related waste and civilian waste. Although many of the issues are similar, in other ways the problems are quite different.

DEFENSE WASTE

Short-term priorities in the early development of atomic energy created significant waste disposal and site cleanup problems later. These priorities included the sense of urgency in developing the atomic bomb during World War II, the pressure to maintain nuclear parity with the Soviet Union during the Cold War, and a lack of outside regulation and government openness about the nation's atomic program. As a result, radioactive waste created by the defense industry was treated, stored, or disposed of in the most expedient way, with little thought for long-term problems.

It was not until the 1970s that federal government management of nuclear facilities came under scrutiny. Reports of high-level liquid radioactive waste leaking from government storage tanks and abandoned uranium mills raised public awareness and concern about nuclear waste disposal. Successful lawsuits, new legislation, and changed policies gradually opened the weapons production sites to state and public review and oversight. The government finally also allocated substantial funds and personnel to develop a plan for the long-term management of defense waste. In 1987, the Department of Energy (DOE) was reorganized to consolidate defense-related waste management programs and to place increased emphasis on site cleanup.

CIVILIAN WASTE

Civilian waste is produced not only by commercial nuclear power plants but also in industrial processes, in medical and biotechnological research, in diagnosing and treating disease (for example, in X-ray use), and in many other ways. For years, users of radioactive materials relied on private sector facilities to dispose of low-level radioactive waste. Meanwhile, most scientists, regulators, and proponents of nuclear-generated electric power thought of high-level waste disposal as a problem that would be solved by future technology.

In the late 1970s, power plant operators realized that serious storage problems for their reactors' spent fuel could emerge by the late 1980s and that some reactors might need to shut down by the mid-1990s unless additional storage became available. At the same time, public concern began to grow. Several states passed legislation prohibiting further nuclear power plant construction until the federal government demonstrated that waste could be disposed of safely and permanently. Other states restricted or prohibited disposal of radioactive waste within their borders. By 1978, only three operating commercial disposal sites remained for low-level waste: at Barnwell, South Carolina; Beatty, Nevada; and Richland, Washington. Governors of these states gave notice that they planned to either close these sites or cut back their operations.

Beginning in the late 1970s, Congress attempted to deal with the issue of radioactive waste. Several pieces of legislation were eventually passed, including the Low-Level Radioactive Waste Policy Act of 1980 and the Nuclear Waste Policy Act of 1982. Both of these laws were substantially amended in the mid-1980s, and problems with the management of civilian nuclear waste disposal remain.

GENERAL ISSUES IN THE MANAGEMENT OF NUCLEAR WASTE

Resolving issues and setting public policy on nuclear waste remain difficult. The responsibility for setting policy is widely dispersed among federal and state governments and agencies. There are complex social issues, such as geographic and generational equity. The effects of low-level radiation on human health are still unknown, as is the long-term behavior of natural or manufactured systems of containment. The issue of terrorism—and fears of a terrorist attack during the transportation of nuclear waste through heavily populated areas—add a new dimension to the discussion.

Some of the issues associated with the management of nuclear waste include minimizing the amount of waste produced. Other decisions also have to be made: how and where such waste should be stored; if and how it should be treated to make it safer to handle, store, and dispose of; when and why waste should be moved; how and by what routes it should be transported; and where and how the waste can be successfully isolated. To answer these questions, attention must be paid to how hazardous the waste is; what level of risk is to be allowed to workers, the public, or the environment; and the costs and benefits of the various methods of management, disposal, and transportation.

The cleanup of already contaminated sites raises additional questions. What is the goal of the cleanup? What eventual uses of contaminated land are achievable or acceptable, and how much money should be spent? Are materials to be removed from the site, and if so, where are they to be taken?

Overall, decisions regarding nuclear waste disposal must be made in a way that incorporates both scientific fact and social values. Should the current waste disposal solutions be used, or should decisions be delayed in the hopes that better technology will be developed? How can the risks to the health of today's workers and public be compared with the risks to the health of future generations?

See also Environment and National Security; Nuclear Weapons

Further Reading

Peterson, Thomas V., and Steve Myers. *Linked Arms: A Rural Community Resists Nuclear Waste.* Albany: State University of New York Press, 2001.

Risoluti, Piero. *Nuclear Waste: A Technological and Political Challenge.* New York: Springer-Verlag, 2004.

NUCLEAR WEAPONS

Weapons of mass destruction (WMD), which convert the energy created by a nuclear chain reaction into an explosion of tremendous force. There are two classes of nuclear weapons: atomic weapons and thermonuclear weapons. Atomic weapons derive energy from fission, the splitting of the nucleus of an atom. Thermonuclear weapons generate energy through fusion, the combining of several atomic nuclei into a single massive nucleus. Both forms of nuclear reaction produce enormous amounts of energy, but fusion creates significantly more than fission. Most of the nuclear weapons in existence today are thermonuclear devices.

Nuclear weapons became central to the Cold War as the two major contenders in the conflict, the United States and the Soviet Union, amassed enormous stockpiles, well exceeding the amount needed to

Japanese surrender forthcoming, Fat Man devastated Nagasaki. The death toll at both cities, from the atomic blasts and the effects of radiation poisoning afterward, is estimated to be as high as 350,000.

The use of nuclear weapons on Hiroshima and Nagasaki remains controversial. The casualties from the bombings are compared with the estimated number of combat deaths the United States would have been forced to suffer in a land invasion. On the other hand, the bombs were dropped to elicit an unconditional surrender from the reluctant and fanatical Japanese military. Some historians contend that the prospect of a Soviet invasion, not the dropping of nuclear weapons, caused the Japanese to surrender. In this interpretation, the use of the atom bomb was primarily motivated by the need to justify the expense of the Manhattan Project and take revenge for Pearl Harbor.

THE ARMS RACE

The United States was the sole atomic power until 1949, when the Soviet Union successful tested its own atomic bomb. Three years later, the United States tested the world's first thermonuclear device. The Soviets followed with a thermonuclear test in 1955. Throughout the 1950s and 1960s, the United States and Soviet Union engaged in a desperate race to surpass one another in the number and destructive power of their nuclear arsenals.

Each side also developed ever-more sophisticated systems to deliver nuclear weapons. In the 1940s and 1950s, long-range bombers were the only means of delivering a nuclear weapon to the enemy's homeland. The development of the intercontinental ballistic missile (ICBM) in the late 1950s and early 1960s made it possible to strike targets thousands of miles away from bases in one's own country. Later developments included the invention of multiple independently targeted reentry vehicles (MIRVs) that allowed a single ICBM to deliver several warheads to different targets.

By the 1970s, both the United States and Soviet Union were willing to address the issue of their runaway nuclear rivalry. In the late 1970s, the Strategic Arms Limitation Talks (SALT) produced the first-ever reductions in the superpowers' nuclear arsenals. These negotiations were followed up in the 1980s by the Strategic Arms Reductions Talks (START). The START treaty continued the arms reduction work begun in the SALT talks.

PROLIFERATION AND NONPROLIFERATION

By the late 1960s, the arms race between the United States and Soviet Union was increasingly being seen as a threat to peace. By 1968, Great Britain, France, and the People's Republic of China (PRC) would also conduct nuclear weapons tests. The rapid growth in the number of nuclear weapons and nuclear states was seen as an alarming development. Existing nuclear powers worried about the possibility of unstable regimes acquiring nuclear weapons. States that could not afford nuclear programs wanted to prevent regional foes from developing them. In 1968, the five nuclear powers, along with most other countries around the world, signed the Nuclear Non-Proliferation Treaty (NPT). The treaty aimed to restrict possession of nuclear weapons to the United States, the Soviet Union, France, Great Britain, and China.

A number of other states, however, have since developed nuclear weapons. India tested a nuclear device in 1974, and Israel is also suspected of having developed nuclear weapons in the 1970s. India's long-time and bitter rival Pakistan announced in 1998 that it had conducted a series of nuclear weapons tests. Six years later, North Korea declared that it possessed several nuclear weapons. Iran is also suspected of developing nuclear weapons, although the Iranian government claims its nuclear program is solely for producing energy. South Africa once had a nuclear program, but dismantled it in the early 1990s.

The collapse of the Soviet Union in 1991 raised fears that impoverished Soviet scientists might sell nuclear secrets, materials, or weapons themselves to rogue states seeking such technology. To prevent that possibility, the United States has worked with Russia and other former Soviet republics to dismantle nuclear weapons in their territory. By 2005, some 5,000 nuclear warheads had been destroyed in the former Soviet Union. Even so, nuclear material has gone missing from some former Soviet republics in central Asia. The location of these states in an area that is home to terrorist groups raises fears about the possibility of terrorists acquiring nuclear weapons.

EFFECTS OF NUCLEAR WEAPONS

Nuclear weapons produce several effects that contribute to their extraordinary capacity for death and destruction. These include blast, radiation, heat, fallout, and nuclear winter.

Blast and Heat

Most of the physical damage caused by a nuclear explosion is a product of the blast itself. The nuclear blast drives air away from the point of the explosion, producing tremendous winds and dramatic changes in air pressure. The force is strong enough to vaporize objects near the center of the explosion. Large objects such as buildings are usually obliterated because of overpressure. Super high-powered winds hurl smaller objects about at great speeds, turning them into deadly projectiles.

Nuclear blasts generate searing heat that can literally melt a person's skin in a matter of seconds. Thermal energy also produces fires from the spontaneous combustion of flammable materials such as wood and paper. Natural gas leaking from lines broken by the blast can be ignited and produce widespread fires. Another serious danger is the possibility of a firestorm, which occurs when hot air rises rapidly and cold air rushes in at ground level to fan the flames even further. These winds are strong enough to cause fire tornados that carry the fire elsewhere. An extremely large firestorm can even create its own weather system, resembling a thunderstorm, driving its spread. Firestorms caused by conventional bombing of the German city of Dresden during World War II were reported to have melted people on the spot.

Fallout, Radiation, and Nuclear Winter

When a nuclear weapon is detonated on or close to the surface of the earth, it digs out a crater. Most of the debris from the crater is flung into the air and returns to the earth in the form of radioactive fallout. Radiation from fallout might cause significant casualties further away from the blast location and hamper cleanup efforts nearer the blast. Some radioactive particles might be flung far up into the stratosphere, returning to earth many years later. Fallout from nuclear weapons tests conducted by the United States and the Soviet Union in the 1950s and 1960s is still detectable today.

Radiation is experienced directly during a nuclear attack. The extremely concentrated radiation produced by a nuclear explosion can kill a victim within hours or days. Those exposed to nonlethal but still highly elevated doses of radiation might develop long-term illnesses from which they never fully recover. A study carried out by the Atomic Bomb Casualty Commission on pregnant women in Hiroshima and Nagasaki found no short-term genetic impact because of radiation. The prospect of longer-term impact however, remains unresolved.

The most serious long-term consequence of a nuclear war is the possibility of a nuclear winter. In this scenario, nuclear blasts would throw up enough dust to block sunlight for a prolonged period of time. Plants deprived of the warmth and sunlight they need to grow would die, leading to massive famine. Eventually, without plants for food or to produce oxygen, all animal life would die as well. Although nuclear winter is still just a theory, it reflects the consensus of most experts on nuclear weapons.

—*William de Jong-Lambert*

See also Arms Control; Arms Race; Atomic Bomb; Cold War; Comprehensive Test Ban Treaty (1996–); Dresden, Bombing of; Fissile Material; Hiroshima; India-Pakistan Rivalry; Intercontinental Ballistic Missiles (ICBMs); Limited Nuclear Option; Limited Test Ban Treaty; Loose Nukes; Los Alamos; Manhattan Project (1942–1945); Mutually Assured Destruction (MAD); Nagasaki; Neutron Bomb; Non- and Counterproliferation; Nuclear Non-Proliferation Treaty (NPT); Oppenheimer, J. Robert (1904–1967); Strategic Nuclear Triad; Tactical Nuclear Weapons; Teller, Edward (1908–2003); Weapons of Mass Destruction (WMD); World War II (1939–1945)

Further Reading

Lambers, William. *Nuclear Weapons*. Cincinnati, OH: Lambers Publications, 2002.

Shambroom, Paul, and Richard Rhodes. *Face to Face With the Bomb: Nuclear Reality After the Cold War*. Baltimore: Johns Hopkins University Press, 2003.

REFLECTIONS

A Nuclear Warrior's View of Nuclear Weapons

What, then, does the future hold? How do we proceed? Can a consensus be forged that nuclear weapons have no defensible role, that the political and human consequences of their employment transcends any asserted military utility, that as weapons of mass destruction, the case for their elimination is a thousand fold stronger and more urgent than for deadly chemicals and viruses already widely declared illegitimate, subject to destruction and prohibited from any future production? I believe that such a consensus in not only possible, it is imperative. . . .

Where do we begin? What steps can governments take, responsibly, recognizing that policy makers must always balance a host of competing priorities and interests? First and foremost is for the declared nuclear states to accept that the Cold War is in fact over, to break free of the attitudes, habits, and practices that perpetuate enormous inventories . . . . Second, for the undeclared states to embrace the harsh lessons of the Cold War: that nuclear weapons are inherently dangerous, hugely expensive, militarily inefficient, and morally indefensible; that implacable hostility and alienation will almost certainly over time lead to a nuclear crisis; that the strength of deterrence is inversely proportional to the stress of confrontation; and that nuclear war is a raging, insatiable beast whose instincts and appetites we pretend to understand but cannot possibly control.

—General Lee Butler, former Commander, Strategic Air Command, in a speech at the State of the World Forum, San Francisco, October 3, 1996.

NUCLEAR WINTER

Theory that nuclear war would result in major climatic and ecological changes. The theory of nuclear winter is attributed to scientist Carl Sagan and four coauthors in the 1983 article, "Global Atmospheric Consequences of Nuclear War," which appeared in the journal *Science*. The article was written when the antinuclear movement was active and when Soviet and U.S. stockpiles of nuclear weapons were abundant. In subsequent years, the article has generally been referred to as TTAPS, an acronym derived from the last initial in each of the author's names.

The article envisions the aftermath of a nuclear war where, depending on the combined yield of the warheads used, a blast would generate significant amounts of dust into the air. The accumulation of dust and smoke into the atmosphere would create a blanket around the earth, preventing sufficient sunlight from entering the atmosphere. The authors argued that the lack of sunlight would precipitate a cooling that would lower the earth's temperature several degrees centigrade in a short period of time. It is believed that the change of one degree could have a serious effect on the environment. The article further posits that the cooling would affect agriculture and animal life, thereby contributing to a greatly diminished ecosystem.

Subsequent to its printing, the nuclear winter theory has been the subject of vigorous debate.

See also Nuclear Weapons

NUNN, SAM (1938–)

Democratic Senator from Georgia known for his long service on the Senate Committee on Armed Services. Born September 8, 1938, in Perry, Georgia, Nunn was the grandnephew of Congressman Carl Vinson of Georgia. He graduated from Emory University in 1961 and received a law degree from the school the following year. While an undergraduate, Nunn served two years in the Coast Guard and served in the Coast Guard Reserve from 1960 to 1968. After admission to the bar in 1962, he worked for the Armed Services Committee of the House of Representatives, but soon had to return to his hometown to help on the family farm.

Nunn entered politics by winning election to the Georgia House of Representatives in 1968. Four years later, he entered the U.S. Senate in a special election to fill a vacancy caused by the death of Senator Richard Russell. His most noteworthy legislative achievements include drafting the 1986 Department of Defense Reorganization Act, and the 1991 Nunn-Lugar Cooperative Threat Reduction Program. The former resulted in the most significant defense reorganization since the National Security Act of 1947; the latter provided incentives for Russia and its former republics to destroy excess nuclear, biological, and chemical weapons. For their pioneering legislation, Senators Nunn and Lugar were nominated for the Nobel Peace Prize in both 2000 and 2001. In addition to the Senate Committee on Armed Services, Nunn also served on the Permanent Subcommittee on Investigations and the Intelligence and Small Business Committees.

Also notable in the career of Senator Nunn was his 1991 vote in opposition to military action against Saddam Hussein's forces in Kuwait. Mr. Nunn himself has stated that this vote ruined an otherwise promising run for the White House on the 1992 Democratic ticket. After the United States emerged victorious from Operation Desert Storm, Senator Nunn withdrew from the presidential race because of the unpopularity of his antiwar stance. Nunn chose not to run for reelection in 1996.

Following his retirement from politics, Nunn practiced law for the firm King and Spalding in Atlanta and has served on many corporate boards. In addition, he serves as cochairman of the Nuclear Threat Initiative (NTI), founded in 2001 to reduce the threat posed to global security by weapons of mass destruction (WMD). Sam Nunn is also a distinguished professor at the School of International Affairs at Georgia Tech University, which bears his name.

See also Goldwater-Nichols Act

OFFENSIVE BIOLOGICAL WEAPONS PROGRAM

Development, stockpiling, and maintenance of weaponized bacteria, virus, or toxin for military purposes. The use of biological weapons was banned by the Convention on the Prohibition of the Development, Production and Stockpiling of Bacteriological (Biological) and Toxin Weapons and on their Destruction, opened for signature in 1972. The Biological Weapons Convention was intended to augment the 1925 Geneva Protocol for the Prohibition of the Use in War of Asphyxiating, Poisonous, or other Gases, and of Bacteriological Methods of Warfare. The convention is the first international disarmament treaty to ban an entire category of weapons. Although more than 100 states have signed, the lack of any verification mechanism makes compliance almost impossible to determine.

Biological warfare is part of the history of colonization and conquest, as invaders have conquered local populations by inadvertently—and deliberately—infecting them with diseases they carry. As a military strategy, the use of biological weapons dates back to the Roman Empire and also was employed during the Middle Ages. Biological warfare was at work during the American Revolution and the Civil War, and earlier, Native Americans were devastated by the diseases brought by Europeans to the New World.

During World War II, the Nazis conducted notorious, horrific experiments on human subjects in concentration camps, involving everything from the deliberate infection of victims with disease to subjecting prisoners to extreme temperatures and other inhumane conditions to test how the human body endures. Unit 731 of the Japanese Imperial Army was also engaged in biological weapons research, including live vivisections and the manufacture of plague bacteria. Meanwhile, the British conducted anthrax experiments off the coast of Scotland, rendering the island test site uninhabitable for decades.

Biological weapons research was conducted throughout the Cold War by both the United States and the Soviet Union. Though nuclear weapons were the focus of contention and agreement, both sides also continued research programs on weaponized disease-causing agents. President Nixon officially disbanded the biological weapons program in the United States in response to public pressure and disgust over the use of chemical weapons in the Vietnam War. The Soviet Union, however, secretly continued to perfect smallpox for dissemination by aerial bombs and missiles. The collapse of the Soviet Union and all that it entailed for the scientific community, including financial hardship and unemployment, has contributed to concern for the fate of materials produced under the program.

In the post–Cold War era, the proliferation of biological weapons and their potential use by terrorists have become matters of deep concern. The past two decades have seen a marked improvement in production techniques for biological agents, resulting in more aggressive disease strains and the use of genetic engineering to turn benign organisms into harmful ones. Genetic engineering can also make disease strains more toxic and robust, thus allowing for a wider range of attack methods. Biological warfare is notoriously difficult to conduct, but scientific advances are making it more efficient and effective. The most important of these advances include the development of agents that are more virulent after deployment, targeting delivery to specific populations, protection for manufacturing personnel against infection, use of genetic engineering to create strains that are harder to detect, and modification of immune systems of target populations to make them more susceptible to infection.

Since the 1990s, more aggressive efforts have been made to establish verification procedures for the Biological Weapons Convention. The United States rejected the convention in 2001, however, on the grounds that it would interfere with legitimate biodefense and commercial activity. Many observers claim that U.S. reluctance to sign the agreement has undermined the treaty's effectiveness.

See also Anthrax; Biodefense/Biosecurity; Biological Weapons and Warfare; Biological Weapons Convention; Bioterrorism; Geneva Conventions; Infectious Disease

Further Reading

Davis, Jim A., and Barry R. Schneider, eds. *The Gathering Biological Warfare Storm.* Westport, CT: Praeger, 2004.

Mangold, Tom, and Jeff Goldberg. *Plague Wars: The Terrifying Reality of Biological Warfare.* New York: St. Martin's, 2001.

United States Government. *21st Century Complete Guide to Bioterrorism, Biological Weapons and Warfare, Germs and Germ Warfare, Nuclear and Radiation Terrorism.* Dulles, VA: Progressive Management, 2001.

OFFICE OF DOMESTIC PREPAREDNESS

Principal component of the Department of Homeland Security (DHS), charged with preventing and responding to acts of terrorism. The Office of Domestic Preparedness (ODP), formerly the Office of State and Local Preparedness, is an agency within the Department of Justice responsible for enhancing the capacity of state and local governments to prevent, deter, and respond safely and effectively to acts of domestic terrorism involving chemical, biological, nuclear, and explosive weapons. In this capacity, the ODP provides training, funds for the purchase of equipment, support for the planning and execution of exercises, technical assistance, and other antiterrorism support to assist states and local jurisdictions.

The September 11, 2001, terrorist attacks on New York and Washington, DC, demonstrated that responding to catastrophic incidents can rapidly deplete local supplies and equipment. The ODP provides grants to first responders to purchase equipment, as well as training and technical assistance. ODP domestic training includes the Homeland Security Assessment and Strategy Technical Assistance; Terrorism Early Warning Group Replication; Interoperable Communication Technical Assistance; Rapid Assistance Team Technical Assistance; General Technical Assistance; Prevention Technical Assistance and Plans; and Planning Synchronization Technical Assistance.

See also Emergency Preparedness and Response; First Responders; Homeland Security, Department of; September 11/ WTC and Pentagon Attacks

OFFICE OF NAVAL RESEARCH (ONR)

Government agency that acts as a liaison between the U.S. Navy and the scientific and technical communities in the United States. The Office of Naval Research (ONR) coordinates, executes, and promotes the science and technological programs of the U.S Navy and Marine Corps through schools, universities, and government laboratories, as well as nonprofit and for-profit organizations. The ONR provides technical advice to the chief of naval operations and the secretary of the navy and works with industry to improve technological manufacturing processes.

The ONR has its roots in the World War II Office of Scientific Research, which established an office in London in 1940 for the exchange of war research between the United States and its allies. In May 1946, the London office became a branch of the Navy's Office of Research and Invention (ORI). Shortly thereafter, Congress transformed the ORI into the Office of Naval Research, with headquarters in Washington and London.

Although the London office had a strong connection to Great Britain, its mission extended beyond that country to survey and report on the rebuilding of Europe and developments in post-Nazi European science. The ONR Tokyo office, opened in 1977, shared a similar mission in Asia. In 1997, the London and Tokyo offices were merged into the present ONR International Field Office, whose scope includes all of Europe, the former Soviet Union, the Middle East, Africa, Northeast and

Southeast Asia, India, Australia, and New Zealand. An additional office was added in Singapore in 2000. Today, the International Field Office provides a single science and technology strategy to its users.

The ONR is responsible for four major programs: Liaison Visits, the Science and Technology Engagement Program (STEP), Conference Support Program (CSP), and Naval International Cooperation Opportunities in Science and Technology (NICOP). These programs range from formal conferences and meetings with science and technical people to programs teaming ONR investigators with academic, industrial, and government laboratories. The end product of these programs is input into the ONR's global database.

See also Science, Technology, and Security; U.S. Navy

OFFICE OF NET ASSESSMENT

Department of Defense think tank created in 1973 and tasked with imagining all possible threats to the national security of the United States. The Office of Net Assessment (ONA) was created in 1973 by President Richard Nixon, who was dissatisfied with the quality of intelligence he was receiving. Nixon created a *net assessment group* in the National Security Council to evaluate intelligence from different agencies about Soviet and Chinese nuclear capabilities. Defense theorist Andrew Marshall was named to head the ONA, a post he has held ever since. The group was transferred to the Department of Defense in 1972.

The ONA arguably has been the most influential organization in shaping American military thinking. Its analyses of U.S. and Soviet military spending in the 1970s convinced U.S. president Jimmy Carter to increase the U.S. military budget during his term in office. During the 1980s, the ONA regularly criticized estimates of Soviet economic strength produced by the Central Intelligence Agency (CIA). The accuracy of the ONA's views was confirmed after the 1991 fall of the Soviet Union. More recently, the ONA pioneered the transformation of the U.S. military using information technology.

One of the tasks of the ONA has been to identify and define major transformations in the conduct of warfare that result when technological developments help cause a fundamental alteration in the conduct of warfare. Such developments are known as revolutions in military affairs, or RMA. The advent of strategic bombing between World War I and World War II is an example of RMA. The development of airplanes capable of carrying large bomb loads and flying far behind enemy lines led military commanders to realize that it was possible to strike at an enemy's homeland, targeting its civilian population as well as the factories that produce war material. This resulted in the creation of new military units and doctrines designed to strike directly at the enemy's capacity to make war and to weaken the morale of its citizens to continue to fight.

In the early 1990s, the ONA identified three areas of technology that provide the basis for the beginning of a new RMA. These include the information revolution, long-range, precision-guided weapons, computer battlefield simulation, and computer-aided design and manufacturing. The ONA also remarked on an apparent trend toward small "special operations" units gradually taking over many functions once performed by "heavy" military formations.

Despite mixed assessments of its work, there is no doubt that ONA has shaped U.S. military planning and strategy for decades. In a sign that ONA is still generating controversy, in 2004 it released a report predicting that climate change could lead to global ecological catastrophe as early 2020. The report warns that such change may well lead to political instability and increase the chances for war and unrest in the near future. This view directly contradicts the views of the administration of President George W. Bush, which discounts the threats caused by global warming.

See also Intelligence and Counterintelligence; National Security Strategy of the United States; Think Tanks

OFFICE OF STRATEGIC SERVICES (OSS) ·

Predecessor of the Central Intelligence Agency (CIA), an office formed during World War II to provide the United States with the ability to conduct intelligence and wage clandestine operations. Led by the colorful William "Wild Bill" Donovan, a lawyer turned military commander who earned a Medal of Honor in World War I, the Office of Strategic Services (OSS) made significant contributions to fighting the Axis forces, including parachuting behind enemy lines and developing spy technology.

In July 1941, President Franklin D. Roosevelt, dissatisfied by the lack of coordination among State Department sources, Army G-2 intelligence, and Naval

Intelligence forces, appointed William Donovan to be coordinator of information (COI). Donovan's job was to direct the nation's first peacetime, nondepartmental intelligence organization, and Donovan pulled together what became known as a "fourth arm" of the military. He combined an odd collection of hand-me-down units from the military and State Department, including intelligence, research, propaganda, subversion, and commando operations, into a unified whole.

The United States' entry into World War II in December 1941 prompted new thinking about the place and role of the COI. This led to the establishment of a new agency, the Office of Strategic Services (OSS), which was formed in June 1942 with a mandate to collect and analyze strategic information required by the Joint Chiefs of Staff and to conduct special operations not assigned to other agencies.

The OSS was soon moved under the Joint Chiefs and some of its original responsibilities were split, with radio broadcasting operations—the Foreign Intelligence Service—becoming part of the Office of War Information. The other responsibilities included the Research and Analysis Branch, which gathered information from unclassified sources such as the Library of Congress; the X-2 Branch (the counterintelligence branch); and the Special Operations Branch, which ran guerrilla operations in Europe and Asia.

As the United States developed its military operations in Europe, OSS operatives played a key role by deploying behind enemy lines and engaging in commando operations and sabotage. At its peak strength in the mid-1940s, the OSS employed 13,000 personnel, the size of an army division. This figure included 7,500 individuals deployed overseas and 4,500 women overall. One prominent woman in the OSS was Virginia Hall, who helped coordinate French resistance fighters prior to D-day and ultimately earned a Distinguished Service Cross, the only one awarded to a civilian woman in the war.

See also Central Intelligence Agency (CIA); Espionage; Intelligence and Counterintelligence; Roosevelt, Franklin D., and National Policy

secretary of defense with policy development, planning, resource management, and program evaluation.

The OSD has several missions, which it pursues in coordination with other elements of the DoD. The main job of OSD is to develop and implement policies in support of United States national security objectives. It also oversees the allocation and management of resources related to DoD plans and programs and serves as the liaison between the DoD and the U.S. intelligence community and other government agencies. Each OSD staff official is responsible for conducting analyses, developing policies, providing advice, making recommendations, and issuing guidance on DoD plans and programs.

The OSD is headed by the secretary of defense and includes the deputy secretary of defense, under secretaries of defense, director of defense research and engineering, assistant secretaries of defense, general counsel, director of operational test and evaluation, assistants to the secretary of defense, and the director of administration and management. The office also includes any other positions created by the secretary of defense to assist in carrying out the OSD's assigned responsibilities.

Until the end of World War II, the military establishment was divided between the Department of War and the Department of the Navy, a framework that caused great inefficiency in the war effort. After the war, Congress passed the National Security Act of 1947, which established a single department for military matters called the National Military Establishment (NME). Two years later the NME was renamed the Department of Defense.

The authority of OSD was strengthened by the Goldwater-Nichols Act of 1986. The act specifies that the U.S. military chain of command runs from the president of the United States to the secretary of defense to the regional military unified commanders, also known as the commanders in chief, or CINCs.

See also Department of Defense, U.S. (DoD); Goldwater-Nichols Act; National Security Act (1947)

OFFICE OF THE SECRETARY OF DEFENSE (OSD)

Government staff responsible for running and managing the Department of Defense (DoD) and assisting the

OFFSHORE BALANCING

Theory of international relations that views multipolarity as an opportunity rather than a threat. Proponents of offshore balancing believe that attempts to maintain

U.S. hegemony as the world's only superpower will lead other states to unite against the United States and ultimately reduce its relative power. Because the United States cannot stop the rise of new great powers, it should aim toward a strategy of *burden shifting,* whereby others will take over responsibility for maintaining regional power balances and quelling problems.

To encourage cooperation in a multipolar world, the great powers would delineate spheres of influence and pledge noninterference in those regions. By pushing for burden shifting and spheres of influence, proponents of offshore balancing hope to dampen the backlash against U.S. hegemony, especially after the launch of the war on terrorism and the Iraq War of 2003. Two leading theorists of offshore balancing are Christopher Layne and Benjamin Schwarz, who supported the idea in a 2002 article in *Atlantic Monthly* titled "A New Grand Strategy." The authors stated that "Although jockeying for advantage is a fact of life for great powers, coexistence, and even cooperation between and among them, is not unusual. Offshore balancing seeks to promote America's relative power and security, but it also aims to maximize the opportunity for the United States to be on decent terms with the other great powers."

See also Balance of Power; Hegemony; Multipolarity

OIL AND NATIONAL SECURITY

The relationship between petroleum, the vital resource fueling the industrialized world (and the American lifestyle), and economic security as a prominent issue of national security (the absence of a threat to American values). Interruption in the supply of oil and other natural resources would have dire economic consequences for the United States and for the entire industrialized world. As a result, the United States and other major oil-importing countries consider the protection of this resource to be a significant concern.

More controversially, dependence on oil imports from unstable regimes and volatile regions, particularly Saudi Arabia and other Persian Gulf states, forces foreign-policy compromises on U.S. policymakers that can also adversely affect national security. For instance, the United States maintains a close alliance based on oil with the autocratic and despotic Saudi regime, despite its nebulous sponsorship of and complicated relationship with radically anti-American Islamic forces.

OIL SHOCKS

Oil has had been a key factor in many of the wars and crises of the 20th century, motivating countries to go to war and determining outcomes. In 1990, for example, Iraqi dictator Saddam Hussein invaded neighboring Kuwait in large part because of a desire to gain access to the country's oil fields. In response, the United States went to war as part of a United Nations (UN) coalition to push back Iraq and restore the oil status quo.

Fears of oil shortage as an issue of U.S. national security stem primarily from the oil shocks of the 1970s. In October 1973, the Arab oil-producing states belonging to the Organization of Petroleum Exporting Countries (OPEC), an international organization that seeks to regulate the price of oil, successfully imposed production restraints and an embargo on the United States and hiked oil prices by 70%. These actions were taken partly in retaliation for U.S. aid to Israel during a joint Egyptian and Syrian offensive known as the Yom Kippur War. It was also a chance for the OPEC cartel to gain leverage over U.S. and international oil companies that were taking a large slice of the profits from the oil-producing countries. (OPEC's first failed attempt at embargo, in 1967, followed Israel's speedy victory in the Six-Day War.)

The effects of the OPEC embargo and price hikes were immediate. By 1973, the United States was importing up to 35% of its oil, as a result of the decline of its own oil production coupled with ever-increasing demand. The oil shortage meant that the United States was effectively held hostage by the Arab nations. Accustomed to an uninterrupted flow of cheap oil, U.S. citizens were suddenly forced to ration everything, from thermostat use to gas consumption, and gasoline lines snaked their way around city blocks. At the height of the crisis, the price of gasoline had risen from 30 cents a gallon to about $1.20. The United States and the entire Western world reeled from a severe recession.

A second energy crisis struck in 1979 in the immediate aftermath of the Iranian revolution. The disruption of Iranian oil exports led to oil shortages, which allowed OPEC to drive up prices once again. Oil lines appeared in the United States as they had six years earlier.

POLICY RESPONSES

Since the economic traumas of the 1970s, America's civilian leadership and military establishment have come to include the concept of economic security within the purview of national-security issues. On December 22, 1975, then-President Gerald Ford signed the Energy Policy and Conservation Act (EPCA), which officially established the Strategic Petroleum Reserve (SPR). This legislation declared that official U.S. policy would be to establish a petroleum reserve of up to 1 billion barrels. In mid-November 2001, President George W. Bush directed the Department of Energy (DOE) to fill the SPR to maximum capacity of 700 million barrels to "maximize long-term protection against oil supply disruptions." As of April 9, 2004, the SPR contained the largest emergency oil stockpile in the world, at 653 million barrels.

Under the EPCA, it is up to the U.S. president to determine that withdrawal of supplies from the SPR is required by a severe energy-supply interruption. Such an interruption is defined as (1) one of significant scope and duration and of an emergency nature; (2) one that may cause major adverse impact on national safety or the national economy; or (3) one that results from an interruption in the supply of imported petroleum products.

STRATEGIC SHIFT

During the Cold War, U.S. national-security strategy was narrowly focused on military power and rivalry with the Soviet Union. Since the collapse of the Soviet bloc, however, U.S. security and defense experts have viewed the Persian Gulf, the Caspian Sea, and the South China Sea as sources of vital oil and natural-gas resources with increased strategic importance. In 1999, the Department of Defense reassigned Central Command to take over senior command authority of U.S. forces in Central Asia, instead of the more peripheral Pacific Command. Central Command oversees U.S. forces in the Middle East and its flow of oil to the United States and its allies.

The strategic reshuffle meant that the vast flow of oil resources from the Caspian basin would now receive the same attention and protection as those in the Middle East. Also in 1999, the National Security Council's annual report stated explicitly that "the United States will continue to have a vital interest in ensuring access to foreign oil supplies," such that the nation "must continue to be mindful of the need for regional stability and security in key producing areas to ensure our access to and the free flow of these resources."

Today, the United States is the world's largest energy producer, consumer, and net importer. Although its own oil reserves rank 11th worldwide, it typically meets around 60% of domestic total gross oil demand with foreign imports (according to 2003 data). In 2003, more than two-fifths of the nation's oil came from OPEC nations. Half of this amount, in turn, derives from Persian Gulf nations, or one fifth of total U.S. oil imports. In 2003, Saudi Arabia, the world's largest oil exporter, was the second-largest supplier of oil to the United States, after Canada.

Today, OPEC controls a smaller share of the oil market than in the 1970s and 1980s. What the United States does not import from OPEC countries such as Saudi Arabia or Iraq, it buys from Canada, Norway, or Mexico. However, oil is a finite resource. Scientists forecast that global oil production will peak in the first decade of the 21st century and decline thereafter. With no corresponding effort to decrease oil consumption, and with global and U.S. demand growing at approximately 2% every year, nations will compete more intensively for resources in the near future. Even as nations around the world search for alternatives, energy prices will likely soar and economies may be plunged into recession.

Some commentators view recent and ongoing turmoil between the United States and Islamic extremists in the Middle East as a predictable consequence of competition over oil. More than two-thirds of the world's remaining oil reserves lie in the Middle East, including the Caspian basin. The United States' dependence on these oil imports makes such regions strategically vital and keeps U.S. military forces tied to the Persian Gulf. Many people also remain concerned that U.S. strategic energy policy has still failed to address larger issues at stake, namely the problem of oil dependence, climate change, and the developing world's lack of access to energy.

See also Middle East and U.S. Policy; Natural Resources and National Security

Further Reading

Deffeyes, Kenneth S. *Hubbert's Peak: The Impending World Oil Shortage.* Princeton, NJ: Princeton University Press, 2003.

Klare, Michael T. *Resource Wars: The New Landscape of Global Conflict.* New York: Henry Holt, 2002.

Yergin, David. *The Prize: The Epic Quest for Oil, Money, and Power.* New York: Free Press, 1992.

OKINAWA

Japanese island that was the site of one of the fiercest battles between Allied and Japanese forces during World War II. The island of Okinawa is now home to one of the largest U.S. Marine Corps military bases.

After the Japanese defeat in World War II, the United States occupied Okinawa and used the island as a major strategic base for American forces in Asia. A presence in Okinawa allowed the United States to project power in Asia and deter communist threats from the Soviet Union and China. In 1960, the United States signed the Treaty of Mutual Cooperation and Security with Japan, which stipulated that the United States would respond to an attack against Japan and placed Japan under the protection of the U.S. nuclear umbrella. The treaty obligated Japan to provide land for U.S. military bases to be financed mainly by the Japanese. Okinawa was the site of the largest and most important of those bases.

Okinawa was officially returned to Japan in 1972, but the United States retained the right to station troops there indefinitely. The Marine Corps base on the island is one of the largest regular marine deployments in the world. There are currently about 20,000 marines stationed in Okinawa in addition to civilian employees and dependents. The total number of U.S. military and civilian personnel has been estimated at 52,000.

The large U.S. military presence on the island of Okinawa has been a source of contention with the local population and has placed strains on the U.S.–Japan security alliance. Because the island of Okinawa is becoming increasingly urbanized, there have been rising complaints from Okinawans over issues including the proximity of the large military facilities to urban areas, as well as environmental problems, training accidents, and crimes committed by U.S. personnel against local citizens. Despite these disputes, the United States is likely to continue to maintain a presence in Okinawa in light of potential trouble spots in East Asia such as Taiwan, China, and North Korea.

See also U.S.–Japan Alliance

OKLAHOMA CITY BOMBING

The 1995 truck bombing of the Alfred P. Murrah Federal Building in Oklahoma City. At the time, the

The Oklahoma City Bombing Memorial, which commemorates the 168 people who were killed when a bomb planted by domestic terrorist Timothy McVeigh and his accomplices destroyed the Alfred P. Murrah Federal Building on the morning of April 19, 1995. Construction of the memorial began in September 1998, and it was dedicated by President Bill Clinton on the fifth anniversary of the bombing, on April 19, 2000. This picture was taken just five days before the June 11, 2001, execution of McVeigh.

Source: Corbis.

Oklahoma City bombing was the most deadly terrorist attack on U.S. soil.

Shortly before 9 a.m. on April 19, 1995, a rented truck packed with 5,000 pounds of explosive material was parked in front of the Alfred P. Murrah Federal Building in Oklahoma City, which housed several federal law-enforcement agencies. The bomb inside the truck consisted of ammonium nitrate fertilizer and nitromethane racing fuel. At 9:05, the bomb exploded, destroying the north face of the nine-story building. After several weeks of search-and-rescue efforts, the final death toll was 168, including 19 children.

Initial reports indicated that the main suspects were individuals of Middle Eastern origin. However, attention turned quickly to Timothy McVeigh, a U.S. citizen known to have far-right antigovernment views. Within 90 minutes of the bombing, an Oklahoma highway patrolman pulled McVeigh over for lack of a license plate and arrested him for possession of an unregistered gun. McVeigh was in police custody when his connection to the attack became known days later. He left a mostly complete paper trail of purchases and rental agreements that tied him to the bombing.

At McVeigh's trial, the U.S. government alleged that McVeigh had sought the help of his friend Terry Nichols. According to the government, McVeigh, Nichols, and other conspirators made preparations in Kansas and headed to Oklahoma with their bomb. Their alleged motive was revenge for a 1993 assault by federal agents on the compound of a religious fringe group called the Branch Davidians near Waco, Texas. April 19 was the anniversary of the raid, which had resulted in the deaths of 80 Branch Davidians. One of the tenants of the Murrah building was the Bureau of Alcohol, Tobacco, and Firearms (ATF), which McVeigh regarded as complicit in the Waco attack.

McVeigh was found guilty of the bombing and received the death penalty for the murder of eight federal law-enforcement officials. He died by lethal injection at the federal penitentiary at Terre Haute, Indiana, on June 11, 2001. An accomplice, Michael Fortier, received a fine of $200,000 and 12 years in prison for failing to notify authorities when he learned of McVeigh's intended attack. Terry Nichols received a life sentence on a manslaughter conviction. He also stood trial in state court at McAlester, Oklahoma, and received a life sentence for 160 murders. A jury deadlock prevented him from receiving the death penalty. The half-destroyed Murrah building was demolished in May 1995, replaced by a memorial and terrorism research center. A museum was dedicated in 2001.

After the bombing, the government changed the protective measures in place around all federal buildings. For example, the close-in parking that allowed McVeigh to park his truck next to the building was eliminated. The bombing further provided a boost to passage of the Antiterrorism and Effective Death Penalty Act of 1996. In February, President Bill Clinton had proposed the Omnibus Counterterrorism Act of 1995, and after the attack he added another $1.25 billion to the package. Congress failed to complete action before the summer recess, but the next year it passed the antiterrorism legislation.

The Antiterrorism and Effective Death Penalty Act weakened habeas corpus by eliminating federal review of state death-penalty cases. It also allowed the U.S. Immigration and Naturalization Service (INS) to hold deportation hearings for any noncitizen who provided material support to terrorist organizations. The act redefined material support to include activities previously assumed to be protected under the First Amendment and froze the assets of any American citizen or organization believed to be an "agent" of a terrorist group. There were no specifications for what constituted an agent. The act served as the legal authority for many of the cases pursued by the Federal Bureau of Investigation (FBI) and the Department of Justice in the aftermath of the September 11, 2001, terrorist attacks on New York City and Washington, DC.

See also Branch Davidians; Terrorism, U.S. (Domestic)

Further Reading

Giordano, Geraldine. *The Oklahoma City Bombing.* New York: Rosen, 2003.

Hamm, Mark S. *Apocalypse in Oklahoma: Waco and Ruby Ridge Revenged.* Boston: Northeastern University Press, 1997.

Marcovitz, Hal. *The Oklahoma City Bombing.* Northborough, MA: Chelsea House, 2002.

OPEC (ORGANIZATION OF PETROLEUM EXPORTING COUNTRIES)

Intergovernmental organization formed to coordinate the petroleum policies of oil-producing nations with a view toward economic stability in the oil market. The Organization of Petroleum Exporting Countries (OPEC) exerts a tremendous influence over world oil supplies and prices. This influence makes it a significant force in shaping the foreign policy of the United States, which imports most of its oil.

In the late 1950s, global oil supplies greatly exceeded the worldwide demand for oil. Prices fell accordingly, and petroleum-producing nations began losing revenue. In 1959, a group of oil-producing countries met in Cairo, Egypt, to find ways to stabilize prices and guarantee steady oil revenues. The following year, five of the nations represented at the meeting—Iran, Iraq, Kuwait, Saudi Arabia, and Venezuela—formed OPEC to obtain for its members the "best possible terms within the postwar petroleum order." By 1971, OPEC had expanded to include Algeria, Indonesia, Libya, Qatar, Nigeria, and the United Arab Emirates.

OPEC engages in collective bargaining in order to stabilize oil production and revenues, and to ensure the highest possible prices for oil. Collective bargaining prevents a "race to the bottom" among producers who might otherwise drop prices to compete for clients. The cartel likewise permits member countries to coordinate their petroleum policies to prevent political conflicts that could cause splits within OPEC. This scheduling and forecasting is important, as OPEC countries possess more than 75% of the world's proven petroleum reserves and produce 55% of all internationally traded oil.

OPEC is governed by a Conference that meets every March and September but that may convene additional meetings as needed. The Conference is advised by a Board of Governors and is supported by a Secretariat, an Economic Commission, and the Ministerial Monitoring Committee. Delegates to the Conference are typically oil, mining, or energy ministers from the member countries. The governing principle of the organization stresses unanimity, and the Conference operates on a one-member, one-vote basis. OPEC members establish quotas to coordinate oil production, but they retain their sovereignty in production matters. Beyond strict oil-production matters, members have established an OPEC Fund for International Development that issues grants and loans to non-OPEC countries.

The stated goal of OPEC is "to promote stability and harmony in the oil market," but this aim is sometimes overridden by political considerations. One of the most prominent examples of this was the Arab oil embargo imposed on the United States after the 1973 Arab–Israeli war. The Arab members of OPEC also substantially decreased exports to other countries, hoping those nations would pressure Israel to return land it captured from Egypt and Syria during the war.

As a result of the embargo, world oil prices nearly quadrupled, affecting vulnerable markets and causing economic hardship. Even today, critics complain that

OPEC's domination of the oil market means that prices are linked to politics rather than to supply and that the cartel's market power represents a risk for other oil producers as well as consumers.

See also Energy Policy and National Security; Middle East and U.S. Policy; Middle East Conflicts (1956, 1967, 1973); Oil and National Security

OPEN DOOR POLICY

Proposed in 1899 by U.S. president William McKinley, policy that aimed to guarantee to all countries equal economic access to China. The Open Door policy was focused on increasing U.S. regional power in East Asia and China.

At the end of the 19th century, China was in political isolation and economic trouble. No major powers recognized China as a sovereign nation, and most of them were claiming extraterritorial rights on its land and exploiting its natural resources. The United States had become an imperial power in East Asia after the acquisition of the Philippines from Spain. However, it was excluded from the sphere of influence of major powers in China.

In the fall of 1898, President William McKinley stated his desire for the creation of an "open door" that would allow all major powers to access the Chinese market. In 1899, Secretary of State John Hay sent notes to France, Germany, Great Britain, Italy, Japan, and Russia, asking them to guarantee equal economic access to China and to preserve Chinese territorial integrity. The goal of such a policy was to put all imperial countries, including the United States, on an equal level of influence over China. No country formally agreed to Hay's policy, each of them stating that they could not commit themselves until the other countries had complied. However, in March 1900, Hay announced that an agreement had been reached. Only Russia and Japan complained.

The Open Door policy was challenged from the beginning. In 1900, Russia exercised almost exclusive influence in Manchuria, a region of northeastern China. In 1915, Japan presented to China the Twenty-One Demands, which included the provision that other powers be barred from further territorial concessions in China. Japan also insisted on control over China's military, commercial, and financial affairs, a demand dropped under U.S. pressure. A series of secret treaties that promised Japan control over German possessions in China at the end of World War I further weakened the Open Door policy.

The increasing disregard of the policy spurred the United States to call a conference on the Limitation of Armaments in Washington, DC, in 1921. The conference produced the Nine-Power Treaty, which guaranteed the integrity and independence of China and reaffirmed the Open Door policy. The treaty was signed by the United States, Belgium, China, France, Great Britain, Japan, Italy, the Netherlands, and Portugal. However, with the 1931 Japanese seizure of Manchuria, the open door was definitely compromised. China would not be recognized as a sovereign state until after World War II.

See also China and U.S. Policy

OPEN SKIES TREATY

International agreement that allows signatory nations to conduct unarmed aerial observation flights over the territory of other participating members. Designed to enhance confidence and security, the Open Skies Treaty gives each party the right to gather information about the military forces and activities of other parties.

The original open-skies concept was proposed by U.S. president Dwight D. Eisenhower to Soviet Premier Nikita Khrushchev in 1955. At the time, the Soviets rejected the concept, and it lay dormant for a generation. In May 1989, the initiative was reintroduced by President George H. W. Bush and signed on March 24, 1992, in Helsinki, Finland. The U.S. Congress ratified the treaty in 1993. The treaty entered into force by January 1, 2002, when it received final ratification by the members of the North Atlantic Treaty Organization (NATO).

The main provision of the Open Skies Treaty allows each member state to observe military forces and actions in the territories of other members by permitting the installation of photographic and advanced sensory equipment on aircraft and satellites. Images collected by a member state are available to any other member willing to pay the costs of reproduction. The treaty also ensures that all surveillance equipment covered under the treaty will be available to all participants in the regime. Signatories agree on an annual quota of observation flights each member state is willing to receive and send out. The treaty covers the national territories—land, islands, and the internal and territorial waters—of all the member states. It is also of unlimited duration and open to other states based on certain stated qualifications.

Provisional application of portions of the treaty took place between 1992 and 2002, and formal observation flights have been in place since August 2002. Since the signature of the Open Skies Treaty in 1992, the security environment in Europe has changed significantly. Nevertheless, Open Skies is the most wide-ranging international effort to date to promote openness and transparency of military forces and activities. It thus remains an important element of the European security structure, along with the Treaty on Conventional Armed Forces in Europe (CFE) and the Vienna Document 1999 agreement on confidence- and security-building measures (CSBMs) under the auspices of the Organization for Security and Co-operation in Europe (OSCE).

See also Intelligence and Counterintelligence; Spy Satellites; Treaties

OPERATION DESERT SHIELD
See GULF WAR (1990–1991)

OPERATION DESERT STORM (1991)

The combat phase of the American-led campaign that inflicted a debilitating defeat on Iraq and liberated Kuwait in the period from January to March 1991. Operation Desert Storm required a month of aerial bombardment followed by a swift thrust by land forces, mostly mechanized. Although most fighting took place in Iraq and Kuwait, a brief incursion into Saudi Arabian territory, as well as ballistic missile attacks upon Saudi Arabia and Israel, contributed to heightened tensions. This operation followed Operation Desert Shield, which was the initial response to the Iraqi seizure of Kuwait in August 1990, deploying forces in and near Saudi Arabia and the Persian Gulf to counter further Iraqi moves, or to resist attack by Iraqi forces.

During Operation Desert Shield, the United States and its allies sent forces to the Persian Gulf and the eastern Mediterranean to defend Saudi Arabia, control the gulf, and prepare for the recapture of Kuwait. The head of the U.S. Central Command, General Norman Schwarzkopf, had focused considerable energy upon arraying overwhelming naval and air superiority in the region, accompanied by a logistical buildup calculated to give the coalition forces a comfortable military balance and margin of security. The required 60-day supply of ammunition, tens of thousands of hospital beds, and thousands of tons of spare parts were either in place or placed in the long supply lines extending to bases in Germany, Spain, the United Kingdom, and the United States.

A presidential order by President George H. W. Bush on November 8, 1990—which called for an effective doubling of the ground forces slated for the offensive—reflected a fail-safe strategy calculated in the Pentagon and agreed to by General Schwarzkopf. The British contingent swelled to an armored division, and a second heavy corps was ordered to the region from the U.S. garrison in Germany. An additional Marine Corps division and amphibious brigade, as well as additional air and naval forces, swelled the U.S. contingent to a total of some 540,000 troops, 6 aircraft carriers, 4,000 tanks, 17,000 helicopters, and 1,800 fixed-wing aircraft.

Important combat forces also were drawn from Egypt (armored corps) and France (armored division and 60 aircraft). Although a Syrian armored division deployed and prepared for action, it was not used, in part because it had equipment identical to that of the Iraqi army. Saudi Arabia, the host nation for most of the allied forces, provided several brigades of ground-combat troops, combat aircraft, and the all-important supply and transportation services required by all the contingents.

THE AIR CAMPAIGN

The air war segment of Operation Desert Storm began on January 17, 1991, with a predawn-attack helicopter strike on the outermost Iraqi radar systems, followed by waves of cruise missiles and stealth aircraft sent against Iraqi air defenses and command and control systems. The classic U.S. air doctrine of "turning out the lights" consisted of destroying the communications and data nodes of the opposing forces and suppressing antiaircraft sites.

Once those goals were accomplished, conventional fighter-bomber and strategic-bomber attacks could occur in relative safety with large volumes of high-explosive bombs. The air attack would also include significant numbers of precision-guided munitions (PGM), which used terminal guidance to destroy high-value targets and those considered too close to the civilian population for conventional attack.

After several successive nights of methodical air attack, the known key Iraqi military and government command and control centers; communications centers; air bases; and suspected sites for storing and manufacturing nuclear, chemical, and biological weaponry had all been destroyed or neutralized. The priority of the air offensive then turned to the tactical units of the Iraqi army, which was dug into positions facing the Kuwaiti–Saudi border, as well as the prize target: Iraqi Republican Guard forces being held back in operational reserve. As the bombing destroyed bridges over the Tigris and Euphrates rivers, Iraqi supply lines evaporated because all road traffic from Iraq to the frontline units was blocked. Meanwhile, on the front lines, all types of U.S. and coalition aircraft struck to achieve the 50% diminution of Iraqi forces in the field stipulated by General Schwarzkopf as his requirement.

The air war of Operation Desert Storm would have achieved its objectives sooner but for the key distraction of the Iraqi bombardment of Israel by medium-range ballistic rockets, the so-called Scuds, which were really improvised medium-range ballistic missiles fashioned from tactical-range rockets. Although the rocket attacks, begun on January 17, did not contain much-feared chemical or biological munitions, they nonetheless provoked considerable tension in both Israel and Saudi Arabia.

Modified U.S. Patriot antiballistic missiles seemed to be effective in stopping most of the Iraqi Scuds. Later analysis, however, revealed that the Scuds, rather than being destroyed by Patriot missiles, were breaking up in final trajectory as a result of faulty design. In any event, a considerable portion of the allied special-forces patrols and tactical air power had to be pulled from their tactical and strategic missions and directed against the SCUD launching sites in the western desert of Iraq.

THE GROUND CAMPAIGN

On February 23, 1991, the much-anticipated ground war of Operation Desert Storm began with nearly simultaneous attacks by three U.S. and two Arab mechanized corps across the Saudi frontier into Iraqi-held territory, including Kuwait. Previously, both sides had sparred with ground forces. For instance, between January 23 and February 10, 1991, U.S. Marines made a few artillery raids against key Iraqi positions, and the Iraqis launching an ambitious attack across the Kuwait–Saudi border on January 29–30, intending to disrupt coalition preparation and morale in what was known as the Battle of Khafji.

In the Battle of Khafji, three Iraqi brigades, perhaps precursors of a full three-division attack, attempted an incursion into allied lines—one by amphibious end-around, one at the border town of Khafji, and the other two against desert outposts covered by the First Marine Division. Allied air reconnaissance, using radar and the JSTARS (Joint Surveillance Target Attack Radar System) airborne ground detection system, detected these movements. As a result, the amphibious effort was destroyed almost before it had begun, the outpost incursion was defeated overnight, and the Khafji battle became a testing ground for the Saudi and Gulf states contingents assembled on the eastern coast of Saudi Arabia, to retake it. They took Khafji quickly, with strong allied air and artillery support, and the incident revealed for the first time the ineffectiveness of the Iraqi army, even when it achieved an element of tactical surprise.

No effective forces lay before the allied corps sweeping into the Iraqi desert and Kuwaiti oil fields, merely third-rate Iraqi infantry divisions filled with conscripts terrorized by weeks of allied bombing and shelling. Moreover, the minefields and field fortifications so tenaciously constructed by the Iraqis in the Desert Shield phase of the conflict had deteriorated from lack of maintenance and bombardments, holding the coalition forces up less than half a day, for the most part.

From east to west, the U.S. 18th Airborne Corps, 7th Corps, Joint Forces Command West (Saudi and Egyptian), 1st Marine Expeditionary Force, and Joint Forces Command East (Saudi and Gulf states) advanced on February 23–24, 1991, against the demoralized Iraqi forces. The U.S. 18th and 7th Corps swept around the exposed inland flank and began to annihilate the Republican Guard units, which were outclassed thoroughly by U.S. and British technical ability to fight at night and in low visibility.

Meanwhile, the Joint Forces and U.S. Marine commands advanced frontally into Kuwait, eliminated a few weak counterattacks, and entered Kuwait City on February 26. In a mere 100 hours, the Iraqi army was in full retreat across the Euphrates River, totally at the mercy of allied air attacks. President Bush declared a cease-fire on the next day, February 27, 1991, and a negotiated armistice took effect on March 3.

The offensive actions of Operation Desert Shield succeeded handily in defeating Iraqi forces and restoring Kuwait to its emir. The offensive crippled Iraqi military power, forcing a political solution to Iraqi threats in the region. United Nations inspection teams later certified the destruction of prohibited munitions and weapons, and allied (later Anglo-American) air patrols were established over the northern and southern sectors of Iraq to deny Iraqi use of airspace from which they could threaten their minority populations and neighboring countries.

See also Chemical Weapons; Cruise Missile; Gulf War (1990–1991); Operation Desert Storm (1991); Precision-Guided Munitions; Stealth Technologies

Further Reading

Friedman, Norman. *Desert Victory: The War for Kuwait.* Annapolis, MD: Naval Institute Press, 1991.
Atkinson, Rick. *Crusade: The Unknown Story of the Persian Gulf War.* Boston: Houghton Mifflin, 1999.

OPERATIONS OTHER THAN WAR (OOTW)

Activities involving the use of the military but that do not necessarily involve armed clashes between two organized forces. Operations other than war (OOTW) include activities such as providing support for civilian authority, emergency evacuations of noncombatants from war zones, antidrug operations, and disaster and humanitarian assistance.

Despite its name, OOTW can also include military operations or the use of troops and military equipment to perform security and peacekeeping functions. These include activities such as combating terrorism, ensuring no-fly or no-go zones, protecting shipping and air lanes, making military shows of force, carrying out preemptive strikes and raids, and providing support to insurgents.

According to the government's Joint Doctrine for Military Operations Other Than War, the principles used in OOTW are simply an extension of the military's war-fighting doctrine. Military OOTW doctrine has six basic principles: (a) every operation should be directed at a clearly defined and attainable objective; (b) all efforts must be directed to a common purpose; (c) security is extremely important, that is, the enemy should never have a military, political, or intelligence advantage; (d) OOTW may require restraint in applying military power; (e) the force must persevere with its mission and stay focused on the long-term goal; and (f) operations must be seen as legitimate by the government and people of the country where they are taking place.

One of the main distinctions between combat operations and OOTW is that considerations other than military victory often are of primary importance in OOTW. The goal of combat is to defeat the enemy's forces as quickly as possible and conclude peace on the terms most favorable to one's own side. However, the goals of OOTW are not always as clear. These goals may include deterring potential enemies, supporting local authorities, and providing humanitarian assistance all at the same time. All of these objectives must be taken into consideration when planning OOTW.

Operation Restore Hope, the U.S. effort to provide famine relief to Somalia in the early 1990s, offers an example of the complex nature of many OOTW. At the time, Somalia was a country without a working central government that was ruled by a variety of armed warlords. The country's political chaos led to a breakdown in food production and distribution, resulting in a devastating famine that threatened the lives of millions of Somalis. Although many countries and international aid agencies sent food and relief supplies, most of these were seized by warlords before they could reach the general public.

The operation began on December 9, 1992, as U.S. Marines landed in Somalia and took control of major airports, seaports, and food distribution points in order to facilitate the delivery of relief supplies. The force of some 38,000 troops patrolled the area in and around the capital Mogadishu, safeguarding relief operations, escorting convoys, and searching for weapons. Troops also repaired more than 1,200 miles of roads, drilled wells to provide fresh water, rebuilt hospitals and schools, and treated thousands of Somalis for everything from bullet wounds to typhoid. Although the international effort to rebuild the central government failed, Operation Restore Hope saved countless lives and provided much-needed assistance to ordinary Somalis.

Operation Restore Hope reflects the three main political objectives of all OOTW. The first is to deter war by intervening to protect U.S. interests. The second is to establish an overseas presence in order to demonstrate U.S. commitment to its allies, to lend credibility to U.S. alliances, to ensure regional stability, and to provide the United States with access to and influence with foreign governments. The third is to respond to crises, whether military or humanitarian. The government considers the attainment of these objectives a major contribution to the national security of the United States.

See also Doctrine; Peacekeeping Operations; Somalia Intervention (1992)

OPPENHEIMER, J. ROBERT (1904–1967)

Scientist, professor, and director of the Manhattan Project, which developed America's first atomic bomb. Born into a wealthy Jewish American family in New York City on April 22, 1904, Robert Oppenheimer was to become known as the father of the A-bomb.

From an early age, Oppenheimer distinguished himself as a brilliant thinker and intellectual. After graduating from Harvard College in 1925, Oppenheimer continued his studies at Cambridge University in England and at Gottigen University in Germany, where he earned his Ph.D. Following his academic pursuits, Oppenheimer returned to the United States in 1929 to teach at the University of California, Berkeley, and at California Institute of Technology.

Despite early successes as a professor and scholar in quantum theory, Oppenheimer is best known for his work on the U.S. atomic bomb project. Following the creation in 1941 of the Manhattan Project—the atomic-bomb program—Oppenheimer was initially brought in to calculate the amount of uranium needed to sustain a chain reaction for an atomic bomb. Soon after, however, Oppenheimer was named the director for the Manhattan Project. The project accelerated under his guidance as he assembled the top theoretical scientists in the country to discuss the atomic program.

Although Oppenheimer is considered the father of the atomic bomb, his reaction to its testing and subsequent use on the Japanese cities of Hiroshima and Nagasaki is well documented. As a result of these bombings, Oppenheimer became an activist for international controls on atomic energy and was opposed to the development of a potentially more powerful weapon, the hydrogen bomb.

At the end of his life and career, Oppenheimer was subjected to increased scrutiny as a former communist sympathizer. During the height of the Red Scare in the 1950s, awareness of his attraction to leftist politics early in his life led to the loss of his security clearance and thus a limitation on the work he could do in the atomic-energy field. He continued to teach and write at Princeton University until his death from throat cancer in 1967.

See also Atomic Bomb; Manhattan Project (1942–1945)

ORDER OF BATTLE

Organizational tool used by military leaders to analyze the composition of enemy units. An order of battle describes the kind of forces one might encounter in an engagement with any particular enemy. This information is used in planning U.S. military strategy and tactics with regard to different potential foes.

The U.S. Army breaks down enemy orders of battle according to several different factors, including numerical strength, level of training and technology employed, combat tactics, and combat effectiveness. Order-of-battle analysis also examines enemy force composition, that is, the command structure and organization of enemy headquarters units and subunits. It also considers the locations of enemy units and other factors including the personalities of opposing commanders and the battle history of individual units.

American military intelligence calls for each U.S. combat unit to maintain an order of battle for enemy units two echelons down. In other words, a U.S. division should monitor enemy battalions, a U.S. brigade should monitor opposing companies, and a U.S. battalion should monitor enemy platoons. This intelligence practice has been in place since first recommended by General George S. Patton during World War II.

See also Combat Effectiveness; Intelligence and Counterintelligence; War Planning

ORGANIZATION FOR SECURITY AND CO-OPERATION IN EUROPE (OSCE)

Pan-European security organization dedicated to conflict prevention, crisis management, and postconflict rehabilitation in Europe. The Organization for Security and Co-operation in Europe (OSCE) is the largest regional security grouping in the world, with 55 member states from Europe, Central Asia, and North America.

The OSCE approaches security with broad definitions and includes issues such as human rights and economic cooperation as key components in the promotion of peace and stability. Although it conducts peacekeeping and conflict-resolution operations, it does not employ force to accomplish its objectives. The OSCE is based on a concept of consensus-based decisions whereby all member states have equal status. Because the organization has no legal standing under international law, these decisions are politically but not legally binding.

The Soviet Union floated the idea of a pan-European security organization in the 1950s, but Soviet attempts to exclude North American countries—and later Soviet aggression in central Europe—derailed those early plans. The idea was revived during the early 1970s, and in 1973, countries from Europe and North America—including the United States—formed the Conference for Security and Co-operation in Europe (CSCE). This organization served as a predecessor to today's OSCE.

The collapse of communism at the end of the 1980s caused a rethinking of the role of the CSCE. Absent the threat of a Soviet invasion of Western Europe, the CSCE sought a new mandate. In November 1990, this mandate was expressed in the Charter of Paris for a New Europe. Under the charter, CSCE members agreed to protect human rights and fundamental freedoms such as freedom of thought, freedom of conscience, freedom of religion or belief, freedom of expression, freedom of association and peaceful assembly, and freedom of movement. The CSCE officially became the OSCE in January 1995. Since that time, the OSCE, once seen as merely setting standards to promote its broad concept of security, has moved toward a robust presence in the field. It has launched more than 20 peacekeeping and security missions throughout the former Soviet Union and the former Yugoslav republics.

With operations winding down in parts of the Balkans, more OSCE resources have been transferred to the Caucasus and Central Asia, which are seen as breeding spots for terrorism. Still, some security analysts believe that major international powers continue to underutilize the potential of the OSCE, to the detriment of making inroads on the root causes of terrorism and organized crime. These issues received renewed emphasis following the terrorist attacks of September 11, 2001, as OSCE officials reaffirmed the organization's comprehensive security approach, designed to tackle the underlying causes of terrorism and not just the results.

See also Cooperative Security; Regionalism; Terrorism, War on International

ORGANIZATION OF AMERICAN STATES

Intergovernmental organization designed to address security issues, settle disputes among member nations, and promote democracy throughout the Western Hemisphere. During World War II, the majority of nations in the Western Hemisphere agreed to defend one another from any potential attacks by German or Japanese forces. This cooperation was the direct result of President Franklin D. Roosevelt's Good Neighbor policy, an assurance that the United States would no longer interfere in the internal affairs of Latin American countries. After the war, the nations of the Western Hemisphere hoped to strengthen this newfound sense of cooperation, leading to the creation of the Organization of American States (OAS) in April 1948.

The organization was designed to ensure the region's collective security, peacefully settle disputes between member nations, and promote trade throughout the region. A General Assembly, consisting of one representative from each member, was created to oversee the organization and vote upon its activities. To fund the organization, each member was required to pay dues based upon the size of its economy.

The member nations also signed a nonbinding agreement called the *American Declaration of the Rights and Duties of Man.* The document enumerated the political and civil rights that member nations were expected to grant their citizens. The United States had wished to list the spread of democracy as the foremost goal of the organization. However, many of the Latin American nations harbored bitter memories of past United States incursions into countries such as Panama and Haiti. Therefore, the OAS resolved not to topple any existing government, even if human-rights violations were involved.

This resolution, however, was soon ignored. In 1954, the OAS granted the United States permission to overthrow the Marxist government in Guatemala. The vote in the General Assembly was sharply divided; those opposed to the overthrow noted that the Guatemalan government was democratically elected. In 1959, a much stronger consensus was formed to eliminate the brutal dictatorship of Rafael Trujillo in the Dominican Republic. Led by the United States, the OAS enacted an economic boycott that smothered the Dominican economy until Trujillo was killed in an uprising.

This success convinced OAS members that intervention in the internal affairs of individual nations was sometimes justified. An effort was therefore made to outline when such intervention was permissible. In 1960, the OAS formed the Inter-American Commission on Human Rights. Consisting of seven members, the commission compiles reports outlining its judgments of both the level of democracy and human-rights conditions in each nation. Based on these reports, the commission recommends whether the OAS should take any action against offending members. In 1969, the commission's authority was increased when the Inter-American Court was formed. This body possesses the power to impose economic penalties upon nations that suppress human rights.

Despite bestowing this additional authority on the OAS, many members condemned the United States' invasion of Panama in 1989. In the wake of the invasion, the General Assembly struggled to further clarify when military action could be taken against a member nation. In 1991, the assembly issued the Declaration of Santiago, a document that specifies five criteria for the use of military intervention. Most of the criteria concern the overthrow of a legally elected leader or the use of violence against innocent civilians. Since the declaration was adopted, the OAS has successfully intervened during uprisings in Haiti, Peru, Guatemala, and Paraguay.

The OAS originally consisted of 21 member states but has since expanded to include 35 nations. Under its guidance, democracy has become much more widespread throughout the Western Hemisphere, and the number of corrupt or oppressive governments in the regions has been reduced.

See also Good Neighbor Policy; Interventionism; Latin America and U.S. Policy

ORGANIZED CRIME

Unlawful activities systematically planned and carried out by highly organized associations of individuals. In addition to designating a type of action, the term *organized crime* also can, and often does, refer to the organizations that are responsible for illicit acts.

MAIN CHARACTERISTICS

The difficulty in clearly defining the concept of organized crime comes from the ambiguity of the term *organized.* For example, how organized does a criminal outfit need to be to be considered an agent of organized crime? Most people who have studied the phenomenon agree that, at the very least, an organized-crime group has to maintain a clear hierarchy among its members and function according to a set of enforceable rules and regulations. A city gang, therefore, which temporarily groups a few youths involved in illegal activities, does not constitute organized crime.

The primary goal of organized crime is economic profit. Organized crime does not traditionally espouse and fight for a particular political ideology. Thus, terrorist organizations like Hamas and al-Qaeda are not usually considered organized-crime groups, even if they are well organized and engage in illegal activities. Organized-crime groups may acquire political power to ensure prosperity for their members, but they do not generally perceive political power as a goal in itself.

Organized-crime groups have a limited, highly specialized membership and are characterized by a carefully thought-out division of labor. As in any legal business enterprise, every member knows his or her place in the organization and will undertake specific duties on a regular basis. Unlike legal businesses, however, organized crime shows a willingness to resort to violence and bribery to achieve its goals.

The continued existence of an organized-crime group does not rely on specific individuals. In other words, in this kind of a group, everybody is replaceable. Even if the leader of the outfit dies or goes to jail, the organization is designed to promptly find somebody to take over. Organized crime, therefore, is characterized by permanency, as much as by its economic priorities, lack of political ideology, hierarchy, and specialization.

METHODS

By definition, organized crime is involved in illegal activities, and its members run the risk of being apprehended by the police. Secrecy and loyalty to one's peers, therefore, are an unquestionable necessity. Such behavior is often supported both by one's respect for a tradition and by one's fear of violent retribution in case of disobedience.

The illegal activities in which organized crime is involved are as numerous as they are diverse. Traditionally, organized-crime groups run operations such as auto theft, narcotics production and trafficking, counterfeiting, economic fraud, gambling, robbery, extortion, loan sharking, money laundering, smuggling, and prostitution. In recent years, organized crime has followed the diversifying strategies of business corporations, establishing overseas branches and identifying new types of potential enterprises. Sophisticated operations such as identity theft, online extortion, and stock market fraud have in many cases become the primary source of income for transnational organized-crime outfits.

Being able to function in more than one country not only provides access to new markets but also allows one to escape police investigators, who are frequently hampered by limited jurisdictions. Often, organized-crime outfits will run legitimate businesses in parallel with their illegal enterprises. This practice lends the enterprises an aura of respectability and serves as a means to launder illegally obtained money.

HISTORY OF ORGANIZED CRIME IN AMERICA

Groups exhibiting some characteristics of organized crime have been active in the United States as far back as the 18th century. Pirates, whiskey bootleggers, and smugglers were common in the colonial period. However, the phenomenon is generally said to have taken its present form in the late 19th century, with the association of corrupt politicians and street gangs.

New York City was the primary venue for early organized-crime groups, due to its many economic opportunities and the easy availability of poor young immigrants willing to break the law in order to come up in the world. With money acquired through activities such as illegal gambling, prostitution, and extortion, New York crime lords were able to buy themselves protection from police and political pressure. By the early 1900s, newly arrived Italian immigrants organized into crime outfits, which later gave rise to the famous Mafia families. The Prohibition era of the 1920s saw an explosion in the number and sophistication of organized-crime groups, which acquired immense wealth—and notoriety—from bootlegging.

In the 1970s, confronted with a rapidly expanding collection of organized-crime syndicates, federal legislators passed a series of laws designed to make it easier to prosecute suspected organized-crime members. By the early 1980s, legislation such as the Racketeer Influenced and Corrupt Organizations Act (RICO) succeeded in significantly reducing, but not eliminating, the influence of organized-crime outfits.

THE ITALIAN MAFIA

Between 1875 and 1920, southern Italy was one of the most important sources of immigrants for the United States in general and New York City in particular. With immigrants seeking freedom from persecution and better lives came characters who had been involved in illegal extortionist organizations back in Italy, such as the Ndragheta in the city of Calabria and the Cosa Nostra in Palermo. The term *Mafia* later came to designate all Italian American organized-crime groups, regardless of origin. These groups found in the immigrant masses both a convenient target for extortion and a permanent source for recruiting organized-crime members.

By the early 1900s, dozens of gangs operated from the midst of the approximately half a million Italians living in New York City. In the decades to follow, famous mafiosi such as Salvatore Maranzano, Giuseppe Masseria, Lucky Luciano, Joseph Bonanno, Frank Costello, Vito Genovese, Thomas Lucchese, and Joseph Profaci would forge alliances and vie for preeminence in the city. In Chicago, another breeding place for the Italian Mafia, "Scarface" Al Capone achieved unrivaled notoriety through his impressive bootlegging operation.

In the early 1980s, the Mafia became the target of crippling blows from prosecutors aided by legislation such as RICO, as well as by the increasing public interest in gangster activities. At present, Mafia control over organized crime is fiercely challenged by relatively new organized-crime groups, such as the Russian mob, South American drug cartels, and East Asian gangs.

THE RUSSIAN MOB

The demise of the Soviet Union in 1991, as well as the subsequent economic depression that engulfed the former Soviet states, set off a wave of immigration to the United States. Coming from a society with little respect for the law, some of the ex-Soviet immigrants saw organized crime as an opportunity to dramatically improve their economic fortunes. As a result, cities including New York, Philadelphia, Los Angeles, Chicago, and Baltimore saw the emergence of dozens of organized gangs whose members came from the former Soviet Union.

The preferred activities of the Russian mob are drug trafficking, prostitution, smuggling, auto theft, financial fraud, extortion, and contract assassination. Among these, financial fraud is probably the most profitable occupation, with the Russian mob believed to be the beneficiary of many large-scale embezzlement schemes. In addition, the group is thought to control hundreds of banks used to launder illegally obtained money. Russian organized-crime outfits have recently become the target of intense investigation, as they are believed to be able and willing to sell nuclear and biological weaponry acquired from poorly guarded sites in the former Soviet Union. The Russian mob is currently said to be operating in nearly 60 countries around the world.

EAST ASIAN GANGS

East Asian organized crime came to the United States mainly from China (including Hong Kong) and Japan. The Chinese Triads and the Japanese Yakuza are perhaps the best-known Asian crime organizations that are currently active in the United States.

The Triads are organizations initially formed in China in the 17th century and are characterized by strong loyalty among their members and willingness to resort to extreme violence. As with the other ethnically based organized-crime groups, the Triads entered the United States in the midst of the immigrant waves of the late 19th and early 20th centuries.

Their preferred activities center around illegal gambling, prostitution run from massage parlors, extortion (often aimed at fellow Chinese business owners), armed robberies, drugs, and contract murder.

The name *Yakuza* describes a variety of criminal organizations of Japanese origin. These groups are highly organized and are often based on a family system, much like the traditional Italian Mafia. In the United States, where it is deeply involved in financial fraud, the Yakuza does not shy away from drug dealing, weapons trafficking, extortion, and prostitution. Exceptionally high levels of sophistication and almost impenetrable structures make the Chinese Triads and the Japanese Yakuza two of the most effective and dangerous kinds of organized crime in contemporary America.

DRUG CARTELS

Organized crime is heavily involved in the narcotics business. A large share of the fabrication, transportation, and commercialization of illegal drugs has traditionally been in the hands of South American crime lords, particularly those operating from or connected to the country of Colombia. The Medellín and Cali drug cartels, in particular, long controlled the drug supply to cities such as New York, Miami, Los Angeles, and Houston. Drug cartels employ thousands of people in both North and South America. With the help of well-organized and generously financed networks, they are able to ship huge quantities of illegal drugs to the United States every year. Once inside the United States, the drugs are usually sold to other organized-crime groups.

In an effort to thwart drug-smuggling operations, the United States has worked with the Colombian government to annihilate the drug supply at its source. To this end, the United States has provided Colombia with extensive military and financial assistance and has sought the extradition of captured drug lords. Nevertheless, the South American drug cartels remain the most affluent organized-crime outfits in America.

CURRENT CONCERNS

In the aftermath of the September 11, 2001, attacks on New York City and Washington, DC, organized crime has come under serious scrutiny for its potential to collaborate with ideologically driven terrorist organizations such as al-Qaeda. Given the increasing sophistication of organized-crime operations and their immense breadth of resources, terrorist leaders such as Osama bin Laden are likely to see great advantages in establishing commercial relations with organized-crime groups in the United States. From the Russian mob's expertise in smuggling nuclear and biochemical warfare agents to the availability of East Asian gangs to provide contract assassins, organized-crime groups perform many activities that may appeal to a well-funded terrorist organization in need of logistical and material help.

Technological advances that have facilitated communication and trade across borders have made such cooperation easier. Today, organized-crime groups can operate in many different countries, making them a more difficult target for national police forces. In response, law-enforcement institutions across the globe are making great efforts to coordinate their activities and thus acquire the same flexibility and effectiveness that have kept transnational organized-crime and terrorist groups in business for decades.

—Razvan Savii

See also Biodefense/Biosecurity; Border and Transportation Security; Drug Cartels; INTERPOL; Narcotics, War on

Further Reading

Abadinsky, Howard. *Organized Crime.* 7th ed. Belmont, CA: Wadsworth/Thomson Learning, 2003.

Kenney, Dennis J., and James O. Finckenauer. *Organized Crime in America.* Belmont, CA: Wadsworth, 1995.

Ryan, Patrick J., and George E. Rush, eds. *Understanding Organized Crime in Global Perspective: A Reader.* Thousand Oaks, CA: Sage, 1997.

OTTAWA LANDMINE TREATY

International agreement banning antipersonnel land mines. Officially titled the Convention on the Prohibition of the Use, Stockpiling, Production and Transfer of Anti-Personnel Mines, the Ottawa Landmine Treaty marks the first time that a conventional weapon in widespread use has been outlawed by a majority of world nations.

Military experts believe that, over the past 25 years, more than 50 countries have manufactured as many as 200 million antipersonnel land mines. The leading producers have been China, Italy, the former Soviet

Union, and the United States. Antipersonnel land mines have been used in countless conflicts throughout the 20th century, and millions remain buried on former battlegrounds. These mines continue to be a daily threat in scores of countries. This ongoing danger to civilians was a significant factor leading to the treaty. Opponents of antipersonnel land mines maintain that the weapons violate an important rule of warfare, in that they are incapable of distinguishing between soldiers and civilians. Moreover, unlike other types of weapons, land mines remain a danger in the areas where they are deployed long after a cease-fire has been called or a conflict has ended.

The impetus for the eventual elimination of antipersonnel mines began with a 1994 speech delivered by U.S. president Bill Clinton to the United Nations. Nevertheless, the United States is not one of the 150 signatories of the treaty. The United States's reluctance to ratify the Ottawa Landmine Treaty stems largely from the unwillingness of the international community to give the United States a so-called Korea exemption. In order to protect South Korea from a possible North Korean invasion, the United States maintains some 40,000 troops and tens of thousands of land mines along the Korean Peninsula's demilitarized zone. The United States considers these mines part of its security guarantee for South Korea in particular as well as a key part of overall U.S. tactical military strategy.

The Clinton administration pledged that the United States would sign the treaty by 2006 if it could identify and deploy an alternative to land mines. In March 2004, however, the administration of President George W. Bush announced that the United States had effectively abandoned that pledge, though it would significantly increase its financial contribution to mine-elimination programs beginning in 2005. The United States has not deployed antipersonnel land mines since the Gulf War of 1991.

United States attitudes and actions in regard to the treaty are contradictory. On the one hand, the United States is not a signatory and is actively developing new types of land mines. On the other hand, the United States has given more money to other countries for demining operations than has any other nation. It has also destroyed more mines—some 3 million—than any other country.

The treaty has had mixed results in controlling the production, deployment, and removal of land mines. As of 2002, the estimated annual number of deaths from land mines decreased from about 26,000 before the treaty went into effect to between 15,000 and 20,000 deaths afterward. The treaty has also resulted in modest reductions in land mine production and sales. However, 16 countries—including the United States—still count land mines among their tactical weapons, and mine-clearing operations have only barely scratched the surface of the problem. The United Nations estimates the number of land mines in Afghanistan alone at 5 to 10 million.

See also Arms Control; Land Mines; Treaties

OVERSEAS DEPLOYMENT
See CONVENTIONAL FORCES IN EUROPE TREATY (1990)

P

PACIFISM

Theory that peaceful rather than violent relations should govern human behavior and that disputes should be resolved through negotiation. Pacifism is not only a response to war but also a response to domestic injustices and government repression.

PACIFIST THEORY

Philosophers draw a distinction between two forms of pacifism: absolute pacifism and conditional pacifism. Each of these forms of pacifist theory has two basic expressions based upon the individual's motivation for pacifist behavior. For some people, pacifism is driven by a moral imperative; for others, it is based on more practical considerations.

The basic premise of absolute pacifism is that one must never use or support the use of force, regardless of circumstances. In deontological pacifism, this is an absolute moral duty, regardless of the immediate consequences of refraining from violence. For example, deontological pacifism might involve refusing to inflict harm on someone to prevent another person (or even oneself) from being injured or killed. Consequentialist pacifism also absolutely forbids the use of violence, but not from an abstract moral or ethical perspective. The consequentialist opposes violence because he or she believes that the evil resulting from it outweighs any good that it might achieve.

Absolute pacifism is an exceedingly difficult philosophy to put into practice. Very few people are willing to passively submit to a violent assault or stand by while a friend or loved one is attacked. Historically, absolute pacifism has a mixed record of success. The charismatic Indian leader Mohandas K. Gandhi successfully used nonviolent resistance to lead India to independence from Great Britain in 1947. However, his campaign took years and led to the death and injury of many Indians at the hands of British colonial troops and police. Civil-rights leader Martin Luther King Jr. led a successful nonviolent crusade for African American rights in the 1950s and 1960s. However, throughout most of history, significant political or social change has been accomplished through or accompanied by force.

In contrast to absolute pacifists, conditional pacifists believe that violence is necessary and permissible under certain circumstances. Conditional pacifists hold that a violent response is sometimes needed to prevent or redress a greater evil, such as threats to one's own or another person's life or health. In conditional deontological pacifism, however, one must consider whether the duty to use violence to right a wrong conflicts with other moral duties. For example, some people argue that aggressors forfeit their rights when they attack others, so any measures to prevent their aggression are justified. The conditional deontological pacifist would disagree with this position, asserting that even aggressors have basic rights that must be respected and that restrain one's actions toward them.

Conditional utilitarian pacifism, on the other hand, examines the use of violence from a results-oriented perspective. That is, it asks whether using violence will produce more morally favorable results than refraining from violent behavior. The utilitarian pacifist believes that the use of force is justified if it results in a greater good. Examples would include self-defense or intervening to prevent an innocent person or persons from being harmed. Conditional pacifism is more common than absolute pacifism and much easier to put into practice. For example, many people opposed to violence in the course of daily life have felt the need to take up arms to defend themselves and their country in times of war.

ROOTS OF PACIFISM

Pacifism is an ancient philosophy whose roots span the continents of Asia and Europe. In India, the spiritual leader Siddhārtha Gautama, known as the Buddha, began preaching a nonviolent philosophy well before 500 BCE. His ideas found wide acceptance throughout Asia and eventually developed into the religion known today as Buddhism. By the early 21st century, there were approximately 350 million Buddhists worldwide. Ancient Greek histories from the 400s BCE record a pacifist protest against the Peloponnesian War in the city of Thásos. The ancient Greek comedy *Lysistrata,* from the same time period, centers around the refusal of the women of a city to sleep with their husbands when the men insist on war with a neighboring city.

Jesus of Nazareth is often cited as an advocate of nonviolence, and some Christian sects do espouse pacifist doctrines. The Quakers, Amish, Mennonites, and Universalist Unitarians are the most avowedly pacifist Christian denominations. Many Christians, however, dispute the contention that Jesus was an absolute pacifist or that he opposed the use of force in all circumstances. The Roman Catholic philosopher St. Thomas Aquinas developed what is known as the *just war theory,* which states that violence is justified in situations where doing nothing would result in a greater wrong than using force.

For some Protestant Christian sects, such as the Mennonites and Quakers, pacifism became a tool of political resistance. As religious minorities, these sects were often persecuted in Europe, where most nations had an official, state-supported religion. Members of these minority denominations practiced peaceful noncooperation, refusing to abandon their faith but renouncing violent opposition to the state church. Many of these sects took part in the settlement of North America in hopes of escaping religious persecution. They formed the core of what would later become the U.S. pacifist movement.

For many centuries, pacifism remained a minority sentiment espoused primarily by specific religious communities. However, developments during the 1800s spurred a wave of more popular pacifist feelings, particularly in Europe. The bloody French Revolution of the 1790s, and the Napoleonic Wars that engulfed Europe in the early 1800s, raised general revulsion on the Continent at the waste and destruction of war. Peace societies, antislavery societies, and decolonization societies sprang up throughout Europe in the mid-1800s, and the first widespread calls for arms control and disarmament came at this time.

PACIFISM IN THE UNITED STATES

Historically, the pacifist movement was less robust in the United States. Although a small and struggling nation at the beginning of the 19th century, by 1850, the United States had expanded to fill North America. Much of its territory was gained by conquest—the Mexican War of 1846 added the entire American Southwest and most of the Pacific coast to the country—and "pacified" during a subsequent military campaign against Native Americans. The fact that the nation had earned its independence by force of arms also fostered the notion that violence was an acceptable solution to political disputes.

It took the disaster of 500,000 American deaths in the Civil War to stir strong pacifist feelings in the United States. The Northern public, in particular. found the toll of battle terrible. Throughout 1863 and even into 1864, there was a strong sentiment in the North to sign a peace treaty and end the war, even if it meant losing the Southern states to secession. Union general Ulysses S. Grant's grim campaign of spring 1864, which resulted in staggering casualties on both sides, horrified many Americans. In the end, however, President Abraham Lincoln stuck with Grant, realizing that his bloody strategy would eventually wear out the numerically inferior Southern forces.

For the next 50 years, American pacifist feelings found expression in U.S. isolationism. In the latter half of the 19th century, the United States concentrated on developing its vast and almost untapped domestic resources, largely continuing its historic policy of avoiding involvement in international politics. This isolationism began to change with the Spanish-American War of 1898, in which the United States gained possessions in Cuba, Puerto Rico, and the Philippines.

However, even as the United States was taking its first steps toward empire, it was trying to avoid military confrontations. The country remained out of European conflicts, and its president on the eve of World War I was a man with strong pacifist leanings, Woodrow Wilson.

PACIFISM IN THE 20TH CENTURY

By the early 1900s, it appeared that the antiwar movement in Europe had achieved some lasting results. With the exception of several regional wars in the Balkans, Europe had been at peace since 1870. The Great Powers of Europe—Great Britain, France, Germany, Austria-Hungary, and Russia—competed for colonial, economic, and diplomatic influence, but they managed to avoid coming to blows. Although pacifism certainly played little part in their colonial policies, the most powerful European nations seemed to share an aversion to conflict among themselves. Among many Europeans there was a sense that Western culture had developed to a point where peace between so-called civilized nations was inevitable.

Europe's apparent calm was shattered by the outbreak of World War I in 1914. The savagery with which civilized nations fought one another dispelled the notion that peace was inevitable. For many people, the war confirmed their suspicion that pacifism was wrong-headed and dangerous. They argued that German aggression proved peace could be maintained only by force. On the other hand, the unprecedented carnage of that war—the first fought with modern weaponry such as the machine gun, tank, and airplane—eventually led many others to the opposite conclusion. They said that the war proved the futility of combat. Millions had died in a war that, at least on the western front, was fought over a narrow strip of muddy wasteland. The conflict was dubbed "the war to end all wars" because many observers believed it showed that modern war was too costly even to contemplate.

In the United States, isolationism and pacifism combined initially to keep the country out of the war. Despite numerous German provocations, including the sinking of American merchant and passenger ships by German U-boats, the United States refused to become involved. As they read reports of the battles in Europe, most Americans felt they were wise to stay out of the fray. However, repeated German transgressions against U.S. sovereignty finally convinced

President Wilson to declare war in 1917. Although the United States participated in the fighting for less than a year, its fresh manpower and industrial might made a critical difference in the outcome.

Pacifism was ascendant in Europe after World War I, as most of the countries devastated by the war looked to rebuild their societies. Many Germans, however, were disillusioned with losing the war and the humiliating peace agreement forced upon their country. When the Nazis came to power in the early 1930s, they sought to rebuild Germany's military and restore German political power by force. Great Britain and France, still haunted by their huge manpower losses in World War I, sought to deter the Germans from using force to achieve their goals. However, neither country was willing to stand up to German provocations, even the German invasion of Czechoslovakia in 1938. Only with the German attack on Poland in September 1939 did France and Great Britain finally declare war on Germany.

As in World War I, the United States at first remained neutral in World War II, although the government did provide nonmilitary assistance to Great Britain. It was only after Japan attacked the U.S. naval base at Pearl Harbor, Hawaii, in December 1941, that the United States entered the war. The drive to defeat the Axis powers, and the subsequent threat of Soviet communism after the war, dampened pacifist sentiments in the United States during the 1940s and 1950s. During the Red Scare of the 1950s, pacifists who opposed the U.S. Cold War military buildup were often labeled communists or communist sympathizers.

The civil-rights movement and the Vietnam War provided new life to the pacifist movement in the United States. The leaders in the fight for civil rights for African Americans espoused principles and practices of nonviolence in their confrontations with local political and law-enforcement officials. Television images of peaceful protesters being attacked by police dogs or sprayed with fire hoses generated sympathy for the civil-rights cause. The willingness of civil-rights leaders to suffer abuse, jail, and even death to advance their cause peacefully eventually won the day and resulted in far-ranging civil-rights legislation in the 1960s.

Opposition to the Vietnam War offered another venue for advocates of pacifism. As the war dragged on, U.S. objectives—not to mention prospects for victory—seemed increasingly unclear to many Americans. An antiwar movement that began on college campuses in the mid- to late 1960s spread to the general population by the early 1970s. Whereas there had been conscientious objectors (those who refuse to perform military service for religious reasons or reasons of conscience) in previous conflicts, their numbers rose dramatically during the Vietnam War. For the first time in history, large numbers of Americans felt that their country was engaging in an immoral war. Antiwar pressure at home, combined with military stalemate in Vietnam, forced an end to U.S. involvement in 1973.

The experience of Vietnam led to wariness on the part of U.S. officials to commit the country to another land war, but it did not result in a strong surge of pacifism. As one of the world's two superpowers, the United States remained engaged in international affairs and did not shy from the threat of force. During the 1980s, the administration of President Ronald Reagan adopted a policy of fostering counterrevolutionary movements in left-leaning and communist countries. However, the government preferred to support indigenous groups such as the Nicaraguan contras, rather than commit U.S. forces overseas.

Iraq's invasion of Kuwait in 1990 led to a change in U.S. posture. Assembling a broad international military coalition, the United States led an allied response that pushed Iraqi forces from Kuwait and crippled Iraq's once-mighty army. The episode did much to restore the U.S. public's faith in the ability of military force to accomplish positive goals. The collapse of the Soviet Union in 1991 and the subsequent end of the Cold War also raised hopes that military might in the future could be used for constructive purposes such as peacekeeping. During the 1990s, the United States dispatched military forces on several United Nations and NATO (North Atlantic Treaty Organization) peacekeeping missions.

Unfortunately, the widely anticipated peace dividend from the end of the Cold War never materialized. Ethnic conflicts, civil war, and the rise of international terrorism have accompanied the demise of Soviet communism. The September 11, 2001, terrorist attacks on New York City and Washington, DC, ended any notion that the world was entering an era of peace.

In the uncertain environment of the war on terror, those who advocate pacifism are often looked upon suspiciously or contemptuously. Many Americans feel that pacifist sentiments undermine the national will and national security at a time when the country is threatened by violent extremists. Some even claim that opposing U.S. foreign policy gives aid and comfort to U.S. enemies and is thus treasonous. These are not new arguments, but they are widely accepted. Today, as in the past, pacifists face the challenge of upholding their moral beliefs while supporting the national interests of their country.

See also Antiwar Movement; Just War Theory; Vietnam War (1954–1975)

Further Reading

Brock, Peter, and Nigel Young. *Pacifism in the Twentieth Century.* Syracuse, NY: Syracuse University Press, 1999.
Charles, J. Daryl. *Between Pacifism and Jihad: Just War and Christian Tradition.* Nottingham, UK: InterVarsity Press, 2005.
Fiala, Andrew G. *Practical Pacifism.* New York: Algora, 2004.

PANAMA CANAL TREATY
See TREATIES

PANAMA INTERVENTION (1989)
See LATIN AMERICA AND U.S. POLICY

PATRIOT MISSILE

Propelled weapon that achieved fame and notoriety during the first Gulf War in 1991, when it had limited success against Iraqi Scud missiles. The purpose of the Patriot missile is to detect, track, and destroy incoming enemy missiles, but in one notorious incident, a software failure resulted in the deaths of 28 American soldiers in Saudi Arabia. The outcome of a congressional inquiry into the incident suggested that the Patriot missiles were not as successful as they had been widely reported to be. The effectiveness of the Patriot is central to wider debates concerning the development of the so-called Star Wars defense system, which would be capable of destroying nuclear weapons in space before they can reach the United States.

RESEARCH AND DEVELOPMENT

The Patriot missile is a guided missile that was conceived in the 1960s and put into development for anti-aircraft use in the 1970s. The Patriot system consists of a combined transporter-launcher carrying 32 missiles, hauled by a trailer. A separate trailer transports radar and other electronic equipment that controls the missiles. The launchers can be up to a kilometer away from the radar and control hub, to which they are linked by microwave signals.

The trailer-mounted radar scans the horizon with a thin beam, flicking between thousands of locations each second. Once something is detected, a message is sent to the control center. It is possible for Patriot to track up to 100 targets. It is also possible for the system to be automated, although an operator is capable of overriding it. The control computer tells the launcher when to fire, at which point two missiles are fired in rapid succession to improve the probability of a hit. The Patriot is 5 m long, reaches supersonic speed almost immediately after being launched, and ultimately accelerates to five times the speed of sound.

PERFORMANCE CONTROVERSY

During the first Gulf War in 1991, the success rate of the Patriot in intercepting Iraqi Scud and Al-Hussein missiles was put at 80% in Saudi Arabia and 50% in Israel, according to U.S. Army figures. The reason the Patriot was said to be more successful in Saudi Arabia than in Israel had to do with the fact that in the former, missiles were aimed at military targets in the desert, whereas in the latter they were aimed at civilian populations. Also, reports on the performance of the Patriot in Saudi Arabia were conducted by the U.S. military and censored in the press, and in Israel the Patriot's effectiveness was monitored by Israel Defense Forces, and press coverage was not censored. Serious doubts about the Patriot were raised in a 10-month investigation by the House Subcommittee on Government Operations, where expert testimony indicated that the Patriot's actual success rate was likely only 10%, and possibly zero.

The controversy surrounding the Patriot missile has continued with the recent U.S. invasion of Iraq in 2003. The Patriot was implicated in the downing of a British Royal Air Force Tornado jet fighter during the invasion, and follow-up investigations on the downing of other British pilots blame the Patriot system. The U.S. Army, however, has not publicly acknowledged any serious flaws, despite published reports that computer program errors caused allied aircraft to be identified as incoming enemy missiles, triggering automatic targeting.

Other reports, warning of repeat friendly-fire incidents, describe soldiers forced to rely on cell phones to verify the authenticity of targets. The Patriot's radar systems are said to produce numerous false indicators and "ghost" incoming enemy missiles. Patriot missiles are currently possessed by the United States, Germany, Belgium, the Netherlands, Israel, Greece, Japan, Saudi Arabia, Kuwait, and Taiwan.

See also Ballistic Missiles; Gulf War (1990–91)

PATTON, GEORGE (1885–1945)

United States general who achieved near-legendary fame in World War II, leading U.S. field armies in North Africa and Europe. Known as Old Blood and Guts, Patton's fiery and unusual character, combined with a high degree of professional insight and competence, made him well respected by friends and enemies, both foreign and domestic.

Born in San Gabriel, California, Patton grew up in a wealthy Southern California family and attended both Virginia Military Institute and West Point, taking his commission in the Army in 1909. He served initially in the cavalry branch, excelling in horsemanship, athletics, and most military skills. Shamelessly romantic in his quest to be a heroic soldier, Patton immersed himself in military history and lore. Outwardly brusque and tough-minded, he inwardly harbored insecurities and sensitivities that he strived to conceal from the public.

Luck also favored Patton, beginning with his participation in General John Pershing's Mexican Expedition of 1916, which gave Patton a future patron, contact with motor vehicles in military operations, and his first encounter with publicity. Promoted quickly to colonel during World War I, Patton formed the Army's Tank Corps with the assistance of Major Dwight D. Eisenhower, who remained behind in the United States while Patton took command of the first U.S. tank units in combat in France.

Peacetime boded ill for Patton, and he languished in several posts after World War I, always able, thanks to his family fortune, to entertain well and keep a fine stable of horses. He graduated from all the Army staff courses and continued to study history and military affairs, being equally at home with concepts of mechanization in the Army as well as furnishing the design of the last U.S. cavalry saber to be adopted. By 1939, however, the 54-year-old colonel feared that his opportunity to perform great feats had passed him by.

The U.S. entry into World War II gave Patton another opportunity to excel, and he was not found wanting. In command of an armored division, he trained it in the Carolina Maneuvers of 1941, demonstrating to all his incredible energy and zeal. His public persona by now had been purposely molded into his ideal of a modern warrior, and he used his various personal connections well, gaining command of the Western Task Force, which he landed on the Atlantic coast of Morocco in the North Africa landings of November 1942. Patton quickly succeeded to the command of the U.S. II Corps in the Tunisian Campaign and formed the Seventh Army for the invasion of Sicily. There he impetuously converted a supporting operation for the British Eighth Army into an Anglo-American race for the Straits of Messina and military honors that almost neglected the enemy situation. Ironically, in midst of his first clear operational victory, his public and military reputation almost collapsed because of incidents in August 1943, in which he slapped enlisted soldiers.

After the invasion of Normandy in June 1944, Patton's mission was to transport his Third Army to France and use it to break out of the Normandy landing region, spearheading the U.S. forces engaged in defeating the German forces in France. This he did with the greatest aplomb, outmaneuvering the Germans and pushing his forces in a madcap race to the Franco-German border. The Battle of the Bulge (December 1944–February 1945) gave Patton his greatest moment in command, redeploying his army on short notice, saving the Belgian town of Bastogne and assisting in the final rout of the Germans. Ironically, Patton died in a traffic accident after the war, having achieved his greatest vainglorious hopes. His memory remains as an icon of aggressive and competent command in battle.

See also Amphibious Warfare; Bulge, Battle of the; Eisenhower, Dwight D., and National Policy; Tanks; U.S. Army; World War II (1939–1945)

PEACE CORPS

Federal agency whose mission is to increase mutual understanding and friendship between the United States and other nations. Peace Corps volunteers undertake a variety of programs to improve the quality of life of people in developing countries. These have traditionally included educational and agricultural programs, but in recent years they have been expanded to include programs aimed at developing businesses, as well.

In a speech at the University of Michigan on October 14, 1960, presidential candidate John F. Kennedy challenged his student listeners to work in less-developed countries and embark on an adventure that would serve mankind. Three weeks later, in another speech, he dubbed the program the Peace Corps. During the first months of his administration, newly elected President Kennedy consolidated numerous previous discussions about a secular volunteer corps into a plan of action.

On March 1, 1961, Kennedy issued an executive order creating the Peace Corps. The law establishing the Peace Corps gave the agency a mandate to "promote world peace and friendship."

The Peace Corps had two primary stated goals. The first was to promote economic development in developing nations and help those "struggling to break the bonds of mass misery" to help themselves. The second goal of the Peace Corps was to generate a mutual understanding between Americans and citizens of developing countries, in hopes that this would launch a "new relationship" between the United States and the developing world.

The philanthropic mission of the Peace Corps was complemented by a significant foreign-policy agenda. Kennedy and his advisers believed that the United States had to "do better" as it competed with the Soviet Union for the loyalties of the newly decolonized third-world nations. Responding to the needs of the newly independent countries would prevent them from being seduced by communism. Moreover, the administration felt that it had to respond effectively to decolonization and the possibility that instability in former colonies may threaten U.S. interests. The Peace Corps, with its anti-imperialist ethos, advanced both understanding and U.S. foreign policy in many cases. The organization was sometimes able to rise above political realities to earn the respect of the people it served.

Peace Corps volunteers receive three months of training in their host countries, learning the local culture and acquiring needed skills they may lack. After volunteers complete their training, they spend 24 months living in communities in a developing nation, working in the fields of education, health, business development, agriculture, the environment, and youth programs. The agency has also recently begun to send volunteers to assist in short-term disaster-relief efforts.

The Peace Corps is open to any U.S. citizen at least 18 years of age, and there is no upper age limit. Many older and retired individuals volunteer their time and expertise to the Peace Corps. The agency currently sends volunteers to work in 69 countries on five continents. Since the organization's founding in 1961, 170,000 volunteers have worked in 136 countries.

See also Humanitarian Aid; Kennedy, John F., and National Policy

PEACEKEEPING OPERATIONS

Multinational forces dispatched by the United Nations Security Council to observe, monitor, report on, and, in the post–Cold War era, enforce cease-fires established in the wake of inter- and intranational conflicts. Peacekeeping operations have been launched in a number of regions in the world over the course of the past half century.

HISTORY OF MULTINATIONAL PEACEKEEPING

The United Nations (UN) was founded in the wake of World War II to establish a system of collective security to address interstate conflict and to "save succeeding generations from the scourge of war." The UN Charter empowers the United Nations, through the Security Council, to take actions it deems necessary to address situations that pose a threat to international peace and security, manifested in conflict among nations. The council's practice of dispatching missions, known as *peacekeeping operations,* to conflict situations, is founded in this provision.

The first peacekeeping operations dispatched by the United Nations were cease-fire monitoring missions. These first took place at the conclusion of the Arab-Israeli War of 1948, and the second followed the cessation of fighting between India and Pakistan in 1949 over the state of Jammu and Kashmir. For the next 40 years, peacekeeping operations would follow the formula set down in these initial efforts. Missions

required not only the consent of the two states involved in the conflict but also that of the then two rival superpowers engaged in the Cold War—the United States and the Soviet Union. Because both nations possessed veto power in the Security Council, it was impossible to dispatch a mission into conflicts in which the combatants were proxies for either superpower.

The collapse of the Soviet Union in 1991 ushered in a new era in the development and practices of peacekeeping. The end of direct U.S.–Soviet rivalry, and unrest caused by ethnic tensions in formerly Soviet-controlled states, led to greater cooperation in the Security Council. Both the number and the nature of peacekeeping missions intensified in the 1990s. Without the constant threat of an automatic veto by one of the superpowers, the Security Council's ability to dispatch peacekeeping missions expanded significantly.

The United Nations defines peacekeeping today as "a way to help countries torn by conflict create conditions for sustainable peace." This definition reflects the evolution that has taken place within peacekeeping since its first days, when missions were limited to observing preestablished cease fires or pacts. It recognizes the fact that more than simple monitoring is required to establish and maintain peace in complex conflict situations. Planners and reviewers at all levels in the United Nations recognized the fact that addressing conflict successfully and sustainably requires a more complex and multifaceted approach. This realization produced today's more diverse peacekeeping missions, which incorporate conflict resolution, diplomacy, development work, and human-rights and truth commissions into the process.

ISSUES IN PEACEKEEPING

Under the UN Charter, member states of the United Nations agree to provide resources in the form of armed forces, money, and rights of passage to missions deemed necessary by the Security Council. In this way, all member states have the ability and the duty to participate in peacekeeping operations. Generally, missions are composed of multinational forces under rotating command.

The Security Council first looks to regional organizations to put together and man peacekeeping missions. Despite some drawbacks, it is a widely recognized principle that a regional solution to problems is usually preferable to the introduction of outside actors who may lack the cultural, geographic, and historical familiarity and sensitivity that regional forces possess. For example, in 1993 the Organization of American States was dispatched to handle the crisis in Haiti pursuant to the military coup in that country, before UN-sanctioned U.S. intervention finally reinstated the democratically elected leader.

However, problems can arise when a regional force is used to handle a conflict. The 1991 intervention by the military arm of the Economic Community of West African States (ECOWAS) in the Sierra Leonean civil war offers an example of the potential difficulties. Problems arose when ECOWAS became partial in the conflict, to the extent that it was viewed by some as another party in it and no longer a neutral observer force. This is a danger when the party sent in to mediate a conflict has a stake in its outcome, as most neighboring states do when a conflict occurs in their geographic vicinity.

Rules of engagement are also a topic of constant review. Although most missions in the first few decades limited the United Nations *blue helmets* to engaging only when under attack, this policy has many critics. Indeed, it has had disastrous results in the past. The most recent and egregious example of UN troops' failure to engage at a level proportionate to the situation is the Srebrenica massacre of 1995. In this incident, UN peacekeeping troops failed to prevent the summary executions of more than 7,000 Muslim men and boys in UN-designated safe areas during the Balkan conflict.

U.S. INVOLVEMENT IN PEACEKEEPING

Like many industrialized Western nations, the United States has infrequently participated in UN peacekeeping operations. Troop contributions by developing states are disproportionately high, for a number of reasons. For one, financial compensation is provided to contributing states, which is a greater incentive for poorer countries than wealthier ones. Another reason for the United States' reluctance to participate in peacekeeping operations is the aversion to suffering casualties in regions of the world where the United States has no significant political interests. This reluctance is sometimes referred to as the *Mogadishu factor.*

In 1993, 18 U.S. soldiers were killed during a UN mission in Somalia. The mission began as a humanitarian effort to secure UN food deliveries to famished populations. However, humanitarian relief efforts were hampered by the actions of local warlords, who seized relief shipments and either sold them or used them to buy the loyalty of other Somalis. The relief effort eventually turned into an attempt to apprehend a prominent local warlord, Mohammed Farah Aideed.

On October 3, U.S. forces were lured into an ambush in the Somali capital of Mogadishu. Two Black Hawk helicopters carrying U.S. troops were downed by local militias armed with rocket-propelled grenade launchers. The pilot of one helicopter was taken hostage for 11 days, and bodies of dead U.S. soldiers were dragged through the streets by cheering crowds. This incident fueled already existing domestic distaste for U.S. participation in multinational efforts under the auspices of the United Nations, where goals do not pertain to specific U.S. interests.

The United States is, on the whole, opposed to putting its troops under the command of other states. When it commits a large number of troops to a UN operation, the United States maintains command control or delegates control only to trusted military allies, such as other NATO (North Atlantic Treaty Organization) members. The United States maintained command control over its troops when it participated in large UN operations in Korea in 1950 and in the Persian Gulf War of 1991. In fact, although critics cite the Mogadishu tragedy as evidence of UN command failure, the troops involved were under U.S. control, not that of the UN or any other member state.

See also Bosnia Intervention; Collective Security; Humanitarian Intervention; Interventionism; Kosovo Intervention; Regionalism; Somalia Intervention (1992); United Nations; UN Peacekeeping; UN Security Council;

Further Reading

Bellamy, Alex J., Paul Williams, and Stuart Griffin. *Understanding Peacekeeping.* Cambridge, UK: Polity, 2004.

Cassidy, Robert M. *Peacekeeping in the Abyss: British and American Peacekeeping Doctrine and Practice After the Cold War.* New York: Praeger, 2004.

PEARL HARBOR

Surprise attack responsible for bringing the United States into World War II. The attack on Pearl Harbor by Japan on December 7, 1941, was famously described by U.S. president Franklin Delano Roosevelt as a "date which will live in infamy." The slogans "Remember Pearl Harbor!" or "Remember December 7th" became central to U.S. propaganda as the United States entered the war more than two years after it had begun in Europe.

United States–Japanese relations had been deteriorating as Japan expanded its empire into China in the years before the outbreak of war in Europe. As the ally of Nazi Germany, Japan felt confident enough to seize French Indochina and threaten Britain's Pacific colonies, as well. The United States responded with an oil and steel embargo against Japan. The positioning of ships in Pearl Harbor, closer to Japan than to the west coast of the United States, was also a deliberate action to draw Japan's attention to the United States and its power.

The battleships USS *West Virginia* (foreground) and USS *Tennessee* sit low in the water and burn after the Japanese surprise attack on Pearl Harbor on December 7, 1941. The *West Virginia* sank after the attack, and more than 100 of her officers and men were killed. Five crewmen aboard the *Tennessee* were killed, but the ship survived the attack, was repaired, and saw active duty in the Pacific during World War II.

Source: Corbis.

On the morning of December 7, 1941, the Japanese embassy in Washington, DC, received the final part of a 14-part message from Tokyo, stating that diplomatic relations with the United States were going to be ended. The message was decoded by U.S. code breakers. Tokyo further directed its embassy to deliver the message to the White House at 1:00 p.m. eastern time. However, the military in Pearl Harbor, on the Hawaiian island of Oahu, were advised too late of the Japanese message, and the Japanese attacked Pearl Harbor at 7:55 a.m. Hawaii time. Although the message was meant to be delivered just before the attack, it was in fact delivered well after the attack had begun, adding to U.S. outrage.

Approximately 100 U.S. battleships, destroyers, cruisers, and support ships were present in Pearl Harbor at the time of the attack. The nearby U.S. Army airfield, Hickam Field, was attacked simultaneously, and 18 bombers, fighters, and attack bombers were destroyed or damaged without having a chance

to take off. More than 188 U.S. aircraft were destroyed, and more than 2,400 Americans were killed. Japanese losses were comparatively minimal—a total of 29 Japanese aircraft were shot down, and possibly 100 Japanese pilots perished.

The attack on Pearl Harbor consisted of two strikes, the second of which completed the mission. The Japanese had considered a third strike, as well, which would have been devastating and greatly delayed the ability of the U.S. Navy to recover. However, Japanese admiral Chuichi Nagumo decided against this third strike, and at 1:00 p.m. Hawaii time, the Japanese planes returned home.

The purpose of the attack on Pearl Harbor was to strike a crippling blow to U.S. naval power in the Pacific. However, one of the primary objectives—to sink U.S. aircraft carriers—was not accomplished, because none were present at the time of the attack. As the war continued, the importance of aircraft carriers (rather than battleships) to naval warfare became increasingly apparent.

Despite the devastation of the attack, the United States quickly recovered. Except for five ships, every ship sunk or damaged at Pearl Harbor was repaired to sail again. Meanwhile, the U.S. Navy went on to sink every one of the Japanese aircraft carriers, battleships, and cruisers that participated in the attack.

The treachery of the Pearl Harbor attack also generated tremendous resentment in the United States toward the Japanese. The subsequent internment of Japanese Americans has been partially attributed to anger over Pearl Harbor. False claims of espionage and collaboration with the enemy were leveled against many Japanese Americans.

Despite numerous investigations, including joint hearings by the U.S. Congress in 1946, many questions about the Pearl Harbor attack have remained unresolved. A number of conspiracy theories have emerged, for example, that have questioned whether President Roosevelt or other U.S. officials may have known of the plan in advance, but let it happen so it would galvanize public opinion to go to war.

At the time, Pearl Harbor was the largest mass use of aircraft carriers in an attack, the farthest-range naval attack, and the largest air attack against a naval target. The assault on Pearl Harbor was also an important factor in the establishment of the United States Central Intelligence Agency, which was intended, among other things, to prevent future sneak attacks like the one at Pearl Harbor.

See also Japanese Internment; Roosevelt, Franklin D., and National Policy; World War II (1939–1945)

Further Reading

Iriye, Akira. *Pearl Harbor and the Coming of the Pacific War: A Brief History with Documents and Essays.* New York: Bedford/St. Martin's, 1999.

Prange, Gordon W., Donald M. Goldstein, and Katherine Dillon. *December 7, 1941: The Day the Japanese Attacked Pearl Harbor.* New York: McGraw-Hill, 1988.

Prange, Gordon W., Donald M. Goldstein, and Katherine Dillon. *Pearl Harbor: The Verdict of History.* New York: McGraw-Hill, 1986.

PENETRATING MUNITIONS

Ammunition capable of penetrating hardened targets such as tanks or bunkers and causing more serious internal damage than conventional munitions. Penetrating munitions come in a variety of forms, including artillery shells, bombs, rockets, and missiles.

The earliest penetrating munitions were developed in rudimentary form during World War II. Allied forces used powerful *dambuster* bombs in an attempt to penetrate the concrete structures of dams along the Rhine River. By collapsing the dams, the Allies hoped to flood important industrial and agricultural regions of Germany, hampering its war effort. Although the bombs did breach some dams, the widespread damage anticipated by the Allies failed to occur.

Today's penetrating munitions awaited technological developments that allowed for more precise targeting and better penetration of hard surfaces, thereby increasing their effectiveness during conflict. Tungsten, a superhard metal, has been used in penetrating munitions since the 1960s. More recently, penetrating artillery and armor-piercing rounds have been designed using depleted uranium, or DU, a radioactive material that is extremely dense. The invention of microelectronics and laser guidance enabled the incorporation of sophisticated targeting systems inside shells and bombs. These targeting systems produced a revolutionary improvement in the ability to strike an intended target.

Penetrating artillery shells and antitank weapons typically consist of a long, thin rod called a *fléchette* surrounded by a casing (or sabot) that allows the round to fit into the barrel of the firing weapon. After the round is fired, the sabot falls away and the fléchette continues to the target. Upon impact, the nose of the fléchette splits in a way that allows it to remain sharp. The energy released at impact disintegrates the fléchette as it bores through the surface of the target. This disintegration creates a hot ball of dust and gas that ignites upon contact with the air inside the vehicle, killing its crew and igniting the ammunition and fuel.

Another type of penetrating munition is the so-called bunker-buster bomb. The bunker buster is similar in configuration to penetrating shells, with a long, narrow body. The bunker buster is loaded with explosives and equipped with a fuse that delays its explosion until after the bomb penetrates its target. More complicated weaponry can even count the number of floors in a building or bunker it has penetrated and, after a specified number, detonate the explosives. Because it is dropped from extremely high altitude, a bunker buster must be laser-guided to its target by the pilot of the aircraft. Bunker busters were used extensively during the U.S. invasions of Afghanistan in 2001 and Iraq in 2003.

See also Antitank Missiles; Science, Technology, and Security

PENTAGON

Located in Arlington, Virginia, headquarters of the U.S. Department of Defense. The term *Pentagon* refers to both the building itself and to the military establishment headquartered there. The Pentagon is the center of military power in the United States.

THE BUILDING AND ITS HISTORY

The Pentagon, which lies across the Potomac River from Washington, DC, is the world's largest office building. It consists of five concentric rings, designated A, B, C, D, and E, each five stories high. Each ring occupies an area large enough to contain the U.S. Capitol building. The Pentagon covers a total area of 29 acres and contains 3,705,793 square feet of office space, three times the floor space of the Empire State Building. Despite its size, the Pentagon is efficiently designed. Although the building contains some 17 miles of hallways, it takes no more than seven minutes to walk between any two points inside.

The Pentagon's tremendous size is a product of the enormity of the role it was built to fulfill. United States involvement in World War II put a tremendous strain on the then-existing Department of War, whose personnel were spread across 17 different buildings in Washington, DC. The Pentagon was designed to consolidate departmental personnel in a central location to increase efficiency.

The original plan for the building, developed by Brigadier General Brehon B. Somervell, took less than four days to conceive. The building was intended to be a three-story facility meant to house 40,000 people. General Somervell, however, ignored President Franklin D. Roosevelt's stated size preferences and began construction on a five-sided building much larger than had been anticipated. The number of stories was increased to four, and then finally five.

Construction on the Pentagon began on September 11, 1941, and was completed less than two years later. The project was subject to the same wartime rationing requirements as every other initiative; thus, concrete ramps substituted for elevators to connect floors. Even so, 13,000 workers were employed in its construction, and the building cost $80 million when it was completed in 1943.

Since its completion, the Pentagon has acquired tremendous symbolic importance as the headquarters of the U.S. military. For many, it stands as a symbol of American power and stability; for others, it symbolizes a U.S. overreliance on military force to advance national interests. The depth of feeling stirred by the Pentagon has been expressed by a number of acts intended to deface or destroy it. Pig's blood was thrown on the Pentagon during Vietnam War protests, and in the 1960s, the radical antigovernment Weather Underground group successfully bombed a women's bathroom in the building. The Pentagon was one of the main targets of the September 11, 2001, terrorist attacks on New York City and Washington, DC, placing the building at the center of the war on terror.

THE PENTAGON AS AN INSTITUTION

The spread of War Department personnel across Washington, DC, was a metaphor for the lack of coordination among the U.S. armed forces. During the war, it became clear that Army, Navy, and Air Force units had to work together closely to be effective. However, the military was plagued by interservice rivalries over allocation of resources and command responsibility. In 1945, President Harry S. Truman proposed unifying military planning and command in a Department of National Defense. The thought of concentrating so much power and authority in one department was worrisome to many military commanders and members of Congress. However, Truman's views won out, and the National Security Act of 1947 combined the Department of War, the Navy Department, and the Department of the Air Force into a new Department of Defense. The civilian head of the department, the secretary of defense, was given authority over all branches of the U.S. military.

The Department of Defense is made up of the U.S. Army, Navy, Air Force, and Marine Corps, as well as noncombat agencies such as the Defense Intelligence Agency and the National Security Agency. The Department of Defense also has authority over the U.S. Coast Guard during wartime; during peacetime, the Coast Guard is under the Department of Homeland Security. The Joint Chiefs of Staff—a panel composed

An aerial view of the Pentagon, the headquarters of the U.S. Department of Defense and the nerve center for U.S. military command and control. Virtually a city within itself, the Pentagon is the biggest office building in the world, housing approximately 23,000 military and civilian employees, as well as about 3,000 nondefense support personnel. Built between September 1941 and January 1943, the Pentagon covers a total of 583 acres and contains more than 3.7 million sq ft of office and storage space. The five-story building contains 17.5 mi of corridors, and each of its five outer walls measures 921 ft.

Source: Corbis.

of the top-ranking officers of each service—is responsible for military planning and serve as the president's military advisers. Though the chairman of the Joint Chiefs of Staff is by law the highest-ranking military officer in the United States, neither the chairman nor the various chiefs of staff are in the chain of command. The chain of command for the U.S. military begins with the president and extends through the secretary of defense to various regional commanders.

THE SECRETARY OF DEFENSE

The secretary of defense is the Pentagon's primary representative to the federal government and the citizens of the United States. The office has evolved in the context of military priorities and challenges to U.S. security. The first secretary of defense, James V. Forrestal, served from 1947 to 1949, the early years of the Cold War. His tenure was marked by the formation of the Eastern bloc and the establishment of NATO (North Atlantic Treaty Organization). Forrestal also served as secretary of defense during the Berlin airlift

and the initiation of the Marshall Plan for European postwar recovery.

Louis A. Johnson, who succeeded Forrestal, was known for his thriftiness, espoused in slogans such as one that claimed the American taxpayer received "a dollar's worth of defense for every dollar spent." Fiscal practicality was, however, soon confronted by the realities of the Korean War. Johnson also presided over serious dissent among branches of the armed services with regard to spending priorities. The essence of the debate concerned the best approach to confronting the numerical superiority of Soviet ground forces and the practicality of atomic deterrence.

Initial setbacks in Korea provoked Johnson's resignation, and he was replaced by George C. Marshall, author of the Marshall Plan. Marshall oversaw a massive expansion of the military in response to what he perceived as the aggressive willingness of communist states to wage war. Despite these efforts, Senator Joseph McCarthy accused Marshall of being soft on communism. The attacks on Marshall backfired; McCarthy's performance during Senate hearings into communist influence in the army turned the U.S. public against him and his mania for seeing communists around every corner. Marshall received the Nobel Peace prize in 1953 for his fundamental role in rebuilding war-torn Europe.

One of the most controversial secretaries of defense was Robert S. McNamara, who served in that position from 1961 to 1968, the longest consecutive tenure in the office. McNamara presided over the increase in U.S. involvement in Vietnam during the administration of John F. Kennedy. A proponent of the use of force in Southeast Asia, McNamara was retained by Kennedy's successor, Lyndon B. Johnson. Many years later, McNamara repudiated his earlier views on Vietnam, saying that U.S. involvement in the conflict was a mistake.

Donald Rumsfeld, who served as secretary of defense under President Gerald R. Ford in the mid-1970s and 25 years later under President George W. Bush, has also been a divisive figure. Under President Bush, Rumsfeld formulated a new military doctrine that emphasized reliance on technology, overwhelming airpower, and the use of small, specialized ground forces rather than large troop formations. This approach flew in the face of the existing Powell Doctrine, devised by former chairman of the Joint Chiefs of Staff Colin Powell. The Powell Doctrine argued that U.S. forces should not enter any engagement without overwhelming superiority of forces on ground, sea, and air.

Rumsfeld's ideas were put to the test in the invasions of Afghanistan in 2001 and Iraq in 2003. In Afghanistan, the United States relied heavily on U.S. special-operations forces supported by local militia. Iraq featured a conventional ground attack carried out by a relatively small force of about 150,000 troops. In both cases, the initial assaults were extremely successful in overwhelming the military opposition. However, in Afghanistan, U.S. forces failed to capture the leaders of the terrorist group al-Qaeda, for whom they were searching, and since the end of fighting, much of the country has come under the control of local warlords. In Iraq, U.S. troops, limited in number, have been unable to control a postwar insurgency that has claimed thousands of U.S. and Iraqi lives.

SCANDAL AND CONTROVERSY

The central role of the Pentagon in defense and national security has also placed it at the center of related scandals and controversies. Two of the most notorious were the Pentagon Papers incident and the Iran-Contra scandal. Both revealed extensive deceptions of the American public by top-ranking administration officials.

The Pentagon Papers

The Pentagon Papers are a 7,000-page history of U.S. involvement in Vietnam since the end of World War II. The papers were leaked, first to the *New York Times,* by Department of Defense employee Daniel Ellsberg and published in 1971. Among other things, the papers revealed that Presidents Lyndon B. Johnson and Richard Nixon did not believe the war was winnable, despite public statements and increased commitment of troops by both administrations. These revelations undermined the already deteriorating public credibility of the government over the Vietnam War. The publication of the papers also provoked the anger of President Nixon.

The Nixon administration was successful in obtaining a federal court injunction, forcing the *Times* to cease publication. It was the first incidence in U.S. history of prior restraint of publication for national-security reasons. The *Washington Post,* however, soon began publishing the papers, as well, and refused a request from the assistant attorney general to cease and desist. The Justice Department once again sought an injunction, but this time they were refused. The Supreme Court ultimately ruled against the government and held that the injunctions were unconstitutional. The Pentagon Papers have been regarded historically as an important instance of the tensions between respecting the First Amendment versus the necessity of protecting national security.

The Iran-Contra Affair

The Iran-Contra affair once again placed the Pentagon at the center of questions concerning checks and balances on presidential power. In 1985, Secretary of Defense Caspar Weinberger agreed to give Iran U.S.-made antitank missiles in return for the release of a prominent American hostage held by Iranian sympathizers in Lebanon. This agreement led to another deal, involving the sale of anti-aircraft missiles to Iran, in which President Ronald Reagan chose to ignore rules requiring him to notify Congress beforehand.

These activities culminated in presidential approval of a plan to sell arms to Iran in exchange for the release of hostages. The funds received from the sales were subsequently (and secretly) used to fund anticommunist rebels in Nicaragua, known as the *contras.* Several government officials, including National Security Advisor John Poindexter, were convicted on several counts of conspiracy, but their convictions were ultimately overturned. The scandal raised numerous issues, among them the proper role of the executive branch in defense and security policy initiatives.

The Pentagon Papers and Iran-Contra scandal highlight one of the main criticisms of the Pentagon: the secrecy and lack of accountability that often spring up around issues of military policy. Because the president appoints the secretary of defense, Pentagon policies naturally tend to reflect the priorities and concerns of the administration. Critics argue that this close tie to the president allows political considerations to intrude on prudent military planning. It may also prevent military leaders from speaking out against policies or decisions that are not in the best interests of the United States.

—William de Jong-Lambert

See also Department of Defense, U.S (DoD); Joint Chiefs of Staff; National Security Act (1947); Pentagon Papers; September 11/ WTC and Pentagon Attacks

Further Reading

Smith, Major General Perry M. *Assignment—Pentagon: The Insider's Guide to the Potomac Puzzle Palace.* New York: International Defense, 1989.

Goldberg, Alfred. *The Pentagon: The First Fifty Years.* Washington, DC: The Historical Office of the Secretary of Defense, 1992.

Locher, James R., III, and Sam Nunn. *Victory on the Potomac: The Goldwater-Nichols Act Unifies the Pentagon.* College Station, TX: Texas A&M University Press, 2002.

PENTAGON PAPERS

Secret government study about America's involvement in the Vietnam War, the release of which sparked an unprecedented legal battle between the administration of President Richard Nixon and the national media (particularly the *New York Times* and the *Washington Post*). Commissioned in 1967 by then-Secretary of Defense Robert S. McNamara, the Pentagon Papers examined the decision-making process behind U.S. participation in the war in Vietnam.

Researched and written under utmost secrecy, the Pentagon Papers were supposed to provide posterity with a candid account of the context surrounding the U.S. decision to go to war in Vietnam. Instead, thanks initially to a former government official and to the *New York Times,* the papers were partially revealed, in 1971, to the American public, whose attitude toward the Vietnam War was already rapidly deteriorating. The disclosure of the study (first by the *Times* and subsequently by the *Washington Post* and other publications) led to a string of high-profile legal confrontations between the federal government and the press.

CONTENTS OF THE STUDY

Robert S. McNamara had been serving as secretary of defense for six years under two presidents (John F. Kennedy and Lyndon Johnson) when he asked 35 Pentagon officials and civilian experts to undertake an in-depth study of U.S. involvement in Vietnam since the end of World War II. The task took one year to complete (from 1967 to 1968) and yielded 47 volumes of documents, including both copies of official memoranda (4,000 pages) and the researchers' own analyses (3,000 pages).

Preoccupied solely with establishing the facts related to Vietnam, the researchers wrote their assessments without any consideration for the government's official perspective on historical (and contemporary) events. The uproar that the papers subsequently brought about when they were leaked to the press is rather easy to understand in light of the study's revelations.

The information unearthed by the researchers showed that the U.S. government had repeatedly misled the American public with reference to its handling of the initial stages of the conflict in Vietnam—that is, from early 1964 to the spring of 1965, before U.S. ground troops landed in South Vietnam. Even as administration officials were publicly denying reports of conducting extensive hostile actions in the region, the Pentagon was engaged in ground-troop deployments in South Vietnam and was conducting air strikes in Laos. In addition, contrary to official government pronouncements, the U.S.-backed South Vietnamese government was described as an "emerging fascist state," and the communist movement was shown to enjoy a huge popularity in both South Vietnam and North Vietnam.

LEAKING THE PAPERS

Upon its completion, the study was kept under close guard and only 15 copies were made. Two of these copies ended up in the vaulted archives of the RAND Corporation, an organization that had been closely associated with the Pentagon.

Prior to being one of McNamara's 35 researchers, one of RAND's employees, Daniel Ellsberg, had worked for the U.S. Department of Defense in Vietnam, studying potential conflict-resolution options. Ellsberg became disenchanted with the American involvement in the conflict, and soon after the completion of the study, he decided to take the initiative and change the state of affairs.

Thanks to his status at RAND, Ellsberg was able to make additional copies of the study. He eventually provided the *New York Times* with some of the documents in question, and the newspaper began publishing them on June 13, 1971. After the *Times* had published three installments of the papers, the Justice Department obtained a temporary restraining order, arguing that, should publication continue, "the national defense interests and nation's security will suffer immediate and irreparable harm."

Because of the court order, the *Times* was forced to halt publication of the Pentagon Papers, but the *Washington Post* concomitantly began to publish excerpts of the study. The extensive legal wrangling that ensued between the government and the newspapers became the most famous instance in U.S. history of governmental efforts to prevent the press from publishing disturbing information. On June 26, 1971, the Supreme Court took up the case and heard oral arguments from all parties. Several days later, the Court decided that the government could not stop the newspapers from printing the study.

CONSEQUENCES

The legal outcome of the battle between the government and the press and its implications regarding press freedom probably constitutes the most significant consequences of the entire Pentagon Papers incident. However, the case had several other far-reaching reverberations, as well. Daniel Ellsberg's prosecution for theft and espionage became a frequent reference in law manuals, in part because of the government's ill-advised tampering with the court proceedings (by illegal wiretapping and suppressing evidence). A few years after the Supreme Court ruling, more of the same governmental misconduct led to the Watergate scandal, which eventually cost Richard Nixon the presidency.

The publication of the Pentagon Papers also convinced an already increasing number of Americans that the war in Vietnam was being mishandled and even manipulated by the executive branch of government for purely political purposes. Following massive popular demonstrations against the war, President Ford announced the end of U.S. involvement in the Vietnam War on April 23, 1975.

To this day, every aspiring American journalist studies the *New York Times'* legal battle with the government over its publication of secret documents. Moreover, the ethical issues arising from Ellsberg's alleged illicit actions and the subsequent breach of national security will probably continue to be dissected by both scholars and journalists for years to come.

See also Civil Liberties; Civil–Military Relations; Classification; Denial; Vietnam War (1954–1975)

Further Reading

Ellsberg, Daniel. *Secrets: A Memoir of Vietnam and the Pentagon Papers.* New York: Viking, 2002.

Rudenstine, David. *The Day the Presses Stopped: A History of the Pentagon Papers Case.* Berkeley: University of California Press, 1996.

Salter, Kenneth W. *The Pentagon Papers Trial.* Berkeley, CA: Editorial Justa, 1975.

Wells, Tom. *Wild Man: The Life and Times of Daniel Ellsberg.* New York: Palgrave, 2001.

REFLECTIONS

An Assault on Democracy

That is what is so chilling: the contempt for public opinion, the ready recourse to the press as an instrument for misleading the public; the easy arrogance with which these men arrogated to themselves decision which no government ought to take without the knowledge, let alone consent, of the people; the contempt for Congress as yet another inconvenience to be dealt with, when necessary, with blithe duplicity.

—Excerpt from a *Washington Post* editorial, June 17, 1971

PEOPLE'S REPUBLIC OF CHINA
See CHINA AND U.S. POLICY

PERESTROIKA

Program of economic, political, and social retooling unveiled by Soviet leader Mikhail Gorbachev in 1986. Thereafter, the word *perestroika,* or restructuring, was added to the modern lexicon. Perestroika, along with Gorbachev's policy of *glasnost,* or openness, became the unintended catalyst for the dismantling of the Union of Soviet Socialist Republics.

For much of its 70-year existence, the Marxist–Leninist–Stalinist totalitarian state known as the Soviet Union had towered over the majority of nations in military and industrial might. In its waning decades, however, the USSR was swaying and heaving under the strain of an outmoded economic system and industrial infrastructure. The Soviet economy had been stagnating since the 1960s. In order to continue competing with its political rivals in the West, the Soviet economy would need drastic restructuring. Hoping to make his nation's economy more efficient, Gorbachev put his faith in his program of reform and adjustment known as *perestroika*.

The main aim of perestroika was to gradually transform the old state-managed command economy into a demand economy that heeded market signals and vested more authority in managers at the enterprise level. The program encouraged limited private ownership and profitability. Reactions to the new policies were contentious and, at times, violent.

In the conflict between the old order and emerging market forces, the communist system of centralized power and privilege continued to hold on. As a result, the new policies produced no economic miracles. Instead, shortages of goods developed, civic order declined, and ethnic rivalries erupted. Perestroika ultimately failed because its measures were too timid, its timing was too late, and its hopes were too grand. Moreover, when more radical changes were made, they often had adverse effects.

After much early hope, Gorbachev failed to bring significant change and lost the support of the Soviet people. His belief that the system could be gradually reformed, as well as his attempt to straddle the line between conservatives and radicals, cost him his political base.

On August 19, 1991, conservative elements in the government launched an abortive coup d'état to prevent the signing of a new union treaty. In the aftermath of the coup, Boris Yeltsin, president of the Russian republic, ascended to power as head of the nation. Under his leadership, Russia embarked on even more far-reaching reforms: The Soviet Union broke up into its constituent republics, and the Commonwealth of Independent States (CIS), a loose federation of former Soviet republics, arose to take its place.

See also Soviet Union, Former (Russia), and U.S. Policy

PLO (PALESTINE LIBERATION ORGANIZATION)

Umbrella group of various Palestinian nationalist organizations dedicated to the establishment of an independent Palestinian state. Founded in 1964 with the support of the Arab states, the Palestine Liberation Organization (PLO) has become the most important representative of the Palestinian people.

A union among different groups with diverse ideologies and priorities, the PLO has undergone extensive transformations over time. One of the most significant of these was the PLO's official 1993 acceptance of the right of Israel to exist as a nation, established by decree in 1948. Until his death in 2004, the one constant within the PLO had been its chairman, Yasir Arafat, leader and founder of Fatah, the most powerful group within the PLO. In 1994, following extensive negotiations with Israel, Arafat formed the Palestinian Authority, which was slated to become the legitimate government of a future independent Palestinian state.

CONSOLIDATION

The establishment of the PLO in 1964 was a long-awaited effort on the part of some of the most influential Palestinian nationalist groups to pool their resources and political power with the aim of fighting and destroying the nation of Israel. Three years after the PLO's inception, in 1967, Israel fought the successful Six-Day War against the combined forces of Egypt, Syria, Jordan, Iraq, and Kuwait, leaving the Jewish state in control of the Gaza Strip and the West Bank, two areas heavily populated by Palestinians.

At that time, events that brought the PLO to the forefront of the Middle Eastern conflict began to rapidly succeed each other. In July 1968, the PLO drafted its official charter, which called for the elimination of Israel from the Middle East and declared that the only way to establish an independent Palestinian state was through armed struggle. The same year, a relatively powerful guerrilla movement called Fatah joined the PLO. Its leader, Yasir Arafat, quickly came to dominate the organization, acquiring in 1969 the position of chairman of the PLO's executive committee. Meanwhile, the various organizations making up the PLO stepped up their guerrilla activities against the Jewish state.

INTERNATIONAL RECOGNITION

In addition to fighting Israel, the PLO soon found itself in conflict not only with Israel, but also with Jordan, which had for years hosted the organization's command center. Feeling threatened by the increasing influence of Palestinians in Jordan's internal affairs, King Hussein of Jordan forced the PLO out of the country. The organization relocated to Lebanon, from where it continued to stage attacks against Israel.

By the early 1970s, the PLO was hard at work acquiring much-needed international legitimization. Its efforts were rewarded in 1974, when the United Nations officially recognized the organization and granted it observer status. The same year, the Arab countries proclaimed the PLO to be the sole legitimate representative of the Palestinian people. Successful on the international scene, the PLO now has to face an offensive by its opponent, Israel, which in 1982 invaded Lebanon with the stated aim of annihilating the PLO guerrillas.

Once again, the PLO went on the move, relocating its headquarters to Tunisia. Within five years, however, the world's attention focused on the Gaza Strip and the West Bank, where hundreds of Palestinian youth clashed with Israeli troops in an uprising that came to be known as the first *intifada* (an Arabic word meaning "shaking off"). Although the PLO was not initially the moving force behind the events, it quickly moved to take control of (and credit for) the Palestinian revolt.

THE OSLO ACCORDS

The intifada continued intermittently for six years. During that time, Yasir Arafat proclaimed an independent Palestinian state composed of the two embattled territories—the West Bank and the Gaza Strip—and officially repudiated terrorist acts. Although the move was well received internationally, relations with the West (and much of the Arab world) took a turn for the worse in 1990, when Arafat gave his political support to the Iraqi dictator Saddam Hussein, who had just invaded Kuwait.

Finally, after prolonged secret negotiations between the PLO and Israel, the PLO signed the Oslo Accords in the presence of U.S. president Bill Clinton. In a dramatic transformation of its initial goal to destroy the Jewish state, the PLO renounced its claim to the territory on which Israel had been founded in 1948 (not including the Gaza Strip, the West Bank, and East Jerusalem). In its turn, Israel agreed to withdraw gradually from the Palestinian territories and gave the Palestinians limited autonomy over the areas of Jericho and Gaza.

AN UNCERTAIN FUTURE

One year after the ground-breaking Oslo Accords, Arafat created the Palestinian National Authority (PA) to administer the autonomous territories, which by 1995 also included parts of the West Bank. The PLO leader was soon after elected president of the PA, and his associates controlled the organization's legislative body.

Within a few months, the PLO removed from its charter all articles that called for the destruction of the state of Israel. Arafat also began a series of face-to-face negotiations with successive Israeli leaders, but the proceedings were hampered by repeated acts of terrorism, including suicide bombings, in the streets of Gaza and the West Bank, as well as by severe ideological differences.

A second intifada erupted in 2000, further obstructing the peace process. Israel ceased to recognize Arafat as a legitimate and credible negotiation partner and isolated him in his compound in the West Bank city of Ramallah. Under pressure from the international community, Arafat appeared to reform the Palestinian Authority and delegated some of his powers. In November 2004, Yasir Arafat died in a hospital in Paris.

Arafat's successor as leader of the PLO, Mahmoud Abbas, has sought to end the violence between Palestinians and Israelis and to move forward toward peace and independence for Palestinians. At present, however, the PLO's key objective, the creation of an independent Palestinian state, remains unaccomplished.

See also Arab-Israeli Conflict; Hamas; Intifada; Middle East and U.S. Policy; Middle East Conflicts (1956, 1967, 1973)

Further Reading

Nassar, Jamal R. *The Palestine Liberation Organization: From Armed Struggle to the Declaration of Independence.* New York: Praeger, 1991.

Norton, Augustus R., and Martin H. Greenberg. *The International Relations of the Palestine Liberation Organization.* Carbondale: Southern Illinois University Press, 1989.

Rabie, Mohamed. *U.S.-PLO Dialogue: Secret Diplomacy and Conflict Resolution.* Gainesville: University Press of Florida, 1995.

POLICE ACTION

An isolated undertaking, military in nature, intended to curb either an insurgency within a state's own borders or by one state against another when that state is in violation of international treaties or norms or is found to have engaged in an act of aggression. Under international and domestic laws, military action can be undertaken by a state either pursuant to a declaration of war against another state or as a police action. In the United States, the Constitution requires that a declaration of war against another state be approved by Congress. Absent a declaration of war, however, the president can order military action by virtue of his powers as commander in chief of the armed forces.

In terms of international law, police actions are permissible under two circumstances. Initiating military action against a state—thus infringing upon its political and territorial sovereignty—is permissible under international law only when that state has perpetrated an act of aggression against another state or when it has otherwise posed a threat to international peace and security and a collective decision has been made by the United Nations to curb this action. One other instance in which a police action is permissible is when a state acts in self-defense against imminent attack by another state, which is deemed the aggressor even if it has not yet attacked. In the post–Cold War era, these lines have been blurred to occasionally include the permission of territorial and political infringement upon states whose governments perpetrate atrocities against their own people, but this is a developing issue. In the post–September 11, 2001, era, these guidelines have become even murkier as states militarily pursue individuals they deem terrorists within the borders of other states.

Even before today's global issues challenged the parameters set up by the UN Charter and other instruments of international law, military activity between states never quite fit neatly within the framework set up by those treaties and pacts. That is, most military activity takes place outside of the context of a declaration of war.

In U.S. history, examples of such incidents abound and include the Korean War, the invasion of Grenada, the Gulf War of 1991, and U.S. involvement in the Balkan wars of the 1990s.

Arguably the most infamous police action undertaken by the United States is the Vietnam War. Like the Korean War, the Vietnam conflict was fueled by the tensions of the Cold War, and U.S. involvement in it was intended to curb the spread of communism in Southeast Asia. The conflict was prolonged far beyond initial expectations, snowballing and drawing the United States further and further into the quagmire, despite growing antiwar sentiment at home calling for extraction from the region.

POLITICAL ASSASSINATION

The purposeful killing of foreign political or military leaders. Although political assassination is prohibited

by executive order, the United States has attempted to use assassination as a policy tool in peacetime and in war. Longstanding moral objections to assassination also have made policymakers wary of using it as a weapon of foreign policy. However, contemporary trends in international politics, especially the rise of terrorism and the proliferation of weapons of mass destruction, suggest that assassination may become a more tempting policy option in the future.

THE USE OF ASSASSINATION IN HISTORY

Until the beginning of the 17th century, assassination was widely accepted as a political device. As late as 1516, English scholar and statesman Sir Thomas More defended the ethics and practicality of political assassination. More was in the mainstream of thought; from the medieval period through the counter-Reformation (ca. 1200–1650), the practice of assassinating rulers or leaders was used with little reservation.

The Protestant Reformation and resulting Catholic counter-Reformation in the 1500s and early 1600s brought a religious dimension to politics that fueled the use of assassination. Monarchs during this time often viewed their foreign counterparts not merely as political rivals but also as heretics. Thus, King Phillip II of Spain, a Catholic, tried repeatedly to assassinate Protestant monarchs such as Holland's William of Orange and Queen Elizabeth I of England. The Vatican took part in such activities, as well, publicly supporting the assassination of Elizabeth.

Political and legal theorists began to codify the prohibition on assassination in the late 16th and 17th centuries. Anticipating the approach of the nation-state, Italian jurist Alberico Gentili wrote in 1598 that European leaders who used assassination might find it used against themselves. He also tied public security to the safety of public leaders. The rise of the nation-state system in the mid-17th century introduced a new norm against political assassination. Because the state system was defined by its political leaders, international order depended on mutual respect for their lives. Because the Great Powers each had an interest in maintaining the existing political order, this tacit agreement reduced the likelihood of any established state resorting to assassination, thus promoting the safety of all their leaders. Assassination remained a domestic problem, but it rapidly declined as a tool of foreign policy.

In the mid-1700s, Swiss legal scholar Emmerich de Vattel gave voice to the prevailing view of assassination.

De Vattel expressed revulsion at the "infamous and execrable" practice of assassination and warned policymakers that any leader who resorted to killing political rivals would be "regarded as an enemy of the human race." At roughly the same time, on the other side of the Atlantic Ocean, Thomas Jefferson wrote that assassination was a product of the Dark Ages, and he applauded civilization for moving forward.

Despite these strong condemnations of assassination, scholars disagree on the historical strength of the norm against political killing. Those who feel that the norm largely has been upheld point out that state-supported international assassination virtually disappeared by the 19th century. Other scholars contend that leaders weigh many factors in making decisions, and that assassination simply came to be seen by decision makers as a less effective political tool. They argue that the apparent norm against assassination was nothing more than a decision to choose options perceived to be better.

Notwithstanding the continuing debate over the power of norms in international politics, the historical record suggests that the informal ban on political assassination had important consequences for the modern state system. Even though a number of political assassinations occurred during the 20th century, there were striking examples of restraint. Perhaps the most telling was in 1938, when British leaders apparently rejected a plan to kill Adolf Hitler, calling it "unsportsmanlike."

During the early Cold War, U.S. policymakers had a freer hand in conducting covert operations, some of which involved assassination attempts on foreign leaders. Because the Soviet threat appeared grave, the Central Intelligence Agency (CIA) was given considerable discretion in its foreign activities. For example, the CIA targeted Cuban leader Fidel Castro after he became a Soviet ally. The CIA arranged a variety of operations, including a plan to kill Castro by using a ballpoint pen that concealed a poisonous hypodermic needle.

The United States also has been accused of planning and participating in assassinations of political leaders in Asia and South America. In 1963, for example, South Vietnamese president Ngo Dinh Diem was assassinated by army generals dissatisfied with his rule, apparently with the approval of the U.S. ambassador Henry Cabot Lodge. In later decades, U.S. leaders strenuously denied involvement in such assassinations. These denials implied a fear of exposure, suggesting that U.S. policymakers were constrained by the general objections to assassination.

The prolonged war in Vietnam, and episodes such as the assassination of South Vietnamese leader Ngo Dinh Diem, caused Congress to look more closely at U.S. covert action. Congress demanded greater oversight and sought to rein in the morally questionable practices of the CIA, including assassination. An executive order prohibiting assassination, authorized by President Gerald R. Ford in 1976, was in a sense the culmination of these reforms. From the end of the Vietnam War to the end of the Cold War, few policymakers in Washington were willing to publicly challenge the ban.

The objection to political assassination survived into the 1990s. During the first Gulf War in 1991, Saddam Hussein's close control over Iraqi military operations gave rise to advocates of *decapitation* strategies. They held that killing key officials would critically disable the Iraqi fighting machine. Here, the norm against assassination came in direct opposition with the military obligation to defeat the enemy. Still, the norm against assassination held. President George H. W. Bush declared, "We're not targeting any individual," and U.S. general Norman Schwarzkopf argued, "That's not the way we fight wars anyway."

THE ASSASSINATION CONTROVERSY

In recent years, the debate over the legality, morality, and effectiveness of political assassination has returned. Evidence suggests that the historical norm against assassination may be eroding. Some analysts argue that state leaders who harbor terrorists should not enjoy protection against assassination. In addition, the proliferation of weapons of mass destruction means that individual leaders can cause astonishing levels of death and destruction. Because more power is wielded by a few individuals, political assassination may seem like the best way to avert potential danger.

Political assassination as a tactic of foreign policy is tempting for several reasons. First, assassination may help influence the behavior of a target state by removing an unfriendly leader. This outcome assumes that the leader's immediate subordinates are more amenable to one's demands. It also assumes that they are likely to be frightened into cooperation by the killing of their leader. Second, the threat of political assassination may give pause to leaders of other states who would challenge U.S. interests. The emphasis on regime change in the foreign policy of President George W. Bush suggests that the United States is trying to coerce leaders of rogue states with direct threats.

Political assassination is also tempting because it may shorten an ongoing war by debilitating enemy command and control. Ending a war would spare the trouble of launching a costly ground invasion and compel surrender. Finally, assassination may have preventive value if targeted leaders seek to acquire weapons of mass destruction or attack American interests. Such rationales are more tempting if the target state is tightly controlled—the greater the degree of centralization, the greater the potential benefits of assassinating the leader.

Despite these incentives, there are two main reasons why political assassination remains controversial. First, Executive Order 12333 makes it unacceptable for any individual employed by or acting on behalf of the United States government to "engage in, or conspire to engage in, assassination." The order, originally signed by President Ford in 1976, has been renewed by every subsequent administration.

The second reason why assassination is problematic and controversial is that it has a dubious record of success. In rare circumstances it has achieved its operational and political objectives; more often, however, it has not. A study by the RAND Corporation analyzed nearly two dozen assassination attempts between 1943 and 1999. It concluded that these attempts were utterly fruitless; there were no successful direct attacks on foreign political heads of state. In rare cases, U.S. support for coups had helped topple undesirable governments. However, even then, the deterrent and coercive goals of leadership attack were hard to achieve. The RAND study found that invasion and occupation was a more reliable strategy for attaining such objectives.

There are other reasons why political assassination is controversial. Some observers question the morality of targeted killings, especially when the target is a democratically elected leader. In addition, opponents of assassination argue that the norm against political killings helps to protect American leaders. Should that norm erode, foreign adversaries may use the threat of assassination as a way to counter U.S. conventional military might.

ISSUES

Targeting Osama

Can the United States legally assassinate Osama bin Laden? Should assassination become a feature of the war on terrorism?

President Gerald Ford explicitly prohibited assassination amid public pressure to reign in "rogue" intelligence operations abroad. Signed in February 1976, Executive Order 11905 states, "No employee of the United States government shall engage in, or conspire to engage in, political assassination." The prohibition

remains in force, but the September 11 attacks rekindled the debate over the appropriateness of assassination.

Supporters of the ban note that the war on terror is essentially a war of ideas. Reducing the danger of terrorism requires improving America's reputation abroad. The resort to assassination–even against the most notorious terrorist leaders–would make the United States appear hypocritical. It cannot promote democratic ideals if it uses targeted killing as a tool of foreign policy. In addition, supporters argue that assassination remains contrary to domestic and international law.

However, the Executive Order does not offer a precise definition of assassination, leaving much room for interpretation. It fails to distinguish between peacetime and wartime assassination, and it is unclear whether leaders of transnational groups are protected. Thus, the Bush administration has argued that targeting al Qaeda leaders is constitutional because the prohibition does not apply to wartime or to actions taken against nonstate terrorists.

Advocates also contend that assassination is justified on moral and strategic grounds in the continuing war on terrorism. Some of these arguments were made even before 9/11. In early 2001, Representative Bob Barr (R-GA) introduced legislation that would overturn the executive prohibition on assassination. The Terrorist Elimination Act of 2001 implicitly challenged the morality of the ban, noting that "present strategy allows the military forces to bomb large targets hoping to eliminate the terrorist leader, but prevents our country from designing a limited action, which would specifically accomplish that purpose." It also argued that prohibiting assassination limits the "swift, sure and precise action needed by the United States to protect our national security."

—Joshua Rovner

See also Central Intelligence Agency (CIA); Covert Action; Covert Operations; Executive Orders

Further Reading

Hosmer, Stephen T. *Operations Against Enemy Leaders.* Santa Monica, CA: RAND, 2001.

Pape, Robert A. *Bombing to Win: Air Power and Coercion in War.* Ithaca, NY: Cornell University Press, 1996.

Richelson, Jeffrey T. *A Century of Spies: Intelligence in the Twentieth Century.* New York: Oxford University Press, 1995.

Thomas, Ward. *The Ethics of Destruction: Norms and Force in International Relations.* Ithaca, NY: Cornell University Press, 2001.

POLITICAL CULTURE
See STRATEGIC CULTURE

PORTLAND SIX

Group of six Portland Muslims convicted on charges of aiding al-Qaeda. The six Portland, Oregon, natives were indicted in October 2003 on charges of conspiracy to provide material support to terrorists, conspiracy to contribute services to al-Qaeda and the Taliban, and conspiracy to wage war against the United States. Following the terrorist attacks on the World Trade Center and the Pentagon on September 11, 2001, the Portland Six traveled to China in order to make their way into Afghanistan via Pakistan, where they were denied visas. The group members planned to fight alongside the Taliban against the U.S. military.

Members of the Portland Six pled guilty to money-laundering charges, plotting to fight for the Taliban, and conspiracy and weapons charges in connection with the plan to go to Afghanistan. Following their guilty pleas, they were sentenced to prison terms ranging from 4 to 18 years.

The Portland Six indictments are notable as some of the earliest cases of the USA PATRIOT Act being implemented for domestic security concerns. The PATRIOT Act, enacted shortly after September 11, gives law-enforcement agencies wide-ranging powers to investigate and prosecute terrorists within the United States. In the Portland Six case, prosecutors had broad authority to issue national warrants and gain access to information they previously did not have.

See also Al-Qaeda; September 11/WTC and Pentagon Attacks; Taliban; Terrorism, War on International

POSITIVE SUM GAME

A game-theory term that refers to situations in which the total of gains and losses is greater than zero. A positive sum occurs when resources are somehow increased and an approach is formulated in which the desires and needs of all concerned are satisfied. One example would be when two parties both gain financially by participating in a contest, no matter who wins or loses. Positive sum outcomes occur in instances of distributive bargaining where different interests are negotiated so that everyone's needs are met.

In contrast to the positive sum game are the zero sum game and the negative sum game. The term *zero sum game* refers to situations in which the total of wins and losses adds up to zero: One party benefits at the direct expense of another. The term *negative sum game* describes situations in which the total of gains and losses is less than zero. The only way for one party to maintain the status quo is to take something from another party. It is in the context of negative sum games that the most serious competition tends to occur.

Further Reading

Kriesberg, Louis. *Constructive Conflicts: From Escalation to Resolution.* New York: Rowman & Littlefield, 2002.

POTSDAM CONFERENCE (1945)

From July 16 to August 2, 1945, the final meeting of the Big Three Allied powers (the United States, the United Kingdom, and the Soviet Union), which presaged the opening of the Cold War. Called to determine the details of the occupation of Germany and Austria, the terms to be imposed upon Japan, and other aspects of the postwar world, the Potsdam Conference demonstrated the tensions always present in the Allied camp.

As agreed to by Big Three leaders Truman, Churchill, and Stalin at the conference, Germany, Austria, and their capital cities were divided into separate occupation zones, and reparations in kind were to be taken from each zone. Germany was to be occupied and reformed under the concept of the five Ds: demilitarization, de-Nazification, democratization, decentralization, and deindustrialization. No attempt to redraw the map of Europe was attempted at the meeting, except to clarify the German–Polish border as the Oder and Neisse rivers and to apportion part of former East Prussia to the Poles. The purpose of the Soviet occupation of the remaining countries in Eastern Europe was characterized as assisting in the democratic reorganization of those states. The conference called upon Japan on July 26 to surrender unconditionally, and in a secret codicil, the Russians promised to enter the war against Japan three months after the defeat of Germany.

By the end of the Potsdam meeting, the United States had tested successfully the first atomic bomb, and the Russian participation in the war against Japan became less significant. However, President Harry S. Truman indicated to Soviet marshal Joseph Stalin that his country had a new weapon of remarkable power and would use it shortly to end the war. This was the beginning of a nascent policy of atomic diplomacy, in which the United States hoped to intimidate the Soviet Union into a more favorable postwar posture.

Although the usual protocols of solidarity emerged from the Potsdam Conference, the wartime alliance was essentially over. Although the Cold War was not yet inevitable, the Soviet Union was not going to open its political, social, and economic system to the West and still feared capitalist encirclement as before the war. The presence of the Red Army in eastern and central Europe served Russian security interests well, and to Russia the language of democratization in the postwar administration signified the establishment of governments friendly to the USSR. Russia entered the war against Japan as promised in August 1945 and stripped reparations from Germany with considerable enthusiasm. Atomic diplomacy failed to shock the Russians at Potsdam, because their espionage system had already informed Stalin of U.S. progress with the A-bomb, and the Russian program to develop the bomb was well underway.

Postwar cooperation continued to remain unlikely between the East and West, largely because of divergent national interests, rather than because of specific problems encountered at Potsdam. If the conference failed to unite a world left devastated and divided, such may have been beyond the normal range of diplomacy. Potsdam, like the previous 1945 Yalta Conference, soon became a rallying point for national political debates in each country, where opposition groups asserted that their political leaders had been duped by the other signatories of the agreements. As a result, peace treaties ending World War II required decades to resolve, and to this day they remain unsigned between Russia and Japan.

See also Atomic Bomb; Cold War; Espionage; Grand Strategy; Soviet Union, Former (Russia), and U.S. Policy; Stalin, Joseph (1878–1953); Truman, Harry S., and National Policy; World War II (1939–1945); Yalta Conference (1945)

POWELL, COLIN (1937–)

Soldier and statesman best known for his role as chairman of the Joint Chiefs of Staff (from 1989 to 1993) and as secretary of state in the first administration of President George W. Bush. Following retirement from the United States Army and prior to his public service, Powell served on the board of America Online. He also founded America's Promise, a non-profit organization for children, in 1997.

Colin Luther Powell was born on April 5, 1937, in the Bronx, New York, to Luther and Maud Powell, immigrants to the United States from Jamaica. He attended the City College of New York, where he participated in the Reserve Officers' Training Corps (ROTC) and earned a bachelor's degree in geology in 1958. During his military career, Powell also earned a master's degree in business administration from George Washington University.

MILITARY CAREER

When Second Lieutenant Powell graduated college in 1958, he began a military career that would span 35 years, include two wars, and culminate in his appointment as a four-star general, the highest military rank in the country. As a junior officer, Lieutenant Powell served stateside as well as in Germany and did two one-year tours in Vietnam as a captain and later as a major.

During his first tour in Vietnam, Captain Powell served as an adviser to the Army of the Republic of South Vietnam. Major Powell's second Vietnam tour, as deputy assistant chief of staff of the 23rd Infantry Division, was marred by what some see as an attempt to cover up the My Lai massacre in an investigation of a letter written by a witness to the killings.

Later tours of duty included service as a battalion commander in Korea, study at the prestigious National War College in Washington, DC, and command of the 2nd Brigade of the 101st Airborne Division. As a brigadier general, Powell served as assistant commander of the 4th Infantry Division. In 1986, Powell returned to Germany as commander of V Corps, a position he held for only five months.

General Powell returned to Washington in 1987 to serve as national security advisor under President Ronald Reagan. Although he played an instrumental role in the Iran-Contra affair, Powell escaped close scrutiny and was subsequently promoted to four-star general and appointed chairman of the Joint Chiefs of Staff in 1989. It was in this post, which he held until his retirement in 1993, that Powell became a household name for his command of the military during 1991's Operation Desert Storm.

In the months leading up to the 1991 invasion of Iraq, Powell gained a reputation as a dovish, even-headed military leader who rarely advocated use of force as the first solution to international conflict. In advocating his so-called Powell Doctrine of diplomacy—sanctions and a steady buildup of forces in Kuwait—Powell found himself in opposition to most officials in the administration of President George H. W. Bush. Once Operation Desert Storm began, however, Powell developed a reputation for fierce loyalty in not attempting to undermine a policy he disagreed with after it was implemented.

CIVILIAN CAREER

Following his retirement from the military in September 1993, Powell embarked on a public-speaking career with audiences across the United States and abroad. In 1995, he finished writing his autobiography, *My American Journey,* which soon became a best seller.

The former general was sought after by both the Democratic and Republican parties and eventually declared himself a Republican. Although he was touted as a possible opponent to Bill Clinton in the 1996 presidential election, he declined to run for office and devoted himself to campaigning for Republican candidates.

The following year, Colin Powell founded America's Promise, an organization devoted to building a better future for children through community involvement. Powell encountered controversy again in his career while serving on the board of America Online, a company that merged with Time Warner in 2000. Powell's son, Michael, was the only member of the Federal Communications Commission who urged that the merger be approved without scrutiny. Controversy arose as a result of the alleged conflict of interest.

POST 9/11

Also in 2000, Powell served as foreign-policy adviser on the presidential campaign of then Texas governor George W. Bush, son of his previous commander in chief during Desert Storm. After Bush emerged victorious, few were surprised when Powell was appointed the 65th secretary of state, thereby becoming the highest-placed African American public official in U.S. history.

The September 11, 2001, terrorist attacks on the United States thrust Secretary of State Powell onto center stage. Powell was charged with securing the cooperation of foreign nations in the war against terror, and he presented the case against Saddam Hussein's regime in Iraq to the United Nations Security Council in February 2003. Although successful in gaining the support of numerous allies for regime change in Afghanistan, the United States did not succeed in garnering support for a Security Council Resolution authorizing use of force against Saddam Hussein and his alleged weapons of mass destruction.

Powell's reputation was somewhat tarnished by his role in "selling" the Iraq War of 2003 to the American people and the world, and he chose not to continue as secretary of state after President George W. Bush was reelected in 2004. Since his resignation and return to private life, Powell has begun to offer cautious criticism of some of the foreign-policy decisions of the Bush administration concerning the move toward war with Iraq.

—*Daniel P. McDonald*

See also Department of State, U.S.; Gulf War (1990–1991); Iraq War of 2003; Joint Chiefs of Staff

Further Reading

Powell, Colin L., with Joseph E Persico. *My American Journey.* New York: Random House, 1995.

POWER, WORLD

A state whose political, economic, and military influence extends worldwide and affects other states and global dynamics. Throughout history, a number of states have served as what might be considered world powers: the ancient Roman Empire, Spain in the 16th century, and France and Great Britain in the 18th and 19th centuries. After World War II, the two greatest world powers were the Soviet Union and the United States, both of which were considered superpowers because of their strength and influence.

CONTEMPORARY EVOLUTION OF WORLD POWER DYNAMICS

At the time of the American Revolution, the world's major powers were Great Britain and France. Until the turn of the 19th century, the United States generally took an isolationist stance in its foreign policy and global posture. The relatively new nation focused its energies internally, forging westward, building domestic industry, and bolstering and protecting economic markets. However, at the end of the 1800s, a shift in the U.S. global position occurred. The expansion of the U.S. Navy, the annexation of Hawaii, and U.S. engagement in the Spanish-American War transformed the United States into a power on a multipolar world stage.

By the early 20th century, Great Britain and France had been joined on the world stage not only by the United States but also by rapidly industrializing societies in Germany and Japan. However, two world wars within the span of 30 years devastated the traditional European powers and broke the military power of Japan. By the end of World War II, the Soviet Union emerged as a new force in world politics, joining the United States as the only truly global powers. For 45 years after World War II, a delicate and often dangerous bipolar rivalry known as the Cold War persisted between the two superpowers. The collapse of the Soviet Union in 1991 produced today's unipolar system with the United States as the world's sole superpower.

Several factors have combined to put and keep the United States at the top of the global power pyramid. These include military superiority, trade volume and economic strength, and political influence. These sources of power enable, supplement, and advance one another, helping to sustain the preeminent U.S. position in world affairs.

The United States military is the largest and most technologically advanced in the world. In addition, no other state has as many military personnel stationed in as many foreign bases as the United States. Some of the roles performed by the U.S. military abroad include ensuring the security of other states, enforcing bilateral security agreements with other states, training other states' armies and specialized units, protecting U.S. interests internationally, stabilizing areas subject to tenuous and delicate political or military situations, and helping to patrol the borders of states whose own armies require reinforcement.

By virtue of this military superiority, the United States sets the standard for NATO (North Atlantic Treaty Organization) military capabilities. Whereas Western European states are as developed in other sectors as the United States, they typically do not put as much emphasis on armament and military development as does the United States. As the leading military power, then, the United States armed forces set the bar for NATO's military standards. Because NATO is a military alliance whose member states contribute troops to create a collective force, interoperability is essential. Therefore, all members' armies must be mutually standardized to some degree. Before being considered for membership, aspirant states must ensure that their militaries will be able to fit into this fold.

The United States' political heft can be seen in many ways. Two manifestations of its global political influence are its status as a member of the Permanent Five (P5) on the United Nations Security Council and its influential and enormous global diplomatic corps. Both work to extend American influence and power abroad.

The U.S. position among the P5 gives it veto power and thus allows it to maintain control over most significant initiatives undertaken by the United Nations. Because the Security Council dispatches peacekeeping operations, any military undertaking initiated and approved by the United Nations must be approved by the states that have P5 status. This power has many implications, as evidenced by the fact that it essentially paralyzed the Security Council during the Cold War years. That is, most conflicts in the world during the Cold War years were proxy to the larger tensions of the communist–capitalist rivalry and were therefore of interest to the opposing superpowers. As both were members of the P5, both could veto Security Council actions that were contrary to their national interests.

POWER AND RESPONSIBILITY

The place of the United States as a world power has always had implications for its national security. For instance, despite strong isolationist sentiment at home, the United States eventually became involved in both world wars after initial hedging. Although the specific circumstances that drew the United States into each of those wars were different, the fact remains that lesser powers would not find themselves in positions that virtually mandated that they actively join in large global conflicts.

Later, during the Cold War years, the U.S. status as one of two superpowers had obvious implications for its national security. Aside from perpetually being on some degree of nuclear alert, U.S. Cold War superpower status had the direct result of forcing the United States' involvement in military engagements it otherwise never would have entered. Both the Korean and Vietnam wars were conflicts that the United States entered for the purpose of balancing Soviet global influence.

The conclusion of the Cold War left the United States as the sole superpower in a world that saw many regions suddenly subjected to security vacuums. Although it spread instability in some ways, the Cold War also suppressed many conflicts that simmered under the surface of American or Soviet control. When the influence of the superpowers was lifted or withdrawn, many states were suddenly left with regional, ethnic, and national conflicts previously obscured by the ideological cover provided by the Cold War. This change made the 1990s a tumultuous decade.

One example of such conflict was the series of wars in the Balkans resulting from the breakup of the former communist state of Yugoslavia. Cobbled together after World War I from several countries of varied ethnicity, Yugoslavia had always been torn by internal rivalries. Its post–World War II communist leader Josip Tito, used force to keep a lid on these tensions for decades. With the demise of communism in Eastern Europe, several Yugoslavian provinces declared independence. Some of these new states saw rival ethnic groups renew old hatreds; others were the targets of attempts by the Yugoslav government to prevent secession. Conflict raged for several years before Western powers, led by the United States, intervened militarily under the auspices of NATO.

The September 11, 2001, terrorist attacks on New York City and Washington, DC, redefined the U.S. role as a world power. By subsequently declaring itself the leader in the war against terror, the United States has essentially committed to a global military presence for an indeterminable period. Given the amorphous and decentralized nature of terrorist organizations, the United States may itself wage this war for a very long time.

American troops are currently engaged in counterterrorism-related missions in Afghanistan, several Southeast Asian states, the Caucasus, and central Europe. In the aftermath of the invasion of Iraq in 2003, foreign terrorists have established a presence on Iraqi soil, adding another major front to the war on terrorism. This war has additional implications for U.S. national security, in that the threat to domestic soil is more tangible and realistic since the attacks of September 11. Critics of America's aggressive campaign against terror in other global regions argue that it will reinvigorate those seeking to attack the United States and that it will increase the threat to Americans both on U.S. soil and internationally.

See also Balance of Power; Bipolarity; Cold War; Communism and National Security; Great Power Rivalry; Hegemony; Hyperpower; Multipolarity; New World Order; Realpolitik; Superpower; Terrorism, War on International

Further Reading

Hook, Steven W. *U.S. Foreign Policy: The Paradox of World Power.* Washington, DC: CQ Press, 2004.

Nye, Joseph S. *Soft Power: The Means to Success in World Politics.* New York: PublicAffairs, 2004.

Zimmerman, Warren. *First Great Triumph: How Five Americans Made Their Country a World Power.* New York: Farrar, Straus & Giroux, 2004.

PRECISION-GUIDED MUNITIONS

Explosive devices delivered to their targets by the use of highly accurate electronic guidance devices. Precision-guided munitions are called *smart bombs,* whereas normal bombs that rely solely on gravity to reach their targets are referred to as *dumb bombs.*

Precision-guided munitions have several advantages over conventional dumb bombs. A smart bomb's high degree of accuracy means that an attacker virtually can be assured of hitting the target. It also means that one needs fewer weapons to take out critical targets. Also, because of its accuracy, a smart bomb can carry a smaller explosive charge than dumb bombs.

Much of the damage done by conventional bombs results from the combined force of near misses and impacts on noncritical areas of a target. Thus, dumb bombs must contain large explosive charges to do significant damage. A single smart bomb with a smaller charge, precisely placed at the weakest point of a building or right on top of a bunker, can be much more effective than many more powerful dumb bombs dropped on the same target.

Another advantage of smart bombs is that they produce a limited amount of collateral damage—that is, damage that affects nearby nontargeted areas. When dumb bombs are dropped, a certain percentage will miss their target entirely and fall in surrounding areas, producing collateral damage. Smart bombs, with their greater accuracy and smaller explosive charge, reduce both the chances and the severity of such damage. However, in the event that its guidance system malfunctions, a smart bomb is much more unpredictable than a dumb bomb. Conventional bombs that miss their targets will still fall in the general area; a malfunctioning smart bomb is likely to fall many miles from its intended target with no way to predict where it will land.

Three types of guidance devices control most precision-guided munitions: television, laser, and satellite. Television-guided weapons were first developed during the Korean War and later perfected in the 1960s. The *fire-and-forget* camera bomb features a television camera that transmits an image back to the aircraft that drops it. The bomb itself is equipped with steering fins controlled remotely by the pilot or copilot of the aircraft, who uses a joystick to direct the bomb to its target. The U.S. Air Force made extensive use of television-guided weapons in the latter stages of the Vietnam War because of public criticism of collateral damage from U.S. bombing.

The U.S. Air Force developed the first laser-guided bomb in 1968. However, these weapons did not enter common use until the invention of the microchip in the 1970s made their guidance devices significantly smaller. A laser bomb is guided by a laser beam that "paints" (illuminates) its target. The laser that produces the beam (called the *target designator*) is mounted either on an aircraft or at a ground site of some type and is aimed by a remote operator. Sensors on the bomb detect the "painting" on the target and direct the bomb to that spot. One weakness of laser-guided bombs is that that they are limited to targets in range of friendly target designators. In addition, they cannot function in weather conditions that obscure the sensors' ability to see the "paint."

A satellite-guided weapon receives signals from orbiting satellites that direct it to its target. These satellites are part of the Global Positioning System (GPS), which circles the earth and provides extremely accurate data about the location of specific points on the ground. When a target is identified, its location is fed into computers aboard GPS satellites. The satellites then locate the point identified as the target and send a signal that guides the bomb directly to that spot. Satellite-guided weapons operate in all conditions and require no remote operator to guide them once released.

Satellite weapons have two main drawbacks. First, it is possible to jam a GPS signal. To address this problem, every satellite-guided bomb stores a map of the target location in its computer memory. In case it loses the GPS signal, the bomb relies on this inertial navigation. However, active GPS guidance is much more accurate than inertial navigation. The second drawback is that the guidance is only as good as the information provided to the satellites. It is up to military intelligence to provide accurate information beforehand about the location of targets.

In recent years, as at the end of the Vietnam War, U.S. military actions in the Middle East have been tempered by concerns about the political consequences of collateral damage. These fears contributed to the widespread use of smart bombs in the Gulf War of 1991 and the Iraq War of 2003. In each case, the U.S. military claimed that the use of precision-guided weapons significantly reduced the amount of suffering among Iraqi citizens. Critics, however, maintain that many of the so-called precision munitions missed their targets and caused extensive collateral damage.

See also Cruise Missile; Science, Technology, and Security; Smart Bomb

PREEMPTION

Use of force by one state against another to prevent a potential attack or counter a perceived threat. The accepted norms of international relations give states the right to defend themselves when attacked. However, a state that faces an imminent threat to its security is not required to wait for an aggressor to strike before taking action. Preemption thus becomes an extension of the right of self-defense, but only if unprovoked aggression is imminent.

Arguably, Israel's strike against the Egyptian air force that began the 1967 Six-Day War was justifiably preemptive. Israel had reason to fear that the Egyptians were planning to attack, making its strike a necessary act of self-defense. The Israeli bombing of Iraq's nuclear reactor at Osirak in 1981, however, is not considered preemptive, because the reactor was under construction and did not present an immediate threat.

Preemption has developed into a foreign policy under U.S. president George W. Bush. He first alluded to preemptive action in an address at the U.S. Military Academy at West Point on June 1, 2002. In that address, Bush asserted that the Cold War doctrines of deterrence and containment were outdated and ineffective in the aftermath of the September 11, 2001, terrorist attacks on the World Trade Center and the Pentagon. He stated, "If we wait for threats to fully materialize, we will have waited too long. We must take the battle to the enemy, disrupt his plans, and confront the worst threats before they emerge." Bush described an altered international sphere where threats had to be eliminated before given a chance to effectively form and threaten nonaggressors.

The 2003 National Security Strategy of the United States stated, "We must be prepared to stop rogue states and their terrorist clients before they are able to threaten or use weapons of mass destruction against the United States and our allies and friends." The document outlined a preemptive strategy to combat weapons of mass destruction, a threat the president argued must be defended against before it is unleashed. In the report, the president asserted that the United States would act preemptively if it deemed a perceived threat to be imminent.

The Bush administration applied this doctrine of preemption to Iraq in its argument for deposing Iraqi dictator Saddam Hussein. The administration alleged that Saddam had amassed weapons of mass destruction (WMD) and that he was developing a nuclear weapons program. U.S. Secretary of State Colin Powell presented a case for disarming Saddam Hussein before the UN Security Council in February of 2003. Powell maintained that Saddam's past history of aggression indicated that the Iraqi leader was willing to use WMD to achieve his goals. The secretary of state characterized Iraq as an immediate threat to its neighbors and to the United States.

The announced policy of preemption was widely criticized, both in the United States and abroad. Many Americans were uncomfortable with the idea of the United States starting a war before it was attacked. The notion seemed at odds with the country's principle of mutual respect for the sovereignty of nations. To many Americans, the idea of preemption was disturbingly reminiscent of the Japanese sneak attack on Pearl Harbor, which brought the United States into World War II. That event became a metaphor for treachery for many Americans, who were concerned that the United States was now adopting something disturbingly similar as national policy. Some critics have also voiced the fear that the administration's aggressive policies may result in increased terrorist attacks against Americans.

Critics of preemption became more vocal in the wake of the Iraq War of 2003, when U.S. forces failed to find any evidence of either WMD or nuclear-weapons facilities in Iraq. This pointed out one of the great dangers of preemption—the possibility that the supposed target state is not actually being targeted. Many experts now believe that Iraq ended its WMD programs and destroyed any WMD stockpiles after the Gulf War of 1991. They think that Saddam continued to pretend to possess such weapons in order to maintain his image as a powerful and dangerous force in the region.

The failure of U.S. intelligence to determine the true state of affairs in Iraq led to an attack that arguably could not be considered truly preemptive. This danger continues to exist with regard to states such as Iran, which the Bush administration listed among the so-called Axis of Evil, along with North Korea and Iraq. Iran's nuclear capabilities are unclear, and it resists international inspection of its nuclear program. Since the invasion of Iraq, there has been much speculation about a preemptive U.S. strike against Iran. As of early 2005, the Bush administration denied having any immediate intention to attack Iran. However, it also refused to rule out the possibility of action to compel Iran to abandon its nuclear ambitions.

See also Bush Doctrine; Bush, George W., and National Policy; Containment and the Truman Doctrine; Deterrence; Intelligence and Counterintelligence; Iraq War of 2003; Preemptive Force; Preemptive War Doctrine; Saddam Hussein; Terrorism, War on International

Further Reading

Beestermoller, Gerhard, and David Little, eds. *Iraq: Threat and Response.* New Brunswick, NJ: Transaction, 2003.

Clarke, Richard. *Against All Enemies: Inside America's War on Terror.* New York: Free Press, 2004.

Daalder, Ivo H., and James M. Lindsay, eds. *America Unbound: The Bush Revolution in Foreign Policy.* Washington, DC: Brookings Institution, 2003.

Elshtain, Jean B. *Just War Against Terror: The Burden of American Power in a Violent World.* New York: Basic Books, 2003.

Woodward, Bob. *Plan of Attack.* New York: Simon & Schuster, 2004.

PREEMPTIVE FORCE

Emergency measure taken with the aim of preventing an imminent, and otherwise unavoidable, attack. The idea of preemptive force is usually employed in a military context, whereby a state claims its right to launch an offensive on a potential enemy *before* that enemy has had the chance to actually implement a plan of attack. The advantage of preemptive strike is rather obvious; by being the first to act decisively, one renders the enemy unable to carry out aggressive intentions. There are also several disadvantages, however, to this strategy. For one, the threatened state might be wrong in its assessment of the threat and launch an unwarranted destructive attack. Second, the use of a preemptive force by one state might set a precedent that would lead to widespread abuse of the preemptive option.

BASIC CONDITIONS

Although scholars and politicians sharply disagree on the ultimate legitimacy of the use of preemptive force, most do tend to agree on several fundamental prerequisites for a specific attack to even be conceived as a potentially justifiable preemptive strike. First, the attack has to come as a reaction to a perceived threat that is both absolutely credible and immediate. Second, the state that reacts to the threat needs to be sure that a preemptive attack is the only effective way to defend itself. Third, the preemptive action needs to be proportionate in scope and potential for destruction with the perceived threat.

One problem, however, is the ambiguous concepts on which these three conditions rest. How credible is credible enough? What does *immediate* mean? What are the measurements by which one assesses the potential for destruction of an event that has not yet taken place?

INTERPRETING THE UN CHARTER

Article 51 of the UN Charter is widely perceived as being extremely relevant to the question of preemption, as it explicitly protects "the inherent right of individual or collective self-defense if an armed attack occurs against a member of the United Nations."

Opponents of the strategy of preemption argue that the article clearly conditions a defensive action on the previous occurrence of an attack, not on the perception of the possibility for an attack. Supporters of the strategy, however, point out that Article 51 does not use the phrase "if and only if an armed attack occurs," therefore leaving the door open for other instances when preemptive force can be used legitimately.

In 2002, President George W. Bush presented the American people with a new National Security Strategy. According to it, the rise of terrorism and the increase in the availability of weapons of mass destruction have changed the international climate to such an extent that the United States now reserves the right to launch a preemptive attack on an enemy "even if uncertainty remains as to the time and place of the enemy's attack." That right was invoked most recently in the Iraq War of 2003, and it remains a highly controversial concept.

See also Declarations of War; First Strike; Interventionism; Terrorism, War on International

Further Reading

Gaddis, John Lewis. *Surprise, Security, and the American Experience.* Cambridge, MA: Harvard University Press, 2004.
Prebeck, Steven R. *Preventive Attack in the 1990s?* Maxwell Air Force Base, AL: Air University Press, 1993.

PREEMPTIVE WAR DOCTRINE

Policy that proposes waging war in an attempt to avoid an imminent attack or to gain a strategic advantage over an impending threat. The main aim of a preemptive attack is to gain the advantage of initiative by using military force before the opponent does. A typical example of a preemptive strike is an attack against enemy troops massed at a state's border ready to invade.

The *Dictionary of Military Terms,* the official dictionary of the U.S. Department of Defense, defines *preemption* as "an attack initiated on the basis of incontrovertible evidence that an enemy attack is imminent." It defines *prevention* in different terms. A preventive war is "initiated in the belief that military conflict, while not imminent, is inevitable, and that to delay would involve greater risk." This apparently was the logic that led to the war in Iraq in 2003.

There are several examples of preemptive attacks throughout the history of warfare. In 1587, English privateer Sir Francis Drake, under the order of Queen Elizabeth I, launched a preemptive attack to destroy the Spanish armada of King Philip II of Spain while it was still anchored in the Spanish port of Cádiz. Prussia's invasion of Saxony and Bohemia in 1756 as Austrian, Russian, and French troops were plotting to attack is also considered a preemptive strike. Preemption was also a strong motive behind the rush to war by Germany, Russia, and France at the outbreak of World War I in 1914, the Chinese intervention in Korea in 1951, and the Israeli strike against Egypt, Syria, and Jordan's forces that were gathering on Israel's borders in 1967.

Preemptive war is often confused with preventive war, and, in fact, a thin line divides the two. Academics define the difference between preemption and prevention solely in terms of time frame. Scholar Robert Jervis, for example, in the November/December 2002 issue of *Foreign Policy,* defined preemption as "an attack against an adversary that is about to strike," whereas preventive attack "is a move to prevent a threat from fully emerging." Although preventive attack is generally considered to violate international law and to fall short of the requirements of a just war, preemptive war is usually thought to be more acceptable.

Specifically, a preemptive attack is believed to be justifiable if it meets the criteria that Secretary of State Daniel Webster spelled out in 1837. According to his strict conditions, a threat must be "instant, overwhelming, leaving no choice of means or no moment of deliberation" for this type of attack to be permissible.

In contrast, the U.S. National Security Strategy document issued in September 2002 argued that the conditions that justify military preemption must be revised. According to this document, the old standard in international law that states can legally order preemptive strikes only when faced with an imminent threat is too restrictive. Instead, it argues that the anticipatory action is justified even if uncertainty remains as to the time and place of the enemy's attack, because the possibility of a terrorist attack with weapons of mass destruction makes the risk of waiting too high.

Before President George W. Bush's National Security Strategy of 2002, the United States had not engaged in a preemptive military attack. The nation had not attacked another country prior to being attacked itself or before U.S citizens were attacked—with one exception. The Spanish-American War represents the sole instance, when the United States initiated hostilities against Spain in 1898 in order to compel that nation to grant Cuba independence. Some have argued that the Cuban Missile Crisis of 1962 also had elements of preemption, but it did not actually include a preemptive military attack by the United States.

The 2002 national security document states that the United States will exercise the right to act preemptively in the event of deadly challenges to its people or to allies emerging from rogue states or terrorist groups. The document states that, "Given the goals of rogue states and terrorists, the United States can no longer rely solely on a reactive posture as we have in the past. The inability to deter a potential attacker, the immediacy of today's threats, and the magnitude of potential harm that could be caused by our adversaries' choice of weapons, do not permit that option."

Although to some observers this so-called Bush Doctrine calls for preventive rather than preemptive attacks, the final result does not change: The United States will act against emerging threats before they are fully formed. According to this approach, an adversary that cannot be deterred and whose attacks cannot be defended against must be stopped before it gains the capability to do harm. This is how President Bush defined preemption, which is considered the only way to be proactive in the face of two new serious threats—terrorism and rogue states.

See also Bush, George W., and National Policy; Preventive War; Terrorism, War on International

PREPOSITIONED EQUIPMENT

Military material that is stored in forward bases or forward-deployed ships and is available for immediate use in a theater of operations. The concept of prepositioning equipment makes preparing for a conflict situation much easier and faster because only troops and limited amounts of equipment must be flown in. During the Cold War, the U.S. rivalry with the Soviet Union created a need to respond to Soviet military challenges, particularly in Europe and the Middle East. At this time, most prepositioned U.S. equipment was stationed at land bases in Europe.

During the 1980s, the army recognized that their existing prepositioning strategy did not provide sufficient flexibility to meet challenges in places far from U.S. land bases. At this time, the military greatly expanded the seaborne prepositioning of equipment. During the Iraq War of 2003, the Army and Marines were helped immensely by the existence of ship-based prepositioned equipment, including most of the combat equipment used to fight the war. Congressional testimony later on, however, revealed some problems with older equipment and a lack of some supplies—problems that were overcome largely because of a long lag period between the movement of troops and the launching of the war.

The 1991 collapse of the Soviet Union led to changes in U.S. prepositioning strategy. Troop reductions occasioned by the end of the Cold War have forced the Department of Defense to rely even more heavily on prepositioned equipment. Much equipment remains in Europe, but many items have been moved to potential trouble spots in the Persian Gulf, the Indian Ocean, Korea, and the Pacific. As the military continues to transform and to adapt more mobile and technologically advanced models of warfare, planners will also need to consider changes in the use of prepositioned equipment in favor of less expensive and more effective options.

See also Forward Basing

PRESIDENTIAL DECISION DIRECTIVES (PDDs)

Issued by the president of the United States, types of executive orders for which different presidents have used a variety of names. The Truman and Eisenhower administrations issued National Security Council policy papers, which made policy recommendations on various topics pertaining to U.S. security. A less formal system was initiated by the Kennedy administration, and both John F. Kennedy and his successor Lyndon B. Johnson referred to them as National Security Action Memoranda (NSAMs).

Later, Richard Nixon and Gerald Ford called them National Security Decision Memoranda (NSDMs), and the system put in place by the Nixon administration served as the model for the Ford, Carter, and Reagan administrations, as well. This system functioned according to the issuance of two series of documents: study directives and decision directives. Study directives were commissioned by the National Security Council or other government agencies to carry out studies to produce data to be used in decision making. Decision directives served the purpose of stating the decision made on the basis of the study directives, and allocated tasks to specific agencies for implementation.

Jimmy Carter used the name Presidential Directives (PDs), and Ronald Reagan called them National Security Decision Directives (NSDDs). President George H. W. Bush called them National Security Directives (NSDs), and Bill Clinton used the title Presidential Decision Directives (PDDs). George W. Bush uses the term National Security Presidential Directives (NSPDs). The Presidential Decision Directives are issued with the advice and consent of the National Security Council, and because they pertain to vital areas of national security, they are often classified.

Different administrations have relied to greater and lesser degrees on Presidential Decision Directives for formulating national-security policy. The Carter and George H. W. Bush administrations produced a relatively small number (63 and 79, respectively), at a rate of 16 to 20 per year, in contrast to the Nixon, Ford, and Reagan administrations, which produced more than 40 per year.

Although Presidential Decision Directives do not account for all aspects of executive policy, they do provide a timeline of the major issues dealt with by various administrations. For example, National Security Action Memorandum No. 271, issued by the Kennedy administration, referred to "Cooperation with the USSR on Outer Space Matters." Later, National Security Study Directive 5-83, issued by the Reagan administration, was concerned with the development by NASA of a permanently manned space station. Presidential Review Directive NSTC-3, "Global Positioning System Policy Review," issued by the Clinton administration, paved the way for commercial and civilian use of the Global Positioning System (GPS).

The subject and uses of Presidential Decision Directives thus change and evolve in response to current events. Presidential Directive NSC-63, issued by the Carter administration, on the Persian Gulf security framework, was a response to the Soviet invasion of Afghanistan and the Iran-Iraq War. The purpose was to account for the numerical superiority of Soviet forces in the region by making the Soviet Union aware that it would face economic and diplomatic sanctions if it intervened. Moreover, it declared: "An attempt by any outside force to gain control of the Persian Gulf region will be regarded as an assault on the vital interests of the United States. It will be repelled by any means necessary, including military force."

In the wake of the September 11, 2001, attacks, President George W. Bush initiated the use of Homeland Security Directives, to be issued by the president of the United States in concert with the Homeland Security Council, which was in itself created by the first directive. The next Presidential Decision Directive issued by the Bush administration altered immigration policies in response to the war on terrorism.

Further Reading

Hogan, Michael J. *A Cross of Iron: Harry S. Truman and the Origins of the National Security State, 1945–1954.* New York: Cambridge University Press, 2000.

Simpson, Christopher. *National Security Directives of the Reagan and Bush Administrations: The Declassified History of U.S. Political and Military Policy, 1981–1991.* Boulder, CO: Perseus Books, 1995.

PREVENTIVE DEFENSE STRATEGY

Post–Cold War guide to national-security strategy that emphasizes the absence of a major, traditional military threat on the scale of the Soviet Union and seeks to prevent similar threats from emerging in the future. Articulated in the late 1990s by former Secretary of Defense, William J. Perry, and former Assistant Secretary of Defense for International Security Policy, Ashton B. Carter. Although preventive defense is defined as a broad politico-military strategy that draws on political, economic, and military instruments, the role of the Defense Department, and of contacts between military establishments, is central.

Preventive defense acknowledges the post–Cold War status of the United States as the dominant military force in the world and stresses the need for American foresight and vision in planning for the prevention of future threats to national security. To fulfill its mission, preventive defense focuses on nurturing cooperative security relationships with Russia and the states of the former Soviet Union, engaging a rising China, reducing and safeguarding nuclear arsenals, and countering the proliferation of weapons of mass destruction (WMD). Preventive defense stresses prevention over the Cold War objectives of containment and deterrence, and argues for maintaining an important peacetime military establishment and diplomatic engagement.

According to Perry and Carter, preventive defense strategy hierarchically outlines different types of threats to U.S. national security. The A-list threats are described as imminent military threats, on the scale of the former Soviet Union, that could threaten the survival of the United States. Preventive defense strategy recognizes five dangers that, if ignored and mismanaged, have the potential to become A-list threats: a chaotic, unstable, and potentially aggressive Russia; loosening of control over nuclear arsenals by Russia and the states of the former Soviet Union resulting in nuclear proliferation among rogue states and terrorists (*loose nukes*); an emerging and potentially adversarial China; proliferation of weapons of mass destruction; and "catastrophic" terrorism.

Threats to U.S. interests, but not necessarily to American survival, constitute a B-list of dangers and include contingencies such as the Persian Gulf and North Korea. The C-list of threats is defined as important contingencies that indirectly affect U.S. national security but that do not directly threaten U.S. interests. These third-tier threats include conflicts such as those in Kosovo, Bosnia, Somalia, Rwanda, and Haiti. Preventive defense calls for continuing to maintain a strong military to deal with these important B- and C-level threats while focusing mainly on A-level dangers.

Preventive defense strategy is based on strong interpersonal relationships between political and military leaders and makes use of a nongovernmental *track-two* dialogue to promote international cooperation and security partnerships. Track-two dialogue includes efforts to influence public opinion among the civilian populations of countries in conflict so that political leaders can more easily make compromises. Military-to-military contacts, in the form of joint training and exercises, confidence-building measures, and consultations, are central to the preventive defense strategy. According to Carter and Perry, in their book *Preventive Defense: A New Security Strategy for America,* defense cooperation with the Russian, Chinese, and European militaries through military-to-military relationships can lessen their propensity to threaten U.S. national interests. Carter and Perry also maintain that military-to-military links can help resolve difficult diplomatic and political issues. A main mechanism for engaging Russia according to preventive defense strategy is the complete and unfettered implementation of the military provisions of both the Partnership for Peace and the NATO-Russia Founding Act. The centrality of the Defense Department in the formulation and implementation of such broad security policies, and the "defense diplomacy" advocated by preventive defense, raises the issue of civil–military relations.

Preventive defense strategy argues that in the post–Cold War world, the United States cannot afford to elaborate a defense strategy based on B- and C-level threats. Major regional contingencies around which defense planning is centered—specifically, conflicts in Iraq and North Korea—do not constitute grave dangers to U.S. survival. Preventive defense stresses programs designed for shaping the environment and hedging for the long term against the failure of its initiatives. It seeks to maintain force structure and readiness for potential regional conflicts but stresses investing in preventive programs that engage Russia and China and that guard against proliferation of weapons of mass destruction and asymmetrical threats to U.S. power and survival.

Further Reading

Carter, Ashton B., and William J. Perry. *Preventive Defense: A New Security Strategy for America.* Washington, DC: Brookings Institution, 1999.

PREVENTIVE WAR

Attacking an enemy now in order to avoid the risk of war under worsening circumstances later. A preventive war occurs when a state attacks another and claims preventive self-defense.

Preventive war and preemptive war differ in the certainty of an attack. Whereas a preemptive war concerns an imminent attack, preventive war takes place with no military provocation. States generally justify preventive war by claiming that the enemy may attack in the future. Therefore, a preventive strike is necessary in order to prevent a worse outcome in the future. For example, Israel launched a preventive strike against the Iraqi Osirak nuclear facility in 1981 in an attempt to prevent Iraq from developing a nuclear capability and threatening Israel at some future date. Additionally, during the Cold War, U.S. officials contemplated attacking the USSR and China before they could develop strong nuclear capabilities.

Although the U.S. National Security Strategy issued by President George W. Bush in September 2002 discussed preemptive attack, it in fact proposed a preventive doctrine. The definition of preemptive action in the document was quite broad. In the letter accompanying the document, President Bush wrote that the United States must be ready to wage war against emerging threats before they are fully formed. Terrorists and rogue states with weapons of mass destruction cannot be contained by deterrence. Because terrorists are fanatics and rogue states are willing to take what would normally be considered unacceptable risks, deterrence that is based on rational reactions does not work. Defense also may not be possible, as the September 11, 2001, terrorist attacks proved. Thus, the United States must be ready to strike first.

Preventive war represents an alternative to deterrence. If a country has no confidence in deterring an adversary with its military or diplomatic might, preventive war becomes the least bad option. Harvard professor Graham Allison was quoted by David Sanger in the *New York Times* in 2002, describing the logic of preventive war: "I may some day have a war with you, and right now I'm strong and you're not. So I'm going to have the war now." In fact, preventive wars typically are initiated by dominant powers. In 1912 the chief of staff of the German army, Helmut von Moltke, opposed a diplomatic solution to the Balkan crisis because he believed that Germany still had a military advantage over France and also over Russia, which was rapidly modernizing its army and could pose a future threat to Germany.

This logic is similar to the rationale behind the 2003 U.S. attack on Iraq. The Bush administration claimed that the reconstituted Iraqi nuclear program would have threatened U.S. interests in the Middle East and that Iraq would eventually attack U.S. territory. The United States also claimed that Iraq was ready to use biological and chemical weapons. On the basis of these impending threats, the United States attacked Iraq as a preemptive strike in March 2003. Following the overthrow of dictator Saddam Hussein's regime, evidence showed that the Iraqi threat was less immediate than the Bush administration had claimed. However, President Bush later maintained that the war in Iraq was justified on the grounds that Saddam Hussein might have someday been able to develop nuclear weapons. Based on this justification, the invasion would constitute a preventive war. Preventive wars are based on long-term calculations about power relations and are attractive to countries that are in a dominant position and seek to stop a rising adversary.

Critics argue that preventive wars are rarely necessary, because deterrence can be effective. Moreover, many threats are often exaggerated. German chancellor Otto von Bismarck called preventive wars "suicide for fear of death." Although the disparity of power between the United States and its enemies means that death is probably no longer a likely outcome, the argument for preventive war still faces some major challenges. First of all, preventive war is based on information about the future threats that sometimes might not be accurate. As the case of Iraq showed, Saddam Hussein's program to develop weapons of mass destruction had been overestimated. Second, motives for preventive war involve predictions about threats that have still to materialize. No one knows how a state, which may be perceived as a threat today, will act tomorrow. Libya, for example, once a leading rogue state, is no longer viewed as a threat. Fortunately, leaders are aware of these limitations and generally are hesitant to resort to the preventive use of force.

See also Bush, George W., and National Policy; Preemption; Preemptive War Doctrine; Terrorism, War on International

Further Reading

The National Security Strategy of the United States of America. September 2002. http://www.whitehouse.gov/nsc/nss.html.

PRISONER OF WAR (POW)

In an armed conflict, a participant who is captured and held by an enemy. The United States uses the term *prisoner of war* (POW) to refer only to its own soldiers, or soldiers of its allies, who are captured by an enemy. Prisoners of war taken by the United States are referred to as *enemy prisoners of war* (EPW).

Soldiers are the individuals most likely to become prisoners of war, although the third Geneva Convention does define other categories entitled to POW status. These include members of other militias and other volunteer corps, including those of organized resistance movements who are commanded by someone responsible for their subordinates. In order to be eligible for protection under the Geneva Conventions, such individuals must be represented by a sign, symbol, or insignia; carry arms openly; and conduct their operations according to the laws of war.

United States Marines assigned to the Third Light Armored Reconnaissance Battalion lead rescued U.S. prisoners of war (POWs) off a Marine Corps KC-130 Hercules cargo aircraft in April 2003. The flight transported the POWs from an airfield near Baghdad to Kuwait following U.S. military actions in support of Operation Iraqi Freedom, the war that deposed Iraqi dictator Saddam Hussein. Every major conflict in history has had prisoners of war, many of whom were not fortunate enough to be rescued.

Source: U.S. Navy.

Other individuals who receive POW status include members of armed forces who profess allegiance to a government or authority, even if that authority is not recognized by the power that captures them. Those who take up arms spontaneously to resist invading forces and who obey the laws of war, even if they have not organized themselves into regular army units, also receive POW status. Unarmed noncombatants captured during a conflict are covered by the fourth Geneva Convention.

The POW issue has taken on different dimensions in different conflicts. Treatment of POWs became more significant in the aftermath of World War II, when the Nazi death camps were opened up in central Europe. The brutal treatment by the Nazis toward enemy combatants and their slaughter of more than 6 million Jews and members of other groups formed the critical part of the prosecution's case at the Nuremberg war trials. Horrific medical experiments carried out on human subjects, gassing, forced labor, and complete disregard for sanitation set a new standard of inhumanity.

The fact that Nazi atrocities had occurred despite Red Cross inspections raised questions about the ability to assure the humane treatment of prisoners. The Nazis, however, were selective in what they showed to the inspectors. In addition, the Red Cross has pointed out in its own defense that its primary goal was maintaining access to the camps. They argued that far more people might have suffered if the camps had been closed completely.

A significant number of veterans from the Korean War and the Vietnam War believe that the U.S. government has not done everything it should to account for those taken prisoner and those whose status is missing in action (MIA). This issue is particularly central to the Vietnam conflict, where certain groups have even gone so far as to accuse the government of covering up evidence of remaining prisoners. The POW/MIA issue has had a recurrent impact on popular culture, where movies, books, and other media feed an appetite for conspiracy theories and rescue scenarios. One school of critical thought suggests that these narratives are manifestations of the fact that the

United States was forced to retreat from Vietnam. These critics say the stories serve the purpose of portraying an alternative type of victory, or re-fighting the war with a revised outcome.

Questions concerning the meaning and definition of POW status have become particularly pertinent in the context of the war on terror declared by President George W. Bush following the September 11, 2001, terrorist attacks on New York City and Washington, DC. A number of individuals taken into custody by the United States military during the war in Afghanistan were not granted POW status by the U.S. government. These prisoners are held in a special detention facility at the U.S. Naval Base in Guantánamo Bay, Cuba.

The Bush administration argues that because this base is not on U.S. territory, the detainees are not subject to U.S. laws regarding the treatment of POWs. In addition, the administration asserts that the prisoners' status as suspected terrorists exempts them from the conditions of the Geneva Conventions. This policy has drawn great criticism, particularly in light of revelations about the abuse of prisoners held by the U.S. military in Abu Ghraib prison in Iraq. Photographs became public of soldiers subjecting prisoners to humiliation and inhumane conditions; the fact that these activities took place in one of Saddam Hussein's former prisons had a galvanizing effect on world opinion.

See also Afghanistan, War in; Geneva Conventions; Legal Ramifications of National Security; Terrorism, War on International

Further Reading

Riconda, Harry, P. *Prisoners of War in American Conflicts.* Lanham, MD: Scarecrow Press, 2003.
Vance, Jonathan F., ed. *Encyclopedia of Prisoners of War and Internment.* Santa Barbara, CA: ABC-CLIO, 2000.
Yarbrough, Steve. *Prisoners of War.* New York: Knopf, 2004.

PRISONER'S DILEMMA

A game concept that analyzes the losses and gains from conflict and cooperation between any two or more players, people, or other variables in a given situation. The word *game* is used here as a scientific metaphor for a much wider range of human interactions in which the outcomes depend on the interactive strategies of two or more persons who have opposing, or at best mixed, motives. Thus, the concept borrows mainly from political science and from game theory—a distinct and interdisciplinary approach to the study of human behavior founded and first written about by the mathematician John von Neumann in 1928.

HISTORY OF THE CONCEPT

The concept of *prisoner's dilemma* is a product of the Cold War. In 1950, scholars Merrill Flood and Melvin Dresher at the RAND Corporation were grappling with the arms race between the United States and the Soviet Union. They posed a hypothetical situation in which two partners in crime are caught by the police, who do not have sufficient proof to convict them. Each individual is thus presented with a matrix of options.

In this matrix, if both prisoners cooperate by not saying anything, they are both rewarded at an equal, intermediate level because of insufficient proof. If only one prisoner defects, he receives the highest level of payoff by going free, while the other player faces the most unfavorable outcome of many years in prison. Finally, if both prisoners defect, each receives an intermediate, rather than maximum penalty, due to the in-built *confession dividend* in the matrix that they both receive. Thus, defection is seen as the best option for either player. The dilemma resides in the fact that each prisoner has a choice between only two options, but neither individual can make a good decision without knowing what the other one will do. The concept thus presents a curious struggle between individual and collective interests.

The concept assumes that the synergistic effect of cooperation will be smaller than the gains made from defection. Many people have argued that this assumption is not valid in many real-life situations, in which the absolute benefits from synergetic cooperation outweigh gains from noncooperation for any single party involved. The assumption, however, becomes more realistic if it takes into account that the synergy takes some time to get realized. In short-term decision making, which is the context in which prisoner's dilemma was initially studied, the actors supposedly do not have any specific expectations about future interactions or collaborations.

In the 1950s and 1960s, several studies of the prisoner's dilemma were performed in which two players acted out a prisoner's-dilemma-type situation repeatedly. Researchers seemed to explore all elements of the dilemma during this period, but a clear strategy did not emerge. As a result, by the 1970s, the prisoner's dilemma fell out of favor among researchers.

However, the question of when to be nice and when to defect was important considering that many business decisions fall into the category of prisoner's dilemma and a great deal of money would be at stake. In search of this elusive strategy, in the early 1980s, the political scientist Robert Axelrod organized a series of computer tournaments. The simplest strategy submitted, "TIT for TAT," won in two successive computer tournaments and basically illustrated that one should cooperate while confronting an opponent on the first round and for the following rounds simply do what the other player did in the round before.

After further analysis, Axelrod finally came up with four maxims to choose an effective strategy. These included not being the first to double-cross; defending yourself but being forgiving; not being envious (if someone has more than you, not getting provoked into a double-cross action); and being clear (making sure that the opponent understands the consequences of his or her actions). Axelrod wrote about this strategy and the prisoner's dilemma in his groundbreaking 1984 book *The Evolution of Cooperation.*

PRINCIPLE OF SUBOPTIMIZATION AND TRAGEDY OF THE COMMONS

In rational decision making, a person makes a decision that is best for him or her, whatever another individual chooses. Thus, in the prisoner's-dilemma framework, it follows that if both decision makers were purely rational then they would never cooperate. The paradox, however, emerges because if both actors are rational, then both will decide to defect and neither of them will gain anything. However, if both irrationally decide to cooperate, both will gain something. This seeming paradox can be formulated more explicitly through what is known as the *principle of suboptimization.*

The principle of suboptimization states that trying to maximize the gains of one person in a group, in general, does not necessarily lead to global optimization or gains for the group as a whole. This is because there is also interaction between the decision challenges of each of the subsystems or people in the group, and the combination of the optimal decisions for each person will be different from the optimal decision for the global problem or the group as a whole. The concept derives from the more basic systemic

principle that maintains that the whole is more than the sum of its parts. The problem of suboptimization underlies most of the problems appearing in evolutionary ethics, which tries to achieve the utilitarian aim of greatest good for the greatest number.

Another, more dramatic implication of the problem of suboptimization is what bioethicist Garrett Hardin called *the tragedy of the commons.* The phrase emphasizes the inherent friction between finite resources and the pressure put on them by the potential gain for one or a few by following an economically rational but selfish mode that assures maximum possible benefit (in the short run) by overutilizing or monopolizing the use of the common resource, eventually leading to its total exhaustion.

RELEVANCE IN GEOPOLITICS

When Axelrod's book, *The Evolution of Cooperation,* first appeared in 1984, it was seemingly read largely as a manual for dealing with the arms race, which at the time was very much on the minds of leading military strategists and makers of foreign policy. During the Cold War, the United States and the Soviet Union each adopted double-crossing strategies and built up large stockpiles of nuclear weapons. Fortunately, this game of prisoner's dilemma never reached the final round, although there were many moments that came to the brink. More recently, Axelrod's book and the concept of prisoner's dilemma have been rediscovered by individuals interested in emergence, social software, and other such areas.

See also Arms Control; Arms Race

Further Reading

Axelrod, Robert. *The Evolution of Cooperation.* New York: Basic Books, 1984.

Poundstone, William. *Prisoner's Dilemma.* New York: Doubleday, 1992.

REFLECTIONS

No Solution

At the end of a 1964 article on the future of nuclear war, J. B. Wiesner and H. F. York concluded that

Both sides in the arms race are confronted by the dilemma of steadily increasing military power and steadily decreasing national security. *It is our considered professional judgment that this dilemma has no technical solution.* If the great powers continue to look for solutions in the area of science and technology only, the result will be to worsen the situation.

PRIVACY ACT

Passed in 1974, legislation that restricts the dissemination of personal information by federal agencies and requires that when information is collected, the individual be told of the ways in which the information could be used. The Privacy Act was passed in the wake of the abuse of Internal Revenue Service (IRS) and Federal Bureau of Investigation (FBI) records by the administration of President Richard Nixon. The act created checks on the transfer of personal information between agencies. The law provided for 12 exceptions, including one that permits law-enforcement agencies to obtain records without a subpoena and another that allows federal agencies to share any information for routine uses after publishing in the Federal Registry a statement of their intent to release such information.

The Freedom of Information Act (FOIA), a companion to the Privacy Act passed in 2000, allows individuals the right to see the contents of files maintained about them by federal executive branch agencies, such as the FBI, the State and Defense departments, and the IRS. Files maintained by Congress, the judicial system, and state governments are not covered by this law, although many states and courts have similar access rules for their files.

Critics of the Privacy Act claim that the law is out-of-date and does not allow for modern information-sharing technologies. In the wake of the September 11, 2001, terrorist attacks, there have been calls to reduce access to public information, citing the use of FOIA requests by people with links to terrorist groups to obtain blueprints for public buildings and power plants, and other sensitive data.

See also Freedom of Information Act (1967); Nixon, Richard, and National Policy; Pentagon Papers; Privacy Rights

PRIVACY RIGHTS

The right to be left alone without unwarranted intrusion by government, media, or other institutions or individuals. Although the Bill of Rights and the U.S. Constitution guarantee the right to life, liberty, and the pursuit of happiness, it was not until the 1965 U.S. Supreme Court decision in *Griswold v. Connecticut*—which overturned a state law making the sale and use of contraceptives a criminal offense—that a modern privacy doctrine emerged. The extent of the right to privacy and its basis in constitutional law remain contested despite the fact that all recently confirmed U.S. Supreme Court justices have affirmed their belief in that right.

The right to privacy is a relatively new constitutional issue. With the exception of *Meyer v. Nebraska* (1923)—a court case that voided a state law prohibiting teaching of foreign languages in elementary schools—the major privacy cases have been decided in the last 40 years. These cases concern sexual activity, marital and family rights, abortion, and the right to die. More recently, of course, they involve issues pertaining to national security.

For example, in one of the most controversial decisions in the history of the nation, *Roe v. Wade* (1973), the Supreme Court voided state laws that made most abortions criminal offenses, on the grounds that such laws violated the Fourteenth Amendment, which some jurists have interpreted as protecting the right to privacy. The right to privacy concerning sexual matters in *Griswold* was cited as a precedent in the decision in *Roe v. Wade.*

Ultimately, the U.S. Supreme Court ruled in *Roe v. Wade* that the Fourteenth Amendment included the qualified right to terminate a pregnancy in the first trimester, at the judgment of the woman and her physician. In the second and third trimesters, the states were given some latitude in regulating abortions to protect the life and health of the woman. Despite upholding the woman's right to privacy in having an abortion, the high court gave the states the ability to supersede that right later in the pregnancy, to sustain the state's right to protect health. Thus, the right to privacy in this case is defined but not absolute.

Modern technology has made credit, medical, and other data readily available and extremely marketable commodities, raising new issues and concerns about the individual's right to privacy. The recently created Do Not Call registries are designed to protect the individual's right to privacy from intrusive telemarketers. However, businesses argue that the registries are an unfair limitation on their right to commerce.

See also Freedom of Information Act (1967); Nixon, Richard, and National Policy; Pentagon Papers; Privacy Act

Further Reading

Spaeth, Harold, and Edward Smith. *The Right to Privacy.* New York: HarperCollins, 1991.

PRIVATIZATION

The economic process of transferring property from public ownership to private ownership, sometimes called *denationalization.* Privatization is the process by which economic activity (the production of goods or services) is removed from the government sector of the economy and placed in the private sector. The reasoning behind privatization is that the market environment of the private sector will force business enterprises to respond to market signals and stimuli and become more efficient.

Privatization is frequently associated with industrial or service-oriented enterprises, such as mining, manufacturing, or power generation, but it can also apply to utilities, such as land, roads, energy providers, telecommunications, or rights to water. In recent years, government services such as health, sanitation, prison facilities, and education have also been targeted for privatization in many countries, including the United States.

According to proponents of privatization, in addition to making enterprises more efficient, privatization policies help to establish a free market as well as foster capitalist competition. The absence of competition, critics of state ownership argue, puts management of state-owned firms under no pressure to produce goods and services that consumers demand and to provide them at lower cost. Moreover, state companies often supply their products and services without direct charges to consumers. Therefore, even if they want to satisfy consumer demands, these firms are unaware of what consumers want because consumption reflects only the availability of goods, not consumer preferences.

Although nationalization (governmental acquisition and management of assets) was common during the immediate post–World War II period, privatization became a more dominant economic trend during the 1980s and 1990s, especially within the United States and the United Kingdom. In these countries, the experience of economic recession in the 1970s catapulted the conservative political parties of Prime Minister Margaret Thatcher and President Ronald Reagan to power. Both leaders called for less government regulation and more business.

Meanwhile, at the World Bank (the post–World War II donor organization for the reconstruction and development of economically distressed countries), developmental economists began to depart and free-trade advocates took control of economic policy at multinational lending organizations. These free-trade advocates became known as *neoliberals* because of their belief in liberal trade policies and their disdain for intervention into economic affairs by national governments.

Believing firmly in the efficiency of the market, the neoliberals scorned the developmentalist theories of government-led planning, which they claimed encouraged protectionist policies and placed the world economy at risk. Reducing barriers to trade and capital flows, it was reasoned, would generate a cycle of economic growth and a sustained attack on poverty. Furthermore, as the world witnessed the disintegration of the Soviet Union in 1991, the failure of the Communist Party trumpeted proof for neoliberals that governments were fallible and that the market was not.

In the case of Eastern Europe, however, the haste to transform economies and transfer state-owned property to the private sector resulted in disastrous consequences. Reformers felt pressured to put in place the rudiments of a middle class in order to avert the return to communism. Private property, it was believed, would help accomplish this by buttressing an economic order that would install an indigenous middle class and redistribute national wealth more evenly.

Unfortunately, the process of property transferal often became mere schemes that put property back in the hands of former communists, placed it under the control of criminal elements, and disenfranchised the very population that privatization was designed to benefit. This situation seemed to confirm the original fears of socialists, that entrusting private businesses with control of essential services would reduce the public's control over them and result in corruption.

The problems in these Eastern European economies were not all the result of privatization. More than 40 years of central planning, along with supply and price controls, posed a perilous set of difficulties. Decades of low wages meant that little wealth was available for investment, no stock markets existed to ease the transfer of property, and indigenous banking systems were not yet sufficiently organized to deal with the pace and turbulence of global financial markets.

In addition, there were no laws to protect or even permit private ownership, nor were there the supporting infrastructure of contract law, an equitable tax code, and financial support services such as the accounting profession. Furthermore, as the burden for transforming the economy was placed upon this newly developing private sector, local industries, which were hastily subject to competition from abroad and conventional lending practices, began to fail. Local firms were in their developmental stages and not prepared to meet the demands of global competition.

These same problems have applied to the developing world, as well. In addition to societies in the process of making the transition to market economies, the economies of lesser-developed countries (LDC) are often ill-prepared to contend with the onslaught of the competitive global market. Privatization in today's economy also means an environment of ceaseless movement of financial capital, demands for tight credit controls, and the exposure of local industry to free-trade policies.

As a result of these conditions, competition from exports has systematically wrought unemployment and poverty in many underdeveloped areas of the world. Many national economies, despite receiving large financial-assistance packages, have suffered harshly rather than prospered. Some experts estimate that as much as 50% of government revenues in such countries go toward the repayment of the national debt. In some cases, this could represent as much as one-fifth to one-quarter of total export earnings to a national budget.

To many, it has become obvious that privatization and free-trade policies alone are not universal solutions to the problems of transition societies, developing economies, and deficit-ridden industrialized nations. Because the economic playing field is not completely level, many neoliberal economists now believe that some degree of regulation is desirable if free trade and privatization are going to be part of the foundation of the new global economic order.

See also Development, Third-World; Globalization and National Security

Further Reading

Gilpin, Robert. *Global Political Economy.* Princeton, NJ: Princeton University Press, 2001.

Sassen, Saskia. "Global Cities and Survival Circuits." In *Global Women: Nannies, Maids, and Sex Workers in the New Economy.* Barbara Ehrenreich and Arlie Russell Hochschild, eds. New York: Henry Holt, 2003.

PROCUREMENT
See DEFENSE BUDGETING

PROHIBITION ON WEAPONIZING SPACE

International ban on the deployment of weapons systems in outer space. As a result of the military utility of space, the ban on weaponizing space is considered a key principle of arms control.

The power to project force capabilities anywhere in the world with weapons from space decreases the security of all nations and increases the threat of space becoming a battlefield. An extended military conflict in space would likely hinder the use of space for commercial and scientific purposes thereafter. Concern about the future capabilities of state militaries to launch weapons of mass destruction or target enemy troops from outer space have led technologically advanced countries, principally the United States and the Soviet Union, to agree in a series of treaties to limit the use of space for military purposes.

The U.S.–Soviet space race of the late 1950s and 1960s provided the impetus for prohibiting weapons in space. The 1957 Soviet launch of *Sputnik,* the world's first artificial satellite, raised fears that the United States was falling behind the Soviet Union in science and technology. The United States responded with more aggressive efforts to accelerate its own space program. By the early 1960s, these efforts led to concerns on both sides that space might be the next frontier of conflict in the Cold War. In 1963, U.S. president John F. Kennedy and Soviet premier Nikita Khrushchev signed the Limited Test Ban Treaty, which placed a de facto moratorium on the use of space for military purposes. The treaty banned the testing of nuclear weapons in space and initiated successive negotiations on the military use of space.

In 1967, the United States and the Soviet Union were two of several nations to sign the Outer Space Treaty. The agreement prohibited member states from carrying, installing, or stationing weapons of mass destruction in space. Member states were also forbidden to establish military bases and conduct military maneuvers in space. By assenting to the Outer Space Treaty, the superpowers indicated their willingness to cooperate on space matters and arms control.

Five years later, the signing of the Antiballistic Missile (ABM) Treaty marked the high point of

U.S.–Soviet cooperation in space. Under the bilateral treaty, both countries were forbidden from deploying or testing ABM systems or components in space. The treaty also prohibited the parties from interfering with each other's national technical means of verification, or spy satellite programs. The treaty remained binding until both countries agreed to withdraw from it in 2002.

Although the ABM Treaty was considered successful at halting space weaponization by the superpowers, it failed to address U.S. concerns about a preemptive attack aimed at disabling U.S. military and civilian satellites. Because satellite systems can easily be tracked, they are vulnerable to being attacked with conventional or nuclear weapons. The U.S. interest in pursuing active-defense systems and hardening satellite targets indicates that the United States will continue to advance its already superior space program. As long as the United States remains the only country to possess the technological capabilities to weaponize space, it will likely retain space superiority for decades to come.

Although few countries possess space programs, the prohibition on weapons in space remains a centerpiece of international arms-control agreements. By agreeing not to allow the stationing and deployment of weapons from space, states hope to quell a possible space arms race. However, despite international cooperation in this endeavor, U.S. superiority in space technology means that it will not likely be deterred from using space for supporting its military capabilities.

See also Antiballistic Missile (ABM) Treaty; Limited Test Ban Treaty; Satellite Reconnaissance; Space Race; Space-Based Weapons; Sputnik; Spy Satellites; Treaties

Further Reading

Pike, John. "The Paradox of Space Weapons." In *Stockholm International Peace Research Institute Yearbook 2003*. Oxford, UK: Oxford University Press, 2003.

Stares, Paul B. *The Militarization of Space*. Ithaca, NY: Cornell University Press, 1985.

PROJECT VENONA
See ESPIONAGE

PROPAGANDA

Mass suggestion or influence through the manipulation of symbols and of individuals. Like other forms of persuasion, propaganda aims to communicate a point of view in a way that leads the target audience to adopt that point of view, doctrine, or practice as its own. Propaganda differs from other forms of persuasion, in that it is typically one-way communication that is carefully controlled, systematic, sustained, and well organized, often intended to damage an opposing viewpoint.

PROPAGANDA CONCEPTS AND TECHNIQUES

Propaganda relies on two basic psychological principles to achieve its purposes: cognitive dissonance and rationalization. First articulated in the 1950s, cognitive dissonance is said to occur when a person simultaneously holds two inconsistent beliefs, such as an aversion to killing versus the need to take up arms to defend one's country. Over time, this state of inconsistency becomes so uncomfortable that individuals strive to reduce the conflict in the easiest way possible. In doing so, they will artificially alter one or both cognitions to make them fit together more easily. For example, people historically have justified and provided legal sanction for taking life during wartime, even though they condemn and punish it in times of peace.

Propagandists also rely upon what is commonly referred to as *the rationalization trap*. The trap is set by intentionally arousing a person's feelings of cognitive dissonance by threatening his or her sense of self-esteem or security. It is then sprung by offering a single solution to reduce the dissonance. In times of armed conflict, one of the most common methods of reducing dissonance is through dehumanization. For example, most people are reluctant to treat others inhumanely. To overcome this hesitation, a propagandist might portray a particular group of people as so dangerous that to offer them any consideration or humane treatment would be a threat to national security. Dehumanizing a group in this way makes it easier for members of the propagandist's target audience to maltreat members of that group.

Scholars began systematic investigation into the use of propaganda during the 1930s and 1940s. Following an extensive examination of World War I propaganda, the U.S. Institute for Propaganda Analysis in 1938 suggested that nearly all propaganda relied upon one or more of several standard communicative devices. These included name-calling (applying a negative label without evidence); the glittering generality (applying a positive label without evidence); transfer (associating an untested idea with a group that possess a positive popular image, often through the use of symbols); the testimonial (using the image of a person or persona to promote an idea, often through quotations or photographs); the plain folks device (appealing through an emotional association with the average citizen); card-stacking (using deception through underemphasis and/or overemphasis of selected evidence); and bandwagoning (appealing to the desire to be associated with the popular opinion or the behavior of the majority).

BRIEF HISTORY OF U.S. PROPAGANDA

Propaganda played an extremely significant role in spreading support for independence in the American colonies. The Committee on Correspondence, a loose-knit group that traveled along the east coast promoting revolutionary ideas, represents one of the earliest effective examples of political *spin*—reporting and discussing current events with a partisan slant. At the same time, Thomas Paine's fiery leaflet *Common Sense,* one of the first widely disseminated pieces of American propaganda, both riled and rallied readers with its impassioned arguments for independence from England.

During the 19th century, propaganda provided a spur to expansion of the nation as well as to civil war. To justify the forcible removal of Native Americans from their lands, the U.S. government promoted a popular image of Native Americans as treacherous and dangerous savages. The campaign against the Indians was promoted as a crusade to "civilize" the frontier and Christianize the "heathens." During the Civil War, each side portrayed its enemy as the champion of an immoral cause. Supporters of slavery raised images of free blacks running rampant, killing and raping whites. Opponents portrayed all slave owners as cruel and heartless taskmasters who beat and took advantage of their slaves.

However, it was not until the 20th century that propaganda became an integral tool of U.S. policy. Woodrow Wilson was arguably the first U.S. president to use propaganda systematically to advance both a national agenda and a particular worldview. In 1917, Wilson launched the Committee on Public Information (CPI), which was charged with spreading Wilson's secular ideology—the need for U.S. involvement in World War I and the desire to establish a postwar

League of Nations—to a particularly isolationist American public. The CPI employed posters, films, a newspaper-style publication (*The Official Bulletin*), and so-called four-minute men—citizens who were specially trained to give compact, concise oral presentations supporting Wilson's agenda.

World War II brought propaganda to an entirely new level of importance and sophistication when German Nazi leader Adolf Hitler and propaganda minister Joseph Goebbels mastered the delicate art. Their success in using propaganda to garner public support for Nazi policies was derived from a deep understanding of the inherent strengths and effective application of propaganda. They understood that the government must have access to intelligence concerning public opinion and that propaganda must be planned and executed by a single authority. In addition, they realized that the intended consequences of the propaganda must be considered well in advance and it must be carefully timed to provoke a response from the audience.

The German Ministry of Propaganda utilized the cinematic talent of actress and director Leni Riefenstahl, whose films *Triumph of the Will* and *Olympia* glorified the Nazi cause and demonstrated the power of ceremony and spectacle in swaying public opinion. To combat German propaganda efforts, President Franklin Roosevelt and U.S. general George Marshall recruited famed Hollywood director Frank Capra to produce a set of films known as the *Why We Fight* series. In producing these films, Capra incorporated much of Riefenstahl's footage into a package that effectively turned Nazi propaganda against itself. The film provided a powerful argument for U.S. involvement in the war to fight Nazism.

CONTEMPORARY PROPAGANDA: PUBLIC DIPLOMACY

Though still prevalent, the use of propaganda has become more nuanced since the end of World War II. In 1953, President Dwight D. Eisenhower established the United States Information Agency (USIA), an independent foreign-affairs agency with the mission of promoting U.S. national interests through a wide range of overseas programs. Today, USIA maintains 190 posts in 142 countries, operates the federal government's educational and cultural exchange (known as the Fulbright Program), broadcasts a number of radio and television programs, including Voice of

America and Radio Free Asia, and coordinates the dissemination of pro-U.S. materials to international audiences.

In 2002, President George W. Bush established a new propaganda arm for the U.S. government, the White House Office of Global Communications. The office has the mission of advising the president and other senior government leaders as to how best to utilize U.S. government communication resources effectively and consistently. It is also charged with promoting the interests of the United States abroad, preventing misunderstanding of U.S. aims and intentions, building support among allies, and informing international audiences of U.S. values and virtues.

These propaganda vehicles and processes are often labeled as efforts of so-called *public diplomacy*, a term first used by Edmund Gullion of the Fletcher School of Law and Diplomacy at Tufts University in 1965. According to Gullion, public diplomacy deals with the cultivation by governments of public opinion in other countries, and the interaction of private groups and interests in one country with those of another. Central to public diplomacy is the transnational flow of information and ideas that ultimately influence public attitudes on the formation and execution of foreign policies.

Public diplomacy continues to be a major part of the Bush administration's efforts to fight global terrorism. As stated in the most recent National Security Strategy of the United States of America, "We will also wage a war of ideas to win the battle against international terrorism. Our immediate focus will be those using effective public diplomacy to promote the free flow of information and ideas to kindle the hopes and aspirations of freedom of those in societies ruled by the sponsors of global terrorism."

—*Bryan M. Baldwin*

See also Capra, Frank (1897–1991); Cinema and the Military; Media and National Security; Psychological Warfare (PSYOPS); Public Diplomacy

Further Reading

Bernays, Edward. *Propaganda.* New York: Ig, 2004.
Cornebise, Alfred. *War as Advertised: The Four Minute Men and America's Crusade, 1917–1918.* Philadelphia: American Philosophical Society, 1984.
Pratkanis, Anthony, and Elliot Aronson. *Age of Propaganda: The Everyday Use and Abuse of Persuasion.* New York: W. H. Freeman, 2001.

SECRETS REVEALED

The Four-Minute Men: General Suggestions to Speakers

The speech must not be longer than four minutes, which means there is no time for a single wasted word.

Speakers should go over their speech time and time again until the ideas are firmly fixed in their mind and can not be forgotten. This does not mean that the speech needs to be written out and committed [memorized], although most speakers, especially when limited in time, do best to commit.

Divide your speech carefully into certain divisions, say fifteen seconds for final appeal; 45 seconds to describe the bond; fifteen seconds for opening words, etc., etc. Any plan is better than none, and it can be amended every day in the light of experience.

There never was a speech yet that couldn't be improved. Never be satisfied with success. Aim to be more successful, and still more successful. So keep your eyes open. Read all the papers every day, to find a new slogan, or a new phraseology, or a new idea to replace something you have in your speech. For instance, the editorial page of the *Chicago Herald* of May 19 is crammed full of good ideas and phrases. Most of the article is a little above the average audience, but if the ideas are good, you should plan carefully to bring them into the experience of your auditors. There is one sentence which says, "No country was ever saved by the other fellow; it must be done by you, by a hundred million yous, or it will not be done at all." Or again, Secretary McAdoo says, "Every dollar invested in the Liberty Loan is a real blow for liberty, a blow against the militaristic system which would strangle the freedom of the world," and so on. Both the *Tribune* and the *Examiner,* besides the *Herald,* contain President [Woodrow] Wilson's address to the nation in connection with the draft registration. The latter part is very suggestive and can be used effectively. Try slogans like "Earn the right to say, I helped to win the war," and "This is a Loyalty Bond as well as a Liberty Bond," or "A cause that is worth living for is worth dying for, and a cause that is worth dying for is worth fighting for." Conceive of your speech as a mosaic made up of five or six hundred words, each one of which has its function.

Get your friends to criticize you pitilessly. We all want to do our best and naturally like to be praised, but there is nothing so dangerous as "josh" and "jolly." Let your friends know that you want ruthless criticism. If their criticism isn't sound, you can reject it. If it is sound, wouldn't you be foolish to reject it?

Be sure to prepare very carefully your closing appeal, whatever it may be, so that you may not leave your speech hanging in the air.

Don't yield to the inspiration of the moment, or to applause to depart from your speech outline. This does not mean that you may not add a word or two, but remember that one can speak only 130, or 140, or 150 words a minute, and if your speech has been carefully prepared to fill four minutes, you can not add anything to your speech without taking away something of serious importance.

Cut out "Doing your bit." "Business as usual." "Your country needs you." They are flat and no longer have any force or meaning.

Time yourself in advance on every paragraph and remember you are likely to speak somewhat more slowly in public than when you practice in your own room.

There are several good ideas and statements in the printed speech recently sent you. Look it up at once.

If you come across a new slogan, or a new argument, or a new story, or a new illustration, don't fail to send it to the Committee. We need your help to make the Four-Minute Men the mightiest force for arousing patriotism in the United States.

—U.S. Committee on Public Information, 1917
Four-Minute Men Bulletin #1

PROTECTIVE GEAR

Equipment worn to shield oneself from physical threats, including gunfire; other munitions; and exposure to chemical, biological, or radiological agents. Protective gear includes body armor such as helmets and bulletproof vests, as well as garments to guard against biological and chemical attack.

Armor is one of the oldest battlefield technologies, although historically only the wealthy could afford the best protective gear. During the Middle Ages, for example, infantry rarely wore steel armor. Most often they used heavily padded cloth or hardened leather to protect their most vulnerable areas. The evolution of

firearms led to the gradual abandonment of armor by the 1700s. By this time, muskets capable of piercing steel plate at a considerable distance made heavy armor obsolete. Even hardened helmets disappeared from most armies.

The evolution of military technology, particularly the growing destructive power of artillery, led to the reintroduction of helmets by the late 19th century. However, other forms of armor remained the province of specialized units; bomb-disposal personnel, for instance, have long worn heavy protective gear. However, combat soldiers remained mostly unprotected until the development of body armor that was light enough to wear for extended periods of time yet effective against modern small-arms fire.

The invention of Kevlar, a lightweight mesh-weave fiber that is stronger than steel, led to the first modern bulletproof vests in the mid-1970s. By the 1980s, the U.S. Army began issuing Kevlar body armor to its frontline units. In the late 1990s, the Army replaced the Kevlar vests with the Interceptor Multi-Threat Body Armor System. The Interceptor has ceramic inserts that can stop, shatter, and catch the standard 7.62 mm rounds used in most military rifles. Protective vests like the Interceptor are designed to absorb the impact of a bullet and spread it out over a wider area, hopefully preventing it from penetrating the body.

Small-arms and other conventional munitions are no longer the only threats a soldier can expect to face on the battlefield. Modern biological and chemical weapons can kill just as effectively as bombs and bullets if delivered accurately. Army units are issued *battle dress overgarments*—protective suits to wear over their regular battle gear—in case of biological or chemical attack. These garments are designed to shield the skin from biological and chemical agents and contain filters to prevent inhalation of contaminants.

In the early 2000s, the U.S. Army began replacing its existing protective overgarments with the Joint Service Lightweight Integrated Suit Technology, or JSLIST. Although the suits were billed as an improvement over existing technology, the Army has struggled with problems of procurement and inventory control. A Pentagon audit in 2002 found than many of the suits are not complete. Another study showed that the suits do not perform well when soaked in sweat or seawater. As a result, the military is currently considering a replacement for the JSLIST.

See also Biological Weapons and Warfare; Science, Technology, and Security

PSYCHOLOGICAL WARFARE (PSYOPS)

A variety of techniques that seek to influence the emotions, attitudes, and behavior of selected audiences in support of political and military objectives. Psychological warfare, also known as psychological operations (PSYOPS), usually connotes nonlethal attempts to gain advantage over the enemy. Techniques include dropping leaflets, airing radio and television broadcasts, and using loudspeakers. Psychological warfare may be conducted independently or as a *force multiplier* that compounds the effects of conventional military actions.

PSYOPS campaigns can be specifically tailored according to the target audience. Operations against enemy soldiers, sometimes called *battlefield PSYOPS,* seek to lower morale and encourage surrender. Psychological warriors often use threatening leaflets to scare the enemy in advance of an attack, often combined with other messages that offer incentives for defection. *Consolidation PSYOPS* have a different audience—noncombatants. Civilians play an important role in war; they work in factories that produce weapons and equipment, they provide support to enemy political leadership, and they offer refuge to enemy fighters. Consolidation operations seek to reduce that support and encourage civilians to accept defeat after fighting has ended. Finally, PSYOPS are used to try to retain the support of allies and sympathizers.

In addition to the benefits PSYOPS can yield on the battlefield, some U.S. commanders believe that PSYOPS help avoid killing foreign civilians. The killing of civilians, often referred to as *collateral damage,* risks damaging the reputation of the country responsible and undermines political objectives in the theater of operations. Civilian casualties also may reduce support for the war effort within the country that perpetrates the killings. For these reasons, contemporary U.S. PSYOPS often encourage local populations to stay out of harm's way during violent conflicts. During the 2003 U.S.-led invasion of Iraq, for example, military aircraft broadcasted messages encouraging Iraqi civilians to stay indoors as American armored columns passed through their towns or neighborhoods. Millions of leaflets dropped on Iraq carried the same message.

Psychological warriors trace their intellectual lineage to the ancient Chinese strategy text *The Art of War,* most likely written during the 400s BCE. The authors (probably a collection of philosophers writing under the pseudonym Sun Tzu) argued that "subjugating the enemy's army without fighting is the true pinnacle of excellence." However, PSYOPS have only recently received significant formal attention from Western military planners.

The United States established a psychological warfare section in the War Department during World War I but made no effort to continue PSYOPS research in the interwar period. In World War II, the Army established the Psychological Warfare Division (PWD) in Europe. Its mission was to disseminate "propaganda designed to undermine the enemy's will to resist, demoralize his forces and sustain the morale of our supporters." However, as happened at the end of World War I, organized psychological warfare units mostly disbanded after 1945.

The Korean War was a watershed for psychological warfare. After re-creating units to drop leaflets and conduct loudspeaker PSYOPS, the Army established the Psychological Warfare Center at Fort Bragg, North Carolina, where it has been headquartered ever since. At the same time, the government funded extensive academic research on communications. Scholars eagerly participated in this effort, viewing psychological warfare as more humane than conventional conflict. A torrent of studies appeared on the nature of psychological coercion. In the 1970s, however, many Americans began to view PSYOPS with skepticism. The Vietnam War experience made the public less willing to support Cold War actions abroad. Covert wars, propaganda, and psychological warfare all fell into disrepute.

At a deeper level, scholars have argued that there is a natural tension between PSYOPS and democracy. This tension arises because the deception involved in PSYOPS stands in direct contradiction to democratic values such as truth and transparency. The strength of any democracy is the people's ability to make informed decisions about the government. A government that routinely engages in large-scale deception and psychological manipulation can shield itself from the public scrutiny required for healthy democracy. It is also difficult to maintain strategic coherence in a pluralistic society. In other words, planners find it hard to project a single message as long as there are dissenting views.

Nonetheless, the United States continues to employ psychological warfare against its enemies. During Operation Just Cause in 1989, U.S. special forces used loudspeakers and radio broadcasts to disorient General Manuel Noriega of Panama and his staff. In Operation Desert Storm in 1991, the U.S.-led coalition dropped an estimated 29 million leaflets on Iraq. According to one report after the war, many Iraqi soldiers waved these leaflets at coalition troops to indicate their desire to surrender. The war against the Taliban in Afghanistan in 2001 saw extensive use of leaflets, as well as more than 800 hours of radio broadcasts from U.S. military aircraft.

More recently, the U.S.-led invasion of Iraq in 2003 incorporated a host of PSYOP tactics and witnessed two significant developments in the practice of psychological warfare. First, PSYOP planners adopted the language of public diplomacy, using terms such as *truth-telling* and *credibility* instead of *influence* and *coercion*. Previous doctrinal statements had been far more blunt. Second, planners carefully coordinated PSYOPS with conventional missions. For example, warning leaflets often landed just ahead of conventional strikes.

The United States not only has used psychological warfare but also has been a target of it. In fact, some analysts worry that foreign states may use PSYOPS and other kinds of information operations increasingly as a way to mitigate the overwhelming military advantage of the United States. This kind of asymmetric strategy emerged during the war in Kosovo in 1999. During that war, NATO (North Atlantic Treaty Organization) initiated a bombing campaign to end Serbian aggression against ethnic Albanians in the Serbian province of Kosovo. To counter this campaign, the Serbs sought to generate public pressure in the Balkans to end the bombing. The Serbs took control of regional television and radio stations, broadcasting messages critical of NATO and printing anti-NATO posters and leaflets.

The Abu Ghraib prison scandal in Iraq revealed the ugly side of PSYOPS. Prisoners in U.S. custody at the facility were subjected to sexual humiliation, physical abuse, and psychological intimidation, such as threats of being killed and simulated drownings. The scandal raised serious questions about the morality, wisdom, and effectiveness of such methods. The U.S. Constitution forbids the use of "cruel or unusual punishments" on U.S. citizens, and the Geneva Conventions restrict the use of force on prisoners of war. In addition, most experts agree that information gained through such methods is rarely reliable. Political observers also note that using such methods on Muslim detainees—the majority of whom officials admit are not guilty of any crime—harms the image of the United States among the very people it is trying to win over in the war on terrorism.

Despite continued faith in psychological warfare, both in the United States and abroad, it remains difficult to measure the actual effects of these techniques. War is a highly charged environment, and many factors influence the emotions and behaviors of participants. Combat causes huge psychological impact, whether or not psychological warfare is employed. Thus, it is hard to disentangle the unique effects of PSYOPS from the typical psychological effects of warfare itself.

See also Constitution of the United States; Geneva Conventions; Legal Ramifications of National Security; Prisoner of War (POW); Propaganda; Terrorism, War on International

Further Reading

Barnett, Frank R., and Carnes Lord, eds. *Political Warfare and Psychological Operations: Rethinking the US Approach.* Washington, DC: National Defense University Press, 1989.

Simpson, Christopher. *Science of Coercion: Communication Research and Psychological Warfare, 1945–1960.* New York: Oxford University Press, 1994.

Sun Tzu. *Art of War.* Translated by Ralph D. Sawyer. Boulder, CO: Westview Press, 1994.

PUBLIC DIPLOMACY

Government-sponsored efforts to communicate directly with foreign publics, often bypassing normal channels of formal diplomacy. Public diplomacy includes all official efforts to convince targeted sectors of foreign opinion to support or tolerate a government's strategic objectives. Methods include statements by decision makers, purposeful campaigns conducted by government organizations dedicated to public diplomacy, and efforts to persuade international media to portray official policies favorably to foreign audiences.

There are two basic kinds of public diplomacy. The first is *branding* or *cultural communication,* in which the government tries to improve its image without seeking support for any immediate policy objective. States use branding strategies to foster a better image of themselves in the world. Ideally, branding creates general goodwill and facilitates cooperation across a variety of issues. It also helps to maintain long-term alliance relationships and undermine enemy propaganda.

During the Cold War, for example, the United States used public diplomacy to persuade European audiences that the foundations of democratic government and capitalist enterprise were superior to Soviet alternatives. The Voice of America broadcast directly into the Warsaw Pact nations of Eastern Europe to dispel myths about the West. At the same time, the U.S. State Department built and maintained reading rooms in Allied nations, replete with books about American history and culture. The department hoped that exposure to American principles and ideas would reinforce broad support for U.S. policies.

The second type of public diplomacy includes various strategies designed to facilitate more rapid results—a category sometimes called *political advocacy*. Although branding or cultural communication is meant to affect long-term perceptions, political-advocacy campaigns use public diplomacy to build foreign support for immediate policy objectives. States sometimes encourage foreign publics to support their own leaders when they cooperate with the sender's policy, or oppose their leaders when they do not. Sometimes states need to quickly convince foreign audiences to support costly alliance military strategies. Foreign leaders may want to cooperate with alliance plans but fear domestic reprisal for agreeing to unpopular actions. Under these conditions, public diplomacy may help those leaders cooperate by reducing the threat of backlash at home.

Kuwait's efforts to gain U.S. popular support for an attack against Iraq in 1990 illustrate this kind of political advocacy. In late 1990, Kuwait hired an American public-relations firm to convince U.S. voters that liberation from the dictator Saddam Hussein was worthwhile and morally correct. Americans had mixed feelings about intervention, and most voters knew little about Kuwait. President George H. W. Bush rightfully worried that he lacked the public mandate to act firmly against Iraq. Kuwait therefore undertook a carefully orchestrated political-advocacy campaign to demonstrate the scope of Saddam's cruelty and gain American sympathy.

In other cases, states use public diplomacy to discredit adversaries. Nations tacitly or explicitly urge foreign publics to oppose leaders who do not share the sender's strategic interests. This strategy has two goals. First, it attempts to encourage cooperation by pressuring recalcitrant foreign leaders who rely on popular support. Second, when prospects for a change in policy are minimal, it encourages foreign audiences to revolt against their leaders. Neither strategy has a long history of success, probably because public-diplomacy campaigns are often received with skepticism. In addition, leaders who are the targets of such campaigns can limit and distort outside information before it reaches the public.

Skeptical commentators have suggested that *public diplomacy* is simply a euphemism for propaganda. Scholars sometimes use the terms interchangeably because, in practice, it is difficult to distinguish one from the other. Professional diplomats recoil at this suggestion, however, because of the negative connotations associated with propaganda. However, the difference between the two can be tenuous. For this reason, public diplomats actively work to avoid the perception that they are mere purveyors of propaganda.

In the years before World War II, for example, Great Britain waged a quiet but effective campaign to rally U.S. popular support for its cause. Many Americans felt that Britain had exaggerated the German threat in World War I and had needlessly drawn the United States into that conflict. Hence, British public diplomats slowly cultivated their message while being cautious not to rouse accusations of propaganda. To do so, they built relationships with members of the U.S. press corps, who had more credibility with American audiences. They also restricted direct broadcasts from the British Broadcasting Company into the United States.

Today, public diplomacy has important implications for the war on terrorism. Improving the image of the United States may reduce the legitimacy of terror among disenchanted audiences in the Middle East and elsewhere. Although public diplomacy may not fully reduce negative images, it may reduce hatred so that terrorists are no longer glorified as martyrs. Thus, public diplomacy, if effective, will make violence against civilians an unacceptable form of protest.

Since the September 11, 2001, terrorist attacks against the World Trade Center and the Pentagon, analysts have offered a number of proposals to reinvigorate American public diplomacy. Some have argued that the United States ought to study the efforts of private marketing firms experienced in shaping public preferences. Others feel that government-owned and operated media, such as the U.S.-based Arabic-language television station Al-Hurrah, are the best way to disseminate U.S. public diplomacy. Despite differences over approach, all policy analysts believe that public diplomacy can assist in the war on terrorism by reducing the sources of recruitment for terrorist organizations.

See also Democracy, Promotion of, and Terrorism; Media and National Security; Propaganda; Psychological Warfare (PSYOPS); Terrorism, War on International; Voice of America

Further Reading

Cull, Nicholas John. *Selling War: The British Propaganda Campaign Against American "Neutrality" in World War II.* New York: Oxford University Press, 1995.

Independent Task Force on Public Diplomacy. *Finding America's Voice: A Strategy for Reinvigorating U.S. Public Diplomacy.* New York: Council on Foreign Relations, 2003.

Lennon, Alexander T. J., ed. *The Battle for Hearts and Minds: Using Soft Power to Undermine Terrorist Networks.* Cambridge: MIT Press, 2003.

Manheim, Jarol. *Strategic Public Diplomacy and American Foreign Policy: The Evolution of Influence.* New York: Oxford University Press, 1994.

Tuch, Hans J. *Communicating with the World: U.S. Public Diplomacy Overseas.* New York: St. Martin's, 1990.

PUBLIC HEALTH, NATIONAL SECURITY AND

Preventing disease and promoting and defending public health in the maintenance of U.S. national security. Attention to public health is a crucial facet of national security at a time when biological and chemical agents can more easily be used as weapons against populations.

The anthrax attacks in the United States, which followed the September 11, 2001, terrorist attacks against the World Trade Center and the Pentagon, highlighted the increased threat to public health in the age of international terrorism. Letters containing anthrax spores that were mailed to offices of several government officials and members of the media claimed five victims. These events were by far the most serious and frightening incidences of terrorist-related threats to public health. In addition, U.S. intelligence programs report biological weapons have been developed in foreign countries and include not only anthrax but smallpox, botulism, bubonic plague, and the Ebola virus. These diseases are all communicable and potentially deadly.

Large-scale violent acts also have public health implications not related to direct injury to the victims. There are many residual effects that must be dealt with. When whole buildings are destroyed—as happened with New York's World Trade Center in the September 11 attack—sanitation and sewer systems may fail, spreading disease and contaminants much farther than the primary site of destruction. Chemicals, such as the freon used in cooling systems, may release into the air, causing serious health effects on nearby populations. The very real nature of the threat has heightened awareness of the need for increased emphasis on safeguarding public health as a part of national-security policy.

OFFICIAL RESPONSES

In October 2001, President George W. Bush created a new cabinet-level government agency called the Department of Homeland Security (DHS), dedicated specifically to ensuring the safety of U.S. citizens within the nation. Part of the mission of the DHS was to develop a comprehensive national strategy against potential terrorist threats or attacks that might have an impact on public health concerns. These concerns include the availability and adequacy of vaccinations, the training of health care personnel, public health surveillance capabilities, hospital capacity, and the coordination of containment of biological threats.

The U.S. public also began to look at the maintenance of public health not only as a critical issue in a time of crisis but also as a good to strive for to prevent catastrophe nationwide. If widespread disease disabled a significant number of people, it would also reduce the ability of survivors to respond effectively to such an attack. Responding after the fact in a haphazard, uneducated manner would not only be unwise but could prove deadly.

In November 2001, the U.S. Health and Human Services Department created a new office called the Office of Public Health Preparedness (OPHP). The purpose of OPHP is to direct the efforts by the Department of Health and Human Services to prepare for, protect against, respond to, and recover from all acts of bioterrorism and other public health emergencies affecting the civilian population. The OPHP also serves to coordinate all activities within the Health and Human Services Department related to such activities. The office works with all health and human service agencies to enhance the response to any possible biological incidents in the future.

Dr. D. A. Henderson, who was later appointed as the first director of the OPHP, testified before the U.S. Senate Foreign Relations Committee just five days before the September 11, 2001, attacks. Speaking on the need for better biodefense preparation, he stated, "Nothing in the realm of natural catastrophes or man-made disasters rivals the complex problems of response that would follow a biological weapons attack against a civilian population. The consequence of such an attack would be an epidemic and, in this country, we have had little experience in coping with epidemics. In fact, no city has had to deal with a truly serious epidemic accompanied by large numbers of cases and deaths since the 1918 influenza epidemic."

CURRENT POLICIES

Current U.S. efforts to safeguard public health combine public education about potential threats and implementing increased strategies to prevent such threats from materializing. In Fort Campbell, Kentucky, researchers are experimenting with a new procedure to develop a treatment for anthrax from the blood of people who are already vaccinated against it. The DHS and private groups including the American Red Cross have been encouraging families to make plans and prepare emergency kits that include food and water, flashlights, battery-powered radios, and anything else they might need for up to three days in case of a power outage. In addition, they are emphasizing that schoolchildren should talk to their parents about where to go and how to maintain contact if the power and phone lines go out. By targeting school-children in a public education program, they are in turn hoping to raise the consciousness of their parents to better prepare the public in a time of national disaster that may affect public health.

Hospitals across the United States are also increasing their awareness and preparedness for a public health threat. Stanford University School of Medicine has established a Bioterrorism and Emergency Preparedness Task Force to deal with events such as those following the September 11 attacks. This task force has developed clinical pathways, medical diagnosis information, and other treatment recommendations that are intended for the use of physicians and other health care providers in the event of a threat to the public. Understandably, the recent events of terrorism in the United States have increased awareness of the need for national security regarding public health, not only in a reactive manner but, more important, in a proactive one. By implementing these measures, great headway can be made in preventing a mass outbreak of disease that would cripple the United States and its ability to defend itself against future terrorism.

See also Anthrax; Biodefense/Biosecurity; Bioterrorism; Emergency Preparedness and Response; Homeland Security, Department of; Infectious Disease; Terrorism, War on International

Further Reading

Committee on Assuring the Health of the Public in the Twenty-First Century and The Institute of Medicine. *The Future of the Public's Health in the Twenty-First Century.* Washington, DC: National Academies Press, 2003.

Novick, Lloyd F., ed. *Public Health Issues Disaster Preparedness: Focus on Bioterrorism.* Bedfordshire, UK: Aspen, 2003.

PUEBLO INCIDENT

Incident in which communist North Korea seized the intelligence ship USS *Pueblo* in international waters in January 1968. One American sailor was killed and 82 captured.

Originally an Army supply vessel that was retired in 1954, the ship was converted into a spy ship in 1966 and served as part of Operation Clickbeetle, a joint mission of naval intelligence and the National Security Agency, intercepting and gathering signals communications. On January 23, 1968, North Korean boats surrounded the ship, which was in waters off the eastern coast of the country, and escorted it to shore. The *Pueblo*'s captain stalled for time, attempting to have the crew destroy classified documents; the Koreans then fired from short range, killing one sailor and wounding four others, and boarded the ship.

Although the U.S. government initially claimed the intelligence losses were not significant, historians today believe otherwise; they believe that the North Koreans were sending important information about communications technology to Moscow. The military planned various scenarios for recovering the ship and its crew, but President Lyndon Johnson opted for a diplomatic solution, fearing any other intervention would lead to the loss of American lives with little likelihood of rescuing the imprisoned sailors. During their ordeal, the sailors were tortured and forced to appear in public to confess their crimes. Only late in the year was a deal finally worked out in which the United States would sign a letter of apology admitting to having violated North Korean waters and promising never to do so again. On December 23, the letter was signed and the crew released. The ship remained in North Korean hands.

PUSAN PERIMETER

Defensive cordon formed by U.S. and South Korean troops around the city of Pusan in southeastern South Korea during the early phases of the Korean War. At the end of World War II, the Korean peninsula was divided into northern and southern halves separated at the 38th parallel. North Korea was a communist dictatorship, closely aligned with the Soviet Union and communist China. South Korea was a capitalist country nominally under the protection of the United States. However, in January 1950, U.S. Secretary of State Dean Acheson excluded South Korea from the postwar defensive perimeter that the U.S. had established to prevent the spread of communism in Asia.

North Korean leader Kim Il Sung saw this as an opportunity to unite the Korean Peninsula under his rule. On June 25, 1950, the North Korean army stormed across the border and overwhelmed the poorly equipped and trained South Korean troops, who were joined by UN forces and U.S. forces hastily rushed in from Japan. The defenders were quickly pushed back into a defensive perimeter around Pusan.

Throughout August, the North Koreans launched a series of intense attacks on the Pusan perimeter. On August 4, North Korean troops crossed the Naktong River roughly 60 miles northwest of Pusan, nearly wiping out the U.S. and South Korean defenders. In an attack on August 24, the North Koreans nearly overran an American force of 20,000 men some 30 miles west of Pusan. In early September, a limited communist breakthrough 60 miles north of Pusan forced South Koreans to abandon their headquarters at Taegu. However, UN troops, reinforced by well-trained American infantry, did not break under the North Korean assault.

On September 15, 1950, an amphibious landing by U.S. and South Korean forces at Inchon Harbor relieved the siege of the Pusan perimeter. The invasion, led by U.S. general Douglas MacArthur, opened up a second front behind North Korean lines that forced the overstretched communist forces to retreat in order to avoid being encircled. The stand at Pusan was just the first act in a bitter three-year struggle. However, it demonstrated how hard the United States would fight to prevent a communist takeover of South Korea.

See also Cold War; Communism and National Security; Containment and the Truman Doctrine; Inchon Landing (1950); Korea, North and South; Korean War; MacArthur, Douglas (1880–1964)

PUTIN, VLADIMIR (1952–)

Former Soviet intelligence agent who succeeded Boris Yeltsin as president of the Russian Federation in 2000. Putin has been a controversial figure whose assurances of democratic sympathies stand in contrast to the authoritarianism of many aspects of his administration.

Born in Leningrad on October 7, 1952, Putin received a law degree from Leningrad State University in 1975. After graduation, he began a 15-year career with the foreign intelligence arm of the KGB, the Soviet secret police. Upon the collapse of the Soviet Union in 1991, he continued in the service of the KGB's successor in Russia, the FSB. Putin served as head of the FSB from 1998 to 1999. In August 1999, Russian president Boris Yeltsin appointed Putin to be Russian prime minister. Four months later, Yeltsin resigned and named Putin as his interim successor. Elections held in March 2000 confirmed Putin as Russia's new president. In March 2004, Russian voters overwhelmingly reelected him to a second term.

After amicable relations under Yeltsin, the tone of the Russia–U.S. relationship has changed under Putin. Whereas Yeltsin worked hard to erase all vestiges of communist influence, including symbols and songs from the Soviet past, Putin has been more open to allowing their return to Russian society. In 2004, Putin went so far as to declare the collapse of the Soviet Union a "national tragedy on an enormous scale." At the beginning of his first term in office, U.S. president

George W. Bush established what seemed to be a good rapport with Putin. Bush met with the Russian leader and declared, "I looked the man in the eye. I was able to get a sense of his soul."

Since that time, Putin's policies have often proven vexing for the United States. For example, Putin was critical of the expansion of the North Atlantic Treaty Organization (NATO) and European Union into formerly Soviet-dominated countries in Eastern Europe, moves strongly supported by the United States. To counter Western influence in the nations surrounding Russia, Putin moved aggressively to forge closer ties with other members of the Commonwealth of Independent States (CIS), a loose federation of countries composed of the independent republics of the former Soviet Union. Putin has also increased Russian political influence over its western neighbors in Ukraine and Belarus, a step that has put his government at odds with the Bush administration, which accused Russia of interfering in Ukraine's 2004 presidential elections. Putin's opposition to the U.S.-led invasion of Iraq in 2003 has also been a source of strain on U.S.–Russian relations.

Putin has come under fire for the increasingly antidemocratic manner in which he has handled political criticism and opposition. As president, he has led a high-profile campaign to prosecute businessmen who control the Russian media and powerful Russian industries. Critics of Putin claim the trials of these so-called oligarchs, who were accused of tax evasion and other financial misdeeds, were merely an excuse for Putin to seize control of the Russian media and economy. Indeed, by 2005, most of the media outlets in Russia were state controlled. The state also held significant financial interests in Russian oil, gas, and other industries.

Putin has shown little tolerance for dissent from his political views. Former Prime Minister Mikhail Kasyanov, who opposed some of Putin's prosecutions and state interference in Russian business, was sacked by Putin a month before the March 2004 elections: Putin dismissed Kasyanov and his entire cabinet and appointed Vikton Khristenko as prime minister. A week later, Putin dismissed Khristenko in favor of Mikhail Fradkov. The seemingly offhand manner in which Putin changes the government when it impedes his plans is a worrisome sign for the Russian republic.

Developments in late 2004 brought an even sharper turn toward authoritarianism in Russia. In the wake of a school hostage crisis that left hundreds of Russian students dead and injured, Putin moved to give himself even greater powers in the name of national security and fighting terrorism. He announced that regional governors would no longer be popularly elected, but instead would be appointed by the president and approved by regional legislatures. He also supported a plan to elect parliamentary deputies by party, rather than choosing individual candidates to fill the seats.

The Bush administration sees both of these moves as further attempts by Putin to consolidate power in the president's hands. The U.S. government openly worries that Putin is dragging Russia back into the autocracy of the Soviet era. Putin denies this is the case, justifying his actions by saying that he is trying—like his U.S. counterpart—to do whatever is necessary to combat terrorism. He also points to the strength of his showing in the 2004 elections as proof that the Russian people support his ideas. According to the current Russian constitution, Putin is not eligible to run for a third term in office in 2008. Western observers are waiting to see if he will try to amend the constitution before that time to continue his time in power.

See also Commonwealth of Independent States; Soviet Union, Former (Russia), and U.S. Policy; Terrorism, War on International; Yeltsin, Boris (1931–)

QUADRENNIAL DEFENSE REVIEW (QDR)

Administration report, released every four years, that is a crucial element in ongoing national security and military reforms aimed at identifying new threats and developing new strategies to combat those threats. In response to what critics perceived as the slow pace of reform at the Pentagon in the years following the end of the Cold War, the U.S. Congress passed the Defense Authorization Act in 1997. The Act mandates that each new administration conduct a comprehensive examination of the nation's defense strategy, force structure, force modernization plans, infrastructure, budget plans, and other elements of the defense program and policies. This is the Quadrennial Defense Review (QDR).

Each Quadrennial Defense Review must define current threats, suggest strategies to foil those threats, and propose the required military forces. The first QDR was the third major strategic reassessment of the force structure of the armed forces in a decade, following the base force assessment in the administration of President George H. W. Bush and the bottom-up review of the administration of President Bill Clinton.

According to the Defense Authorization Act, the pace of global change required a new and comprehensive assessment of the defense strategy of the United States and the force structure of the armed forces needed to meet the threats to the nation in the 21st century. Critics, however, charged that neither the first QDR nor the National Defense Review, a Congress-appointed independent body that evaluated the QDR, went far enough in challenging ingrained security policy. In particular, these critics were concerned about the need to fight two regional wars almost simultaneously and maintain the forces necessary to do so.

See also Bottom-Up Review

R

RADAR (RADIO DETECTION AND RANGING)

Remote detection system used to locate and identify objects. Radar relies on sending and receiving electromagnetic radiation, usually in the form of radio waves or microwaves. Electromagnetic energy moves in waves at or near the speed of light. The wavelength of an electromagnetic wave determines some of the characteristics of the wave. Gamma rays and X-rays have very short wavelengths and can penetrate solid objects. Longer wavelengths such as radio waves or microwaves tend to be reflected by solid objects and are more effective for radar.

Radar creates an electromagnetic energy pulse that is focused by an antenna and transmitted through the air. This focused wave is called the *signal*. Objects in the path of the signal, called *targets*, scatter the electromagnetic energy. Some of this scattered energy is reflected or bounces back toward the radar. This is called an *echo*. The receiving antenna (which is usually the transmitting antenna as well) gathers this radiation and feeds it to a device called a *receiver*. The receiver reports the return and, depending on the sophistication of the device, simply reports the detection or analyzes the signal for more detailed information.

Radar can determine a number of properties of an object, including its distance, speed, direction of motion, and shape. Radar can detect objects in the dark, beyond a line of sight, and in diverse weather conditions. Even though radio waves and microwaves reflect better than other electromagnetic waves with shorter lengths, only a minute fraction of the radar signal is reflected back (about a billionth of a billionth). This low return requires the radar system to transmit high amounts of energy in the signal.

Radar has many applications, from meteorology to speed limit enforcement. Air defense and tactical military operations are dependent upon airborne and ground-based radar installations to track threats and coordinate attacks. Radar is integral to air and sea navigation, defense, improving traffic safety, and providing scientific data. Air traffic control is highly dependent on large networks of ground-based radar systems.

Meteorologists use radar to observe and forecast the weather. Recent improvements, such as Doppler radar, have been effective for providing tornado, hurricane, and other types of severe weather warnings. Radar is also employed in climate research, for mapping the surface of the earth from orbit, in remote sensing applications, and for investigating the surface of other planets and asteroids.

Radar systems perform the same basic tasks, but the manner in which these are operationalized affects the systems' parts. Pulse radar, for example, sends out bursts of electromagnetic waves at intervals. This requires a method of timing that bursts from the transmitter, causing this type of radar to require a more complex transmitter. Continuous wave radar sends out a continuous signal to obtain detailed information about the target—about its speed and direction, for example. Because this type of radar is more dependent on the return, or echo, it requires a more complex receiver.

See also Distant Early Warning (DEW) Line

RADIO FREE EUROPE

Radio broadcasting organization created by the U.S. government to provide information and political commentary to the people of communist Eastern Europe and the Soviet Union. In the absence of unbiased media in the communist countries, Radio Free Europe provided its estimated 35 million listeners with news from around the world and, more important, from their own countries. Due to its largely successful efforts to outwit communist censors and reach its listeners on a daily basis, Radio Free Europe is credited with having contributed significantly to the demise of communist regimes throughout Eastern Europe and the Near East.

Radio Free Europe first began transmitting from its headquarters in Munich, Germany, on July 4, 1950, to a Czechoslovakian audience. Soon, its target was enlarged to include most of the Soviet-dominated countries, across 13 time zones. The station was funded by the U.S. Congress through the Central Intelligence Agency (CIA). However, the fact of CIA involvement was kept secret until the late 1960s for fear of Soviet retaliation.

The CIA ended its involvement in Radio Free Europe's financing and operation in 1971, and control was transferred to a Board for International Broadcasting appointed by the U.S. president. Four years later, in 1975, Radio Free Europe was merged with a similar broadcasting organization named Radio Liberty, creating what is still called Radio Free Europe/Radio Liberty (RFE/RL). Despite the termination of CIA involvement in Radio Free Europe, the Soviet Union continued its attempts to jam the station until 1988.

Following the end of the Cold War in 1989, the role of RFE/RL has changed in many of its target countries. The station is now officially allowed to operate in most of the states it broadcasts to, with the exception of Belarus, Turkmenistan, Tajikistan, and Iran. RFE/RL currently has bureaus in 23 countries throughout Eastern Europe, the former Soviet Union, and the Middle East. In 1995, its headquarters moved to Prague, Czech Republic.

RFE/RL broadcasts in more than 20 different languages, including lesser-known tongues such as Bashkir, Circassian, Tatar, and Chechen (all spoken in the Russian Federation). It does not broadcast in English at all. Nineteen of the languages in which it broadcasts are spoken by Muslim communities, ranging from Kosovo (in the Balkans) to Iran (in the Middle East). In addition to providing its listeners with local news and information, RFE/RL aims to assist countries that are in transition in developing their civil societies (including the media) and guarding against the resumption of totalitarian rule.

See also Communism and National Security; Eastern Bloc; Iron Curtain; Propaganda; Psychological Warfare (PSYOPS); Voice of America

Further Reading

Mickelson, Sig. *America's Other Voices: The Story of Radio Free Europe & Radio Liberty.* New York: Praeger, 1983.

Puddington, Arch. *Broadcasting Freedom: The Cold War Triumph of Radio Free Europe and Radio Liberty.* Lexington: University Press of Kentucky, 2000.

Urban, George R. *Radio Free Europe and the Pursuit of Democracy: My War Within the Cold War.* New Haven, CT: Yale University Press, 1998.

RADIOLOGICAL DISPERSION DEVICE (RDD) OR DIRTY BOMB

A device that uses conventional high explosives to disperse highly dangerous radioactive materials, such as the isotopes americium, cobalt 60, and cesium 137, which are well-suited for radiological weapons because of their availability and the length of time they remain radioactive.

Experts believe that terrorists could assemble a radiological dispersion device (RDD), or dirty bomb, in a matter of weeks, and the idea that terrorists might one day try to detonate such a device is one of the greatest fears in the war on international terrorism. Responding to possible threats at the New Year's Eve celebrations in New York City in 2004, the Federal Bureau of Investigation (FBI) and other federal agents were armed with small radiation detectors and patrolled Times Square on the lookout for a terrorist dirty bomb. Terrorists could also achieve the results of a dirty bomb attack without the actual use of explosives. Radiation could be released using smoke or aerosols to mask the attack.

According to the Center for Technology and National Security Policy at the National Defense University (NDU), a successful dirty bomb attack in

New York or Washington, DC, would kill dozens of people, sicken thousands, and contaminate an area the size of the Washington Mall. In the aftermath of the attack, buildings would have to be razed, and debris—including more than three feet of topsoil—would have to be removed and taken to a protected area. Estimates on the economic impact of such an attack using a dirty bomb range as high as $40 billion.

An NDU report calls for a number of steps to defend the United States against an attack with an RDD or dirty bomb. These steps include the deployment of more decontamination equipment, the stockpiling of medication, the implementation of national standards for emergency response, better disaster coordination, and insurance reform to buffer the economy from dirty bomb attacks.

See also Homeland Security; Terrorism, War on International

Further Reading

Zimmerman, P. D., and C. Loeb, *Dirty Bombs: The Threat Revisited*. Washington, DC: National Defense University, 2004.

RAND CORPORATION

A U.S. think tank organization established following World War II to offer independent research and analysis to the U.S. military.

On May 14, 1948, Project RAND (a contraction of the term *research and development*) broke away from its parent company, the Douglas Aircraft Company of Santa Monica, California, and became an independent nonprofit organization. The project was dedicated to furthering and promoting scientific, educational, and charitable purposes for the public welfare and security of the United States.

The RAND Project was an outgrowth of discussions that involved the U.S. War Department, the Office of Scientific Research and Development, and industry leaders. These groups saw a need for a private organization to connect military planning with research and development decisions in a postwar period in which peace might not be permanently assured. Covert foreign policy became an early specialty of RAND policy analysts.

Since its establishment, approximately two-thirds of RAND's research has involved national security

issues. The remainder of the research conducted by the organization is devoted to issues concerning health, education, civil and criminal justice, labor and population studies, and international economics.

Today, RAND boasts achievements in its contributions to the U.S. space program, digital computing, and artificial intelligence. The organization also has expertise in child policy, civil and criminal justice, education, environment and energy, health, international policy, labor markets, national security, population and regional studies, science and technology, social welfare, terrorism, and transportation.

See also Think Tanks

RAPID DEPLOYMENT FORCE (RDF)

An elite formation of troops designed to move greater distances in a shorter time than conventional military formations. The U.S. military has long used rapid deployment forces as a way to move troops quickly to trouble spots. However, the expansion of U.S. security interests after World War II increased the need for a force that could be quickly dispatched anywhere around the world. This led to the creation of the U.S. Rapid Deployment Joint Task Force.

The concept of light, mobile special forces can be traced to military formations popularized in the 18th century. The French army of that time created light cavalry units called hussars to carry out fast strikes on enemy targets. During the Napoleonic Wars of the early 1800s, many European armies used special light infantry formations as scouts and sharpshooters on the fringes of the main formations. These units went by various names, depending upon their nationality. For example, such forces in German and Austrian armies were often called *Jaeger*, or hunter, battalions. These units typically consisted of irregular troops who could live off the land and were not as dependent as regular conscripts were on direct control by senior staff officers.

During the American Revolutionary War, the Continental Congress established the U.S. Marine Corps as a rapid deployment force for use against British troops. The Marines continued to serve in this capacity after the United States won its independence in 1784. In the early 1800s, the Marines were sent to North Africa in response to Barbary pirates who were attacking U.S. shipping in the Mediterranean. During the Mexican War, U.S. Marines invaded the Mexican port of Veracruz to pave the way for the U.S. victory over Mexico.

The Marines remained the sole U.S. rapid deployment force for many years. However, this changed following the Allied victory in World War II and the rise of communism as a global challenge to U.S. interests. Immediately after the war, the United States viewed Western Europe and the Korean Peninsula to be the main areas of potential overseas military confrontation. During the decades following the war, political and military rivalry between the United States and the Soviet Union spread across all the world's continents. The Middle East, Africa, and Southeast Asia joined Europe and Korea as potential trouble spots. The United States thus faced the need for combined land, sea, and air forces that could respond to threats in any of those places at a moment's notice.

In 1977, a U.S. government study called for the creation of a multiservice force that could be rapidly deployed outside the operational regions of the North Atlantic Treaty Organization (NATO) and Korea. That year, U.S. President Jimmy Carter directed the military to establish a force that could project U.S. power quickly and decisively. The 1978 seizure of American hostages in Iran, and the Soviet invasion of Afghanistan the following year, stimulated and justified the formation of the Rapid Deployment Joint Task Force (RDJTF) in 1980.

Originally established as part of the U.S. Readiness Command, the RDJTF was made a separate force in 1981, reporting directly to the Joint Chiefs of Staff. Headquartered at MacDill Air Force Base in Tampa, Florida, the RDJTF was responsible for planning, training for, and carrying out rapid U.S. responses to threats against vital national interests. The focus of the RDJTF was on the Middle East, particularly the Southwest Asia-Persian Gulf region. In 1983, the RDJTF was replaced by the formation of the U.S. Central Command, or CENTCOM. Like the RDJTF, CENTCOM has no permanent forces assigned to its control. When an emergency arises that requires a military response, available forces from the four service branches and the U.S. Coast Guard are assigned to CENTCOM control.

The United States is not the only country that maintains rapid deployment forces. Russia, Great Britain, France, and Germany all have similar units. According to some military analysts, post–Cold War budget pressures on national militaries will make rapid deployment forces more important in the future. Indeed, not only are many larger nations upgrading their rapid deployment forces but a number of smaller states such as South Africa, Brazil, and Malaysia have also begun to form similar units. NATO has also established a large-scale rapid deployment force, known as the Allied Rapid Reaction Corps (ARRC). These developments reflect the importance of flexibility and speed in modern military operations.

See also CENTCOM; Special Forces; U.S. Marine Corps

Further Reading

Allen, Patrick. *Rapid Reaction Forces*. Shrewesbury, UK: Airlife Publishing, 2002.

Matsumura, John et al. *Lightning Over Water: Sharpening America's Light Forces for Rapid Missions*. Santa Monica, CA: RAND, 2001.

REAGAN DOCTRINE

Term used to characterize the policy of the administration of President Ronald Reagan (1981–1988), which aimed to support anticommunist insurgents globally.

Ronald Reagan, who held strong anticommunist views, was elected President of the United States in November 1980. The former actor had become embroiled in disputes over the issue of communist influences on the film industry when Reagan was president of the Screen Actors Guild in the mid-1950s.

In his 1985 State of the Union address, President Reagan reasserted his vehement anticommunist stance when he called on Congress and the American people to stand up to the Soviet Union, which Reagan termed the *Evil Empire*. As early as 1983, the Reagan administration had articulated a shift in U.S. policy in a series of national security directives, which identified turning back Soviet expansionism as a central priority of U.S. foreign policy.

In a policy break from the doctrine of containment established by President Harry S. Truman, Reagan sought to turn back what he termed Soviet aggression on every continent. Based on the *Roll Back* strategy advanced by Secretary of State John Foster Dulles in the 1950s, the Reagan Doctrine sought actively to reduce the influence of the Soviet Union beyond its borders.

Reagan differed from Dulles in that the president relied primarily on overt material support of anticommunist insurgents attempting to oust Soviet-backed regimes. The Reagan administration sought to rebuild the credibility of the U.S. commitment to resist Soviet encroachment on the interests of America and its allies and support third-world states willing to resist or oppose Soviet initiatives hostile to those interests.

Under the Reagan Doctrine, the Reagan administration provided overt and covert support to several anticommunist insurgents. In Nicaragua, the administration supported the Contra movement in an effort to force the leftist Sandinista government from power. In Afghanistan, the United States provided material support to Afghan rebels, known as the mujahideen, to help them end Soviet occupation in Afghanistan.

See also Cold War; Iran-Contra Affair; Reagan, Ronald, and National Policy; Soviet Union, Former (Russia), and U.S. Policy

Further Reading

Hahn, Walter F., ed. *Central America and the Reagan Doctrine.* Lanham, MD: University Press of America, 1987.

Scott, James M. *Deciding to Intervene: The Reagan Doctrine and American Foreign Policy.* Durham, NC: Duke University Press, 1996.

REAGAN, RONALD, AND NATIONAL POLICY

The foreign policy agenda advanced by Ronald Reagan (1911–2004), 40th president of the United States, calling for active American confrontation with the Soviet Union, a significant expansion of U.S. military capacity, a renewed offensive on communist insurgencies in third-world nations, and the development of a controversial space-based missile defense system—an agenda often identified by the moniker peace through strength.

Ronald Reagan took office in the winter of 1981, intent on establishing a new aggressive plan of action for U.S. involvement in the Cold War. Beginning with the administration of President Richard Nixon, and continuing through those of Presidents Ford and Carter, the American approach to its Soviet adversary had become one of détente, or a gradual thawing of tensions and deescalation of military conflicts. Reagan's fierce anticommunist position (originating from his

experience as the president of the Hollywood Screen Actors Guild, 1947–1952 and 1959–1960), combined with a renewal of Cold War pressures brought on by the Iranian Revolution of 1979 and the Soviet invasion of Afghanistan in 1980, set the stage for the dramatic shift in U.S. foreign policy.

Reagan believed wholeheartedly that the Soviet Union, with its planned economy and state-sponsored socialist system, would be unable to stand toe-to-toe with the United States simultaneously on every front—most notably the arms race, the battle for economic supremacy, and the ongoing war of competing ideologies. Moreover, Reagan maintained that the United States had a moral obligation to combat the Soviet Union, a regime he once famously referred to as the Evil Empire.

As such, Reagan initiated an enormous $800 billion defense buildup, secured passage of a radical series of tax cuts (in which the top tax rate was reduced from 70% to 28%), and funded anticommunist military uprisings in such nations as Nicaragua, Angola, and Afghanistan. Reagan's programs, though arguably contributing to the demise of the Soviet Union, saddled the United States with more than $2 trillion in debt.

Among President Reagan's most controversial proposals was the development and eventual deployment of a space-based missile-defense system. This Strategic Defense Initiative (SDI) was dubbed *Star Wars* by critics who maintained that not only was such a program too far-fetched (both in terms of cost and technology), but that it was also in direct violation of America's legal commitment to the Antiballistic Missile (ABM) Treaty of 1972.

SDI ultimately led to the breakdown of a series of groundbreaking arms-limitation talks between Reagan and Soviet Premier Mikhail Gorbachev in Reykjavik, Iceland, in October of 1986. Prior to discussing SDI, Reagan and Gorbachev had agreed in Iceland to immediately limit their respective nuclear forces to 1,600 delivery vehicles and 6,000 warheads, reduce all strategic strike forces by 50% over the first five years of any agreement, eliminate all stockpiles of nuclear ballistic missiles over a 10-year period, and remove large amounts of nuclear munitions from Europe and parts of Asia in the interim. As a concession, Premier Gorbachev wanted the Reagan administration to effectively end its pursuit of SDI. Reagan countered by offering to share SDI technology with the Soviet Union; Gorbachev balked. In a moment of genuine brinkmanship, Reagan ultimately refused to concede SDI and walked away from the talks altogether. Many felt that Reagan was playing a very dangerous game, but others point to Reykjavik as the defining foreign policy moment of his eight-year presidency. Reykjavik set the stage for U.S.-Soviet agreement on the Intermediate-Range Nuclear Forces (INF) Treaty signed in December of 1987, as well as the Strategic Arms Reduction Treaty (START I) signed in July of 1991. The Soviet Union dissolved five months after the START I treaty was ratified.

Reagan's support of anticommunist efforts in third-world nations tarnished his reputation as both a proponent of democratization and a law-abiding citizen. American efforts in Nicaragua, Afghanistan, Angola, and elsewhere were often conducted in concert with highly questionable resistance leaders. Moreover, critics claimed that Reagan's interference in the domestic affairs of other nations would ultimately lead to an anti-American backlash from the third world.

The administration's most damaging move came in its decision to secretly sell weapons to Iran (which needed to arm itself in its ongoing war with Iraq) and channel the proceeds to anticommunist Contras in Nicaragua. Although Reagan was ultimately absolved of any of the legal charges levied against him in the so-called Iran-Contra affair, the scandal raised serious questions about both his leadership and ability to speak truthfully to the American people.

A controversial and colorful figure to be sure, Ronald Reagan presided over one of the most precedent-setting periods of American foreign policy history. Much of what he accomplished—for better or for worse—has set the stage for the international environment of the 21st century.

See also Arms Control; Arms Race; Cold War; Communism; Communism and National Security; Democratization; Gorbachev, Mikhail; Grenada Intervention; Iran-Contra Affair (1985–1986); Nuclear Weapons; Reagan Doctrine; Reykjavik; Soviet Union, Former (Russia), and U.S. Policy; Strategic Defense Initiative (SDI)

Further Reading

Scott, James. *Deciding to Intervene: The Reagan Doctrine and American Foreign Policy*. Durham, NC: Duke University Press, 1996.

Shimko, Keith. *Images and Arms Control: Perceptions of the Soviet Union in the Reagan Administration*. Ann Arbor: University of Michigan Press, 1991.

REFLECTIONS
The Flourishing of Democracy

The objective I propose is quite simple to state: To foster the infrastructure of democracy—the system of a free press, unions, political parties, universities—which allows a people to choose their own way to develop their own culture, to reconcile their own differences through peaceful means.

This is not cultural imperialism; it is providing the means for genuine self-determination and protection for diversity. Democracy already flourishes in countries with very different cultures and historical experiences. It would be cultural condescension, or worse, to say that any people prefer dictatorship to democracy. Who would voluntarily choose not to have the right to vote, decide to purchase government propaganda handouts instead of independent newspapers, prefer government to worker-controlled unions, opt for land to be owned by the state instead of those who till it, want government repression of religious liberty, a single political party instead of a free choice, a rigid cultural orthodoxy instead of democratic tolerance and diversity?

—U.S. President Ronald Reagan
Speech to the British House of Commons, 1982

REALISM

Political theory that conceives of world affairs as a struggle for power among nations. Realism discounts moral considerations in foreign policy, and asserts that a state can achieve security only by amassing power. States project power mainly by relying on force or the threat of force.

Variations of realist theory have dominated the study of international relations since World War II, especially in the United States, in which realism also influenced policymakers. Rival theories question realism's most fundamental assumptions. Yet realism remains relevant, even in an interdependent world plagued by nonstate threats, such as the international terrorist group al-Qaeda.

According to realists, the struggle for power among nations is rooted in human nature. When nations find that their interests coincide, they collaborate. However, when nations' interests clash, rivalry and conflict ensue. To survive, states must follow national interests by maximizing their power.

Realists admit that skilled diplomacy can achieve mutual accommodation, but they reject idealist visions of durable peace, trust, and cooperation among countries. Realists are skeptical about the possibility of moral progress or human improvement; they believe that wars are bound to occur because of an innate lust for power and because there is no overarching authority to impose peace. Relations among states are inherently competitive, especially in the field of military security.

PROPONENTS

Realism rose to the fore after World War II, but its origins can be traced back to the 5th century BCE. The ancient Greek historian Thucydides attributed the Peloponnesian War (between Athens and Sparta) to the growth of Athenian power and the fear that it evoked in Sparta. In his *Melian Dialogue*, Thucydides observed that the strong do what they will; the weak do what they must.

Realist themes resurfaced in *The Prince* (1513), a treatise on princely rule by Renaissance Italian political leader Niccolò Machiavelli. Dismissing all ethical considerations, Machiavelli focused on the strength of the ruler as the prime factor for successful government.

In the 1930s, British political scientist and historian Edward H. Carr argued for *realism* in the study of international relations. Carr advocated realism as an antidote to what he saw as utopianism or wishful thinking in the League of Nations and in U.S. President Woodrow Wilson's ideal of self-determination for all nations.

Realism was most compellingly systematized by the German-born American political scientist Hans Morgenthau in *Politics Among Nations* (1948). Morgenthau argued that political leaders could deduce rational and objectively correct policies from the immutable laws of nature that govern politics. He conceived of power as the principal goal in international relations, and he defined the national interest in terms of power. Morgenthau's views inspired generations of scholars and practitioners of international politics in North America and Western Europe.

ASSUMPTIONS

Realist theory assumes that the state is the most important actor in world affairs. It discounts other actors above the state level (such as the European Union or the United Nations) and below the state level (such as terrorist networks, multinational corporations, and ethnic minorities within states). The state is also assumed a single unit (ignoring divisions among government bureaucracies such as the State Department and the Pentagon) that acts based on a rational calculation of costs and benefits. From a realist point of view, the international system is one of anarchy, with no authority capable of enforcing rules on sovereign states.

In realist thought, relations among states are considered naturally conflictual, and the outcome of international relations is dictated by differences in the relative level of military and economic power. World affairs are defined by security competition among sovereign states under the chronic threat of war. According to realists, states claiming to promote universal values such as democracy or peace are concealing their self-interest, in fact. State leaders cannot be expected to adhere to the moral rules that normally bind individuals because state leaders have only one goal: the survival of the state.

CRITICISM

According to critics, realism is too narrowly focused on power politics and the causes of conflict, ignoring broader social, economic, and environmental issues. Most critics agree that the world is indeed anarchic, but they point to the development of a complex interdependence and at least the idea of an international community.

Critics of realist thought also claim that states are no longer alone on the world stage. Their borders are increasingly permeable, and other actors have gained importance, including supranational organizations, multinational corporations, and terrorist networks.

The realist emphasis on sovereign states is falling behind the times, as virtually no government can now claim absolute control over its territory, in the face of globalization. Modern communications technology, global financial markets, and a shared environment contribute to interdependence, making it practically impossible to guarantee the security of one state without also ensuring the security of other states. Institutions, rather than states, can best address the problems of an emerging global village. Institutions promote trust and mitigate the effects of international anarchy.

State preferences are determined not only by military and economic capabilities but also by culture and ideology. States have largely lost the incentive for territorial expansion because knowledge resources are becoming more important than natural resources for generating power and prestige.

Critics of realism also draw attention to examples of cooperation among countries beyond a narrowly defined self-interest. Such cooperation is possible because states, which are motivated by human wants and needs, strive for absolute (rather than relative) gains.

Critics also take issue with realism's exclusion of ethical and sociopsychological dimensions. Realism cannot explain the growing salience of moral imperatives such as human rights. Moral restraint and responsibility affect the struggle for power among states. Realism cannot fully account for the complexity of the contemporary world, in which power is exercised in many dimensions, not only among independent states.

NEOREALISM

U.S. political scientist Kenneth Waltz updated realist theory in the late 1970s, founding the school of neorealism, or structural realism. Waltz attempted to provide a coherent theoretical framework to explain behavior in the international system, especially the consequences of major shifts in the balance of power, recurring patterns of interaction, and similar behavior by disparate states.

Instead of referring to human nature, Waltz focused on the anarchic characteristics of the international system. He assumed that the ultimate state interest was not power but security. According to Waltz, the maximization of power often ensures security, but in some cases, it might trigger an arms race, as happened in the Cold War.

As a theory, realism gave form and structure to the study of international politics. As a worldview, it offered insight into diplomacy and statecraft, especially for practitioners of *realpolitik* (an expansionist national policy having as its sole principle the advancement of the national interest). Despite its limitations, realism remains relevant today, even in a globalized world in which multiple actors strive for various goals, of which military power is only one.

See also Geopolitics; Globalization and National Security; Interdependence; Machiavelli, Niccolò (1469–1527); Morgenthau, Hans (1904–1980); Realpolitik

Further Reading

Carnegie Council on Ethics and International Affairs. "What Does Ethics Have to Do with International Affairs?" FAQ. http://www.carnegiecouncil.org/page.php/prmID/16

Cook, Thomas I., and Malcolm Moos. *Power Through Purpose: The Realism of Idealism as a Basis for Foreign Policy*. Baltimore, MD: Johns Hopkins University Press, 1954.

Daalder Ivo, H. "Are the United States and Europe Heading for Divorce?" *International Affairs* 77 no. 3 (2001): 553–567. http://www.brookings.edu/views/articles/daalder/divorce.pdf

Herz, John H. *Political Realism and Political Idealism*. Chicago: University of Chicago Press, 1951.

Machiavelli, Niccolò. *The Prince*. New York: Penguin, 1975.

Morgenthau, Hans J. *Politics Among Nations: The Struggle for Power and Peace*, 5th ed., revised. New York: Alfred A. Knopf, 1978. http://www.mtholyoke.edu/acad/intrel/morg6.htm

Waltz, Kenneth N. *Theory of International Politics*. New York: Random House, 1979.

REFLECTIONS

Realism

[I]t appears to me more appropriate to follow up the real truth of a matter than the imagination of it; for many have pictured republics and principalities which in fact have never been known or seen, because how one lives is so far distant from how one ought to live, that he who neglects what is done for what ought to be done, sooner effects his ruin than his preservation; for a man who wishes to act entirely up to his professions of virtue soon meets with what destroys him among so much that is evil.

—Niccolò Machiavelli
The Prince, 1513

The concept of interest defined as power imposes intellectual discipline upon the observer, infuses rational order into the subject matter of politics, and thus makes the theoretical understanding of politics possible.

—Hans J. Morgenthau
Politics Among Nations, 1948

REALPOLITIK

Term of German origin that refers to international relations based upon the advancement of national interest and calculation of power. Realpolitik is a central principle of political realist thought and a reference to power politics among states.

In the arena of international relations, political realist thought emphasizes the constraints placed upon politics by human nature and the nonexistence of a dominant international governing body. These conditions combine to transform international relations into a realm of actors motivated by power and interest.

Realists assert that human nature remains unchanged since the days of classical antiquity and is, at its core, egoistic and thus inclined toward immorality. According to realpolitik, the nonexistence of a dominant governmental body in international relations results in anarchy in the international arena. The concept also holds that, within states, human nature usually is tamed by hierarchical political authority and rule. In international relations, anarchy not merely allows but encourages the worst aspects of human nature to be expressed.

The Prince, written by the Renaissance Italian political leader Niccolò Machiavelli, is universally acknowledged as a classical political work that espouses realpolitik behavior. In the book, Machiavelli discusses how to gain, maintain, and expand power. Any means necessary to achieve the desired end—security of the state—are justified.

Other realist political philosophers include the ancient Greek historian Thucydides and the 17th-century English philosopher Thomas Hobbes. Hobbes concluded that humanity's natural condition is a state of war, but a superior power dominating the actions of individuals can impose constraint and social structure, thus allowing humanity's escape from anarchical existence. According to Hobbes, hierarchical political authority awes humanity into submission and peace.

See also Hobbes, Thomas (1588–1679); Machiavelli, Niccolò (1469–1527); Realism

Further Reading

Donnelly, Jack. *Realism and International Relations.* Cambridge, UK: Cambridge University Press, 2000.
Viotti, Paul R., and Mark V. Kauppi. *International Relations Theory: Realism, Pluralism, Globalism, and Beyond.* Boston: Allyn and Bacon, 1999.

REGIONALISM

Political philosophy that emphasizes the primacy of the interests of larger regional groupings over those of individual states. Regionalism stands in contrast to nationalism, in which the interests of the nation-state are considered paramount.

Nationalism has been the preeminent force in international relations for hundreds of years. The Peace of Westphalia that ended the Thirty Years' War in 1648 formally established the nation-state system as the accepted political order in Europe. That conflict was the culmination of several large and myriad smaller religious wars stretching over more than a century. Westphalia established the principle that rulers had the right to determine what religion would be observed in their territories. By extension, it recognized the sovereignty of established states and condemned interference in their internal affairs.

Regionalism is largely a product of forces shaping the world since the early 20th century, including decolonization and globalization. After World War II, newly independent nations in Africa and Asia created several regional political and economic organizations, such as the Organization of African Unity (OAU) and the Regional Cooperation for Development (RCD). These organizations had ambitious goals based on a perceived sense of shared interest among former colonies. National interests, however, often overrode regional priorities, checkering the groups' records of achievement.

The OAU was established in 1963 by 23 African states seeking to end the remaining colonialism in Africa and to promote peace and economic development on the continent. The OAU had some modest successes in promoting economic liberalization in Africa, but it failed to prevent or mitigate scores of regional wars and the rise of authoritarian regimes throughout the continent. The OAU was disbanded in 2002 and replaced by a new organization named the African Union (AU).

The AU has shown a greater willingness to intervene in the affairs of member states than did the OAU. In May 2003, an AU force composed of troops from South Africa, Ethiopia, and Mozambique was dispatched to Burundi to enforce peace agreements in the wake of Burundi's recently ended civil war. The AU also sent 300 observers to monitor ethnic violence in the Darfur region of Sudan and is now considering the deployment of peacekeepers to the area.

Iran, Turkey, and Pakistan formed the RCD in 1964 to liberalize and promote trade among the three countries. However, the member states could not develop a mutually acceptable mechanism for expanding trade or mobilizing regional resources. Political instability following the 1979 Iranian revolution caused the RCD to suspend operations until 1985. At that time, a new group, the Economic Cooperation Organization (ECO), arose from the old RCD. In 1990, following the collapse of Soviet communism, seven newly independent states in Central Asia and the Caucasus joined the ECO.

The goals of ECO incorporate both economic and social objectives. Economic goals include promoting sustainable development in member states, removing trade barriers and promoting regional trade, developing transportation and communications links among member states and with neighbor states, developing economic liberalization and privatization, and mobilizing the region's resources (particularly energy) to increase regional economic power. Social objectives of ECO include cooperating to control regional drug trafficking, having mutual ecological and environmental protection, and strengthening cultural ties among the people of the region.

Globalization—the growing worldwide economic, political, and social interconnectedness—has also provided a strong impetus toward regionalism. This has found its most prominent expression in a surge of regional economic and trade agreements since the 1990s. The increased internationalization of business caused by improvements in transportation and communications has led neighboring countries to create regional trade zones to protect themselves against economic competition from other regions. Pacts such as the 1993 North American Free Trade Agreement (NAFTA) among the United States, Canada, and Mexico have facilitated lower trade barriers among neighbors and political allies.

Europe has taken regionalism a step further with the adoption of the euro as the common currency by 12 members of the European Union (EU), a supranational organization that attempts to coordinate the economic policies of member countries. The EU has existed formally since 1992, but Western European nations have instituted informal organizations for similar purposes since the 1950s. However, the introduction of the euro marked a radical abandonment of one of the historic hallmarks of national sovereignty: a separate currency.

By discontinuing their own currencies in favor of the euro, the 12 EU states that form the so-called Economic and Monetary Union (EMU) have committed to an unprecedented experiment in regionalism. Sharing a common currency means that the economic health of each member can significantly affect that of all the others. EMU members agree to work through the EU parliament to resolve differences or disputes over economic policy, marking a shift from national toward regional control over internal state affairs. Some EU states, most notably Great Britain, have resisted joining the EMU for fears of losing control over their national economic fortunes.

The long-term goal of the EU is the political integration of Europe, in part motivated by a desire to act as a counterweight to the economic and military power of the United States. After one-half century of close interdependence between Europe and the United States during the Cold War, the partners in the Cold War Atlantic Alliance are still political allies, but they are also competitors for global economic and political influence. Both the EU and NAFTA reflect the rise of regionalism as a political and economic force gradually supplanting national rivalries as a focus of international relations.

See also Globalization and National Security; Nationalism; Nation-State; New World Order

Further Reading

Mittelman, James. *The Globalization Syndrome: Transformation and Resistance.* Princeton, NJ: Princeton University Press, 2000.

Rosenau, James, N. *Distant Proximities: Dynamics Beyond Globalization.* Princeton, NJ: Princeton University Press, 2003.

REPUBLIC OF CHINA ON TAIWAN

Political self-designation for the island commonly known as Taiwan.

Although its international legal status is unclear, the Republic of China on Taiwan functions as an independent state, electing its own leadership and managing its own internal and external affairs. Its neighbor to the west, the People's Republic of China (PRC), claims Taiwan as a province and considers the Taiwanese government to be illegal. Since 1949, Taiwan and China have developed an uneasy standoff, occasionally trading provocations but never engaging in open warfare.

Complex political and economic issues have vested other world powers, notably the United States and Japan, with an interest in the conflict. Such outside forces exert a considerable measure of influence over the actions of both Taiwan and China.

ROOTS OF THE CONFLICT

The history of Taiwan is as complicated as its present political situation, with the island changing hands several times over the past five centuries. After decades of Spanish and Dutch rule, China annexed large parts of Taiwan in the late 1600s. Two centuries later, in 1895, following the Sino-Japanese war, control over Taiwan passed to Japan. Despite Taiwanese resistance, the Japanese dominated the island for the next 50 years. In 1945, at the end of World War II, a defeated Japanese Empire returned Taiwan to China.

The Chinese, however, were experiencing a political crisis at the time. The country's loyalties were divided between followers of Nationalist Party leader Generalissimo Chiang Kai-shek and Communist Party leader Mao Zedong as China plunged into civil war. Chiang, who had fought both Japan and the Chinese communists on the mainland, faced his first challenge in the form of a revolt by the indigenous Taiwanese, which the Nationalists rigorously repressed. The United States and other western powers recognized Chiang as China's legitimate ruler, whereas the Soviet Union supported the Chinese communists.

While battling the communists, Chiang reestablished Chinese administration in Taiwan. However, the Nationalist Party on the island proved to be thoroughly corrupt, and in 1947, the generalissimo had to call in troops to crush a Taiwanese revolt. As chance would have it, two years later Chiang lost his struggle with the communists and was forced to evacuate to Taiwan with more than one million supporters. The generalissimo's presence on the island and the threat of a powerful Communist Chinese neighbor seeking reunification sent shock waves through Taiwan's already tumultuous political life.

From Taiwan, the generalissimo still claimed to represent the legitimate government of all Chinese people. He considered Mao's communist regime to have usurped his legitimate rule. For its part, Communist China, formally known as the People's Republic of China (PRC), perceived Taiwan as a renegade province and reserved the right to take whatever measures it thought necessary to reunite the island with the mainland.

Taiwan's Nationalist government, however, had more to worry about than PRC threats. In 1947, frustrated by the corruption that plagued a government run by Chiang's imported mainlanders, the Taiwanese rose up once again. The revolt was again suppressed and Chiang declared martial law, a condition that stayed in effect for the next 40 years. During this time, no opposition party legally could be formed, and the government ruled with an iron fist. Throughout this period, the Nationalists continued to espouse the goal of reuniting island and mainland under Nationalist rule. At the popular level, however, a Taiwanese identity, distinct from a Chinese identity, began to appeal to an increasing number of islanders. That sense of identity eventually changed the Taiwanese public's perspective on the desirability of joining the mainland under one government.

CHANGING DIRECTION

In the late 1960s, Taiwan's economy started growing at a rapid pace. By the early 1980s, the phenomenon came to be known as the Taiwanese miracle. The booming economy, coupled with the end of martial law and the subsequent democratization of the political process in the late 1980s, contributed significantly to the gradual transformation of the Taiwanese attitude toward mainland China.

In March 1991, Taiwanese President Lee Teng Hui announced that his government no longer claimed the territory of mainland China, as the generalissimo and his successors had done for over 40 years. This did not placate the PRC, however, which continued to express frustration at what it perceived to be the island's dangerous drift toward independence. In 1996, China staged live-ammunition war games just off the coast of Taiwan—a not-so-subtle warning against a unilateral declaration of Taiwanese independence. Just three years later, Taiwanese President Lee raised the political stakes by speaking on the record of the need for a "state-to-state" relationship with China. Taiwan now contemplated a choice between two policy options that were equally distasteful to China: supporting the ambiguous yet relatively stable status quo or supporting a drive for outright independence.

The dilemma, however, did not affect Taiwan and China only. Other world powers with serious interests in the region wasted no time in getting involved in the conflict. As early as 1971, the United Nations General Assembly officially recognized the PRC as the sole legitimate representative of the Chinese people. A year later, the United States officially acknowledged Communist China's position that Taiwan was a part of its territory. Because China refuses to establish diplomatic relations with countries that recognize Taiwan's statehood, the United States does not currently have an embassy on the island. However, the U.S. government maintains the American Institute in Taiwan, which plays the role of America's official representative to the island.

As a matter of official policy, the United States is neutral in regard to questions of Chinese reunification and Taiwanese independence. Successive American administrations have regularly disapproved of any potential Taiwanese declaration of independence. However, the Taiwan Relations Act of 1979 allowed the island to buy sophisticated American armament, which would allow it to defend itself efficiently against a potential Chinese attempt to achieve unification by force.

Should the PRC attempt to invade the island, it would face well-armed Taiwanese forces potentially aided by an American military that is anxious about China's increasing influence in Asian and global affairs. The Chinese government, aware of this fact and cognizant of U.S. anxieties, has proposed a peaceful reunification within the one-China, two-systems framework. The policy would allow Taiwan to maintain a measure of political and economic autonomy. Taiwan would be able to continue deciding its own policies, except those that deal with matters of diplomacy and national defense. Similar policies were adopted with regard to Hong Kong and Macau, former European colonies returned to Chinese control in recent years.

The Taiwanese government does not agree with the proposed solution, and local politicians declare themselves in favor of outright independence from time to time. These declarations incense the communist government, which typically responds with threats or provocative actions. As of 2005, the conflict remains unresolved, with the main actors (Taiwan, China, and the United States) deadlocked in a situation that arguably each resents and finds uncomfortable. Nevertheless, the status quo seems to be the only conceivable situation in which the contenders do not feel compelled to resort to aggressive, even military, measures.

—*Razvan Sibii*

See also China and U.S. Policy; Communism and National Security; Geopolitics; Mao Zedong (1893–1976); Sovereignty

Further Reading

Brown, Melissa J. *Is Taiwan Chinese? The Impact of Culture, Power and Migration on Changing Identities.* Berkeley: University of California Press, 2004.

Lijun, Sheng. *China's Dilemma: The Taiwan Issue.* New York: I. B. Tauris Publishers, 2001.

Zagoria, Donald S., ed. *Breaking the China-Taiwan Impasse.* Westport, CT: Praeger, 2003.

RESERVE FORCES

Component of the U.S. military consisting of individuals who train and serve part-time. The U.S. Army, Navy, and Air Force all maintain reserve forces.

The reserve consists of both soldiers who have retired from active military duty as well as individuals who enlist directly into the Reserve. Reservists typically spend one weekend per month in inactive duty training and two consecutive weeks of active-duty training each year. Reserve forces are divided into two components: the Selected Reserve and the Individual Ready Reserve. The Selected Reserve is the primary pool from which the armed forces draw reserve personnel. Those who train on weekends or who are on full-time support status make up the Selected Reserve. The Individual Ready Reserve consists of retired former soldiers and other standby forces.

Many critical support capabilities are located either exclusively or primarily in the reserves. The Army Reserve, for example, contains all the services training divisions, railway units, enemy prisoner of war (POW) brigades, and chemical brigades. It also has most of the Army's civil affairs; psychological operations; medical and transportation units; and a large portion of its public affairs, engineer, and power projection assets. All the Army's bridging capability is also assigned to reserve units.

The Army and Navy reserve forces both began as informal support units that were later institutionalized by the U.S. Congress. The Naval Reserves can trace their origin to the actions of American citizens who took to the seas to harass British shipping during the Revolutionary War. State naval militias provided a reserve force of sorts for the United States throughout the 19th century, but by the outbreak of World War I, it was clear that the navy required a more formal reserve system. On March 3, 1915, U.S. President Woodrow Wilson signed legislation creating a naval reserve force.

The Army Reserve formally came into being at about the same time as the Naval Reserve. Like the Navy, the Army relied heavily on state militias and volunteers to serve as a reserve force. Their training and readiness, like that of naval militia members, was uneven and often of dubious quality. In 1908, the U.S. Congress authorized the Army to create a reserve corps of medical officers. Four years later, the Army Appropriations Act created the Regular Army Reserve. The National Defense Act of 1916 formed the Reserve Officer Training Corps (ROTC); a year later the Medical Officers Corps was incorporated into the Regular Army Reserve to form what is now the U.S. Army Reserve.

The U.S. Air Force Reserve is the youngest of the reserve forces, created as a result of the National Defense Act of 1947. It was officially designated an agency of the Air Force on April 14, 1948. It did not become a separate command (the status of the Army and Navy Reserves) until 1997. The Air Force Reserve participated in the Berlin airlift that relieved the Soviet blockade of West Berlin in 1949. Since that time, Air Force Reserve units have seen action in the Gulf War of 1991 and the Iraq War of 2003, and participated in many humanitarian and disaster relief efforts.

The collapse of the Soviet Union in 1991 brought significant changes to the reserves' force structure. These changes placed reserve forces directly in the line of fire. Reserve units were used extensively in the Gulf War of 1991, the Bosnia Intervention of the mid-to-late 1990s, and the Iraq War of 2003. Reserve units are also among the first-line defense against terrorist attacks on the United States. The Civil-Military Cooperation Program uses Army Reserve expertise to help communities plan for and respond to such attacks.

At the beginning of the 21st century, U.S. reserve forces have assumed a greater responsibility for national security than ever before. The Army Reserve was deployed 10 times between 1991 and 2003; by contrast, it had been mobilized only 9 times in its previous 75 years of existence. In addition, the reserves have played an unprecedented role in the 2003 Iraq War. The subsequent U.S. occupation has stretched the reserves to the limits. Force limitations have prevented many reserve units from rotating out of combat or compelled them to return much more quickly than normal. Some military experts have warned of the threat of breaking the reserve forces by relying too heavily on them for front-line duty. This has sparked debate about

a return to the draft, but the administration of President George W. Bush has opposed that idea.

See also All-Volunteer Force; Conscription/Volunteer Force; Gulf War (1990–1991); Iraq War of 2003; National Guard; Reserve Officers' Training Corps (ROTC)

Further Reading

McPherson, Cameron. *Life in the Navy Reserves*. Victoria, BC: Trafford Publishing, 2003.
Moskos, Charles C., ed. *The Postmodern Military: Armed Forces After the Cold War*. New York: Oxford University Press, 1999.

RESERVE OFFICERS' TRAINING CORPS (ROTC)

Elective military education program at a college or university that leads to a commission as an officer in the U.S. armed forces. Reserve Officers' Training Corps (ROTC) programs are offered by the Army, the Air Force, and the Navy (including the Marine Corps). ROTC is one of the three programs of commissioned officers in the military, along with the service academies and officer candidate schools.

Established in 1916, ROTC was created as a way to expand the pool of candidates for the military officer corps beyond the students at the sometimes-clannish service academies. The ROTC program also brought the military and its officers to high schools and colleges throughout the country, a move that developed and cemented ties with local communities. As of 2004, ROTC programs existed on more than 1,000 campuses in the United States and accounted for 60% of all officers in the U.S. armed forces.

For its members at colleges or universities, ROTC provides tuition, fees, and a small stipend, as well as uniforms and military gear. Cadets are organized into military units in which they have the opportunity to exercise leadership skills as they move through the four-year program. Experienced military officers and noncommissioned officers serve as mentors and guides to ROTC cadets. ROTC cadets also participate in supplementary activities, including rappelling, learning to pilot planes, and attending military schools such as Airborne and Ranger training.

Military training in ROTC occurs year-round, but summer is when most tactical training takes place.

Spread over two summers, this tactical training includes a basic session covering soldier training and tasks and an advanced session emphasizing leadership training and skills. Depending on the needs of the military, graduates of ROTC can serve in active-duty units or be assigned to reserve duty.

See also All-Volunteer Force; Reserve Forces

REVOLUTION IN MILITARY AFFAIRS (RMA)
See OFFICE OF NET ASSESSMENT

REYKJAVIK

Summit meeting held in October 1986 between U.S. President Ronald Reagan and Soviet Premier Mikhail Gorbachev, the aim of which was to discuss the placing of limitations on the strategic arms of each nation. Following a summit meeting in Geneva, Switzerland, in November 1985, Ronald Reagan and Mikhail Gorbachev met in Reykjavik, Iceland, to discuss the possibility of strategic arm reductions. Only the second meeting between the two world leaders, they approached the talks with diverse agendas.

Reagan staked his presidency on his commitment to opposing the Soviet Union at every opportunity. The White House believed that American supremacy was key to U.S. survival, and it was thought that an accelerated arms race would cause irreparable harm and place tremendous pressure on a faltering Soviet economy.

Meanwhile, Gorbachev was basing his presidency on the dual reform programs of *perestroika* and *glasnost*. For much of its 70 years, the Soviet state towered over the majority of nations in military and industrial might. In its waning decades, however, the Soviet Union was faltering under the strain of its outmoded economic system and industrial infrastructure. To compete against political rivals in the West, the Soviet economy and society would need drastic restructuring.

However, Gorbachev could not afford to continue down the path to reform without assurances about national security. He needed an arms limitation treaty to accomplish this. Reagan, on the other hand, was gradually being perceived as an extremist hard-liner bent on the destruction of the Soviet Union. To allay such fears, Reagan would appear open to negotiations and was thus willing to attend summit meetings.

The two leaders met in Reykjavik from October 11 to October 16 to discuss arms limitations. During the exchange of proposals, it became clear that the sticking point was the space-based missile defense system known as the Strategic Defense Initiative (SDI), or Star Wars, under consideration by the United States. President Reagan refused to limit SDI research and technology to the laboratory. Gorbachev, however, would not accept anything less than a ban on missile testing in space. Despite the failure to reach an agreement on this issue, both sides felt that the meeting was a success and that it opened the way for further progress.

Gorbachev later remarked that he and President Reagan had had real conversations about key issues during the Reykjavik meeting. For this reason, he considered the meeting a turning point in the Cold War.

See also Arms Control; Summit Conferences

RIO PACT

Mutual defense agreement signed in 1947 by the United States and 19 Latin American countries. Under the terms of the Rio Pact, an attack against any of the signatory nations is regarded as an attack against all. The pact provides for all signatories to send troops in defense of any member that is the target of foreign aggression.

The Rio Pact was both an extension of the Monroe Doctrine of the 19th century and a product of the 20th century Cold War. The Monroe Doctrine, outlined by U.S. President James Monroe in 1823, declared the western hemisphere off-limits to European intervention. It stated that the United States would regard any attempt by foreign powers to interfere in Latin America to be an act of aggression against the United States. The Monroe Doctrine, however, was a unilateral declaration by the United States. It reflected a desire to create an exclusive U.S. sphere of influence in the western hemisphere rather than a collective statement of solidarity among western nations.

Fears about the spread of Soviet communism after World War II led the United States to seek a more active alliance with other Western-Hemisphere nations. Thus, on September 2, 1947, the United States and 19 Latin American countries signed the Rio Pact, which created a hemisphere-wide security zone. Under the pact, members agreed to refrain from aggression against each other, as well as to defend one another from outside aggression. The Rio Pact authorizes the use of force to resist aggression if two-thirds of the members vote to do so. Each member nation, however, must consent to the use of its troops in any military action. The Rio Pact was the first formal regional defense agreement concluded under the terms of Article 51 of the United Nations Charter. It also served as a model for the North Atlantic Treaty that created the North Atlantic Treaty Organization (NATO) in 1949.

As the perceived Soviet threat to the Western Hemisphere decreased, the Rio Pact became less important for U.S. foreign policy. For example, Argentina invoked the pact in 1982 to obtain U.S. assistance in the Falklands War against Great Britain, but the United States backed the British in that conflict. However, after the September 11, 2001, terrorist attacks against New York City and Washington, DC, some Western-Hemisphere nations—particularly Brazil—have talked of reviving the Rio Pact in response to the threat of international terrorism. These suggestions have been met with a positive response from the administration of U.S. President George W. Bush.

See also Cold War; Collective Security Communism and National Security; Latin America and U.S. Policy; Monroe Doctrine (1823); Regionalism; Treaties

RISK ASSESSMENT

The process of weighing the potential benefits and drawbacks of a course of action to determine whether to undertake that action. Risk assessment is the initial step in the risk management process and the one that is perhaps not only the most difficult to execute but also most subject to error. The individuals charged with shaping and executing U.S. national security policy constantly engage in risk assessment. Every decision they make that affects the security of the country contains both possible benefits and potential risks. Through risk assessment, decision makers determine whether the potential benefits of the policy outweigh the accompanying risks. After the risks of a course of action have been identified and weighed, decision

makers formulate policy based on their assessment of risk versus reward.

CHALLENGES IN RISK ASSESSMENT

One of the first challenges in risk assessment is identifying all the possible risks and benefits of a course of action. Often a policy can lead to unforeseen consequences that change the final balance of risk and reward. For example, when the Soviet Union invaded Afghanistan in 1979, the United States decided to provide weapons and training to the Afghan defenders. With U.S. support, the Afghans eventually defeated the Soviet invasion. However, U.S. policymakers failed to anticipate that many of the same Afghan fighters would later form the core of the international terrorist group al-Qaeda. Members of al-Qaeda members turned U.S. training and weaponry against their former sponsors, and the group has become one of the principal threats to U.S. security interests.

Another obstacle to accurate risk assessment is weighing the relative importance of the severity of a risky outcome versus the possibility that such an outcome will occur. Which should be granted higher priority when determining policy: a risk that potentially could result in a large loss but has a low probability of occurring, or one that is more likely to happen but would result in a lower potential loss? Making such a determination accurately might require more time and resources than are available to policymakers. These restrictions can contribute to faulty risk assessment and thus faulty decision making.

CASE STUDY: THE BAY OF PIGS

A study of the 1961 Bay of Pigs invasion offers some insights into the difficulties and pitfalls of risk assessment. It also highlights the role of outside factors such as political pressure that can affect the risk assessment process. The failed U.S.-backed invasion of Cuba illustrates how failing to assess adequately the potential risks of a policy can lead to disaster in its implementation.

Background of the Invasion

When communist guerrilla leader Fidel Castro overthrew Cuban dictator Fulgencio Batista in 1959, U.S. leaders were stunned and dismayed. The U.S. government had supported Batista because of his strong anticommunist and pro-United States policies. The presence of a communist, anti–United States regime less than 100 miles from the United States was seen in Washington as a serious threat to U.S. national security. Castro increased U.S. fears when he signed economic and defense agreements with the United States' strategic rival, the Soviet Union. In response to these developments, the administration of U.S. President Dwight D. Eisenhower began to formulate plans to invade Cuba and topple Castro.

The Eisenhower administration worked on plans for the invasion throughout 1960, using the Central Intelligence Agency (CIA) to recruit and train an army of Cuban exiles for the mission. The initial plan called for an amphibious landing near the Cuban city of Trinidad, supported by U.S. air power. The administration hoped the invasion would lead to a popular uprising on the island that would force Castro to flee Cuba.

After John F. Kennedy became the U.S. president in 1961, he approved Eisenhower's plan with several modifications, including moving the invasion site to the Bay of Pigs. The original site was chosen because it was closer to the area in which most of the active anti-Castro forces in Cuba were located. The new location was chosen because the tides there were more favorable for an amphibious landing.

On April 15, 1961, U.S. planes bearing the markings of the Cuban Air Force bombed airfields in Cuba. The following day, some 1,500 Cuban exiles landed on the southern coast of Cuba at the Bay of Pigs. It soon became clear, however, that the plan was going quite poorly. Cuban resistance to the invasion was much tougher than expected, and the hoped-for local uprisings never occurred. Some of Kennedy's military advisers recommended using U.S. air support to help the troubled invaders, but Kennedy refused. He did not want to risk revealing U.S. involvement in the invasion, even though (unknown to Kennedy) the Soviet Union was aware of the plan before the invasion ever started. The invading forces lost some 90 men before surrendering on April 19.

Lessons for Risk Assessment

In hindsight, both the Eisenhower and Kennedy administrations made several erroneous assumptions in assessing the risks of an invasion of Cuba. Perhaps the most significant was their conviction that an invasion would lead to massive anti-Castro sentiment in Cuba. The success of both U.S. plans depended upon the invasion stimulating an anti-Castro uprising.

Although there was a strongly anti-Castro faction on the island, the United States overestimated both its numbers and its influence. By changing the landing site from Trinidad to the Bay of Pigs, the Kennedy administration reduced the already-slim chances of such an uprising occurring.

A second major failure of risk assessment was the belief that the invading forces would be able to support themselves after they landed. U.S. planners believed that the exile army could live off the land with help from the local population. They envisioned the invaders sweeping across Cuba, receiving support and additional recruits from Cubans who wanted to depose Castro. As it turned out, the invaders were no match at all for the Cuban defenders. Only the use of U.S. air power could have saved the invasion from total failure at the start, but political considerations prevented President Kennedy from providing overt U.S. military support. If Kennedy had been aware that the Soviet Union knew of the invasion plans, he may have been less reluctant to use U.S. air power. Lacking that knowledge, Kennedy's desire to keep U.S. involvement a secret sealed the fate of the invasion.

It is clear that both U.S. administrations involved in planning the Bay of Pigs made several errors in risk assessment. They overestimated the likelihood of popular support for the invasion while underestimating the risks should that support fail to materialize. They also placed too much hope for success on the anticipated popular uprising in Cuba. The decision to conceal U.S. involvement meant using a hastily assembled and trained force of amateurs to carry out the invasion. Neither administration properly assessed whether such a ragtag force could succeed against the Cuban army, which U.S. leaders considered inconsequential. This faulty assessment of the relative military capabilities of both sides also contributed to the failure of the invasion.

MODERN FAILURES IN RISK ASSESSMENT

Despite the lessons taught by the Bay of Pigs invasion, U.S. planners have repeatedly made similar mistakes in risk assessment. For example, the U.S. involvement in Vietnam was based upon the assessment that it was riskier to allow South Vietnam to become communist than to commit U.S. troops to defend the pro-West South Vietnamese government. However, the U.S. defeat in Vietnam did not lead to a communist takeover throughout Southeast Asia, as U.S. leaders had predicted. Thirty years after the war, Vietnam is one of only two communist nations in Southeast Asia, and it enjoys friendly relations with the United States.

Flawed risk assessment also contributed to the difficulties faced by occupation forces in Iraq following the 2003 U.S. invasion of that country. Certain elements within the administration of President George W. Bush argued that the Iraqis would welcome invading forces as liberators, and that the country would return to normalcy soon after the invasion. Based on this assessment, they ignored warnings by uniformed military leaders that the U.S. was not committing sufficient troops to maintain order after the invasion. As a result, the occupying forces found themselves unable to deal with widespread looting in the wake of the invasion and unprepared for the guerrilla insurgency that began soon after the fall of the Iraqi regime.

These more recent examples show that despite the vast intelligence resources available to modern national leaders, risk assessment is still a difficult and inexact art. As the world grows increasingly complex and interrelated, predicting all the potential risks, rewards, and consequences of national security policies becomes more difficult. The potential for unforeseen consequences of an action are perhaps greater now than ever. This means that national security planners must be given—and use effectively—as many resources as possible to help assess the risks of U.S. national security policy.

—John Haley

See also Afghan Wars; Bay of Pigs; Iraq War of 2003; Threat Assessment; Vietnam War (1954–1975)

Further Reading

Turner, James T., and Michael G. Gelles. *Threat Assessment: A Risk Management Approach.* Binghampton, NY: Haworth, 2003.

ROGUE STATE

Nation that rejects international law and the conventions of the international community. Rogue states are feared and condemned in the international community (or, at least, other states feel uneasy about their leadership) because they reject international accountability. Their decision-making behavior does not follow traditional, recognized patterns, and it is hard to predict what they will do.

CHARACTERISTICS OF A ROGUE STATE

Numerous behaviors lead the international community to categorize a nation as a rogue state. Some of these pertain to a nation's treatment of its own people, whereas others pertain to its relations with other nations. Often, a combination of both domestic and international outrages can lead to a nation's appellation as a rogue state.

Nations that flagrantly commit human rights abuses against their own citizens or maintain repressive ideologies while ignoring the condemnation of the international community are classified as rogue states. For example, when South Africa was under white minority rule it ignored decades of United Nations Security Council resolutions and international sanctions aimed at its apartheid policies. Under Fidel Castro, Cuba continues to deny its citizens the kinds of rights guaranteed under the First Amendment to the U.S. Constitution.

Other rogue states include North Korea, in which Kim Jong Il (and his father before him) has reduced the nation to extreme poverty while building up an offensive military-industrial complex. Under Saddam Hussein, Iraq was criticized for gassing its Kurdish population and for torturing its citizens. The Taliban government in Afghanistan was criticized for its authoritarianism, in particular its oppressive gender policies, restrictions of free press, and human rights violations.

The Iranian government under the leadership of its fundamentalist Islamic mullahs continues to face similar criticisms. So, too, does the government of Sudan, which in recent years tacitly or overtly supported the displacement and extermination of hundreds of thousands of its black citizens by paramilitary groups loyal to the government.

Although the states mentioned here are often classified as rogue states, other nations engaged in similar activities or abuses might not be classified the same way. This may be the result of political sympathies or because those nations are in the process of attempting to improve freedoms for their citizens.

Numerous kinds of offenses against the international community render a nation a rogue state. Nations that deliberately or illegitimately harm their neighbors; nations that deliberately and consistently flout international law, conventions and norms; and nations that persist in acting unilaterally, without the support of the community of nations, are called rogue states. An example of international harm was the Iraqi invasion of Kuwait in 1990.

Violations of international law and conventions by rogue states are numerous. The United States feels significant threat from such nations, particularly those that are state sponsors of terrorism or provide support to terrorists. For example, Afghanistan under the Taliban government refused to surrender the perpetrators of the September 11, 2001, terrorist attacks. Rogue states can be havens for anti-West terrorist organizations as well; rogue governments have usually declared some form of opposition to the West and are unlikely to examine terror activities too closely.

The pursuit of weapons of mass destruction outside of great power approvals or treaty-based agreements is frowned upon by the international community and contributes to the status of a rogue state. Iran, Libya, and Syria have offensive biological weapons in violation of international treaties, whereas Cuba, North Korea, and the Sudan are suspected of developing them. Several of these states are also developing long-range missiles that could pose a threat to neighboring countries.

THE UNITED STATES AS A ROGUE STATE

One nation consistently identified as a rogue state by some nations is the United States. The United States frequently violates international law and conventions and engages in unilateral action. Its violations of international law include the My Lai massacre during the Vietnam War and the mining of Nicaragua's harbors in the 1980s. The United States also has blatantly intervened in numerous states and ousted (or supported the ousting) of democratically elected governments. In so doing, the United States has violated the sovereignty of other nations. In many cases, the United States has also installed or supported dictators, including the shah of Iran, Pol Pot of Cambodia, Joseph Mobutu of Zaire (now the Democratic Republic of the Congo), and General Augusto Pinochet of Chile.

To the dismay of the international community, the United States refuses to participate in a number of treaty-based international organizations, such as the International Court of Justice and the International Criminal Court. Although the government cites reasons of national security, it has not signed conventions that otherwise have considerable worldwide support, including the 1997 convention on land mines. The United

States has withdrawn from the 1972 Antiballistic Missile (ABM) Treaty and the Kyoto Protocols.

Unilateral action (often considered reckless by the international community) is another characteristic of a rogue state, and it is one more reason why many classify the United States as a rogue nation. Its near-unilateral regime changes in Afghanistan and Iraq, while removing totalitarian regimes, were criticized for their one-sided approach. Since 1945, for example, the United States has attempted to destroy more than 30 national-populist movements with economic and diplomatic pressures or with intervention by the Central Intelligence Agency (CIA).

CONSEQUENCES OF ROGUE STATUS

Rogue states lose a number of benefits by going their own way. Belonging to the community of nations confers some legitimacy, whereas rogue states suffer in the eyes of public opinion. Many states will, and do, refuse to maintain normal diplomatic relations with these states, resulting in political isolation. Because these states frequently refuse to participate in (or are not invited to attend) international conventions, they lose representation in conferences and agreements of worldwide importance.

Many nations refuse to engage in trade with rogue states or they can launch economic sanctions against them. Not only does the rogue state in question lose the opportunity to purchase cheaper or different products from other countries, it is forced to attempt to produce almost everything it needs itself. This task can be difficult because some countries do not have the resources needed to produce advanced technologies, pharmaceuticals, and so on. Overall, rogue states, despite their ability to act without international accountability, lose the opportunity to interact meaningfully with other states, often rendering them pariahs on the world stage.

See also Axis of Evil; Unilateralism

ROOSEVELT COROLLARY

Informal addendum to the Monroe Doctrine articulated by President Theodore Roosevelt stipulating American involvement in Latin America.

In a 1904 address to Congress, President Theodore Roosevelt asserted the right of the United States to exercise international police power and intervene in

Latin America if European debt collectors interfered in the Western Hemisphere. This declaration by the president became known as the Roosevelt Corollary to the Monroe Doctrine because of its implicit warning to Europeans to stay out of Latin America.

Written in 1823, the Monroe Doctrine was a response to increasing European involvement in the affairs of Latin American countries. It cautioned Europeans from any ambitions to colonize Western-Hemisphere territories because this would represent "an unfriendly disposition toward the United States."

The Roosevelt Corollary is notable because it reasserts the Monroe Doctrine. However, it provides justification for U.S. intervention in the western hemisphere. It also rationalizes a U.S. international police role to stabilize Western-Hemisphere countries when deemed necessary.

The Roosevelt Corollary emerged in a climate of increasing European involvement in debt collection in the Western Hemisphere, primarily in the Dominican Republic and Haiti. Both Haiti and the Dominican Republic amassed substantial foreign debt in the late 19th century. The dictator of the Dominican Republic, Ulises Heureaux, in an attempt to prevent his country from falling into bankruptcy, entered into corrupt and complex refinancing schemes with European nations, skimming millions of dollars for himself. Under Heureaux's regime, the Dominican Republic found itself bearing the burden of the crippling debt owed to French and English creditors. Following his assassination in 1896, the Dominican Republic was too weak financially to repay these creditors, and in response, the French and English governments positioned warships in the Caribbean.

These French and English warships signified a European presence that threatened to displace the significant economic and political interests of the United States in the region. Thus, Roosevelt reacted by creating the corollary to the Monroe Doctrine to make clear the U.S. position on European interference.

Similarly, using the justification for intervention outlined in the Roosevelt Corollary, the United States encouraged the Dominican government to seek U.S. assistance for the collection of duties and debt repayment. As a result, the United States assumed responsibility for customs collection in the Dominican Republic. Despite suspicions that Roosevelt and the United States had territorial ambitions in the Western Hemisphere, the president maintained that his sole motive was the recovery of the Dominican economy.

However, scholars have debated whether President Roosevelt's intentions were purely benevolent. In fact, subsequent to the debt crisis in the Dominican Republic, the United States intervened about a dozen times with military force in Latin America. Roosevelt himself avowed that his aim of reasserting the Monroe Doctrine was not for the purpose of U.S. territorial expansion into the region as many critics suggested, but rather an acceptance of responsibility to the United States' neighbors to the south.

However, Theodore Roosevelt's presidency suggests a highly assertive approach to Latin America and the Caribbean. While limiting European interests in the region, Roosevelt worked aggressively to promote U.S. interests in Latin America, including his ambitious project for the Panama Canal. Working to link the Atlantic and the Pacific oceans, Roosevelt supported Panama's separation from Colombia to facilitate the construction of the canal.

See also Latin America and U.S. Policy; Monroe Doctrine (1823); Panama Canal Treaty; Roosevelt, Theodore (1858–1919)

ROOSEVELT, FRANKLIN D., AND NATIONAL POLICY

Thirty-second president of the United States (1933–1945), who served longer than any U.S. president and presided over a period that included the Great Depression and World War II. The policies and decisions of President Franklin D. Roosevelt (1882–1945) had an enormous impact on the future of the United States, both domestically and internationally, and thereby forever affected its national security policies.

President Franklin Delano Roosevelt's views of national security changed significantly over the course of his four terms in office. Domestic economic difficulties were the most serious threat facing the nation when Roosevelt was first elected in 1932. This led him to focus on U.S. domestic problems and to avoid entanglement in European disputes that were threatening to lead to war. By the start of his fourth term, however, Roosevelt was one of the principal leaders of the Allied forces fighting Nazi Germany. During his presidency, Roosevelt thus was forced to move from a philosophy of defense to one of offense to respond to Japanese and German aggression.

When Roosevelt became president in 1933, U.S. foreign policy was one of isolationism. At that time, the United States perceived no significant foreign threats to its security. The armed forces of France and Great

Franklin Delano Roosevelt at the Yalta Conference (1945), flanked by British prime minister Winston Churchill and Soviet premier Joseph Stalin.

Source: Library of Congress.

by providing arms through the so-called cash and carry program, but the nation was not prepared to commit troops or declare war on the Axis powers. At the same time, however, Roosevelt took steps to prepare the country for the possibility of war. After the German conquest of France in 1940, he increased the size of the U.S. Army to 375,000 troops because of German progress in Europe. The year before, he launched the Manhattan Project to develop a nuclear weapon in response to warnings that the Germans were working on such a device.

As German successes mounted, Roosevelt became concerned about the ability of Great Britain, Germany's sole remaining opponent, to hold out. Still, he knew there was little enthusiasm in the United States for entering World War II. In 1940, Roosevelt implemented the Lend-Lease program that supplied weapons and other supplies and equipment to Great Britain to forestall victory by the Axis forces. However, this policy was subject to much criticism from U.S. isolationists. Roosevelt also deepened U.S. involvement in the Atlantic by increasing the Navy's patrols there and by ordering its ships to fire on German U-boats.

The decision about going to war was taken out of Roosevelt's hands on December 7, 1941, when Japanese aircraft attacked the U.S. naval base at Pearl Harbor, Hawaii. Several days after the attack, German leader Adolf Hitler, in a surprising move, declared war on the United States. Within a week, the United States had gone from noninvolvement in foreign conflicts to engagement in a war that spanned most of the globe.

After the United States' entry into World War II, Roosevelt's national security policy focused completely on winning the war in Europe and in the Pacific. To that end, he allied the United States not only with Great Britain but also with the Soviet Union, despite ideological differences and widespread anticommunist sentiment in the United States.

Britain, and the intervening Atlantic Ocean, seemed to isolate the United States from Germany. Although Japan was considered a dangerous rival, it was occupied with a land war in China. In addition, Japan's limited access to important military resources, such as oil and rubber, checked its expansionist tendencies. The Soviet Union, although it was an ideological opponent, was not a serious military rival and was more concerned with internal matters than with foreign policy.

Roosevelt's primary challenge when elected in his first term was to lead the country to economic recovery from the depths of the Great Depression. A stock market crash in 1929 caused widespread bank failures in the early 1930s. Countless families lost their savings, and thousands of businesses went bankrupt, throwing millions of Americans out of work. When Roosevelt was elected, one out of every four Americans was unemployed. During his first two terms in office, Roosevelt refused to become deeply involved in the European affairs, despite increasing pleas from France and Great Britain.

With the outbreak of hostilities in Europe in 1939, Roosevelt decided to walk a fine line between isolationism and interventionism. He made it clear that the United States would help the European democracies

Toward the end of his presidency, Roosevelt concentrated not only on the war effort but also on ensuring peace afterward. This led him to champion the creation of an international organization for collective security. Roosevelt died in April 1945, just months after his fourth inauguration. Although he had articulated no clear vision for the world following the war, he clearly felt that international cooperation was critical for maintaining international stability. He also believed that the great powers, with the creation of an international organization such as the League of Nations, could play a constructive role in preventing future conflict in their respective regions of the world.

See also Isolationism; Lend-Lease; Manhattan Project (1942–1945); Pearl Harbor; World War II (1939–1945); Yalta Conference (1945)

Further Reading

Black, Conrad. *Franklin Delano Roosevelt: Champion of Freedom.* New York: Public Affairs, 2003.

Larrabee, Eric. *Commander in Chief: Franklin Delano Roosevelt, His Lieutenants, and Their War.* Annapolis, MD: Naval Institute Press, 2004.

Young, Nancy Beck, ed. *Franklin D. Roosevelt and the Shaping of American Political Culture.* Armonk, NY: M.E. Sharpe, 2001.

ROOSEVELT, THEODORE (1858–1919)

Twenty-sixth president of the United States; also a noted author, explorer, and political reformer. Theodore Roosevelt was born on October 27, 1858, in New York City. After graduating from Harvard University in 1880, he briefly attended Columbia Law School before abandoning law to pursue politics. In 1881, Roosevelt was elected as a Republican to the New York State Assembly at age 23. In the Assembly, he incurred the wrath of the Tammany Hall politicians who controlled New York City politics. Roosevelt fought bills that would enrich Tammany Democrats, their supporters, and business trusts.

POLITICAL ADVANCES

In 1889, three years after unsuccessfully running for New York City mayor, Roosevelt was appointed to the Civil Service Commission in Washington, DC. He returned to New York City in 1895 as Police Commissioner, a post he held until he was appointed Assistant Secretary of the Navy two years later. Roosevelt rose to national prominence during the 1898 Spanish-American War. He organized the First U.S. Volunteer Cavalry that fought Spanish forces in Cuba, returning home a hero.

Roosevelt was elected governor of New York in 1898, earning a reputation as a political reformer and staunch opponent of corruption and monopolistic business practices. In 1900, Republican presidential candidate William McKinley named Roosevelt as his running mate in the upcoming election. Less than a year later, McKinley was assassinated and Roosevelt became the (then) youngest president in U.S. history. Roosevelt was handily reelected in 1904.

Among Roosevelt's accomplishments were dissolving several large companies for violating antitrust laws, intervening in the 1902 coal strike, and securing the passage of the Elkins Law (1903), which denied rebates to favored corporations. Roosevelt also extended the jurisdiction of the Interstate Commerce Commission, obtained passage of the Food and Drug Act, created the Department of Commerce and Labor, and initiated several laws protecting workers.

Roosevelt was an avid environmentalist who limited mining and lumber operations that were exhausting natural resources at an alarming rate. He set aside millions of acres of land for public use, creating several national parks. He also championed seminal conservation legislation, including the Reclamation Act of 1902.

FOREIGN AFFAIRS

Roosevelt increased the power of the presidency in the foreign affairs arena as well. He coined the phrase walk softly and carry a big stick, which aptly describes his foreign policy. This was especially true in the Western Hemisphere, where he sought to solidify the position of the United States as a world power.

Potential European intervention in South America and the Caribbean led Roosevelt to formulate what is known as the Roosevelt Corollary to the Monroe Doctrine. This stated that the United States had a direct interest and obligation to impose order in the affairs of Latin American countries. The concept of *dollars for democracy* was born during Roosevelt's tenure, a policy of using financial incentives to U.S.-friendly regimes in Latin America.

A typical example of Roosevelt's Latin American policy was his action in response to Colombia's refusal to ratify the Hay-Herran Treaty in 1903. The treaty recognized the independence of the territory that is now Panama, which was in rebellion against Colombia. Roosevelt dispatched the warship USS *Nashville* to prevent Colombian troops from landing in Panama, thus assuring the success of the Panamanian revolution. Roosevelt quickly extended diplomatic recognition to the new republic, and soon afterward construction of the Panama Canal began, thus providing a financial boon to the new nation.

Roosevelt was proactive in world affairs as well. He is credited with opening U.S. relations with China and he was awarded the 1906 Nobel Peace Prize for organizing the conference that ended the Russo-Japanese War in 1904. Roosevelt was an ardent supporter of the World Court at The Hague, the Netherlands, and was an effective diplomat. In 1907, he made a gentleman's agreement with the Japanese to discourage emigration of laborers to the United States, thus reducing tensions created by several anti-Japanese laws passed by the California legislature.

LATER CAREER

In 1908, Roosevelt practically ordained his successor as president, William Howard Taft. However, Roosevelt felt betrayed by many of Taft's policies, especially his lenient attitude toward corrupt business practices. Thus, Roosevelt ran as a third-party presidential candidate on the Progressive (or Bull Moose) Party platform in 1912. Many Republicans voted for Roosevelt instead of Taft, splitting the Republican vote and assuring the election of Democratic nominee Woodrow Wilson. Four years later, Roosevelt made a final unsuccessful bid for the Republican nomination for president.

During his remarkable career, Roosevelt found time for big game hunting and exploration, most notably a 1913 trip to the Amazon, during which the River of Doubt was renamed *Rio Teodoro* in his honor. He was also the author of some 40 books. His most famous work is a four-volume set titled *The Winning of the West*. Roosevelt also authored books on politics, hunting, the military, biographies of American politicians, and exploration. His autobiography was published in 1913.

See also Monroe Doctrine (1823); Panama Canal Treaty; Roosevelt Corollary; Spanish-American War (1898)

Further Reading

Grondahl, Paul. *I Rose Like a Rocket: The Political Education of Theodore Roosevelt.* New York: Free Press, 2004.

RUBY RIDGE

In August 1992, incident in which FBI agents and federal marshals engaged in an 11-day standoff with self-proclaimed white separatist Randy Weaver, his family, and a friend named Kevin Harris, in a remote cabin in Ruby Ridge, Idaho. Weaver's wife, Vicki, his 14-year-old son, Sammy, and U.S. Marshal William Degan were killed during the siege. Harris and Weaver were injured. A Justice Department review and Senate hearings were critical of the way the Federal Bureau of Investigation (FBI) handled the case.

Randy Weaver was a former Army engineer with special forces training. His wife and children—Sammy, Sara, and Rachel—moved in 1983 to a cabin he built on Ruby Ridge in Idaho, about 40 miles from the Canadian border. Another daughter, Elisheba, was born there, and Harris joined the family later.

Weaver's troubles with the federal government began when he attended several meetings of the white supremacist group the Aryan Nation at the group's compound in Hayden Lake, Idaho, in the late 1980s. Weaver was not a member of the Aryan Nation, but he shared a similar ideology. At one of the meetings, Weaver befriended an informant of the Bureau of Alcohol, Tobacco and Firearms (ATF), who purchased two sawed-off shotguns from Weaver in October 1989.

When Weaver refused to become an informant for the ATF, federal agents pursued a weapons charge against him. A magistrate released Weaver after his arrest, setting a trial date for February 19, 1991. The trial was then moved to February 20, but a probation officer sent a letter to Weaver, incorrectly stating that the trial date was March 20. When Weaver failed to appear for trial, the court issued a bench warrant for his arrest. Weaver was subsequently indicted by a federal grand jury for failing to appear at trial.

On August 21, 1992, the situation turned violent. Weaver's dog discovered federal marshals hiding on the Ruby Ridge property. Federal marshal Art Roderick shot the dog. Sammy Weaver returned fire and was shot in the back by Federal Marshal Larry Cooper, who later claimed the shooting was accidental. Soon after, Harris killed Deputy Marshal William Degan in an armed exchange that included Randy Weaver.

After the shootings, the federal marshals requested assistance from the FBI, which dispatched its elite Hostage Rescue unit to Ruby Ridge. (The Justice Department investigation conducted after the incident was critical of the FBI for failing to gather sufficient intelligence and for not ordering the residents of the cabin to surrender before engaging them in a firefight.)

On August 22, FBI sniper Lon Horiuchi, hiding about 200 yards from the cabin at Ruby Ridge, fired two rounds. The first shot hit Randy Weaver in the arm. The second shot was meant for Harris, but struck Vicki Weaver in the face while she held her infant daughter behind the front door of the cabin. Vicki Weaver died soon after, but her body remained in the cabin for 11 days.

Weaver and Harris finally surrendered to the federal officers about a week later. They were charged with a host of crimes, including murder, conspiracy, and assault. An Idaho jury acquitted Harris of all charges. Weaver was convicted of failing to appear for the original firearms charge.

The Justice Department inquiry—differing from a separate FBI report—concluded that FBI agent Hourichi's second shot was unconstitutional because Harris and Weaver were running for cover and could not be considered imminent threats. The inquiry further alleged that Hourichi unnecessarily endangered others by firing at the door of the cabin. The agent was later acquitted of manslaughter charges brought by Boundary County, Idaho, prosecutors.

Federal investigators ruled that there was insignificant evidence to charge Larry Potts, then deputy director of the FBI, and other top officials with conspiring to cover up the botched operation. In 1995, the government settled a lawsuit brought by Randy Weaver and his three surviving daughters.

See also Federal Bureau of Investigation (FBI); Militia

Further Reading

Bock, Alan W. *Ambush at Ruby Ridge: How the Government Set Randy Weaver Up and Took His Family Down.* Irvine, CA: National Book Network, 1995.

Walter, J. *Ruby Ridge: The Truth and Tragedy of Randy Weaver.* New York: HarperCollins, 2001.

RUDMAN-HART COMMISSION

See NATIONAL SECURITY, U.S. COMMISSION ON (USCNS)

RULES OF ENGAGEMENT

Directives meant to describe the circumstances under which ground, naval, and air forces will enter into and continue combat with opposing forces. Formally, rules of engagement refer to the orders issued by a competent military authority with reference to when, where, how, and against whom military force may be used. Rules of engagement are part of a general recognition that procedures and standards are essential to the conduct and effectiveness of civilized warfare. These rules have implications for what actions soldiers may take on their own authority and what directives may be issued by a commanding officer.

Rules of engagement must be consistent, attempt to account for expected scenarios, and reflect an understanding of both the political and military aspects of a given situation. They might describe points with regard to dealing with unarmed mobs, the property of local civilians, the use of force in self-defense, the returning of hostile fire, the taking of prisoners, the level of hostility (that is, whether the country is at war), as well as a number of other issues.

The notion that war should be regulated has a long history in international treaties and agreements, the most significant being the Geneva Conventions, which regulate the treatment of prisoners and civilians in time of war. However, rules of engagement are a more modern concept. They are the product of fears concerning the possibility of nuclear warfare, advances in telecommunications, the role of the media in modern conflicts, and the increased use of military forces in a peacekeeping role.

During the Cold War, both superpowers realized that the potential advantages of attacking were not worth the consequences of retaliation. The possibility that a minor incident could result in nuclear warfare inspired a need to establish procedures defining allowable actions. At the same time, technological advances allowed for greater possibilities in monitoring what was taking place on the battlefield, tightening the chain of command. These same advances also created a more prominent role for the media. The tendency of war correspondents to make political leaders responsible for military excesses, first clearly evident in the Vietnam War, led to greater concern for regulating events on the ground.

The Vietnam War has since become a commonly cited example to describe the problems of requiring soldiers to fulfill an ambiguous set of objectives. It was also during this time that the acronym ROE (for rules of engagement) became broadly familiar. However, the concept of a standing order not to return fire without a clear target began with the U.S. intervention in Lebanon in 1958. The subsequent U.S. intervention in the Dominican Republic in 1965–66 also required restraint, and American soldiers became increasingly familiar with ROE. The standard operating procedures imposed on U.S. troops during the Vietnam War resulted in accusations that domestic concerns were inhibiting the military's freedom of operation.

Since the bombing of a U.S. Marine headquarters in Beirut, Lebanon, in 1983, a caveat has been added to the ROE, stating, "Nothing in these rules limits your right to exercise your inherent right of self-defense." There was also the development of peacetime rules of engagement (PROE), which differentiated between hostile acts versus intent, and also emphasized proportionality—that a response must be appropriate to the level of threat.

In 1994, PROE was replaced by Joint Chiefs of Staff standing ROE (JCS SROE), which instructs that use of force must also be consistent with international law. The two commonly recognized ROE are standing ROE (SROE), which refers to situations in which the United States is not actually at war and thus seeks to constrain military action, and wartime ROE (WROE), which does not limit military responses to offensive actions.

See also Geneva Conventions; Military Doctrine

Further Reading

Biddle, Stephen D. *Military Power: Explaining Victory and Defeat in Modern Battle.* Princeton, NJ: Princeton University Press, 2004.

Echevarria, Antulio Joseph. *Clausewitz's Center of Gravity: Changing Our Warfighting Doctrine—Again!* Carlisle, PA: Strategic Studies Institute, U.S. Army War College, 2002.

RUMSFELD, DONALD (1932–)

An experienced Washington insider, appointed secretary of defense in 2001 by President George W. Bush. Donald Rumsfeld previously occupied that office from 1975–1977, and his early handling of the Defense Department as an experienced administrator later deteriorated under the pressure of serious national defense issues.

Born in 1932, Donald Henry Rumsfeld grew up in Chicago, Illinois, and graduated in 1954 from Princeton University. He served briefly in the Navy as an aviator and then began pursuing political aspirations. Starting as a staffer to members of Congress from Ohio and Michigan in 1958 and 1959, he took a three-year break as an investment broker in Chicago before winning election to Congress as a Republican from Illinois in 1962.

In 1969, Rumsfeld resigned his congressional seat to join the White House staff of President Richard Nixon. He served as special assistant for economic opportunity for less than a year before becoming an adviser to the president for the next three years. Appointed Ambassador to the North Atlantic Treaty Organization (NATO) in 1973, Rumsfeld departed the White House just before the Watergate scandal reached crisis level.

During the administration of President Gerald Ford, Rumsfeld served as chief of staff before becoming secretary of defense in 1975. In 1977, Rumsfeld removed himself from government for several years, serving as a corporate CEO. However, he sometimes also served on special commissions, such as arms control adviser (1983–84), presidential envoy to the Middle East (1983–84), and chairman of the Commission to Assess United States National Security, Space Management, and Organization (1999–2001). This last group recommended in its January 11, 2001, report that the United States needed a ballistic missile defense program, effectively reviving the moribund Strategic Defense Initiative (SDI)—the so-called Star Wars of the administration of President Ronald Reagan.

While in the business world, Rumsfeld retained close enough connections with Republican party members to win a nod from Vice President Dick Cheney in 2000 for the defense cabinet post in the newly formed cabinet of President George W. Bush. Because the Bush administration had few defense policy initiatives in mind besides missile defense and the substitution of advanced technology war fighting systems for programmed defense expenditures (the so-called Transformation Defense Initiatives), Rumsfeld was ideally suited for the chief defense position.

However, the military service chiefs soon registered dismay with Rumsfeld's single-minded approach to defense programming. The money needed to revive ballistic missile defense programs and kick start the ill-defined Transformation Defense Initiatives would leave little for the desired modernization and operations budgets that were already in the defense plans but lacked sufficient funding to accomplish. In addition, Rumsfeld displayed a sense of intellectual and managerial superiority as a former defense chief, seen as arrogance by some, an attitude that left the service chiefs and their staffs baffled.

After only six months of mutual discomfort, the Pentagon had to respond to the September 11, 2001, attack by terrorists upon the United States. It became necessary to correct homeland defense weaknesses while also devising a campaign to occupy Afghanistan and eradicate the terrorist centers there. Additionally, the Defense Department had to expand the scope of military operations to plan the defeat and occupation of Iraq within a year of initiating operations against Afghanistan.

Defense spending soared under these wartime conditions, and at first, it seemed as if the conventional force modernization would be funded after all. However, the nation's deepening economic crisis, national debt, and unending demands for military operations after the poorly planned Iraq campaign made program cuts seemingly inevitable. By mid-2004, Rumsfeld's originally confident management style met with heavy criticism, although he continued to enjoy the strong support of President Bush.

See also Afghanistan, War in; Bush, George W., and National Policy; Cheney, Richard (1941–); Civil-Military Relations; Defense Budgeting; Department of Defense, U.S (DoD); Iraq War of 2003; Office of the Secretary of Defense (OSD); Pentagon; Terrorism, War on International

S

SADDAM HUSSEIN, (1937–)

President of Iraq from 1979 to 2003. Saddam Hussein was born April 28, 1937, to a poor family near Tikrit, Iraq. He joined the Ba'ath Party at the age of 20 and participated in the party's coup on July 17, 1968. Saddam rose to the top of the party, assuming the Iraqi presidency in 1979. From 1980 to 1988, he oversaw the Iran-Iraq War, a protracted conflict remembered for the indiscriminate use of chemical weapons by both sides. In 1991, Saddam invaded Kuwait, setting off the first Gulf War.

Under his repressive dictatorship, the economic and human rights conditions deteriorated for average Iraqi citizens. Saddam used chemical weapons against the Kurdish populations in northern Iraq and brutally squelched an uprising by the Shia Iraqis in the southern part of the country. Throughout the 1990s, Saddam refused to fully cooperate with the international community and its inspectors to eliminate the threat of chemical weapons under his control. The resulting sanctions only exacerbated the plight of most Iraqis.

In 2003, acting on the belief that Saddam still possessed chemical and biological weapons, was attempting to develop nuclear weapons, and had friendly relations with the international terrorist group al-Qaeda, a U.S.-led coalition invaded Iraq to liberate its citizens. Saddam was captured by U.S. forces on December 13, 2003. Currently, the former dictator is awaiting trial in an Iraqi court.

See also Gulf War (1990–1991); Iraq War of 2003

SALT I AND II
See STRATEGIC ARMS LIMITATION TALKS (SALT)

SATELLITE RECONNAISSANCE

Use of satellites equipped with photo-optic, electro-optic/infrared, or radar technology to provide detailed reports of geographical areas, military installations and activities, troop positions, or other picture-based intelligence. Satellite reconnaissance relies on data provided by image intelligence (IMINT) satellites, which operate in low, near-polar orbits at an altitude of between 500 and 3,000 km and maintain the same orbit around the earth. They make about 14 revolutions per day and scan a new swath of ground with each orbit.

The IMINT satellites depend on three general technologies. Using *photo-optic* technology, an image is recorded on film, which must then be retrieved, processed, and analyzed. Because there is a one-to-three-day time lag from the time the data is requested to the time the image can be used, photo-optic satellites are more useful for strategic planning than for tactical combat situations. Photo-optic satellites cannot penetrate clouds or darkness and can be fooled by camouflage.

Electro-optic/infrared (EO-IR) satellites provide full-spectrum photographic imagery, including infrared. Images from EO-IR satellites can be further sharpened and defined through digital enhancement. Although IR sensors can spot heat sources at night,

The northern VIP palace of former Iraqi leader Saddam Hussein, which was looted and vandalized by Iraqis during the Iraq War in 2003. Located in the city of Mosul, the palace, one of many owned by Saddam Hussein, was occupied by the 101st Airborne Division as a command-post headquarters after U.S. forces captured the city. The occupation of the palace and its grounds was part of a shifting of operations from Baghdad, the Iraqi capital, to Mosul to help ensure the security of that city. The entire site, which occupies 2.6 square miles, includes several palaces and other residences as well as three lakes and artificial waterfalls.

Source: U.S. Army.

they cannot spot vehicles or aircraft on the ground once their engines are cold. Like photo-optic satellites, EO-IR satellites are unable to penetrate clouds and darkness and are only slightly less likely to be fooled by camouflage. IR sensors can also be fooled by dummy heat sources and can be blocked to some degree by special IR-netting.

In satellites using *radar* technology, an image is created by high-energy radar pulses reflected off the earth's surface. Synthetic aperture radar technology, a technique used to generate radar images in fine detail, allows imaging at any time of day or night. Long wavelengths allow penetration of cloud cover and imagery even in dusty conditions. Doppler-radar technology is used to spot movement of ships and aircraft, and ground moving-target indication (GMTI) radar is useful for detecting ground movement of vehicles. Radar ocean reconnaissance satellites (RORSAT) are primarily used over oceanic regions to search for shipping. Resolution is not as good with radar satellites as

with photo-optic or EO-IR satellites, however, and analyzing the imagery requires a higher level of skill. Images can also be subject to noise due to backscatter (a form of electronic static) caused by unfavorable conditions such as rough seas or nearby large, metallic surfaces. Radar satellites are also susceptible to active jamming.

One of the most significant advances in IMINT technology has had to do not with the platform in space but with the manipulation of the digital data derived from these satellites. The National Imagery and Mapping Agency, which was set up to centralize the research, development, and analysis of satellite imagery, can now configure data in three-dimensional format. These so-called *envisions*, computer- generated 3D animations of terrain and landscapes, are valuable not just in warfare but also in mission rehearsals of military and intelligence operations. The animations can help policymakers gain both diplomatic leverage in negotiations and understand problems faced by peacekeepers or soldiers prior to deployment.

The National Reconnaissance Office (NRO), established in 1960, is the U.S. government agency responsible for designing, building, and operating U.S. reconnaissance satellites. The NRO is a separate operating agency of the Department of Defense (DoD) and is jointly managed and staffed by the DoD and the Central Intelligence Agency (CIA). The Director of Central Intelligence establishes the NRO's data collection priorities and requirements.

In addition to the DoD and the CIA, other government agencies that work closely with the NRO in maintaining the U.S. satellite reconnaissance program include the National Security Agency, the National Geospatial-Intelligence Agency, the Defense Intelligence Agency, the Central MASINT (measurements and signatures intelligence) Office, and the United States Space Command. In addition, six Congressional committees oversee NRO programs and activities. The NRO is funded through the National Reconnaissance Program, part of the National Foreign Intelligence Program. In recent years, the NRO has implemented a series of actions declassifying some of its operations. In December 1996, for the first time, the NRO announced the launch of a reconnaissance satellite in advance.

National and military leaders rely on data from reconnaissance satellites to provide warning of potential military aggression, monitor weapons of mass destruction programs, track terrorists, enforce arms control and environmental treaties, and assess the impact of natural and man-made disasters. Advances in weaponry, space, communications, and information technology have made possible near real-time information support for military personnel, arms proliferation issues, and counterterrorism efforts.

In 1996, in response to a recommendation from an independent panel of experts from the defense, intelligence, and corporate sectors, the NRO adopted a goal of devoting 10% of its budget to research and development. Technology-sharing programs were also developed with the Department of Defense and with NASA. Two recent technological advances were the Geosynchronous Lightweight Technology Experiment (GeoLITE) and the Space Technology Experiment (STEX). GeoLITE explored advanced satellite communications methods and STEX demonstrated multiple leading-edge spacecraft technologies.

Additional new technologies significantly advanced civil and military space programs and had commercial benefits as well. These include visual display technology for high definition television (HDTV), optical instruments for personal camcorders, advanced integrated circuit chips and micro devices for personal computers, communications technology for the Internet, and imagery exploitation technology for medical screening.

See also Defense Intelligence Agency (DIA); Geopolitical Intelligence; Geospatial Mapping; Intelligence and Counterintelligence; Radar (Radio Detection and Ranging); Science, Technology, and Security; Spy Satellites

SCHELLING, THOMAS (1921–)

Distinguished university professor and professor of economics who, using game theory, contributed to the development of such concepts as bargaining and strategic behavior applied to diplomacy of war and peace. Schelling's research interests include military strategy and arms control, conflict and bargaining theory, nuclear proliferation, energy and environmental policy, climate change, smoking behavior, international trade, and ethical issues in policy and in business.

Born in 1921, Schelling earned a degree in economics at the University of California, Berkeley in 1944, before starting his career at the U.S. Bureau of the Budget. He worked with the Marshall Plan to rebuild Europe between 1948 and 1951 and then joined the Executive Office of the President at the White House, where he served until 1953. In 1951, Schelling obtained a Ph.D. in economics at Harvard University.

In 1953, Schelling joined Yale University as professor of economics. Five years later, in 1958, he moved to Harvard, where in 1969 he became Lucius N. Littauer Professor of Political Economy at the John F. Kennedy School of Government. At Harvard, Schelling also directed the Institute for the Study of Smoking Behavior and Policy from 1984 to 1990. In 1990, he joined the Maryland School of Public Affairs at the University of Maryland.

In his 1960 work, *The Strategy of Conflict,* Schelling pioneered the study of bargaining and strategic behavior. The book was considered among the most influential on strategic studies since 1945. Schelling studied strategy and bargaining situations in international conflict by applying game theory. He saw bargaining as a game in which it is important to think what the opponent can do, how one can react, and how the opponent will react to one's behavior. In these situations, threats and promises may have important strategic effects.

According to Schelling, a threat is a communication of one's incentives, designed to impress on another party the automatic consequences of an action. For example, a threat of retaliation may prevent a country from starting a war, or, in an economic context, it may prevent a company from starting a competitive price war. The efficacy of a threat depends to large extent on its credibility, which is built on the incentives of the player who threatens to carry out the threat. In this context, reputation plays an important role. It tells if one should believe that a player keeps his promises. A threat without credibility has no strategic value.

Schelling further developed these concepts in *Strategy and Arms Control,* published in 1961. In

1966, in his work, *Arms and Influence,* he applied these notions to military power and the diplomacy of war and peace. In his 1978 work, *Micromotives and Macrobehavior,* Schelling analyzed how minor decisions of individuals may interact in such a way that they have serious consequences at the macro level.

During his career, Schelling was elected to numerous prestigious institutions, including the National Academy of Sciences, the Institute of Medicine, the American Academy of Arts and Sciences, the American Economic Association, and the Eastern Economic Association. He also served as chairman of the advisory committee of the Institute for Social and Economic Policy in the Middle East at Harvard University and as a member of the Board of Trustees of the Albert Einstein Institution, a nonprofit organization devoted to the study of nonviolent political action.

See also Brinkmanship; Deterrence; Strategic Culture; Zero Sum Game

SCHWARZKOPF, NORMAN
See GULF WAR (1990–1991)

SCIENCE, TECHNOLOGY, AND SECURITY

The exploitation of science and technology in the furtherance of the U.S. national security interests. Science and technology (S&T) development is obviously crucial to national security issues and to the international diplomatic agenda of the United States. The U.S. government, through the Department of State, frequently interacts with other governments under conditions in which technological capabilities are central to the deliberations. In addition, new technologies and scientific advances are critical to the maintenance of U.S. intelligence, military efforts, and antiterrorism strategies.

THE DEPARTMENT OF DEFENCE (DOD)

Most of the science and technology efforts that are critical to national security are conducted by the U.S. Department of Defense (DoD). Anita Jones, Director of Defense Research and Engineering for DoD, reported that in 2005 the DoD funded 16 percent of the total federal investment in research and development. These activities include basic research, applied research, and development of advanced technology. Currently, most of the DoD emphasis is on the development of advanced technologies. The department dominates federal investment in areas including computer science; materials; electrical, mechanical, and civil engineering; and mathematics.

The DoD science and technology effort involves numerous agencies. These include the Defense Advanced Research Projects Agency (DARPA), which developed the computer networking technology that led to creation of the Internet; the Defense Technical Information center (DTIC), which is responsible for the transfer of information among DoD personnel, defense contractors and potential contractors, and other government agencies; and the Information Science and Technology Directorate, which is responsible for exploring new technologies and determining the department's technology needs.

Responsibility for overseeing the DoD's technology efforts rests with the director of Defense Research and Engineering in the Office of the Secretary of Defense. Individual research initiatives are managed by the Service Research Offices, which include the Army Research Office (ARO), the Office of Naval Research (ONR), the Air Force Office of Scientific Research (AFOSR), the Defense Advanced Research Projects Agency (DARPA), the Ballistic Missiles Defense Organization (BMDO), the National Security Agency (NSA), and the Army Corps of Engineers (COE). The director of research also coordinates basic research activities with the National Science Foundation (NSF) and other federal departments and agencies.

THE STATE DEPARTMENT

The Department of State is responsible for ensuring that S&T considerations are integrated into U.S. foreign policy. It is also charged with identifying and exploiting opportunities for international cooperation involving the U.S. science community. Science and technology play a critical role in foreign policy discussions of topics such as nuclear nonproliferation, arms control, the use of outer space, population growth, adequate and safe food supplies, infectious diseases, energy resources, and the competitiveness of industrial technologies.

The Department of State has several internal departments involved in S&T issues. The Arms Control and Disarmament Agency is responsible for building sound science into national security policies such as arms control, export controls, and nonproliferation. The Bureau of Oceans and International Environmental and Scientific Affairs (OES) often leads international negotiations on issues such as the building and operation of an international space station or controlling substances that deplete the stratospheric ozone layer and cause global climate changes. OES has negotiated international umbrella agreements to create a network of advisory and regulatory mechanisms to protect oceans and fisheries.

A 1999 report by the National Academy of Sciences and the National Research Council made several recommendations to improve government collaboration with the scientific community. Among these suggestions was the appointment of a science and technology advisor with direct access to the secretary of state and other senior officials. The adviser leads a department-wide initiative called "Science and Diplomacy: Strengthening State for the Twenty-First Century." Its core objectives include increasing the number of scientists in the department and exposing lay personnel to S&T issues; building partnerships with the S&T community, other government agencies, and foreign partners; providing the department with accurate advice on emerging S&T; and creating an environment that fosters proactive decision making, as opposed to reactive crisis management, on S&T issues.

THE CENTRAL INTELLIGENCE AGENCY

The exploitation of science and technology has always been a significant element of Central Intelligence Agency (CIA) activities. The CIA's S&T efforts have been responsible for the design and operation of some of the United States' most important spy satellites and for the U2 and A-12 spy planes. The agency is heavily involved in the collection of signals intelligence (SIGINT) and helped pioneer the technical analysis of foreign missile and space systems. Its satellites and SIGINT activities are vital to intelligence analysts in assessing the capabilities of foreign weapons systems. It is also responsible for a number of scientific advances—including a key component of heart pacemaker technology—that have been made available for medical and other purposes.

The CIA's S&T efforts have also led to some less noble activities. Among the CIA's early scientific interests were special interrogation methods, including the use of drugs and chemicals, hypnosis, and isolation. Experiments in the 1950s led to the suicide of Frank Olson, an Army scientist, after he was given LSD without his knowledge as part of a CIA program. Poison pens and exploding seashells were designed in futile attempts to assassinate Cuban leader Fidel Castro. The CIA funded the attempts of alleged psychics to report on activities at Soviet military facilities by "viewing" those activities from California and sought to employ cats and birds for intelligence collection—in one case implanting assorted equipment in a cat to turn it into a mobile, controllable, bugging device.

SCIENCE AND TECHNOLOGY POST–SEPTEMBER 11

Since the terrorist attacks on September 11, 2001, the challenge of balancing the nation's national security with the openness required for the advancement of science has become increasingly complicated. This has led to several changes in the treatment of visiting scientists as well as government procedures for dealing with technology firms.

Due to concerns about terrorism, foreign students and scholars in S&T fields are finding it increasingly difficult to obtain visas to study or work in the United States. The USA PATRIOT Act of 2001 and the Enhanced Border Security and Visa Entry Reform Act of 2002 tightened both the requirements and the enforcement of entry procedures for foreign visitors. In 2001, the Student and Exchange Visitor Information System was created to allow officials to maintain up-to-date information on foreign students and exchange visitors in the United States. Various surveys conducted since 2001 have indicated declines in the number of foreign students enrolling in U.S. educational institutions. Increased security has even kept many foreign students and scholars from attending brief academic meetings in the United States.

The two main restrictions scientists and their institutions are encountering in contracts and grants in the post–September 11 era are tighter prepublication reviews and background checks on foreign collaborators. The federal government is now more likely than previously, to intervene in "sensitive but unclassified" research, implementing procedures such as requiring special permits and clearances for all projects with foreign workers. Since September 11, the scientific community also must seriously consider whether and to what extent to restrict the publication of certain studies that may compromise national security.

Critics of such measures argue that the free flow of ideas and unhindered exchange of information is vital for the health of the scientific community. They worry that these restrictions will hamper the creativity and vitality of U.S. scientists. Supporters of the restrictions point out that the unprecedented ease with which dangerous technology information can be acquired or spread requires caution to avoid having it fall into the wrong hands. The resolution of this debate is certain to have a significant effect on the conduct of U.S. scientific and technological research in the 21st century.

See also Defense Advanced Research Projects Agency (DARPA); Dual-Use Technology; Information Warfare; Nanotechnology; Signals Intelligence (SIGINT); Spy Satellites

Further Reading

Burgleman, Robert, Clayton M. Christensen, and Steven C. Wheelwright. *Strategic Management of Technology and Innovation.* New York: McGraw-Hill, 2003.
Skolnikoff, Eugene B. *The Elusive Transformation: Science, Technology, and the Evolution of International Politics.* Princeton, NJ: Princeton University Press, 1994.

SEA-LAUNCHED BALLISTIC MISSILES (SLBMs)

In the event of a nuclear war or other threat to U.S. national security, missiles capable of being launched from nuclear submarines. Nuclear submarines form one-third of the strategic nuclear triad, along with land-based missiles and bombers. The advantage of launching missiles from submarines is that the missiles may be dispersed across a wide area, making it essentially impossible to destroy them all at once. The disadvantage is that communication with nuclear submarines enables the detection of the submarine's location; also submarine-launched missiles are less accurate than those launched from land.

Sea-launched ballistic missiles are carried by Ohio class, Trident submarines, the largest submarines deployed by the U.S. Navy, second in size only to Russian Typhoon submarines. These submarines,

specifically designed for extended patrols at sea, are equipped with Trident Intercontinental Ballistic Missiles (ICBMs), which are designated as sea-launched ballistic missiles (SLBMs).

Missile launch from a submarine occurs below the ocean's surface. However, the missile never makes contact with the water because it is surrounded by a bubble of gas. Gas pressure ejects the missile from its launch tube within the submarine. The first Trident was deployed in 1979, and the first Trident II in 1990; the Trident II is expected to be in service until the year 2020.

See also Ballistic Missiles; Submarines

Further Reading

Mosher, David. *Rethinking the Trident Force.* Washington, DC: Congressional Budget Office, 1993.
Spinardi, Graham, with Steve Smith, Thomas Biersteker, Chris Brown, Phil Cerny, and A. J. R. Groom, eds. *From Polaris to Trident: The Development of U.S. Fleet Ballistic Missile Technology.* New York: Cambridge University Press, 1994.

SEA WARFARE
See ANTISUBMARINE WARFARE (ASW); SUBMARINE WARFARE

SEALIFT

Maritime transportation of equipment and troops to sustain and augment military forces deployed overseas during war or peacetime. During wartime, as much as 95% of the equipment needed for fighting forces to operate at the battlefronts is transported by sea. Sealift has several key advantages over airlift, the other key method for transporting troops and materiel.

Unit for unit, ships involved in sealift have a greater capacity than transport aircraft. Ships can also preposition at a friendly port or at sea near an area of potential conflict. Furthermore, ships that travel in international waters do not require permission to operate from foreign governments.

In the United States, the Military Sealift Command (MSC) is responsible for all stages of sealift. Its responsibilities include planning, requisition of crews and ships, and execution of its duties in support of U.S. forces around the globe.

STRATEGIES

The Military Sealift Command embraces three operational strategies in its mission of maritime transportation of military cargo in both peacetime and wartime. The first of these strategies is *prepositioning,* the strategic location of transport ships, manned with necessary logistical support, near a crisis area. A second strategy, *surge shipping,* is the transportation of urgently needed supplies and equipment, such as tanks and helicopters, in the critical early stages of a conflict. *Sustainment shipping,* the third strategy, provides a constant supply pipeline by transporting the weapons, food, and other equipment needed by forces in the field to sustain the conflict.

FORCE STRUCTURE AND SIZE

The MSC, which employs roughly 7,500 personnel worldwide, is headquartered in Washington, DC, and has area commands in Norfolk, Virginia; San Diego, California; Naples, Italy; and Yokohama, Japan. Most of its personnel are assigned to seagoing jobs, and approximately 4,700 are civilian employees of the federal government. MSC ships are crewed by civilians, but manpower may be augmented by naval reservists during wartime.

The Military Sealift Command currently operates about 120 ships worldwide, with an additional 100 ships in reserve status. These include government-owned ships and privately owned charters. In addition, the MSC also commands hospital ships, fast sealift ships, which transport armored equipment to combat theaters in minimal time, and maritime prepositioning ships, which are positioned at overseas strategic locations and contain equipment and supplies for the support of armed forces in areas of conflict.

The MSC also commands the Naval Fleet Auxiliary Force (NFAF), which deploys nearly 40 ships around the world in direct support of U.S. naval ships. The NFAF ships conduct towing and salvage operations in addition to their central responsibility of underway replenishment.

HISTORY

Maritime transportation of supplies and equipment in support of forces deployed overseas is as old as sailing itself. Ancient Egyptian vessels plied the Nile River, transporting troops and supplies in periods of external conflict and civil war. Roman galleys crossed the Mediterranean Sea, transporting diplomats, troops, and supplies to distant colonies. The conquest of England by William the Conqueror in 1066 is a notable early example of a successful sealift operation.

In the 20th century, both World Wars saw sealift operations take the form of convoy systems to transport equipment and supplies to an embattled Europe. Despite threats from German U-boats, tens of millions of tons of supplies crossed the Atlantic. The U.S. island-hopping campaign against Japanese forces in the Pacific is an example of sealift operations on an epic scale. During World War II, the industrial might of the United States was transported across two oceans to vanquish two powerful, committed enemies.

Although four separate government agencies controlled sealift for the United States in World War II, sealift command functions were combined in 1949 under the Military Sea Transportation Service (MSTS). The MSTS was renamed the Military Sealift Command (MSC) in 1970.

During Operation Desert Storm in the Gulf War, the MSC distinguished itself by undertaking the largest sealift operations of any coalition nation. More than 12 million tons of equipment—including tanks, helicopters, and supplies—were delivered to the combat zone in support of forces charged with expelling Iraqi forces from occupied Kuwait.

Military Sealift Command ships also took on the task of delivering humanitarian aid during the ill-fated Somalia intervention of 1992 to 1994. Today, the MSC continues to supply U.S. fighting forces in the aftermath of the Iraq War of 2003, with equipment and supplies ranging from ammunition to helicopters.

The rise of international terrorist groups as a threat to national security has led to an emphasis on the importance of rapid response airlift as a means to counter terrorist organizations. Nevertheless, the United States and its allies still find themselves in sustained stability maintenance and combat operations in both Afghanistan and Iraq. Both of these undertakings serve to underscore the continued need for sealift to sustain prolonged deployments of large numbers of troops to any corner of the world.

See also Airlift; Military Sealift Command (MSC)

SECRET SERVICE

Federal agency, originally founded to combat counterfeiting, best known for its role in protecting the president of the United States. In recent years, the scope of Secret Service duties has broadened to include fighting electronic crime.

The Secret Service, created as part of the Treasury Department in 1865, is the oldest general law enforcement agency of the U.S. government. Established to halt the spread of counterfeit currency, the agency's responsibilities were expanded in 1867 to investigating any attempts to defraud the government. Targets of early Secret Service investigations included the Ku Klux Klan, smugglers, mail robbers, and bootleggers.

The Secret Service provided occasional protection for presidents beginning in 1894 with President Grover Cleveland. However, it was not until the 1901 assassination of President William McKinley that the agency was assigned to protect the president full time. In 1922, Congress created the White House Police at the request of President Warren G. Harding. Eight years later, this force was placed under the supervision of the Secret Service. It was renamed the Executive Protection Service in 1970 and its jurisdiction was extended to include protection of foreign diplomatic missions on U.S. soil. Over the years, Secret Service protection was extended to the president-elect, vice president, former presidents, major presidential and vice presidential candidates and their immediate families, as well as visiting heads of state and their spouses.

Laws enacted in the 1980s and 1990s expanded the purview of the Secret Service into the areas of electronic fraud, bank fraud, and overseas counterfeiting operations. The Telemarketing Fraud Act and the Identity Theft and Assumption Deterrence Act, both enacted in1998, provided the Secret Service with a mandate against computer fraud. The agency's jurisdiction was expanded by the USA PATRIOT Act of 2001, which increased the Secret Service role in investigating criminal computer activities. In this role, the Secret Service has established nationwide electronic task forces to combat computer crimes.

On March 1, 2003, the Secret Service became part of the newly created Department of Homeland Security (DHS). This is a signal of the importance that the U.S. government places on computer and electronic crime. Adding the Secret Service to DHS, a cabinet-level department, puts the agency in direct touch with the president and at the center of the war on international terrorism.

See also Computer Security; Homeland Security, Department of; Terrorism, War on International

SECURE SECOND STRIKE

A term dating from the Cold War, also known as *counter-force*, which refers to the ability to strike an enemy's population centers with nuclear weapons, after having first attacked missile silos and nuclear bases. The desirability of the secure second-strike option partially explains the extraordinarily high number of nuclear weapons maintained by both the United States and the Soviet Union during the arms race.

Secure second strike was a concern that followed the massive retaliation doctrine (also known as nuclear utilization theory) and ignored the implications of mutually assured destruction (MAD). The policy of the United States in the early 1950s was that the country should be prepared to respond to security threats with nuclear weapons. This policy was established in the context of the recognition of the overwhelming superiority of Soviet conventional forces.

By the early 1960s, the U.S. defense establishment realized that the most likely outcome of the outbreak of nuclear war would be the elimination of both sides. This understanding came to underpin the maintenance of the balance of power and negotiation of peace agreements between the United States and the Soviet Union to reduce their nuclear arsenals. The secure second-strike doctrine was criticized by most experts for failing to recognize that the number of weapons unleashed in such a scenario would automatically make life impossible throughout much of the world.

See also Arms Race; First Strike; Mutually Assured Destruction (MAD); Nuclear Deterrence; Nuclear Weapons.

Further Reading

Cordsman, Anthony H. *Strategic Threats and National Missile Defenses: Defending the U.S. Homeland.* Westport, CT: Praeger, 2001.

Larsen, Jeffrey A. *Arms Control: Cooperative Security in a Changing Environment.* Boulder, CO: Lynne Rienner, 2002.

Lennon, Alexander T. J. *Contemporary Nuclear Debates: Missile Defenses, Arms Control, and Arms Races in the Twenty-First Century.* Cambridge, MA: MIT Press, 2002.

SECURITY DILEMMA

Security problem encountered among states of roughly equal power, states that may get involved in an arms race and then be unable to disengage. Security dilemmas are possible when states are most concerned with their own security and with their relative power position in the international system. When this is the case, even peaceful states with no expansionist or aggressive ideas may be drawn into the dilemma. A security dilemma—and the arms race, which is tied to it—can occur without any participant desiring it.

The security dilemma begins when one state tries to improve its power position relative to one or more states by acquiring more arms. Its purpose—whether offensive or defensive—is unimportant; it has the same effect. This state, either seeking to grow more powerful or defend against another state, gains an advantage over its rivals or neighbors. These states, which are always protecting their own security, grow nervous because the first state has the means of violence and domination available. The increase in the first state's security causes a corresponding decease in the security of its rival or neighboring states.

To protect itself, each rival state will begin to acquire new weapons. The problem, however, is that offensive and defensive weapons are often indistinguishable, and the new weapons begin to look suspicious and menacing to the first state and to the other neighbors. Suspicions multiply, and the states begin to acquire more and more arms, resulting in a theoretically infinite game of one-upmanship. Security dilemmas lead almost inevitably to arms races, in which rival states race to acquire more and better weapons.

The security dilemma exists because both acquiring more arms *and* not acquiring more arms will not increase the country's security. In acquiring more arms, a state simply induces its rivals to buy more as well; in not acquiring more arms, the state faces a risk of military defeat by its enemies.

The security dilemma played itself out in accordance with the theory during the Cold War. Each time either the United States or the Soviet Union gained a slight advantage in the types of weapons, the other tried to match the first country or turn the advantage around. Thus, the Soviet Union raced to obtain nuclear weapons to catch up to the United States; the United States and the Soviet Union raced to develop space-based strategic weaponry. The same pattern occurred with regard to the number and location of weapons each acquired. Both countries became embroiled in an arms race; the United States placed missiles in Eastern Europe; and the Soviet Union attempted to place missiles in Cuba.

Security dilemmas do not necessarily need to be related to arms, nor do they necessarily depend on the actions of more than one country—though that is usually the way it happens. A country can create its own security dilemma, as did the European colonial powers and Japan in the 1930s, to some extent. Insecure economically, each of these powers sought to expand its territorial base to gain control of more resources. The English, French, and Belgians moved into Africa; the Japanese moved into China. As each country acquired control of more territory, it had more territory to defend, causing each to try to expand further to secure the previously conquered territory, rendering the country perpetually insecure.

The security dilemma can be ameliorated. At some point, each country will decide that continuing to expand its arsenal is simply too costly—or it will simply run out of resources to build the arsenal. In either case, the nation will start to seek other solutions to increase its power. One solution is forming an alliance with another country. Cooperation does leave the country vulnerable to cheating, but the country accepts this risk rather than going on alone. Rival or neighbor states may (and probably will) feel threatened by the alliance, and will form their own alliances, gradually creating a balance of power. Once balance is achieved, both sides will realize there is nothing to be gained from attack and there will be an absence of war. Nineteenth-century Europe realized this solution.

Seemingly unrealistic, another solution to the security dilemma has been effective nonetheless. A state with a strong neighbor, with whom it cannot effectively compete, may attempt to enter into heavy economic cooperation with the neighbor it fears. Economic cooperation leads to interdependence and significantly raises the costs of attacking the weaker neighbor. Some argue that France began trading heavily with Germany after World War II for this reason.

A third solution is that one country's resources will simply give out over time, and the country will drop out of the race altogether. Since there is little need for states of vastly unequal power to compete with one another, they may both escape from the security dilemma. This occurred at the end of the Cold War, when the economic infrastructure of the Soviet Union could no longer sustain the arms race with the United States.

A fourth way to ameliorate the security dilemma is for a state to try to acquire weapons that are used specifically for defense and deterrence. At the same time, it should announce that it is obtaining these weapons purely for defensive purposes. Although such an action may not solve the security dilemma, it may render it less dangerous.

See also Arms Race

SELECTIVE SERVICE

Federal agency created to administer the nationwide military draft in the United States. The agency oversees the military registration of draft-age (18- to 25-year old) males, even though the U.S. government has not conducted a draft since 1973.

The Selective Training and Service Act of 1940, signed into law by President Franklin D. Roosevelt, created the country's first peacetime draft. It also formally established the Selective Service System as an independent federal agency to administer the draft. The Selective Service was established to provide a means to call up troops quickly in the event of war. With Europe already engulfed in World War II and Japan making threatening moves in the Pacific, Roosevelt wanted to beef up the unprepared U.S. armed forces.

The end of World War II did not bring with it the end of the draft, as the Soviet Union arose to challenge U.S. political and military power. The United States retained the draft after the war to maintain a large standing army that could counter potential Soviet aggression. However, public sentiment turned against the draft during the Vietnam War. The availability of deferments that seemed to favor the wealthy and powerful spread a perception that the poor were shouldering more than their fair share of the burden in Vietnam. That perception, combined with the general unpopularity of the war, led Congress to refuse to extend the draft law in 1973.

Since that time, the United States has had an all-volunteer military. In 1975, President Jimmy Carter suspended the requirement that draft-age males register for service but reinstated the law in 1980 after the Soviet Union invaded Afghanistan. In the event that a military draft is enacted, the Selective Service System will manage the process and run an Alternative Service Program for individuals classified as conscientious objectors.

Almost all noncitizens living in the United States, including illegal aliens, refugees, and those with permanent residency status are required to register with the Selective Service. Full-time military personnel are not required to register, but members of the Reserve and National Guard not on full-time active duty must do so. Conscientious objectors must also register; however, if the draft is instituted, they have the opportunity to file for an exemption from military service on religious or moral grounds. Individuals who are hospitalized or incarcerated are required to register within 30 days after they are released. Disabled men who are not institutionalized and are capable of leaving their homes must also register. The Selective Service requires the disabled to register even if their disability would excuse them from service because it does not have the authority to classify an individual as disabled. Only the military has that authority.

Changes made since the end of the Vietnam War are designed to make the draft more equitable, should it be necessary. These include stricter guidelines for educational deferments and a revised lottery system designed to provide for less uncertainty. As of early 2005, many military experts were warning that continued overcommitment of U.S. armed forces would eventually force the United States to resume the draft. The administration of President George W. Bush declared that it had no plans to reinstate the draft, but some observers feel that it may be just a matter of time.

See also All-Volunteer Force; Conscription/Volunteer Force

SEPTEMBER 11/WTC AND PENTAGON ATTACKS

Series of terrorist strikes in which Islamic fundamentalists hijacked four American planes and crashed them into New York City's World Trade Center and the Pentagon building outside Washington, DC. The terrorist attacks, which claimed nearly 3,000 lives, were the most deadly foreign attack on U.S. soil since the War of 1812.

The operation was carried out by 19 members of the international terrorist network al-Qaeda, headquartered at the time in Afghanistan. In the wake of the attacks, President George W. Bush announced a worldwide assault on terror, which significantly changed the tone and nature of U.S. foreign and domestic policy. These changes have generated criticism from many quarters.

A SUCCESSION OF TRAGEDIES

According to evidence uncovered in 2005, planning for the September 2001 terrorist attacks began as early as 1996. The culmination of those plans occurred early on the morning of Tuesday, September 11, 2001. Soon after takeoff, American Airlines Flight 11 from Boston to Los Angeles was hijacked and, at 8:46 a.m., the hijackers crashed it into the north tower of the World Trade Center (WTC) in New York City. Eighteen minutes later, the south tower of the World Trade Center was hit by another commercial airliner, United Airlines Flight 175, which had been commandeered shortly after American Airlines Flight 11.

In little more than a hour, both towers collapsed from structural meltdown caused by burning aviation fuel. At least 20 other buildings around the WTC complex were damaged from the impacts and the subsequent explosions. The planes carried over 150 passengers and crew members, and more than 2,600 additional people died at the site. That total included some 400 firefighters, paramedics, and police officers who had rushed to the area to save the people trapped inside the skyscrapers.

At 9:43 a.m., shortly before the WTC towers collapsed, a third hijacked airliner slammed into the western side of the Pentagon building in Washington, DC. American Airlines Flight 77 had been on route from Washington's Dulles Airport to Los Angeles, and was carrying 64 persons. A fourth hijacked plane—United Airlines Flight 93—never reached its intended target, later believed to be the Capitol building in Washington, DC. Following a struggle between the hijackers and some of the passengers, the airliner crashed in rural southwest Pennsylvania.

The North Tower

American Airlines Flight 11 was hijacked by five individuals who had received prior training in Afghan terrorist camps. The hijacker who piloted the plane was Mohammed Atta, believed to have been the ringleader and coordinator of the entire operation. On September 11, Flight 11 took off from Boston at 7:59 a.m. The hijacking apparently started about 15 minutes later, when two of the hijackers stabbed flight attendants who were preparing to serve breakfast.

The hijackers quickly gained access to the cockpit, and Atta, who had been trained as a pilot, took the controls. Meanwhile, four other terrorists used irritant sprays to push the passengers toward the rear of the plane. Two flight attendants, Betty Ong and Amy Sweeney, managed to phone the authorities on the ground and alert them of the crisis, but the plane could not be stopped.

Forty-seven minutes after takeoff, American Airlines Flight 11 crashed into the WTC north tower. Within 10 minutes of impact, access to and from the skyscraper's upper section was cut, and the encroaching fire forced several individuals to jump from the burning building to their deaths. At 10:29 a.m., the north tower collapsed, killing hundreds of people, World Trade Center workers and rescuers alike.

The South Tower

The south World Trade Center tower was hit by United Airlines Flight 175, which had been hijacked by five citizens of the United Arab Emirates and four Saudi Arabians. Half an hour after the 8:14 a.m. takeoff, the pilots reported receiving a suspicious transmission from another plane. That plane was later identified as Flight 11, which was being hijacked at that very moment. Minutes afterwards, their own aircraft was taken over.

The hijacking operation on Flight 175 followed roughly the same pattern as the one on Flight 11. Several crew members were stabbed, and the terrorists kept the passengers under control by resorting to irritant sprays and bomb threats. Once again, some passengers managed to phone family members and tell them about the unfolding crisis.

At 9:03 a.m., Flight 175 hit the south tower of the World Trade Center. Many people in the building heard an earlier explosion from the direction of the north tower, but they were unaware that it had been caused by a plane crash. A few minutes before the south tower was hit, the occupants were told to begin an orderly evacuation. The order had been given because the burning north tower was endangering the entire complex, not in anticipation of a possible second plane impact. This fortunate coincidence likely saved many lives in the south tower. Nevertheless, more than 1,000 first response personnel had arrived on the scene before the second skyscraper collapsed, and many were trapped when the south tower disintegrated at 10:05 a.m.

The Pentagon

As Americans were trying to recover from the shock of the attacks on New York, they discovered that

Family members and onlookers watch a hearing of the 9-11 Commission (officially known as the National Commission on Terrorist Attacks Upon the United States) in New York City on May 18, 2004. The bipartisan commission, created by Congress in late 2002, was charged with preparing a full and complete account of the circumstances surrounding the September 11, 2001, terrorist attacks, including the government's preparedness for and the immediate response to the attacks. The commission also provided recommendations designed to guard against future attacks.

Source: Getty Images.

the terrorists were not content to restrict themselves to one city. Soon after takeoff from Washington, DC, five people took over American Airlines Flight 77. At least three were veterans of multiple Islamic holy wars in Central Asia. However, the story of the hijacking of American Airlines Flight 77 reads a little differently than those of the New York planes. Unlike the terrorists who seized planes in New York, the Washington hijackers used box cutters instead of knives, and they employed no irritant sprays or bomb threats. They were also less aggressive toward the passengers, and did not harm any of them prior to crashing the plane.

When Flight 77 ceased communication with the ground towers, some dispatchers realized that the plane had been hijacked. However, many believed that it was the plane that hit the south tower of the World Trade Center. Instead, at 9:37 a.m., the plane turned around and flew back toward Washington, crashing into the western side of the Pentagon building and killing 125 people inside. Fighter jets from nearby Langley Air Force Base had been scrambled in response to the hijacking, but they were still some 150 miles away when the crash occurred.

Pennsylvania

Four planes were hijacked on September 11, 2001, but only three crashed into buildings. The fourth, United Airlines Flight 93, crashed in a field in Somerset County, Pennsylvania, following a pitched struggle between passengers and hijackers. The crisis on board Flight 93 began 46 minutes after takeoff. The operation did not go as planned from the very beginning. Gaining access to the cockpit proved harder than the hijackers thought, and ground controllers were able to listen to noises of a struggle and shouts of "Mayday" through an open radio channel. Unlike the other three hijackings, there were only four terrorists on Flight 96, which may have contributed to their inability to carry out the plan in its entirety.

As with the other flights, some passengers were able to communicate by phone with family members, who told them what had happened in New York City. Aware that their plane was probably meant to be used in a similar manner, the passengers decided to fight the hijackers. At 9:57 a.m., a fight erupted onboard the plane. Shortly after 10 a.m., with passengers storming the cockpit, the hijackers crashed the plane in a field southeast of Pittsburgh. It was later revealed that Vice President Dick Cheney had given permission for fighter jets to shoot down Flight 93, but confusion in the chain of command prevented the order from being carried out.

A CHAIN OF FAILURES

As soon as the initial shock passed, important questions began to flood the government, the intelligence community, and the media. How could a handful of crudely armed individuals execute such a devastating attack? Why weren't they stopped before they could carry out their plan? Were they contemplating similar attacks in the future? How could the country protect itself against such attacks?

In the wake of the terrorist attacks, the U.S. Congress convened a special commission to study the attacks and determine what factors allowed the plot to proceed undetected. According to the commission's official report, the hijackers were able to prepare and execute their grim undertaking because of widespread "failures of imagination, policy, capabilities, and management" on the part of various U.S. authorities whose role it was to prevent such an event from happening.

The commission report cited failures of imagination that prevented the top echelons of the intelligence community—notably the Central Intelligence Agency (CIA) and Federal Bureau of Investigation (FBI)—from conceiving of the possibility that a terrorist network based in the rugged mountains of Afghanistan would be able to plot such a complex operation. Moreover, failures of policy denied such institutions as the CIA and the FBI the ability to share information on suspect activity inside and outside the United States.

The report also cited failures of capability that allowed the terrorists to enter the country and prepare their plan in relative comfort—including taking flight lessons and moving money around—out of the sight of the police and the FBI. Finally, failures of management prevented federal field agents with legitimate suspicions or even some knowledge of potential attacks to properly communicate with their superiors. All of these failures ultimately conspired with decades-old instability in Middle Eastern politics to produce one of the most traumatic events in modern American history.

INSTITUTIONAL RESPONSES

Public and institutional criticism of intelligence and security failures prior to the September 11 attacks led to a dramatic restructuring of the U.S. national security apparatus. In 2002, a new cabinet-level Department of Homeland Security (DHS) was created to coordinate efforts to prevent terrorism on U.S. soil. In an attempt to centralize authority for domestic security matters, the DHS assumed authority over many formerly independent government agencies, including the Secret Service and the Immigration and Naturalization Service. The DHS was given responsibility for protecting U.S. cities and vital infrastructure from terrorist threats and monitoring the flow of people and goods across U.S. borders.

The intelligence community was also restructured because of the congressional committee's findings. A new director of national intelligence position was created in 2004 to coordinate intelligence gathering and sharing between federal agencies. The heads of the CIA, FBI, State Department, and military intelligence services are required to provide copies of the information they collect to the director of national intelligence. This allows the director to gain a comprehensive overview of U.S. intelligence rather than the views of a single agency.

A less popular institutional response to the attacks was the passage of legislation abridging certain civil liberties in the name of combating terrorism. In the months following the attacks, many terrorist suspects were arrested and held without charges in federal facilities. Detainees were routinely denied the right to see attorneys and their whereabouts were often kept secret. These actions outraged many Americans, who complained that they violated basic constitutional guarantees against illegal seizure. The passage of the USA PATRIOT Act, which broadened federal investigatory and police powers, was protested by many citizens. In March 2005, the Montana State Senate voted 88-12 to condemn the act as un-American.

However, many supporters of the Patriot Act and similar laws believe that such measures are necessary to stop terrorism. They feel that Americans must give up some of their accustomed liberties to ensure the safety of the country against terrorist attack. The debate over security versus freedom is fiercely contentious, and has become one of the most significant issues to arise from the September 11 attacks.

—Razvan Sibii

See also Afghanistan, War in; Al-Qaeda; Bin Laden, Osama; Bush, George W., and National Policy; Homeland Security, Department of; Intelligence and Counterintelligence; Iraq War of 2003; Legal Ramifications of National Security; Middle East and U.S. Policy; Terrorism, War on International; Terrorists, Islamic

Further Reading

Brill, Steven. *After: The Rebuilding and Defending of America in the September 12 Era.* New York: Simon & Schuster, 2003.

Clarke, Richard A. *Against All Enemies.* New York: Free Press, 2004.

Fouda, Yosri, and Nick Fielding. *Masterminds of Terror. The Truth Behind the Most Devastating Attack the World Has Ever Seen.* Edinburgh, UK: Mainstream Publishing, 2003.

War on Terrorism

The consequences of the September 11 events are as numerous as they are wide-ranging. A few hours after the attacks in New York City and Washington DC, President George W. Bush announced his administration's decision to annihilate not only the individuals directly responsible for the terrorist attacks—Osama bin Laden and his al-Qaeda associates—but also those governments who gave them aid.

The United States quickly acted on that decision. On October 7, 2001, U.S. and British forces attacked Afghanistan, which had acted as a host for al-Qaeda training camps. Less than three years later, the United States also attacked Iraq, partly on the pretext that Iraqi ruler Saddam Hussein supported al-Qaeda. Both operations were presented as milestones in the newly declared War on International Terrorism. Although the former regimes of both countries were swiftly overthrown, the considerable numbers of U.S. troops required for postwar occupation have experienced unrelenting armed resistance.

SHERMAN, WILLIAM TECUMSEH (1820–1891)

In the American Civil War, union general known for destroying southern infrastructure during his infamous March to the Sea in 1864. Sherman's direct targeting of the enemy's means of production marked the first large-scale implementation of the strategy of *total war*.

William Tecumseh Sherman was the son of an Ohio judge who died when William was nine years old. The young Sherman was raised by a neighbor who served as a U.S. senator and who later obtained a commission for Sherman to the U.S. Military Academy at West Point. Sherman graduated from West Point in 1840 and subsequently served in the Mexican War. In 1852, he resigned his commission and became a banker in San Francisco and New York before practicing law in Leavenworth, Kansas. In 1859, Sherman took a post as head of Louisiana's state military academy. He resigned the position when Louisiana seceded from the Union in January 1861.

Upon the outbreak of the Civil War, Sherman accepted a commission as a colonel in the U.S. Army. He commanded a Union brigade at the first battle of Bull Run in July 1861 and was promoted to brigadier general in August of that year. At his own request, Sherman was removed from field command due to personal problems, including drinking. He was placed in charge of a military department in Kentucky but returned to combat in April 1862 as a division commander under General Ulysses S. Grant at the Battle of Shiloh. The following month Sherman was promoted to major general, and, in July, his troops occupied Memphis, Tennessee. In the spring and summer of 1863, Sherman participated in Grant's Vicksburg campaign, which cut the Confederacy in two and helped hasten the defeat of Southern forces in the west. He led the U.S. 15th Corps in the Union assault on Vicksburg in July 1863.

In October 1863, Grant was named supreme commander in the west, and Sherman succeeded him as commander of the Army of Tennessee. Between November 1863 and February 1864, Sherman's troops conducted a successful campaign against Confederate forces in the Deep South, destroying vital Southern transportation and supply links. When Grant was appointed to command the Army of the Potomac in March 1864, Sherman was named supreme commander in the west.

Over the next five months, Sherman laid down a fierce siege against Atlanta that culminated in the city's surrender on September 2, 1864. On November 15, Sherman burned most of the city a day before setting out on his historic March to the Sea. With some 60,000 troops and little opposition, he used a scorched earth strategy to decimate the Southern infrastructure. Sherman's strategy was to demoralize enemy combatants and noncombatants alike by destroying everything in his path. Houses, farms, factories, railroads, harbors, food supplies—nothing was spared from looting, burning, or spoilage.

Sherman's tactics represented a radical departure from the way wars had been fought in the previous century. Retreating armies had used scorched earth tactics to deny food and other supplies to invaders, but advancing forces had never adopted it as a conscious strategy. Attackers routinely pillaged territories they invaded and tried to live off the land when possible, and the destruction of property to spread terror among the populace is as old as war itself. However, Sherman's deliberate and systematic destruction of every functional part of Southern society was something entirely new in warfare.

The path of destruction continued from Atlanta to Savannah, Georgia, which fell to Sherman's forces on December 21, 1864. Sherman continued up the coast into South Carolina, ravaging Charleston and raining devastation on the home state of Southern secession. By the spring of 1865, Sherman's troops had advanced through South Carolina into North Carolina, driving the remaining Confederate forces from the south while Grant closed in from the north. On April 9, 1865, Confederate commander in chief General Robert E. Lee surrendered to Grant's forces, ending the war.

In 1869, Grant was elected president of the United States and Sherman was promoted to succeed him as commander of the U.S. Army. During the 1870s, Sherman led U.S. forces in the Indian Wars against Native American tribes in the western United States. He applied the same scorched earth tactics in these campaigns that he pioneered on the March to the Sea. Despite his ruthless campaigning, however, Sherman spoke out against government maltreatment of Native Americans who settled on reservations.

Sherman retired from the Army in 1884 and settled in New York City. Friends and supporters tried to urge him to run as a Democratic candidate in that year's presidential election. However, he resisted their attempts to draw him into politics with the now-famous quote, "If nominated I will not accept, if elected I will not serve." Sherman died in 1891 and was buried in St. Louis, Missouri.

See also Tactics, Military

Further Reading

Barney, William L. *William Tecumseh Sherman*. The Reader's Companion to American History. New York: Houghton Mifflin, 1991.

SIGNAL CORPS

Combat support branch of the U.S. Army whose mission is to manage all aspects of communications and information systems support. The primary competency of the Signal Corps is in the management and maintenance of communications and information systems from domestic Army bases to forward deployed combat areas.

The Signal Corps was officially established as a branch of the U.S. Army in March 1863. The evolution of the Signal Corps' mission and methods to carry out that mission has reflected the advance of technology in the United States. At its inception during the Civil War era, the Signal Corps used semaphore—a flag signaling system. By the end of the Civil War, however, the corps was using the telegraph to communicate from coast to coast.

By the late 19th century, the Signal Corps was employing the telephone, heliograph, and observation balloons in wartime. Because of its expertise in ballooning, the Signal Corps was tasked with control of early aviation technology and the development of military aircraft, including the first procurement of an army aircraft purchased from the Wright brothers in 1908. The Signal Corps relinquished control of aviation in 1914 when the Air Corps was established as a separate branch of the military.

During World War I and World War II, the Signal Corps was responsible for implementing and designing radio technology in support of the war effort. In subsequent years, the Signal Corps continued to develop radio, radar, and sonar technology to enhance its communications ability.

The contemporary mission of the Signal Corps includes the management of all modern telecommunications and information systems. This includes the maintenance and management of computer systems, Internet and local area networks, and voice and data communications. In the modern age of technological warfare, the Signal Corps continues to play a central role in defending and promoting U.S. national security.

See also Computer Security; Radar (Radio Detection and Ranging); Science, Technology, and Security; Signals Intelligence (SIGINT); U.S. Army

SIGNALS INTELLIGENCE (SIGINT)

Intelligence gathering by interception of communications, lasers, or radio signals. Signals intelligence (SIGINT) became a critical tool for military intelligence gathering with the development of wireless communications in the late 19th century. Nearly all militaries deploy units that specialize in SIGINT, and the U.S. National Security Agency (NSA) specializes in this field of intelligence. SIGINT often involves encryption (coding) and cryptanalysis (decoding), since sensitive diplomatic and military communications are usually encrypted.

TYPES OF SIGINT

There are five types of signals intelligence. Communications intelligence (COMINT) is the interception, processing, and analysis of communications from foreign sources. These include voice messages, Morse code, or Teletype messages that may or may not be encrypted. COMINT often involves interception of diplomatic communications.

Electronic intelligence (ELINT) is the interception of signals from military and civilian hardware that is not used for traditional forms of communication, such as radar. Interception of signals from air defense radars allows analysts to discern their operating characteristics and devise ways for friendly aircraft to avoid detection. ELINT may also involve interception of signals from navigation and weapons tracking systems on aircraft, vehicles, or ships.

Radar intelligence is the detection of enemy aircraft or missiles and their operational characteristics by means of radar. Whereas ELINT scans enemy radar signals to gather information, radar intelligence collects data by sending out radar signals of its own.

Nonimaging infrared intelligence employs sensors that can detect the presence and movement of an object by its temperature. This type of intelligence gathering may be used at night or in other situations in which the detection of enemy forces by visual means is difficult.

Laser intelligence involves the interception and analysis of laser communications. Laser intelligence has been critical in the development of precision-guided munitions, or smart bombs. A laser called a target designator shoots a laser beam at a target and sensors in the smart bomb pick up and follow the beam to the target. Because this is a relatively new field of SIGINT, many activities remain classified.

HISTORY OF SIGINT

Signals intelligence is as old as the history of human conflict. Leaders in the American War of Independence, for example, employed relatively simple codes and ciphers as well as invisible ink in their communications. Encrypted British communications, intercepted and deciphered by the Americans, helped seal the fate of the British at the Battle of Yorktown in 1781.

However, the ability to act quickly on signals intelligence became possible only with the advent of wireless communications toward the end of the 1800s. Letters or battle plans inadvertently captured in combat may have been days or weeks out of date. Radio or telephone intercepts, on the other hand, provide current information and the technology to communicate them instantly to military commanders. As a result,

SIGINT came to occupy a central role in the wars of the 20th century.

In World War I, the failure of the czar's forces to protect their communications led to a catastrophic Russian defeat at the hands of the Germans at the Battle of Tannenburg in 1914. On the other side of the Atlantic, the 1917 interception of the German Zimmerman telegram by the United States contributed significantly to the U.S. decision to enter World War I on the side of the Allies. The telegram outlined a German offer to annex large parts of the United States to Mexico if Mexico entered the war on the side of Germany.

The use of signals intelligence in World War II has been well documented. Perhaps most well known is the American breaking of the Imperial Japanese Navy code JN 25. The U.S. ability to read Japanese messages allowed the U.S. Navy to inflict a decisive defeat on Japanese forces at the Battle of Midway in 1942.

During the Cold War, the United States and Soviet Union both employed SIGINT to gather intelligence on the military capabilities and diplomacy of friends and foes. Both, however, also found that there were limits to SIGINT. The U.S. Army in Vietnam and the Soviet Army in Afghanistan both encountered irregular forces that did not rely heavily on electronic signals to communicate. Such situations reinforced the need for other forms of intelligence gathering, particularly human intelligence (HUMINT).

Today's war on terror presents similar challenges to signals intelligence. Threats to national security now are as likely to come from terrorist groups or other nonstate actors using less conventional forms of communication such as cell phones, Internet chat rooms, and messages circulated through underground audio or videotapes. These new forms of communication require new responses from those responsible for U.S. signals intelligence.

See also Cryptology; Human Intelligence (HUMINT); Intelligence and Counterintelligence; Science, Technology, and Security

SINGLE INTEGRATED OPERATIONAL PLAN (SIOP)

The U.S. strategic warfighting plan for the use of nuclear weapons. The Single Integrated Operational

Plan (SIOP) is one of the most highly classified of all government documents.

The SIOP is the culmination of a long process that begins with the president of the United States, who provides the U.S. Department of Defense (DoD) with a conceptual guide for the use of nuclear weapons. The DoD converts that information into the Nuclear Weapons Employment Policy, a list of objectives, specific targets, and operational constraints. The Joint Chiefs of Staff then rework that list into the Joint Strategic Capabilities Plan. The U.S. Strategic Command uses the Joint Strategic Capabilities Plan to compile the SIOP, which contains the specifics of targeting orders, scheduling, and needed weapons. A new SIOP is approved each year, even if it is not fundamentally different from the previous year's plan.

The first SIOP was approved in late 1960 as an attempt to develop a more systematic approach to the various targets for potential U.S. nuclear strikes. It was also a response to advances in technology that improved the U.S. ability to hit a broader range of targets. Recently declassified documents indicate that outgoing President Dwight D. Eisenhower and other top officials believed that the first SIOP went too far. The plan called for multiple nuclear strikes against military and urban-industrial targets in the Soviet Union, China, and their allies. The initial SIOP also tried to unite the various nuclear forces of the U.S. Air Force, Navy, and Army into a synchronized format.

Since those early years, various SIOPs have been developed. SIOPs focused on counter-force strategy from the early to mid-1960s, deterrence and more flexible responses with limited nuclear options in the mid-1970s and early 1980s, and again on counter-force strategy in the mid- to late 1980s. The number of targets has dropped dramatically since the collapse of the Soviet Union in 1991.

The existence of SIOP was not publicly acknowledged for more than a decade, and many details about SIOP remain shrouded in mystery. From the beginning, a special information category—extremely sensitive information (ESI)—has been attached to the SIOP. The U.S. government is understandably cautious about revealing details of its nuclear strategy, even though some observers feel that American citizens should be aware of their country's nuclear intentions.

See also Nuclear Utilization Theory; Nuclear Weapons; Strategic Nuclear Triad

SMALL-SCALE CONTINGENCIES

Military operations that require fewer preparations than major war and whose missions include humanitarian and peacekeeping operations. Small-scale contingencies (SSC) are not defined or limited by a single military operation but rather include varying degrees of military participation. These include limited strikes, evacuation operations, enforcing no-fly zones, and peacekeeping and humanitarian affairs missions that may require military intervention. These missions are referred to by several terms including operations other than war (OOTW) and major operations other than war (MOOTW).

U.S. military planning is derived from two primary sources: the Quadrennial Defense Review prepared by the Department of Defense every four years, and the National Security Strategy developed by the White House at its discretion, generally every few years. In 1997, the Quadrennial Defense Review required the military to build up sufficient resources to meet demands for stability and support operations and to fight two major theater wars while simultaneously intervening in small-scale contingency operations. This was the first official inclusion of SSCs in national defense planning.

Small-scale contingencies require more planning than stability and support operations, but not nearly as much as a major theater war. The Quadrennial Defense Review and other analyses guide planning for SSC missions. They also focus on maintaining flexible, rapidly deployable forces that can meet the requirements for a variety of situations. The U.S. military, however, has been criticized for a sluggish transition to the peacekeeping and humanitarian mission. United States forces are still ill trained to handle these missions on a large scale. Partly for this reason, SSC planning has emphasized the need to prepare the military appropriately for the peacekeeping aspect of its mission.

One unique characteristic of small-scale contingency operations is that their desired outcome and duration are not always clearly defined. Some of the more recent examples of U.S. small-scale contingency operations have included both short- and long-term missions. Following the 1991 Gulf War, the United States established no-fly zones in northern and southern Iraq to protect ethnic minorities from air attacks by Iraqi dictator Saddam Hussein. Projected to last several months, their enforcement ended only after the U.S.-led invasion of Iraq in March 2003. From 1992 to 1994, the U.S. military conducted Operation Restore Hope in Somalia, a military-humanitarian effort to provide food and health assistance to Somalis. In the Balkans, the 1995 Implementation Force/Stabilization Force (IFOR/SFOR) was an SSC projected to last for one year. Ten years later, the United States was still involved in the mission.

Small-scale contingency operations, while focused on humanitarian and peacekeeping efforts in recent years, still occasionally require the U.S. military to exercise its military might. Some of the more traditional military roles assigned to SSCs include carrying out military exercises in the Taiwan Straits, participating in multinational force deployments in Haiti, and enforcing a naval embargo on Bosnia.

See also Humanitarian Intervention; Military Doctrine; National Security Strategy of the United States; National Security Strategy Reports; Operations Other Than War (OOTW); Peacekeeping Operations; Quadrennial Defense Review (QDR)

with guided aircraft during World War I. The first successful guided-bomb experiments took place during World War II. Greater sensitivity to civilian casualties during the Vietnam War led to the development of more sophisticated smart bomb technology. It was not until the Gulf War of 1991, however, that smart bombs received the most attention.

See also Global Positioning System (GPS); Precision-Guided Munitions

Further Reading

Latham, Robert. *Bombs and Bandwidth: The Emerging Relationship Between Information Technology and Security.* New York: New Press, 2003.

Myers, Lawrence. *Smart Bombs: Improvised Sensory Detonation Techniques and Advanced Weapons System.* Boulder, CO: Paladin Press, 1990.

SMART BOMB

Guided munitions that achieve a greater degree of accuracy and cause less collateral damage. Features that distinguish smart bombs from ordinary bombs are an electronic sensor system, a control system, and adjustable flight fins for guidance.

The three primary types of smart bomb technology are TV/IR-guided bombs (television/infrared), laser-guided bombs, and Joint Direct Attack Munition (JDAM) bombs. The TV/IR-guided bombs essentially operate like a remote-control glider, with a remote operator steering the bomb to a given target. Laser-guided smart bombs are guided by an operator, who directs the bomb to the target via laser light. The disadvantage of both of these systems is that the bomb sensor must maintain visual contact with the target and may be diverted by cloud cover or other obstacles.

The JDAM bomb avoids this problem by using Global Positioning System (GPS) technology to orient itself. Before dropping the bomb, the attacking aircraft uses its own GPS receiver to locate the target on the ground. This information is fed to the JDAM's computer just before launch and the JDAM's GPS receiver processes signals from GPS satellites to steer the bomb toward its target.

Technological advances toward the development of more accurate smart bombs dates back to experiments

SOMALIA INTERVENTION (1992)

Military operation mounted by the United States as part of a wider international humanitarian and peacekeeping effort that started in the summer of 1992 and ended in the spring of 1995. The intervention in Somalia was an extremely complex enterprise. It has remained in the mind of many Americans mainly because of one major incident that took place on October 3 and 4, 1993: namely the so-called Battle of Mogadishu, in which 18 U.S. soldiers and hundreds of Somali militia and civilians were killed. What started as a humanitarian operation aimed at channeling food supplies to the famished Somali population ended in a bloody fight that wrought even more chaos on an already embattled country.

HISTORICAL BACKGROUND

The politically-charged events that foreshadowed the 1992 intervention in Somalia arguably go back to 1991, when Somali dictator Mohammed Siad Barre was overthrown in a military coup staged by a coalition of opposition warlords. As soon as the warlords saw themselves in power, the two most powerful—Ali Mahdi and Mohammed Aideed (who would later play a crucial role in the Battle of Mogadishu)—began fighting among themselves.

The incessant conflict led to the destruction of the country's agriculture and, by way of consequence, to nationwide famine. By the fall of 1991, the United Nations estimated that 4.5 million Somalis were on the brink of starving to death. Under international pressure, the warring factions, including General Aideed, agreed to a cease-fire, allowing UN observers to enter the country and organize a humanitarian effort there.

In April 1992, the UN humanitarian effort, known as Operation Provide Relief, arrived in Somalia. However, the undertaking proved to be extremely difficult, as various Somali militia disregarded the cease-fire and engaged in extensive fighting as well as in large-scale hijacking and looting of international food convoys.

In his last weeks in office, President George H. W. Bush proposed to the United Nations that American combat troops be sent to Somalia to protect aid workers. The United Nations accepted Bush's proposal, and on December 9, 1992, around 25,000 U.S. troops began arriving in Somalia.

FIGHTING AIDEED

Almost from the very beginning, just like in the case of the humanitarian effort, the military operation was beset with difficulties. The lack of a national Somali leadership, as well as the daily mayhem in the streets of the capital city of Mogadishu, bedeviled the security operation. Unsatisfied with the mission's results, the new U.S. president, Bill Clinton, ordered the number of U.S. troops reduced.

By June 1993, only 1,200 American combat soldiers remained in Somalia, aided by troops from 28 other countries acting under the authority of the United Nations. The already unstable situation on the ground took a sharp turn for the worse when 24 Pakistani soldiers were ambushed and killed while inspecting a weapons storage facility. The United Nations unofficially blamed General Aideed's militia for the operation, and passed a resolution calling for the apprehension of those responsible for the massacre.

During the next two weeks, U.S. and UN troops attacked objectives associated with Aideed's forces, without succeeding in capturing the general. On August 29, more than 400 elite U.S. Delta Force troops flew into Somalia on a mission to apprehend Aidid. The ensuing Battle of Mogadishu was to become a symbol for the entire Somali operation.

A LOST CAUSE

On October 3, 1993, the U.S. elite forces staged their sixth attempt to arrest or annihilate General Aideed and his top lieutenants. The objective was the Olympic Hotel in Mogadishu, where the targets were thought to be meeting.

The mission, however, did not go as planned. The troubles began when one of the six Black Hawk helicopters that transported the Delta Force soldiers was shot down near the hotel. Rushing toward the site of the crash to rescue the crew, other U.S. troops came under a heavy barrage of fire. Hundreds of Somali fighters filled the streets, and the U.S. soldiers became trapped.

After 17 hours of continuous fighting, the surviving U.S. troops were finally rescued by an international force. The battle left 18 U.S soldiers dead and 84 wounded. On the Somali side, at least 300 people were wounded, many of them civilians caught in the crossfire. Although the mission was technically successful—as several high-ranking Aideed associates were apprehended—it was widely perceived as a failed operation due to its high cost in human lives.

Soon after the incident at Mogadishu, President Clinton pulled all of the American troops out of Somalia. A year later, in the spring of 1995, UN troops followed suit, leaving the country engulfed in clan warfare. General Aideed died of bullet wounds in 1996, but the internal strife in Somalia continued. To this day, the Somali national government operates from exile because of the unsafe conditions inside the country. Somalia remains one of the poorest countries in the world.

See also Humanitarian Intervention; International Peacekeeping and Overseas Deployment; Peacekeeping Operations

Further Reading

Bowden, Mark. *Black Hawk Down: A Story of Modern War.* New York: Atlantic Monthly Press, 1999.

Casper, Lawrence E. *Falcon Brigade: Combat and Command in Somalia and Haiti.* Boulder, CO: Lynne Rienner, 2001.

Clarke, Walter, and Jeffrey Herbst, eds. *Learning From Somalia: The Lessons of Armed Humanitarian Interventions.* Boulder, CO: Westview Press, 1997.

SOUTHEAST ASIA TREATY ORGANIZATION (SEATO)

Anticommunist alliance among Australia, France, Great Britain, New Zealand, Pakistan, the Philippines, and the United States. The Southeast Asia Treaty Organization (SEATO) was created to halt the spread of communism among the nations of Southeast Asia.

SEATO was established September 8, 1954, with the signing of the Southeast Asia Collective Defense Treaty. The treaty was promoted by the Western powers when France withdrew its colonial army from Vietnam. An integral part of the treaty was the Pacific Charter, affirming the rights of Asian and Pacific people to equality and self-determination. The stated goals of SEATO were to increase economic, social, and cultural cooperation among the member countries. Civil and military organizations were also established under SEATO and headquartered in Bangkok, Thailand.

SEATO sanctioned the use of U.S. forces in Vietnam, although France and Pakistan withheld their support. Many critics, in fact, saw the organization as a way to legitimize U.S. participation in Vietnam among Southeast Asian publics. Without the unanimous support of all of the member nations, however, SEATO was precluded from intervening in the fighting in Laos and Cambodia.

Pakistan withdrew from SEATO in 1968; and, with the withdrawal of U.S. forces from Vietnam in 1974, SEATO lost much of its reason for existence. The following year, in 1975, France suspended financial support for the alliance. By that time, the alliance was seriously weakened, and SEATO was officially disbanded on June 30, 1977.

See also Alliances; Collective Security; Communism and National Security; Treaties; Vietnam War (1954–1975)

SOVEREIGNTY

Institution in international relations that affirms a state's legitimate domestic and international autonomy; also an organizing principle of modern international relations.

Most often applied to states, sovereignty is a complex and evolving concept. Modern-state sovereignty originated in the 1648 Peace of Westphalia, the agreement that ended the Thirty Years' War in Europe. This war of religion had torn Europe apart and made political reorganization desirable. Thus, the treaty signed by the Western European powers represented a rejection of a hierarchical system in which they were subject to the pope and the Holy Roman emperor. It established, instead, a system of territorial nation-states. The new states were capable of exercising supreme authority within their territories and acting (theoretically) as equal actors in the international realm.

The system of mutual recognition of sovereign states forms the basis for modern international relations. This institution, however, depends heavily on recognition, de facto control, and legitimacy. For a system of sovereign states to endure, each state must accept the others as legitimate political and territorial entities with their own identities, power, and interests.

Sovereignty can therefore be very controversial; breakaway nations or states must be acknowledged by other entities before they can claim sovereign authority or participate (legally) in international relations. To gain acknowledgment—which can be quite difficult—states must be able to exert domestic sovereign control. Merely claiming to rule without the power, resources, or political will to substantiate the claim is insufficient. Would-be sovereign states generally must also demonstrate that they rule legitimately.

As it developed, sovereignty was understood as existing on two separate levels—internal and external. Internal sovereignty means that a state has certain spatial and political characteristics. A sovereign state is a territorial entity with clearly delineated borders. The state has ultimate authority within its borders over people, material resources, and domestic affairs, and is not subject to a higher power. Importantly, this authority is regarded as legitimate.

External sovereignty has intertwining political, territorial, and legal characteristics. The sovereign state is independent of all external authority and represents an autonomous unit; it has a political identity. In principle, it is free from the interference of other states in the conduct of its own domestic and international affairs; and it is thus responsible for its own security as well.

It is understood, therefore, that each state has a right and responsibility to protect and defend the integrity of its borders. As such, a sovereign state is seen as having a legitimate right to use force to resist direct invasion or indirect attempts at control. Sovereign states are therefore legitimate actors in international politics, with the power to formulate foreign policy, conclude treaties and trade agreements, form alliances, and wage war.

Sovereignty also has legal implications. For all states, sovereignty represents *standing* in international law. States may, rightfully, enter contracts, sue one another and be sued in international courts, conduct diplomatic negotiations, and so forth. They may also claim jurisdiction in international disputes. In the special case of failed states, the principle of sovereignty can be a safeguard against total disintegration. While a functioning government may not exist, previous recognition of sovereignty is generally a guarantee that a state will continue to survive, in a de jure sense, as a sovereign nation. The institution of sovereignty thus normalizes relations between states. In its political and legal manifestations, it provides an organizing principle for the contemporary international system.

See also Power, World

SOVIET UNION, FORMER (RUSSIA), AND U.S. POLICY

The impact of the policies of the Union of Soviet Socialist Republics (USSR) on U.S. national security from the time of the Russian Revolution in 1917 to the collapse of the Soviet Union in 1991. Relations between the United States and the Soviet Union not only dominated the foreign policy of both nations for decades but also had a great impact on domestic policy and life in both countries. The rivalry drew the countries into an arms race and military conflicts that cost trillions of dollars and claimed tens of thousands of lives.

EARLY HISTORY

The Soviet Union arose from the chaos of postrevolutionary Russia in the later stages of World War I. In February 1917, with the war going badly for Russia, a popular uprising forced Czar Nicholas II to abdicate the Russian throne. He was replaced by a provisional government that continued the war against Germany. Six months later, Bolshevik rebels led by Vladimir Ilyich Ulyanov—better known as Lenin—overthrew the provisional government. Lenin signed a peace treaty with Germany in March 1918 and set up a revolutionary communist form of government.

Lenin, however, had opposition both at home and abroad. The less-revolutionary Mensheviks, who had been partners in the provisional government, were unwilling to accept Lenin's leadership. They soon began an armed resistance to Bolshevik rule, setting off a civil war. The Bolsheviks' revolution also caused great concern among the Western Allies in the war against Germany—the United States, Great Britain, and France. These states were shocked by the coup against and subsequent murder of the czar. Lenin's withdrawal of Russia from the war and his establishment of a hard-line communist government was more than the Allies could take.

After defeating Germany in late 1918, the Western Allies sent troops and equipment to support the Mensheviks in the Russian Civil War. This began a period marked by simultaneous civil war and foreign incursion to which the Bolsheviks responded with a set of policies known collectively as War Communism. It was also a time of economic experimentation, as Lenin centralized the Russian economy. The government in Moscow took ownership of all private enterprises, including farms. Moscow set agricultural and industrial production quotas and state bureaucrats managed the Russian economy.

By 1920, the Bolsheviks had prevailed in the civil war, but Lenin's policies had been disastrous for the Russian economy. Realizing the weaknesses of economic centralization, Lenin introduced the New Economic Period (NEP)—market-friendly measures designed to encourage private ownership and foreign investment in the country—in 1921. During this period, U.S. firms, including General Electric, Ford, and Westinghouse, entered the Soviet market. This move toward capitalist economic philosophy encouraged Western politicians who had grown increasingly concerned about the direction of Lenin's rule.

In 1922, the former Russian Empire was formally renamed the Union of Soviet Socialist Republics. (The name Soviet was taken from the Russian word for a local worker's council. Such councils were the backbone of the Bolshevik movement during the revolution.) Lenin did not live to see the Soviet Union rise to its eventual status as a world superpower. His death in 1924 set off a struggle between his old ally and revolutionary partner Leon Trotsky and the general secretary of the Soviet Communist Party, Joseph Stalin. Although clever and brutally efficient, Stalin was not one of Lenin's favorites. In a political testament dictated before his death, Lenin advised other communist leaders to "think about a way of removing Stalin from that post [general secretary]."

THE USSR UNDER STALIN

Stalin eventually won the power struggle with Trotsky, forcing Trotsky to leave the country in 1928. Having consolidated his power, Stalin set about reversing many of Lenin's policies. In 1929, Stalin scrapped the NEP and set out to build a modern society that was economically self-sufficient. The Soviet economy, again disdainful of private ownership, was directed by a series of five-year plans that controlled production schedules and consumption patterns. Virtually all aspects of Soviet life came under the direction and watchfulness of the state.

By the early 1930s, the Soviet Union was boasting impressive economic numbers. Industrial goods were being produced in astonishing volume and military output had reached great heights. In some categories, Soviet production led the combined efforts of the rest of the world. Stalin's forced industrialization and militarization of the Soviet state accomplished rapid economic development and accrued tremendous power to the Communist Party.

In achieving these numbers, however, the Soviet government resorted to a policy of systematic repression and brutality. Stalin used state propaganda organs to whip up fear of foreigners and suspicion of Western capitalist society. He portrayed the Soviet Union as an island of communist progress surrounded by evil capitalist forces waiting to destroy the Soviet Union. To maintain an iron control over the populace, Stalin resorted to purges, massive arrest and deportation of political opponents, and forced migration of entire peoples to break up their political power. He even implemented policies designed to create famine in areas opposed to his rule.

The rise of a strong, anticommunist German state in the 1930s posed a serious challenge to Stalin. The purges had decimated the Soviet military, which although large, was poorly trained, poorly equipped, and poorly led. On the eve of Germany's 1939 invasion of Poland, which started World War II, Stalin signed a nonaggression pact with Germany's leader, Adolf Hitler. The Nazi-Soviet pact bought Hitler peace on his eastern front so he could turn his attention to France in 1940. It also gave Stalin time to rebuild the Soviet officer corps and modernize his army. The agreement between such bitter ideological enemies stunned the rest of the world.

After overrunning France, Hitler turned on Stalin. He broke the nonaggression pact by invading the Soviet Union in 1941 and driving deep into the country. Over the next four years, the Soviet population would suffer terribly from war and Nazi brutality. By the end of the war in 1945, some 30 million Soviet soldiers and civilians had lost their lives, and much of the country was devastated by incessant fighting. The wholesale destruction of Soviet industry and agriculture led the U.S. intelligence community to conclude that the Soviet Union would be unable to mount any major military operations for the next 15 years.

The memories of German invasions in 1914 and 1941, and Western intervention in the Russian Civil War, left Stalin more paranoid than ever about the need for security from foreign threats. He refused to withdraw his army from the Eastern European countries that Soviet troops occupied as they drove Nazi forces back to Germany. In these countries, the Soviet Union set up communist governments whose policies were aligned with those of the Soviet Union. Eastern Europe thus formed a buffer zone between the Soviet Union and the West and created a closed economic area for Soviet exploitation. The presence of the Soviet Red Army in Eastern Europe left the Western powers few options but to accept the situation or attack the Soviet Union.

Relations between the United States and the Soviet Union were tense throughout the Stalin era, but they grew increasingly confrontational after World War II. In June of 1948, the Soviets imposed a blockade of Western traffic in and out of the Allied-controlled zone of the German capital, Berlin. The Soviets hoped to dislodge the Western Allies from the city, which was completely enclosed within the Soviet-occupied eastern portion of Germany. The Allied powers responded with an airlift that forced the Soviets to abandon the blockade by May of 1949.

CONTAINMENT

The Berlin blockade signaled the formal beginning of an extended period of U.S.-Soviet political and military rivalry known as the Cold War. During this time, the United States adopted a policy toward the Soviet Union known as containment, first articulated by U.S. diplomat George Kennan.

One of the main architects of U.S. foreign policy, Kennan recognized that the Soviet state commanded the loyalty of its people by raising the constant threat of invasion and by arguing that only a highly centralized and militarized state could protect the country from foreign takeover. Kennan asserted that the Communist Party successfully used these ideas to demand sacrifice and allegiance of the Soviet people at the cost of personal liberties and a better quality of life. He also predicted that this constant fortress mentality, if denied an outlet, would eventually push the Soviet system to the brink of collapse. His idea, then, was to defeat communism by containing it to the Soviet Union if possible.

Kennan advised the United States to identify and defend only its most vital spheres of interest. These would be major centers of industrial power, such as Western Europe and Japan. By opposing the Soviets at every vital strategic point, Kennan calculated that the West's material, ideological, and strategic advantages would eventually win out in a war of attrition. Built into the strategy, too, were opportunities to allow the Soviets an honorable way out rather than the sole option of warfare.

A group of U.S. policy analysts known as *idealists* felt that containment did not go far enough in meeting the Soviet challenge. They complained that losing even peripheral interests meant a loss to Western industry of clients in the developing world. These losses also represented psychological defeats in the ideological struggle between communism and capitalism. Because of these concerns, containment underwent intellectual revision in a 1950 National Security Council directive known as NSC-68.

This NSC-68 document called for a massive U.S. military buildup to counter Soviet aggression. Believing that the Soviets understood raw force only, the idealists claimed aggression by the Soviet Union had to be met on a worldwide basis with military might, no matter the cost. The strategy outlined in NSC-68 placed the world on the brink of nuclear holocaust and paved the way for an intense period of domestic U.S. anticommunism in the 1950s. The decade saw the United States fight a Soviet-backed North Korean invasion of South Korea, as well as the beginnings of U.S. military involvement to oppose communist influence in Vietnam.

POST-STALINISM

Stalin's death in 1953 set off another struggle for Soviet leadership that was eventually won by Nikita Khrushchev. In a reversal of policy, Khrushchev denounced Stalin's brutalities and the cult of personality that had grown up around Stalin. Khrushchev promoted political reform and moved to soften relations with the West. He characterized the United States as a rival rather than an enemy, a move that angered many hard-line Soviet communists as well as the Soviet Union's ally, Communist China.

Khrushchev reopened high-level dialogue with the United States to ease the strain in relations that had heightened during the final days of the Eisenhower administration. However, when the Soviets downed an American U2 reconnaissance plane flying over the Soviet Union, tensions between the superpowers rose once again. The situation was eventually defused, and President John F. Kennedy's administration believed that Khrushchev desired a period of calm in foreign affairs to gain time to make economic progress at home and solidify his political base.

Superpower relations again took a dangerous turn in October 1962, when President Kennedy discovered that the Soviet Union was building secret missile bases in Cuba. The United States imposed a naval quarantine of Cuba and demanded the removal of all Soviet missile bases from the island. Khrushchev threatened to launch tactical nuclear weapons against Western Europe in the event of a U.S. invasion of Cuba. For seven days, the world teetered on the brink of a nuclear war. The deadlock in the Cuban Missile Crisis, as it was called, was finally resolved when the Soviets agreed to remove their missiles from Cuba.

The Cuban Missile Crisis marked the depth of Cold War animosity between the United States and the Soviet Union. It also ushered in an extended period during which superpower relations made little progress. Khrushchev's ouster as Soviet leader in 1964, and the eventual succession of hard-liner Leonid Brezhnev, further lowered expectations for a thawing in international affairs. Every positive development, such as the 1968 signing of the Nuclear Non-Proliferation Treaty, seemed to be balanced by a setback, such as the Soviet invasion of Czechoslovakia that year. Fading hopes for improved relations were further undercut by the 1968 election of President Richard Nixon, a longtime staunch anticommunist.

FROM DÉTENTE TO PERESTROIKA

Despite his reputation as a Cold War warrior, President Nixon sought to improve U.S.-Soviet relations. Rather than any desire to create an environment of general good will, Nixon was motivated by the recognition that the two nations had specific areas of mutual interest. The resulting relaxation of tensions between the superpowers was known as détente. The Strategic Arms Limitation Treaty signed at the 1972 Moscow summit meeting represented the application of détente in an area where both powers shared similar interests—the reduction of the threat of nuclear war.

President Nixon was convinced that the time of U.S.-Soviet bipolar world dominance was ending and that a multipolar world order was rapidly approaching. He anticipated a deepening split in Chinese-Soviet relations and saw China as an emerging global power. Sensing this change in political dynamics, and realizing that the United States did not have the resources to sustain its current level of global commitment, Nixon embraced a strategy called triangular diplomacy. To this end, Nixon pursued the opportunity to establish relations with the People's Republic of China as a way to pressure the Soviet Union to adopt less confrontational policies.

The United States continued to pursue a policy of détente after Nixon resigned the presidency in 1974. His successors, Gerald Ford and then Jimmy Carter, continued to negotiate arms control treaties with the Soviet Union while avoiding military confrontation. The 1979 Soviet invasion of Afghanistan, however, spelled the end of détente. President Carter withdrew U.S. athletes from the 1980 Summer Olympic Games in Moscow to protest the Soviet invasion. Carter's successor, Ronald Reagan, presided over a renewed era of U.S.-Soviet hostilities.

President Reagan believed that the United States could deal effectively with the Soviet Union only from a position of U.S. strength. He called for massive investments in defense and proposed the development of a high-tech missile defense system nicknamed Star Wars. American military expansion was matched by Soviet defense spending, which put great strains on the Soviet economy. The occupation of Afghanistan was also becoming a serious burden on the Soviet Union. Despite years of fighting and massive Soviet casualties, Afghan rebels still successfully resisted Soviet forces. Like the United States in Vietnam, the Soviet Union became bogged down in a guerrilla war in Afghanistan that was growing increasingly unpopular among the Russian people at home.

Brezhnev's neglect of domestic affairs and obsession with military and technological rivalry with the United States brought the Soviet Union to a time of crisis in the mid-1980s. His death in 1982 was followed by a period of political jockeying by members of the Soviet leadership. In 1985, Mikhail Gorbachev emerged as the victor in the contest for power. Gorbachev inherited a country whose economy had been severely weakened under Brezhnev's rule and a populace that was growing ever more restive in the face of shortages of food and consumer goods.

To ease the burden on the weak Soviet economy, Gorbachev supported an end to the nuclear arms race, as well as a reduction in conventional arms. He opened a dialogue with Western leaders, emphasizing the shared benefits of reducing stockpiles of intercontinental ballistic missiles (ICBMs). In 1987, the United States and Soviet Union signed the Intermediate Nuclear Forces (INF) arms limitation treaty. Two years later, the Soviet Union pulled its troops out of Afghanistan.

Domestically, Gorbachev instituted the twin programs of *glasnost* (openness) and *perestroika* (economic reform). Glasnost was an effort to reveal the terrible secrets of the Soviet past that had been hidden by previous regimes, and to promote more openness, or transparency, in government. It was an attempt to win the confidence and trust of a public that had been motivated for decades by lies and intimidation. Perestroika represented a restructuring of the Soviet economy to promote private investment and reverse policies that had hindered productivity.

Though Western leaders praised these strategies as a welcome move toward democracy, they produced domestic troubles for Gorbachev. Perestroika failed in its attempt to reform Soviet economic policies by not completely abandoning central planning. Glasnost, meanwhile, set off demands for independence in many Soviet republics and brought to the surface local ethnic and religious tensions that had been repressed under Soviet rule.

As Gorbachev's reform drive stalled, both reformers and conservatives roiled in discontent. An attempted 1991 coup by communist hard-liners unleashed massive street protests in Moscow. Poorly coordinated and lacking support from the military, the coup soon collapsed. Boris Yeltsin, president of the Russian Republic, led the resistance in the capital and helped reinstall Gorbachev into power. However, the coup irreparably damaged Gorbachev's credibility, and he resigned as president of the Soviet Union on December 25, 1991. Gorbachev turned power over to Boris Yeltsin, who announced the dissolution of the Soviet Union the next day.

POST-SOVIET RUSSIA

The Union of Soviet Socialist Republics was replaced by a new entity, the Commonwealth of Independent States (CIS). The CIS is a loose alliance composed of 12 of the 15 newly independent former Soviet republics. (The Baltic states of Estonia, Latvia, and Lithuania chose not to join the CIS.) The Russian Federation, successor state to the former Russian Federated Soviet

Republic, assumed the seat in the United Nations that had been held by the Soviet Union. As the largest and most populous of the former Soviet republics, the home of the former Soviet capital Moscow, and the inheritor of most of the Soviet Union's military might, Russia is looked on as the successor to the Soviet Union.

In Russia, Yeltsin adopted a policy of aggressive desovietization, reversing Soviet economic and political policies, removing former Soviet officials from power, and even outlawing symbols of the old regime. He began a thorough privatization of the Soviet economy, auctioning off state-owned enterprises and breaking up the nation's collectivized farms. These policies were popular in the West and among much of the Russian public. However, Yeltsin's reforms brought significant instability to a society that had resisted change for almost 75 years.

The privatization of Russian industry was accompanied by charges of massive corruption, as a few well-connected businessmen were able to purchase valuable assets for a fraction of their true value. The explosion of unrestrained capitalist sentiment in Russia led to the rise of organized crime and an unprecedented level of crime and violence. Yeltsin also faced domestic political challenges, including an armed uprising in the province of Chechnya. Civil wars in neighboring countries such as Georgia and Armenia also threatened Russian political stability.

Throughout the 1990s, Yeltsin maintained a close political and personal relationship with U.S. President Bill Clinton. The United States supported Russian economic and political reforms, even though it opposed Yeltsin's use of force in Chechnya. Despite reservations about some of Yeltsin's policies, the Clinton administration saw him as a valuable ally.

At home, however, Yeltsin was growing less popular as his economic shock therapy drove more and more Russians into poverty. The failed Soviet policies had to be corrected, but doing so meant dismantling the social safety net that once supported most Russian citizens. The state was forced to lay off thousands of workers and had difficulty paying those it kept. Soldiers often went months without pay, prompting discontent and leading to a rash of desertions. With little prospect of income from state-funded research work, Russian weapons scientists often turned to selling their expertise to other nations, thus raising concerns about rogue states or terrorist groups obtaining nuclear weapons from cash-strapped former Soviet republics.

RUSSIA UNDER PUTIN

In 2000, Vladimir Putin, former head of the Soviet secret police (KGB) and an unabashed Russian nationalist intent on restoring Russia's stature as a world power, was elected to succeed Yeltsin as president of Russia. While most Russians were glad to be rid of Soviet rule, they lamented the decline of Russia's international prestige following the collapse of the Soviet Union. Putin seized on that sentiment in his presidential campaign, announcing support for rebuilding Russia's security services, a vigorous nationalist foreign policy, and market-friendly economic policies.

When President George W. Bush announced an international war on terrorism following the September 11, 2001, terrorist attacks on the World Trade Center and the Pentagon, Putin quickly aligned Russia with the Bush program. Additionally, Putin has been much more aggressive than Yeltsin in repressing Chechen independence and replying to terrorist attacks in Russia. In the three years following September 11, Putin ordered military assaults to resolve terrorist hostage crises that took place in a Moscow theatre and in a school in Russia's Caucasus region.

Putin's willingness to settle matters with force troubles some U.S. observers, as does his increasing tendency toward authoritarianism—bypassing the Russian parliament and dismissing political appointees who oppose his policies. In 2005, he amended the Russian constitution to replace the system of popularly elected regional governors to one in which the president appoints the governors, significantly increasing the power of the president and the central government at the expense of local populations.

Putin also embarked on a highly publicized and widely criticized anticorruption campaign that involved prosecuting prominent Russian businessmen for fraud and tax evasion. Many observers called the charges politically motivated and saw them as a way to return control of critical industries such as oil and gas to the state. They also felt that Putin used the defendants, who were highly unpopular with the Russian public, as scapegoats for his own inability to make progress in revitalizing Russia's economy.

As of early 2005, the U.S. relationship with Russia was ambiguous. Putin is first and foremost committed to advancing Russian interests and bolstering Russian power and prestige. In some cases, such as in the war on terrorism, those goals coincide with the objectives of U.S. national security. In others, however, they lead to significant differences of opinion between the United States and Russia. For example, Russia's long-standing political and economic ties to Iraq contributed to Putin's refusal to join the U.S.-led invasion of that nation in 2003. The United States and Russia are no longer bitter ideological foes as they were during the Cold War. However, they remain rivals for geopolitical influence in a complex and competitive world.

—Jack A. Jarmon

See also Arms Race; Cold War; Commonwealth of Independent States (CIS); Communism; Communism and National Security; Containment and the Truman Doctrine; Cuban Missile Crisis; Détente; Geopolitics; Nixon, Richard, and National Policy; Putin, Vladimir (1952–); Reagan, Ronald, and National Policy; Terrorism, War on International; Union of Soviet Socialist Republics (USSR); World War II (1939–1945); Yeltsin, Boris (1931–)

Further Reading

Cameron, Fraser. *U.S. Foreign Policy After the Cold War.* London: Routledge, 2002.

Hanson, Philip. *The Rise and Fall of the Soviet Economy: An Economic History of the USSR, 1945–1991.* New York: Longman, 2003.

Suny, Ronald Grigor. *The Soviet Experiment: Russia, the USSR, and the Successor States.* New York: Oxford University Press, 1997.

SPACE RACE

Cold War competition between the United States and the Soviet Union to gain technological superiority and achieve historic firsts in the field of space flight and exploration. The space race served political goals as well as scientific ones. The superpowers viewed their accomplishments in the space race as a public measure of the relative strengths of the capitalist and communist systems. Beyond that, the competition for superiority in outer space rapidly accelerated development of many areas of high technology that have since become an integral part of modern society, most notably computers and telecommunications.

SPUTNIK AND EXPLORER

The beginning of the space race traditionally dates to the launch of the Soviet Sputnik satellite on October 4, 1957. The Sputnik was the first artificial satellite placed into Earth's orbit by humans. However, both the United States and Soviet Union had been working seriously on the problem of space flight since the end of World War II. The defeated Germans had made significant progress in this area during the war, developing the world's first ballistic missile, the V-2 rocket.

After the war, both sides scrambled to acquire the services of as many former German rocket scientists as possible. The United States seemed to fare much better in this effort, capturing the head of the V-2 program, Dr. Werner von Braun, and many of his top assistants. Yet, despite this head start, work on a U.S. rocket capable of leaving the earth's atmosphere was slow and filled with setbacks. Meanwhile, the Soviets were making steady progress that eluded the notice of U.S. intelligence services.

The Sputnik announcement shocked and stunned the United States. The Soviet Union not only had managed to launch a rocket into outer space, it had also successfully placed a satellite into Earth orbit. By contrast, the U.S. space program was marked by a series of spectacular failures, as several rockets exploded on or shortly after launch. These failures appeared to be an indictment of the relative weakness of U.S. science education. In the wake of the Sputnik launch, U.S. President Dwight D. Eisenhower spearheaded a movement to place greater emphasis on teaching science in American schools.

In December 1957, the Soviets launched a second Sputnik satellite into orbit, this one carrying a live dog, named Laika. The move seemed to confirm the total Soviet dominance in the space race. The United States, however, was not willing to concede defeat so easily. On January 31, 1958, a Mercury Redstone rocket carried the first U.S. satellite, *Explorer I*, into orbit. On its flight, *Explorer I* discovered the Van Allen radiation belt that surrounds Earth. This marked the first practical use of an orbiting satellite; neither Sputnik had performed any scientific functions.

The success of *Explorer I* brought renewed confidence to the U.S. space program and served notice that both sides were willing to devote substantial economic and political resources to the space race. Later that year, the United States authorized the establishment of a separate government agency—the National Aeronautics and Space Administration (NASA)—to coordinate the nation's space exploration efforts. The race for space had begun in earnest.

MANNED FLIGHT

When John F. Kennedy became president of the United States in 1961, he set the nation a goal of putting men on the moon and returning them safely by the end of the decade. Kennedy issued his challenge just a month after Soviet cosmonaut Yuri Gagarin became the first human to fly in space on April 21, 1961. Gagarin made a single orbit of the earth in a flight that lasted just 108 minutes. Three weeks later, astronaut Alan Shepard became the first American in space, although his Mercury spacecraft did not achieve orbit. The first American to orbit the earth was John Glenn, who achieved that feat in February 1962.

The Soviet Union recorded a string of other firsts during the early days of human space flight. In August 1962, the Soviets launched the first spacecraft to carry more than one person into space. In June 1963, Soviet cosmonaut Valentina Tereschkova became the first woman in space. Soviets made the first flight without spacesuits in 1964, and cosmonaut Aleksei Leonov made the world's first spacewalk outside of a spacecraft in 1965.

While the Soviets were making headlines with these pioneering accomplishments, the United States was working methodically toward achieving the goal set by President Kennedy. In 1961, NASA established the Apollo program to develop the technology needed for a lunar landing. Two years later, it launched Project Gemini, which sent astronauts into orbit to perform tasks that would help prepare them for the duties they would face on a moon flight. The Gemini and Apollo programs carried out more than 20 space flights in preparation for a manned flight to the moon. On July 20, 1969, *Apollo 11* landed on the moon and astronaut Neil Armstrong became the first human to set foot on the lunar surface.

POST-APOLLO DEVELOPMENTS

Most observers felt that the U.S. moon landing ended the space race with a decisive American victory. The Soviet Union never matched the feat, instead concentrating on the development of orbiting space stations, such as the Salyut series and *Mir*. The United States sent several more Apollo missions to the moon, but made no further plans for human exploration of other planets. The formal end of the space race occurred with the 1975 joint Apollo-Soyuz mission, in which U.S. and Soviet spacecraft docked, or joined, in orbit while their crews visited one another's craft and performed joint scientific experiments.

After this time, the goals of the two space programs diverged sharply. The Soviets focused on space stations, while the United States pursued development of the space shuttle, a reusable orbital vehicle, formally known as the Space Transportation System (STS). The intense head-to-head competition that marked the peak years of the space race gave way to an acknowledgment that space exploration was no longer considered a matter of critical political importance.

The challenges of conquering space, however, did produce lasting scientific results. Computer technology, for example, advanced at an astronomical rate during the space race. Spacecraft required computers powerful enough to control complex functions yet small enough to fit on board a cramped capsule. The needs of the space program also led to a host of breakthroughs in electronics, telecommunications, guidance, and remote control systems. Much of the technology that runs modern society was developed and perfected because of the space race.

Of course, space flight also led to the development of intercontinental ballistic missiles (ICBMs) capable of delivering nuclear warheads thousands of miles away. The guidance systems developed for space flight increased the accuracy of ICBMs, allowing pinpoint delivery of nuclear warheads to distant targets. Many of the electronics pioneered in space flight have since found extensive military uses. The legacy of the space race is thus very mixed. It has, for better or worse, had a significant impact on life in the 21st century.

See also Ballistic Missiles; Cold War; Intercontinental Ballistic Missiles (ICBMs); Science, Technology, and Security; Sputnik

Further Reading

Collins, Martin J. *Space Race: The U.S.-USSR Competition to Reach the Moon.* Petaluma, CA: Pomegranate Communications, 1999.

Scott, David, and Aleksei Leonov. *Two Sides of the Moon: Our Story of the Cold War Space Race.* New York: Thomas Dunne Books, 2004.

Van Allen, James A., Matt Bille, and Erika Lishock. *The First Space Race: Launching the World's First Satellites.* College Station, TX: Texas A&M University Press, 2004.

REFLECTIONS

Nuclear Weapons and the Space Race

During their competition for outer space sovereignty, the United States and the Soviet Union promoted the idea that countries were willing to devote significant economic and political resources to the space race. With the resulting advanced technology, each nation also amassed huge arsenals of nuclear weapons, creating a legacy of the space race that many believe no longer serves U.S. interests or national security.

What steps can governments take, responsibly, recognizing that policymakers must always balance a host of competing priorities and interests? First and foremost is for the declared nuclear states to accept that the Cold War is in fact over, to break free of the attitudes, habits, and practices that perpetuate enormous inventories, forces standing alert, and targeting plans encompassing thousands of aimpoints. Second, for the undeclared states to embrace the harsh lessons of the Cold War: that nuclear weapons are inherently dangerous, hugely expensive, militarily inefficient, and morally indefensible; that implacable hostility and alienation will almost certainly over time lead to a nuclear crisis; that the strength of deterrence is inversely proportional to the stress of confrontation; and that nuclear war is a raging, insatiable beast whose instincts and appetites we pretend to understand but cannot possibly control.

—General Lee Butler
Former Commander, Strategic Air Command
Speech given at the State of the World Forum
San Francisco, October 3, 1996

SPACE-BASED WEAPONS

Weapons deployed from space. Space-based weapons fall into three general categories—those that defend against ballistic missiles, those that attack or defend satellites, and those that attack terrestrial targets. Currently in these categories, land-based systems are the only weapons to have been deployed. To defend against space-based weapons, two types of land-based systems have been tested—antisatellite weapons (ASATs), which have been under development since the 1960s, and ground-based lasers that impair or disable satellites.

Outer space has been used for military purposes—such as reconnaissance missions or targeting—since the launch of the first Sputnik by the Soviet Union in 1957. In 1959, the UN General Assembly set up the Committee on the Peaceful Uses of Outer Space (COPUOS) to promote international cooperation in space. Shortly after the Sputnik launch, the fear of

bombardment satellites prompted both the Soviet Union and the United States to research space weapons for defensive and offensive purposes. While the development of submarine-launched ballistic missiles served to limit offensive space weapons, research into defensive space weapons continued.

In the 1960s, antisatellite (ASAT) weapons were developed to disable enemy satellites. These early antisatellite weapons consisted of missiles packing high explosives and shrapnel; kinetic weapons were investigated later. Although many ASAT weapons tested by both the United States and the Soviet Union failed to perform as expected, and treaties were signed to limit the deployment of space weapons, research into new weapons systems continued.

In the late 1990s, the U.S. Army began work on the kinetic energy antisatellite system (KEASAT), which fires a multitude of pellets to slow down enemy satellites, forcing them to burn up in the atmosphere. Ground-based lasers have also been successfully tested. In 1997, the U.S. military tested a chemical laser against a satellite, temporarily disabling its optical sensors. Russia was known to have tested such weapons as well.

The weaponization of space is controlled through a number of norms and treaties, most notably the 1967 Outer Space Treaty, which prohibits the deployment of weapons of mass destruction in space and was signed by 97 countries, including the United States. The treaty bans weapons of mass destruction, defined as "nuclear weapons or any other kinds of weapons of mass destruction," from space. However, it does not prohibit the launching of ballistic missiles, such as ICBMs, through space. What constitutes a weapon of mass destruction is also under debate, and so many experts feel that the Outer Space Treaty is outdated.

The second most important treaty that pertains to space weapons is the Antiballistic Missile (ABM) Treaty. Signed by the United States and the Soviet Union in 1972, the ABM treaty constrained each country's antimissile defense to two fixed, ground-based defenses of 100 missile interceptors each. The ABM treaty also prohibited interference with monitoring satellites. Concerns that a nationwide defense system would spur a renewed arms race caused the Soviet Union and the United States to reduce the number by half. Both sides reasoned that a nuclear first-strike policy was unacceptable and, ultimately, that remaining vulnerable to each other's offensive nuclear weapons, while maintaining a policy aimed at deterrence, was the lesser of two evils.

However, research into space weapons continued in the 1970s and 1980s. In March 1983, President Ronald Reagan announced the development of the Strategic Defense Initiative (SDI). The program, which became known as Star Wars, sought to present the end to nuclear weapons through perfect, space-based defense. However, SDI was fraught with political and scientific difficulties. Notable scientists argued that with cheap technologies, such as multiple dummy warheads, an opponent could easily overwhelm a missile defense space weapon, thwarting the weapon's capacity to respond to real danger.

Many defense experts consider the ABM treaty to be a Cold War leftover that is dangerously outdated. In January 1999, the administration of President Bill Clinton approached Russian president Boris Yeltsin with a request to amend the Antiballistic Missile (ABM) Treaty to permit U.S. deployment of a limited National Missile Defense (NMD) system aimed at protecting U.S. territory from missile attacks by rogue nations.

In 2001, President George W. Bush met with Russian President Vladimir Putin to promote a reduction of nuclear weapons and abandon the framework of the ABM treaty. Both sides agreed to cooperate in the development of national missile defense systems, symbolically ending the ABM treaty. The collapse of the ABM treaty is illustrative of the move to test and deploy space-based weapons.

In addition to the costs of developing space-based weapons, many predict that the development of such weapons will launch a renewed race to weaponize space with China. However, should the United States decide not to put weapons in space, Moscow and Beijing might still pursue antisatellite technologies of their own.

Critics argue that the risks of weaponizing space far outweigh the benefits. First and foremost, inexpensive antisatellite technology—such as ground-based lasers or nuclear missiles—could incapacitate space weapons as well. The stakes are high. As of January 2004, some 600 operational military and commercial satellites were in orbit, and the U.S. Space Command estimated that by 2010, nearly 2,000 satellites would be operational and in orbit. The United States also spends large sums on commercial space uses and even more on military uses in space.

Proponents of space weapons argue that the U.S. investment and reliance on satellites makes protection of those assets a necessity. Given recent public statements and military assessments, the deployment of space weapons has the air of inevitability, causing some to suggest the need for revamping the Outer Space Treaty. Current military plans, such as the Air Force's Vision 2020, outline the need for weapons to defend those assets and, probably, conduct offensive operations in space.

Many different types of weapons are envisioned, some as simple as jamming technologies that can be directed from orbit to others that focus lethal energy or employ kinetic weapons that are dropped on their targets. In the near term, space weapons will include hypersonic bombers that could attack targets anywhere in the world within a matter of hours.

See also Antiballistic Missile (ABM) Treaty (1972); Missiles; Strategic Defense Initiative (SDI)

Further Reading

Preston, Bob, Dana J. Johnson, Sean Edwards, Michael Miller, and Calvin Shipbaugh. *Space Weapons Earth Wars.* Santa Monica, CA: RAND Corporation, 2002.

SPANISH-AMERICAN WAR (1898)

Between the United States and Spain (April 21– August 12), brief war fought mainly in the Spanish colonial territories of Cuba and the Philippines and considered a turning point in the history of U.S. foreign relations. Victory in the Spanish-American War quickly went to the United States, and peace negotiations resulted in U.S. control over Cuba, and the annexation of Puerto Rico, Guam, and the Philippines. The Spanish-American War turned the United States into a world power, as it removed Spain from the Western Hemisphere and established an important U.S. presence in the Pacific.

Cuban revolutionaries had been fighting Spanish colonialists since the 1860s. U.S. public support for the Cuban cause grew as the rebels gained ground in the late 1890s. The U.S. press strongly promoted intervention on behalf of Cuba and published accounts of Spanish concentration camps and of the destruction of U.S. property on the island. Expansionist politicians, U.S. business interests, and general public opinion also favored war against Spain and urged a reluctant President William McKinley to intervene on behalf of Cuba.

On February 15, 1898, the U.S. battleship *Maine*, which had been sent to Havana Harbor to protect U.S. citizens and property, was hit by an explosion and sunk, killing more than 250 men. Although a thorough investigation eventually concluded that technical problems had caused the explosion, the U.S. public and Congress concluded that the Spanish had attacked the *Maine* and as a result, prowar sentiment in the United States was further incensed.

The U.S. Congress began preparations for war as President McKinley demanded that Spain grant Cuba its independence and withdraw from the island after U.S. mediation. Spain refused and declared war on the United States on April 24; Congress then issued an April 21 retroactive declaration of war on Spain.

The ensuing conflict was tilted in favor of U.S. forces. Admiral George Dewey led a quick and easy naval victory over the Spanish fleet in Manila Bay, Philippines. With the help of Filipino forces, U.S. land forces soon occupied Manila and the whole island of Luzon. War was also waged in Cuba, where 16,000 U.S. troops, including Theodore Roosevelt's Rough Riders, captured Santiago by July 17. The island of Puerto Rico was quickly occupied in August. An armistice was signed on August 12, 1898.

The Treaty of Paris peace agreement was ratified by the U.S. Senate on February 6, 1899. Although Cuba was now free, the United States forced the Cuban Constitutional Convention to accept the Platt Amendment, which, among other provisions, gave the United States the power to intervene in Cuba to protect Cuban sovereignty. The Platt Amendment also established a 99-year lease of the naval base at Guantánamo in Cuba, and it forced enactment of programs to make Cuba more attractive to U.S. investors. Puerto Rico also was annexed by the United States as an *unincorporated territory,* and its inhabitants were not made U.S. citizens until 1917. Guam also was ceded to the United States as part of the peace agreements that ended the war.

U.S. commercial and military interests also led to a demand for the annexation of the Philippines. The strategic importance of a Manila base allowed easier access to Chinese trading ports and would prevent U.S. commercial rivals France, Germany, and Great Britain from seizing the islands. Philippine rebels fighting Spanish colonialists had initially welcomed and fought alongside the U.S. troops. However, when it became clear that the United States was not leaving the islands, fierce fighting erupted between the rebels and U.S. troops and lasted through 1901. Lower-level conflict continued until 1913.

The Spanish-American War led to charges that President McKinley's foreign policy was expansionist and promoted U.S. imperialism. In response, a large and significant anti-imperialist movement soon emerged in the United States among middle-class and wealthy professionals, including large numbers of women. Many historians have argued that the Spanish-American War was really about the United States seeking markets for U.S. goods rather than land or the responsibility of subjugating foreigners.

See also Interventionism; Isolationism

Further Reading

Bradford, James C., ed. *Crucible of Empire: The Spanish-American War and Its Aftermath.* Annapolis, MD: Naval Institute Press, 1993.

Freidel, Frank B. *The Splendid Little War.* Springfield, NJ: Burford Books, 1958.

May, Ernest. *Imperial Democracy: The Emergence of America As a Great Power.* New York: HarperCollins, 1973.

Trask, David. *The War with Spain in 1898.* Lincoln, NE: University of Nebraska Press, 1997.

SPECIAL FORCES

Elite military units specially organized and trained to conduct unconventional warfare, usually behind enemy lines. Special operations forces (SOF) work in small units and the selection process for SOF operators is extremely demanding. SOF units use their specialized skills to gain an advantage over numerically superior adversaries, using surprise to exploit weaknesses in an opponent's defenses. Other distinctive characteristics of SOF units include self-sufficiency and the ability to operate under a variety of conditions. Special forces often possess unique language skills and traditionally have trained and worked with indigenous forces.

MISSION AND ORGANIZATION

The line between conventional and unconventional operations is often fuzzy. In practice, it is sometimes difficult to isolate missions that are the unique purview of special forces. This is because conventional forces also operate in hostile environments and perform many of the same missions as SOF units. U.S. military doctrine tries to clarify the distinction by declaring that SOF units operate in "hostile, denied, or politically sensitive areas." In other words, SOF is used in places where it is not feasible to apply overt conventional force.

Special Forces Missions

The U.S. Department of Defense distinguishes nine principal SOF missions. These include direct action, special reconnaissance, foreign internal defense, unconventional warfare, counterterrorism, psychological operations, civil affairs, counterproliferation, and information operations.

Direct actions include guidance for precision weapons systems, mine warfare, and personnel rescue. Special reconnaissance involves human intelligence gathering in hostile or denied areas. Foreign internal defense means helping foreign host governments fight domestic insurgents. Unconventional warfare is composed of a range of activities including sabotage and guerrilla warfare. Counterterrorism relies on intelligence gathering and preemptive strikes. Psychological operations help missions succeed by influencing the emotions or objective reasoning of targets. Civil affairs are efforts to encourage and maintain positive interaction with local military and civilian officials. Counterproliferation involves intelligence gathering to stem the spread of weapons of mass destruction. Finally, information operations target enemy command and communications networks.

In addition to the nine principal SOF missions, there are six collateral missions. These include coalition support, combat search and rescue, counterdrug activities, countermine activities, foreign humanitarian assistance, and security assistance. The last category is *special activities,* or covert missions that are not publicly acknowledged by the United States. Such activities require presidential approval and strict congressional oversight.

Special Forces Organization

Each military service has its own dedicated special forces. The United States Special Operations Command (SOCOM) oversees the SOF of all services. These forces usually are deployed to regional combatant commands, but also may be integrated into a number of different command authorities depending on location and the nature of the deployment.

Contemporary Army SOF units include, among others, Army Special Operations Forces (Green Berets) and Rangers. Delta Force is a more recent addition, created in the late 1970s as a counterterrorism unit proficient in civilian rescue. Air Force parachute-rescue jumpers (PJs) act as ground-based forward air controllers and specialists in combat search and rescue. Navy SEALs are experts at underwater demolition and amphibious infiltration. Marine Force Recon is an elite unit, even though elitism is anathema to corps culture. Although these units each have different specialties, all operatives undergo thorough military training and pride themselves on flexibility and adaptability.

HISTORY OF U.S. SPECIAL FORCES

Units resembling special forces have existed for centuries. In 1756, British Major Robert Rogers organized a battalion to act as both a reconnaissance and strike force against French and Indian enemies in North America. This group ranged through the New England wilderness and took the name Rogers's Rangers. During the American War for Independence, U.S. commanders Ethan Allen and Francis Marion formed small groups of militia to perform surprise attacks on British forces. Confederate cavalry led by Nathan Bedford Forrest became adept at infiltrating Union lines during the American Civil War and wreaking havoc in rear areas. Merrill's Marauders, an aggressive cavalry unit from Texas, also earned a reputation for harrying Union supplies and communications.

The modern origins of SOF, however, lie in World War II. U.S. Army Ranger battalions trained with the British Special Air Service and operated behind Japanese lines in the Philippines, during the invasion of Italy, and on the D-day landings at Normandy. World War II also gave birth to the Office of Strategic Services (forerunner of today's Central Intelligence Agency), U.S. Navy Frogmen, and Air Commandos. These groups eventually evolved into the modern Army Special Forces, Navy SEALs, and Air Force special operators, respectively.

Special forces have been involved in most U.S. combat operations since World War II. In some cases, they played crucial roles, such as in the invasion of Panama in 1989. Special forces have also been subject to a good deal of political controversy. Before Vietnam, for example, the Army Green Berets enjoyed wide popularity. But accusations of torture and executions during the war sullied their reputation and increased tension between SOF and conventional forces.

Special forces historically have also dealt with acrimony from within the conventional military establishment. Conventional force commanders, who often believe that victory is the result of the application of overwhelming force, tend to view SOF with skepticism. Special operations such as sabotage and psychological warfare play only a minor role in conventional military doctrine. In addition, SOF units break from standard military practices, sometimes eschewing rank and uniform codes. Because conventional officers do not always understand the role of special forces, they occasionally mistrust the SOF operators under their command.

Special forces are important in the ongoing debate over military transformation. Advocates believe that the United States should make greater use of its highly trained special forces. They argue that the United States currently has less need to rely on conventional units because it is unlikely to face an enemy of comparable military strength for decades. Special forces, by contrast, are ideal for the asymmetric confrontations more typical of the 21st century. The speed and flexibility of SOF allows them to track clandestine adversaries, and their language skills assist coordination with local forces. Some defense analysts, however, worry that too much faith is being put into SOF capabilities. They argue that the United States still needs large conventional forces if it wants to pursue an assertive foreign policy.

See also Asymmetric Warfare; Conventional Forces in Europe Treaty (1990); Covert Action; Covert Operations; Green Berets; Psychological Warfare (PSYOPS)

Further Reading

Marquis, Susan L. *Unconventional Warfare: Rebuilding U.S. Special Operations Forces*. Washington, DC: Brookings Institution Press, 1997.

McRaven, William H. *Spec Ops: Case Studies in Special Operations Warfare: Theory and Practice*. Novato, CA: Presidio Press, 1995.

Paddock, Alfred H., Jr. *U.S. Army Special Warfare: Its Origins*. Lawrence, KS: University Press of Kansas, 2002.

Southworth, Samuel A., and Stephen Tanner. *U.S. Special Forces: A Guide to America's Special Operations Units, The World's Most Elite Fighting Force*. Cambridge, MA: De Capo Press, 2002.

SPUTNIK

The world's first artificial satellite, launched by the Soviet Union on October 4, 1957. The Sputnik program (*sputnik* roughly translates into "fellow traveler") comprised four separate launches.

At a weight of 184 pounds, *Sputnik 1* was sent into space from the Soviet Union's desert rocket testing facility near Tyuratam in the Kazakh Republic. The satellite was designed to relay information about the upper atmosphere back to Earth. The launch of *Sputnik 1* came as a surprise to the United States and created a sense of panic among many experts because it was believed that the Soviets could soon deploy a nuclear missile into space that would be capable of reaching the United States. Thus, far from being heralded as a great scientific achievement, *Sputnik 1* shattered Americans' sense of security and technological superiority.

President Dwight D. Eisenhower was not very concerned with the Soviets being the first into space, but he missed the significance of the event to ordinary Americans. Technology had been a decisive factor in World War II, and fears that communists had taken the technological lead had Americans greatly concerned. After the launch of the 1,120-pound *Sputnik 2* in November 1957, anxieties skyrocketed. Finger pointing among U.S. government officials and military departments led to debate over an ostensible technology gap between the United States and its archrival, the Soviet Union.

Sputnik 2 was also another first for space science—the satellite carried the first live passenger into orbit, a dog named Laika. The third Russian attempt to launch a satellite was a failure, although the fourth attempt was another success. Designated *Sputnik 3*, the satellite was powered by solar panels and returned geophysical data for over two years.

Although the post-Sputnik confidence crisis was largely the work of politicians and fanned by the media, public reaction to the Soviet launches prompted a deeply introspective period in the United States, followed by action to remedy the purported technology gap. It appeared that the Soviet Union had taken the lead in science education, and so such education in the United States received greater attention, particularly precollege physics and elementary-school science. Educators worked with prominent scientists to shape curricula that were to have far-ranging effects on U.S. technological, scientific, and industrial advances.

In 1958, Congress passed the National Defense Education Act (NDEA), which drastically changed the federal government's role in education and provided grants and loans to public and private schools, as well as individuals, for programs in mathematics, foreign language studies, and science. In response to the Soviet challenge, Congress also passed the National Aeronautics and Space Act (1958), creating the National Aeronautics and Space Administration (NASA); in that same year, the Department of Defense formed the Defense Advanced Research Projects Agency (first called ARPA). Numerous projects and agencies were advanced. The space race began with Sputnik. Eleven years later, after the launch of the first Sputnik, the United States became the first to put a man on the moon.

See also Defense Advanced Research Projects Agency (DARPA); Eisenhower, Dwight D., and National Policy; National Defense Education Act (NDEA); Soviet Union, Former (Russia), and U.S. Policy; Space Race

SPY SATELLITES

Use of space satellites to spy on other nations and provide intelligence that might be crucial to a nation's security and other interests. Military strategists have always sought higher ground to look down on enemies, and spy satellites afford just such a unique position.

There are two basic types of spy satellites—those that eavesdrop on communications for signals intelligence, or SIGINT, and those that generate high-quality image intelligence, or IMINT. SIGINT satellites detect and intercept radio, mobile telephone, and data transmissions for the National Security Agency (NSA). Signals intelligence satellites cannot intercept communications carried over landlines, however. The United States operates signals intelligence satellites in geostationary, elliptical, and low Earth orbits.

IMINT satellites return images to the National Imagery and Mapping Agency (NIMA) and fall into three general categories—radar imaging, optical imaging, and a combination of the two. Radar imaging satellites use radio (microwave) signals to scan the earth, while optical satellites use mirrors to gather light for photography. Radar imaging satellites generate a microwave beam, bounce it off an object, receive the echo, and then reconstitute the information into a picture. A relatively new technology is synthetic aperture radar (SAR) satellites, which are unhindered by darkness or bad weather. Optical imaging suffers from the inability to see through clouds, a shortcoming overcome by space-based imaging radar.

All imaging satellites suffer from relatively short windows of opportunity in which to take images. However, due to various technological advances, spy satellites can now remain over an area for about 10 minutes. With enhancements in optical and radar technology, satellite developers hope to place satellites at higher orbits so they can take pictures for longer durations. Imaging quality has also been greatly enhanced. Early optical imaging satellites produced photographs that ranged in resolution down to about two meters. The current generation of U.S. spy satellites is reportedly able to identify objects on the ground as small as 10 centimeters.

The National Reconnaissance Office (NRO) operates satellites for the U.S. military and the intelligence community, while U.S. reconnaissance satellites are launched by the Air Force. The NRO designs, builds, and operates the nation's reconnaissance satellites, and supplies data to the Central Intelligence Agency (CIA) and the Department of Defense (DoD). The first spy satellite program in the United States was named Corona. Corona was designed to take photographs over the Soviet Union and China, replacing the dangerous U2 flights over the territory of those two nations. U2 flights had been ongoing since 1956, but Soviet radar systems had soon proven better able to track the planes than originally thought.

With the fallout from the U2 spy plane incident of 1960, in which Air Force pilot Gary Powers and his plane were shot down over the Soviet Union, a better way of seeing Soviet installations had to be found. Satellite photography proved to be the way. After taking the photographs, the satellite would jettison the developed film back to Earth.

After several rocket failures, Corona made its first successful flight and film return in August 1960. Bringing back the first images of Earth from outer space was no small achievement. Of the first 30 Corona missions, only 12 were considered successes. Camera systems such as those employed in Corona continued in use until the 1980s, after which image data began being beamed directly to Earth.

Spy satellites return enormous amounts of data. While the exact amount of image data collected by spy satellites is classified, experts estimate that orbiting satellites each day produce hundreds of terabytes of data. By comparison, the entire text holdings of the Library of Congress constitutes roughly 20 terabytes.

Since the end of the Cold War, the data from spy satellites has been used in operations throughout the world. However, all this data needs to be processed, examined, and ultimately put to use by people. A classic example of duping U.S. spy satellites is India's nuclear test of 1996.

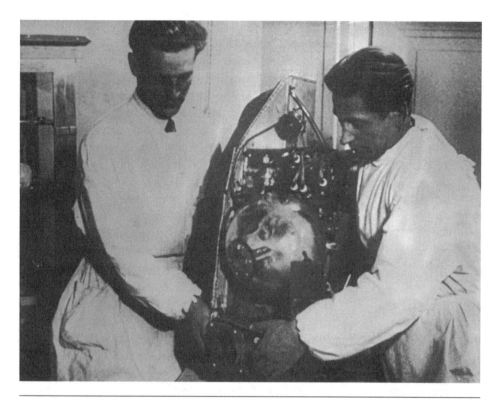

Soviet scientists checking the chamber containing the dog Laika in preparation for the launch of *Sputnik 2*, the second of a series of Sputnik spacecraft sent into Earth orbit. Launched on November 3, 1957, *Sputnik 2* carried Laika aloft to an altitude of 1,060 miles and circled the earth at about 18,000 miles an hour. The first living being to leave Earth and travel to outer space, Laika, a female part-Samoyed terrier, survived in orbit only a day or two before thermal problems in the spacecraft killed her. Nevertheless, the mission provided Soviet scientists with important data on the behavior of a living organism in a space environment.

Source: Corbis.

India put its nuclear testing equipment underground after a story reported that U.S. spy satellites were monitoring their activities. Through charting satellite orbits and cleverly avoiding activity while satellites were overhead, India was able to conduct its test in secrecy.

In recent years, the use of SIGINT to track terrorists has become one of the highest priorities. According to intelligence reports, signals intelligence satellites monitored the whereabouts of Islamic terrorist Osama bin Laden and his satellite and mobile phone communications. Field reports have confirmed satellite intelligence of his general location on a number of occasions.

In addition to the intelligence uses of spy satellites, the media has been quick to take advantage of declassified and unclassified imagery produced by these satellites. The French SPOT (Satellite Pour l'Observation de la Terre, or Earth observation satellite) series of surveillance satellites mainly serves commercial customers. A SPOT satellite observed the Soviet nuclear reactor accident in Chernobyl. On February 22, 1995, President Bill Clinton signed an executive order directing the declassification of intelligence imagery acquired by the first generation of U.S. photoreconnaissance satellites. The National Imagery and Mapping Agency leads U.S. government efforts to declassify and release formerly secret images. Much of that data is now used commercially.

The future development of satellite technology promises even greater resolution and signals techniques. Additional challenges include the hardening of spy satellites against attack and the development of redundant systems to ensure information availability. Future Imagery Architecture (FIA) is a National Reconnaissance Office plan to develop small-satellite technology for a new generation of spy satellites in what analysts believe is the largest intelligence-related contract ever. The supersecret project for the National Reconnaissance Office is estimated to be worth up to $25 billion over two decades, and FIA projects it will be designed to operate effectively for the next few decades.

See also Intelligence and Counterintelligence; Signals Intelligence (SIGINT)

Further Reading

Gaffney, Timothy. *Secret Spy Satellites: America's Eyes in Space.* Berkeley Heights, NJ: Enslow Publishers, 2000.

STALIN, JOSEPH (1878–1953)

Soviet dictator and despot famed for his brilliant tactics, brutal methods, and police-state totalitarian rule.

Stalin was a secretive figure, a man who obscured his past as much as possible, rendering even his birth date a matter of dispute.

Stalin was born Iosif Dzhugashvili in 1878 (he claimed 1879) to poor parents in Georgia, then part of Greater Russia, or the Russian Empire. He attended a strict religious seminary in Tiflis, then became involved in politics. Between 1902 and 1917, Stalin was arrested for revolutionary activity, was exiled within the Russian Empire, and escaped repeatedly.

He first used the pseudonym Stalin—signifying *man of steel*—in 1912, signing that name to an editorial for the newspaper *Pravda*. He used multiple aliases over the years, but eventually settled on Stalin in 1913. Possessed of an excellent memory, a gift for intrigue, and ruthlessness, Stalin came to dominate the Soviet Union for many years.

Stalin became the general secretary of the Soviet Communist Party in 1922, and thereafter used that position to build a support base. When Soviet revolutionary leader Vladimir Lenin died in 1924, Stalin defeated Leon Trotsky—a gifted orator and political philosopher and Stalin's greatest rival—for leadership of the Communist Party. Stalin successfully portrayed Trotsky as a counterrevolutionary and enemy of the Soviet Union, and forced him into exile.

Stalin thus emerged as Lenin's successor, surprising many party members who saw him as an excellent organizer but not a visionary. He worked hard to promote his legitimacy in the eyes of the party and the public, stressing his devoted adherence to Leninism. Stalin went so far as to have history rewritten to make the roles of his adversaries less, and his own revolutionary role greater.

Once in power, Stalin implemented his vision to the detriment of the people. He forced collectivization in agriculture, a move that was both unpopular and unproductive, and led, moreover, to a massive famine. He emphasized military buildup in his first Five-Year Plan, created the first modern command economy, and steered the country toward industrialization. Nevertheless, his rule heartened Russia in the early 1930s. His vision was the dawn of hope after the previous decades of unrest, civil war, and famine. His popularity gave rise to a Stalinist cult of personality.

Stalin was a leader who, like the Machiavellian princes he admired, was more feared than loved. Terror was a fundamental part of the regime, at no time more so than during the purges of 1936–1938. Paranoid and focused on maintaining power, Stalin instituted the so-called Great Terror to rid the country of "anti-Soviet elements." He instituted show trials to make an example of those who had "strayed" and become "traitors." Victims of Stalin's ruthlessness often were sent to prisons or labor camps, known as *gulags*. Millions perished, including ordinary citizens, top party members, and many of the original Bolshevik revolutionaries. Many of these individuals were killed because of their dissent or imaginary crimes against the state, or because they represented threats to Stalin's own power.

Stalin's international politics tended to be opportunistic. In 1939, he formed an alliance with Nazi leader Adolf Hitler against the "capitalist-imperialist victors of World War I," an alliance formalized by the 1939 Nazi-Soviet Nonaggression pact. However, when Hitler launched Operation Barbarossa against the Soviet Union in violation of the alliance, Stalin formed an uneasy Grand Alliance with the United States and Great Britain. After World War II ended, this alliance collapsed with mutual distrust and the intensification of power rivalries and the fall of the Iron Curtain.

Stalin's emphasis on nationalism and active promotion of expansionist interests of the Soviet Union made him very popular in the postwar environment within his country. Though increasingly glorified in the Soviet Union toward the end of his life, Stalin died after a stroke, morose and alienated, on March 5, 1953.

See also Cold War; Potsdam Conference (1945); Soviet Union, Former (Russia), and U.S. Policy; World War II (1939–1945); Yalta Conference (1945)

STAR WARS/MISSILE DEFENSE
See STRATEGIC DEFENSE INITIATIVE (SDI)

STEALTH TECHNOLOGIES

Techniques, designs, and materials employing scientific advances for deceiving radar or other means of detection. Some techniques used in stealth technology can be as simple as pigments that make it hard to see objects against their background or applying materials that absorb radio waves. Others may involve complicated designs to scatter enemy radar signals, confuse infrared detectors, or cloak electromagnetic energy.

While radar-absorbing coatings had been in use since World War II, better stealth designs were made possible by computers. In the early 1970s, the Defense Advanced Research Projects Agency (DARPA) began work on stealth technologies aimed at reducing an object's radar cross section (RCS), or the measure of radio waves reflected back to their point of origin. Diamond-shaped objects proved most able to reduce the RCS, so much so that some planes appeared invisible to conventional radar. Just as looking in a mirror reflects your image, flat perpendicular surfaces returned radio waves directly to the radar antennas.

Stealth technologies are used primarily in aircraft and ships and have proven successful in warfare. During the 1991 Gulf War, the F-117A Nighthawk was heavily used and suffered no losses. Since its debut in 1982, only one Nighthawk aircraft has been lost in combat, and the U.S. Air Force intends to continue flying the planes well into the next decade. However, critics maintain that stealth aircraft are susceptible to low-cost defensive measures, such as the 1960s era missile launcher that brought down a Nighthawk over Yugoslavia in 1999.

Most stealth aircraft fly at subsonic speed to avoid the attention generated by a sonic boom, making the aircraft vulnerable to attack by faster flying jets as well. The high price of development and maintenance of stealth aircraft is also a concern. The B-2 bomber, which reportedly has the RCS of an aluminum marble, became a byword for cost overruns, and the high-tech Joint Strike Fighter (JSF), whose RCS is near that of a golf ball, is currently $1 billion over cost due in large part to its stealth features. Costly radar-absorbing paints and tapes must be regularly reapplied and the planes themselves must be sheltered from the weather.

Stealth aircraft are often painted in dark colors to blend with the night sky, although advances in materials science may make it possible for planes to change color on the fly. Electrochromic polymers are similar in principle to the technology found in some new car mirrors that sense bright lights and darken accordingly. Such technology may work its way onto stealth aircraft and ships of the future.

See also Defense Advanced Research Projects Agency (DARPA); F-117A Stealth Fighters; Joint Strike Fighter; Radar (Radio Detection and Ranging)

Further Reading

Evans, Nicholas D. *Military Gadgets: How Advanced Technology Is Transforming Today's Battlefield . . . and Tomorrow's*. Englewood Cliffs, NJ: Prentice Hall, 2004.

Friedman, George, and Meredith Friedman. *The Future of War: Power, Technology, and American World Dominance in the Twenty-First Century*. New York: St. Martin's Press, 1998.

STINGER MISSILES

Portable guided surface-to-air missile system. The FIM-92A Stinger Weapons System is effective against low-altitude airborne targets including fixed-wing aircraft, helicopters, unmanned drones, and cruise missiles. The Stinger, launched from a portable shoulder mount, is a fire-and-forget weapon that uses passive infrared targeting and an advanced navigation system. The Stinger can be launched from field vehicles, such as the Bradley Infantry Fighting Vehicle or HMMWV (Hum-Vee) Avengers, attached to a helicopter, or by a soldier using a disposable launch tube and reusable stock.

The Stinger missile replaces the Redeye, the first lightweight shoulder fired surface-to-air missile, which was developed in the 1960s and adopted for combat use by the U.S. Marines in 1966. The first Stingers, which featured advanced targeting and navigation systems, were introduced in 1982.

With a range of five miles, the Stinger can hit targets flying as high as 11,500 feet. Stinger are extremely accurate, and once launched, the five-foot long, 22-pound missiles travel at 1,500 mph. Stingers use sensors that look for the infrared light (heat) produced by the target's engine. The missiles carry identification friend or foe (IFF) technology, which enables them to identify the ultraviolet shadow of the target and use that information to distinguish the target from other heat-producing objects in the area.

The missile operator (typically a two-man detail, though a single person can operate the system) simply centers the target in a digital display. While the missile is flying, the on-board guidance system will keep the target centered and make necessary course corrections.

Stinger missiles are manufactured by Prime-Hughes Missile System Company and have a replacement cost of $38,000. U.S. forces currently have an inventory of about 13,400 Stingers, primarily for use in protecting combat soldiers in the field from airborne enemies.

The terrorists who shot down Pan Am Flight 800 off Long Island in 1996 were believed to have used a Stinger missile. The Central Intelligence Agency (CIA) provided Stinger missiles to Afghan insurgents in the late 1980s for use against Soviet helicopters during the Soviet occupation and war in Afghanistan.

See also Missile Technology Control Regime (MTCR); Missiles

STRATEGIC AIR COMMAND

U.S. military command whose role was critical to providing a deterrent threat against the Soviet Union during the Cold War in support of U.S. nuclear strategy. Headquartered at Offutt Air Force Base in Omaha, Nebraska, the Strategic Air Command (SAC) was the component of the unified command plan charged with organizing, training, equipping, administering, and preparing strategic air forces for combat. Most importantly, SAC controlled most U.S. nuclear weapons as well as the air delivery systems, bombers, and missiles capable of delivering those weapons.

The Strategic Air Command was critical to the U.S. deterrent policy against the Soviet Union during the Cold War. The task of the Strategic Air Command was to provide strategic nuclear bombing depth to the U.S. nuclear arsenal. The SAC was central to deterrence policy, as it strengthened U.S. capabilities to deliver a costly blow to the Soviet Union. Specifically, the Strategic Air Command oversaw the bombers capable of carrying nuclear payloads with the intent of strategically bombing Soviet cities. Because of its central role in the nation's nuclear strategy, SAC received a significant portion of the U.S. defense budget.

The Strategic Air Command was first established in 1946 as a part of the larger U.S. Army Air Corps. However, with the establishment of the Air Force as a separate branch of the armed forces, and the advent of the Cold War, the Strategic Air Command soon took on a new and important role.

The Strategic Air Command grew significantly following the discovery of a so-called *bomber gap* in the 1950s, in which U.S. intelligence reported significant Soviet bomber superiority. Because of this, President Dwight D. Eisenhower ordered the immediate production of more bombers. As was later discovered, the bomber gap did not actually exist, because the Soviets flew their bombers in loops to convey the picture that they had greater numbers of bombers.

It was under Eisenhower's administration that the Strategic Air Command grew most significantly in both size and importance. Under his administration, the New Look concept was forwarded, positing that U.S. forces would be reliant on nuclear weapons as a deterrent and air power as a strategic advantage. It was at this point that the Air Force began developing numerous bombers to deliver strategic nuclear weapons and serve a reconnaissance role in detecting Soviet military power and intentions.

Along with overseeing the strategic bombing capability, the Strategic Air Command oversaw long- and medium-range missile development as well. In this respect, SAC facilitated the development and maintenance of U.S. intercontinental ballistic missiles (ICBMs) and intermediate-range ballistic missiles (IRBMs).

Although headquartered at Offutt Air Force Base, SAC maintained several forward operating bases, including bases overseas in countries such as England. These bases were important to the nuclear mission—in the event that war with the Soviet Union broke out, forward-based bombers would be significantly closer and more easily able to strike the Soviet Union. Similarly, planning for SAC increasingly focused on spreading SAC assets to several different areas to lessen their vulnerability and limit the possibility of having one strike disable the Strategic Air Command. As such, SAC bombers were deployed to well over 50 domestic and overseas locations.

With the fall of the Soviet Union in 1991 and the culmination of the Cold War, the fear of nuclear war and the need for major nuclear deterrence capabilities came to an end. In 1992, the Strategic Air Command was decommissioned and, in its place, the Strategic Command was created. The Strategic Command assumed many of the previous SAC responsibilities, but also absorbed U.S. military space operations.

See also Bomber Gap; Cold War; Deterrence; Eisenhower, Dwight D., and National Policy; Strategic Command, U.S.

STRATEGIC ARMS LIMITATION TALKS (SALT)

From 1969 to 1979, negotiations between the United States and the Soviet Union that resulted in treaties (SALT I and SALT II) to reduce the proliferation of nuclear arms. SALT I is an acronym for the first series of Strategic Arms Limitation Talks held from 1969 to 1972 between the United States and the Soviet Union. The talks resulted in a number of agreements reducing the offensive nuclear arsenals of the two superpowers. A second round of talks (SALT II) occurred between 1972 and 1979 and focused on curtailing the manufacture of strategic nuclear weapons.

SALT I (1969–1972)

The late 1960s was a period of change in the character of the nuclear arms race between the United States and the Soviet Union. The Soviets were deploying heavy land-based intercontinental ballistic missiles (ICBMs) as well as ICBMs launched from submarines (SLBMs) at a rate of about 200 per year beginning in 1968.

Meanwhile, the U.S. nuclear arsenal had remained at 1,054 ICBM and 656 SLBM since 1967, but the United States was deploying more multiple independently targeted reentry vehicle (MIRV) warheads that enabled a single missile to attack as many as 10 separate targets. The United States had a substantial lead in long-range bombers as well. Both nations had developed and deployed antiballistic missile systems.

Essentially, the arms race was moving toward a stalemate as both nations had the capability to destroy one another several times over. On November 17, 1969, representatives of the superpowers held the first of a series of negotiations in Helsinki, Finland. Further sessions alternated between Helsinki and Vienna, Austria.

After protracted negotiations, the United States and Soviet Union reached an agreement on antiballistic missiles in May 1971. The negotiations ultimately culminated in the Antiballistic Missile Treaty and the Interim Agreement Between the US and the USSR on Certain Measures With Respect to the Limitation of Strategic Offensive Arms (the so-called SALT I treaties). U.S. President Richard Nixon and Soviet Premier Leonid Brezhnev signed the treaties in Moscow on May 26, 1972. In the treaties, both sides agreed to reduce the number of ICBMs and ABMs, but the United States refused to reduce the number of MIRV warheads.

SALT II (1972–1979)

Presidents Gerald Ford and Jimmy Carter were less successful than President Nixon in the subsequent Strategic Arms Limitation Talks (SALT II), which lasted from 1972 to 1979. President Ford and Secretary of State Henry Kissinger met with Brezhnev and agreed to reductions in the number of missiles, but Soviet treatment of its Jewish citizens chilled relations between the superpowers. When President Carter proposed even deeper cuts, Brezhnev refused.

Threatened by improved U.S. relations with China and a deteriorating economy, Brezhnev finally met with President Carter in Vienna in 1979 and the leaders signed a treaty. The SALT II treaty limited each nation to 2,250 nuclear missiles with no more than 1,320 MIRVs. The U.S. Senate balked at the treaty, however, and when the Soviets invaded Afghanistan in 1979, U.S.-Soviet relations again deteriorated.

The U.S. Senate never ratified the treaty, although both nations honored its terms. In 1982, President Ronald Reagan announced a new round of negotiations, the Strategic Arms Reduction Talks (START), to replace the SALT treaties. START resulted in subsequent agreements to reduce nuclear weapons.

See also Arms Control; Carter, Jimmy, and National Policy; Cold War; Ford, Gerald R., and National Policy; Intercontinental Ballistic Missiles (ICBMs); Kissinger, Henry (1923–); Multiple Independently Targetable Reentry Vehicles (MIRVs); Nuclear Weapons; Reagan, Ronald, and National Policy; Strategic Arms Reduction Talks (START)

STRATEGIC ARMS REDUCTION TALKS (START)

Disarmament agreements that began in Geneva in 1982 (START I) and continued with two further treaties (START II and START III) after the collapse of the Soviet Union in 1991. These Strategic Arms Reduction treaties took place between the United States and the Soviet Union until 1993, when the former Soviet republics of Kazakhstan, Ukraine, and Belarus joined Russia in the talks. The breakup of the Soviet Union in 1991 delayed the implementation of the START I agreement by three-and-a-half years.

START I dealt with offensive weapons and was finally signed in 1991, just before the collapse of the Soviet Union. START II focused on the elimination of heavy intercontinental ballistic missiles (ICBMs) and multiple warhead ICBMs. START II was ratified by the U.S. Senate in 1996 and by the Russian Duma in 2000. START III is currently under negotiation between the United States and the Soviet Union.

Enforcement of the treaties is dependent on extensive data exchange, notifications, on-site inspections, and continuous monitoring activities. A projected START IV agreement would involve all declared nuclear nations and would have the goal of substantially reducing global warhead levels. A central concern of nations in the post–Cold War era is the issue of weapons proliferation and the maintenance of large arsenals, for which the collapse of the Soviet Union is seen as an important contributing factor.

See also Arms Control; Treaties

Further Reading

Goldblat, Jozef. *Arms Control: The New Guide to Negotiations and Agreements.* Thousand Oaks, CA: Sage Publications, 2002.

U.S. Arms Control and Disarmament Agency. *Arms Control and Disarmament Agreements: Texts and Histories of the Negotiations.* Washington, DC: Government Printing Office, 1996.

Wainhouse, David W. *Arms Control Agreements: Designs for Verification and Organization.* Baltimore, MD: Johns Hopkins University Press, 1992.

STRATEGIC BOMBING

Military approach involving bombing that is intended to destroy a nation's ability to wage war. Strategic bombing targets features of infrastructure—such as factories, railways, and refineries—that are essential for the production and supply of war materials. The strategy of strategic bombing is a part of total war, a concept that refers to the enlistment of the sum total of a society's resources to aid in a conflict.

Strategic bombing was developed during World War I. Although, initially, aircraft were only used in the war for surveillance purposes, they soon were being used in offensive operations as well. Bomb squadrons began conducting missions farther from the front lines for the purposes of causing indirect harm to military targets. This evolved, during the interwar period, into recognition of the value of strategic bombing. Technological developments during that time, such as extended aircraft flight and the ability to reach higher altitudes, also made the strategy more feasible.

At the start of World War II, all nations' air forces had a policy of attacking military targets only. That changed, however, once the German Luftwaffe began conducting air raids on British cities, including London. As a result, strategic bombing became a fundamental part of military combat. The purpose of strategic bombing was not only to undermine industrial production but also to demoralize the population. Thus, civilian populations suffered to a degree that was unprecedented. Meanwhile, as more and more planes were shot down, both sides began adopting a policy of night raids, which, while less accurate, were safer for bomb crews.

The most significant episode of strategic bombing during World War II was the dropping of the atomic bombs on Hiroshima and Nagasaki in 1945. The United States had already used conventional bombing raids to devastate civilian centers in both Germany and Japan. However, the use of atomic weapons raised the stakes of dropping bombs from the sky and thus had a permanent impact on the conduct of war and international relations in the post–World War II era.

Nuclear warfare quickly developed into an arms race for weapons that did not require planes for delivery. The focus of international relations shifted to missiles and defense systems meant to destroy incoming nuclear missiles. However, bombers did remain one-third of the strategic nuclear triad, due to the greater flexibility they offered in the event of heightened tensions and a potential conflict. Unlike a missile, a bomber could be retrieved. Also, unlike missile silos where the missiles were launched, bombers were mobile and thus less vulnerable to attack. They were also more accurate than the missiles launched from nuclear submarines.

Aside from the altered implications of bombing campaigns initiated by the introduction of nuclear weapons, the increased media exposure of modern warfare also had an impact on strategic bombing. Bombing campaigns were an essential element of U.S. strategy during the Vietnam War, and these campaigns gained a reputation for being unacceptably indiscriminate. For example, the administration of President Lyndon Johnson implemented Operation Rolling Thunder, which was meant to be a ceaseless and relentless bombing campaign against North Vietnam. The bombing campaign, however, was ultimately regarded as ineffective, and it also added to the catalogue of images broadcast back to the United States showing civilian casualties. The total-war aspects of strategic bombing, in effect, became part of what depleted support for the Vietnam conflict back in the United States.

Nevertheless, strategic bombing has continued to play an important role in U.S. military strategy. The first Gulf War (1991) against Iraq began with an air campaign called Operation Desert Storm, aimed at paving the way for the ground campaign that followed. The intervention of the North Atlantic Treaty Organization (NATO) in former Yugoslavia in 1999, led by the United States under President Bill Clinton, also involved a bombing campaign that was essential to the success of the operation. Most recently, U.S. Defense Secretary Donald Rumsfeld famously referred to the "Shock and Awe" to be produced by the air offensive at the beginning of the invasion of Iraq in 2003.

See also Air-Land Battles

Further Reading

Gentile, Gian P. *How Effective Is Strategic Bombing? Lessons Learned from World War II to Kosovo.* New York: New York University Press, 2000.

Knell, Hermann. *To Destroy a City: Strategic Bombing and Its Human Consequences in World War II.* Cambridge, MA: De Capo Press, 2003.

Smith, John T. *Rolling Thunder: The Strategic Bombing Campaign, North Vietnam 1965–1968.* London: Crecy Publishing, 1995.

STRATEGIC COMMAND, U.S.

Military command established in 1992, which is one of nine U.S. military commands under the Department of Defense (DoD). The primary responsibility of the U.S. Strategic Command (USSTRATCOM) lies in providing early warnings of attacks against the United States. It also works to prevent the proliferation of weapons of mass destruction (WMD).

The USSTRATCOM has its origins in the establishment of the U.S. Air Force's Strategic Air Command (SAC) at the beginning of the Cold War. Due to the development of nuclear capabilities by the Navy, the Joint Strategic Target Planning Staff (JSTPS) was formed in 1960 to work with SAC to develop the Single Integrated Operational Plan (SIOP)—a nuclear war plan at the strategic level.

In June 1992, immediately following the end of the Cold War, the JSTPS and SAC were eliminated and USSTRATCOM was established to respond to the changing global political reality. In October 2002, USSTRATCOM was combined with the U.S. Space Command. This change reflected the current push toward restructuring the military to respond to the changing nature of security threats.

In January 2003, new duties were assigned to the U.S. Strategic Command: C4ISR (otherwise known as command and control, communications, computers, intelligence, surveillance, and reconnaissance, and global strike), Department of Defense Information Operations, and missile defense integration. The current mission of the USSTRATCOM is to establish and provide the full spectrum of global strike and coordinated space and information operations capabilities to meet national security objectives. The mission of USSTRATCOM is also to provide operational space support, integrated missile defense, global C4ISR, and specialized planning expertise.

The headquarters of USSTRATCOM is located in Nebraska at the Offutt Air Force Base. Located elsewhere in the country are other operations centers. Located in Arlington, Virginia, the Joint Task Force-Global Network Operations (JTF-GNO) of the USSTRATCOM acts to secure the information network of the Department of Defense. The Cheyenne Mountain Operations Center, at the Cheyenne Mountain Air Force Station (CMAFS) in Wyoming, provides a real-time view of what is occurring in space. At Lockland Air Force Base in Texas, USSTRATCOM's Joint Information Operations Center (JIOC) helps to incorporate Information Operations (IO) into various military actions and plans.

The USSTRATCOM is headed by a member of the U.S. armed services who acts as the commander of various assigned forces from the four branches of the U.S. military. Approximately 2,500 personnel, coming from both military and civilian sectors, work at USSTRATCOM headquarters. Below the central command are smaller units, each assigned various tasks such as plans and policy, manpower and personnel, capability and resource integration, and global operations. Below global operations are subsections that focus on logistics, intelligence, C4 systems, and current operations.

Under USSTRATCOM are several task forces assisting it in carrying out its assigned mission. The intercontinental ballistic missiles network is one example of a resource under the USSTRATCOM. Other task forces include ballistic missile submarines, aerial/refueling submarines, and reconnaissance aircraft and strategic bombers. The Army Space and

Missile Defense Command (SMDC), and Army Forces Strategic Command (ARSTRAT) are commands within the army that provide support for USSTRATCOM. Within the Air Force, the Strategic Air Forces (STRATAF) and the Air Force Space Command occupy the same role. The U.S. Marines also have a specific command, the Marine Forces Strategic Command (MARFORSTRAT), to facilitate the use of marine forces under the command of USSTRATCOM. Within the U.S. Navy, it is the Naval Network Warfare Command (NETWARCOM) that controls the naval resources used by USSTRATCOM.

With the emerging new threats that impact the national security of the United States, USSTRATCOM strives to provide the necessary capabilities to protect the United States and its citizens. USSTRATCOM protects U.S. national security using deterrence, and it works to prevent surprise attacks. The command also provides strategic support to military campaigns, such as Operation Iraqi Freedom. The USSTRATCOM will likely play an even more significant role in the future, especially as space warfare technology develops.

See also Space-Based Weapons; Strategic Nuclear Triad

STRATEGIC CULTURE

How states go about viewing national security issues and concerns. A direct descendant of political culture, strategic culture is based on the idea that a national style derives logically from the concept of political culture. Grounded in the study of anthropology, political culture says we can understand a particular group by looking at their norms, practices, and values. From that theory comes the notion that a particular culture should encourage a particular style in thought and action. Applied to national interests, including national security, strategic culture suggests that there is a distinct U.S. strategic culture, a distinct Russian strategic culture, and a distinct Chinese strategic culture.

All of these cultures are based on particular ways of thinking and acting on national security issues. For example, a Chinese strategic culture might be based on the political ideas of China as a protective and closed civilization. From that might come a reliance on more regional and defensive methods and technologies. By contrast, the U.S. strategic culture may be based on notions of using many resources and using overwhelming combat power to obtain a victory. This might be based on the experiences of the United States in World War I and World War II, as well as in decisive victories such as in Grenada (1983), Panama (1989), and the Gulf War (1991).

Jack Snyder, one of the prominent theorists in the area of strategic culture, has noted that the socialization process in a particular strategic culture not only inculcates the culture but also provides a basis for seeing future actions. This worldview, in turn, shapes the possibility of reforms and changes. Strategic culture thus has an effect on the development of strategy and tactics in a particular country.

The theory of strategic culture has been criticized as being too determinative and for failing to recognize the role that factionalism and factions play in any society, including the national security and military communities. Yet, it is clear that the culture of anything has an effect on it, its development, and its responses. As a result, experts generally include strategic culture as an element for consideration in any discussion of strategy.

STRATEGIC DEFENSE INITIATIVE (SDI)

During the administration of President Ronald Reagan, a research and development program, initiated to build a space-based antiballistic missile defense system. The Strategic Defense Initiative (SDI) program sought to end the threat of nuclear missiles through a perfect, space-based defense, but it was fraught with political and scientific difficulties.

SDI became known by the moniker Star Wars after President Reagan's March 1983 speech declaring the U.S. ambition to make nuclear weapons "impotent and obsolete" through space-based laser interceptors. The ambitious SDI concept originally entailed the use of high-powered X-ray lasers to shoot down enemy missiles. Such lasers required an enormous amount of energy to produce, so much so that the use of atomic energy was considered the only feasible energy source.

Initial estimates for the power required to instantly destroy warheads ranged from 100 to 1,000 megawatts for up to 2,000 seconds, comparable to the power generated hourly by a nuclear power plant. Later designs incorporated the use of kinetic weapons or missiles to hit incoming missiles. Last resort ground-based interceptors were also designed. In discussion with Ronald Reagan,

Edward Teller, who along with Richard Garwin is credited with the creation of the hydrogen bomb, advocated the use of X-ray lasers as interceptors to shoot down incoming missiles. Teller's vision convinced Reagan that such a system was both feasible and highly desirable.

Critics maintained that SDI was technically unworkable and that it would alter the balance of power that had kept the world's superpowers in check. Many scientists argued that with cheap technologies, such as multiple dummy warheads, an opponent could easily overwhelm a missile defense space weapon, thwarting the weapon's capacity to respond to real danger. Cruise missiles, which do not enter space, and unmanned planes were also of concern.

Treaties would also have had to be renegotiated if SDI was implemented. The Antiballistic Missile Treaty held the United States and the Soviet Union to a small number of ground-based missile defenses. Signed by the United States and the Soviet Union in 1972, the ABM treaty constrained the antimissile defenses of each country to two fixed, ground-based defenses of 100 missile interceptors each. Concerns that a nationwide defense system would spur a renewed arms race caused the Soviet Union and the United States to reduce the number by half.

Both sides reasoned that a nuclear first-strike policy was unacceptable and that ultimately, remaining vulnerable to each other's offensive nuclear weapons, while maintaining a policy aimed at deterrence, was the lesser of two evils. The Outer Space Treaty of 1967 also prohibited the deployment of space-based nuclear weapons, and so tests of such weapons could not be carried out without pulling out of the treaty.

In response to U.S. research, the Soviet Union began work on its own version of SDI. Some experts now reason that the enormous financial burden placed on the Soviet Union due to SDI helped speed the downfall of communism, and so the indirect benefit of SDI was that the United States outspent the Soviets in an economic war.

Work on SDI was discontinued after the end of the Cold War and the breakup of the Soviet Union, although research into ground-based interceptors continued. Under the Reagan administration, actual expenditures on SDI amounted to approximately $30 billion. During the administration of President Bill Clinton, missile defense received continued funding under what some dubbed the Son of Star Wars program, or National Missile Defense (NMD).

With the apparent demise of the ABM treaty, the administration of President George W. Bush is funding the development of the less-costly NMD system. Such a system, if successful, would be deployed at several locations throughout the United States and, potentially, in allied countries. As of 2004, a defense system that employs early warning radar and consists of 10 missiles to intercept nuclear ballistic missiles had been deployed in Alaska. Additionally, another 10 missiles will be deployed in California, and by the end of 2005, 10 more will be placed in Alaska.

The goal of the NMD system is what is known as *layered defense,* which would provide multiple opportunities to shoot down an enemy missile along its entire flight path. Ballistic missiles can be attacked in any of four phases—the boost phase, postboost phase, midcourse phase, and terminal phase. During the boost phases, missiles are at their most vulnerable. However, attacking a missile at the boost phase poses daunting challenges. First and foremost, the threat must be detected within moments.

Another antiballistic missile technology under development is the airborne laser, which is currently conceived of as a fleet of 747s outfitted with chemical lasers that would be deployed in 2008 or 2009. Adding another layer to the defense will be the Kinetic Energy Interceptor program. This initiative is aimed at deploying a boost-phase intercept capability by the year 2008. The concept of using unmanned aerial vehicles (UAVs) to counter ballistic missiles during their boost phase is also being considered.

Unlike the huge numbers of missiles that SDI would have had to field, the primary mission of National Missile Defense is the defense of the United States against a limited strategic threat, such as that posed by a rogue nation or terrorist organization. Critics maintain that the cost (currently at more than $8 billion per year) is too high and that the risk of missile attack is too low to justify NMD's continued development.

A recent report by a team of economists found that the cumulative cost of a missile defense system—including boost-phase, midcourse, and terminal defenses as called for by the Bush administration—could be between $800 billion and $1.2 trillion. According to the Center for Defense Information, over $100 billion has been spent on SDI and NMD since President Reagan first advanced the program.

As with SDI, critics argue that simple countermeasures could be designed to thwart the NMD system. While Russia has agreed to allow the development of NMD, some experts suggest that the system might compel China to increase its nuclear arsenal, which in turn could cause India and Pakistan to increase theirs as well.

See also Ballistic Missiles; National Missile Defense; Reagan, Ronald, and National Policy; Space-Based Weapons

Further Reading

McMahon, K. Scott. *Pursuit of the Shield.* Lanham, MD: Rowman & Littlefield Publishers, 1987.

STRATEGIC FORCES

Military units capable of destroying large-scale targets from extremely long ranges. In modern military parlance, strategic forces typically refer to units that provide nuclear strike capability. These forces take three forms: land-based intercontinental ballistic missiles, sea-launched ballistic missiles, and long-range strategic bombers.

HISTORY OF U.S. STRATEGIC FORCES

Limits on transportation technology prevented the development of true strategic forces until quite recently. The invention of the airplane first provided military commanders with the ability to deliver a significant blow deep behind enemy lines. Perhaps the first truly strategic military forces were the Allied long-range bombers of World War II. Flying in fleets of up to 1,000 planes, U.S. and British bombers wrought extensive damage on Germany's industry as well as its civilian population. This bombing campaign contributed significantly to the Allied victory in the war in Europe and proved the value of strategic forces in modern warfare.

During World War II, the bombers were one of several branches of the United States Army Air Force (USAAF), which was part of the U.S. Army. In March 1946, the USAAF was divided into three branches: Air Defense Command (ADC), Tactical Air Command (TAC), and Strategic Air Command (SAC). The primary missions of SAC were to conduct long-range offensive operations in any part of the world, either independently or in cooperation with land and naval forces; and conduct maximum-range reconnaissance over land or sea, either independently or in cooperation with land and naval forces.

During the late 1940s and early 1950s, SAC bombers were considered the United States' strategic front line of defense against possible Soviet aggression. However, the development of the intercontinental ballistic missile (ICBM) in the late 1950s radically changed the nature of strategic forces. An ICBM could be launched from a base thousands of miles away from its intended target and, unlike a bomber, could not be shot down once in flight. Advances in miniaturization and missile guidance technology during the 1960s and 1970s made ICBMs more powerful and more accurate. By the mid-1970s, a single land-based ICBM could deliver multiple nuclear warheads accurately to many separate targets. Both the United States and the Soviet Union built and deployed thousands of land-based ICBMs.

The late 1950s also witnessed a revolution in sea warfare that produced the world's first nuclear powered submarines. Capable of staying at sea for months at a time—and almost undetectable underwater—nuclear subs soon became the newest addition to U.S. strategic forces. By the mid-1960s, submarines were being outfitted with sea-launched ballistic missiles (SLBMs) that could be fired from hundreds of feet below the surface of the ocean. Like land-based ICBMs, SLBMs have ranges measured in the thousands of miles. Because they are virtually undetectable, ballistic missile subs are almost ensured of surviving a nuclear first strike by an enemy nation. This made them perhaps the most valuable strategic weapon for both the United States and the Soviet Union during the period of the Cold War.

MODERN U.S. STRATEGIC FORCES

As of the early 21st century, U.S. strategic forces were composed of the so-called *strategic nuclear triad* of strategic bombers, land-based ICBMs, and submarine-based SLBMs. Until 1992, these three components of U.S. strategic forces were under separate areas of command. Through SAC, the USAAF had responsibility for strategic bombers. In 1947, the USAAF became a separate military service, the United States Air Force (USAF), with SAC as one of its main components. The USAF was also in charge of land-based ICBM operations. The U.S. Navy had command authority over the nation's ballistic missile submarines.

In 1992, the U.S. Department of Defense placed all three parts of the nuclear triad under a single command—the U.S. Strategic Command (STRATCOM). This change was prompted by the recent collapse of the Soviet Union and a subsequent shift of focus from strategic nuclear weapons to terrorism and rogue states as the main threats to U.S. national security. Consolidating the nation's strategic forces was intended to streamline intelligence gathering and help coordinate planning for U.S. strategic defense policy. Since 2002, STRATCOM has also included the U.S. Space Command, which is in charge of U.S. military efforts in space.

U.S. strategic force doctrine has evolved along with the changing mission of STRATCOM. During the Cold War, strategic deterrence was based on massive nuclear retaliation in case of a first strike by either side. The doctrine of mutually assured destruction (MAD) called for each side to have enough nuclear weapons to survive an attack and launch an equally devastating counterattack. Nuclear weapons were both the offensive threat and the defensive response.

The collapse of the Soviet Union in 1991 dramatically changed the threat of nuclear war between the superpowers, causing the U.S. government to reevaluate the role of strategic forces in U.S. national security policy. In 2002, a U.S. Nuclear Posture Review called for expanded nuclear deterrence, but also included recommendations for nonnuclear options as well as active and passive defenses to meet strategic threats. The use of nuclear weapons thus is no longer the sole focus of U.S. strategic force planning.

See also Ballistic Missiles; Bomber Gap; Cold War; Conventional Forces in Europe Treaty (1990); First Strike; Intercontinental Ballistic Missiles (ICBMs); Limited Nuclear Option; Multiple Independently Targetable Reentry Vehicles (MIRVs); Mutually Assured Destruction (MAD); Nuclear Deterrence; Nuclear Weapons; Sea-Launched Ballistic Missiles (SLBMs); Secure Second Strike; Strategic Air Command; Strategic Bombing; Strategic Command, U.S.; Strategic Nuclear Triad; Submarines

Further Reading

Buchan, Glenn. *Future Roles of U.S. Nuclear Forces: Implications for U.S. Strategy.* Santa Monica, CA: RAND, 2004.
Moody, Walton S. *Building a Strategic Air Force.* Washington, DC: Government Reprints Press, 2001.
Woolf, Amy F. *U.S. Nuclear Weapons: Changes In Policy and Force Structure.* New York: Novinka Books, 2005.

STRATEGIC NUCLEAR TRIAD

Three major types of nuclear weapons systems in the strategic forces of the United States; consisting of land-based missiles, strategic bombers, and submarine-based missiles. The purpose of maintaining the triad is to create a flexible series of policy options in the event of a nuclear crisis. The various programs that make up the triad have a variety of strengths and weaknesses that account for, and are reinforced by, one another.

Land-based missiles are the most accessible from the command perspective because of the simplicity of communications and officers with access to firing circuits. They are subject to the greatest degree of control and promise great accuracy once fired. Their greatest disadvantage lies in the fact that their locations are fixed; thus they are easily targetable. More important, once launched they cannot be recalled. Thus, their use requires extremely high levels of assurance.

Unlike missiles, bombers can be recalled, and their location is not fixed, making them less vulnerable to attack. Their disadvantage relative to missiles, however, lies in the slow delivery time entailed by bomber-based nuclear weapons.

The submarine-based missiles are the safest part of the nuclear triad in terms of their relative invulnerability to a first strike. The mobility of the submarine forces, in addition to the near impossibility of hitting them all at once, makes them the most survivable. The disadvantage, however, is that it is nearly impossible to maintain two-way communications with a submarine without revealing its location. Because the location of the submarine and its relative motion at the time of launch are more difficult to determine, the missiles are less accurate.

The strategic nuclear triad has provided the foundation of U.S. nuclear strategy since the early 1960s.

Further Reading

Buchan, Glenn. *Future Roles of U.S. Nuclear Forces: Implications for U.S. Strategy.* New York: RAND, 2004.
Evaluation of the U.S. Strategic Nuclear Triad: Hearing Before the Committee on Governmental Affairs. Washington, DC: GPO, 1994.
Shambroom, Paul. *Face to Face with the Bomb: Nuclear Reality after the Cold War.* Baltimore, MD: Johns Hopkins University Press, 2003.

STRATEGIC OFFENSIVE REDUCTION TREATY (SORT)

Signed in Moscow in 2002, agreement between the United States and Russia to reduce offensive nuclear weapons. According to the provisions of the Strategic Offensive Reduction Treaty (SORT), U.S. President George W. Bush and Russian President Vladimir Putin agreed that both countries would reduce their strategic nuclear warheads to a level between 1,700 and 2,200 by December 31, 2012. This level is nearly two-thirds lower than the current level of nuclear warheads in each country. SORT is part of a broad array of cooperative efforts announced between the two countries in the aftermath of the Cold War.

The reductions stipulated by SORT were first announced by President Bush in 2001 during a summit held in Washington, DC, and at Crawford, Texas, with President Putin. The treaty was later ratified by both the U.S. Senate and the Russian Duma. The earlier-negotiated Strategic Arms Reduction Talks (START) of 1991 continues unchanged, and the verification procedures begun by START are to provide the foundation for these same processes with SORT. Immediate implications for the U.S. arsenal are to include the retirement of Peacekeeper ICBMs and the conversion of nuclear submarines to conventional use. Some of the warheads removed from deployment are to be used as spares, some will be stored, and some will be destroyed.

See also Arms Control; Soviet Union, Former (Russia), and U.S. Policy; Strategic Arms Reduction Talks (START)

SUBMARINE WARFARE

The use of diving craft, usually armed with underwater weapons, in combat operations. Although initially ineffectual because of their primitive designs, submarines developed into highly effective combat vessels, capable of sinking the largest surface ships and causing severe strategic and economic disruption in modern war. Ironically, the submarine menace attracted a great deal of attention since World War II, but the end of the Cold War has returned submarines almost to an auxiliary role similar to the era of its origins.

EARLY DEVELOPMENTS

The primitive submersible torpedo boats built at the beginning of the 20th century offered few portents for the future. Short ranged, unstable, blind, dangerous to operate, and pitifully under armed, these vessels nevertheless employed the new torpedo (torpedo first meant a sea mine) as main armament and thus could sink the grandest warship then afloat under certain circumstances.

Accordingly, the sole role assigned to these early submarines was the defense of harbors and coastlines against conventional blockades that navies had been using since the 16th century. Russian submarines kept the otherwise victorious Japanese navy clear of Vladivostok during the 1904–1905 Russo-Japanese War, for example. However, the threat of surface torpedo boats had already caused naval doctrine to change by then, introducing the distant blockade tactic, where fleets covered enemy coasts from hundreds of miles away, leaving coast defenses with little to accomplish.

The technical improvements to the submarine before 1914 sufficed to make it a formidable threat against warships on patrol and merchant ships, although their poor handling characteristics kept them out of fleet actions of the day. The submarines of World War I sank all classes of warships, driving blockading units far offshore, and the warfare potential of the submarine advanced it to the major naval problem of the day.

Initially, the submarine was expected to follow the rules for seizure of shipping established by the 1899 Hague Convention. Under such rules, a submarine was expected to stop a merchant vessel by surfacing to signal or fire a shot across its bow, after which the merchant ship would be seized as a prize of war or sunk after the crew had been ordered into lifeboats and safeguarded. Of course, submarines had minimal crews and accommodations, making the detachment of crews to take captured merchant ships or the embarking of their crews an absolute impossibility. The surfacing of a submarine before an unidentified merchant vessel also made it vulnerable to attack by ramming or concealed armament, not to mention nearby escorting warships and aircraft.

The tempting targets posed by Allied commerce—and the limited results offered under conventional attacks permitted by the rules of the Hague Convention—pressured the German navy to opt for unrestricted submarine warfare in World War I. The German government authorized this on two occasions—January 1915 to May 1916 and May 1917 to November 1918—the latter becoming the key cause of the U.S. declaration of war against Germany in April 1917. This calculated risk on the part of Germany almost brought Britain and Italy to economic collapse, but the improved weapons and detection equipment of antisubmarine craft and ships, and the use of convoys to pass more ships through the submarine zones under escort, resulted in the defeat of the German submarine campaign.

THE WEAPONS MATURE

During the interwar period, navies counted on improved submarines to render good service in fleet reconnaissance, attack of the opposing battle lines, and attrition by attacking naval vessels outside ports and in transit. Attacking merchant vessels counted for less, given the problems of World War I and the continuation of Hague Convention rules treating the attack of commerce. Even the German navy, resurrected under the 1935 Anglo-German Naval Agreement, relegated its submarine force to auxiliary functions. The Japanese navy, however, considered the submarine an integral unit supporting the battle fleet, as did the U.S. Navy.

The coming of World War II found the German navy unready for confrontation with its opponents on the high seas, and it quickly converted its strategy to target shipping (commerce warfare), using unrestricted submarine warfare. The U.S. Navy, damaged by the Japanese attack on Pearl Harbor, opted for unrestricted submarine warfare as its only effective offensive measure.

Japanese submarines, technically inferior in several respects to Western craft, scored few successes against U.S. naval vessels and never waged a dedicated campaign against commerce. Thus, the key submarine campaigns of the war were the two commerce warfare campaigns of the United States and Germany, in which the former succeeded beyond all expectations and the latter narrowly failed as the Allies mounted a massive antisubmarine campaign that still saw over 21 million tons of shipping lost in the process.

The postwar and Cold War situation saw the Soviet navy developing the world's largest submarine force, although this had been the case, unrecognized, before World War II. The members of the North Atlantic Treaty Organization (NATO), faced with the apparent threat of the Soviet force, converted their submarines largely to antisubmarine missions, made possible with technical advances in detection, fire control, and weapons technology. Few Russian naval surface targets could be expected in a NATO-Warsaw Pact war, but submarines did perform reconnaissance in each other's inland waters and harbors.

The development of nuclear-powered submarines armed with long-range torpedoes and missiles allowed the return of antiship and fleet support missions to the world's submarine flotillas. Nuclear submarines had the speed and endurance to operate with fleet units, providing scouting and antisubmarine support, as well as attacking opposing fleet units. The end of the Cold War left these concepts untested, but the submarines of each side had already registered their abilities to track and follow opposing fleet units. Submarines also continued to perform clandestine reconnaissance and landing of agents, as they had since World War I.

A final evolution in submarine warfare was the strategic bombardment mission. German submarines had experimented with rocket launching during World War II, and the Japanese had built submarine carriers for launching torpedo-armed floatplanes against the Panama Canal at the end of that war. U.S. and Russian submarines became launch platforms for early cruise missiles in the 1950s, and then became part of their strategic forces, employing submarine launched ballistic missiles (SLBMs) in the 1960s. The stealth, security, and reliability of SLBMs have made them a permanent part of the U.S., Russian, French, Chinese, and British naval forces in the present day.

The contemporary state of naval forces and doctrine still holds many roles for the submarine, but few of these correspond to the original tasks or the missions that the vessels performed in their heyday. The narrowing probability of conventional warfare between great and medium-sized powers, which still have submarines in their arsenals, has relegated submarine forces to strategic missile-launch duty, on one extreme, and clandestine reconnaissance and agent landing, on the other. Neither mission will demand flotillas the size of previous epochs.

See also Antisubmarine Warfare (ASW); Ballistic Missiles; Cruise Missile; Sea-Launched Ballistic Missiles (SLBMs); U.S. Navy; World War I (1914–1918); World War II (1939–1945)

Further Reading

Freidman, Norman. *U.S. Submarines Since 1945*. Annapolis, MD: Naval Institute Press, 1994.

Parrish, Thomas. *The Submarine: A History*. New York: Viking, 2004.

SUBMARINES

Craft and ships designed to operate underwater for at least useful intervals of time, usually employing underwater weapons or equipment. In less than a century, the clumsy and unsafe submersible torpedo boat had become the terror of the seas once forecast by writer Jules Verne.

Beginning as a crude invention barely suitable for the defense of harbors and coastlines, the submarine boat has evolved through several generations of technological advances. In all generations, however, the vessels have made special demands on their personnel for training and psychological preparation. Many navies eschewed the submarine for that reason, but an effective submarine force marks a first-rate navy, even in current times.

THE SUBMERSIBLES

The early submersibles were simple ballasted and sealed launches or diving bells that merit attention only as precursors or novelties prior to the development of effective war machines. For example, a Confederate submersible named the *Hunley* sank the Federal steam sloop USS *Housatanic* on February 17, 1864, during the American Civil War, but it operated as a low-lying torpedo boat, incapable of submerged operations.

Several notable boats performed marginally satisfactory sea trials in the last decades of the 19th century. But, in 1899, John P. Holland invented the first successful submarines for the United States. He is rivaled only by the Spaniard Isaac Peral for the title of father of the modern submarine. After a brief dalliance with a group of Irish rebels, for whom he built three unsuccessful submersible rams, Holland joined a New York iron works as a draftsman and designed his first submarine torpedo boat in 1888. That was the same year in which Peral finished the first practical submarine, which was not adopted by the Spanish navy. Finding his own financiers, Holland formed his own company in 1893, but his first successful submarine is considered the *Holland No. 6* boat, commissioned in 1900 as the U.S. Navy's first submersible. Holland designs found favor in navies overseas, including those of England, Japan, and Russia.

In the early 20th century, all major and several minor navies placed submarines in service. Some, like the British Royal Navy, viewed the submarine with both disdain and fear because of its potential to upset the naval balance. The boats placed in service in the first decade of the century remained crude, dangerous to operate, and limited to coastal defense. However, the introduction of the diesel engine for surface propulsion, and the gyroscope for underwater navigation, enabled the next generation of submarines to perform very well against defenseless surface ships in early World War I.

Although still more like their submersible predecessors than like modern submarines, owing to their limited endurance and speed underwater, the submarines of World War I scored spectacular successes in the war against both warship and merchant ship targets. Although hopes that the submarine could contribute to fleet actions proved false, the destruction of merchant shipping by World War I submarines seriously threatened both Great Britain and Italy during the war. The swift development of hydrophones and depth charges to detect and attack submarines enabled the antisubmarine forces of World War I to eventually gain the upper hand, especially when the Allies organized merchant shipping convoys and laid extensive mine barrages to bar submarines from the high seas.

SUBMERSIBLES TO SUBMARINES

The period between World War I and World War II saw feverish developments of submarine designs and concepts, reflecting the experience of World War I and the emerging technologies. Attempts to control submarines through disarmament and law of war conventions would have little effect in the second world conflict, however.

Several threads of development may be discerned—coastal defense boats of around 250 tons displacement, a standard oceangoing submarine in the 700-to-1,000 ton range, and submarine cruisers in the 2,000-to-3,000 ton range. The latter category included amazing designs of submarines built to carry large-caliber guns, aircraft, and mines, in addition to large propulsion plants and large fuel storage to permit worldwide deployments. Again, hopes ran high that battle fleets could be supported offensively by submarines operating with them or defensively by submarines establishing screens to detect and attack approaching enemy fleets before surface actions began.

World War II saw the submarine reach its maturity as a commercial raider and as a valuable fleet auxiliary.

The nation's newest and most advanced nuclear-powered submarine, the PCU *Virginia*, Portsmouth, Virginia, in August 2004, on its way to the Norfolk Naval Shipyard after completing sea trials. The *Virginia* is the only major naval vessel designed with the post–Cold War security environment in mind. As such, it embodies the fighting and operation capabilities required to dominate the coastlines while maintaining undersea dominance in the open oceans.

Source: U.S. Navy.

Incremental improvements in the design and construction of the submarines gave them much better underwater speed, endurance, diving and sea-keeping capabilities, fire control, torpedoes and mines, optics, and sound detection and ranging equipment, including the new sonar devices.

Although the U.S. Navy developed outstanding 2,000 ton submarine designs for long-range patrols against fleets and convoys in the Pacific, greatly aided by the Allied radar advantage, it was the German navy that made significant developments in underwater performance. These improvements set the postwar trends for developing the first true submarines. The German type XXI and XXIII boats used high capacity batteries, air induction snorkels, hulls without appendages, and improved underwater fire control systems that gave them underwater performance superior to surfaced operations. With the type XVI boat, the use of hydrogen peroxide as a combination fuel and oxygen source offered near independence of action while operating submerged at high speeds and high endurance. On the other extreme, the Japanese produced the first primitive strategic submarine, the I-400 class submarine aircraft carrier, designed to strike the Panama Canal with three floatplanes each.

In the immediate post–World War II period, the world's major navies adopted most German innovations for modernizing their older submarines and designing newer ones, aided by improvements in welding and steel alloys. Deck guns and other drag-producing items disappeared, but hydrogen peroxide fuel proved infeasible, owing to its volatility. The U.S. Navy first turned to nuclear power plants to achieve true submarine performance, allowing the boats to operate underwater for long periods.

Nuclear reactors produced steam to drive propulsion turbines and operate auxiliaries that permitted endurance limited only by crew stamina and supplies. The Russian, British, and French navies joined the nuclear submarine club with a few others in process. Other navies opted for quieter conventional submarines better suited for inland and shallow waters. Nuclear power permitted the construction of much larger and more capable boats than ever before. The large power reserves of the nuclear plants allowed the installation of large active and passive sonar equipment, fire control computers, and weapons.

Many different submarine designs emerged from the shipyards, but they eventually settled into two basic designs—an attack submarine with from 4,000 to 10,000 tons of displacement, used to attack other ships and submarines, and the strategic submarine of 6,000 to 22,000 tons, able to fire ballistic or other types of guided missiles, whether submerged or surfaced, against land targets. The development of submarine-launched cruise missiles for attacking ship and land targets blurred the differences between attack and strategic submarines to some extent.

By the early 1980s, the submarine had become the weapon of dominant sea power, and each contending navy feared opposing submarines more than any other threat. Since then, however, the high cost of operating, maintaining, and manning submarines has placed severe limitations on the size of modern flotillas, especially in the cases of the nuclear-powered craft.

See also Antisubmarine Warfare (ASW); Sea-Launched Ballistic Missiles (SLBMs); U.S. Navy; World War I (1914–1918); World War II (1939–1945)

Further Reading

Friedman, Norman. *Submarine Design and Development.* Annapolis, MD: Naval Institute Press, 1984.
Parrish, Thomas. *The Submarine: A History.* New York: Viking, 2004.

SUEZ CANAL CRISIS (1956)

In the fall of 1956, the surprise military intervention in Egypt by France and Great Britain to seize control of the Suez Canal. The Suez Crisis demonstrated the continuing diplomatic role of spheres of influence, uncomfortably parallel to the suppression of the Hungarian Revolt in the same year by the Soviet Union. U.S. attempts to draw Egyptian interests toward the West by economic means foundered with disputes over the Aswan Dam project and Egyptian dallying with Soviet aid. The resulting chaos of the Canal crisis effectively ended the postwar solidarity of the Western powers.

Western enmity toward the government of Egyptian President Gamal Abdul Nasser rose with the failure of negotiations over the building of the Aswan High Dam on the Nile River in July 1956. The subsequent embracing of the Soviet Union and Warsaw Pact nations by Nasser, and his nationalization of the Suez Canal Company, brought France and Britain together in plotting a military seizure of the canal.

The Israelis made a fitting ally for France and Great Britain, as they were anxious to weaken or destroy the Nasser regime. Accordingly, Israel invaded the Sinai Peninsula with the bulk of its army on October 29, 1956, fighting through the passes and approaching the Suez Canal. Meanwhile, the British and French declared that they would enforce a UN cease-fire resolution by landing and separating the forces along the canal.

Under air and naval supremacy, France and Britain landed troops at Port Said and Port Fuad on October 30 and began to occupy the entire Canal Zone. U.S. President Dwight D. Eisenhower was greatly angered by the effrontery of the Anglo-French moves, which were made without informing the United States.

Furthermore, the incident removed the spotlight from the Soviets and their behavior in the revolt in Hungary.

Pressure from the United Nations, especially from the Soviet Union and United States, forced the Anglo-French attackers to break off the action and evacuate their forces, ending this peculiar intervention on December 22, 1956. The Israeli forces withdrew separately in March 1957, having administered a moral and physical blow to the Egyptian army.

The military difficulties and diplomatic morass that subsumed the British and French in the Suez Canal incident signaled the end of postwar British and French independence of action outside of their standing alliances. Meanwhile, the United States gained a new antagonist in Egypt and became further embroiled in the problems of the Middle East. U.S. intervention in Lebanon in 1958 may be considered a direct outgrowth of the Suez episode. Moreover, the continuing bargaining with Saudi Arabia over economic and defense issues crossed with American-Israeli relations, became more serious, and drew the United States deeper into the Gulf region.

The arms race also accelerated in the region because of the Suez incident, with the United States and Soviet Union the leading suppliers of arms for their respective clients there. For the Israelis, the tonic of military success was soured by the diplomatic actions that, in their view, had denied them the fruits of military victory.

The Six-Day War of 1967 redressed that failure a decade later by creating a crisis covering a unilateral Israeli offensive that carried their forces to the banks of the Suez Canal and forced the closing of this vital Egyptian waterway and financial treasure for more than seven years. However, the Egyptian army then astounded the world with its surprise crossing and reoccupation of the Suez Canal zone on October 6, 1973, eliminating many of the Israeli fortified outposts that had been mistakenly considered impregnable.

The Egyptian forces dug in and repulsed both air and armored counterattacks of the Israelis with layered air defenses and antitank guided missiles. However, Egyptian attempts to enlarge their zone and relieve pressure on their Syrian allies led to heavy losses and opened the way for an Israeli counteroffensive, crossing the canal and threatening both Cairo and Suez.

Israel and Egypt signed a cease-fire agreement in November 1973 and peace agreements on January 18, 1974. The Israelis withdrew to the Sinai passes, and Egypt placed only reduced forces on the east bank of the Suez Canal. Israel eventually relinquished the Sinai to Egypt in return for a permanent peace settlement in 1979.

See also Arab-Israeli Conflict; Cold War; Eisenhower, Dwight D., and National Policy; Interventionism; Middle East and U.S. Policy; Middle East Conflicts (1956, 1967, 1973); Soviet Union, Former (Russia), and U.S. Policy

Further Reading

Gorst, Anthony, and Lewis Johnman. *The Suez Crisis.* London: Routledge, 1997.

Louis, William Roger, and Roger Owen, eds. *Suez 1956: The Crisis and Its Consequences.* Oxford, UK: Clarendon Press, 1989.

SUICIDE BOMBING

Most prevalent today in the Middle East, armed violence, generally involving civilians, in which the perpetrator is prepared to lose his or her own life in the attack. Since the term implies the existence of a bomb of some sort, suicide bombing per se has only become possible in the modern era with the advent of explosive materials.

The idea of intentionally sacrificing one's life to harm one's enemies is probably as old as warfare itself. In recent decades, however, suicide bombing has been associated primarily with three main phenomena—the Japanese kamikaze attacks of World War II, the terrorist attacks against the United States on September 11, 2001, and the violent Palestinian struggle against Israel.

Insofar as terrorism is a concept that describes violence aimed primarily at instilling fear into a group of people, not all forms of suicide bombing are terrorist, although they are all vicious in nature. Some have argued that suicide attacks against strictly military targets (such as the World War II kamikaze strikes) do not qualify as terrorist acts since their primary goal is to physically destroy an armed opponent and not to terrorize a civilian populace. All suicide bombing, however, owes its effectiveness to the absolute determination of the perpetrator to accomplish his or her deadly mission at all costs.

HISTORY OF SUICIDE BOMBING

The term "suicide bombing" entered the media vocabulary in the early 1980s, when members of the Lebanese terrorist organization Hezbollah began to detonate bombs after infiltrating enemy compounds in Beirut, Lebanon, killing themselves in the process. The most infamous of these attacks occurred at a Marine barracks in Beirut on October 23, 1983, and left 241 U.S. military personnel dead. War historians subsequently connected Hezbollah's technique with the famous kamikaze attacks perpetrated at the end of World War II by the Japanese air force and navy against American warships in the Pacific.

Since the 1980s, suicide bombing has been adopted by many armed groups, notably Hamas, Islamic Jihad, the al-Aqsa Martyrs Brigade (all in Palestine), and the Tamil Tigers (in Sri Lanka). On September 11, 2001, 19 Arab men hijacked four commercial planes and piloted them into selected buildings in the United States in a suicide bombing of unprecedented scale, killing themselves and almost 3,000 other people. In recent years, more than 20 countries across the globe have experienced suicide bombings.

As a military tactic, suicide bombing is more likely to be employed in asymmetric warfare—that is, in a conflict between two unequal forces. A perpetrator who does not have to worry about a postoperation escape plan is an enemy that cannot be deterred by the threat of imprisonment, torture, or death. For that reason, antiterrorist specialists have long been frustrated in trying to formulate a coherent strategy to neutralize the devastation wrought by suicide bombers. Most experts agree that the only way to guard against such attacks is to prevent potential perpetrators from acquiring what is, arguably, a death wish.

PROFILE OF A SUICIDE BOMBER

Due to the extensive media coverage of the countless suicide attacks that have occurred in the past two decades in the Middle East, the words "suicide bomber" immediately bring to mind a militant Islamic fundamentalist. Fighting against an Israeli army that is vastly superior in weaponry and organization, for example, Palestinian militants have increasingly resorted to suicide attacks, aimed at striking fear into the hearts of the Jewish civilian population of Israel.

During the 1990s, when such attacks began to multiply, the typical suicide bomber was a highly religious man between the ages of 18 and 23, single, with a high school education. In more recent years, however, this profile has lost its relevance to counterterrorist specialists, as different categories of people (including women, teenagers, and college graduates) have chosen to become suicide bombers.

Suicide attacks, however, do retain a religious dimension as most bombers consider themselves to be future martyrs (called *shaheed* in Arabic) engaged in a holy war, or jihad. Since the Koran explicitly forbids suicide, the bombers interpret their self-sacrifice as merely a radical military technique, and not a purposeful destruction of their God-given life.

Drawing from the testimonies of prospective suicide bombers, it has been possible to identify a handful of justifications or rationalizations for their drastic actions. The most important motive, at least as far as Palestinian militants are concerned, is the perceived heavenly reward promised to everyone who dies fighting the holy war against the enemies of the Islamic faith. Revenge is also often invoked as an important reason for committing an act of suicide bombing.

This form of armed violence has many wealthy supporters in the Middle East, terrorists who guarantee a prospective suicide bomber that his or her family will receive a large financial reward after the mission is successfully accomplished. Although money is never mentioned as the primary reason for perpetrating such attacks, it undoubtedly helps the recruitment of potential martyrs. Successful (and hence dead) suicide bombers are celebrated as fallen heroes, and their families enjoy an enhanced social status within their communities.

TRAINING AND INDOCTRINATION

Islamic suicide bombers are typically drafted from mosques and youth centers. While seeking fanatical single-minded individuals, recruiters do not, however, enlist what psychologists would describe as mentally unstable, suicidal personalities. Once a prospective bomber joins the cause, he or she undergoes a long period of preparation, which includes many hours of religious indoctrination. Reportedly, some recruits have been asked to lie in empty graves for hours so that they can see for themselves how peaceful a so-called righteous death can be. They spend progressively less time with their families and friends, and concentrate almost obsessively on spiritual preparation for the attack.

Suicide bomber *handlers*—that is, the organizers of the suicide attacks—do not give the bombers the details of their missions until days before they are sent out to seek their targets. The weapon of choice is usually an explosives-laden belt, which can be wrapped around the bomber's body and hidden by loose clothes. The organizers of suicide bombings are extremely media-conscious, making sure that the death of their martyrs attracts a lot of publicity through massive destruction and loss of human life, and through the selection of highly symbolic targets (as in the case of the September 11, 2001, terrorist attacks on the World Trade Center and the Pentagon).

In recent years, it has become a tradition for prospective Palestinian suicide bombers to write or videotape a testimony before setting out to accomplish their mission. The videotaped recordings are usually rife with religious and military symbols. The subsequent death of the bomber is often celebrated as a happy event in his or her community, as this particular kind of sacrifice is thought to be pleasing to God. Given the inefficacy of deterrents, as well as the sense of moral superiority and religious accomplishment that prospective perpetrators typically acquire, suicide bombing remains extremely difficult to counteract, even by powerful, well-organized militaries.

See also Hamas; Intifada; Kamikaze; September 11/WTC and Pentagon Attacks

Further Reading

Axell, Albert, and Hideaki Kase. *Kamikaze: Japan's Suicide Gods*. London: Pearson Education Limited, 2002.

Human Rights Watch. *Erased in a Moment: Suicide Bombing Attacks Against Israeli Civilians*. New York: Human Rights Watch, 2002.

Reuter, Christoph. *My Life as a Weapon: A Modern History of Suicide Bombing*. Princeton, NJ: Princeton University Press, 2002.

Victor, Barbara. *Army of Roses: Inside the World of Palestinian Women Suicide Bombers*. Emmaus, PA: Rodale Press, 2003.

SUMMIT CONFERENCES

Meetings between or among the heads of rival or enemy powers in an attempt to satisfy mutual demands through negotiation rather than warfare. Summit conferences are not just meetings between heads of state. A true summit requires powers that are more or less evenly matched and rulers who have the power and prestige to make major decisions on the spot with the authority to carry them out afterwards. A practical agenda for a summit meeting must be devised ahead of time, and those involved must not only have agreed on some subjects to discuss, but those on which they are willing to make compromises or concessions.

The modern era of the summit conference began in 1938, when British Prime Minister Neville Chamberlain, Italian leader Benito Mussolini, and French Premier Edouard Daladier met with Nazi leader Adolf Hitler in an attempt to avert war on the European continent. In the end, in exchange for Hitler's promise to avoid further aggression, Churchill, Mussolini, and Daladier agreed to allow Hitler to control the German-speaking border regions of Czechoslovakia, thus effectively eliminating Czechoslovakia as a military power. Unfortunately, for those who hoped this would keep the peace, Hitler reneged on the agreement within months, sending troops into Prague, and then invading Poland. The result was World War II.

In the modern era, summits continued to make sense as a means of gaining concessions from other nations. Modern methods of communication and travel make it relatively easy for leaders to cover large distances quickly if they wish to talk things over in person. Because they do not have to be absent or out of touch for long periods, heads of state can risk travel in a way that would have been unthinkable in an earlier era.

A series of summit meetings among the leaders of the victorious Allies of World War II—the United States, the Soviet Union, and Great Britain—were held to decide how to carve up what was left after the war. The first of these summit meetings was held in occupied Teheran, Iran, in 1943. In 1945, Allied leaders met again at the Crimean summer resort of Yalta. Later that summer, when a third meeting was held in Potsdam, Great Britain's presence was largely irrelevant, and the summit primarily consisted only of the two superpowers—the United States and the Soviet Union.

Summit conferences have remained an important part of international diplomacy since the end of World War II. In the modern era of mass media, a summit conference always leads to banner headlines, television specials, photo opportunities, and a lot of print and broadcast commentary.

During the Cold War, U.S. presidents from Dwight Eisenhower to Ronald Reagan met their Soviet counterparts from Nikita Khrushchev to Mikhail Gorbachev at summits held in places from Glassboro, New Jersey, to Reykjavik, Iceland. Although they sometimes came to agreement on practical details, such as reductions in the number of ballistic missiles held by each country, arguably these summit meetings had no true effect on the course of the Cold War.

The last of the summit meetings held between the two superpowers was in Reykjavik, Iceland, in 1987. At that summit conference, Russian leader Mikhail Gorbachev and U.S. President Ronald Reagan came close to agreement on a massive disarmament plan. At the same time, however, for all intents and purposes the Soviet Union was already disintegrating.

Although currently without a comparable superpower with whom to negotiate, the United States has remained an active participant in the summit meetings of other nations. In particular, the United States has played an important mediator role in summits designed to negotiate an end to the Israeli-Arab conflict. This role began in September 1978, when President Jimmy Carter met with Egyptian president Anwar Sadat and Israeli Prime Minister Menachem Begin at Camp David, where they agreed to what is known as the Camp David Accords—a framework for peace in the Middle East. In July 2000, President Bill Clinton, Israeli Prime Minister Ehud Barak, and Palestinian leader Yasir Arafat, along with other officials and technical advisers, met at Camp David to negotiate a final settlement of the Palestine-Israel conflict based on the Oslo accords. The negotiations ended in failure in 2005, however, when the sides could not agree about the issue of Jerusalem.

Other nations also continue to hold summit conferences. For example, Arab heads of state have held a number of summits, with the primary goal of determining strategy toward Israel. These Arab League summit meetings began in Khartoum, Sudan, in 1964, and have been held as recently as 2002.

—Laura Kittross

See also Arab-Israeli Conflict; Camp David Accords; Middle East and U.S. Policy; Potsdam Conference (1945); Reykjavik; Soviet Union, Former (Russia), and U.S. Policy; World War II (1939–1945); Yalta Conference (1945)

SUN-TZU (300s BCE)

Chinese general who lived in the fourth century BCE and authored the military treatise *The Art of War,* which contains strategic principles still employed today. Sun-Tzu lived in the Chinese state of Wu, located in modern Shandong Province, during the fourth century BCE. This period in Chinese history is known as the Warring States Period. At that time, a cluster of states in southern China battled frequently for control of the region's plentiful natural resources. The price for defeat was steep; the population of a losing state was commonly slaughtered or enslaved.

When Sun-Tzu became commander of Wu's military, he was well aware of the perils of military defeat. But he also recognized that Wu was positioned to dominate the region. The state of Chou, which had long controlled the surrounding states, was in a period of steep decline. Wu and another state, Yüeh, both possessed the strength to succeed Chou as the region's power. Sun-Tzu thus crafted a strategy designed to elevate Wu's standing in the region while avoiding a potentially devastating confrontation with Yüeh. Sun-Tzu charted this strategy in his famous book *The Art of War*.

The Art of War outlined several key principles. First, Sun-Tzu contended that the decision to initiate a war is the gravest choice a nation can make. Therefore, war must be pursued only when a nation is threatened. Once a nation has decided to engage in a war, it must carefully plan its overall strategy. This planning includes a meticulous observation and assessment of the enemy. Sun-Tzu demanded that his military commanders evaluate the enemy's numbers, the ability of the enemy's forces, its level of discipline, the reputations of its leaders, its supplies, and even whether the enemy preferred to fight in good or bad weather.

Sun-Tzu next listed the rules for confrontation once war became imminent. A direct battle must never occur, Sun-Tzu cautioned, unless the enemy has definitely fielded the weaker force. Otherwise, an army must maneuver itself into a position to attain victory. First, the enemy must be deceived so that it underestimates its opponent's strength. Next, it must be craftily led into terrain that will hamper its movements. Subsequently, guerrilla attacks can be used to weaken the enemy once it has been placed in a defenseless position. Once the enemy has been significantly weakened, it can be exploited by striking at its most vulnerable points. Overall, Sun-Tzu advised that fighting should occur only when victory is assured.

The Art of War has gained adherents through successive centuries. The text gained new pertinence in the 20th century when Chinese revolutionary Mao Zedong followed its principles to lead the communist takeover of China. Aware of Mao's success, the Vietcong adopted Sun-Tzu's guerilla tactics in its battles against the United States during the Vietnam War.

The *Art of War* has even influenced recent U.S. military strategy. While serving as head of the Joint Chiefs of Staff, General Colin Powell devised a policy known as the Powell Doctrine. The doctrine stated several firm principles: The United States should engage in military action only when the mission's purpose is clearly stated and the mission is of vital importance to national security; the United States must enter the battle with the clearly superior force; and a clear end to the mission must be declared. Echoes of Sun-Tzu's advice about the gravity of war and the need to ensure victory resound throughout the Powell Doctrine and explain the U.S. desire to maintain a military that is far superior to any other in the world.

See also Guerrilla Warfare; Powell, Colin (1937–)

Further Reading

Halberstam, David. *War in a Time of Peace*. New York: Scribner, 2001.
Sawyer, Ralph D. Introduction to *The Complete Art of War*. By Sun-Tzu and Sun Pin. Boulder, CO: Westview Press, 1996.

SUPERPOWER

Uniquely powerful nation, with superior military, economic, and political strength. At the close of World War II, two nations emerged from the wreckage as superpowers—the United States and the Soviet Union. With most of their infrastructure still intact, and in possession of significant arsenals, these two countries were poised for rivalry. Relations soured as both countries laid claim to spheres of influence, and superpower rivalry became superpower hostility, with significant impact on the rest of the world.

Superpowers enjoy a natural claim to world leadership because they have substantial *hard* and *soft power*. They can enjoy maximum benefits by employing both. Hard power includes coercive power—both military and economic. Military might is important, but international law, customs regarding legitimate use, and the high cost of use (in terms of the loss from trade) render it best employed as a deterrent for superpowers. Hard power is also economic power; superpowers can create incentives or economic punishments that force other states to follow its lead. Soft power—state charisma, or leadership by example—can make leadership from superpowers more palatable and legitimate to other countries and render the use of hard power unnecessary.

With their overwhelming strength, superpowers enjoy certain privileges and hegemonic power relationships. Due to their superior strength, superpowers essentially dictate the world security climate. In a bipolar system, any agreements that rival superpowers reach (on arms control, for example) are necessarily binding on every other country. The lack of an agreement may have even greater effects: Alliance with one power or the other can make even small or weak countries into legitimate military targets.

Moreover, superpowers—because of their overwhelming military strength—have the capacity for mutual annihilation, and so they generally prefer not to go to war with one another. As a result, superpowers sometimes diffuse conflict by playing out their hostilities by proxy in small nations (as was the case in Korea and Vietnam).

There are, however, certain responsibilities that accompany such power. Superpowers, even more than great powers, have some obligation to maintain international peace and security. In a bipolar world system, some tension and conflict is expected. Nevertheless, because of their overwhelming power and influence, superpowers are obliged—morally and in their own interests—to prevent conflicts in their spheres from escalating. Even more important, rival superpowers are obligated to regulate their own behavior to protect life itself—the former Soviet Union had, and the United States still has, the capacity to destroy the world through nuclear holocaust. A sole superpower also has a responsibility to protect peace and security through self-regulation, and not to abuse its power.

Like great powers, superpowers have the ability to intervene (for humanitarian purposes or in their own interest) in interstate and intrastate conflicts. Both the United States and the Soviet Union were extremely active in third-party conflicts during the Cold War. Since the collapse of the Soviet Union in 1991, the United States has led numerous interventions—some with the support of the world community (as in the first Gulf War) and some without (as it instituted regime change in Iraq in 2003). The legitimacy of preemptive warfare, particularly when practiced by a superpower against a weak state, is hotly contested.

The rights and duties of a lone superpower like the United States are still being determined. Among the issues under contention are whether such a nation has the right to impose its will on other countries because of its strength; whether it has the right to preemptive defense; whether it has a duty to intervene in humanitarian crises, and whether it has a duty to assert responsible leadership even at a cost to itself and its own security.

See also Bipolarity; Cold War; Great Power Rivalry; Hyperpower; Soviet Union, Former (Russia), and U.S. Policy

SUPREME COURT, ROLE OF U.S.

Role in national policy of the highest court in the United States, which has jurisdiction to hear certain cases that may affect national security issues. Under Article III of the U.S. Constitution, the U.S. Supreme Court shares jurisdiction with lower district courts to hear all cases arising under the Constitution, U.S. laws, treaties of the United States, and between U.S. citizens and foreign states. The Court is granted original jurisdiction—the power to be the first court to try a case and make findings of fact—over "all Cases affecting Ambassadors, other public Ministers and Consuls." U.S. Congress has also given district courts original jurisdiction to decide civil cases involving the U.S. Constitution, federal laws, and treaties. Thus, the U.S. Supreme Court is vested with constitutional and statutory power to decide cases concerning national security.

Despite its jurisdiction, the Supreme Court generally has been reluctant to decide on cases involving national security. Instead, it has chosen to abstain from such cases and has based these decisions on constitutional and political limitations. The judicial doctrines primarily relied on by the Supreme Court to abstain from national security cases are the political question doctrine, standing, and ripeness. These doctrines are important to issues involving national security not because they limit the Supreme Court's role, but because they force the U.S. Congress and the president to carry out their war power duties.

POLITICAL QUESTION

The U.S. Supreme Court may decline to rule on disputes when it decides that the resolution of an issue is better left to the political branches of the government. This political question doctrine, when relied on by the Court, renders an issue nonreviewable. The U.S. Congress and the president—with the intention that the result will better reflect the will of the people—must instead decide the issue. Legal scholars disagree, however, on how the Court decides that the question is political and whether it is then required or optional to abstain.

The political question doctrine was first expressed by Chief Justice John Marshall in *Marbury v. Madison* (1803) and later reexamined in *Baker v. Carr* (1962). The Court rarely relies on the doctrine and has only invoked it twice in cases relating to national security. In *Gilligan v. Morgan* (1973), a group of students sought a declaratory judgment allowing for federal judiciary assessment of the Ohio National Guard's "training, weaponry, and orders" to determine whether force would inevitably be used against the students at Kent State University. The Court held that the Constitution gave power of control of the National Guard to Congress.

The Court invoked the doctrine again in 1979, when Arizona Senator Barry Goldwater challenged President Jimmy Carter's decision to withdraw from the mutual defense treaty with Taiwan without Senate authorization. Although the Constitution requires the "advice and consent" on making treaties, it is silent on the unilateral abrogation of treaties. Senator Goldwater's claim was held to be not proper for judicial resolution by four members of the Supreme Court because it was deemed a political question. A fifth member of the Court agreed that the case should be dismissed but concluded instead that the case was not ripe for review.

STANDING

A plaintiff has standing if he or she is qualified to assert or enforce legal rights in a court of law. To demonstrate standing in a federal court, a party must show three things. First, a plaintiff must show *injury in fact*—that is, a violation of a legally protected interest—that is specific and actual or imminent. Second, the plaintiff is required to explain a *causal connection* between the injury and the conduct in dispute. Finally, the plaintiff must demonstrate that a favorable decision by the court will *redress* his or her injury. However, if the Court dismisses a lawsuit based on standing, it does not mean that the case is not justifiable. It may merely suggest that the wrong plaintiff brought the suit.

In cases involving national security, the Court has held that a plaintiff who is merely a concerned citizen lacks standing to initiate a lawsuit unless Congress statutorily grants the person standing and the plaintiff is within the zone of interest. The Court has held that a plaintiff may have taxpayer standing, but only if the claim challenges specific constitutional limitations of the government's taxing and spending powers. For example, in *Schlesinger v. Reservists Committee to Stop the War* (1974), members of an antiwar group who opposed United States involvement in Vietnam brought an action against the secretary of defense and three service secretaries on behalf of all citizens and taxpayers, challenging the membership of members of Congress in the reserves. The Court held that the group did not have standing to sue the secretaries because the injury they argued to have suffered was an abstract injury rather than a concrete injury. In addition, the plaintiffs also lacked taxpayer standing because they failed to demonstrate a logical nexus between their claim and their status as taxpayers.

RIPENESS

Finally, the Supreme Court may temporarily avoid adjudication if it holds that the issues in a case are not ripe for review—that is, if the Court holds that future events will alter the issues in the case and will render the case irrelevant. A court's reliance on the ripeness doctrine does not completely bar an issue from being heard in court. The Court has merely determined that it is not the right time for the case to be heard. The doctrine is relied on in cases involving national security if parties in the case seem to be seeking only an advisory opinion and not the resolution of an actual and specific legal case.

In *Dellums v. Bush* (1990), the Court ruled that the case was not ripe for review. The case involved the deployment of U.S. troops to the Persian Gulf prior to the 1991 war against Iraq. The plaintiffs were 53 members of the House of Representatives and one member of the Senate. They claimed that the president did not have the authority to deploy U.S. troops because the power to declare war is reserved to Congress. The Court held, however, that although the plaintiff had standing to request an injunction stopping the deployment, the case was not ripe for judicial review because the issue had not first been brought to a vote in Congress. The Court held that it would be premature to decide on the issue of whether a declaration of war is required if Congress itself has not yet determined that a declaration is necessary. The Court did not offer guidance on how or when the case would be ripe for review.

TERRORISM CASES

After the terrorist attacks of September 11, 2001, and the war in Afghanistan, the administration of President George W. Bush implemented a series of controversial antiterrorism policies. The first issue brought before the Supreme Court concerning the antiterrorism policies involved the detention of 660 men from 40 countries who were captured during the course of the campaign in Afghanistan by the U.S. military. The men had been held for over two years at the U.S. Navy Base in Guantánamo Bay, Cuba. In *Rasul et al. v. Bush* (2004), the Court held that because Guantánamo Bay is under the exclusive jurisdiction and control of the United States, U.S. courts have jurisdiction to consider legal challenges surrounding the detention of the foreign nationals captured abroad by the U.S. military in connection with ongoing hostilities. The Court also considered the fact that the plaintiffs, two Australians and twelve Kuwaitis, were not nationals of any country that the United States was at war with and that they denied any acts of aggression against the United States. The Court also noted that the men had not been charged with any crime and did not have access to any tribunal.

The *Rasul* case remains one of the few cases that the Supreme Court has agreed to hear involving the antiterrorism policies of the federal executive branch. The two other cases—*Hamdi v. Rumsfeld* (2004) and *Rumsfeld v. Padilla* (2004)—both involved U.S. citizens. Similar to the ruling in *Rasul*, the Court held in *Hamdi* that the plaintiff must be given access to the U.S. court system. In *Padilla*, the case was sent back to the lower court because the plaintiff lacked standing.

The limited role of the Supreme Court in matters of national security is apparent from its refusal to hear most cases involving the issue. The Court has, for the past two centuries, relied on constitutional limitations and political constraints to avoid ruling on national security issues. The recent terrorism cases mark a shift in the types of national security issues being brought before the Court, primarily issues of civil liberties and consideration of international law.

See also Constitution of the United States

Further Reading

Dycus, Stephen, Arthur L. Berney, William C. Banks, and Peter Raven-Hansen. *National Security Law,* 3rd ed. New York: Aspen Law & Business, 2002.

Henkin, Louis. *Foreign Affairs and the Constitution,* Mineola, NY: The Foundation Press, 1972.

SURFACE TO AIR MISSILE (SAM)

Radar or infrared guided missile fired from a ground position to intercept and destroy enemy aircraft or missiles. Surface to Air Missiles (SAMs) were developed to protect ground positions from hostile air attacks, specifically high-altitude bombers flying beyond the range of conventional antiaircraft artillery.

During the 1950s and 1960s, batteries of Nike-Ajax and Nike-Hercules SAMs provided strategic air defense against Soviet ICBMs and long-range bombers. Following agreements between the Soviet Union and the United States to limit strategic nuclear devices and the subsequent dismantlement of the Soviet Union into independent republics, research focused on the development of short-range, lighter, and more portable SAMs to protect ground troops. An important development among hand-held SAMs is integrated fire-control systems for ground units, which can separate friendly aircraft from hostile aircraft.

Since 1970, almost all the major industrial nations have developed tactical weapons to protect ground troops from air attack. Hand-held antiaircraft missiles using optical sighting and infrared homing devices like the Stinger missile have been used effectively against fighters and helicopters in conflicts in Afghanistan, Iraq, and other areas.

The United States provided anti-Soviet forces in Afghanistan in the late 1980s with Stinger missiles, which were an effective defense against Soviet helicopters attacking mountain positions. Muslim extremist groups have retained some of these weapons and acquired new SAMs, a situation that poses a significant terrorist threat at the current time.

A SAM was fired on an Israeli airliner in Africa in 2003. Insurgents also have downed a number of U.S. aircraft during Operation Iraqi Freedom using handheld surface to air missiles. Recent homeland security advisories have directed domestic airports to increase security around their perimeters to prevent a SAM missile from being launched at commercial airliners departing or arriving at U.S. airports.

See also Missiles

SURGE CAPACITY

The ability of a system to expand rapidly, beyond its normal capacity, to meet increased demands made because of unexpected emergencies or disasters. Surge capacity has been a traditional concern of the military, given the ambiguities of war and war fighting. It is also a concern in times of peace.

A significant reason for having a military surge capacity is that if the nation ever requires a large increase in military capabilities due to a rapid change in the security environment, it can do so. Thus, in part, this argument has justified having more military bases and posts than might otherwise be efficiently operated. For example, after major wars, U.S. military planners have sought to build surge capacity into the support structures. This would, and does, include plans for calling up and supporting military reserves and National Guard forces to active duty, both in the United States and overseas.

While surge capacity has been a concern of the military and national security, it also has become a concern of other nonmilitary systems. These systems may be directly or indirectly affected. For example, in the case of bioterrorism, a bioterrorist attack would test the surge capacity of the health care system by increasing demand for qualified personnel, medical care, and public health. Other examples would include first-responder systems (police, fire, and emergency systems), communications systems (telephone, cell phone, and Internet systems), and transportation systems (such as the Civilian Air Backup System, which supports military deployments like recent ones to the Gulf and Iraq).

See also Bioterrorism; First Responders

SUSTAINABLE DEVELOPMENT

Form of development that ensures that economic growth, rising living standards, and other types of development can be maintained for the current and for future generations. Sustainable development is domestically acceptable, economically sound, eco-friendly, and culturally sensitive. It embraces the regular types of development—economic, political, social infrastructure, health, and education development—and makes certain that progress in these areas can be continued. Moreover, it includes the replenishment and development of cultural and social resources as well as traditional material ones. It is a form of development that tries to improve the present without compromising the future. The principle of sustainable development recognizes that today's human beings deserve a reasonable standard of living and that future generations should be given the same opportunity.

Development projects that are prompted by outsiders require local acceptance. They should be culturally, socially, and ethically appropriate for the region. Projects might be well intended, and indeed productive, but if they do not obtain buy-in from those in charge, they are not sustainable. As much as possible, however, sustainable development projects and ideas should come from the people (who are most aware of their own needs) and should be run and maintained by them. It is their participation, zeal, and long-term commitment that will keep a particular program running.

Economic sustainability is a major concern. It includes protecting natural and physical resources, as well as implementing sound policies that protect a nation's capital and goodwill resources. In developing countries—which tend to rely heavily on primary economic activities, such as agriculture and extraction—protecting natural resources is very important. Sustainable development argues for crop rotation (which depletes the soil less) and fallowing (allowing the soil to rest).

Sustainable development argues against monocropping, in which farmers plant all their fields with a single cash crop such as peanuts or soybeans. Not only does such monoculture deplete soil, it is economically risky. A farmer is not guarded against loss if the crop is destroyed; and if the market price for the crop is low, the farmer may not be able to earn enough to feed his family—especially as some cash crops, like cotton, are not food. In terms of other natural resources, sustainable development argues against practices like deforestation (particularly in old-growth forests) and overfishing, and it argues in support of replanting and responsible harvesting.

It is likewise important for developing countries to protect their other resources, such as their infrastructure, machinery, and technology. Sustainable development includes the creation of a technological cadre—machinists, technicians, engineers—who have the knowledge and skill to design, build, maintain, and repair infrastructure and other elements of society.

Past agricultural development projects, while well intended and productive, were stopped because local people had not been trained in how to fix broken tools or equipment.

Sound economic policies can help sustain all kinds of development within a state. It includes basic maintenance of economic machinery—not overspending; investing income, loan, and grant monies prudently; and keeping the money supply at appropriate levels to prevent inflation or deflation. Privatization, which is occurring in developing countries and is often mandated as part of the loan policies of the International Monetary Fund (IMF), must be pursued appropriately. The rate at which privatization occurs should not produce excessive unemployment, and it should give the population enough time to learn about private business management. Openness to foreign investment may help grow the economy, but it should be introduced at sustainable levels.

One of the most significant factors affecting sustainability and closely aligned with economic sustainability is *environmental protection.* Many developing countries have significant renewable and nonrenewable natural resources, such as good soil, timber, fish, minerals, oil, or gas. If harvested or developed too quickly, even normally renewable resources may be depleted. Results may include soil erosion or degradation, loss of soil fertility, deforestation, desertification, and imbalances in local ecosystems that result in an eventual loss of biodiversity. Extracting nonrenewable sources too quickly may also result in ecologic damage (such as from mining operations set up with insufficient attention to the environment).

There are economic arguments against environmental damage as well. In the case of renewable resources, exhausting them too quickly may endanger their capacity to reproduce themselves. Selling off limited resources quickly may result in lower prices and an ultimate loss to the developing country. Sustainable development, then, is ecologically friendly, ensuring that renewable resources are able to regenerate themselves, and that nonrenewable resources are not parted with too quickly,

nor extracted at a cost to the environment. Protecting the environment as a whole—particularly special ecological zones like the rainforests—is also economically important because of the rise of ecotourism.

The human component of sustainable development is important as well. To make other development practices more effective, population levels need to be addressed. Many developing countries have large populations, and large populations, particularly those in large metropolitan areas, tend to put significant pressure on resources. Sustainable development thus includes maintaining the population at a sustainable level. Education about family planning options may help families make informed decisions about reproduction. Improved health care may also help families stay smaller. Some families currently have many children because they know that not all will survive until adulthood; the ability to treat childhood disease particularly may slow population growth naturally.

Sustainable cultural and social development is likewise important to creating a stable society with a higher standard of living. Social development includes reducing social ills, like murder, rape, arson, and other violent crimes; theft; alcohol and substance abuse; juvenile delinquency, and so forth. These things may be countered in part by poverty reduction, which stems in part from economic development, job creation, and government welfare benefits. Health education and access to health care can also reduce these ills.

Social development likewise includes granting access to basic education for boys *and* girls of all socioeconomic strata. In a globalizing world, cultural development means concerted efforts to preserve the unique traditions of a nation's peoples, reinforcing identities, and creating social order. It includes the preservation of historical legacies for the future—historic sites, monuments, and religious edifices—as well as local language, customs, and ideals.

See also Development, Third-World

T

TACTICAL NUCLEAR WEAPONS

Small nuclear warheads intended for use in a battlefield situation or a limited strike. Tactical nuclear weapons, also referred to as *battlefield nukes*, are less powerful than the strategic nuclear warheads mounted on intercontinental ballistic missiles. They are meant to devastate enemy targets in a specific area without causing widespread destruction and radioactive fallout.

The United States began developing lightweight nuclear warheads in the 1950s. One of the first such devices was the W-54 warhead, whose explosive force, or yield, varied from 0.1 to 1 kiloton (a kiloton is a force equal to 1,000 tons of TNT). By comparison, the atomic bombs dropped on Japan in World War II had yields of 12 to 25 kilotons. The W-54 was the main warhead used on the Davy Crockett nuclear recoilless rifle, a portable warhead launcher that was crewed by a single soldier. The Davy Crockett could deliver a warhead to a target up to 2.5 miles away.

During the 1960s, the U.S. Navy and Marines collaborated on development of a tactical nuclear device called the Special Atomic Demolition Munition (SADM). The project called for a two-man crew to parachute from an aircraft carrying a portable warhead similar to the W-54. The crew would place the weapon in a harbor or other target reachable by sea. They would then swim to a small craft waiting offshore to pick them up. The nuclear device was set to explode after the crew was safely out of the blast area.

During the Cold War, both the United States and the Soviet Union manufactured and deployed tens of thousands of tactical nuclear weapons. These included nuclear artillery shells, nuclear antiaircraft missiles, and nuclear antitank rounds. However, none were ever used in combat. For destroying small targets, modern conventional munitions were found to be just as effective as nuclear weapons. The only advantage of nuclear weapons in a tactical situation is that one warhead can be used in place of many conventional explosives. In addition, neither of the superpowers was willing to risk unleashing all-out nuclear war by employing battlefield nukes.

Since the end of the Cold War, however, Russia has developed a much more open attitude toward the use of tactical nuclear weapons. This change stems largely from the deterioration in Russian conventional forces following the 1991 collapse of the Soviet Union. The cash-strapped Russian military sees tactical nuclear weapons as a cost-effective way of defending Russian interests in the post-Soviet era. By contrast, the United States unilaterally destroyed its tactical nuclear arsenal after the fall of the Soviet Union, and Congress passed legislation forbidding the testing, development, and stockpiling of nuclear warheads with yields of less than 5 kilotons.

See also Nuclear Utilization Theory (NUT); Nuclear Weapons; Reagan, Ronald, and National Policy; Soviet Union, Former (Russia), and U.S. Policy

TACTICS, MILITARY

Specific methods used to engage and defeat an enemy in combat. Tactics stand in contrast to strategy, which is the military's overall plan to achieve its objectives.

The history of U.S. involvement in World War II offers an example of the differences between strategy and tactics. In 1941, Japan planned to seize much of Southeast Asia to secure much-needed supplies of oil and rubber. Knowing that the United States would oppose this plan, Japan adopted the strategy of crippling the United States' ability to respond to Japanese invasions in the region. The tactics they employed to achieve their objective included a surprise air attack on the U.S. fleet in Pearl Harbor, Hawaii, and an amphibious assault on U.S. Army forces in the Philippines. The Japanese attacks brought the formerly neutral United States into World War II.

TYPES OF TACTICS

Military tactics can be classified into several categories, including offensive tactics, defensive tactics, and tactics of deception. The tactics one chooses to employ depend upon the military situation and the composition of one's forces. In fact, an army's makeup is often a reflection of the types of tactics it prefers to use. An army consisting mainly of light and mobile units will be more likely to employ tactics that emphasize speed and flexibility. By contrast, an army made up primarily of heavy units will probably prefer tactics that rely on massive firepower and strength of numbers for success.

Offensive Tactics

The oldest and simplest offensive tactic is the frontal assault—a straightforward charge into known enemy positions. The frontal assault typically relies on sheer numbers and firepower to overwhelm the defenders. There is no pretense of deception or question about where the main attack will take place.

Until quite recently, the frontal assault was the preferred offensive tactic in most combat situations. However, the increasing accuracy, range, and dependability of firearms since the mid-1800s have made the frontal assault nearly obsolete. The use of the machine gun in World War I made frontal assaults on prepared defensive positions almost suicidal.

Flanking and encirclement maneuvers offer an alternative to the risks of a frontal assault. A flanking attack is one that strikes an enemy from the side rather than the front. A flank attack is usually preceded by a holding attack—a limited assault on the front of the enemy line meant to draw the defender's attention. While the opponent is busy dealing with the holding attack, the real assault comes from the side, with the goal of surprising the defenders and throwing them into confusion. The troops conducting the holding attack then press their assault, driving the defenders back from both the front and side.

In an encirclement, the attacking force completely surrounds its enemy, cutting off the opponent's lines of communication, supply, and retreat. Many times, an encircling army does not need to make a concerted attack on the opposing force to destroy it. By denying the encircled enemy access to vital supplies such as food, medicine, and ammunition, the attackers are often able to compel the defender to surrender with limited use of force. Encirclement requires a very mobile and well-coordinated army that can get around an enemy position and maintain its own supply lines while doing so. The increasing use of tanks and other mechanized vehicles in the mid-20th century made encirclement a much more common military tactic.

The reconnaissance in force is an offensive tactic that combines two goals—assaulting an enemy position and gathering military information. Like other offensive tactics, a reconnaissance in force aims to capture territory and kill enemy troops. However, these goals are secondary to the objective of gathering battlefield intelligence to help plan military operations in the area. A related but smaller-scale operation is called a *raid* or *patrol*. Patrols are typically carried out by small units that attempt to quickly infiltrate enemy positions, capture prisoners for interrogation, and return with a minimum of casualties.

Defensive Tactics

Basic defensive tactics can be classified generally into two categories: static defense and mobile defense. Static defense relies on heavily defended forward lines, typically supported by strongpoints such as fortifications and bunkers. Static defenses are designed to repel even the strongest frontal assault. The strategic placement of strongpoints is meant to reduce the chances of flanking or encirclement of defenders by enemy forces. Static defensive positions are designed so that adjacent units have lines of fire that allow them to support one another.

The advent of the tank and airplane as weapons of war rendered purely static defensives obsolete against modern armies. For example, in the 1930s France built an enormous series of complex fortresses along its eastern border to prevent a German invasion. When the Germans did invade in 1940, they simply drove around the northern flank of this so-called Maginot Line. German forces did assault the Belgian fort at Eben Emael during their invasion. Although the fort was considered the strongest in the world, German air bombardment and parachute landings on the fort forced its surrender in less than a day.

Mobile alternatives to static defense include the defense-in-depth and the fighting withdrawal. In defense-in-depth, only a portion of a defender's army occupies positions on the front line. Additional lines of defense are located behind the front line. If attackers breach the first line of defense, the defenders fall back to join troops already in the next line back. The defense-in-depth forces attacking troops to make a series of assaults on prepared positions rather than allow them to achieve a significant breakthrough with a single victory. Defense-in-depth also continually forces attacking troops to face fresh defenders.

In a fighting withdrawal, defending forces establish temporary positions that they gradually abandon in the face of superior attacking forces. As they retreat, defending forces look for good defensive positions where they can make stands and inflict casualties on the attacker. However, no position is considered too valuable to abandon in order to preserve the defending force. Fighting withdrawals are meant to slow the pace of an attack without committing to a static defense.

A fighting withdrawal often turns into a counterattack, in which units that were on the defensive move over to the offensive. Counterattacks usually occur when an attacking force is tired or has overstretched its supply lines. In this weakened state, it is much more vulnerable to being attacked and defeated by the opposing force.

Deception Tactics

As their name suggests, deception tactics are meant to confuse an enemy or provide it with false information about one's own strength, position, or intentions. Some deceptive tactics are extremely old, whereas some are products of modern technology.

Camouflage—concealing troops from the enemy by making them hard to distinguish from their surroundings—has been used since ancient times. German tribes fighting against the legions of the Roman Empire often concealed their ranks by carrying tree limbs or other forms of vegetation. Native Americans achieved a reputation among Europeans for the "ungentlemanly" way they concealed themselves behind trees or

other forms of cover during combat. These tactics contrasted sharply with European warfare of the 18th century, in which armies fought each other in the open, methodically advancing on enemy lines in the face of defending fire.

Camouflage clothing, however, is a relatively new development in warfare. Ancient and medieval armies, being composed mainly of citizens conscripted to serve in times of war, had no regular uniforms of any type. They simply wore their everyday attire into battle. In contrast to today's uniforms, early modern armies often wore brightly colored uniforms so that it was easy to distinguish one side from the other. The great amounts of smoke produced by early firearms limited visibility on the battlefield, making it difficult for leaders to identify troops in drab clothing. The invention of more powerful, smoke-free propellants for firearms eliminated much of the visibility problem. By the early 20th century, most armies adopted uniforms that were camouflage or dull-colored; providing one's troops with concealment against enemy fire had become a greater challenge than distinguishing them from the opponent.

Misdirection is an important deception tactic often used by attacking forces. Misdirection involves making an opponent think one is going to strike in a certain place, while actually striking someplace else. Prior to the Allied invasion of German-occupied France during World War II, U.S. military intelligence pulled off one of the greatest misdirection operations in history.

The Germans suspected that the Allied forces would land either at Normandy or the Pas de Calais, both in France. The latter site was considered more likely because it was closer to Allied bases in England. The Allies chose to invade at Normandy, but they created an entire fake army in England across from the Pas de Calais to convince the Germans that the landing would occur there. Made up of dummy tanks, trucks, and planes, as well as fake radio traffic, the phantom army held the Germans' attention. Even after the real landings occurred, German commanders were reluctant to send reinforcements to Normandy, as they were convinced that the attack there was only a diversion. They were still sure the real invasion would come at Pas de Calais. By the time the Germans realized they had been deceived, the Allied forces were successfully ashore.

MODERN TACTICAL DOCTRINE

As warfare has evolved and become more complex, so have military tactics. In the not-too-distant past, military tactics were largely restricted to battlefield activities—the positioning and use of large-scale troop formations. Over time, however, tactics have been devised for actions involving even very small numbers of troops and situations not directly related to battle. Current military doctrine specifies tactics for storming individual buildings or even rooms, securing an area following combat, and dealing with local insurgencies in occupied areas.

Comparing the composition of early-21st-century U.S. armed forces with those of World War II reveals signs of both continuity and change in U.S. military tactics. During World War II, the U.S. military was a mass force of millions of conscripts, organized into large-scale heavy fighting units. The U.S. military at that time leaned heavily on tactics that made use of massive firepower and the ability of the U.S. economy to produce seemingly unlimited amounts of war materiel. It also employed advanced technology to great effect, pioneering the use of strategic air warfare and making great advances in radar, communications, and weapons technology. The U.S. Army was the world's first completely mechanized force, relying solely on trucks and other self-propelled vehicles to transport ground troops. By contrast, even the sophisticated German Wehrmacht (which consisted of the navy as well as the army) used horses extensively for transport until the end of the war.

The modern United States military, by contrast, is a much smaller volunteer army composed of professional soldiers for whom the military is a career. Instead of relying on large troop formations and overwhelming logistical superiority, it employs tactics that emphasize mobility and the efficient application of force. Hundreds of bombers were needed to destroy a target in World War II, but the modern U.S. military can do the same job using a relative handful of unmanned cruise missiles. The sheer weight of arms used by the United States in World War II has given way to precision accuracy and greater explosive power concentrated in fewer munitions. Even more so than its World War II counterpart, the modern U.S. military relies heavily on technologically sophisticated military hardware to defeat its enemies.

The changes in U.S. force composition and tactics since World War II are also a result of changes in the global political situation. Throughout most of the Cold War period, the United States believed that the next major war, should one occur, would take place in Europe. Both U.S. and Soviet military planners envisioned that

such a conflict would entail large tank battles in the same vein as those fought during World War II. However, such massive armored conflicts never materialized.

The shooting conflicts fought during the Cold Wars were mostly brush wars—engagements fought between relatively small forces in jungles or other areas not conducive to conventional military tactics. Even the large-scale conflicts of the era, such as the Vietnam War and the Soviet War in Afghanistan, were won by the triumph of unconventional guerilla warfare over conventional military tactics. By the time of the collapse of the Soviet Union in 1991, the United States had begun to significantly reshape its forces to reflect this reality.

By the late 1980s and early 1990s, it had become clear that the primary military threats in the near future would likely arise in regions more remote from U.S. bases in North America and Europe. At this time, the United States accelerated its transformation from a heavy-unit-based force to one focused on mobility and rapid-deployment capability. As of the early 21st century, this transformation was still underway. Donald Rumsfeld, secretary of defense under President George W. Bush, is a staunch proponent of a leaner and more flexible military. Rumsfeld's views increase the likelihood that future U.S. military tactics will show an even greater emphasis on small-scale operations.

—*John Haley*

See also Air-Land Battles; Blitzkrieg (Lightning War); Carpet Bombing; Counter-Force Doctrine; Decoys; Forward Basing; Military Doctrine; Psychological Warfare (PSYOPS)

Further Reading

Biddle, Stephen. *Military Power: Explaining Victory and Defeat in Modern Battle.* Princeton, NJ: Princeton University Press, 2004.

Ferris, John R., et al. *World History of Warfare (Tactics & Strategies).* Lincoln: University of Nebraska Press, 2002.

Wiest, Andrew, and M. K. Barbier. *Strategy and Tactics: Infantry Warfare.* St. Paul, MN: Motorbooks, 2002.

TAILHOOK SCANDAL

In 1993, scandal involving naval and marine officers. The Tailhook Association is a private organization that sponsors the Tailhook symposium, a reunion of former marine and navy flyers that began in 1956. Members of Tailhook also include defense contractors, and the U.S. Navy and contractors provide significant support to the meetings. By 1992, the Tailhook Association boasted 10 corporations and 15,000 individual members.

In 1993, Navy lieutenant Paula Coughlin claimed on ABC News that the Tailhook convention that she attended had included a gauntlet of officers who groped her and made questionable comments as she attempted to get through. Her revelations brought forth other women, who indicated that similar indignities had happened to them at Tailhook conventions.

Admiral John W. Snyder, for whom Coughlin was an aide, acknowledged her report, noting that such behavior was the natural consequence of getting naval aviators drunk. Coughlin filed charges and, when her case moved slowly, she went public with her allegations. A seven-month investigation by the Naval Criminal Investigative Service and Inspector General uncovered 140 cases of misconduct against 80 to 90 female victims.

As a result of the investigation, the secretary of the navy, H. Lawrence Garrett III, ordered the services to take disciplinary action against 70 individuals. Fifty were participants in the gauntlet, and 6 had obstructed the investigation. When witnesses placed Garrett and his chief of naval operations (CNO), Frank Kelso, near the gauntlet, the secretary resigned and the CNO retired early.

As the Tailhook story spread, senior officers retired or had their careers ruined. Defenders of the Tailhook Association attacked Coughlin's credibility, but she and other victims maintained that allegations were true. She and six other victims sued the association, which settled out of court. Coughlin resigned her commission in 1995.

Kelso and Garrett had previously worked to better women's status and opportunities in the navy, but the Tailhook scandal ended both their careers. In 1994 the aircraft carrier USS *Dwight D. Eisenhower* became the first combat ship to accommodate women. That happened shortly after the 1994 Tailhook convention.

Other careers were affected by the scandal. Admiral Snyder was relieved of duty, and three other admirals were censured. Thirty more admirals got letters of caution. More than three dozen lower-grade officers received letters of caution or fines. Of the 117 officers implicated in the scandal, only 10 were junior grade.

The Tailhook scandal brought sexual harassment and sexual crimes in the military from out of the shadows. In the aftermath, military women began speaking out about the abuses that had occurred since the active recruitment of women with the end of the draft in 1973. The increasing presence of women in greater numbers in the new unisex military placed great stress on the old-line traditional military. To many, the Tailhook events were the logical outcome of such stresses breaking through under the weakening influence of excess alcohol.

As a result of Tailhook, the other armed services became more aware of the problems of sexual harassment and more aggressive in dealing with it, but not particularly more successfully. The army weathered a number of scandals in the 1990s, and as of 2004, the Air Force Academy had not yet overcome the stigma of periodic flare-ups of sexual harassment and sexual crimes against women.

A decade after the Tailhook scandal, traditionalists in the military continued to fault Coughlin for damaging the image of the armed services, accusing her of seeking her own advantage at their expense. Moreover, women continue to struggle for unqualified acceptance within the armed forces.

See also Gender Issues; U.S. Navy

Further Reading

Office of the OSD Inspector General. *The Tailhook Report: The Official Inquiry Into The Events Of Tailhook '91."* New York: St. Martin's, 1993.

Vistica, Gregory L. *Fall from Glory: The Men Who Sank the U.S. Navy.* New York: Simon & Schuster, 1995.

Zimmerman, Jean. *Tailspin: Women at War in the Wake of Tailhook.* New York: Doubleday, 1995.

TAIWAN RELATIONS ACT

A 1979 congressional act that ensured the continued protection of Taiwan after the United States had normalized relations with Communist China.

On December 15 1978, President Jimmy Carter announced that the United States planned to normalize relations with the People's Republic of China. Beginning in January 1979, the United States would grant the Communist Chinese republic full diplomatic recognition. Negotiations between the two nations had secretly occurred since the administration of President Richard Nixon. During these deliberations, the Chinese government had made three consistent demands: that the United States would end its diplomatic recognition of Taiwan, that it would withdraw from the 1954 Mutual Defense Treaty it had signed with Taiwan, and that all U.S. military forces would depart from Taiwan.

Carter realized that a bipartisan group of congressmen, known as the China Lobby, would vehemently protest the Chinese demands. These congressmen strongly supported Taiwanese independence and argued that an independent Taiwan was vital to U.S. security interests in Asia. However, Carter viewed China as an emerging world power; in his view, a steady relationship with China was far more important than guaranteeing Taiwan's freedom from Chinese control. Therefore, when Carter made his announcement, he acceded to the Chinese demands, but to appease his congressional opponents, he stipulated that the Taiwanese question must be settled peacefully and that the United States would retain the right to supply Taiwan with weapons for defensive purposes. He also created the American Institute in Taiwan, a nonprofit corporation that would be used to conduct informal relations with Taiwan.

The U.S. Congress, however, was not satisfied with either Carter's ambiguous assurance that the Chinese would not invade Taiwan or with the nation's new informal arrangement with Taiwan. Both the House of Representatives and the Senate began drafting bills that would ensure America's continued protection of Taiwan. The outcome of these bills was the Taiwan Relations Act.

On March 19, 1979, a congressional conference committee met to reconcile the differences between the House and Senate bills. The committee ultimately emerged with a compromise that contained several key provisions. First, the bill demanded that the future of Taiwan be resolved peacefully and urged the president to seek a Chinese renunciation of force. Second, the bill noted that any threat against Taiwan would be considered a matter of security for the United States. Next, the bill confirmed that the United States could supply Taiwan with the weaponry necessary for its self-defense. Finally, the bill stipulated that the president and Congress would jointly determine what weapons would be sold to Taiwan.

Not surprisingly, China vociferously protested the bill, even threatening to withdraw from its newly normalized relation with the United States. But the congressional leadership correctly guessed that the Chinese government was bluffing; the Chinese wanted the new diplomatic relationship as badly as the Carter administration did. The true threat came from Carter's veto pen. Carter received the bill on March 30. He expressed his displeasure with the bill by waiting until April 10 to sign it, the last day before the bill would have automatically become law. He also declined to hold a public signing ceremony, instead signing the bill late at night.

In retrospect, Carter's displeasure seems highly misplaced. Since the Taiwan Relations Act was passed, the United States has strengthened its relationship with the People's Republic of China. Although China's relationship with Taiwan has not been resolved, the act has prevented China from directly using force against the island. The act has also prevented Taiwan from aggravating the Chinese by declaring its independence. In over two decades, democracy has flourished in Taiwan and U.S. security interests in the region have been maintained.

See also Carter, Jimmy, and National Policy; China and U.S. Policy

Further Reading

Koenig, Louis W., James C. Hsiung, and King-yuh Chang, eds. *Congress, the Presidency, and the Taiwan Relations Act.* New York: Praeger, 1985.

Lee, David Tawei. *The Making of the Taiwan Relations Act: Twenty Years in Retrospect.* Oxford, UK: Oxford University Press, 2000.

TALIBAN

Government of Afghanistan between 1996 and 2002, which was dominated by an extreme Sunni Muslim political-religious ideology. The Taliban ("seekers") began as a small movement of religious students in Kandahar around 1994. At that time, Afghanistan was a failing state, rendered unstable by war with the Soviets followed by a civil war as various indigenous movements and leaders fought for control of the government. None gained full popular support; and in Kandahar, these turf battles left the city in a state of virtual anarchy. The religious students in the city reacted to the corruption and infighting by advocating a strong, Islamic-based intervention.

The Taliban was overwhelmingly a movement of Pashtun peoples, though it did include other ethnic groups. Its major sources of coherence were a strict, radical, Sunni interpretation of Islam and devotion to the idea of an archetypal Islamic state. Their call for security and order, and the end of corruption, was widely attractive. The Taliban gained recruits from among university students and ex-military officers, but particularly from among those educated in *madrassas* (religious schools) in refugee camps in Pakistan. They gradually took control of Afghanistan from 1994 to 1997, seizing abandoned equipment and seeking recruits as they went. The Taliban came to power in 1996 after seizing the Afghan capital of Kabul in September of that year and creating a ruling establishment. They ultimately controlled nearly 90% of the country.

Although they gained quick victories in the field, the Taliban had focused only on military campaigns and had little experience with civil government or foreign policy. The internal decision-making process and the chains of command were deliberately unclear, informal, and secretive. The Taliban tabled discussion of foreign affairs until stability could be achieved. Moreover, the Taliban attracted the attention of aid agencies and watchdog groups because of their human-rights violations, particularly against Shiite Muslims, members of other minority sects, and women. The Taliban did, however, restore order to much of the country by implementing the Islamic rule of law known as *sharia*.

Once in power, the Taliban began to enforce their narrow, puritanical interpretation of Islam, repudiating all elements of modern Western rationalism. The Taliban strongly regulated appropriate behavior. They issued edicts for proper appearance (long beards and turbans for men, burkas for women). They banned women from working, except within the health sector (a woman's duty was to bring up the next generation of Muslims) and closed girls' schools (pending the creation of a suitable curriculum). Because many women were teachers, boys' schools were often closed as well because of a lack of teachers. The Taliban also strongly condemned inappropriate behavior: The implementation of the sharia meant that adulterers were stoned and thieves had their hands cut off. The Taliban also banned music, games, and any representation of the human or animal form as being contrary to Islam. Later, the Department for the Promotion of Virtue and the Prevention of Vice acted as a religious police to enforce these decrees.

A Taliban militia member manning antiaircraft artillery in Afghanistan in 1995 during the period of civil strife between the Taliban rebels and government forces. In the fall of 1996, the Taliban finally managed to take the Afghan capital of Kabul and consolidate their power. After taking Kabul, the Taliban leaders began to institute their rigid and uncompromising fundamentalist brand of Islam.

Source: Corbis.

The Taliban in Afghanistan became a rogue regime, openly flouting international conventions and harboring radical elements, such as members of the international terrorist group al-Qaeda. Following the September 11, 2001, terrorist attacks against the United States, the United States appealed to the Taliban to extradite some of the known ringleaders, including al-Qaeda leader Osama bin Laden. When the Taliban refused, the United States launched a military campaign against Afghanistan on October 7, 2001, to induce regime change and unearth the terrorists.

The Taliban government officially capitulated to U.S. forces in January 2002, but many of their leaders remain at large.

See also Afghanistan, War in; Al-Qaeda; Terrorism, War on International

TANKS

Tracked, heavily armored combat vehicles that can destroy enemy forces by direct fire. Most tanks in use today are main battle tanks (MBT), which have heavier armor and a larger-caliber main gun than other types of tanks. Tanks have seen action across the globe in every major combat engagement since World War I. Since their development, the vehicles have improved greatly in speed, armament, armor, and size.

TYPES OF TANKS

The main battle tank (MBT) is the most powerful direct-fire land-based weapon. An example of this firepower is the 120mm main gun mounted on the U.S. M1 Abrams tank. Although MBTs are employed mainly to fight other MBTs, they can also be used against other targets, such as infantry troops.

The term *main battle tank* is used to distinguish this type of vehicle from lighter, less expensive tanks, generally used in airborne and amphibious operations, as well as older tanks. One such smaller tank is the so-called tankette, a small tank, usually without a turret, that carries a crew of two and has one or two machine guns. Tankettes were produced mainly in Great Britain in the 1930s, and production of the vehicles ceased with the onset of World War II as the tankette's limited usefulness and vulnerability to more powerful tanks became apparent.

Light tanks are small and designed for speed. They have been used in a scouting role and to strike vulnerable areas of enemy formations. Some were even light enough to be airlifted into battle. Most saw action in World War I and World War II, but the M551 Sheridan tank employed by the U.S. Army saw action in Vietnam and Operation Desert Storm.

Medium-sized tanks were the predecessors of today's MBTs. Examples of these tanks include the M4 Sherman and M48 Patton tanks of the United States and the Russian T-34 tank. Heavy tanks were designed to break through enemy formations with their powerful guns and armor. The tanks are no longer in use, however, due to their lack of speed and high cost. Notable examples of the heavy tank are the PzKfw V and VI tanks built and used by the Germans during the World War II.

Another type of tank is the infantry tank. Originally developed during World War I by the British and French, this type of tank was slow and heavily armored. These features suited its main purposes, which were to clear battlefields of obstacles and to protect advancing friendly troops. Examples of the infantry tank are the British Mk II Matilda and the Mk IV Churchill, both of which served with distinction in World War II.

Developed by the Germans in World War II, tank destroyers usually consisted of an antitank gun mounted on an existing tank chassis. Tank destroyers combined powerful main guns (usually over 75mm) with speed, but they were lacking in armor. Although designed to destroy other tanks, tank destroyers were eventually superseded by the more capable medium tank. Examples of tank destroyers include the Russian SU-85 and the German Rhinoceros, which combined a Panzer chassis with an 88mm gun.

TANK ARMOR

The MBT is the most heavily armored vehicle in any modern army. Its armor protects the crew as well as the vehicle itself from penetrating rounds fired from other tanks, antitank guided missiles fired from infantry or aircraft, and antitank mines. Designers of MBTs must find the right balance between armor and weight, because it would be impractical to attach heavy armor to every part of the tank. Usually the front of the chassis and turret front are the most heavily armored, and the sides and turret top have the lightest armor.

Several types of armor are used in different modern MBTs. Passive armor is made up of layers of steel, metallic alloys, and ceramics. Another type of armor is reactive armor, so named because it explodes outward and away from the crew on contact with an incoming mortar round. One of the most effective types of armor is British Chobham armor, used in construction of British Challenger and American M1 Abrams tanks. This type of armor consists of spaced ceramic blocks wrapped in a resin fabric between layers of conventional armor.

TANK ARMAMENT

The history of tank armament follows the development of increasingly large-caliber guns with longer ranges. The British "Little Willie" of 1916 carried 57mm guns and machine guns, and the German Panzer IV tank of World War II had a 75mm main gun. The American M48A5 tank of the 1950s had a 105mm main gun with a range of 2,000 yards.

The main guns of modern MBTs generally measure 120mm for American and European models and 125mm for Russian models, and they fire high-explosive penetrating rounds at ranges of over 2,000 yards. Most MBTs also have a small-caliber machine gun mounted coaxially with the main gun. Many tanks also have a machine gun mounted on the turret roof for use against aircraft as well as enemy troops.

Soldiers of the First Infantry Division's Second Battalion, Third Brigade Combat Team, heading back to their base in Iraq in M1 Abrams tanks after fighting with Iraqi insurgents in July 2004. The backbone of U.S. armored forces, the M1 Abrams provides enough mobile firepower to destroy any opposing armored fighting vehicle in the world, while providing protection for its crew in any conceivable combat environment. During the Iraq War, the M1 Abrams easily countered Iraqi forces and dismantled them.

Source: U.S. Army.

HISTORY OF TANKS AND TANK WARFARE

The tank was originally developed by the British in World War I for the purpose of overrunning enemy trenches in Europe. The term *tank* was used so that factory workers would think they were producing mobile water tanks rather than an entirely new type of weapon.

The first tank prototype was tested in September 1915, and the first British MK1 tanks saw action at the Battle of the Somme in September of the following year. Although most of these early tanks broke down, at the Battle of Cambrai, British tanks succeeded in breaking through German positions. World War I also witnessed the first tank-against-tank battle, when German and British tanks squared off in April 1918.

Between World War I and World War II, the tank began to take its modern shape, with a lower profile,

a compact hull, and a turret in place of the earlier rhomboidal form. The 1930s saw the development of the German Panzer and Soviet T-34 tanks, both of which would play a prominent role in the approaching war.

World War II introduced the term *blitzkrieg* to military history. This tactic, which stressed combined attacks of infantry, tanks, and air support, allowed the Germans to sweep quickly across Europe with devastating success. Although early German Panzers were actually inferior to some tanks in the British and French arsenals, blitzkrieg and the unprecedented use of communication radios in German tanks ensured victory.

Although far superior to the American M4 tank, later Panzer and Tiger models were outnumbered by the Americans and British coming from the west and from Russian T-34s coming from the east. Although tanks were used by the Americans and Japanese in the fighting in the Pacific, jungle terrain somewhat limited their range and usefulness.

The Korean War once again proved the usefulness of tanks. Because of reluctance on the part of the great powers to cross the nuclear threshold in Cold War conflict, North Korean T-34 tanks faced off against U.S. Sherman and Patton tanks as well as the British Centurion. Due to the entrenched nature of the Korean War, however, tanks did not serve in an assault role with infantry but were essentially long-range, heavy-caliber snipers used to fire against enemy positions.

Tanks served in a limited support role in the Vietnam War, and many experts proclaimed them to be obsolete following heavy Israeli losses at the hands of anti-tank guided missiles in the 1973 Yom Kippur War. However, Operation Desert Storm in 1991 proved once again not only the potential effectiveness of tanks in an assault role but also the superiority of U.S. and European tank design over older Russian models in Iraqi hands.

TOWARD THE FUTURE

The end of the Cold War raised questions regarding the relevance of the main battle tank. The threat of a Soviet invasion of Europe subsided with the political collapse of the Soviet Union in 1991. Moreover, unconventional security threats requiring unconventional responses have since arisen in every corner of the world. In 1989, for example, rapid reaction forces toppled the dictatorship of Manuel Noriega in Panama, and the tank played a limited role in toppling the Taliban in Afghanistan in 2001. Tanks also played little more than an ancillary role in the Iraq War of 2003 and the occupation of Iraq that followed. The MBT has yet to establish a steady role in this new age of asymmetrical warfare, and its future is far from certain.

—Daniel P. McDonald

TELLER, EDWARD (1908–2003)

American physicist who played an instrumental role in developing the hydrogen bomb. Edward Teller was born in Hungary, where he received his Ph.D. from the University of Leipzig in 1930. He came to the United States in 1935 to teach physics at George Washington University. In 1939, he watched Albert Einstein sign a letter urging President Franklin D. Roosevelt to develop the atomic bomb. He became an American citizen in 1941 and worked on the Manhattan Project, which successfully detonated the first nuclear weapon in New Mexico in July 1945.

Following the bombings of Hiroshima and Nagasaki at the end of World War II, Teller became an advocate of bigger and stronger nuclear devices and critical of the reticence of Manhattan Project scientists to develop such weapons. His criticism of Robert Oppenheimer, the physicist who headed the Manhattan Project, and Teller's subsequent call for a new laboratory to develop more potent nuclear weapons, alienated Teller from many of his colleagues.

After World War II, Teller served as a professor of physics at the University of Chicago, and he was also associated with the thermonuclear research program at Los Alamos National Laboratory. Teller was instrumental in the development of the first hydrogen bomb, which was detonated on November 1, 1952. As a result, he is often called the Father of the Hydrogen Bomb, an appellation he reportedly disliked. In 1952, Teller became a professor at the University of California and cofounder and director of the Lawrence Livermore Laboratory. In 1960, he resigned from the laboratory to devote time to teaching and research. In 1962, he received the Enrico Fermi Award for his contributions to the development, use, and control of nuclear energy.

Teller was a staunch supporter of President Ronald Reagan's so-called Star Wars space-based missile defense system and an advocate for new and more potent weapons systems as a means to maintain peace. He opposed several treaties aimed at reducing the spread of nuclear weapons. Teller worked in his office at the Livermore lab several days a week until his death at the age of 95.

See also Atomic Bomb; Hiroshima; Manhattan Project (1942–1945); Reagan, Ronald, and National Policy

TERRORISM See TERRORISM, U.S. (DOMESTIC)

TERRORISM, U.S. (DOMESTIC)

Systematic assaults within the United States for the purposes of creating fear and influencing government policy. Terrorist acts may consist of kidnapping, bombing, murder, attacks with chemical or biological weapons, blackmail or any number of other types of activities meant to coerce by causing, or threatening to cause, harm. There is a long history of terrorism carried out on U.S. territory; however, the attacks on the World Trade Center in New York City and the Pentagon near Washington, DC, on September 11, 2001, focused an unprecedented level of public attention on terrorism. Since that time, U.S. foreign policy has been specifically focused on fighting the war on terrorism.

DEFINING TERRORISM

One of the problems with describing domestic terrorism is deciding what terrorism is. Terrorism is typically portrayed in the media and popular culture as the strategy of a weak, marginalized minority seeking to impose its beliefs on a wider population. Terrorist activities are covert and isolated because the interests represented are not shared by the majority of the world's inhabitants.

If the question is tactics and interests, however, then it is also possible to understand the founding of the United States as a terrorist act. At the time of the American Revolution, the Continental Army represented desires in conflict with those of the large Loyalist population, upsetting the British colonial system. As far as military strategy was concerned, the Continental Army frequently employed guerrilla tactics to compensate for the advantages of the professional British troops, which the latter derived from representing an established government with a sizable treasury.

Additionally, there are critics who argue that the United States is itself the most powerful terrorist regime in existence today. Examples cited to substantiate this view include anticommunist activities of the Central Intelligence Agency (CIA) in Central America during the 1980s and the dropping of atomic bombs on Hiroshima and Nagasaki at the end of World War II. The latter has been referred to by some critics as the greatest terrorist act in human history. Citing these examples, then, it is possible to say that the identity of a terrorist can be defined as dependent upon who is being terrorized.

Whatever position one takes on the question of terrorism and the identity of the terrorist, terrorist activities conducted within the United States can, for practical purposes, be described as acts by individuals opposed to the United States or to U.S. government policy. Though current concerns with terrorism are centered on Islam and the activities of Muslims, terrorists throughout U.S. history have represented a variety of causes and interests. These have ranged from abolitionism, anarchism, libertarianism, socialism, and communism, to anticapitalism and opposition to U.S. military activities overseas.

TERRORISM IN THE UNITED STATES BEFORE 9/11

The question of slavery was the source of a number of violent incidents within the United States, even before the outbreak of the Civil War. The passage of the Kansas-Nebraska Act in 1854 meant that new states entering the Union were allowed to decide whether or not slavery would be legal within their borders. This made these states grounds for conflict between pro- and antislavery groups. The conflict grew so violent that the terms *bleeding* or *bloody* Kansas have been adopted to describe the sequence of violent events that took place between 1854 and 1856. The activities of both sides may also be described as terrorist, in that they involved violence and intimidation in order to influence a political outcome.

Among the more well-known individuals involved on the antislavery side in Kansas was radical abolitionist John Brown. Brown later became famous for his raid on Harpers Ferry, Virginia, in 1859, when he and a group of abolitionists attempted to seize the local armory for the purpose of arming local slaves. Brown's raid was initially successful, but a raid by U.S. Marines resulted in the deaths of a number of his men, and Brown himself was brought to trial on charges of treason and later hanged.

One of the most important acts of terrorism in U.S. history was the Haymarket bombing, which took place in Haymarket Square, Chicago, on May 4, 1886. The bombing occurred during an anarchist rally organized to protest the killings of four people the day before, when police opened fire on a strike at the McCormick Harvesting Machine Company. Police arrived to disperse the rally, and eight were killed when a bomb was thrown among them. The police responded by opening fire, killing several and injuring nearly a hundred more. The Haymarket bombing triggered a panic that soon spread across the country. Socialism and anarchism were associated with immigrant labor, and hundreds of radicals were quickly rounded up. Though no one was ever charged with throwing the bomb, eight anarchists were put on trial, all but one of whom were German immigrants. Three ended up with life imprisonment, four were hanged, and one committed suicide.

The trial of the anarchists in the Haymarket bombing is typically regarded as an extremely biased manifestation of paranoia regarding immigrants and the supposed threats to social and political order they had brought with them from Europe. It was also a precursor to future "red scares," the most well known of which took place at the height of the Cold War in the context of McCarthyism.

Another significant terrorist act involving an anarchist was the assassination of President William McKinley in 1901. McKinley was assassinated by Leon Czolgosz, son of Russian-Polish immigrants, whose motivation for his act was protesting the injustices of capitalism. Nearly a decade later, in 1910, the headquarters of the *Los Angeles Times* was bombed by two union leaders, killing 21 people. The perpetrators ultimately pleaded guilty, but at their trial they were defended by famed lawyer Clarence Darrow.

The first terrorist act that specifically targeted the U.S. public, serving to provoke fear in the innocent bystander, was the Wall Street bombing of 1920. The bombing involved a horse-pulled wagon passing by a lunchtime crowd, loaded with 100 pounds of dynamite and 500 pounds of steel shards. Seventy people were killed and 300 were injured. Eastern European and Italian anarchists were suspected in the bombing, but the crime was never solved. The Wall Street bombing remained the most significant bombing attack on U.S. soil until the Oklahoma City bombing, 75 years later.

A source of domestic terrorist activity during the 1950s was Puerto Rican nationalism. The desire for an independent Puerto Rico resulted in the attempted assassination of President Harry S. Truman, in 1950, and the wounding of five congressmen in 1954. In the former incident the assassins were unsuccessful, and in the latter the terrorists were brought to trial and convicted.

Terrorist fears have frequently been associated with foreigners, immigration, and foreign cultures. The use of the word *terrorism* originally derived from the period known as "the Terror" during the French Revolution, which inspired fear in the established aristocracies across Europe. The notion of terrorism and terrorist activities was also closely associated with the activities of the Russian intelligentsia, including the assassination of Czar Alexander II in 1881, the failed 1905 Revolution, and the then-epitome of left-wing radicalism, the Bolshevik Revolution.

Although considered mainly a crime of foreigners or immigrants, a number of significant terrorist attacks on U.S. soil have been carried out by U.S. citizens, against U.S. citizens, for purposes unrelated to any foreign ideology. In 1963, for example, a member of the Ku Klux Klan, Robert Chambliss, opposed to civil rights for African Americans, murdered four girls by setting off a bomb in a Baptist church in Alabama. Chambliss was initially found not guilty, thanks in part to the intervention of FBI Director J. Edgar Hoover. Public outrage, however, inspired by the atrocity, helped pass the Civil Rights Act of 1964. Fourteen years later, Chambliss was finally convicted, as were two of his accomplices in 2000.

Anger over the Vietnam War motivated the activities of the Weather Underground, a splinter group of the Students for a Democratic Society (SDS). The Weathermen were responsible for blowing up a monument to victims of the above-mentioned Haymarket bombing in Chicago as a kickoff to the so-called Days of Rage in October of 1969. The subsequent riot in Chicago's business district led to shootings and scores of arrests.

The next year, the Weathermen declared war on the U.S. government in response to the shooting of a Black Panther and carried out bomb attacks on the Capitol and the Pentagon. The group dissolved over the course of the 1970s, and very few members ever did jail time. One member, in an unfortunately timed interview with the *New York Times* on September 11, 2001, described the aesthetic quality of bomb explosions and regretted that the group had not been successful in carrying out more.

The activities of the Symbionese Liberation Army (SLA), including murders, robberies, and extortion, were considered significant acts of domestic terrorism during the 1970s. The SLA achieved particular notoriety with the kidnapping of newspaper heiress Patty Hearst, who later became a member of the organization that had abducted her. Hearst was ultimately captured and sentenced to prison. She is considered a textbook example of the so-called Stockholm syndrome, in which victims identify with, and become allies of, their captors.

The activities of Theodore Kaczynski (also known as the Unabomber) may also be defined as terrorist, although his political motivation was not dissatisfaction with the government as much as the conditions of modernity. Between 1978 and 1994, Kaczynski sent a number of bombs to individuals and locations he considered responsible for technological development.

Kaczynski's neo-Luddite opinions, as expressed in a manifesto published in the *Washington Post* and the *New York Times,* consisted of dystopian predictions for the future of complex societies.

The worst terrorist attack in U.S. history, prior to the September 11, 2001, attacks, was the bombing of the Alfred P. Murrah Federal Building in Oklahoma City, Oklahoma. The attack took place on April 19, 1995, and was carried out by militia member Timothy McVeigh, with the help of two accomplices, Terry Nichols and Michael Fortier. The attackers exploded a pickup truck containing a bomb at around 9:00 a.m., just after parents had dropped their children off in a day care center located in the building. The explosion killed 168 people.

McVeigh was apprehended less than an hour after the explosion. At his trial, the prosecution asserted that the attack was motivated by the FBI assault on the headquarters of the Branch Davidians in Waco, Texas, in 1993. The latter incident had helped fuel anti-government sentiment among libertarians nationwide. McVeigh was sentenced to death, Fortier received 12 years in prison and a $200,000 fine, and Nichols received life imprisonment.

SEPTEMBER 11, 2001

The attack on the World Trade Center in New York City in 2001 had been preceded by an earlier attack and a bomb plot eight years before. In 1993, terrorists attempted, unsuccessfully, to bring down the Twin Towers with a bomb inside a van parked in the underground garage. The explosion resulted in the deaths of six people and caused significant structural damage. The attack had a significant effect on public fears concerning terrorist attacks, particularly once the New York City landmark bomb plot was uncovered several months later. The latter plan was to involve the destruction of the United Nations building, Lincoln Tunnel, Holland Tunnel, George Washington Bridge, and the New York City headquarters of the FBI.

The events of September 11, 2001, are significant in a number of ways. Not only were they the most significant terrorist attacks ever carried out on U.S. soil, but they were also among the best-documented tragedies in U.S. history. The collapse of the World Trade Center was broadcast live on television, narrated by reporters who were still not quite sure what the attacks were and who was responsible. The impact of the number of casualties, nearly 3,000, was compounded by the dramatic circumstances of their deaths—hijack victims, trapped office workers, and first responders attempting to rescue bystanders. The two targets in the 9/11 attack—the World Trade Center and the Pentagon—were symbols of American power and affluence.

Responsibility for the 9/11 terrorist attacks was claimed by Osama bin Laden and his al-Qaeda terrorist network. Bin Laden is a citizen of Saudi Arabia, as were nearly every one of the terrorists who took part in the attacks. At the time, bin Laden was sheltered by the Taliban regime in Afghanistan, a fundamentalist Muslim government that the United States had earlier supported in its opposition to the Soviet Union. When the Taliban refused to give up bin Laden after the 9/11 attacks, the United States invaded Afghanistan. That invasion was followed two years later by an invasion of Iraq in 2003, under the pretext that Saddam Hussein had links with al-Qaeda and possessed weapons of mass destruction that he planned to use in terrorist attacks against the United States. Neither of these accusations has ever been proven.

Public anxiety over terrorism was heightened in the weeks after September 11, when letters containing anthrax were sent to media offices and two U.S. senators. The identity of the senders has never been determined, nor is it known whether the anthrax attacks were related to the attacks on the World Trade Center and the Pentagon. However, all of these incidents, occurring in quick succession, created concern, fear, and paranoia among many Americans.

Significant domestic measures taken in response to the September 11 terrorist attacks include the establishment of the Department of Homeland Security and the implementation of the Homeland Security Advisory System, which is a color-coded terrorist-threat alert meant to inform the public of the current likelihood of a terrorist attack.

—William de Jong-Lambert

See also Al-Qaeda; Bin Laden, Osama; Homeland Security Advisory System (Color-Coded Alerts); Homeland Security, Department of; Oklahoma City Bombing; September 11/WTC and Pentagon Attacks; Terrorism, War on International; Terrorists, Islamic

Further Reading

Laqueur, Walter. *A History of Terrorism.* New Brunswick, NJ: Transaction, 2001.

Sinclair, Andrew. *An Anatomy of Terror: A History of Terrorism.* London: Macmillan, 2003.

TERRORISM, WAR ON INTERNATIONAL

Ongoing United States–led international campaign aimed at apprehending or destroying individuals and groups judged to have been involved in the planning or the execution of acts of terrorism. The war on terrorism was declared by President George W. Bush soon after the terrorist attacks against the United States on September 11, 2001. The campaign has so far included a wide range of aggressive measures, from military action against Afghanistan and Iraq, to financial restrictions against countries or groups thought to harbor terrorists, to legal initiatives and enhanced intelligence-gathering operations.

In the evening of September 11, 2001, President Bush announced his intention to launch a long-term offensive—a war on terrorism—against the individuals who planned the hijackings that were responsible for the 9/11 attacks, as well as the countries that gave them support and shelter. Within less than a month, a U.S.-led coalition began an air assault on Afghanistan, the country that had been sheltering suspected September 11 mastermind Osama bin Laden and his al-Qaeda terrorist organization. A year and a half later, another U.S.-led coalition invaded Iraq, in the second major armed conflict since the war on terrorism began.

Meanwhile, on the financial front, a concerted international effort has blocked numerous financial assets linked to terrorist entities. The United States, as well as many other countries, also has passed an impressive volume of antiterrorist legislation. Since September 11, the list of targets in the war on terrorism has expanded to include not only individuals and groups linked to al-Qaeda, but also other, unrelated groups that have been officially labeled terrorist organizations. The war on terrorism continues around the world and, according to virtually every political and military leader (including President Bush), it is likely to last for generations.

INSTITUTIONAL CHANGES

In analyzing the circumstances of the September 11 terrorist strikes, a special commission (the 9/11 Commission) deplored the "failures of imagination, policy, capabilities and management" that prevented the government from apprehending the attackers while they were still in their planning phase. As early as September 2001, policymakers in Washington, DC, began addressing those problems.

Seven days after the terrorist attacks, in a drastic departure from pre-9/11 legal standards, the Justice Department initiated a series of regulations allowing it to detain noncitizens suspected of terrorist activities for an unspecified period of time. Two weeks later, Congress passed the USA PATRIOT Act, a highly controversial piece of legislation that, among other things, improves the ability of law enforcers to identify, track down, and collect evidence on suspected terrorists operating on U.S. territory. By the end of the year, more than 750 terrorism suspects had been detained by the U.S. authorities. In August 2002, following an earlier presidential order, military tribunals opened in Guantánamo Bay (Cuba), ready to try terrorism suspects being held there. Within less than a year, the U.S. government gained a new executive-level department—the Department of Homeland Security, established by law in November 2002.

FINANCIAL MEASURES

According to the Bush administration, one of the measures taken by the president in the war on terrorism was to direct government agencies to block the flow of money suspected of funding terrorist groups. To that end, three organizations were formed. The first, the Foreign Terrorist Asset Tracking Center, became active less than a week after the 9/11 attacks. It was designed to dismantle terrorist financial bases and shut down their fundraising capabilities by creating financial profiles of known terrorist groups and taking steps to close down their sources of money.

The second institution, Operation Green Quest, sought to encourage the business community to report suspicious financial activity, such as movements of funds originating from or going to countries suspected of aiding terrorist groups. The third organization, the Terrorist Financing Task Force, aimed to prevent individuals from using the U.S. banking system to move money earmarked for terrorist activities. Besides the United States, more than 167 other countries have made efforts to deny alleged terrorists access to money. Since September 11, 2001, the international community has frozen more than $138 million owned or managed by terrorism suspects.

THE WAR IN AFGHANISTAN

Having declared its intention to launch an immediate offensive against both the individuals responsible for the 9/11 terrorist strikes and the countries that harbored them, the Bush administration wasted no time in initiating a war against Afghanistan.

Addressing a Joint Session of Congress on September 20, 2001, President Bush had already identified a group of loosely affiliated terrorist organizations known as al-Qaeda, led by Osama bin Laden, as responsible for the plane hijackings that culminated in the 9/11 attacks. The president had also told Congress that al-Qaeda was based in Afghanistan, a country ravaged by decades of civil war and controlled at the time by a fundamentalist Islamic regime known as the Taliban.

The Afghan government was asked in stark terms to surrender bin Laden and his associates. Faced with a Taliban refusal, the Unites States and its ally, Great Britain, began a bombing campaign over Afghanistan on October 7, 2001. Closely collaborating on the ground with the anti-Taliban resistance, the Allied troops soon captured all of Afghanistan's major cities. The Taliban leader, Mullah Omar, along with Osama bin Laden, managed to disappear, and they have yet to be captured.

THE INVASION OF IRAQ

Afghanistan was not the only large-scale open conflict in the war on terrorism. Less than three years after the beginning of the war in Afghanistan, the United States and Great Britain invaded Iraq. Like Afghanistan, Iraq had been at the center of worldwide attention for decades. Iraqi dictator Saddam Hussein had long been accused of numerous infringements of international law, war crimes against its neighbors Iran and Kuwait, oppression of his own citizens, and illicit development of weapons of mass destruction (WMD). To this long roster, the Bush administration also added the *terrorist* designation despite considerable debate over the purported connection between al-Qaeda and Saddam Hussein.

Having announced in September 2002 the adoption of the doctrine of preemption—which would allow the United States to strike at enemies who pose an immediate threat to the United States but have not yet acted on that threat—President Bush received authorization from Congress to attack Iraq if Saddam Hussein refused to dismantle his weapons-of-mass-destruction programs. On March 19, 2003, despite significant international and domestic opposition, American and British forces invaded Iraq.

After three weeks of fighting, Saddam Hussein's regime was toppled and the allied forces began what was to become a protracted, costly occupation of Iraq. Saddam Hussein was captured in mid-December of 2003. Despite the high-profile arrest, the fighting continued in Iraq, with a daily toll of both Iraqi and allied lives. United States and international investigators failed to find any WMD.

THE INTERNATIONAL DIMENSION

International cooperation in the war on terrorism has been extremely fragmented. In the wake of the September 11 attacks, President Bush told the countries of the world that they had to make a decision—they were either with us, or against us. Bush insisted that the war on terrorism was the world community's fight against the enemies of civilization.

Many of the countries that rallied behind the U.S. cause after 9/11, however, had since then expressed profound disagreements with the Bush administration's handling of the campaign to annihilate terrorist groups around the world. Most notably, many traditional U.S. allies—such as France and India—opposed the war in Iraq. The United Nations Secretary-General Kofi Annan declared the U.S.-led invasion of Iraq illegal and counter to the UN Charter.

Other international actors, however, pledged various kinds of assistance to the United States and its "coalition of the willing." Australia, Italy, Japan, and the Netherlands, as well as around 35 other nations, supported the invasion of Iraq.

TAKING IT GLOBAL

Afghanistan and Iraq have so far been the only two countries attacked under the banner of the war on terrorism. Clashes between U.S. troops (or their allies) and groups accused of terrorist activity have nevertheless taken place around the globe. Dozens of governments received what was, in some cases, unexpected help in prosecuting decades-long regional conflicts against rebel groups.

In April 2002, for example, the United States inaugurated a 20-month, $64 million plan aimed at helping the country of Georgia fight insurgents, and more than 100 U.S. soldiers are currently providing training to Georgian forces. In the Philippines, more than 1,500 U.S. troops are actively assisting the local military in its campaign against the Abu Sayyaf group—an

Islamic fundamentalist militia thought to have ties with al-Qaeda. Iran and North Korea, two of the three countries identified by President Bush in 2002 as being part of an "axis of evil," are coming under much pressure to give up their WMD programs. Pakistan, one of President Bush's most important allies in the war on terrorism, has sent a considerable number of troops to its unruly Northwestern Frontier region with a mission of annihilating al-Qaeda sympathizers. Dozens of other countries are currently receiving financial, military, or intelligence help from the United States.

HIJACKING THE WAR ON TERRORISM?

The war on terrorism did not belong exclusively to the United States. Whereas various states (notably Israel) had traditionally spoke of the militia groups they fought as "terrorists," after the 9/11 attacks, a plethora of nations adopted the terminology of the war on terrorism, to the outrage of some human-rights groups.

Russia's military campaign against Chechen separatists is but one example of this development. In almost every speech delivered by a Russian official on the subject, the Chechens are labeled as terrorists and the Russian government's attempts to subdue them are presented as battles in the war on terrorism. On the other side, certain actions of the Chechen insurgents (such as the August 2004 suicide bombings that brought down two commercial airliners, and the September 2004 hostage crisis in the town of Beslan) have certainly helped the effort of Russian officials to recast the conflict within a war-on-terrorism framework. In South Asia, India's campaign against the Kashmiri militants was also infused by the war-on-terrorism vocabulary, allowing the government to present the clash as part of what President Bush called the "monumental struggle of good versus evil."

SUCCESSES AND CRITICISM

Because of the complexity of the war on terrorism and the multiple fronts on which it is fought, its successes and failures are hard to identify and quantify. The numerous participants flood the media with claims of victory on a regular basis, often in defiance of the reality on the ground. In terms of the military campaign against al-Qaeda, the Bush administration announced in 2004 that two-thirds of the group's known leaders had been apprehended or killed. In

March 2003, Pakistani forces arrested Khalid Sheikh Mohammed, who was suspected of having put together the September 11 plan of attack.

Another high-profile success claimed by the United States was the official renunciation by Libya of its weapons of mass destruction (WMD) programs. Following at least nine months of secret diplomatic talks, Libyan leader Mu'ammar Gadhafi admitted that his country had been trying to develop WMD and pledged to get rid of the WMD technology.

On the other hand, the U.S.-led war on terrorism also has received a lot of criticism because of its aggressiveness, which some countries and human-rights groups call excessive and unwarranted, and its seeming unilateralism. Steeped in controversy, the war on international terrorism is likely to continue shaping world politics for many decades to come.

—*Razvan Sibii*

See also Afghanistan, War in; Bush, George W., and National Policy; Coalition Building; Democracy, Promotion of, and Terrorism; September 11/WTC and Pentagon Attacks

Further Reading

Clarke, Richard A. *Against All Enemies.* New York: Free Press, 2004.
Cohen, David B., and John W. Wells, eds. *American National Security and Civil Liberties in an Era of Terrorism.* New York: Palgrave Macmillan, 2004.
Friedman, George. *America's Secret War: Inside the Hidden Worldwide Struggle Between America and Its Enemies.* New York: Doubleday, 2004.
Woodward, Bob. *Bush at War.* New York: Simon & Schuster, 2002.

TERRORISTS, ISLAMIC

Individuals or groups who use violence in order to advance a political or cultural agenda based on their own interpretation of Muslim religious and social ideology. Islamic terrorism is not a single entity; it consists of many proponents and practitioners using violence to achieve a variety of goals. Many Islamic terrorist groups are devoted to establishing an independent Palestinian state in the Middle East. Many have pledged to destroy the state of Israel. Some seek to overthrow secular governments in the region and replace them with Islamic regimes. Others fight non-Muslim (especially Western) influence in the Middle

East, and still others pursue several or all of these goals at once. One thing these different groups share in common is a willingness to use violence—and often their own suicides—to achieve their ends.

THE MUSLIM BROTHERHOOD

The philosophical roots of Islamic terrorism lie in the Arab nationalist and religious movements of the early 20th century. Perhaps the most influential of these was the Muslim Brotherhood, founded in Egypt in 1928. Members of the Muslim Brotherhood were upset with reforms in the Islamic world following the fall of the Ottoman Empire after World War I. Under its reformist president Kemal Ataturk, Turkey—which had inherited the administrative and political structures of the old Ottoman Empire—became a thoroughly secular state. Ataturk abolished the position of caliph (secular leader of all Muslims) and replaced Muslim religious law with Western-style civil law.

The Muslim Brotherhood saw these moves as a betrayal of Islam to the materialist and secular ideals of the West. However, prior to the 1940s, the brotherhood confined its activities largely to political protest and organization. After World War II, the group's lack of peaceful progress led it to embrace violent action against Egypt's pro-Western government. The brotherhood also took up arms against Israel in the 1948 Arab-Israeli War. In 1954, the brotherhood tried to assassinate Egyptian President Gamal Abdel Nasser. In retaliation, Nasser outlawed the group in Egypt.

Over the next 25 years, the brotherhood spread to other countries in the Middle East and carried out many terrorist acts. It particularly targeted Arab politicians who were seen as too secular or not sufficiently anti-Israeli. The group was very active in Syria until a failed 1980 attempt against the life of Syrian president Hafaz al-Assad. The incident led to an all-out government campaign that decimated the brotherhood in Syria. After the so-called Hama Massacre, the Muslim Brotherhood disappeared as a political force in the region. In the late 1980s it reinvented itself as a religious and social organization that is now seen as a relatively moderate voice in the Islamic world.

THE PALESTINIAN
LIBERATION ORGANIZATION (PLO)

Many young Muslims heard the brotherhood's call for the restoration of what it saw as "pure" Islamic society in the Middle East. Quite a few of these founded their own organizations to pursue violent political change. In the 1970s, several of these groups came together under the banner of the Palestinian Liberation Organization (PLO). The members of the PLO were united by opposition to Israeli occupation of Palestinian lands taken in previous Arab-Israeli wars. They also objected to the denial of Israeli citizenship to Palestinians living in Israel and the so-called occupied territories. The PLO denied Israel's right to exist and called for the establishment of an independent Palestinian state.

Throughout the 1970s and 1980s, groups aligned with the PLO carried out hundreds of terrorist activities. Most of these bombings, shootings, kidnappings, and hijackings occurred in Israel and the Middle East, usually involving the deaths of noncombative civilians. However, the violence frequently spread to surrounding countries in Europe and Africa. In 1972, for example, eight PLO gunmen took Israeli athletes hostage at the Summer Olympic Games in Munich. A gun battle with German police and army units resulted in the deaths of 11 Israeli athletes and five of the terrorists.

During the 1990s, PLO leader Yasir Arafat announced a change in the group's policy. Arafat agreed to recognize Israel's sovereignty if Israel would begin discussions to establish a separate Palestinian state in the occupied territories. Since that time, the Israeli government has recognized the PLO as the legitimate representative of the Palestinian people. The PLO runs a separate political organization within Israel, but the two sides still have not reached final agreement on the date or form of a Palestinian state. Setbacks in the process have led to several uprisings, or *intifada,* by Palestinian terrorist groups such as Hamas and Fatah, which are unhappy with the lack of progress.

AL-QAEDA

The late 1970s saw a shift in the nature of Islamic terrorism, which coincided with two major political events in the Middle East—the toppling of the shah of Iran in 1979 and the Soviet Union's invasion of Afghanistan later that year. The shah of Iran, a staunch ally of the United States, was installed in power as the result of a 1953 coup planned by the Central Intelligence Agency (CIA). His reign was marked by both an enthusiastic embrace of Western ideas and culture, and extreme brutality toward his political opponents. By 1978, radical Islamic college students, led by the exiled cleric Ayatollah Ruhollah Khomeini, were leading public demonstrations against the shah. In February 1979, the protesters forced the shah to flee the country. Shortly thereafter, Khomeini and his followers established an Islamic state in Iran and immediately named the United States as the number-one enemy of Islam. The United States was, in Khomeini's phrase, "the great Satan."

While events in Iran whipped up anti-U.S. sentiment among Muslims, the Soviet invasion of Afghanistan fueled general anti-Western feelings in the Middle East. Many Islamic nations saw the invasion by the officially atheist Soviet Union as yet another attempt by outside powers to force their culture onto Muslims. Among Muslim extremists, anti-U.S. rhetoric merged with anti-Soviet rhetoric in a rejection of all influences that were seen as non-Islamic or anti-Islamic.

The war in Afghanistan attracted many idealistic young Muslims who wished to drive the Soviets from the Middle East. One of these *mujahideen,* or freedom fighters, was Osama bin Laden, the son of a rich and prominent businessman in Saudi Arabia. While fighting the Soviets, bin Laden learned valuable skills and built up a network of committed and fanatical mujahideen. Much of the mujahideen's training and weaponry was supplied by the United States, which was covertly supporting the Afghan resistance against the Soviets. The combination of U.S. support and Afghan troops finally forced the Soviets to withdraw their forces in 1989. However, bin Laden was convinced that the United States was just as dangerous to Islam as the Soviet Union. He dedicated himself to ridding the Middle East of all non-Islamic influences and reestablishing the caliphate.

After the Afghan war, bin Laden used his family wealth to set up a terrorist organization called al-Qaeda ("the base") to carry out attacks on U.S. interests in the Middle East and elsewhere. Al-Qaeda was involved in the 1993 bombing of the World Trade Center (WTC) in New York City; the 1996 attack on U.S. troops in Khobar, Saudi Arabia; the 1998 bombings of U.S. embassies in Kenya and Tanzania; and the bombing of the destroyer USS *Cole* in Yemen in 2000. On September 11, 2001, al-Qaeda carried out the deadliest terror attack ever on U.S. soil, flying jet airliners into the World Trade Center in New York City and the Pentagon near Washington, DC. The attacks caused the collapse of both towers of the World Trade Center and resulted in the deaths of some 3,000 Americans.

Immediately following the September 11 attacks, the United States invaded Afghanistan, whose government was providing bases for al-Qaeda. Although many of the group's important leaders were caught and their bases in Afghanistan destroyed, bin Laden escaped and al-Qaeda survived. Since that time, al-Qaeda has claimed responsibility for a number of other deadly attacks, including a nightclub bombing in Bali in November 2002 and the bombing of commuter trains in Spain in March 2004, which killed hundreds. In the wake of the 2003 U.S. invasion of Iraq, groups affiliated with al-Qaeda have claimed responsibility for many acts of violence against U.S. troops and Iraqi citizens.

The religiously inspired terrorism characterized by al-Qaeda represents a break from the more politically motivated terrorism of the PLO. Establishing independent Arab states in the region is no longer sufficient—modern Islamic terrorists demand that those states reject Western cultural influences and impose Muslim holy law on their citizens. This attitude has alienated many Muslims who might support the group's political goals but who oppose their social agenda. Recognizing this split in Muslim public opinion forms a key part of the current war on terrorism. Western nations are trying to convince average Muslims that the negative image of the West painted by al-Qaeda is incorrect. In this way, they hope to reduce the flow of new recruits attracted by the terrorists' message. At the same time, the United States has committed to combating Islamic terrorists with every weapon at its disposal, including the use of military force.

See also Afghan Wars; Al-Khobar, Attack on U.S. Troops at (1996); Al-Qaeda; Bali, Terrorist Bombing in; Bin Laden, Osama; Iranian Hostage Crisis; Iraq War of 2003; Middle East and U.S. Policy; Moussaoui, Zacarias; September 11/WTC and Pentagon Attacks; Taliban; Terrorism, U.S. (Domestic); Terrorism, War on International; USS *Cole* Bombing

Further Reading

Gabriel, Mark A. *Islam and Terrorism: What the Quran Really Teaches About Christianity, Violence and the Goals of the Islamic Jihad.* Lake Mary, FL: Charisma House, 2002.

Katz, Samuel M. *Jihad: Islamic Fundamentalist Terrorism.* Minneapolis, MN: Lerner, 2003.

Syed, M. H. *Islamic Terrorism.* Delhi: Kalpaz, 2003.

TET OFFENSIVE

Attack staged by North Vietnamese forces, beginning in the early hours of January 31, 1968, during the Vietnam War. The Tet Offensive consisted of simultaneous attacks by 85,000 troops under the direction of the North Vietnamese government. The attack was carried out against five major South Vietnamese cities, dozens of military installations, and over 150 towns and villages throughout South Vietnam. The offensive derives its name from the Vietnamese New Year holiday—Tet—during which the attacks occurred.

In the fall of 1967, the communist Vietcong decided to gamble upon a course of action that would ideally break the stalemate between the United States and North Vietnam. This course of action consisted of a series of widespread and repeated attacks on South Vietnam. For the North Vietnamese government, the best result would be a galvanizing of discontent in the South that would, in turn, enforce the collapse of America's ally, the government and army of South Vietnamese leader Nguyen Van Thieu. The least optimistic result would be convincing the United States that it could not win the war. Many Americans did believe this by the third day of the Tet Offensive attacks.

The Tet Offensive has been seen by many as the turning point in the war. By February of 1968, the U.S. death toll in Vietnam had risen to more than 500 per week. As the death toll rose, U.S. public support declined. Much of the American public viewed the Tet Offensive as a sign of the undying North Vietnamese aggression and will. The place of the U.S. media in fostering and furthering this belief in North Vietnamese strength during that period has been a topic of study and argument.

Whatever the impetus, the American public grew increasingly vehement in its opposition to the continued presence of U.S. solders in Vietnam, and the gulf between what the military saw as the most effective means of fighting the war became even larger from the inevitably politically driven administration.

On March 10, 1968, the *New York Times* ran a story under the headline "Westmoreland Requests 206,000 More Men, Stirring Debate in Administration." This request galvanized the public and convinced them that, rather than a Vietnamization of the conflict, America's involvement was increasing at the cost of American lives in the face of an unfaltering and seemingly unbeatable enemy.

The military, however, unlike the American public, had grown more optimistic following the Tet Offensive. They saw a successful rebuke of the enemies' attacks and an undeniable weakening of communist forces and strength, for the communist forces had suffered heavy casualties. General William C. Westmoreland viewed the post-Tet situation as an opportunity for an American offensive and expansion of the conflict on the ground, to further debilitate the enemy and deny any future resurgence. He renewed a former request for more troops, with the encouragement of the Joint Chiefs of Staff chairman, General Earle Wheeler. His request was initially denied, however—President Johnson did not desire any expansion of the ground war.

Increasingly vocal antagonism against any escalation of U.S. involvement in Vietnam put greater pressure on the Johnson administration and the U.S. Congress. In mid-March, 139 members of the House of Representatives sponsored a resolution asking for congressional review of U.S. policy in Vietnam. Secretary of State Dean Rusk was called before the Senate Foreign Relations Committee and questioned for 11 hours. On March 22, President Johnson decided upon only a small increase of troops. At the same time, the president announced that General Westmoreland would be returning to the United States in midsummer to become chief of staff of the army.

See also Vietnam War (1954–1975)

Further Reading

McMahon, Robert J., ed. *Major Problems in the History of the Vietnam War: Documents and Essays.* Lexington, MA: DC Heath, 1995.
McNamara, Robert S. *In Retrospect: The Tragedy and Lessons of Vietnam.* New York: Times Books, 1995.

THEATER MISSILE DEFENSE

Deployment of nuclear and conventional missiles for the purpose of maintaining security in a specific region, or *theater*. The purpose of theater missile defense is to protect allies from local threats in their region or to address specific security issues and enable credibility in addressing particular threats. Theater missile defense addresses specific defense concerns, which may be unique and vary from region to region.

Theater missile defense primarily refers to defensive, antiballistic missile systems, such as the United

States's Patriot missile. Systems such as the Patriot are designed to intercept incoming ballistic missiles before they can strike their intended targets. During the Gulf War of 1991, the Patriot was employed for theater missile defense in Israel and Saudi Arabia to counter the threat of Iraqi SCUD missiles. Although initial assessments suggested that Patriot missiles were highly effective, later analyses cast doubt on the number of incoming Iraqi missiles actually destroyed by Patriots.

Another important feature of theater missile defense is that it may decrease the likelihood of global nuclear war. A premise of theater missile defense is that limited, winnable nuclear war is possible, and appropriate strategies to account for such an outcome must be devised. The focus of disarmament talks throughout the cold War was primarily intercontinental ballistic missiles (ICBMs). Ballistic and intermediate ballistic missiles were the weapons of theater defense. These weapons did not differ in terms of their destructive power but rather in terms of their range and, thus, their strategic applicability.

Aside from ballistic missiles positioned on allied territory, another important element of theater strategy was tactical nuclear weapons, which are design for attacking nuclear forces in close quarters. Theater nuclear weapons do not have intercontinental range and may consist of long-range to battlefield nuclear weapons, such as land mines, bombs, and artillery shells. This aspect of theater missile defense in Western Europe was of great concern throughout the Cold War because the United States recognized the vast superiority of Soviet ground forces. The only way of meeting a Soviet conventional threat, it was argued, would be to resort to nuclear weapons. The question, however, was whether or not nuclear conflict could realistically be contained.

The issues of theater missile defense and fighting a limited nuclear war influenced both U.S. and Soviet defense policy throughout the Cold War period. The Soviet Union prepared for the possibility of nuclear war by investing in nuclear-proof bunkers for civilians and the maintenance of emergency food stores. Early in the Cold War, U.S. defense policy with regard to nuclear weapons was premised on the idea that fighting and winning a nuclear war was possible. That stance changed in the early 1960s with the recognition of mutually assured destruction (MAD).

Aside from the construction of private bomb shelters, the United States made no preparations to defend the civilian population from a nuclear war. The U.S.

government preferred to imply that they had no first-strike intentions, accepting that a counterattack would easily decimate the civilian population. Another feature of this strategy was targeting Russian population centers rather than military targets. This also made sense, primarily in terms of a counterstrike, rather than a first strike, because it assumed that aiming at military targets would be futile if the missiles were already launched.

A noted disadvantage of theater missile defense is that it requires the placement of nuclear weapons on foreign, allied soil. This placement makes the weapons a highly visible target for antinuclear protestors in countries where sentiment is much more negative toward nuclear weaponry (this was particularly true in Europe). Another element of this antinuclear sentiment was that many Germans, in both East and West Germany, considered their country as a likely ground zero in the event of nuclear war between the United States and the Soviet Union. A commonly predicted scenario was that an attempt to fight a limited nuclear war in Europe, beginning in Germany, would escalate into global nuclear war.

With the end of the Cold War, the center of theater defense has shifted from Western Europe to northeast Asia. This shift is particularly evident as concerns over a potentially hostile North Korean military presence continue to escalate.

See also National Missile Defense; Nuclear Deterrence; Nuclear Weapons; Patriot Missile; Strategic Defense Initiative (SDI) Strategy

Further Reading

Alexander, Brian, and Alistair Millar, eds. *Tactical Nuclear Weapons: Emergent Threats in an Evolving Security Environment.* Dulles, VA: Brassey's, 2003.

Rose, John P. *The Evolution of U.S. Army Nuclear Doctrine, 1945–1980.* Boulder, CO: Westview Press, 1980.

Van Cleave, William R., and S. T. Cohen. *Tactical Nuclear Weapons: An Examination of the Issues.* New York: Crane, Russak, 1978.

THINK TANKS

Nonprofit research organizations engaging in public policy analysis, research, and often advocating solutions. The term *think tanks* describes a wide range of organizations established to assess the validity and utility of the ideas that form the basis for policy. In addition to evaluating ideas, think tanks often develop new concepts upon which future policies might be based.

Some think tanks are strictly nonpartisan, researching policy issues without regard to the political implications of their final analysis. Others view their main purpose as providing intellectual support to politicians or parties. Think tanks—more properly, public-policy research organizations—are ubiquitous in U.S. political life, and many occupy the same sphere of activity as interest groups, media consultants, spin doctors, and political parties.

The term *think tank* first was used during World War II and was applied to a secure room or environment where defense scientists and military planners could meet and confer over strategy. Today, the term is used to cover more than 2,000 U.S.-based organizations that engage in policy analysis and development—as well as at least 2,500 similar institutions worldwide.

Largely the consequence of efforts by leading philanthropists and intellectuals, the first major wave of think tanks in the United States began to emerge at the beginning of the 20th century. These initial enterprises were foreign-policy institutes where scholars and private-sector elites could meet, conduct research, and debate issues. The Carnegie Endowment for International Peace (established in 1910 by Pittsburgh steel baron Andrew Carnegie), the Hoover Institution on War, Revolution and Peace (created by President Herbert Hoover in 1919), and the Council on Foreign Relations (established in 1921) became the leading forums for the exchange of ideas and debate on international subjects in the early 20th century. Later to appear were the Brookings Institution, established in 1927, and the American Enterprise Institute, established in 1943.

Today, with the intensity of the competitive political debate, think tanks have come under as much censure as praise. According to journalist Tom Brazaitis, writing in the *Cleveland Plain Dealer,* modern think tanks are "political idea factories where donations can be as big as the donor's checkbook and are seldom publicized." Another critic has observed that "Think tanks are like universities minus the students and minus the systems of peer review and other mechanisms that academia uses to promote diversity of thought. Real academics are expected to conduct their research first and draw their conclusions second, but this process is often reversed at most policy-driven think tanks."

However, not all assessments of think tanks are negative. Andrew Rich, a political scientist who has studied think tanks, says that they "remain a principal source of information and expertise for policy makers and journalists. . . . Their studies and reports are regularly relied upon to guide and/or bolster members of Congress in their legislative efforts."

THREAT ADVISORY LEVELS

A color-coded indicator of the likelihood of a forthcoming terrorist attack on the United States or its citizens and interests abroad. Introduced by the U.S. Department of Homeland Security in the wake of the terrorist attacks of September 11, 2001, the threat advisory levels function both to alert U.S. citizens to the possibility of attack and to direct federal and state agencies to take enhanced security precautions. The threat advisory level is set by the president of the United States on the advice of the secretary of homeland security.

There are five threat advisory levels: green (low risk of attack), blue (guarded risk of attack), yellow (elevated risk of attack), orange (high risk of attack), and red (severe risk of attack). Each threat level ostensibly adds an additional layer of security and subsumes all of the extra precautions taken at lower threat levels. The Homeland Security Advisory System specifies what precautions should be taken at each threat level.

During a blue condition, federal agencies check communications with designated emergency response and command locations and review emergency response procedures. When the threat advisory is yellow, law-enforcement agencies increase their surveillance of critical locations and coordinate emergency plans with other state and local personnel. During an orange alert, federal agencies take additional precautions at public events and restrict access to threatened facilities. With a red alert, the federal government increases personnel and resource levels to address critical emergency needs, mobilizes specially trained teams, and closes affected public and government facilities.

Critics of the threat advisory system maintain that its five incremental levels hold little practical utility, in that neither the green (low) level nor the blue (guarded) level will ever likely be set. Supporters of the threat advisory system, however, argue that it has been a highly effective tool for raising public awareness at critical moments and for helping governments make opportune policy and resource decisions.

See also Homeland Security; Homeland Security Act (2002); Threat Assessment

THREAT ASSESSMENT

Efforts to identify the precursors of violence through a studied analysis of a perceived or real danger and then initiating an intervention process to stop violent acts before they erupt. Threat assessments are tools that can be useful in any relevant context. However, in the realm of international relations and geopolitics, the concept essentially refers to a situation in which studied and tactical responses are needed to counter threats posed by an individual, group, or country to harm the citizens or territory of another country. The nature of threats may emanate from an armed invasion, a nuclear threat, other weapons of mass destruction (including chemical and biological weapons), and, more recently, terrorism, which may use one or a combination of weapons and other nonconventional methods to attack its chosen targets.

HISTORICAL BACKGROUND

Traditionally, the application of threat-assessment methodology has been more focused on individual systems and has been used primarily by law-enforcement and anticrime branches of government. However, with the onset of globalization, the spread of multidimensional dynamic systems, and the changing nature of domestic and international security threats, an expanded definition of threat-assessment methodology was required to address the new complexities. In this transitional phase, it is recognized that these threat assessments are part of a distinct and ongoing process; to identify new and changing threats effectively, continuous data gathering and analysis (intelligence) are required.

During the Cold War era, the geostrategic and political environment necessitated threat assessments on numerous occasions. The Cuban Missile Crisis of 1962 could well be considered among one of the most notable of these moments, when the United States was brought to the brink of a potential nuclear war because of a real threat posed by the placement of Soviet missiles in Cuba. However, the threat-assessment approach was not very well developed at that time, particularly in national defense and security ranks and institutions. During the past two decades, however, and particularly in the 1990s, this has changed with the unpredictable threat of terrorism across the globe, which has brought unparalleled international attention to the problem.

TERRORISM AND THE THREAT OF TERRORISM

In recent decades, terrorism has struck hard with a new and changing face. The United States has been among the main victims of terrorist attacks, many of which have taken place beyond the territorial boundaries of the nation.

In the past two decades, the United States has suffered the single largest number of terrorist attacks, along with concomitant loss of life and damage to national assets. The targets have included symbols and institutions that represent U.S. power or presence in some way across the globe.

The nature of such attacks is always uncertain, ranging from food poisoning in Oregon, to a truck bomb in Oklahoma, to suicide airline hijackings in New York and Washington, DC, to anthrax-laced letters in the District of Columbia.

In fighting terrorism, or any other threat, some of the questions that arise are: How credible and serious is the threat? To what extent does the threatening source appear to have the resources, intent, and motivation to carry out the threat? Determining the credibility and seriousness of the threat is complicated by the increasingly diffuse nature of attacks. For example, potential adversaries are more likely to strike vulnerable civilian or military targets in nontraditional ways in order to avoid direct confrontation with military forces, or to coerce governments to take some action that they desire, thus winning a symbolic or actual victory.

In terms of the resources available to carry out such acts, terrorists have become more viable today because of porous borders, rapid technological change, greater information flow, and the destructive power of weapons now within the reach of states, groups, and individuals who seek to use them in nondesirable ways. The most difficult elements to measure, however, are intent and motivation, because perpetrators of terrorism are driven by nontangible and immeasurable elements, such as religious fundamentalism or anti-American sentiment caused by past historical events and economic deprivation.

RISK-MANAGEMENT APPROACH

In an effort to combat terrorism, and taking into account the unique nature of the threat posed by it, some U.S. government and intelligence groups and individuals have promoted the adoption of the risk-management approach as an important element in developing national-security strategy. This approach is advocated as a complement to other military and nonmilitary options to fight the danger.

The risk-management approach is a systematic process to analyze threats, vulnerabilities, and the relative importance of assets, in order to better support key decisions linking resources with prioritized efforts for results. The other two components of an effective risk-management approach include a vulnerability assessment and an assessment of criticality (relative importance).

In the context of this approach, a threat assessment is a decision-support tool that helps to establish and prioritize security-program requirements, planning, and resource allocations. In practical terms, this definition of threat assessment implies that intelligence and law-enforcement agencies assess the foreign and domestic terrorist threats to the United States and prioritize them accordingly. The U.S. intelligence community, which includes, among others, the Central Intelligence Agency (CIA), the Defense Intelligence Agency, and the State Department's Bureau of Intelligence and Research, monitors the foreign-origin terrorist threats to the United States. The FBI gathers information and assesses the threat posed by domestic sources of terrorism.

OTHER APPLICABLE AREAS

Several federal government organizations, as well as companies in the private sector, apply some formal threat-assessment process in their programs, or such assessments have been recommended for implementation. For example, the Department of Defense (DoD) uses threat assessments for its antiterrorism program designed to protect military installations. It evaluates threats on the basis of several factors, including a terrorist group's intentions, capabilities, and past activities.

Similarly, the Interagency Commission on Crime and Security in U.S. Seaports reported that threat assessments would assist seaports in preparing for terrorist threats. Additionally, a leading multinational oil company attempts to identify threats in order to decide how to manage risk in a cost-effective manner. Due to the fact that the company operates overseas, its facilities and operations are exposed to a multitude of threats, including terrorism, political instability, and religious or tribal conflict.

Some individuals and groups who have examined threat assessments in detail argue that, although they

are key decision support tools, they might not adequately capture emerging threats posed by terrorist groups. The rationale is that it is practically impossible to identify every threat or acquire complete information even about the threats one is aware of, let alone potential threats. They suggest the adoption of a more holistic risk-management approach that incorporates the two additional assessments of vulnerability and criticality, which can provide a better assurance of preparedness for terrorist and other attacks in general. Regardless, it is becoming clear that, because the United States and the world continue to face increasing danger from terrorism and other such threats, threat assessments will be a necessity, not just an option.

—Divya Gupta

See also Counterthreat; Threat Advisory Levels

Further Reading

Cameron, Gavin. *Nuclear Terrorism: A Threat Assessment for the 21st Century.* New York: St. Martin's, 1999.
Hall, Harold V., ed. *Terrorism: Strategies for Intervention.* New York: Haworth, 2003.

THUCYDIDES

Ancient Greek historian whose main work, *The History of the Peloponnesian War,* was meant to provide future generations with valuable lessons on the causes and dynamics of all violent conflicts. His extraordinary insight into the historical implications of a single, albeit prolonged, armed dispute, as well as his scholarly impartiality, set Thucydides apart even from such illustrious predecessors as the Greek historian Herodotus.

Thucydides was born in the ancient city of Athens around the year 460 BCE to a wealthy, aristocratic family. At that time, Athens was the center of a flourishing empire, kept under tight control with the help of an impressive military force hardly matched by any of the other powers in the region. Around the year 431 BCE, however, these powers rallied around the rival city-state of Sparta. The war that subsequently broke out between the two city-states and their allies—the Peloponnesian War—raged on and off for more than 25 years. The conflict eventually came to an end with the capitulation of Athens.

HIS LIFE

At the outbreak of the Peloponnesian War, Thucydides was in his 20s, possibly already serving in the Athenian army as an infantryman, or hoplite. In 424 BCE, while in his 30s, he was elected general and shared the command of military operations in Thrace, a region northeast of Athens. Unable to deliver the important city of Amphipolis from the hands of a Spartan army, Thucydides was exiled from Athens.

For the next 19 years, Thucydides lived in Thrace, spending much of his time traveling in the Peloponnesian region (southwest of Athens). Thanks to his aristocratic roots and his status as an Athenian exile, Thucydides was able to speak to many of the war's major participants, who provided him with precious information for his history of the conflict. Thucydides was permitted to return to Athens in 404 BCE, at the end of the war, but he returned to Thrace soon after. He spent the rest of his life working on his account of the Peloponnesian War. He died around 401 BCE, possibly by violent means.

THE HISTORY

Thucydides died before he could complete *The History of the Peloponnesian War,* which ends abruptly in the middle of a sentence. The author begins his work by explaining his belief that this particular war is "more worthy of relation than any that had preceded it" (even greater than the Trojan War), mainly due to the high state of military development that both Athens and Sparta enjoyed at the time. Thucydides then lays out the principles on which he sees fit to undertake the writing of his *History.*

According to Thucydides, his aim is to produce a truthful account of the war, avoiding the temptation to blend historical events with myths and legends. In doing so, the Greek historian introduces a term on which all realist theories of international relations have since been founded—the *balance of power.* Thucydides was the first historian to work with the assumption that the rise of a powerful state will, by necessity, be accompanied by constant attempts from other states to arrest that development. Because of the exceptional scholarly rigorousness of his work and the introduction of concepts that are now considered to be political-science fundamentals, many consider Thucydides to be the true father of modern historians.

See also Balance of Power

Further Reading

Abbott, G. F. *Thucydides: A Study in Historical Reality.* New York: Russell & Russell, 1970.

Proctor, Dennis. *The Experience of Thucydides.* Warminster, UK: Aris & Phillips, 1980.

TOMAHAWK CRUISE MISSILES

Land-attack cruise missiles launched from ships or submarines. The BGM-109 Tomahawk flies at low altitudes to strike fixed targets, such as communication and air-defense sites, in high-threat environments and in all weather conditions. The Tomahawk eludes radar detection because of its small cross section and low-altitude operation. A turbofan engine propels the missile after launch, emitting little heat, which makes infrared detection difficult, as well.

Once it reaches land, the Tomahawk uses inertial and terrain-contour-matching (TERCOM) radar guidance. A map is stored on the missile's computer, and the system continually compares the map with the actual terrain to locate its position relative to the target. Similarly, the target is identified from a stored image. As the TERCOM scans the landscape, the Tomahawk missile is capable of twisting and turning like a radar-evading fighter plane, skimming the landscape at an altitude of only 100 to 300 feet.

The Tomahawk is a long-range, highly survivable, unmanned attack weapon capable of pinpoint (nearly 92%) accuracy. During the opening salvos of a regional attack, military planning calls for sea-based Tomahawks to be used to compromise and suppress enemy air operations and defenses. The 20-foot-long missile has a range of about 700 miles. Manufactured by Hughes Missile Systems at an average unit cost of $1.4 million, Tomahawk missiles traveling at 550 mph are capable of carrying conventional, cluster, and nuclear payloads.

Ships and submarines have different weapons-control systems for launching the Tomahawks. A vertical launch system is used on ships, whereas attack submarines can launch the system horizontally by using torpedo tubes or from external launchers attached to the hull.

The first combat test of the Tomahawk system occurred in 1991 during Operation Desert Storm in Iraq. In the war, about 280 Tomahawks were used to destroy hardened targets, such as Iraqi surface to air

The launching of a Tomahawk cruise missile from the USS *Florida* in the Gulf of Mexico in January 2002. The launch was part of Giant Shadow, a Naval Sea Systems Command/Naval Submarine Forces experiment of potential future submarine force capabilities. The event was a milestone in the history of the submarine force—the first time that a Tomahawk missile had been launched from a missile tube of an SSBN class (ballistic missile) submarine.

Source: U.S. Navy.

missile sites, command and control centers, and electrical power facilities; the missiles also are credited with destroying the Iraqi presidential palace.

Operation Desert Storm saw the first coordinated Tomahawk and manned-aircraft strike in history. Since then, Tomahawks have been used extensively in Iraq (January and June 1993), Bosnia (1995), Operation Desert Strike against Libya (1996), Afghanistan (2002), and Operation Iraqi Freedom (2003).

See also Missiles; Operation Desert Storm (1991)

TONKIN GULF RESOLUTION

Resolution that authorized President Lyndon B. Johnson to use whatever force he deemed necessary in Vietnam. This Tonkin Gulf Resolution passed the U.S. Senate on August 10, 1964, with only two dissenting votes.

The Tonkin Gulf Resolution stated that communist Vietnamese naval units had violated the UN Charter and international law by attacking U.S. naval vessels lawfully present in international waters on August 1, 1964. North Vietnamese torpedo boats had attacked the *Maddox,* a U.S. destroyer, in the Gulf of Tonkin on that date. The *Maddox* and another ship reported that they were under attack again three days later. This second attack was incorrect, however, for the sailors misread sonar and radar equipment malfunctioning in heavy seas.

Notwithstanding any possible errors or misjudgments, President Johnson presented the attack to the U.S. Congress as impetus for passing the Tonkin Gulf Resolution. Two days of debate followed, with ultimate passage of the resolution. The Tonkin Gulf Resolution was ultimately repealed by Congress on January 2, 1971.

The purpose of the joint resolution was to promote the maintenance of international peace and security in Southeast Asia. The Tonkin Gulf Resolution depicted the attacks in the Tonkin Gulf as a deliberate and systematic campaign of aggression that the communist regime in North Vietnam was waging against its neighbors. It emphasized that the United States did not contain any territorial, military, or political ambitions in Southeast Asia, but that it desired only that the Vietnamese people should be left in peace to work out their own destinies.

The Tonkin Gulf Resolution granted President Johnson, as commander in chief, the power to take all necessary measures to repel any armed attack against U.S. forces and to prevent further aggression.

See also Johnson, Lyndon B., and National Policy; Vietnam War (1954–1975)

TOTALITARIANISM

A system of government in which a leader (often a charismatic one), supported by a loyal party, dominates all aspects of an atomized society with weapons of propaganda, indoctrination, and terror. Totalitarian regimes since the mid-20th century have included Nazi Germany, Stalinist Russia, and the rogue state of North Korea.

TOTALITARIANISM DEFINED

Totalitarianism is not just a dictatorship or one-party rule, although it may contain aspects of each of these. What distinguishes totalitarianism from other forms of authoritarian rule is that the totalitarian society is one in which the dividing line between the government and society has disappeared. This means that the government controls—through propaganda, indoctrination, and terror—the actions and the psyches of the individuals it rules. It ordains both public and private life, and, at its pinnacle, rules them totally.

Totalitarianism is not politically defined or determined. It may occur in reactionary (rightist) or revolutionary (leftist) states. The two most famous totalitarian states—Nazi Germany and Stalinist Russia—were at opposite ends of the political spectrum but quite similar in their methods of domination. Certain social conditions, rather than political ones, must be met for the implementation of a totalitarian state.

PREREQUISITES FOR TOTALITARIANISM

The totalitarian process requires huge numbers of isolated individuals. Large numbers ensure that people will feel sufficiently superfluous, will not find common interests, and will not suffer total depopulation when the liquidation of classes begins. Therefore, the first and most necessary condition for a totalitarian society is a collapse of a previously existing society of millions—usually a corrupt, hypocritical system. Its breakdown creates the *masses*—enormous numbers of people without common interests. The masses of the new classless society feel adrift, frustrated, powerless, and insecure, having lost their previous sense of identity and place in the social structure. The individual in this society feels superfluous and alone. He or she does not enjoy normal social bonds or human connections, even at the level of the family. Society as a whole becomes atomized and individualized.

The totalitarian movement (which exists before it gains total control and becomes a totalitarian state) stands in opposition to the hypocritical, stable respectability of the previous system. The movement's frank glorification of violence in the service of its ideology is both a contrast to the previous regime and fascinating in its own right. Propaganda attracts attention to the ideology and the power of the movement, ultimately providing a way for the individuals to lose themselves in something greater—something that will be of historical importance. In this context, the huge numbers of isolated individuals find structure and a sense of place in the totalitarian movement. Therefore, totalitarian movements enjoy the confidence of the masses up to the end.

FEATURES OF TOTALITARIANISM

The defining characteristic of totalitarianism is *coerced unanimity*. As totalitarianism involves total control over many aspects of life, coercion must take many forms: ideology, propaganda, indoctrination, and terror. Ideology forms the backbone of the totalitarian movement. Whether focusing on race or class or some other category, the totalitarian party is not designed to promote the interests of a group and therefore never has a specific agenda. It is intended to ponder sweeping ideological questions of importance to the ages, not to everyday life. It is often pseudoscientific, based on "laws" of humanity and human nature. Because only the future can resolve the correctness of the ideological arguments, the use of reason and logic against them becomes useless.

The ideology of totalitarianism is interpreted by a mysterious, and often charismatic, totalitarian leader. This leader is represented as infallible by the party and often speaks prophetically, describing predictable forces of human nature and political relations. To this end, the truth is often adjusted by the party to fit the declarations of the leader, leading to such practices as the rewriting of history (practiced famously by Soviet leader Joseph Stalin). Predictions made by the leader may be actively fulfilled by the party, reinforcing the leader's status. The leader can manipulate the truth and determine what is true; and the party reinforces this truth through repetition.

The totalitarian state has a single mass political party, though only a few are allowed to be full party members (the rest are considered sympathizers). Party control means that *active unfreedom* exists—citizens are continually forced to show their support for the regime and may be punished if they do not. Control is exerted through a party monopoly over armed combat and centralized direction of the economy. It also involves a near monopoly on mass communications (the press, movies, radio).

These technologies are used by the party as means for disseminating propaganda and penetrating the minds of the citizens. Propaganda convinces those who are not sufficiently indoctrinated and those not yet properly subdued, although its primary use is for communication about the state to the outside world. The regime generally uses indoctrination and psychological domination to pacify its population once it has taken control of the government. Individual intellectual, spiritual, and artistic initiatives are actively destroyed.

Despite these psychological attacks, a few dissenters may remain within the totalitarian state. The government actively seeks out these individuals, using its communications base to discredit them. The government aggressively uses technology to infiltrate private lives—to supervise individuals' activities and, later, to organize records and reports on these individuals. With sufficient (or fabricated) evidence, the government proclaims dissenters to be enemies and then purges or eliminates them. In Stalinist Russia, for example, a common practice involved the use of *show trials* in which the guilt of the accused was already decided. The purpose of the trial was to serve as a warning to other potential dissidents.

As the list of real enemies is depleted, other scapegoats or enemies are created to maintain the totalitarian system. These enemies are often found among party members. Personnel are interchangeable and expendable, so members who pose real or imagined threats to the leader are often eliminated.

Ironically, once the population is subdued, propaganda ceases and terror (previously used but held in check) is fully unleashed. Terror is the strongest weapon of the totalitarian state. Its agents are often secret police who inspire terror because they purge enemies of the regime and innocents alike, often indiscriminately.

Terror increases exponentially because of a belief in guilt by association—family members and acquaintances of the accused become suspect. Out of fear, these associates may give (true or false) information to support the accusations, in an attempt to save themselves, resulting in deeper isolation and greater submission to the regime. Over time, whole classes of people—such as peasants in Russia and Jews and other "undesirables" in Nazi Germany—are destroyed, with death tolls running into the tens of millions. The horror of totalitarianism lies in its complete and unremitting domination of an already pacified population.

See also Communism

TRADE AND FOREIGN AID

The relationship between U.S. foreign aid and the growth of international trade in the 20th century. America's advance as an economic and financial world power began with its entry into World War I. By the end of that conflict, the United States had wiped out its foreign debt, strengthened its currency, and become a major player in international financial markets. However, it was not until the conclusion of World War II that the United States fully emerged as the world's premier economic force.

EARLY FOREIGN AID POLICY

The foreign aid policy of the United States and its bureaucracy took form following World War II. By the end of that war, Western fears that the power vacuum of a defeated Germany and an exhausted Britain and France might be filled by an aggressive and unrestrained Soviet Union created great international tension. There was great concern not only that Soviet influence would expand into this political void, but also that a threat to democratic market-oriented economies could arise from within the emerging sociopolitical structure of Western Europe itself.

The experience of the Great Depression, and the possibility of an aggressive military agenda by the Soviet Union, created deep uneasiness among U.S. policymakers. This apprehension toward the market, during the same period in which the Soviet Union was proclaiming remarkable economic numbers with regard to industrial growth, helped propel the communist parties of Italy and France. The anxiety over such circumstances was a driving force behind U.S. foreign policy in the immediate postwar period.

With these circumstances as a backdrop, officials and organizers from various nations met at a conference in Bretton Woods in New Hampshire. The document prepared at this conference, the Bretton Woods Agreement, created three important economic institutions: the World Bank, the International Monetary Fund (IMF), and the General Agreement on Tariffs and Trade (GATT).

The conventional wisdom at the time was that the cause of the Great Depression and World War II was the decline of world trade brought about by "beggar-thy-neighbor" trade policies. This assessment became a guiding principle of political economists in the United States and its allies in the West. Western economists and U.S. policymakers reasoned that a reduction in barriers to trade and capital flows would generate a cycle of economic growth and a sustained attack on poverty, thus making communism less attractive and viable. Although the Soviet Union was invited to join in this process of institution building, Soviet leader Joseph Stalin declined to participate.

Within the economic environment created by the Bretton Woods Agreement, the policies of free trade flourished. The effort to ensure the dominance of U.S. business in the postwar era while containing the advance of communism became the main thrust of U.S. trade policy and foreign-assistance programs.

THE POSTWAR WORLD

In the initial years following World War II, Europe faced tremendous economic plight. The continent suffered not only from a lack of investment capital, but also from a massive U.S. trade surplus that raised the specter of uncontainable inflation. In order to ease these strains on the system, the United States designed and implemented the Marshall Plan to help rebuild Europe's economic infrastructure. Doing so, it was hoped, would stimulate European trade with the world as well as increase intraregional trade among European countries.

Several economic programs and commercial mechanisms were devised to promote these policy aims. The most notable was the invention and placement of counterpart funds. Under this arrangement, U.S. commodities would be delivered to the representatives of the Committee for European Economic Cooperation. These goods were then resold through normal commercial channels, and each recipient government would deposit, in local currency, the equivalent to the amounts received, in grant form, from the proceeds from these sales.

Ninety five percent of the counterpart funds could only be released with the consent of the U.S. government, which directed that the funds be used either for debt retirement or economic stimulus. Additional grants and loans to recipient aid countries enabled European managers to purchase U.S. specialty tools for emerging industries and pay for technical assistance programs for industrial specialists and farmers. The remaining 5% went for overhead costs to cover administrative, acquisition, and procurement expenses and even the cost of postage on privately contributed relief packages.

The Marshall Plan, or the European Recovery Program (ERP), as it was formally called, is commonly viewed as a great success. Between 1947 and 1951, the goal of increased European production was largely fulfilled, and foreign trade expansion, the second priority of the ERP, was also realized. However, inflation and lingering balance-of-payment difficulties undermined the hope of full internal financial stability. These economic problems were mostly due to rearmament policies resulting from the Korean War, which also led to further depletion of Western Europe's gold and silver reserves. As defense budgets expanded, so too did imports of high-cost raw materials. Inflationary pressures returned and private consumption declined, but not before the payment crisis to U.S. industry and agriculture was averted and Europe was put back on its economic feet.

USAID

Building upon the experiences of the Marshall Plan, the U.S. State Department began providing economic aid beyond Europe to third-world allies in the 1950s. In 1961, the U.S. government passed the Foreign Assistance Act (FAA), which established the Agency for International Development (AID) to coordinate humanitarian assistance, business-promotion programs, and developmental and food aid.

With the intent of meeting the communist challenge in these regions, military aid programs for bolstering anticommunist regimes paralleled U.S. economic aid. The main aims of U.S. foreign trade strategy and assistance were to promote the economic interests of corporate America and keep recipient nations under the political influence of Washington.

In the 1960s, the flagship program of U.S. foreign aid was the Alliance for Progress, which supported agrarian land reform and cooperative solutions to rural poverty through more equitable income distribution and economic and social planning in Latin American. A multilateral program, the Alliance for Progress aimed to increase per capita income in Latin American countries by 2.5% a year and gain a commitment from those nations for the promotion and spread of democratic institutions. In this effort, the United States agreed to supply or guarantee $20 billion over 10 years. As part of the assistance package in the Alliance for Progress, the United States contributed programs of military and police assistance to counter communist subversion in Latin America.

By the late 1960s, the Vietnam War had diverted attention and resources away from the Alliance for Progress, and commitments to Latin America were reduced. Most Latin American nations were unwilling to implement needed reforms, and the permanent committee created to implement the alliance was disbanded by the Organization of American States in 1973.

As opposed to the successes of the Marshall Plan, USAID programs were often viewed as a part of the problem rather than the solution. *Tied aid* policies forced a dependence on U.S. commodities, thereby eliminating any option on the part of the recipient country to source supplies from an open and competitive market. Support for free trade unions and other AID-dependent organizations inhibited the development of local, independent organizations. Finally, military aid buttressed repressive regimes and undermined the original pledge to promote and support democratic governance.

SHIFTS IN AID POLICY

The simultaneous complementary and competing forces of economic aid and counterinsurgency programs often led to failure. Such failures led the United States to reconsider and redefine its assistance programs. In the 1970s, U.S. foreign aid policy gave more weight to meeting the basic economic needs of the poor than to implementing developmental strategies. From 1976 to 1980, the administration of President Jimmy Carter stressed human-rights provisions as a way to limit the provisioning of military and police aid to repressive governments.

In the 1980s, the direction of U.S. international assistance shifted again. The experience of the worldwide recession of the 1970s catapulted Ronald Reagan into the presidency. At this time, free-trade advocates took over control of policy, not only in Washington, but also in London and at the World Bank. The emphasis in foreign aid now swung toward using aid to subsidize private-sector development and as a weapon to contain the Soviet Union.

As the strategic focus moved away from basic needs, the Reaganomic belief in the efficiency of free markets linked U.S. assistance with the structural-adjustment programs of the World Bank and the International Monetary Fund (IMF). Under the new policies, states that received IMF loans had to follow a set of strict economic prescriptions. These prescriptions called for monetary stabilization, but at the cost of giving local governments the ability to manage their economy through monetary policy. Hence, the greatest onus for reforming the economy was placed upon the private sector.

As the world witnessed the disintegration of the Soviet Union in the early 1990s, many viewed the failure of communism as proof that governments were fallible and the market was not. Urged on by these events, the World Bank and the IMF blanketed the developing world with template structural adjustment programs.

As a result of these programs, local industries were subject to competition from abroad and conventional lending practices. The aims of these programs were to force the private sector to respond to market signals. Local firms, however, often were not prepared to meet the demands of global competition. Furthermore, indigenous banking systems, particularly in the transition economies of Russia and Eastern Europe, were not yet sufficiently organized to deal with the pace and turbulence of global financial markets.

CRITIQUING THE SYSTEM

Some observers have argued forcefully that capital market liberalization does not always yield the desired fruits. The ceaseless movement of financial capital, demands for tight credit controls, and requirements that local industry be exposed to free-trade policies and foreign competition from exports have all too often contributed to unemployment and poverty in many underdeveloped areas of the world.

As a result of such measures, many economies that received large financial-assistance packages have suffered harshly rather than prospered. In many third-world countries, the situation has developed into what has been described as a debt trap. Experts estimate, for example, that as much as 50% of government revenues in some nations go toward paying off the national debt. In some cases, this represents one-fifth to one-quarter of export earnings to a national budget.

Compounding any current debate on the role and application of foreign aid are the difficulties wrought by religious fundamentalism, global terrorism, the disintegration of the former Soviet Union, and the U.S. deficit. Additionally, rapid economic globalization is overwhelming the structures of many national states.

The financial pressures of national security and parity of the dollar relative to other currency blocs may force the United States to redefine foreign aid within the context of trade once again. Faced with these challenges, the role of the United States as the premiere economic power in the world may undergo reassessment and change. The impact upon future foreign aid policy and international trade relations is thus yet to be determined.

—*Jack A. Jarmon*

See also Alliance for Progress; Foreign Aid; International Monetary Fund (IMF); Marshall Plan; World Bank

Further Reading

Sobol, Robert. *The Life and Times of Dillon Reed.* New York: Dutton, 1991.

Stiglitz, Joseph E. *Globalization and Its Discontents.* New York: Norton, 2003.

Thomas, Caroline. "Global Governance and Human Security." In *Global Governance: Critical Perspectives,* Rorden Wilkinson and Steve Hughes, eds. New York: Routledge, 2002.

Wexler, Imanuel. *The Marshall Plan Revisited: The European Recovery Program Economic Perspective.* Westport, CT: Greenwood Press, 1983.

TRADE LIBERALIZATION

The decrease in trade barriers between countries, including reductions in quotas, tariffs, and nontariff barriers. Reductions such as these are designed to increase trade between nations and encourage economic interconnectedness.

Trade liberalization policies have contributed significantly to increases in international trade; average quotas and tariffs on foreign goods have been reduced from 40% prior to World War II to less than 4% currently. And while overall global output has increased over five

times since the end of World War II, total world exports are now nearly 15 times greater than they were in 1950. This indicates a staggering growth in international trade relative to overall economic output.

INSTITUTIONS DEDICATED TO TRADE LIBERALIZATION

The modern era of global trade liberalization can be traced to the post-World War II period. The most notable step toward liberalizing trade during this period was the establishment of the General Agreement on Tariffs and Trade (GATT). GATT, which was created in 1947 and maintained offices in Geneva, Switzerland, was committed to systematically reducing barriers to international trade. Over a period of nearly five decades, it conducted eight rounds of multilateral negotiations to reduce trade barriers among member states.

The final round of GATT negotiations, the Uruguay Round (1986–93) resulted in the establishment of the World Trade Organization (WTO). The WTO was designed to carry on the work of GATT but had expanded goals that included not just reducing barriers to trade, but fostering global competition. The WTO also promotes the liberalization of trade by serving as a dispute settler for member nations. Additional tasks of the WTO include providing assistance to developing nations as they prepare to enter the global trade arena. The WTO, also based in Geneva, currently has 146 members, with more than a dozen additional states seeking membership.

Domestically, one of the most important institutions committed to trade liberalization is the North American Free Trade Agreement (NAFTA). NAFTA went into effect in 1994 and links the United States, Canada, and Mexico into a free trade zone. Both President Bill Clinton and President George W. Bush have attempted to increase the reach of NAFTA to include much of the rest of Latin America, but protests, both within the United States and from several Latin American governments, have delayed any significant progress on this initiative.

THE THEORY BEHIND TRADE LIBERALIZATION

Liberal trade policies are supported by a belief that a free market system of international trade is best equipped to provide for global economic growth. Proponents of trade liberalization suggest that by removing barriers to trade, states can more efficiently use the resources they have (capital, labor, and so forth) and purchase additional goods and services from other nations at competitive prices. Other arguments made by supporters of liberal trade policies include the potential for decreased international conflict as national economies become more tightly linked. Finally, supporters of trade liberalization often cite the effects of trade liberalization on income; the WTO estimates that aggregate global income may have increased by as much as $519 billion as a result of the Uruguay Round talks.

ISSUES IN TRADE LIBERALIZATION

Trade liberalization is currently a highly controversial topic, as evidenced by the recent protests against the WTO in Seattle, Montreal, and Geneva. Some of the most contentious topics include the differing effects of trade liberalization on the Northern Hemisphere versus the Southern Hemisphere, lingering protectionism among many states, and an ongoing debate between the merits of free trade versus fair trade.

Despite the impressive growth of the global economy often cited by the WTO, there is ample evidence that this economic growth is occurring disproportionately in favor of nations in the Northern Hemisphere. Income disparity between the North and the South has risen precipitously (doubling from a 30 to 1 disparity in 1960, to a 60 to 1 disparity in 1990), suggesting that the economic gains from trade have not been distributed equally among nations in the North and those in the South.

Although many developing countries (particularly in Latin America and Africa) have attempted to liberalize their trade policies and shift economic resources to export-driven activities, heavy debt loads and chronic trade deficits have prevented the realization of many of the purported benefits of trade liberalization. The North/South issue thus remains a fiercely contested topic in discussions of trade liberalization, and many southern countries are working to get a stronger voice in the WTO in an attempt to modify some of the trade liberalization policies supported by the WTO.

Another concern about trade liberalization is that even in this era of free trade, protectionism lingers. Even countries in the North, traditionally the strongest proponents of trade liberalization, have at times resorted to protectionist measures, particularly in agriculture. Subsidies for domestic agriculture, as well as health and quality concerns over imported agricultural products, have contributed to many protectionist measures within the United States, Japan, and Europe. The hypocrisy of these protectionist measures is felt particularly strongly by developing nations, which resent the rhetoric of trade liberalization combined with the practice of certain protectionist policies among those in the North.

Although trade liberalization has guided policymakers for more than 50 years, there are increasing voices in support of fair trade. Supporters of fair trade are concerned about the discrepancies in labor standards, worker rights, and environmental standards between states. Fair trade supporters advocate for a global harmonization of minimum standards for worker rights and environmental protection and are critical of the competitive advantage that many developing nations get through exploiting their workers and/or the environment.

Despite the recent controversy over trade liberalization, it seems that liberal trade policies continue to be supported and advanced by many world leaders. Liberal trade polices, though at times contradicted by instances of protectionism in both the North and South, continue to dominate the arena of international trade. The WTO currently oversees more than 90% of the world's trade, and it is actively working to increase free trade among nations across the globe.

See also Free Trade; General Agreement on Tariffs and Trade (GATT); North American Free Trade Agreement (NAFTA); World Trade Organization (WTO)

Further Reading

Dicken, Peter. *Global Shift.* New York: Guilford, 1998.
Rodrik, Dani. *Has Globalization Gone Too Far?* Washington, DC: Institute for International Economics, 1997.

TRADE WARS

Situation in which countries attempt to protect their own industries and agriculture through mechanisms such as tariffs or subsidies. These actions spark similar retaliation from other countries.

Countries often attempt to protect their industries from cheaper imports or to obtain an advantage in exports to other countries. Subsidies that give an edge in global competition, (such as farm subsidies in the

United States) or the imposition of stiff tariffs on imports from other countries (such as steel tariffs imposed by the United States in 2002) are common mechanisms for gaining such an advantage.

Sometimes it is not clear whether other countries are acting in a protectionist manner, such as when the European Union banned beef from cattle reared using growth hormones in 1999, arguing that such beef was not safe for consumption. In that case, however, the United States, which was the primary country injured by the ban on cattle imports, was allowed by the World Trade Organization (WTO) to impose sanctions on European countries. Such protectionist measures tend to benefit more developed countries and hurt the ability of developing nations to compete in the global economy. However, due to the tendency of other countries to retaliate in response to protectionist measures, often no one truly benefits.

THE WORLD TRADE ORGANIZATION (WTO)

The World Trade Organization (WTO), headquartered in Geneva, Switzerland, and established by the Uruguay Round of the General Agreement on Tariffs and Trade (GATT) in 1994, is the primary regulator of trade disputes in the world. The WTO oversees a huge number of agreements defining the rules of trade between its member states. The WTO replaced several previous attempts at international trade regulation and agreement, such as the International Trade Organization (ITO) and the General Agreement on Tariffs and Trades (GATT). As of December 2004, there were 148 members of the WTO. All WTO members are required to grant one another most-favored-nation status, such that (with some exceptions) trade concessions granted by a WTO member to another country must be granted to all WTO members.

The WTO is a one-vote, one-country organization, which means that the very smallest and poorest countries theoretically have the same influence over trade policies as the largest and most powerful countries. In reality, however, most decisions of the WTO are made by consensus rather than by a vote. The advantage of consensus is that it encourages efforts to find the most widely acceptable solutions. The main disadvantages include the large time requirements and the many rounds of negotiation needed to develop a consensus decision, and the tendency for final agreements

to use ambiguous language on contentious points, making future interpretation of treaties more difficult.

At the heart of the WTO, and most relevant to the issue of trade wars, is its Dispute Resolution Body (DRB). When a member nation feels that it has a cause of action against another member, it may request that a Dispute Settlement Panel (DSP) be established. Panels are required to complete their hearings and present their report within six months, absent extenuating circumstances. Panel reports may be appealed by the countries involved.

The WTO has faced controversy from the very beginning of its existence. It took four months to seat the first director-general, Reanto Ruggiero, primarily because of U.S. fears that an Italian would favor Europe. It took many more months to install the necessary bureaucracy and to implement more than 24,000 pages of agreements that form the framework of the WTO.

In the late 1990s, the WTO became a focus of protests by the antiglobalization movement, which exploded into the public consciousness during the WTO meetings in Seattle, Washington, in 1999. More recently, trade talks collapsed in Cancún, Mexico, in 2003, due to the refusal of some developing countries, led by India, China, and Brazil, to accept proposed decisions unless the European Union and the United States eliminated their agricultural subsidies.

WORLD TRADE BLOCS

Countries have attempted to forge trade links with neighboring countries and to deny access to competing nations. These free-trade zones and trade blocs are one of the major issues currently facing the world trading system. Debate exists as to whether they will lead to increased protectionism, or to the promotion of trade liberalization. The following are some of the major trade blocs in existence.

North American Free Trade Agreement (NAFTA)

The North American Free Trade Agreement (NAFTA) links the United States, Canada, and Mexico in a free-trade zone. The agreement covers environment and labor issues, as well as trade and investment. U.S. unions and environmental groups have argued that these safeguards are too weak.

The United States hopes to expand the agreement to the rest of Latin America by forming the Free Trade Area of the Americas (FTAA) by 2005. However, key countries such as Brazil are skeptical of its benefits. The United States has signed separate free-trade agreements with Chile and with some Central American countries.

The European Union (EU)

The European Union (EU) is now the most powerful trading bloc in the world, with a gross domestic product (GDP) nearly as large as that of the United States. The EU has found it difficult to shed its protectionist past in the area of agricultural imports, but it plans to implement a major reform of its Common Agricultural Policy in January 2005. The creation of the euro as a common currency for EU members has led to even closer economic links for many of the countries in the European Union.

The Cairns Group

Named after the Australian town where the first meeting took place, the Cairns group is made up of agricultural exporting nations. It was formed in 1986 for the purpose of lobbying in world trade talks to free up trade in agricultural products. As highly efficient agricultural producers, the countries in the Cairns group are interested in ensuring that their products are not excluded from markets in Europe and Asia. In addition to Australia, leading member nations of the group include Canada, Brazil, and Argentina.

The Asia-Pacific Economic Cooperation Forum (APEC)

The Asia-Pacific Economic Cooperative Forum (APEC) is a loose confederation of countries bordering the Pacific Ocean that have agreed to facilitate free trade. The 21 members, which account for 45% of the world's trade, include China, Russia, the United States, Japan, Australia, and a number of other smaller countries in Asia and the Pacific region.

See also Bretton Woods Conference; Development, Third-World; Free Trade; General Agreement on Tariffs and Trade (GATT); North American Free Trade Agreement (NAFTA); Trade Liberalization

TRADING WITH THE ENEMY ACT, 1917
See EXECUTIVE ORDERS

TRANSNATIONAL THREATS

Threats to national security that do not originate in nor are confined to a single country. A 2000 study by the RAND Corporation identified four particularly serious transnational threats to U.S. security: terrorism, organized international crime, the spread of radical Islamic politics, and the proliferation of weapons of mass destruction (WMD).

The emergence of transnational threats is a consequence of rapid advances in transportation and telecommunications during the late 20th century. Jet airliners have reduced dramatically the time and effort needed to travel over great distances. Cellular telephones, e-mail, and the Internet have made it much easier for large groups of individuals to communicate across long distances. The ease of travel and communication in the modern world facilitates the ability of criminals and terrorists to operate on a global basis.

Terrorism offers a good example of how modern technological advances have turned a once-local problem into one of international dimensions. Politically motivated violence was not unknown prior to the late 20th century, but it typically took the form of assassinations or attacks on local targets. The groups involved—such as the Serbian Black Hand organization—were usually confined to a single country or geographical area and operated independently of one another. Although they posed a problem for local authorities, such groups rarely spread far from their source or joined forces with other terrorist organizations.

In more recent times, however, terrorist groups from different nations and regions have become much more interconnected. Throughout the 1970s and 1980s, the Palestinian Liberation Organization (PLO) coordinated the activities of nearly a dozen terrorist groups from across the Middle East and North Africa. Since the 1990s, the al-Qaeda international terrorist network has spawned cells that operate in dozens of countries and have carried out many terrorist attacks around the world. Al-Qaeda leaders communicate to their followers via e-mail and the Internet, and through smuggled audiotapes and videotapes. They also use computers to transfer funds from secure bank accounts to operatives worldwide. Before the advent of computers and digital technology, such coordination and global organization were difficult, if not impossible.

The 1991 collapse of the Soviet Union contributed significantly to the increasing number of transnational threats. The Soviet collapse created a host of newly independent nations from the former Soviet republics and led to the emergence of free, more democratic governments throughout Eastern Europe. However, it also stripped away the state-supported Soviet economic system that protected the businesses of these nations from outside competition. Freedom was accompanied by economic depression, as uncompetitive state-owned businesses either were shut down or privatized and dramatically reduced in size.

The post-Soviet economic crisis created an atmosphere in which organized crime flourished. The Russian mafia, virtually unknown in the West before the fall of the Soviet Union, quickly became a scourge of European and U.S. law-enforcement agencies. Since the late 1990s, the Russian mob has dealt heavily in crimes such as computer and financial fraud, human trafficking, and murder for hire on a global scale. The Russian mafia is also suspected of having ties with Middle Eastern terrorist groups such as al-Qaeda, which flourished in heavily Muslim former Soviet republics in the Caucasus and Central Asia after the Soviet collapse.

Economic uncertainty in the wake of the Soviet collapse also raised the possibility that unemployed scientists might seek to earn cash by selling chemical, biological, or nuclear secrets to terrorists or rogue states. With most state-funded research canceled or severely curtailed, scientists in many former Soviet republics were forced into poverty. Some sought to raise money by offering their expertise to groups or states that wished to acquire WMD. In many former republics, the materials used in the construction of nuclear weapons were poorly guarded and monitored. Parts of the stockpiles of nuclear materials in these nations remain unaccounted for.

In the United States, the National Coordinator for Security, Infrastructure Protection, and Counter-Terrorism is responsible for coordinating the nation's efforts to counter and respond to transnational threats. This official consults with various federal law-enforcement and security agencies to form policies with regard to computer security, protection of critical infrastructure assets, counterterrorism, continuity of government operations, international organized crime, and emergency preparedness against the use of WMD. The Department of Homeland Security also tackles many of these same issues.

The revolution in computer and communications technology shows little signs of slowing, which means that transnational threats are likely to grow in significance in the foreseeable future. Effectively combating these threats will require a high level of international cooperation, especially the sharing of information between countries that can help track terrorists and organized-crime groups. The same technology that made transnational threats possible will be integral to protecting against them.

See also Al-Qaeda; Asymmetric Warfare; Globalization and National Security; Nuclear Proliferation; Organized Crime; Soviet Union, Former (Russia), and National Security; Terrorism, Islamic; Terrorism, War on International

Further Reading

Mandel, Robert. *Deadly Transfers and the Global Playground: Transnational Security Threats in a Disorderly World.* New York: Praeger, 1999.
Williams, Phil, ed. *Russian Organized Crime: The New Threat (Transnational Organized Crime)*. London: Frank Cass, 1997.

TRANSPORTATION AND NATIONAL SECURITY
See BORDER AND TRANSPORTATION SECURITY

TRANSPORTATION COMMAND (TRANSCOM), U.S.
See DEPARTMENT OF DEFENSE, U.S. (DoD)

TRANSPORTATION SECURITY ADMINISTRATION

A U.S. agency, created following the September 11, 2001, terrorist attacks on the World Trade Center and the Pentagon, that is charged with developing policies to ensure the safety of U.S. air traffic and other forms of traffic. The mission of the Transportation Security Administration (TSA) is to protect the transportation systems of the United States, while ensuring freedom of movement for people and commerce. Airport security and preventing aircraft hijacking are important concerns of the TSA.

The public face of the Transportation Security Administration is seen in the form of uniformed screeners at airports as part of airport security. Screeners examine both passengers, through a rigorous screening process including X-rays, and luggage, through larger screening machines. Screeners and some of their administrative procedures, including the list of banned items (which has included items such as fingernail clippers and knitting needles), have been subject to criticism. Overall, Americans and other foreign travelers have accepted increased security measures, as expressed by the TSA, as part of the post-9/11 world.

The TSA is also concerned with threats—such as shoulder-fired missiles—at and around airports and the profiling or screening of passengers, sometimes using computers and information technologies. The policies and actions of the Transportation Security Administration have been and will continue to be subject to executive, legislative, and judicial scrutiny.

See also Homeland Security

TREASON

Attempting to overthrow the government to which one owes his or her allegiance or assisting that government's enemies. The history of treason is populated by numerous infamous names, including Benedict Arnold, Guy Fawkes, Julius and Ethel Rosenberg, and John Walker Lindh.

The history of the crime of treason is a long one. As early as 1350, the English Statute of Treason distinguished between two forms of treason—petty and high. Petty treason was the murder of one's lawful superior, including when a wife killed her husband or a servant killed his master. High treason, on the other hand, dealt with acts that were serious threats to the stability or continuity of the state. It included attempts to kill the king, the act of counterfeiting coins, or waging war against the state. In the 18th century, high treason was further defined as encompassing or imagining the death of the ruler, violating the ruler's companion or heir, levying war against the ruler, and adhering to the ruler's enemies. The punishment for high treason in England, up until 1998, was death.

In the United States, the crime of treason is spelled out in the Constitution. Article III of the Constitution defines treason as levying war against the United States or giving aid and comfort to its enemies. Possible penalties for treason under U.S. law include five or more years in prison, a fine of $10,000 or more, preclusion from holding any public office, and death.

There have been approximately 40 federal prosecutions for treason in the history of the United States and even fewer convictions. Several people were convicted of treason as a result of the Whiskey Rebellion of 1794; they were all pardoned by President George Washington. Perhaps the most noted trial for treason was that of Aaron Burr in 1807. The former vice president was charged with treason on the grounds that he was planning to set up a new nation between Mexico and the area west of the Appalachians. Burr was acquitted due to the lack of the required two witnesses.

The most controversial 20th-century case of treason may have been the case of the Rosenbergs. A husband and wife, Julius and Ethel Rosenberg were convicted in 1951 of conspiring to steal U.S. atomic secrets for the Soviet Union. Although a great deal of debate surrounded their trial and shocking execution, the charge was confirmed years later, at least concerning Julius, by declassified Soviet secret transmissions.

Treason laws are also found in the statues of states. Florida, for example, defines treason as levying war against the state, adhering to its enemies, or giving them aid and comfort. There have been only two convictions for treason at the state level in the United States. Thomas Dorr, leader of a rebellion in Rhode Island in 1842, was tried and convicted of treason against the state. The radical abolitionist John Brown was tried and convicted of treason in Virginia as a result of his raid on a government arsenal in Harpers Ferry, Virginia, in 1859.

The most recent cases of treason have been related to wars, including the U.S. war against Afghanistan in 2001. During Operation Enduring Freedom, while fighting for the Taliban, U.S. citizen John Walker Lindh was captured by U.S. forces and became the subject of a great media blitz. Brought to trial, but not on charges of treason, Lindh eventually pled guilty to lesser charges and is currently serving time in prison in California.

See also Lindh, John Walker

TREATIES

Formal agreements, embodied in a document and binding under international law, between two or more nations in reference to peace, alliance, commerce, territorial agreements, and the like. In the field of foreign affairs, the power of the president under the U.S. Constitution to negotiate and sign treaties is second only to his power as commander in chief. A treaty is negotiated by the president and/or his plenipotentiaries and requires approval by two-thirds of the U.S. Senate before the president may sign the treaty into law.

PRESIDENTIAL POWER

Article II, Section 2, of the U.S. Constitution provides the president with the authority to make treaties, with the consent of the Senate. It was by no means clear at the outset of the Constitutional Convention in Philadelphia in 1787, however, that the treaty power would come to be vested jointly in the president and the Senate. Under the Articles of Confederation, the power to make treaties had been vested in the legislature, and the Virginia Plan seemed to indicate that all powers vested in the Congress under the articles should inhere in the legislature under the new constitution.

Alexander Hamilton appears to have been the first person to suggest, in mid-June 1787, that the treaty power should be held jointly by the legislative and executive branches. As late as early August of that year, it seemed as though the Constitutional Convention was heading toward giving the Senate the power to make treaties.

Skeptics were concerned, however, that the new Senate would be pliant to the states and liable to consummate treaties that were not in the interest of the country as a whole. Various regions also feared being sold out. Southerners worried about the future of navigation rights to the Mississippi River, and New Englanders were concerned about the future of fishing rights to the waters off Newfoundland. James Madison took the position that the president, being the only truly national figure entrusted with guarding the interests of the country, should possess the full treaty power himself.

As with so many other important issues at the Philadelphia convention, the delegates sent the treaty issue to the Committee on Postponed Matters. The committee suggested the essential arrangement and language that would become part of Article II, giving the president the power to make treaties "with the Advice and Consent of the Senate," and specifying that no treaty could be approved without the assent of two-thirds of the senators.

The two-thirds supermajority, put forward as a mechanism to protect regions from having their interests surrendered by treaty, was the object of an amendment that would have required a simple majority vote to approve treaties. Other amendments sought to involve the House of Representatives in the treaty process and to apply the two-thirds supermajority only to treaties that sought to end a war.

Madison offered the lone motion seeking to change the president's role in the treaty process, urging that the Senate should be able to enact peace treaties on its own by a two-thirds vote. Madison believed that a self-interested president might stand in the way of a peace treaty, to maintain his prominence in wartime. But the convention dispatched with his argument quickly when it became clear that Congress could end any war by refusing to fund it.

As the first president, George Washington had to define for posterity what exactly "advice and consent" meant with respect to the treaty process. While negotiating a treaty with the Creek Indians early in his presidency, Washington sought consultation with the Senate. Washington's request, contained in a letter that Vice President John Adams read to the Senate, caught the chamber off guard. When the Senate finally worked through its confusion and responded to the query, an angry Washington found the reply completely inadequate.

In truth, part of the blame was Washington's for having surprised the Senate and expecting a reply too quickly. Nonetheless, Washington thereafter took "advice and consent" to mean that the Senate would simply approve or deny a treaty that the president submitted to it once his administration had finished negotiating it. The precedent stuck, although presidents from time to time have unofficially solicited the opinions and concerns of individual senators on negotiations pertaining to particular treaties and even involved them in the negotiation process. The norm is for ambassadors and diplomats to negotiate a treaty at the president's direction, although he sometimes dispatches diplomatic special agents—chosen by the president alone, without Senate confirmation—on important diplomatic missions abroad.

ROLE OF THE SENATE

Before concluding debate on a treaty and voting on it, the Senate may amend a treaty's text, thus altering its content and necessitating additional diplomacy between the United States and the foreign nation or nations in question. Additionally, the Senate can affix to a treaty reservations that clarify the Senate's understanding of its terms and provisions.

An example of the attachment of reservations occurred with the Panama Canal treaties of 1977–1978, which obligated the United States to turn over the Panama Canal to Panama. President Jimmy Carter had to accept two crucial reservations that the Senate attached to the two treaties. The first reservation reaffirmed the right of the United States to use military force to keep the canal open; the second stated explicitly that the United States did not intend to interfere in Panama's sovereignty. The former reservation was necessary to secure the votes of hawkish senators, whereas the latter was calculated to calm the Panamanian people. Over the course of U.S. history, the Senate has made changes to approximately 15% of the treaties it ultimately approved.

Because a supermajority is required for Senate approval of treaties, the president must be mindful of the idiosyncratic demands of individual senators and also reach out to members of the other party. Senators, keenly aware of their chamber's reputation as the world's greatest deliberative body, tend to have robust egos, a national rather than local orientation, and considerable expertise on foreign policy matters. A certain senator thus may be determined that a treaty reflect his or her personal priorities on its subject matter. In the case of the Panama Canal treaties, President Carter's acquiescence to the reservation concerning the right of the United States to use military force was driven by the concerns of Senator Dennis De Concini, a democrat from Arizona.

Rarely in recent decades has the president's party had a decisive majority in the Senate, and frequently his party has been in the minority. This means that Senate approval of a treaty must be anchored in bipartisan support, which requires the president to bargain for the votes of individual senators, much as he often does on domestic legislation. For example, as World War II drew to a close, President Franklin D. Roosevelt went to great lengths to secure support from senators of both parties for the United Nations. President Woodrow Wilson's complete alienation of Republican senators during his quest to secure U.S. membership in the League of Nations a generation earlier loomed large in Roosevelt's thinking.

Presidents have stirred controversy by attempting to reinterpret the language of treaties in a manner contradictory to the Senate's prior understanding of their meaning. From the Senate's point of view, such a presidential action is little more than an attempt to go around the Senate by amending the treaty in question without the Senate's assent. In 1985, for example, the administration of President Ronald Reagan announced that it had decided to reinterpret the language of the 1972 Antiballistic Missile (ABM) Treaty with the Soviet Union to allow the United States to go forward with research and development on President Reagan's Strategic Defense Initiative (SDI). However, the interpretation of the Senate at the time of the ABM treaty's ratification, and of the three subsequent administrations, was that the treaty forbade development of a space-based antimissile system.

After a protracted struggle with the Senate over the meaning of some of the ABM treaty's crucial terms, the Reagan administration finally tailored its SDI research to conform to the original interpretation of the treaty's language. President George W. Bush finally withdrew the United States from the ABM treaty in 2002, after Russian Premier Vladimir Putin seemed to accept Bush's argument that a space-based antimissile system would not represent a danger to Russia.

The Constitution is silent on the subject of how a treaty may be terminated, but this issue was resolved in the case of *Goldwater v. Carter* (1979). In 1978, President Jimmy Carter moved to establish full diplomatic relations with the People's Republic of China, a policy change that required him to sever the 1954 Mutual Defense Treaty between the United States and the Republic of China (Taiwan). Senator Barry Goldwater of Arizona contended that the Senate had to approve the termination of treaties, and he filed suit in federal court. Ultimately, the Supreme Court let stand a lower federal court decision against Senator Goldwater, thereby setting the precedent that the president can unilaterally abrogate a treaty.

EXECUTIVE AGREEMENTS

By custom and practice, presidents have come to possess the universally acknowledged power to accomplish certain diplomatic objectives through the use of executive agreements rather than treaties. An executive agreement amounts to a handshake agreement between the president and a foreign leader, committing each of them to take specified reciprocal actions. The president's authority to make executive agreements emanates from his powers as commander in chief and chief diplomat, the vesting of executive power in the presidency, existing laws and treaties, and Supreme Court decisions. In *U.S. v. Curtiss-Wright Export Corporation* (1936), the Court memorably referred to the president as the nation's "sole organ" in the routine conduct of foreign policy.

Importantly, executive agreements do not require Senate approval. Because the Constitution does not mention executive agreements, there is no formal demarcation between subject matter that should be handled by treaty and that which should be handled by executive agreement. The decision is up to the president, who is expected to be mindful of the Senate's insistence that core foreign-policy concerns require its imprimatur, and also of the fact that a treaty carries greater legitimacy in domestic and international opinion than an executive agreement.

President Carter's decision to handle the return of the Panama Canal via two treaties was driven by both the subject matter's direct relationship to U.S. national security and also Carter's need to share political responsibility with the Senate for such a controversial policy adjustment. Many executive agreements require subsequent legislation or appropriations to carry them out, and this fact may caution presidents further against attempting to accomplish through executive agreements what would more properly be done through treaties.

Some of the most significant diplomatic actions in U.S. history have been carried out by executive agreement rather than treaty. During the period of the modern presidency, Franklin D. Roosevelt's 1940 exchange of 50 U.S. destroyers for 99-year leases on British bases in the Western Hemisphere stands out as an executive agreement of exceptional importance.

Executive agreements have steadily become much more common than treaties over the past century and a half. By the late 1800s, presidents were concluding more executive agreements than treaties. This imbalance grew in the early decades of the 20th century and skyrocketed during the era of the modern presidency. Between 1939 and 1989, more than 11,500 executive agreements were concluded, compared with just over 700 treaties. However, this ratio of executive agreements to treaties has declined slightly during the presidencies of Bill Clinton and George W. Bush, due mainly to the large number of trade treaties engineered by the former and the decline in foreign-policy multilateralism of the latter. It is too soon, though, to conclude that the larger historical trend has changed fundamentally.

As executive agreements came to be the preferred diplomatic instrument of modern presidents, the potential for misusing them to commit the power of the United States became a real possibility. By the 1970s, the Senate often spent time ratifying treaties dealing with such secondary concerns as international archaeological preservation, aviation, and radio regulation, while presidents concluded secret executive agreements pledging the United Sates to the sharing of intelligence and the use of military force. In the Case-Zablocki Act of 1972, Congress required the president to notify the Senate Foreign Relations Committee and the House Foreign Affairs Committee of all executive agreements within 60 days. In 1977, Congress reiterated its will on this matter, passing legislation requiring the president to inform Congress of any written or oral agreement that could be construed as a formal commitment by the United States.

The greater post-Vietnam scrutiny of executive agreements has not been matched by a significantly greater hesitancy to ratify treaties. Between 1953 and 1989, fewer than 6% of treaties submitted by the president to the Senate were not ratified. Interestingly, when Senate approval is in serious doubt, a president is more likely to withdraw a treaty from consideration at the last moment than let it go down to defeat. For instance, during the same time period, 1953–89, presidents withdrew 17 treaties from consideration by the Senate, whereas the Senate flatly rejected only 2.

Some scholars contend that the required two-thirds majority for Senate approval of treaties is unrealistically high and that it drives presidents to circumvent the Senate by conducting as much of their foreign policy as possible through executive agreements. Experts who take this view argue that a simple majority, which is the metric required in many other countries for approval of treaties, would be much more realistic in an age in which divided party control of government is the norm. Other authorities, citing the Case-Zablocki Act and Congress's general post-Vietnam determination to carefully scrutinize the president's handling of all aspects of foreign policy, believe that the two-thirds threshold should stand. Given the difficulty of amending the Constitution, the prospect of changing the treaty process seems improbable. What is certain in the age of U.S. hegemony, however, is that U.S. presidents will continue to face intricate questions about whether and how to make treaties and secure the support of the Senate for them.

—*Douglas M. Brattebo*

Further Reading

Milkis, Sidney M., and Michael Nelson. *The American Presidency: Origins and Development, 1776–2002.* Washington, DC: CQ Press, 2003.
Pfiffner, James P. *The Modern Presidency.* Belmont, CA: Thomson Wadsworth, 2005.
Pika, Joseph A., and John Anthony Maltese. *The Politics of the Presidency.* Washington, DC: CQ Press, 2004.

TRIAD

A three-sided military-force structure consisting of land-launched nuclear missiles, nuclear missile submarines, and strategic aircraft with nuclear bombs and missiles. The triad was a central element in the U.S. military strategy during the Cold War. The theory underlying the triad was that by having its nuclear assets spread across various weapons platforms, the force was more likely to survive an attack by the Soviet Union and be able to respond to a first strike successfully.

Following the end of World War II, the United States and the Soviet Union entered into the Cold War, a period of increased political, economic, and military tensions. Both sides engaged in a military rivalry, in which initially, the United States sought to balance its nuclear supremacy against the conventional superiority of Soviet troop strength. Later, the Soviet Union acquired nuclear technology—atomic and then thermonuclear weapons. An arms race ensued, and both sides eventually possessed extensive arsenals of nuclear missiles, bombs, and rockets.

The development of political and military strategy in that era included each nation's concern with surviving a first strike by the other. In order to ensure that sufficient nuclear forces survived to conduct a second strike, both the United States and, to a lesser degree, the Soviet Union spread their resources across various weapons platforms. These platforms included rocket-launched nuclear missiles, submarine-launched nuclear missiles, and strategic aircraft with nuclear bombs or nuclear missiles.

For example, the land component of the triad included intercontinental ballistic missiles ranging from the Atlas to Titan to Minuteman, and later, the Peacemaker missile; all were multistage rockets capable of carrying one or more nuclear weapons and guided by highly developed inertial guidance systems. With a range of 8,000 km, these missiles posed a formidable threat to an enemy. The sea component of the triad included older nuclear submarines, as well as more modern Trident submarines carrying sea-launched missiles such as Poseidon C-3s and Trident C-4s. The air component of the triad included bombers such as the old, but still flying, B-52s and newer B-1B bombers, equipped with eight or more nuclear bombs.

The triad still exists as a component of U.S. military strategy, but with reduced nuclear arsenals and inventories. Recent decisions to develop the so-called Star Wars technology, and later a National Missile Defense, will undoubtedly affect the continued reliance on the Triad.

See also Missiles

TRIP WIRE

National Security Strategy (NSS) concept that is analogous to the actions of a land mine. A wire can extend from a land mine and serve as the means to detonate or trigger the explosive in the mine. For instance, in Vietnam, soldiers would employ Claymore land mines along guerrilla trails. If an enemy soldier went down the trail, not paying too much attention, he could trip the wire and cause the mine to go off, killing himself and other members of his unit. In national-security strategy, different things can serve as a trip wire in some form of military action.

During the Cold War, for example, various outposts were considered trip wires for the use of force. In Berlin, Germany, the U.S. stationed an army brigade. Its primary purpose was to serve as a trip wire, setting off war in Germany if the Soviet Union took any sort of action. Likewise, the deployment of the Second Infantry Division to the northern part of South Korea continues to serve as a trip wire. If North Korea crosses the demilitarized zone and engages the Second Division in combat, that action will cause the deployment and employment of additional U.S. and allied military units to the Korean peninsula.

Another trip wire has been the Distant Early Warning (DEW) Line, a deployed early-warning system that tracks missiles or aircraft entering U.S. and Canadian airspace. If any missiles cross that DEW trip wire, a response would occur, including launching U.S. missiles.

Even in the post–Cold War world, the concept of a trip wire is still employed. During the conflicts in Bosnia and Kosovo, the establishment of safe zones in the country served as a trip wire for military action by the North Atlantic Treaty Organization (NATO). When Bosnian forces entered those safe zones, NATO launched air strikes against them. It is likely the tripwire concept will continue to be employed at different levels—strategic, operational, and tactical—in the future and in future conflicts.

See also Distant Early Warning (DEW) Line

TRUMAN DOCTRINE

Cold War position articulated by U.S. President Harry Truman pledging support to countries fighting communism to contain communist expansion. In 1944, British Prime Minister Winston Churchill and Soviet leader Joseph Stalin made a so-called percentages agreement, in which they traded British and Soviet influences in the Balkan and Mediterranean countries. This agreement essentially resulted in the recognition of Romania as part of the Eastern bloc and Greece as part of the West. The British thus retained their traditional influence in Greece, considered the cradle of Western civilization. The British foreign minister had declared this influence crucial to the defense of British mandates in the Middle East and the protection of the British Empire. As a result, the British participated in the Greek civil war, maintaining an active presence until forced to withdraw.

The internal war in Greece had been raging periodically since 1941 among monarchist, republican, and communist factions. The first two rounds of fighting saw little intervention from third parties. In the third round of the civil war, however, the British fought with the republicans against the communists, who were both fighting the monarchists. As the war progressed, the communist-backed Greek Democratic Army (GDA) gained much popular support, control of much of the country, and the wherewithal to proclaim a rival government in 1947. The British, however, could do nothing to prevent the GDA's progress. Extensive domestic fiscal woes had forced them to relinquish their control in the region in late 1946, and they called upon the United States to take their place.

Up to that point, the United States had expressed little interest in the Greek conflict, providing minimal amounts of aid. However, new fears of communist expansion and Cold War politics caused the United States to reassess its position. Notably, the Soviets had sent a letter to nearby Turkey in August 1946, in which they offered to share control and defense of the Turkish Straits. This indirect threat to Turkey's security would have threatened U.S. strategic and economic interests.

Furthermore, the *domino theory,* supported by Undersecretary of State Dean Acheson suggested that a communist takeover in Greece could contaminate neighboring countries in the Middle East and North Africa. It was thus feared that a communist Greece and other Soviet satellites in the region could encircle Turkey and bring it into the Soviet camp. The United States recognized the vital security concerns in the region and felt a need to act decisively.

On March 12, 1947, President Harry S. Truman gave the speech that elucidated a policy that became known as the Truman Doctrine. In his speech, Truman announced that it was the policy of the United States to support free peoples who are resisting attempted subjugation by armed minorities or by outside pressures. The Soviet Union was not mentioned explicitly, but the speech was clearly directed at it.

Truman's speech painted a black-and-white world that pitted democratic freedom against oppressive totalitarianism. The potential conflict was described in ideological language rather than security terminology. The rhetoric Truman used had multiple purposes: to convince a fiscally conservative Republican Congress to support the proposed aid package; to arouse U.S. popular support for cold warfare; and to express a clear doctrine of containment of communism.

Truman called directly for aid for Greece and Turkey—seen as actively battling communist pressures, internally and externally—in the form of food, money, and military support. The majority of hundreds of millions of dollars in aid, in both cases, went to military support. The United States helped modernize the Turkish army, navy, and air force. It took firm control in Greece and advocated a no-compromise solution to the war, supporting the government's call for unconditional surrender. The U.S. involvement in Greece ultimately prolonged and changed the course of the war. It did, however, help to contain the conflict to Greece, so that it did not spread throughout the region.

The United States helped the embattled Greek government roll back the communist insurgency that was supposedly taking direction from Moscow. The movement, however, was not Soviet supported. Ironically, Stalin continued to abide by his agreement with Churchill and actually succeeded in stemming communist Yugoslavia's aid to the Greek rebels. The Soviet Union did not provide a significant amount of aid until after the Truman Doctrine was issued, and then for only six months. Regarding the doctrine as mere propaganda, Stalin did not react strongly to it.

The verdicts on the purposes of the Truman Doctrine are varied. With some justification, it has been described as aggressive containment of a belligerent enemy (the Soviet Union, after all, had installed numerous puppet governments in neighboring Eastern European countries). It also has been seen as justification for hegemonic direct intervention in the politics of other nations (when the United States intervened, the government required State Department approval to conduct its foreign policy and make important decisions).

The Truman Doctrine has also been regarded as an attempt to reestablish a balance of power in Europe and ensure Western European security. Often, it is portrayed as protection of genuine national-security interests. A communist success might, over time, have leaned toward Moscow for support, and a Stalinist-style regime would have threatened U.S. trade and security throughout the eastern Mediterranean region.

The Truman Doctrine—the security-based complement to the Marshall Plan in democratic Western Europe—had far-reaching impacts. It served as justification for Cold War warfare in any region of the world. Moreover, it justified a new U.S. tradition of intervention (outside the Western Hemisphere) when the nation felt that its interests were at stake, ultimately providing the basis for intervention in Korea. The doctrine also changed the face of governance in Greece, turning back the tide of communist successes. The Truman Doctrine also provided an ideological base for the North Atlantic Treaty Organization (NATO) and helped promote the admission of Greece and Turkey into that alliance.

See also Communism and National Security; Doctrine; Marshall Plan; Truman, Harry S., and National Policy

TRUMAN, HARRY S., AND NATIONAL POLICY

Thirty-third president of the United States (1945–1953), who faced the initial challenges of the emerging Cold War between the United States and the Soviet Union. During his administration, President Harry S. Truman (1884–1972) strove to strengthen war-torn Europe, bolster the United States as the defender of the noncommunist world, contain communism, halt the spread of Soviet influence in Europe and Asia, and maintain a superior nuclear arsenal. The unifying theme of Truman's foreign and national security policies was the conviction that the free world must be protected from the Soviet Union and its goal of global domination.

SHAPING THE POSTWAR WORLD

Shortly after the death of President Franklin D. Roosevelt in April 1945, Vice President Truman was sworn in as president, a month before the end of World War II in Europe. Having served only 82 days as vice president, Truman took office with negligible experience in foreign affairs. He had not been privy to any of the policy-making relating to the conduct of the war, and he had been excluded from most foreign-policy meetings. Realizing the extent of his handicap, Truman relied on his advisers, particularly the secretary of state, James F. Byrnes; ambassador to the Soviet Union, Averell Harriman; and Roosevelt's close assistant, Harry Hopkins.

At the Potsdam Conference in Germany in July 1945, with the war in the Pacific still raging, Truman met with Allied leaders Winston Churchill of Great Britain and Joseph Stalin of the Soviet Union. At the conference, the three Allied leaders agreed on the future of a dismantled, disarmed Germany. However, they came into conflict when the issue turned to carving out the lands each would occupy after the war— regions that soon would become their nations' spheres of influence. Truman was adamant that the United States would occupy Japan without Soviet interference, and the Soviets made it clear that they wanted dominion over Eastern Europe.

While Truman was at Potsdam, the United States tested the world's first atomic bomb in New Mexico, in preparation for using two bombs to attack Japan during the last days of the war. The success of the atomic bomb test inspired Truman to envision the

United States as the future guardian of all nuclear arms. However, his faith in U.S. supremacy in nuclear weaponry fell apart when the Soviet Union tested its own atomic bomb in 1949. This event persuaded Truman that the United States must maintain nuclear superiority, a conviction that contributed to the development of the nuclear arms race.

THE TRUMAN DOCTRINE AND MARSHALL PLAN

The cornerstone of Truman's national-security policy was set in place on March 12, 1947, in a speech that outlined the so-called Truman Doctrine. The event inspiring the speech was a civil war in Greece, in which procommunist rebels sought to overtake the repressive right-wing Greek government. With little money and an inadequate military, the Greek government was sure to be overthrown.

Truman and his advisers became convinced that if Greece fell to the rebels, a Soviet-backed communist government would take over. The president thus beseeched Congress for $400 million in economic and military aid for Greece, framing the civil war as a global battle between free (noncommunist) nations and totalitarian (communist) nations. He maintained that if Greece fell to communist rule, then Turkey and the Middle East were in danger, and possibly Europe and the rest of the free world, as well.

In 1947, Secretary of State George C. Marshall pushed for an economic recovery and reconstruction plan for Europe. Known as the Marshall Plan, the project was supported by Truman's belief that Europe must be strengthened to prevent communism and Soviet aggression from gaining a foothold. The Soviet Union insisted that the Marshall Plan was a ruse for the U.S. to control Europe. The Soviets then planned their countermoves accordingly.

Crisis in Berlin

In June 1948, the Soviet Union formed a blockade encircling the city of Berlin, preventing food and other supplies from entering West Berlin. The United States and Great Britain responded by organizing the Berlin airlift, shipping supplies via military aircraft to West Berlin in 1948–1949. In April 1949, the U.S. Senate approved U.S. membership in the North Atlantic Treaty Organization (NATO), in hopes that a strong European military alliance would bolster war-weakened

Europe and prevent the likelihood of Soviet incursions. Truman also wanted to encourage Western Europe to be strongly pro-U.S. in the Cold War.

The successful operation of the Berlin Airlift caused the Soviets to lift the blockade in May 1949. The outcome of the Berlin crisis reinforced the balance of power in Europe, with the Soviet Union in control of Eastern Europe and East Germany, and the United States and its allies protecting Western Europe from Soviet aggression.

Communist China

When Chinese communist revolutionary Mao Zedong ousted nationalist leader Chiang Kai-shek's forces in 1949 and formed the People's Republic of China, Truman refused to recognize the new nation, thus opening the door for the communist Chinese to consider aligning themselves with the Soviet Union. The situation destabilized Asia.

The Soviet Union's entry into the league of nuclear nations and the rise of communism in China, both occurring in 1949, caused Truman in early 1950 to order the National Security Council (NSC) to overhaul the nation's national security policy. With the strong support of Secretary of State Dean Acheson, the new policy document, entitled NSC-68, urged an immediate, dramatic increase in all U.S. military spending, including for nuclear arms. NSC-68 held that the United States must prepare itself to counter the steps the Soviet Union was taking to dominate the world, including the United States. In addition to building a superior military and nuclear arsenal, NSC-68's recommendations called for a campaign to galvanize Americans to support an expansion of the military.

Korea

Several months later, on June 25, 1950, Kim Il Sung, the leader of the Democratic People's Republic of Korea (North Korea), attacked the Republic of Korea (South Korea). Truman responded by immediately engaging U.S. air and naval forces. With the support of the U.S. Congress and the United Nations, U.S. ground troops landed in South Korea.

Truman was adamant that the United States must intervene in Korea to prevent the fall of South Korea to the communist North. Believing that the Soviets intended to control a united communist Korea, Truman was determined that the United States must prevent the Soviets from gaining more territory in Asia. If they succeeded, Truman believed, the Middle East would be the next region to succumb to communism, perhaps followed by Europe. The president agreed with General Douglas MacArthur and his advisers that U.S. troops must not only save South Korea but must also oust the communists from North Korea.

As U.S. forces pressed into North Korea toward the Chinese border, Mao Zedong retaliated by ordering Chinese troops to assist the North Koreans in the fall of 1950. The communists pushed U.S. forces south of the 38th parallel into South Korea. The Korean War arrived at a point of stalemate, with neither side gaining an advantage. Negotiations began, but there was little progress on the Korean front during the rest of Truman's administration.

Truman concluded his presidency in 1952 having achieved an expansion of the U.S. military and nuclear arsenal, which sharply polarized the United States and the Soviet Union and accelerated the arms race. In 1952, as the next election grew closer, President Truman announced he would not seek another term

See also Arms Race; Atomic Bomb; Berlin Airlift; Korean War; Korean War, Entry Into (1950); Marshall Plan; National Security Act, 1947; North Atlantic Treaty Organization (NATO); NSC-68 (National Security Report); Potsdam Conference (1945); Truman Doctrine

Further Reading

Hogan, Michael J. *A Cross of Iron: Harry S. Truman and the Origins of the National Security State.* New York: Cambridge University Press, 1998.

Offner, Arnold A. *Another Such Victory: President Truman and the Cold War, 1945–1953.* Stanford, CA: Stanford University Press, 2002.

TWO-THEATER WAR

Also known as two-major-theater war (2MTW), or major regional conflicts (MRCs), a defense-planning construct used to estimate the size and composition of U.S. forces necessary for optimal military readiness at any given time. The two-theater-war concept holds that the United States should be capable of simultaneously fighting two major conflicts in different parts of the world.

During the administrations of Presidents John F. Kennedy and Lyndon B. Johnson, the Defense Department used a two-and-one-half strategy—the ability to fight two major wars and one limited conflict simultaneously. In the 1960s, this paradigm referred to the ability to confront a Soviet attack in Europe, a Chinese attack somewhere in Asia, and a minor conflict in Cuba.

Fiscal constraints and the war in Vietnam led to a one-and-one-half concept during the 1970s. During the late 1970s and 1980s, President Jimmy Carter used the measure of multitheater war, with the Soviet Union in Europe and the Persian Gulf, and the administration of President Ronald Reagan sized U.S. forces on the basis of an all-out global war with the Soviet Union and its Warsaw Pact allies (an idea known as the Illustrative Planning Scenario). The administration of President George H. W. Bush used a base-force concept built on general capabilities rather than planning based on specific scenarios.

The two-theater-war force-planning mechanism was adopted in 1993 by the administration of President Bill Clinton, and it referred to the readiness to concurrently fight a large, offensive ground war in the Persian Gulf (most likely against Iraq) and another war on the Korean peninsula (against North Korea).

Critics of the two-major-theater-war criterion cite the problem of planning as if one were "fighting the last war." They stress the changing nature of threats to U.S. national security—such as terrorism, the proliferation of weapons of mass destruction among smaller states, and an emerging China. As a result, emphasis is now usually placed on lighter, more flexible, and more mobile rapid-response forces.

The administration of President George W. Bush laid out a slightly modified two-theater-war concept in the 2001 Quadrennial Defense Review. The requirement for the United States to be able to simultaneously fight a war in two critical areas was maintained, and U.S. forces were expected to be able to win decisively in one of those conflicts. A decisive victory is defined as including the potential for territorial occupation and regime change if necessary. Defense of the homeland, forward deterrence in four critical regions of the world (Europe, Northeast Asia, the East Asian littoral, and the Middle East and Southwest Asia), and planning for smaller-scale contingency operations forms part of the new force-sizing construct articulated in the 2001 Quadrennial Defense Review.

See also Quadrennial Defense Review; War Planning

Further Reading

Metz, Steven, ed. *Revising the Two MTW Force Shaping Paradigm.* Carlisle, PA: Strategic Studies Institute, 2001.

TYRANNY

A form of dictatorial, one-person government characterized by injustice and lack of respect for the rights of individual citizens. Tyranny frequently arises out of dissension as another social system is either disintegrating or experiencing internal strife. The potential tyrant may be part of the existing aristocracy and may endeavor to seize control during a power struggle with his or her peers. A tyrant may also be a popular leader or demagogue who already has some support from the masses. In either case, the tyrant helps to overthrow the existing regime and replace it with one-person rule. Tyrants are not subject to checks and balances from other parts of the government and may ignore or reject a previously existing constitution. The tyrant's rule is absolute.

The tyrannical ruler recognizes that he needs a base of support and protection from enemies. He will attempt to please a segment of the population large enough to ensure that his rule will continue unchecked. To gain such support, he maintains a group of loyal and powerful supporters, whom he rewards richly but fundamentally distrusts and keeps at an appropriate distance. As the supporters are entrusted with maintaining his rule, the tyrant will choose to surround himself with powerful, wealthy nobles or military forces. His rule is not based upon a social contract or the consent of the governed; people obey because of fear of punishment.

The tyrant's rule may enjoy broad-based support despite the autocratic nature of his regime, but more often he is despotic and controls the population through propaganda, repression, or fear. He controls political speech (by preventing the formation of a popular representative body) and the media. The citizens' basic civic rights are nonexistent; their human rights are subject to abuse if they are perceived to be enemies of the regime. The tyrannical leader frequently employs a network with secret police, spies, or informers that can be used to find, intimidate, or harm would-be resisters. Moreover, the population living under tyranny is frequently impoverished. Poverty (often induced through taxation) is both a form of control and a means to pay for wars or the tyrant's own private goods.

The tyrant is at all times conscious of the fragility of his regime and uses specific tactics to keep it afloat. He frequently participates in or instigates wars, which simultaneously distract the citizens from domestic problems and keep them preoccupied and prevented from organizing against the ruler. War also ensures that the environment remains unstable and the people continue to feel a need for a leader. To these ends, tyrants may actively cultivate fear of foreign powers and fear of anarchy, leading the populace to the conclusion that tyrannical rule is better than anarchy or domination. Tyrannical rule relies on both domestic and international insecurity and the fear it creates.

U

UNABOMBER (THEODORE J. KACZYNSKI, 1942–)

Person responsible for the worst serial bombing case in U.S. history. On January 29, 1998, Theodore J. Kaczynski, then 55, pled guilty to 13 federal charges involving the bombing deaths of three people and injury of two others. Kaczynski's plea—made two years to the day after a tip by his brother led the Federal Bureau of Investigation (FBI) to Kaczynski's remote Montana cabin—ended the 18-year search for the so-called Unabomber.

Ted Kaczynski, a Harvard-trained mathematician and former professor at the University of California, Berkeley, admitted responsibility for mailing and placing 16 bombs in a string of attacks motivated by his antitechnology beliefs. The attacks began on May 26, 1978, when a security officer at Northwestern University opened a small wooden box he had found in a parking lot. The box contained a bomb and the officer narrowly avoided injury.

Other victims of the Unabomber were not as fortunate. Sacramento computer-store owner Hugh Scrutton; timber lobbyist Gilbert Murray, who also lived in Sacramento; and Thomas Mosser, a New Jersey advertising executive, all died as a result of bombs sent by the Unabomber, Ted Kaczynski. A total of 29 people were injured in the bomber attacks. The identity of the bomber was a mystery for years.

In 1995, the Unabomber promised to suspend his attacks in exchange for the publication in several newspapers of his *Unabomber Manifesto*—a 35,000-word attack on technology. A man named David Kaczynski, who turned out to be the Unabomber's brother, contacted the FBI after noting similarities between the manifesto and letters he had received from his brilliant but reclusive brother. David hoped his actions would spare his brother from the death penalty. That turned out to be the case. In 1998, Ted Kaczynski—the Unabomber—received consecutive life sentences for the attacks and was fined $4.7 million to prohibit him from profiting from Unabomber movies or book deals.

See also Terrorism, U.S. (Domestic)

UNILATERALISM

Foreign-policy strategy in which a sovereign state chooses to pursue its international interests and goals strictly on its own and not in concert or consultation with other sovereign states, international organizations, or nongovernmental organizations (NGOs). Unilateralism is the easiest of foreign-policy options, as it requires no diplomacy, no need to build consensus, and no prerequisite of multilateral support. At the same time, however, unilateral actions often generate a backlash of international anger and accusations of illegitimacy.

The United States has been a major contributor to multilateral and bilateral efforts (for example, it was a charter member of the United Nations), yet the United States has a long history of unilateral engagement. Post–World War II examples of U.S. unilateralism abroad include the Bay of Pigs invasion (1961), the so-called Secret War in Laos (1960s), the Grenada intervention (1983), and the Panama intervention (1989). The United States' unilateralism is also reflected in its abandonment of the 1972 Antiballistic Missile Treaty, its choice not to ratify the Ottawa Landmine Treaty (1999), and its decision to oust the regime of Saddam Hussein in Iraq in 2003 despite widespread international opposition.

Supporters of American unilateralism insist that the United States has the legitimate authority to take whatever actions it sees fit in the defense of its own security. They also claim that, as the world's only current superpower, the United States is obligated to promote and protect democratic regimes throughout the world. Critics of U.S. unilateralism fear that, over the long term, the United States will stray from the rules of multilaterally defined international law, weaken the strength of international institutions, favor military action, and generally raise arguments that international rules place too heavy a constraint on the freedom of the United States to act alone to protect its interests.

In the wake of the terrorist attacks of September 11, 2001, the administration of President George W. Bush signaled a major foreign-policy shift in stating that the United States has the right to pursue unilateral actions against terrorism when acceptable multilateral alternatives cannot be found. Critics of the so-called Bush Doctrine maintain that the need to obtain international support for military ventures constitutes a critical check on the power of individual nations. The doctrine is indicative of the struggle between the need to maintain multilateral international institutions and the desire of nations to pursue their own interests.

See also Bay of Pigs; Bilateralism; Bush Doctrine; Bush, George W., and National Policy; Grenada Intervention; Iraq War of 2003; Multilateralism; Preemption; Preemptive War Doctrine

UNION OF SOVIET SOCIALIST REPUBLICS (USSR)

Also known as the Soviet Union; world's first communist regime and principal rival of the United States during the Cold War.

ORIGINS OF THE USSR

The USSR arose as a result of the collapse of the Russian empire, one of the longest-standing monarchies in Europe. The Romanov family had ruled Russia for centuries, but during the reign of Czar Nicholas II (1894–1917), Russia began to come apart. Economic and political troubles caused popular discontent with the czar's authoritarian rule. Although the 1906 creation of the Duma (parliament) was supposed to give the people a voice in government, real power still lay with the czar.

The outbreak of World War I in 1914 brought Russia and its allies Britain and France into conflict with Germany and Austria-Hungary. The war went badly for Russia, which suffered military defeats on the battlefield and hunger, shortages, and deep political troubles among the civilian population. The February Revolution of 1917 brought rioting in the streets and caused the shaken czar to lose control of the government. Nicholas dissolved the Duma and abdicated his throne, throwing the country into revolution.

With Nicholas gone, the Duma joined with the Petrograd Soviet (worker's council) to form a provisional government, but this was unable to provide real reform. Vladimir Lenin, leader of a radical socialist party known as the Bolsheviks, put forth a program that promised peace, food, land redistribution, and local government. As the populace grew increasingly restless for change, the Bolsheviks staged a coup, seizing power in the October Revolution of 1917. They proclaimed the founding of a new state—the Union of Soviet Socialist Republics—built on the foundations of the fallen Russian empire.

The Bolsheviks set about creating a communist state, abolishing the old imperial regime of classes and titles, prohibiting counterrevolutionary speech and action, and establishing state ownership of land. The workers were to be liberated and united in their common struggle, and land would be given to the poor. The bourgeois and the aristocracy who lived off the labor of others were to be eliminated. The Bolsheviks, however, were not securely in control. Turbulence continued as other groups, notably the less revolutionary Mensheviks, battled Lenin for control. In December 1917, Lenin dismissed the recently formed Constituent Assembly after a vote that did not favor the Bolsheviks, and he used the Cheka (secret police) to quash resistance to Bolshevik control. The country dissolved into a civil war that pitted the Bolshevik *Reds* against the *Whites*—social democrats, more moderate socialists, czarists, and others. The Bolsheviks, with better organization and more military support, eventually triumphed in 1920 and consolidated their control over the USSR.

From the time the Bolsheviks gained power, the Western world looked askance at the Soviet Union. The West was fearful that the communist revolution would spread from Russia to its own countries. Ideologically opposed to communism and fearful of domestic threats to their leadership, western powers including Great Britain, France, and the United States made consistent efforts to balance their power against that of the Soviet Union. On the whole, however, Soviet foreign policy was aimed at counterbalancing the West and protecting the USSR from invasion.

THE USSR BETWEEN THE WARS

Lenin, the charismatic leader of the Bolshevik movement, wasted no time in laying down the political and economic foundations of the USSR. In 1919, he helped establish the Communist International (Comintern), an organization dedicated to promoting future communist revolutions and whose policy was dictated by Moscow. Outlawing private ownership of land, Lenin forced farmers to work on large collective farms in which farmers pooled their resources and planted crops dictated by the government. He also created a centralized, planned economy that gave the state control over industry and the new collectivized farms. Lenin's policies proved to be a disaster; millions of Soviet citizens died during a famine in 1921–22 that is widely blamed on Lenin's collective-farming policies.

The Soviet Union under Lenin was governed by the Central Committee, a relatively small group of senior government officials. Lower-level officials received their orders from the committee, and both were subject to the shadow government of the Communist Party. Joseph Stalin, who became general secretary of the Central Committee in 1924, strongly influenced both it and the Communist Party. Stalin would use this appointment as a springboard to further his political career.

Lenin died in 1924 after a period of deteriorating health. Almost immediately, a battle over who would succeed Lenin flared up among Stalin, Leon Trotsky (a leading organizer of the February Revolution), and Nikolai Bukharin, a general favorite but a poor political infighter. Stalin, who was politically ruthless and brilliant at manipulation, emerged as the new leader. In the years that followed, his former rivals would be among millions of Soviets killed in Stalin's pursuit of absolute power.

Although communist rule was supposed to produce a classless society, the USSR was still marked by haves and have-nots. Stalin used these remaining class distinctions to stir up hostilities between wealthier citizens and the poorer peasants and workers. He then used the resulting social agitation to justify a campaign to purge "bourgeois" elements from Soviet society. In 1928, Stalin organized a series of show trials to eliminate political rivals by trying them on phony charges.

Despite adoption of the 1936 constitution that guaranteed civil rights and the equality of all Soviet people, concentration camps emerged in distant reaches of the country and the regime became increasingly totalitarian. From 1936 to 1938, Stalin instituted the Great Terror to rid the country of anti-Soviet elements. Millions of people were killed or sent to the camps, known as *gulags*. Many of the victims were generals and high-ranking party opponents, including Bukharin. The purge crippled many sectors of Soviet society and proved disastrous for the country's military leadership.

In his efforts to control the Soviet economy, however, Stalin failed to duplicate his mastery of political affairs. His Five-Year Plan, begun in April 1929, was intended to increase the growth of the industrial working class, spur the growth of heavy industry and the military, accelerate the collectivization of agriculture, and create a cultural revolution. The USSR industrialized rapidly in spite of the worldwide Great Depression of the 1930s, yet collectivization again proved a failure and resulted in a famine in 1933.

WORLD WAR II

Stalin was aware that external and internal enemies abounded, especially as Europe moved closer to war in the late 1930s. He also realized that the Soviet armed forces were not ready to face a rearmed Germany. He thus signed a nonaggression pact with German dictator Adolf Hitler in August of 1939. Under the agreement, the USSR agreed not to attack Germany if the Germans went to war with Great Britain and France. In return, when Germany invaded Poland the following month, it ceded the eastern portion of Poland to the USSR. Germany also agreed not to interfere with Soviet expansion in the Baltic states and Finland.

The Nazi–Soviet pact stunned the world, but both parties realized it was merely an alliance of convenience.

German Nazism and Soviet communism were ideological opposites, and each had vowed to destroy the other. Two years later, in June 1941, Hitler discarded the pact and invaded the Soviet Union. The Soviet army, purged of its most senior officers, was overwhelmed by the German invasion. Several million Soviet troops were killed or captured in the next six months. However, the German assault gradually ground to a halt due to the vastness of the Soviet Union and the brutally harsh Russian winter. German forces were stopped just 20 miles from Moscow; they would never get any closer.

The German invasion ended Soviet neutrality in World War II and thrust the Soviet Union into an uneasy grand alliance with the United States and Great Britain. Ideologically, the Western powers were just as far from the USSR as was Nazi Germany. However, Stalin and the Allies had no choice but to work together. Their survival depended upon defeating Hitler; differences between the Allies would have to be settled after the war.

By the end of 1942, German troops were again threatening Moscow and had pushed deep into the southern USSR. By winter, however, the renewed advances had stretched the German army to its limits. The Soviets staged a massive counteroffensive at Stalingrad from November 1942 to January 1943 that destroyed the entire German Sixth Army. The Battle of Stalingrad was a major turning point in the war. From that point on, the Soviet army gradually pushed the Germans back to their own borders. In April 1945 the Soviets launched the final assault on the German capital, Berlin, and on May 8 the Germans finally surrendered.

World War II was both a disaster and a tremendous opportunity for the Soviet Union. The country had suffered some 30 million deaths and millions more casualties, and the years-long fighting had destroyed much of the country's industry and agriculture. At the same time, the Soviet Union had captured all of Eastern Europe during the advance to Germany. Stalin established communist regimes in these nations, creating satellite governments that would take direction from Moscow and that would form a protective sphere of influence to protect the USSR from future invasions.

THE COLD WAR

Disagreements over political and economic doctrines, as well as practical issues such as the future of Germany and the development of the atomic bomb, estranged the

USSR from its World War II allies. The next 45 years would be marked by an intense political and military rivalry between the USSR and the West (particularly the U.S.) known as the Cold War. This period was marked by *proxy wars,* in which the main opponents fought each other through conflicts involving third-party nations. At times, neither nation was directly involved in the fighting. This kind of competition was particularly common during the 1960s and 1970s in Africa, where the United States and USSR frequently supported opposing sides in civil wars. At other times, one of the superpowers fought forces backed by the other, such as in the wars in Korea, Vietnam, and Afghanistan.

Stalin's death in 1953 marked a significant change in Soviet internal and external politics. The new Soviet leader, Nikita Khrushchev, was a devoted communist who began an active campaign of de-Stalinization in the USSR. In his address to the 20th Communist Party Congress—the first since Stalin assumed power—Khrushchev promised to overcome "the cult of the individual and its consequences." Many cases of imprisonment under Stalin's rule were investigated, and thousands of innocent persons were released from the gulags.

During the early years of his tenure as first secretary, Khrushchev's policy of decentralization led to high economic growth rates in the USSR. This growth, and Cold War military competition with the United States, also fueled the Soviet space program. In October 1957, the USSR launched Sputnik, the world's first artificial satellite. The achievement stunned the West and triggered a space race between the United States and the USSR. The political rivalry between the USSR and the West was sharpened in 1955 with the signing of the Warsaw Pact, a military alliance between the USSR and its Eastern European satellites.

These successes were offset by a number of foreign-policy and domestic problems that eventually toppled Khrushchev from power. The Cold War threatened to become hot several times in his tenure, especially during the 1962 Cuban Missile Crisis, when the world came close to nuclear war. Khrushchev was held accountable for the Chinese communists' decision to end their alliance with the USSR, even though relations between the two countries were poor when he took power. Added to these woes were a slowing economy in the early 1960s and highly unpopular state campaigns against religion and subversive writers.

Leonid Brezhnev replaced Khrushchev in 1964, reversed some of Khrushchev's more unpopular reforms, and encouraged recentralization and short-term economic development. As with the policies of previous Soviet leaders, the plan failed to improve the economy but succeeded in consolidating Communist Party control of the Soviet Union. Although the economy declined, the availability of consumer goods and leisure time increased, so it appeared as if the nation was prospering. The illusion of prosperity contributed to a complacent mood in the party leadership. Those previously in power stayed in power, and party leaders grew more rigid and out of touch by the day.

In the foreign-policy arena, Brezhnev embraced a policy of détente, and relations with the West improved. He helped alleviate the arms race by signing SALT I and SALT II arms-limitation agreements with the United States. However, he made a tremendous mistake with his decision to intervene militarily in Afghanistan to support the Marxist faction that had taken power in 1978. The 1979 Soviet invasion would prove as costly to the USSR as the Vietnam War was to the United States. Unable to defeat an elusive enemy in the rugged terrain of Afghanistan, Soviet troops remained mired in stalemate for a decade. The USSR's standing in the international system was substantially damaged by its involvement, and the economic and human costs of the war were enormous.

COLLAPSE OF THE USSR

Although few realized it at the time, the mid-1980s witnessed changes that soon would spell the end of the Soviet Union. Brezhnev's death in 1984, followed by the sudden death of his successor Yuri Andropov, brought Mikhail Gorbachev to power as general secretary in 1985. Gorbachev inherited a nation mired in a bloody war that was straining an already weakened Soviet economy. His response was a risky policy based on three principles: *perestroika* (reform), *glasnost* (openness), and *demokratizatsiia* (democratization), which he hoped would bring new life to the Soviet system. One sign of the new spirit of openness was the Soviet willingness to admit (if belatedly) that a nuclear reactor at Chernobyl exploded in 1985. Under previous Soviet regimes, such an incident would have been hidden from the press and might not have been discovered for decades.

Internationally, Gorbachev made a great deal of headway, meeting with President Ronald Reagan in 1985 to discuss a way to end the arms race. Disarmament programs were initiated under Gorbachev's leadership, and the two leaders agreed to eliminate land-based intermediate- and short-range weapons, efforts that culminated in the Intermediate Range Nuclear Treaty. When popular pressure forced the resignation of communist regimes in Eastern Europe, Gorbachev refused to intervene militarily to prop them up. This decision was cemented by the breakup of the Warsaw Pact in July 1991.

Although these moves were popular outside of the Soviet Union, they alarmed Communist Party hardliners. The Emergency Committee—an eight-man group representing the interests of the party, the Soviet military, and the secret police (KGB)—attempted a coup on August 18, 1991. The organizers seized Gorbachev, who was vacationing on the Black Sea. They also tried but failed to arrest Soviet President Boris Yeltsin, who made his way to the Russian White House and took control of the government. After a tense, weeklong standoff with Soviet troops encircling the building, the coup collapsed.

Gorbachev officially resigned as head of the Communist Party but remained in office as head of state, attempting to keep the Soviet Union together. His efforts, however, were unsuccessful. In December 1991, the Soviet republics of Russia, Ukraine, and Belorussia (which later became the nation Belarus) put forth the Minsk Declaration, which stated that the Soviet Union would be replaced by a Commonwealth of Independent States (CIS). Gorbachev resigned on December 25, and the Soviet Union was officially dissolved on the last day of that year.

The USSR was replaced by 15 successor states: the Russian Federation, Estonia, Latvia, Lithuania, Belarus, the Ukraine, Moldova, Azerbaijan, Armenia, Georgia, Kazakhstan, Uzbekistan, Turkmenistan, Tajikistan, and Kyrgyzstan. Although politically independent, they share membership in the CIS, which coordinates the powers of its member states in areas of trade, finance, lawmaking, and security. Russia, the largest and most populous of the countries that arose from the USSR, remains a world power due to its massive size, abundant resources, and large (if decaying) military.

The breakup of the USSR was accompanied by a brief period of cooperation between the United States and Russia. However, hopes for a closer friendship between the two nations have been frustrated over disagreement about the U.S. invasion of Iraq in 2003, the expansion of NATO into Eastern Europe, and an increasing turn back to authoritarianism under Russian

President Vladimir Putin. The fall of the Soviet Union removed a significant threat to U.S. national security but presented new challenges, as well.

See also Afghanistan, War in; Commonwealth of Independent States (CIS); Cold War; Communism; Eastern Bloc; Glasnost; Gorbachev, Mikhail (1931–); Iron Curtain; Khrushchev, Nikita Sergayevich (1894–1971); Korean War; North Atlantic Treaty Organization (NATO); Perestroika; Soviet Union, Former (Russia), and U.S. Policy; Sputnik; Stalin, Joseph (1878–1953); Strategic Arms Limitations Talks (SALT); Superpower; Vietnam War (1954–1975); World War I (1914–1918); World War II (1939–1945); Yalta Conference (1945); Yeltsin, Boris (1931–)

Further Reading

Hanson, Phillip. *The Rise and Fall of the Soviet Economy: An Economic History of the USSR, 1945–1991.* New York: Longman, 2003.

MacKenzie, David, and Michael W. Curran. *Russia and the USSR in the Twentieth Century.* Belmont, CA: Wadsworth, 2001.

Suny, Ronald G. *The Soviet Experiment: Russia, the USSR, and the Successor States.* New York: Oxford University Press, 1997.

SECRETS REVEALED

Purges and Terror

The brutal and totalitarian techniques perfected by Stalin were initially instituted under Lenin, who established the first concentration camps during his reign. Lenin approved the suspension of civil liberties for *bandits* (those rebelling against Bolshevik leadership), some of whom were shot on the spot without trial. He interned political opponents and dissidents who died by the tens of thousands. Lenin also authorized the judiciary to legalize and justify terror.

Stalin's crimes vary from Lenin's mainly in degree. Millions of people died during Lenin's leadership from purges as well as from famine, war, and disease. However, Stalin was directly responsible for orders that sent millions to death through execution or exile. From 1936 to 1938, the NKVD (People's Commissariat of Internal Affairs), under Stalin's direction, implemented the Great Purges. Stalin himself edited the lists of persons to be purged and arranged show trials for the accused. Branded as enemies of the people, the defendants were made into scapegoats, blamed for undermining the Soviet regime. Notoriously, some of those prosecuted were opposition leaders Zinoviev,

Kamenev, and Bukharin; much of the Red Army general staff; and regional party leadership.

The reasons given for the purges vary. Some cite Stalin's paranoia and perceptions of enemies. Others argue that the problem was systemic—in totalitarian systems, it is necessary to continually turn over the staff to prevent subordinates from becoming too powerful. Still others claim that the purges began as Stalin's attempt to eliminate political opponents but that the program eventually sought to eliminate potential opponents as well as actual ones. Whatever the reasons for them, the purges characterized the historical brutality and inhumanity of the Soviet political system.

UNITED NATIONS

Intergovernmental organization with worldwide membership established to promote international peace and security. The United Nations (UN) is a multilateral institution that helps to establish international norms of conduct and harmonious relations. It promotes national self-determination and mutual understanding and cooperation between countries.

Unlike other organizations and institutions, the United Nations is a forum in which large states and small states can connect on an equal footing. Large states gain recognition as important pillars of international peace and security and can shape policy. Small states that are interested in diplomacy but cannot afford to support embassies in every country, gain access to decision makers from other nations. Moreover, states have a forum in which to address universal issues, build coalitions, and instigate worldwide change.

HISTORY OF THE UNITED NATIONS

During World War II, the United States, Great Britain, the Soviet Union, and China began shaping an agreement for a postwar intergovernmental organization that would succeed the weak League of Nations. They created the major forms of the organization—its aims, structure, and framework—at the Dumbarton Oaks Conference in Washington, DC, in 1944. The new organization would help all nations resist another conflict that plunged the world into war by fostering economic, social, and diplomatic cooperation. Fifty nations completed the agreements forming the United Nations on June 26, 1945, concluding the United Nations Conference on International Organization in

San Francisco. The United Nations Charter was ratified on October 24 (now United Nations Day).

THE COLD WAR

Despite the spirit of cooperation that led to the formation of the United Nations, relations between the United States and the Soviet Union deteriorated quickly after World War II. For the next 45 years, the two powers would compete for global influence politically, militarily, and economically. During this period, known as the Cold War, the United Nations was often unable to function as an effective force for peace. The permanent members of the UN Security Council—China, France, Great Britain, the United States, and the Soviet Union—frequently vetoed actions within their spheres of influence. For example, the Vietnam War was left out of UN security discussions.

Nevertheless, the United Nations did take some significant actions and began defining its scope beyond the charter. It authorized the use of international force for the first time in the Korean War, calling for UN member states to assist South Korea in repelling the North Korean invasion. The mission, conducted largely under U.S. direction, was successful and South Korea remained independent. The UN mission in Afghanistan in the late 1980s accomplished what it set out to do: negotiating a withdrawal of Soviet troops. However, it did not end the fighting between local Afghan factions, nor did it help create lasting stability in Afghanistan.

The United Nations achieved a few notable successes toward the end of the Cold War. The principle of collective security was applied successfully for the first time when a UN force helped repulse Iraq's invasion of Kuwait in 1991, preserving Kuwait's sovereignty. The UN Transition Assistance Group (UNTAG) in Namibia supervised a cease-fire in that nation, promoted stability, and helped the country reach full independence.

POST–COLD WAR DEVELOPMENTS

Ironically, the United Nations has used its enforcement powers more since the end of the Cold War than it did during those years of international tension between superpowers. Since the 1990s, the United Nations has expanded the nature of its peacekeeping operations as well as its social and economic programs. The substantial commitments made to these efforts have produced mixed results.

In 1991–92, the UN Advance Mission in Cambodia (UNAMIC) and the UN Transitional Authority in Cambodia (UNTAC) helped bring peace to much of that country, supervised free and fair elections, and promoted civic participation and human rights. At the same time, it failed to realize a total cease-fire or create a reliable political infrastructure. From 1992 to 1995, the United Nations launched three major operations in Somalia to maintain a cease-fire between warring clans and deliver humanitarian aid. The country had been torn apart by civil war and the collapse of the central government, and conditions were worsened by drought. The UN, although engaged in a peacekeeping mission, became an active belligerent in the conflict. Humanitarian efforts were successful in delivering aid, but UN military forces were unable to impose a cease-fire or disarm the most powerful warlords.

Rwanda proved another problem. There had been a UN presence in Rwanda during the 1994 genocide, which killed around 800,000 Tutsis, but the United Nations refused to give its military commanders in Rwanda the authority to try to stop the killings. In fact, UN troop levels were actually decreased during this time. After the slaughter ceased, the United Nations engaged in some reconstruction work and humanitarian aid.

The Bosnian intervention from 1993 to 1995 was another ambiguous endeavor. The United Nations was reluctant to intervene in a civil war set off by Bosnia's decision to seek independence from Yugoslavia. Despite reports of atrocities and ethnic cleansing of Bosnian Muslims at the hands of Bosnian Serbs, the United Nations took no action for years. Its humanitarian efforts delivered a great deal of aid but did not always get supplies to where they were needed most. United Nations–guarded safe areas, such as Srebrenica, were not secure, and conventional peacekeeping was unsuccessful. The fighting ended only after U.S. and NATO armed forces intervened in the conflict.

Despite hopes that the United Nations could take a more active role in supporting peace in the post–Cold War atmosphere, some of its larger interventions have been ambiguously successful and largely criticized. In many cases, failures were caused by a lack of political, economic, military, and logistical support from the members. The United Nations has had, on the other hand, some important nonmilitary successes. It engaged in human-rights monitoring for the first time in Guatemala and El Salvador in the late 1990s. Election monitoring in Cambodia, South Africa, Kosovo, and East Timor likewise proved successful.

The United Nations has had a great deal of success in less political arenas, such as the promotion of women's rights, the eradication of disease, humanitarian aid, clearing land mines, protecting the environment, and other domains into which it has expanded more recently. Moreover, the United Nations continues to grow and develop, progressively expanding into new areas of international concern.

UN ORGANIZATION

The United Nations is divided into six main bodies—the Security Council, the General Assembly, the Secretariat, the Economic and Social Council (ECOSOC), the Trusteeship Council, and the International Court of Justice. It also includes a large number of subordinate boards and organization. The organizations' structure and responsibilities are spelled out in the United Nations Charter.

The UN Charter

The charter includes several principles necessary to the functioning of the UN. It recognizes the "sovereign equality" of the members; each nation—no matter what its size, population, or power—is considered equal and autonomous. The charter also presumes that nations will attempt to use peaceful means first in settling disputes, directs that all members will respect the sovereignty of each member state, and outlines a system of collective security.

The charter gives the organization four broad missions: "to maintain international peace and security, to develop friendly relations among nations, to cooperate in solving international problems and in promoting respect for human rights, and to be a center for harmonizing the actions of nations." To fulfill these missions, the charter includes provisions for the development of six principal organs: the Security Council, the General Assembly, the Secretariat, the Economic and Social Council (ECOSOC), the Trusteeship Council, and the International Court of Justice.

The Security Council

The Security Council is composed of 15 nations, 5 of which are permanent members: the United States, Great Britain, France, China, and the Russian Federation (although Germany, India, Japan, and Brazil are working to also become permanent members). These so-called P5 members have the right of veto and may block any proposed motion before the council. The other 10 member nations of the Security Council are elected for two-year terms. A successful motion must receive the support of nine members, including all five permanent members. Motions and decisions made by the Security Council are binding on all UN members.

The UN Charter gives the Security Council primary responsibility for maintaining international peace and security. The council is given specific authorization to determine threats to, and breaches of, international peace and security; to call upon conflicting factions to settle disputes peaceably; to implement blockades, embargoes, and sanctions; and to use armed force.

The General Assembly

The General Assembly is permitted to discuss any matter within the scope of the UN Charter. It may also discuss questions of international peace and security and make recommendations to the Security Council on these matters. Specifically, it is entrusted with developing international law, encouraging international cooperation, and promoting human rights.

All members of the United Nations may send up to five delegates to the General Assembly, which operates on a one-nation, one-vote principle. As of 2005, there are 191 member nations in the General Assembly. Votes on important questions—such as the election of non-permanent members to the Security Council, admission of new members to the UN, or approval of the budget—require a two-thirds majority; normal motions require only a simple majority.

The Secretariat

The Secretariat is responsible for the day-to-day operations of the United Nations; the staff for each organ is considered part of the Secretariat. Its head, the secretary-general, is the face of the United Nations and the chief administrative officer of each of the UN organs. The secretary-general has the power to advise the Security Council of threats to international peace and security. Unofficially, these assertions carry a great deal of weight on the international scene in private negotiations or public proclamations.

The Economic and Social Council (ECOSOC)

The Economic and Social Council (ECOSOC) has the power to investigate and make recommendations regarding international economic, social, cultural, educational, health, and related matters. It consists of 54 UN members elected to three-year terms by the General Assembly. Decisions are made by simple majority. The council is also charged with actively promoting respect for human rights. ECOSOC may issue reports and submit its findings on these matters to the General Assembly for consideration.

The Trusteeship Council

The Trusteeship Council consists of those nations that administer trust territories, any of the P5 members not administering trust territories, and elected delegates of other nations. In the aftermath of World War II, the Trusteeship Council looked after territories in transition that were already under UN mandate or that were taken from the losing powers at the end of the war. Today, the Trusteeship Council continues to oversee any territories that members voluntarily place under UN mandate.

The International
Court of Justice (ICJ)

The International Court of Justice (ICJ) is a court used by member states to settle legal disputes. It may decide cases involving member states, and states using the court are obliged to regard its decisions as binding. The ICJ may also give advisory opinions on legal matters at the request of the General Assembly. All member nations are party to the Statute of the ICJ, though non-UN-member states may use the court with the agreement of the General Assembly and the Security Council.

OTHER UN ORGANIZATIONS

The United Nations has a multitude of other programs and organizations not specifically delineated by the UN Charter. These bodies address global issues such as human rights and development, the environment, and trade. They include the United Nations Children's Fund (UNICEF), the Office of the High Commissioner for Human Rights (OHCHR), the United Nations Environmental Programme (UNEP), and the United Nations Conference on Trade and Development (UNCTAD). The United Nations also supports scientific and cultural development and preservation through the United Nations Educational, Scientific,

and Cultural Organization (UNESCO), human health through the World Health Organization (WHO), and financial stability through the World Bank and the International Monetary Fund.

See also Bosnia Intervention; Cold War; Collective Security; Humanitarian Aid; Humanitarian Intervention; Korean War; Kosovo Intervention; League of Nations; Peacekeeping Operations; Somalia Intervention (1992); United Nations Monitoring, Verification and Inspection Commission (UNMOVIC); United Nations Special Commission (UNSCOM); UNOSOM (United Nations Operations in Somalia); UN Peacekeeping; UN Security Council

Further Reading

Muldoon, James. P., Jr. *Multilateral Diplomacy and the United Nations Today.* 2nd ed. Boulder, CO: Westview Press, 2005.
Price, Richard M., and Mark W. Zacher, eds. *The United Nations and Global Security.* London: Palgrave Macmillan, 2004.
Weiss, Thomas G. *United Nations and Changing World Politics.* Boulder, CO: Westview Press, 2004.

REFLECTIONS

Preamble to the UN Charter

We the peoples of the United Nations, determined

To save succeeding generations from the scourge of war, which twice in our lifetime has brought untold sorrow to mankind, and

To reaffirm faith in fundamental human rights, in the dignity and worth of the human person, in the equal rights of men and women and of nations large and small, and

To establish conditions under which justice and respect for the obligations arising from treaties and other sources of international law can be maintained, and

To promote social progress and better standards of life in larger freedom,

AND FOR THESE ENDS,

To practice tolerance and live together in peace with one another as good neighbors, and

To unite our strength to promote international peace and security, and

To ensure, by the acceptance of principles and the institution of methods, that armed force shall not be used, save in the common interest, and

To employ international machinery for the promotion of the economic and social advancement of all peoples,

HAVE RESOLVED TO COMBINE OUR EFFORTS TO ACCOMPLISH THESE AIMS.

Accordingly, our respective governments, through representatives assembled in the city of San Francisco, who have exhibited their full powers found to be in good and due form, have agreed to the present Charter of the United Nations and do hereby establish an international organization to be known as the United Nations.

—Preamble to the Charter of the United Nations

UNITED NATIONS MONITORING, VERIFICATION AND INSPECTION COMMISSION (UNMOVIC)

The successor commission to the United Nations Special Commission (UNSCOM), charged with disarming Iraq of its weapons of mass destruction (WMD) and monitoring Iraq's compliance with United Nations (UN)–mandated weapons restrictions. The United Nations Security Council established the United Nations Monitoring, Verification and Inspection Commission (UNMOVIC) with UNSC Resolution 1284 on December 17, 1999.

The Iraq-Iran War in the 1980s and the Gulf War of 1991 were followed by nearly a decade of efforts by the United Nations Special Commission to address Iraq's weapons program. During this time, the international community was concerned about the capacity of the Iraqi weapons program, particularly its plans to develop chemical and biological weapons. Building on the work of UNSCOM, the United Nations Security Council passed UNSC Resolution 1284 to establish the United Nations Monitoring, Verification and Inspection Commission. The mandate for this new commission was twofold: to disarm Iraq of its unconventional weapons or weapons of mass destruction, which included chemical weapons, biological weapons, and missiles with a range greater than 150 km (90 mi), and to establish a system of monitoring and verification to ensure Iraq's compliance with UN restrictions and prevent future acquisition of prohibited weapons by the Iraqi government.

The United Nations Monitoring, Verification and Inspection Commission is headed by an executive chairman supported by a sixteen-member College of Commissioners who act as advisers. Dr. Hans Blix was nominated for the position of executive chairman of the commission by UN Secretary-General Kofi Annan and confirmed by the UN Security Council in January 2000. The executive chairman is required to report to the United Nations Security Council every three months. The College of Commissioners is comprised of weapons specialists, analysts, scientists, engineers, and operational planners. This body meets four times yearly to brief the executive chairman. Within the UNMOVIC, there are four divisions: planning and operations, analysis and assessment, technical support and training, and information. The UNMOVIC is financed by the UN oil-for-food program.

On September 15, 1998, the Iraqi parliament voted to cease cooperation with the United Nations Special Commission. It was not until December of the following year that a successor commission was established to confront the threat posed by Iraq's weapons program. Despite the creation of UNMOVIC, inspections in Iraq did not resume until the United Nations Security Council adopted UNSC Resolution 1441 in November 2002. This resolution 1441 chastised Iraq for its continued noncompliance with the UNMOVIC. It also insisted that UN inspectors be granted unrestricted access to sites of their choosing throughout the country to confirm Iraq's compliance with disarmament requirements. During the approximately four months UNMOVIC was able to operate in Iraq, inspectors discovered previously undisclosed munitions and munitions components consistent with chemical and biological weapons. The intended purpose of these items has not yet been determined by UNMOVIC.

The UNMOVIC inspectors were withdrawn from Iraq on March 18, 2003, just prior to the U.S. invasion of that country. Dr. Hans Blix subsequently stepped down as the executive chairman of UNMOVIC on June 30, 2003. He was replaced by Demetrius Perricos, under whose chairmanship the commission continues to assess the Iraqi weapons program.

See also Biological Weapons and Warfare; Chemical Weapons; Gulf War (1990–1991); Iraq War of 2003; United Nations; Verification; Weapons of Mass Destruction (WMD)

UNITED NATIONS SPECIAL COMMISSION (UNSCOM)

United Nations (UN) inspection agency established in the wake of the first Gulf War to ensure the elimination of Iraq's supposed ballistic missiles and weapons of mass destruction. Unable to surmount Iraqi obstructions,

UNSCOM became embroiled in disagreements within the UN Security Council over policy toward Iraq. UNSCOM was replaced by another commission in 1999.

The UN Security Council established UNSCOM in April 1991 to conduct on-site inspections of Iraq's biological, chemical, and missile capabilities. The commission had a mandate to monitor the elimination of any discovered weapons of mass destruction, ballistic missiles with a range greater than 150 km, and related production facilities. UNSCOM was also given the task of ensuring that Iraq did not resume the acquisition or production of prohibited weapons. UNSCOM conducted nuclear weapons inspections in Iraq in collaboration with the International Atomic Energy Agency (IAEA).

The twenty members of the commission held full sessions twice a year in New York to discuss policy and to assess results of the inspections. UNSCOM's executive chairman reported directly to UN Secretary-General Kofi Annan. The first executive chairman of UNSCOM was Rolf Ekéus, a Swedish ambassador, who was later succeeded by Australian diplomat Richard Butler.

UNSCOM had an office in New York, staffed by technical experts, analysts, and data processors, and another office in Bahrain, where inspection teams were trained and logistics planned. A third office in Baghdad provided communications support in the field. The commission's operating costs (about $25–30 million per year) were covered by frozen Iraqi assets, receipts from the oil-for-food program, and voluntary contributions from UN member states. The United States and Britain provided aircraft, facilities, equipment, and intelligence about suspected Iraqi weapons sites. UNSCOM inspection teams were staffed by 1,000 individuals from more than 40 countries, although most of the inspectors came from the United States and Great Britain.

UNSCOM's work was to be implemented in three stages, which sometimes overlapped. First, UNSCOM was to gather the information necessary to assess Iraq's chemical, biological, and missile capabilities. Second, the commission was to dispose of any weapons of mass destruction, ballistic missiles, and related facilities, by destroying them, removing them, or rendering them harmless. Third, UNSCOM was to conduct long-term monitoring to verify Iraq's compliance with its obligation not to reacquire banned capabilities. In the pursuit of the first two tasks, UNSCOM

launched more than 250 inspection missions to Iraq. The commission never managed to reach the third stage.

Based on gaps in the weapons inspectors' inventory of Iraqi weapons, UNSCOM demanded an explanation about 550 artillery shells filled with mustard gas, which Baghdad claimed had been lost after the Gulf War. The commission also insisted that Iraq report on the fate of 500 aerial bombs that contained chemical and biological agents. Iraq refused to respond to these inquiries, which were later taken up by UNSCOM's successor, the United Nations Monitoring, Verification and Inspection Commission (UNMOVIC).

Baghdad resented the UNSCOM inspections as an interference in its internal affairs. Iraqi president Saddam Hussein also accused UNSCOM of serving as a cover for U.S. spies. Iraqi officials continually obstructed the searches by UNSCOM investigators, deceiving them through false statements and documents. Inspectors also were subjected to physical threats and psychological intimidation by the Iraqis. In one instance, UNSCOM inspectors had to chase Iraqi trucks hauling electromagnets away from a military base, while guards on the trucks fired over the heads of the inspectors.

Iraq provided to UNSCOM only a portion of its weapons stocks and reportedly retained the production capability and documentation necessary to revive weapons programs when possible. Iraq was also widely suspected of concealing the full extent of its chemical-weapons program, including a VX nerve-agent project. In 1997, Iraq barred UNSCOM inspectors from a new category of sites, those declared to be sovereign presidential palaces. Many of these sites were, in fact, large compounds capable of storing weapons material.

In December 1998, UNSCOM inspectors were evacuated from Iraq on the eve of a U.S. and U.K. bombing campaign. Subsequently, Iraq did not allow UNSCOM investigators to resume their work. Iraq's failure to cooperate caused deep divisions within the UN Security Council, which weakened UNSCOM's political mandate. The council could lift UN economic sanctions against Iraq only after the inspectors declared Iraq free of weapons of mass destruction, which it could not do if it was barred from making further inspections. Finally, in December 1999, the UN Security Council agreed to form a new inspection agency, UNMOVIC, which would maintain political neutrality by abstaining from exchange of information with U.S. intelligence services.

Despite Iraqi obstructions, UNSCOM managed to compile some information about Iraq's capabilities and facilities. It also managed to destroy some banned weapons and facilities. Although UNSCOM did not fully achieve its mission, it set an important precedent and standards for arms control in the future.

See also Iraq War of 2003; United Nations; United Nations Monitoring, Verification and Inspection Commission (UNMOVIC); UN Security Council; Weapons of Mass Destruction (WMD)

Further Reading

Butler, Richard. *Saddam Defiant: The Threat of Weapons of Mass Destruction and the Crisis of Global Security.* London: Ekeus, 2000.
UNSCOM. Basic Facts. http://www.un.org/Depts/unscom/General/basicfacts.html

UN PEACEKEEPING

Military and civilian operations intended to restore or preserve peace in a specific area of conflict. Although peacekeeping is not a prerogative of the United Nations, most often it is carried out by that organization.

United Nations peacekeeping has evolved from small emergency operations to large multidimensional mobilizations. Since 1948, there have been 59 United Nations (UN) peacekeeping operations involving troops from 130 nations. The diversity of the participating forces is reflected by the fact that Canada and Fiji—hardly global military powers—have taken part in almost all UN peacekeeping operations. A total of 1,800 soldiers from more than 100 countries have been killed while serving on peacekeeping missions. Thirty percent of the fatalities occurred in the years 1993–95.

HISTORIC OVERVIEW

The UN Charter does not mention the concept of peacekeeping, nor does it provide specific provisions for implementation. Indeed, peacekeeping was not envisaged as one of the original missions of the United Nations. However, UN Secretary-General Dag Hammarskjöld and Canadian Foreign Minister Lester B. Pearson developed the idea of preventive diplomacy in the 1950s as a concept to limit superpower confrontation. Peacekeeping subsequently became the primary means of preventive diplomacy.

Traditional Peacekeeping

The first UN peacekeeping operation took place in response to the Greek civil war in 1947. This mission was authorized by the United Nations General Assembly rather than the UN Security Council. A second mission occurred in 1948 when the United Nations sent a group of military observers, the UN Truce Supervision Organization, to oversee the cease-fire in the Arab-Israeli conflict. A similar team was sent to the India-Pakistan border in 1949. These operations, the forerunners to traditional peacekeeping, aimed to supervise cease-fires and monitor activities in the territory.

Pearson, who was now the Canadian prime minister, developed the concept of traditional peacekeeping in the 1950s, an achievement for which he was later awarded the Nobel Peace Prize. The goal of traditional peacekeeping is to help war-torn countries create and maintain conditions conducive to long-term, sustainable peace. Traditional peacekeeping generally takes place in the period between a cease-fire in a conflict and a political settlement to the conflict. Secretary-General Dag Hammarskjöld embraced the idea of traditional peacekeeping, which provided the United Nations a new collective security role with peacekeeping at its core.

The first traditional peacekeeping mission was established in 1957 at the end of the Suez Crisis in the Middle East. The second mission, which took place in 1960–64 in Congo (now Democratic Republic of Congo), was larger and more complex. Almost 20,000 troops were deployed, as well as a significant number of civilian staff. This mission was extremely costly. The Soviet Union and France claimed the mission exceeded its mandate and refused to pay their UN dues, provoking a UN funding crisis that has never been fully overcome. As a consequence, peacekeeping expenses were removed from the general UN budget and became part of a separate budget.

Several large-scale traditional peacekeeping missions established in the 1960s and 1970s are still ongoing. These include one launched in Cyprus in 1964, to supervise the cease-fire between Egyptian and Israeli forces in 1973. In general, however, Cold War tensions and rivalries produced dissent in the Security Council over proposed peacekeeping operations, and the number of missions declined significantly.

The only mission authorized in the 1970s was in Lebanon and was deployed between 1974 and 1987.

Wider Peacekeeping

Following the end of the Cold War, peacekeeping operations increased dramatically. The rise in the number of operations reflected the view that in the post–Cold War era, the United Nations could play a relevant role in bringing solutions to regional conflicts.

According to the authors of *Understanding Peacekeeping,* UN peacekeeping operations experienced three different changes between 1988 and 1993. First, there was a quantitative transformation—during these five years the Security Council authorized 20 new missions, more than in the previous 40 years combined. In 1993, 80,000 peacekeepers were deployed on the ground. Second, there was a qualitative transformation. Peacekeeping operations in Cambodia, Bosnia, and Somalia saw an expansion of the traditional peacekeeping mandate to include monitoring elections; training police; and overseeing civil administration, humanitarian aid, and peace enforcement. In contrast to their indifference to peacekeeping in previous decades, the United States and Great Britain became actively involved in these new missions. Finally, peacekeeping expanded to include the promotion of principles such as democracy and rule of law.

In 1992, the United Nations assessed how it could respond to the new challenges of the post–Cold War era. *Agenda for Peace,* authored by Secretary-General Boutros Boutros-Ghali, was the first internal report that proposed ways to strengthen the UN's peacekeeping capacity. The report was optimistic about the organization's ability to match the new challenges, but it called for additional funds and resources that member states, despite their verbal commitments, failed to provide. The *Agenda* also established the Department of Peacekeeping Operations (DPKO) in order to improve the organization's capacities to manage peacekeeping. However, Boutros-Ghali's report failed to address the challenges of expanding traditional peacekeeping in more complex missions and in more dangerous environments, where troops were deployed during ongoing conflicts.

The Retreat

From 1995 to mid-1999, the number of UN peacekeepers on the ground declined sharply, from 80,000 to 12,000. The failure of missions to Somalia, Rwanda, and Bosnia accounted for most of this retreat. In addition, North Atlantic Treaty Organization (NATO) forces took over the peacekeeping responsibilities in the former Yugoslav republics and other missions were closed. These included operations in Mozambique (ended January 1995), Somalia (March 1995), El Salvador (April 1995), and Rwanda (March 1996). The only new peacekeeping operation set up during this time outside the former Yugoslav republics was in Angola.

This period witnessed two of peacekeeping's greatest failures. The genocide in Rwanda in 1995 illustrated how difficult it was for the United Nations to react rapidly to impending crises. In Bosnia, peacekeepers failed to create safe areas to protect civilians from Serbian aggression. The massacre of Srebrenica, where more than 7,000 Muslims were killed, happened under the watch of UN peacekeepers who had neither the mandate nor the resources to intervene.

New Operations

Beginning in June 1999, new missions in Kosovo and East Timor, and expanded missions in Sierra Leone and the Congo, increased again both the costs and personnel deployed in UN peacekeeping operations. From July 1999 to June 2001, overall UN peacekeeping personnel levels increased to 43,000. Several factors account for this new expansion in peacekeeping. First of all, there was a renewed concern with humanitarian problems, which motivated the interventions in Kosovo and East Timor. Also, the merging of security and development agendas, the activism of African states such as Nigeria and South Africa, and the lessons learned from the past induced a rebirth of peacekeeping. East Timor and Kosovo also involved a new level of complexity, with a greater emphasis on civilian administration and state-building.

As of July 2004, 58,741 military and civilian police from 100 different countries are serving in 16 peacekeeping operations, half of which are in Africa. Pakistan is the largest contributor, with more than 8,600 personnel, followed by Bangladesh with 8,200 and Nigeria with 3,500. Other significant contributors are Ethiopia and Ghana, with more than 3,000 troops, along with India, Uruguay, South Africa, and Nepal. The approved UN peacekeeping budget for 2004–2005 is about $2.8 billion, bringing the estimated total cost of peacekeeping operations since 1948 to $31.5 billion. This means that debts incurred by UN peacekeeping operations are higher than debts to the UN's regular budget. By the end of 2004, 15 countries owed more than $1.9 billion in peacekeeping debts. The United States topped the list with a debt of $480 million, and Japan owed the second-largest amount, $176 million.

ESTABLISHING PEACEKEEPING OPERATIONS

The Department of Peacekeeping Operations (DPKO) is responsible for planning, managing, deploying, and supporting all UN peacekeeping operations. Established in 1992, DPKO works closely with the UN Department of Political Affairs and provides executive direction to all UN peacekeeping operations. Each operation requires a new mission, authorized by the UN Security Council, and resources have to be assembled to meet the requirements of the situation.

Authorizing Peacekeeping Operations

There is no standard procedure to establish a peacekeeping operation. However, in most cases, the process starts with consultations among member states, the UN Secretariat, and the parties involved in the conflict, which have to agree on troop deployment. Sometimes, peace agreements require the presence of peacekeepers on the ground.

As soon as security conditions permit, a technical-assessment team travels to the area to analyze the needs for and implications of a UN mission. The secretary-general makes recommendations to the Security Council, taking into consideration the findings of the assessment team. The Security Council must authorize a peacekeeping operation with a resolution that specifies the size and mandate of the mission. Such resolutions require at least 9 out of 15 votes in favor and are subject to veto by the council's five permanent members—China, France, Great Britain, Russia, and the United States.

Planning, Deploying, and Financing Peacekeeping Operations

Planning for political, military, operational, and logistical aspects of the operation involves the secretary-general's special representative, appointed to head the operation, and DPKO. Member states are asked to contribute military troops and civilian police on a voluntary basis. Personnel in peacekeeping operations remain members of their own national service but serve under the operational control of the United Nations. They wear their own uniforms but also wear blue berets or helmets and the UN insignia.

When a significant number of U.S. troops are involved, operational control remains in U.S. hands or in the hands of a military ally such as a NATO member. Because the U.S. president never relinquishes his command authority over U.S. troops, American officers retain authority over their own military forces serving in UN operations.

The time required to deploy a mission depends on the will of member states to provide troops and financial resources. It varies from 24 hours—as happened in 1973 for the UN Emergency Force in the Middle East—to several weeks for more complex missions.

The General Assembly allocates peacekeeping costs based on a special scale that takes into account the relative economic wealth of member states. The five permanent members of the Security Council are required to pay a larger share because of their special responsibility for the maintenance of international peace and security. Member states providing troops or other tangible support for a mission are reimbursed from the mission budget at agreed-upon rates, and this payment creates an incentive for developing countries to contribute to peacekeeping.

MODERN PEACEKEEPING

After 56 years, UN peacekeeping has evolved from little more than short-term policing to complex and multidimensional operations. Lessons learned from the past show that there is no single model for a successful peacekeeping operation, although a clear mandate and adequate resources are considered fundamental elements for an adequate response. Modern peacekeeping doctrine suggests that missions must respond to the needs and aspirations of the local populations and fit the political and socioeconomic dimensions of the territory, country, or region of concern.

—*Francesco Mancini*

See also Bosnia Intervention; Interventionism; Kosovo Intervention; Somalia Intervention (1992); United Nations; UN Security Council

Further Reading

Bellamy, Alex J., Paul Williams, and Stuart Griffin. *Understanding Peacekeeping*. Cambridge, UK: Polity Press, 2004.

Diehl, Paul. *International Peacekeeping*. Baltimore, MD: Johns Hopkins University Press, 1994.

Thakur, Ramesh, and Albrecht Schnabel, eds. *United Nations Peacekeeping Operations: Ad Hoc Mission, Permanent Engagement*. Tokyo: UN University Press, 2001.

UN SECURITY COUNCIL

Organ of the United Nations (UN) that has primary responsibility for the maintenance of international peace and security.

RATIONALE AND ORGANIZATION

After World War II, the victorious Allied powers led an international community of states in forming the global security organization called the United Nations. However, it soon became clear that meetings of the entire membership were neither a speedy nor practical way to address rapidly developing international crises. Thus, the founders of the United Nations created a body known as the Security Council, so that a subset of the membership could quickly come together to attend to crises and formulate responses on behalf of the entire organization. The council was originally composed of 11 members, but added 4 more seats in 1965 in response to a doubling in the United Nation's overall membership since 1951. The council remains at 15 today, although the United Nations has since grown to 192 states.

Council members fall into two broad groups: those that have permanent status, and those with two-year terms. Since the UN's founding, the permanent members have been the United States, Great Britain, France, the Russian Federation (as the successor to the Soviet Union), and China (with the mainland government replacing that of Taiwan in 1971). Collectively referred to as the P5, these states owe their status to their being accepted in 1945 as the postwar great powers (with the United States and the Soviet Union being then, of course, the greatest among the great). The General Assembly, the forum for political meetings of the entire UN membership, elects the 10 term members with due regard for ensuring, as specified in Article 23 of the charter, "equitable geographical distribution." Half of the 10 are replaced each year, and retiring members are not eligible for immediate reelection.

FORMAL POWERS AND FUNCTIONS

The UN Charter assigns the Security Council "primary responsibility for the maintenance of international peace and security." Although the General Assembly also has the authority to consider such matters, the council's primacy is underscored in charter provisions. Article 10 makes clear that the assembly's powers on these issues are advisory only. Article 14 states that the assembly must defer to the council when the latter attends to a specific international dispute or a potential threat to peace and security.

The most significant of the council's enumerated powers fall under Chapters VI and VII of the charter. The former addresses the peaceful settlement of disputes and empowers the council to investigate international disputes or predispute situations and recommend procedures or methods to resolve them. Chapter VII specifies those actions that the council can take or call for when confronted with threats to the peace, breaches of the peace, or acts of aggression. It goes considerably further than Chapter VI in the powers assigned. It gives the council the right to determine the existence of any such threats, breaches, or acts. Once it identifies a threat, the council can call on the parties to take measures to dampen their dispute and give the council time to consider what else should be done.

Should all of these measures prove inadequate, the council can move toward enforcing its decisions. Article 41 gives the United Nations the power to impose nonmilitary means of enforcement, including economic sanctions, severing diplomatic relations, and embargoing transportation, postal, electronic, and other means of communications. Article 42 authorizes the use of armed force by member states on behalf of the organization should lesser actions be deemed inadequate. Chapter VII resolutions are generally regarded as legally binding on the membership.

Consistent with these powers, the charter also states that UN members must accept and carry out decisions of the council. The council can recommend that the General Assembly suspend any member that fails to do so or expel particularly grievous violators of charter principles. The council later can reinstate suspended members on its own should it choose to do so.

Other important assigned council functions include making recommendations to the General Assembly on the appointment of new members to the United Nations and on the appointment of the organization's chief administrative officer, the secretary-general.

Together with the General Assembly, the council also elects the judges of the International Court of Justice, which sits in The Hague.

PROCEDURES AND ACTIVITIES

The council is always on call, and any member state or the secretary-general can bring to its attention a situation that threatens international peace and security. Should it be willing to be seized by the situation, the council usually calls on the parties to resolve their dispute through peaceful means while it awaits a report from the secretary-general on the facts of the matter. It may also call on the secretary-general to use his good offices, or it may directly appoint a special representative (or ask that the secretary-general do so) to mediate between the parties. With their consent, it may, among other things, authorize the dispatch of cease-fire monitors, a civilian peace mission, or a peace-operations force that can assist in establishing conditions conducive to a long-term return to peace. Should such actions not suffice, it can move to the Chapter VII measures outlined above. In unusual circumstances (such as occurred with Iraq's aggression against Kuwait in 1990) or in the face of a humanitarian disaster, it may go so far as to authorize an international military force to use all necessary means to set a situation right.

Although the council conducts some of this business in open session, it also resorts to private meetings and informal consultations. These often allow for more pointed exchanges and dispense with the diplomatic niceties and political rhetoric characteristic of public events. Some informal consultations are considered meetings of council members rather than meetings of the council per se. No official records are kept of such proceedings.

The most solemn expression of the council's will is its passage of a resolution. There must be nine affirmative votes for a proposed resolution to be accepted. On substantive votes, each member of the P5 holds a veto, that is, the right to prevent a proposal's passage. Ceding this privilege to the P5 reflected both the hope that they would see eye to eye on decisions and the recognition that no one can force a great power to accept and implement a decision that it opposes. Without this proviso, it is clear that the P5 would not have signed on to the organization. When a P5 state wishes to make clear its displeasure with a proposal without vetoing it outright, it also has the option (as do other members of the council) of abstaining from the vote.

There has been a very significant decrease in the number of P5 vetoes since the end of the Cold War. From 1946 through 1990, P5 states, especially the Soviet Union, cast an average of five vetoes a year. The average has since dropped to somewhat less than two. The fact remains, however, that the veto is a last-resort measure. Its very threat provides considerable leverage. With that threat, a P5 state can discourage consideration of any issue it wishes to keep off the agenda or cause a proposed resolution to be modified until it meets the state's requirements. There is no indication that the P5 are any less apt to resort to such threats in this era than they were in the past.

Nonmembers of the council can participate in its meetings under specified conditions. In particular, when the council is considering a question, any state within the UN that believes its interests could be affected has a right to address the council, but unless it is already a member, it has no right to vote on a resolution. Conversely, a member of the council that is party to a dispute under consideration by the council must abstain from voting.

Whereas voting constitutes the most formal and public way that the council expresses its will and intent, it also uses less formal presidential statements. Each member of the council takes a one-month turn in the president's chair. Among the president's duties is issuing statements that reflect the sense of the council on questions such as "The Situation in Somalia" or "Threats to International Peace and Security Caused by Terrorist Acts." Such statements are often seen as less binding or more provisional than are resolutions.

THE COUNCIL'S CHANGING SIGNIFICANCE

The significance of the council is a function of what states make of it, and the P5 are ultimately controlling in this regard. The East–West rivalries of the Cold War went far to relegate not only the council but the entire United Nations to the role of bit player and forum for mutual accusations. The end of intense Cold War rivalries, and an accompanying international sense that the UN could be useful, led to greater attention to and reliance upon the organization and particularly on the Security Council as the organ that made things happen.

By several measures, the United Nations clearly has been more active since the end of the Cold War.

The council held 55 formal meetings and 62 informal consultations in 1988, compared to 273 and 259, respectively, in 2002. The council passed an average of 10 to 20 resolutions per year from 1946 through 1988, and about 50 to 70 per year since then. Just 8 presidential statements were issued in 1988; 42 were issued in 2002. The United Nations authorized a total of 46 peacekeeping missions from 1989 through 2004, compared to 13 in its previous 42 years of existence.

The council has also been more active in invoking Chapter VII enforcement measures. Of the 14 cases in which the council has invoked nonmilitary sanctions, 2 occurred before 1990 and 12 occurred thereafter. Similarly, although military enforcement actions were authorized only twice prior to 1990 (with the Korean War and with enforcement of a trade embargo against Rhodesia), they have since been invoked to deal with situations in the former Yugoslav republics, Somalia, Haiti, Rwanda, the African Great Lakes region, Albania, the Central African Republic, Sierra Leone, Guinea-Bissau, East Timor, the Democratic Republic of the Congo, Burundi, Liberia, Ivory Coast, and Afghanistan.

The council's activism has not been without controversy. In particular, states and informed observers have sharply criticized it for authorizing military peace missions that were overly ambitious in their goals and demands despite lacking needed resources. Some of these missions led to the deaths of innocent civilians and to the humiliation and sometimes the death of peacekeepers, as well. Highly publicized problems in Somalia and the former Yugoslav republics, compounded by the council's failure to authorize forceful action at the start of the 1994 Rwanda genocide, threw a pall over the UN's 50th-anniversary celebrations in 1995. Although the council's expressed aims are usually laudatory, council members still do not always follow through to ensure that what they resolve should be done actually can be done.

The greatest dissatisfaction with the council may be among developing states. Many have viewed the council's increased activism as a mixed blessing, because it is they or their neighbors who are often the subjects of council resolutions and sponsored actions. They chafe at control of the council by the P5 in general and by the United States in particular as the sole post–Cold War superpower. Hence, a significant development in the council's history may have been a nonevent. In spite of President George W. Bush's expressed determination to force a final vote authorizing the U.S. attack against Iraq that took place in March 2003, the United States ultimately decided against such a course of action. The Bush administration not only expected vetoes by as many as three of the P5 but also failed to garner positive votes among several term members, as well. That example may foreshadow increased U.S. reluctance to bring future critical issues to the council.

PROSPECTS FOR REFORM

Proposals to reform the council have focused on three features: size, makeup, and the veto power. As the UN's membership has grown, pressure has increased to broaden the council's membership, possibly to 21 or 24 members. The United Nations has also considered creating some kind of a special membership for Germany, Japan, and regional leaders such as Brazil, India, South Africa, or Nigeria. The special membership could take the form of a permanent seat without veto power. However, the veto itself may be in for changes, as well. Some UN members have proposed that it either be done away with or that its use be restricted—for example, only to resolutions that involve Chapter VII. The consensus among informed observers is that the P5 will not restrict their own veto and will be reluctant to grant it to other states. It also seems certain that the council will grow, but whether that growth will involve giving some states a special membership status remains to be seen.

—Donald C. F. Daniel

See also Bosnia Intervention; Cold War; Interventionism; Korean War; Kosovo Intervention; Peacekeeping Operations; Somalia Intervention (1992); United Nations; UN Peacekeeping

Further Reading

Inderfurth, Karl F., and Loch K. Johnson. *Fateful Decisions: Inside the National Security Council.* New York: Oxford University Press, 2004.

MacKenzie, Lewis. *The Road to Sarajevo.* Toronto: HarperCollins, 1994.

Malone, David, ed. *The UN Security Council: From the Cold War to the Twenty-First Century.* Boulder, CO: Lynne Rienner, 2004.

REFLECTIONS

A Peacekeeper's Reaction to Security Council Decisions

And just when it seemed things could not get worse, the Security Council started to make life impossible for UN commanders and troops on the ground in Bosnia.

In late 1992 and early 1993, the Security Council issued resolutions that called for UNPROFOR (the UN Protection Force) to "use such force as necessary to guarantee the delivery of humanitarian aid" and to establish a number of "safe havens" for the Bosnian Muslims. The resolutions were announced with great fanfare in the halls outside the council. Unfortunately, no one had bothered to check the military viability of these resolutions considering the reluctance of potential troop-contributing countries to get more deeply involved in the Bosnian conflict. First, all sides in the Bosnian conflict were interfering with the delivery of aid and, more often than not, using women and children to block roads. Second, safe havens would merely have concentrated the Muslims in seven or eight locations, thereby tacitly encouraging ethnic cleansing and providing the Serbs and Croats with easily identified targets.

—Major General Lewis MacKenzie
Chief of Staff, UNPROFOR

UNMANNED AERIAL VEHICLES (UAVs)

Powered aircraft that are guided without an onboard crew. Unmanned aerial vehicles (UAVs) are used primarily for reconnaissance and gathering intelligence, but the U.S. military has been exploring other ways of using the potential of these craft.

The earliest recorded use of unmanned aerial vehicles occurred during the American Civil War, when both sides tried to use balloons loaded with explosive devices as unmanned flying bombs. The idea was for the balloons to come down inside a supply or ammunition depot and explode. The Japanese repeated this tactic in World War II, sending long-distance bomb-laden balloons over the Pacific toward the United States. Unable to gauge their success, the Japanese called off the project after several weeks.

The United States experimented with early self-propelled UAVs during World War II, modifying aircraft for use as unmanned flying missiles. After World War II, the U.S. military developed target drones—remote-controlled, unmanned aircraft used as targets for missile or air gunnery tests.

During the Vietnam War, advanced aviation technology began to make UAVs more effective. The United States launched large numbers of unmanned drones over North Vietnam for day reconnaissance missions. Known as Firebees, the drones later were used for other military missions, including night reconnaissance, gathering electronic intelligence, eavesdropping on enemy communications, dropping propaganda leaflets, detecting surface-to-air missile (SAM) radar sites, and identifying enemy units.

Since the 1980s, UAVs have been used extensively in recent conflicts in the Middle East. The Pioneer UAV system of the U.S. Navy and Marine Corps has been in operation since 1985 and played a significant role in the 1991 Gulf War. The battleship USS *Missouri* used its Pioneer drones to spot targets for its main guns, which devastated Iraqi defenses off the coast of Kuwait during that war. Following the Gulf War, military officials recognized the worth of the unmanned systems.

The two main U.S. UAVs now in use are the Predator and the Global Hawk. The Predator operates between 15,000 and 25,000 feet and carries three sensor systems—a color video camera and two types of radar. The air force has also placed Hellfire missiles aboard some Predators. In the near future, the Predator may be able to conduct missile attacks on remote targets, mark targets with its laser for other aircraft, or read targets marked by other sources.

Predator does have some drawbacks. For example, it is not an all-weather system. When it was first deployed in the Balkans in the early 1990s, it was found to ice up frequently. As a result of that experience, Predator now employs an anti-icing system. This system allows it to de-ice its fuselage for a short time, but the missile still cannot operate for a long period under icy conditions. The new Predator B has a number of characteristics that will improve its ability to deal with a wider range of environmental events, including icing conditions.

The Global Hawk is a jet-powered UAV first deployed in the skies over Afghanistan in 2002. The Global Hawk operates at around 60,000 feet and carries a package of sensors similar to that of the air force's U-2 spy plane. Although the Predator currently has a more sophisticated system for electronic eavesdropping, tests show the Global Hawk has great potential in this area. The Global Hawk can stay aloft for up to 34 hours, compared to 12 hours for the updated Predator.

The air force and navy are currently designing and testing UAVs for use as weapons platforms. The marine corps has Dragon Eye, a small, hand-launched UAV that can give small-unit leaders a picture of the battleground. Some of the UAVs currently under development will be as small as a human hand. Even though UAVs are increasing their roles in combat, surveillance, and other areas of combat, military strategists are just beginning to understand the impact of multiple UAV on modern airpower doctrine and practice.

See also Cruise Missile; Intelligence and Counterintelligence; Signals Intelligence (SIGINT)

UNOSOM (UNITED NATIONS OPERATION IN SOMALIA)

Two United Nations (UN) peacekeeping and humanitarian missions—UNOSOM I (1992–93) and UNOSOM II (1993–95)—designed to alleviate problems in Somalia created by civil war and drought. UNOSOM I was dispatched by the United Nations in mid-1992. Because the central government had collapsed, the United Nations was unable to seek consent to deploy troops, so the mandate was kept neutral and limited. United Nations personnel were to distribute humanitarian aid to alleviate the drought-created famine. More than 4,000 troops were authorized for the mission, but only 500 were deployed, because local warlords prevented them from moving much beyond the airport in the Somali capital, Mogadishu. Like its successor mission, UNOSOM I suffered from several problems. Troops often refused to accept orders from UN commanders before checking with their own governments, and difficulties with communicating and coordinating activities impeded the mission. The $43 million intervention had few casualties, but its effectiveness was poor.

The failing mission was replaced in December 1992 by a UN-mandated, U.S.-led peace-enforcement mission known as the Unified Task Force (UNITAF). The more heavily armed military personnel of UNITAF had greater success, managing to disarm several of the warring Somali clans. However, the warlords tolerated UNITAF solely because of the U.S. troops' capacity to use force, the limited-time mandate of the mission, and—most significantly—because the operation did not threaten the political balance in the civil war. UNITAF did not last long. On October 3, 1993, an ambush that downed an American helicopter and killed 18 U.S. soldiers shook American public support for the mission. The Americans pulled out of the country by March of 1994.

The United Nations formally returned to Somalia in 1993 with the $1.6 billion mission called UNOSOM II. Twenty-nine countries authorized troops to pursue a highly ambitious mandate—a mandate that went far beyond the limits of traditional, neutral peacekeeping missions. The troops were to restore order to Somalia, disarm Somali civilians, and build the foundation for a stable government. Humanitarian aid, rather than being distributed according to need, was used as a reward for those who supported the mission. Moreover, the attempt to arrest Mohammed Aideed, the most powerful warlord in the nation, was not a neutral act. The ruling warlords were making a lot of money out of the chaotic situation, and they strongly resisted the proposed rebuilding operations.

After planning such an ambitious operation, the United Nations failed to support the mission adequately. The UN resolutions that created the mission were unclear and did not provide for the use of military force. Little attention was given to promoting stable cease-fires or preventing minor incidents from becoming larger ones. Furthermore, the United Nations did not obtain consent for operations from the warring parties in Somalia, a mistake that proved costly. The organization assumed that the UN flag would protect the troops, so they were lightly armed and lacked the equipment necessary in a civil-war zone. There were 110 UN fatalities from hostile acts.

The mission was considered a peacekeeping disaster and was ended in March 1995. UNOSOM II did not—and could not—fulfill its mandate, and the population continued to suffer from all it had endured from 1992 onward. The mission was a further failure for the United Nations because of rampant mismanagement and corruption. Some $3.9 million was lost to theft, $76,000 in cash was lost to mildew, and millions were wasted on overpriced contracts.

The failed missions had substantial repercussions for Somalia and for future peacekeeping missions. First, Somalia remains mired in internal conflict, despite the peacekeepers' efforts; order remains elusive and death tolls continue to rise. Second, the Mogadishu Syndrome—fear of politically unpopular casualties as part of a UN mission—continues to plague planners of peacekeeping missions in the United Nations and particularly in the United States. Third, the blatant failure in Somalia made the international community reluctant to intervene in other civil conflicts; as a result, it failed to stop the genocide in Rwanda in 1994.

See also Humanitarian Aid; Humanitarian Intervention; Peacekeeping Operations; Somalia Intervention (1992); United Nations

URANIUM, DEPLETED

Dense, mildly radioactive metal that is primarily used in the production of U.S. munitions. Depleted uranium (DU) is created as a waste product when the radioactive isotope U-235 is extracted from natural uranium ore. This U-235 uranium is used as a fuel in nuclear power plants and in the production of some nuclear armaments.

Depleted uranium consists of natural uranium minus the U-235 isotope. As a waste product, DU is plentiful and extremely costly to dispose of because of its radioactivity. As a result, arms manufacturers can obtain DU for minimal or even no cost.

Because DU is exceptionally dense, it is used in the production of tank armor, armored clothing, cruise missiles, aircraft, and bombs designed to destroy metal or metal-frame bunkers. It is also manufactured as a coating on ammunition and other armaments. Munitions coated with DU can easily penetrate metal and are readily combustible.

The U.S. defense industry began using DU in 1977, but DU-enhanced armaments were not used in combat until the Gulf War in 1991. They have since been used in the Bosnia and Kosovo interventions, the War in Afghanistan, and the Iraq War of 2003. The benefits of DU on the battlefield were demonstrated in the Gulf War when DU-coated artillery, tank bombs, and ammunition deployed by the United States and coalition forces destroyed at least 1,000 Iraqi tanks. By contrast, not one U.S. DU-coated Abrams tank was knocked out.

Questions have been raised since the Persian Gulf War about the impact of DU on human health and the environment. Some scientists, medical experts, and Gulf War veterans believe that exposure to DU causes a variety of health problems, including cancer. European NATO veterans of the Bosnian conflict have

made similar charges. The U.S. Department of Defense, the U.S. Veterans Administration, the United Nations, and NATO have each conducted investigations exploring these claims. Both the Defense Department and NATO have concluded that the risk to human health from DU is negligible in most cases. In situations of extreme exposure, experts recommend that the involved soldiers receive medical follow-up for evidence of excessive uranium ingestion. Such exposure has occurred when soldiers in armored vehicles accidentally have been hit by DU-coated missiles fired by friendly units and when troops have been involved in clearing away destroyed DU-coated tanks.

Although the U.S. military and many medical experts maintain that DU poses no significant threat to human health, DU in sufficient concentrations can contaminate soil and water supplies. The U.S. Army has estimated that a cleanup of its weapons-testing site at the Jefferson Proving Ground in Indiana, where 77 tons of DU ordnance has been deployed, will cost at least $1 billion. The World Health Organization has also identified a number of locations in Bosnia and Kosovo that require cleanup.

See also Environmental Degradation; Nuclear Waste Disposal; Penetrating Munitions; Protective Gear; Tanks

U.S. AGENCY FOR INTERNATIONAL DEVELOPMENT (USAID)

United States government agency with the explicit dual purpose of advancing America's foreign-policy interests and fostering a better quality of life in less-developed countries. Created in 1961 by an executive order from President John F. Kennedy under the Foreign Assistance Act, the U.S. Agency for International Development (USAID) has philosophical roots in immediate postwar America and the plans to reconstruct Europe. At that time, international development assistance was seen as vital and necessary for U.S. political and economic interests. After the expiration of the Marshall Plan's reconstruction initiative in Europe, the U.S. government created multiple programs to manage international aid monies.

USAID's predecessors—the International Cooperation Administration, the Development Loan Fund, the Export-Import Bank, and the Food for Peace program—were often politically stymied or uncoordinated in their efforts. Thus, USAID was created with a mandate to consolidate these agencies and organize and administer all nonmilitary aid to foreign countries. Although USAID is an independent agency, it is still guided by official policies and it reports to the secretary of state.

USAID works to put policy into practice: The agency promotes global health, economic development, and democracy, and it sponsors related programs in agriculture, education, conflict management, and humanitarian assistance. It is the U.S. agency most actively involved in disaster relief, antipoverty initiatives, and encouraging the growth of good governance, either through its own programs or through nongovernmental partners.

USAID actively sponsors health programs in a number of different arenas: maternal and child health, nutrition, family planning, and the reduction of infectious diseases such as tuberculosis and malaria. A major project involves care for those infected with or affected by HIV and AIDS; to date, in fighting the AIDS pandemic, the agency is the largest donor in any organization, public or private. It also supports the Food for Peace program to bring food to the chronically undernourished.

As a party to the Washington Consensus, USAID supports a neoliberal approach to economic development. The agreement concluded that nations seeking to promote economic growth and end poverty should undergo structural adjustment—in the form of deregulation and privatization of industry. USAID gives advice to governments seeking to promote a business-friendly climate but does not seek to intervene actively in the market. Rather, much of its help includes technical assistance: advising states about the creation of stable fiscal, banking, and trade policies; reliable financial institutions; and private property protections. Programs also include information-technology initiatives and support for education.

USAID likewise has a strong political thrust. The agency is charged with supporting ideas and institutions that lead to stable, peaceable, democratic governance in countries with little prior history of civil society. Specifically, the agency supports the development of the rule of law, the creation of written civil and commercial codes, the protection of human rights, the promotion of free and fair elections, active civic participation by the citizenry, government transparency and accountability, and anticorruption initiatives. The agency also provides education about democracy and democratic practices.

USAID has had some substantial successes. It contributed largely to the worldwide eradication of smallpox and supported agricultural research, which had enormous positive impacts wherever it was implemented. At the same time, the agency has participated in less-successful efforts. Past programs were criticized for ignoring cultural differences and for operating inefficiently in their design and implementation. Aid programs in Israel and Egypt have faced particularly severe criticism regarding their effectiveness. The agency, however, has an active evaluation system that supports organizational learning and development. For instance, to become more attuned to cultural considerations, USAID is developing a "listen to the customer" strategy. In this way, it is improving its ability to advance the interests of the United States and the countries it serves.

See also Foreign Aid; Kennedy, John F., and National Policy; Marshall Plan

U.S. AIR FORCE

Aviation branch of the U.S. military. The U.S. Department of the Air Force was founded by the National Security Act of 1947, signed by President Harry S. Truman. The National Security Act also created the Department of Defense, the Joint Chiefs of Staff, the National Security Council, and the Central Intelligence Agency (CIA). The creation of the U.S. Air Force was thus a feature of the more general consolidation and reorganization of U.S. defense strategy following World War II.

WORLD WAR I AND THE INTERWAR PERIOD

Military aviation finally gained formal status in the United States with the creation of the Aviation Section of the U.S. Army Signal Corps in 1914. The flying unit consisted of 12 officers, 54 enlisted men, and 6 airplanes. By contrast, when World War I broke out in Europe that same year, the German air force consisted of 180 planes, the French air force boasted 136 planes, and the British had 48. Early in the war, airplanes were used solely for reconnaissance. However, the rapid development of airplane design, air gunnery, bombing equipment, and combat strategies and techniques turned the skies into a battlefield. Most of these developments bypassed U.S. military aviation. The United States remained neutral until 1917 and its air-combat readiness lagged well behind. High-ranking U.S. Army officers were still convinced that the airplane's primary military use was to gather intelligence.

The first military use of U.S. airpower actually occurred a year before the nation entered World War I. When Mexican bandit Pancho Villa staged a raid into New Mexico in March 1916, the First Aero Squadron was enlisted to take part in border patrol as a tactical air unit. The squadron also participated in the subsequent U.S. expedition that hunted Villa after he retreated into Mexico.

The United States entered World War I with woefully inadequate military airpower but a tremendous pool of resources that, with guidance from European Allies, could be transformed into a credible force. The U.S. Army Air Service was formed as part of the American Expeditionary Force that was dispatched to Europe to join the fighting. Congress allocated $640 million for aeronautics and airplane production, but all of the planes constructed in U.S. factories were based on British, French, and Italian designs. Because the war ended just a year after U.S. entry, the United States ultimately purchased, rather than built, most of its combat aircraft.

Advances in aircraft technology and air combat doctrine made between World Wars I and II would have important implications for future conflicts. New altitude records were set, the first test jumps were made with parachutes, the first Round-the-Rim (periphery of the continental United States) flight was conducted, and coast-to-coast flight tests were carried out. Speed tests were also conducted to improve flight time, and gyroscopic equipment was installed to control altitude and direction.

With the United States officially uninvolved in foreign wars during this time, American pilots gained experience where they could. Some volunteered their services to fight in the Kościuszko Squadron during the Polish-Soviet War (1921). At home, former World War I ace Billy Mitchell was developing new doctrines for the use of airpower. In 1923, he conducted a demonstration in which he proved that airplanes could sink battleships at sea. Mitchell was furious when his superiors dismissed the significance of the demonstration. United States military leaders still were unable to grasp the full potential of airpower. By the 1930s, European nations, particularly Germany and England, were much further advanced in both aircraft design and air-combat doctrine than the United States.

WORLD WAR II AND THE COLD WAR

World War II began with the German invasion of Poland in 1939. The German air force played a key role in supporting ground forces during the Germans' rapid victories in Poland, Holland, Belgium, and France in the early years of the war. The Germans demonstrated dramatically the value of airpower in modern combat. It soon became clear that command of the skies over the battlefield would be essential to victory.

As in World War I, the United States was at first neutral in the conflict. However, in recognition of the growing importance of airpower, in 1941 the Army Air Corps was renamed the U.S. Army Air Force; two years later it acquired equal status with the army and navy. The United States finally entered the war on December 7, 1941, when Japanese naval air forces attacked the U.S. Pacific Fleet at Pearl Harbor in a real-life application of Mitchell's demonstration nearly 20 years before. However, unlike in World War I, during this war the United States would have ample time to design, build, and make history with its own aircraft.

Airpower played an important role for U.S. operations in both the European and Pacific theaters of combat. United States strategic bombers struck at German and Japanese industrial targets, significantly impairing Axis war production. Reconnaissance aircraft gathered vital intelligence for offensive operations such as the 1944 D-day invasion of France. Fighter-bombers attacked enemy troops and other ground targets, such as railroads and supply depots. By 1944, the Allied forces had uncontested control over the skies on both fronts, with U.S. airpower playing the leading role. Fittingly, airpower ended the war with the dropping of atomic bombs on Hiroshima and Nagasaki.

Airpower also played a significant role in U.S. Cold War strategy. The first postwar test of U.S. air strength came during the Berlin Airlift in 1949. The Soviet Union had blockaded all land routes to the city of West Berlin, which was located in the heart of Soviet-controlled East Germany. In response, the U.S. Air Force flew in thousands of tons of essential supplies such as food and fuel. The success of the airlift ultimately forced the Soviets to lift the blockade.

The importance of the air force to national security was once again demonstrated during the Cuban Missile Crisis of 1962. Air force spy planes provided photographic evidence that the Soviets were planning to install nuclear weapons in Cuba, within quick striking distance of U.S. soil. President John F. Kennedy, acting on this intelligence, ordered a naval blockade of Cuba to prevent the Soviets from sending further missiles to Cuba. Faced with a possible nuclear confrontation over the matter, the Soviets backed down and dismantled the missile sites they had begun to construct on the island.

The role of the air force in Korea and Vietnam is more ambiguous. Particularly in the latter conflict, airpower was associated with some of the worst excesses of the war, such as the dropping of napalm and the relentless bombing of Vietnam, Laos, and Cambodia. Hundreds of thousands of tons of bombs were dropped in Southeast Asia during this time period, and the phrase "bomb them back to the Stone Age" became part of the rhetoric of some of the most virulent war supporters. In this context, attacks from above by pilots who never saw their enemy were considered representative of the anonymity of modern warfare.

Perhaps the most important role the air force played during the Cold War was as a nuclear deterrent to Soviet aggression. A branch of the air force known as the Strategic Air Command was and still is responsible for maintaining and overseeing the U.S. arsenal of strategic nuclear bombers and nuclear-tipped intercontinental ballistic missiles (ICBMs). Although the fall of the Soviet Union in 1991 substantially decreased the chances of nuclear conflict, the air force retains its nuclear strike capability as a deterrent against attacks by other nations on U.S. soil.

POST–COLD WAR ERA

The casualties suffered by the U.S. military during the Vietnam War instilled a reluctance among U.S. leaders to commit ground troops in combat operations. As a result, the most important engagements conducted by the United States military since the end of the Cold War have involved the heavy use of airpower. In some instances, punitive air strikes have been used as a tactic where ground attacks would be logistically difficult or politically sensitive.

The 1991 Gulf War began with air assaults lasting six weeks before troops moved in. Between that conflict and the Iraq War of 2003, the air force maintained no-fly zones inside Iraq as part of the larger strategy of keeping Saddam Hussein's regime isolated. Airpower also played a vital role in U.S. peacekeeping

efforts in the former Yugoslav republics, including airlift operations to provide relief to refugees.

Today the air force is also heavily involved in activities aimed at fighting international terrorism. These include airborne spraying to eradicate narcotics that are a potential source of terrorist funding, and intelligence gathering through the use of spy satellites and unmanned planes called drones. In remote and rugged areas such as the mountains of Afghanistan, airpower can be applied to such tasks more easily and flexibly than can ground troops. The ability to deliver the appropriate amount of force directly to a target quickly and efficiently makes the air force an ideal tool for projecting U.S. power and defending U.S. national security.

—*William de Jong-Lambert*

See also Air Warfare; Atomic Bomb; Berlin Airlift; Bomber Fleet; Cold War; Cuban Missile Crisis; Intercontinental Ballistic Missiles (ICBMs); National Security Act; Nuclear Deterrence; Strategic Air Command; Truman, Harry S., and National Policy; World War I (1914–1918); World War II (1939–1945)

Further Reading

Benton, Jeffrey C. *Air Force Officer's Guide.* Mechanicsburg, PA: Stackpole Books, 2002.

McCarthy, James P., ed. *The Air Force.* Westport, CT: Hugh Lauter Levin, 2002.

Werrell, Kenneth P. *Chasing the Silver Bullet: U.S. Air Force Weapons Development from Vietnam to Desert Storm.* Washington, DC: Smithsonian Books, 2003.

REFLECTIONS

Arguing the Case for Airpower

In January 1921, General Billy Mitchell appeared before Congress to testify about the effectiveness of airpower against ships at sea and to ask to be given a chance to demonstrate his ideas. The following exchange with members of the congressional committee shows the difficulties he faced selling his ideas but also the conviction with which he argued for them.

MITCHELL:	[Our airplanes] can destroy or sink any ship in existence!
CONGRESSMAN BASCOM SLEMP:	If that's true, why aren't you able to convince high-ranking officers of the Army who have the consideration of these problems?
MITCHELL:	We are presenting the situation to you, and we're ready to demonstrate this thing. If you allow no air force, not only will an

	opposing fleet land at will, but their aircraft will fly all over our country.
REPRESENTATIVE THOMAS SISSON:	Should the British example in carriers and a unified air force serve as a model for our country?
MITCHELL:	Yes Sir. I do not consider that the Air Force is to be considered as in any means supplanting the Army. You have always got to come to manpower as the ultimate thing, but we do believe that the air force will control all communications, that it will have a very great effect on land troops and a decisive one against a navy.
SLEMP:	Your argument really leads up to the advocacy of a combined air service.
MITCHELL:	There is no other efficient solution of the air problem. If you scatter the air force around it leads to double overhead, and to a double system of command, and many other difficulties. It has been proven wrong everywhere.
SLEMP:	It seems to me that the principal problem is to demonstrate the certainty of your conclusions.
MITCHELL:	Give us the warships to attack and come and watch it!

U.S. AIR FORCE ACADEMY

Military service academy whose primary function is the development and preparation of officers for air service. In 1948, a board of leading civilian and military educators was appointed to plan a curriculum for an air force academy. The board was headed by then-president of Columbia University Dwight D. Eisenhower. The board's original recommendation was that, during peacetime, at least 40% of the regular officers taken into each branch of the service should be academy graduates. Two years after its creation, the board reached the conclusion that the needs of the air force could not be met merely by expanding other service academies.

The U.S. Congress authorized creation of the Air Force Academy in 1954. On April 1, 1954, President Dwight D. Eisenhower signed the bill establishing the U.S. Air Force Academy. Construction on the facilities began in Colorado Springs, Colorado, in 1955, and the first class of 306 men was sworn in that year. The first class containing women graduated from the academy in 1980. Holly Adams, a member of the academy's 43rd graduating class, was the first female senior class president in Air Force Academy history.

See also U.S. Military Academy; U.S. Naval Academy

U.S. ARMY

Branch of the U.S. military with primary responsibility for land combat. It is the only one of the nation's armed forces able to conduct large-scale land warfare and to seize and occupy territory. These assets make the army one of the principal instruments of U.S. military and national-security policy.

ORGANIZATION

The U.S. Army consists of three branches: the active-duty army, the Army Reserve, and the Army National Guard. Each branch includes both military and civilian personnel. The army is a part of the Department of the Army, which is itself a division of the Department of Defense. The secretary of defense is the civilian officer with direct authority over the U.S. Army.

The active-duty army consists of some 512,000 troops deployed in bases throughout the world. As a result of the 2003 U.S. invasion of Iraq, some 115,000 of those troops are currently stationed in the Persian Gulf region. Most of those are serving in Iraq, although there are significant numbers of soldiers in Kuwait and smaller numbers in other Gulf states, such as Saudi Arabia. The army also stations about 70,000 soldiers in Germany and some 40,000 each in South Korea and Japan.

The Army National Guard and Army Reserve were developed as auxiliary organizations to support the active-duty army. They serve as a pool of trained reinforcements for the army and a ready force to handle emergency tasks, such as providing disaster relief. There are currently about 350,000 troops in the Army National Guard and 200,000 in the Army Reserve. Both the Army National Guard and Army Reserve have been called upon to shoulder a large part of the burden in Iraq following the 2003 war. As of March 2004, approximately 37,000 Army National Guard troops and 17,000 army reservists were serving in the Gulf.

HISTORY

The army has not always held the prominent place in U.S. affairs that it does today. Throughout most of U.S. history, the army has been a small force that was expanded only during times of war. It was not until after World War II that the United States adopted the policy of maintaining a large standing army.

Revolutionary War to Civil War

The U.S. Army had humble beginnings in the American Revolutionary War. The main American force was the volunteer Continental Army, most of whose recruits signed up to receive a cash bonus and a promise of land after the war. The soldiers were inexperienced and ill-equipped and had little or no training for battle. The Continental Army was joined by state and local militia, who were often better equipped and more experienced than the regular army.

The Continental Army lost most of the battles it fought against British regular troops early in the war. Late in 1776, General George Washington adopted a new strategy of avoiding large confrontations in favor of a guerilla war using hit-and-run tactics. These tactics proved successful in frustrating the British army and in convincing France to enter the war against Britain in 1780. The Continental Army's defeat of British forces at Yorktown four years later ensured American independence.

Congress disbanded most of the army after the war, and by 1789, the army had only 800 soldiers. The military weakness of the United States was revealed when the country became involved in the War of 1812. The United States hoped to drive British forces from Canada, but the small and poorly trained American troops were ineffective against British soldiers. The army did win a major engagement at the Battle of New Orleans in 1815, but by and large, the few land combats of the war had no decisive influence on the outcome.

The army remained small in the following decades, but it grew increasingly professional after the establishment of the U.S. Military Academy at West Point, New York. The westward expansion of the United States during this period brought the nation into conflict with Mexico in 1846. The Mexican War (1846–48) was the first conflict fought by the U.S. Army mainly on foreign soil. In a foreshadowing of future wars, the U.S. Army defeated a numerically superior Mexican foe through the use of improved technology and superior tactics.

The Civil War and the Late 1800s

The United States Army entered the American Civil War (1861–65) with its already small core of experienced soldiers divided between Union and Confederate forces. Robert E. Lee, commander of the Confederate Army, and his Union rival in the final years of the war, Ulysses S. Grant, were West Point graduates who had served together during the Mexican War. Many other former U.S. Army officers also served in the ranks of the Confederacy.

Civil War combat was marked by an unprecedented level of death and destruction. Technical improvements in weaponry, combined with a reliance on outdated tactics from an earlier era, produced staggering casualties for both sides. A major battle might claim 10,000 to 20,000 lives and result in many times more casualties. An estimated 600,000 Americans on both sides died during the war, more than the total of all other U.S. wars combined.

The horrible casualties convinced U.S. President Abraham Lincoln that a volunteer army would be insufficient to win the war. In March 1863, the U.S. government declared that all male citizens 20 to 35 years of age, and all unmarried men 35 to 45, were eligible for military service. The measure was extremely unpopular and led to a draft riot in New York City that summer. The Confederate Army was also forced to resort to conscription, which was no more popular in the South than it was in the North.

After the Civil War, most army draftees and volunteers returned to civilian life and the army once again shrunk in size. The army's main missions in the years following the war were the occupation of the former Confederate states and pacifying the Indians on the western frontier. In the South, the army kept order during Reconstruction, the process of rebuilding the South and bringing it back into the Union. Reconstruction officially ended in 1877, when the last federal troops were withdrawn.

During the 1870s and 1880s, the army directed its efforts mainly to fighting Native American tribes who resisted U.S. expansion into their lands. The earliest major battles of the so-called Indian Wars took place in the mid-1850s, and the last occurred in 1877. However, continuing battles with remaining tribes continued throughout the 1880s. By the early 1890s, the last remaining pockets of Native American resistance had been subdued, largely as a result of the efforts of the army.

The Era of Imperialism

By the late 19th century, the United States had grown from a weak agricultural nation to a powerful industrial giant. American companies, eager to find new markets for their goods, drove a new wave of American imperialism. In 1898, the destruction of the U.S. warship *Maine* in Cuba's Havana harbor led the United States to declare war on Spain (which owned Cuba at the time), despite proof of Spanish involvement. During the war, the United States captured Spanish possessions in Cuba, Puerto Rico, and the Philippines. Although the war lacked notable land battles, it marked the Army's first major seaborne deployment on foreign soil. More importantly, it established the United States as a global power with interests far from its own shores.

At the start of World War I in 1914, the U.S. Army consisted of some 98,000 regular troops with an additional 27,000 in the National Guard. It was the largest American peacetime army to date, but it was dwarfed by the major European armies, which numbered millions of soldiers apiece. The United States remained neutral until 1917, finally declaring on war on Germany after repeated German provocations. The U.S. entry was a turning point in the war. A wartime U.S. draft brought hundreds of thousands of fresh troops to the Allied cause and helped to defeat the tired German army. World War I marked the largest U.S. Army mobilization up to that time. More than 4 million soldiers served in the U.S. Army during World War I, and over 50,000 were killed in action.

As after previous wars, the United States rapidly demobilized after 1918, cutting the size of the army to fewer than 100,000 troops. However, by the 1930s, the growing possibility of another European war, and the rise of a militarily aggressive Japanese empire in the Pacific led to an increase in U.S. military spending. This spending was not, though, accompanied by a significant increase in U.S. ground forces. When Japan attacked the U.S. fleet at Pearl Harbor on December 7, 1941, the United States found itself once again at war with an army unprepared for the task. However, outrage at the sneak attack on Pearl Harbor spurred a wave of enlistment in the United States; millions of men volunteered for the army and other branches of the military. Congress reinstated the draft and conscripted millions more.

World War II and Korea

Supported by Allied industrial and technological superiority, the U.S. Army during World War II grew into the most powerful military force in the world. In addition, the army was no longer solely a land-bound force; it relied heavily on airpower during the war. The Army Air Force, separated from the Army Signal Corps between the wars, provided much of the U.S. striking power in World War II. Tactical army fighters and fighter-bombers provided close support for troops in battle, and long-range strategic bombers attacked German and Japanese industry.

The U.S. Army in World War II was also the nation's first fully mechanized army. Troops no longer marched or rode into battle on horseback but were carried by trucks, jeeps, half-tracks, and other motorized vehicles. Combined land-sea-air amphibious assaults throughout Europe and the Pacific also enabled the army to perfect its combined arms tactics. Open terrain in North Africa and Western Europe allowed tank commanders to develop and practice new armored doctrines. The army pioneered the development of new technology, such as radar, field radios, flamethrowers, bazookas, and guided rockets that would change the face of warfare.

At its peak in World War II, the U.S. Army totaled more than 8 million soldiers; 230,000 lost their lives in combat. After the war ended, most draftees and volunteers left the army and quickly returned to their civilian lives. The outbreak of the Korean War in 1950 thus caught the United States unprepared to wage another major land war. President Harry Truman returned to the draft to provide the manpower needed to defend South Korea. Some 2 million Americans would eventually serve in Korea, and 27,000 would die before the war ended in 1953. The United States still maintains a significant military presence in South Korea.

Growing Cold War tensions, exemplified by the outbreak of the Korean War, convinced the U.S. government that the country needed a standing army. After Korea, the United States maintained the largest peacetime army in its history. Large numbers of troops were stationed in overseas hotspots, particularly Germany and South Korea. Basing troops in Germany assured American allies that U.S. troops would meet any planned invasion of Western Europe by the USSR. United States troops in South Korea provided similar security guarantees against North Korean aggression.

Vietnam and Its Aftermath

In the late 1950s and early 1960s, the United States became increasingly involved in affairs in Southeast

Asia. Concerned about a communist takeover of South Vietnam, President John F. Kennedy sent U.S. Army Special Forces overseas in 1961 to support the South Vietnamese Army. By 1963, more than 16,000 American troops and advisers were in the country and some had even taken part in combat. The following year, President Lyndon B. Johnson dramatically increased the number of troops in Vietnam.

In Vietnam, the army relied on airpower and technological sophistication as never before. The war saw the first large-scale use of helicopters to engage enemy troops, carry U.S. soldiers into battle, and evacuate casualties. In response, the less technologically advanced North Vietnamese forces borrowed a page from George Washington, using hit-and-run tactics with devastating effect. By avoiding large set-piece battles, they canceled the U.S. Army's advantage in firepower and frustrated efforts to force the war to a decisive conclusion. American public support for the war gradually eroded in the face of heavy U.S. casualties in a war that seemed to have no prospect for victory. The United States finally pulled out in 1973 after the loss of 50,000 soldiers, more than 30,000 of them from the army.

The defeat in Vietnam had two major effects on the U.S. Army. First, it made American leaders more reluctant to commit troops to combat. The United States turned to the rapid, long-range striking power of the air force and navy to project U.S. power with less risk of casualties. Protests about the unfairness of the draft during Vietnam also put an end to conscription. Even before the last U.S. troops left Vietnam, the draft was abolished and the army became once again an all-volunteer force.

The Post–Cold War Army

Throughout the Cold War, army tactics and strategy were dictated by the need to counter the threat posed by the Soviet Union. The collapse of the Soviet Union in 1991 forced a major reassessment of army priorities. With the disappearance of the Soviet threat, the army reduced its force by about one-third and concentrated on increasing its readiness and modernization. The United States adopted a new strategy of being ready to fight two major conflicts at the same time while still providing troops for disaster relief at home or UN peacekeeping missions abroad.

That same year, during the Gulf War of 1991, the U.S. Army fought its first major engagement since Vietnam. In response to Iraq's invasion of Kuwait in late 1990, U.S. forces led an international coalition to expel the Iraqi forces. Nearly 500,000 U.S. Army troops took part in the campaign, which forced the Iraqis to surrender in just four days. The swiftness and decisiveness of the Gulf War victory restored a great deal of the pride and prestige the army had lost after Vietnam.

With the United States uninvolved in major conflicts during the 1990s, the army was deployed mainly in several UN peacekeeping missions, including those in Bosnia, Kosovo, Haiti, and Somalia. These missions, though important for U.S. foreign relations, were often unpopular with the American public—especially when they resulted in U.S. casualties. Public outcry at the loss of 18 soldiers in Somalia in 1993 led the United States to abandon that mission.

Afghanistan, Iraq, and the War on Terror

Following the September 11, 2001, terrorist attacks on the United States, the U.S. Army was deployed in an overseas war for the first time since 1991. In early 2002, U.S. Army units supported by special-operations troops were sent to Afghanistan. Their objectives were to capture the al-Qaeda terrorists who planned the attacks and to depose Afghanistan's ruling Taliban government, which was supporting the terrorists. The rugged Afghan terrain made operations difficult and offered an almost endless number of hiding places for al-Qaeda forces. Although the army succeeded in toppling the Taliban and installing a democratic Afghan government, it failed to capture most of the senior al-Qaeda leaders or destroy the terrorist organization.

A year later, the U.S. Army led a coalition that invaded Iraq to depose the regime of President Saddam Hussein, who was suspected of concealing weapons of mass destruction. The army overran Iraq in less than a month, sweeping the overmatched Iraqi army from the battlefield. However, in the aftermath of the fighting, Iraqis loyal to the former regime began an armed resistance that soon killed more U.S. troops than had died during the invasion itself. Critics claimed that the army had not committed sufficient forces to secure the peace after winning the war. They faulted civilian leaders for relying on a doctrine that deemphasized the need for troops and relied too much on mobility, speed, airpower, and superior intelligence and communications technology.

The occupation and insurgency in Iraq poses a serious dilemma for the army. To meet troop demands without resorting to a draft, the army has forced soldiers to stay beyond their official discharge dates, a practice called *forced retention.* It has also speeded up troop rotations, so soldiers get less time off before having to return to combat. The war has also stretched the National Guard and Reserves to their limits. In early 2005, the army reported that all three of its branches were significantly below their reenlistment and recruiting goals. Nevertheless, President George W. Bush has vowed not to reinstate the draft. If crises arise in Korea or other global hotspots, that vow may be put to the test.

—*John Haley*

See also All-Volunteer Force; Conscription/Volunteer Force; Conventional Forces; Conventional Forces in Europe; Green Berets; Guerrilla Warfare; Interservice Rivalry; Military Draft; Patton, George (1885–1945); Powell, Colin (1937–); Reserve Forces; Signal Corps; UN Peacekeeping; U.S. Air Force; U.S. Marine Corps; U.S. Navy

Further Reading

Halberstadt, Hans. *Army: The U.S. Army Today.* Bolton, UK: Chartwell Books, 2003.

Morris, James M. *History of the U.S. Army.* Emmaus, PA: JG Press, 2003.

U.S. Army Historical Foundation. *The. Army.* Westport, CT: Hugh Lauter Levin, 2001.

REFLECTIONS

Executive Order 9981: Integration Comes to the Army

On July 26, 1948, President Harry S. Truman issued Executive Order 9981, which led to the integration of African Americans within the ranks of the U.S. Army. The following are excerpts from that executive order:

Whereas it is essential that there be maintained in the armed services of the United States the highest standards of democracy, with equality of treatment and opportunity for all those who served in our country's defense . . . it is hereby ordered as follows.

It is hereby declared . . . that there shall be equality of treatment and opportunity for all persons in the armed services without regard to race, color, religion or national origin. This policy shall be put into effect as rapidly as possible, having due regard to the time

required to effectuate any necessary changes without impairing efficiency or morale.

There shall be created in the National Military Establishment an advisory committee to be known as the President's Committee on Equality of Treatment and Opportunity . . . [which] is authorized on behalf of the President to examine into the rules, procedures and practices of the armed services in order to determine in what respect such rules, procedures and practices may be altered or improved with a view to carrying out the policy of this order.

All executive departments and agencies of the Federal Government are authorized and directed to cooperate with the Committee in its work, and to furnish the Committee such information or the services of such persons as the Committee may require in the performance of its duties.

U.S. ARMY WAR COLLEGE
See WAR COLLEGES

U.S. CENTRAL COMMAND (USCENTCOM)

A regional headquarters responsible for planning and conducting U.S. military activity in northeast Africa and southwest and central Asia. As a unified combatant command, CENTCOM is composed of forces from the army, navy, air force, and marines, and has a broad and ongoing mission. The regional division of commands represented by the Unified Combat Command structure allows U.S. defense planning to be focused on specific regions. CENTCOM is one of nine Unified Combatant Commands that include U.S. Northern Command (NORTHCOM), U.S. European Command (EUCOM), U.S. Pacific Command (PACOM), and U.S. Southern Command (SOUTHCOM), as well as the functionally ordered U.S. Joint Forces Command (JFCOM), U.S. Special Operations Command (SOCOM), U.S. Transportation Command (TRANSCOM), and U.S. Strategic Command (STRATCOM). CENTCOM is headquartered at MacDill Air Force Base in Tampa, Florida. The commander in chief of CENTCOM (CINCCENT) reports directly to the secretary of defense.

CENTCOM has no combat units permanently assigned to it. Instead, all four armed services provide CENTCOM with component commands. These include USARCENT (army), USCENTAF (air force),

USMARCENT (marines), USNAVCENT (navy), and SOCCENT (special operations).

CENTCOM's area of responsibility covers 27 countries from the Horn of Africa to central Asia. CENTCOM's Northern Red Sea and Arabian Peninsula area consists of Egypt, Iraq, Jordan, Lebanon, Syria, and Yemen, as well as the Gulf Cooperation Council (GCC) states of Bahrain, Kuwait, Oman, Qatar, Saudi Arabia, and the United Arab Emirates. United States interests in this area include strategic oil resources and access to waterways such as the Persian Gulf. The Horn of Africa region covered by CENTCOM consists of Djibouti, Eritrea, Ethiopia, Kenya, Somalia, Sudan, and the islands of Seychelles. This region is considered important because it borders the critical sea lines of communication through the Red Sea. CENTCOM's south Asian area comprises Iran, Pakistan, and Afghanistan. Main U.S interests in this region include containing Iranian military expansion and fighting terrorism. The central Asian states included in CENTCOM's area of responsibility are Kyrgyzstan, Kazakhstan, Turkmenistan, Tajikistan, and Uzbekistan. Oil and gas development in the Caspian area are of key importance to U.S. interests in the region.

CENTCOM seeks to enhance U.S. presence in order to maintain stability and regional security in the volatile regions it covers. The free flow of oil and trade, freedom of navigation in the Persian Gulf, and the war on terrorism are key U.S. interests in the region covered by CENTCOM. To fulfill its objectives, CENTCOM maintains an active peacetime politico-military engagement program with countries in its area of responsibility, which include combined exercises and training, humanitarian assistance, and security assistance. In the event of a conflict, CENTCOM is poised to quickly mobilize and respond.

The Defense Department defines CENTCOM's theater strategy as "shaping the Central Region for the 21st Century." CENTCOM's theater goals are grouped into war fighting, engagement, and development categories. War-fighting objectives are the most important and include protection, promotion, and preservation of U.S. interests in the Central Region, such as regional stability, free flow of energy resources, and freedom of navigation; development and maintenance of necessary forces and infrastructure to be able to respond militarily should the need arise; deterrence of conflict through forward presence and joint military exercises; and maintenance of combat readiness to be able to decisively fight and win a conflict should deterrence fail. Engagement objectives include maintenance

and support of coalitions and collective security efforts that support U.S. interests in the region; close relationships with regional political and military leaders; support for regional militaries; and countering terrorism and the threat of weapons of mass destruction. Development goals include prompt response to humanitarian and environmental crises and the maintenance of awareness of regional security, political, social, and economic trends.

Created in 1983 to replace the temporary Rapid Deployment Joint Task Force (RDJTF), the primary mission of CENTCOM originally was to deter Soviet aggression and protect U.S. interests in southwest Asia. CENTCOM has since served as an effective means of projecting U.S. military power to the Gulf region from halfway around the globe. Some recent operations conducted under CENTCOM include the liberation of Kuwait under Operation Desert Storm (1991); humanitarian intervention in Somalia with Operation Restore Hope (1992–93); combating international terrorism in Afghanistan with Operation Enduring Freedom (2001); and the invasion of Iraq and the overthrow of Saddam Hussein with Operation Iraqi Freedom (2003).

See also Counterterrorism; Gulf War (1990–1991); Iraq War of 2003; Middle East and U.S. Policy; U.S. Northern Command; U.S. Pacific Command; U.S. Southern Command

Further Reading

Mendel, William W., and Graham H. Turbiville Jr. *The CINCs' Strategies: The Combatant Command Process.* Carlisle Barracks, PA: Strategic Studies Institute, U.S. Army War College, 1998.

U.S. COAST GUARD

Branch of the U.S. armed forces responsible for coastal defense, maritime security, maritime safety, facilitation of maritime commerce and recreation on the water, and the protection of national resources. In carrying out its duties, the Coast Guard operates in domestic waters, off the coast, and internationally.

The Coast Guard has its roots in the late-18th-century establishment of the Revenue Cutter Service. or, as it was also known, the Revenue Marine. This service was initially responsible for protecting the collection of federal revenue, preventing smuggling, and enforcing trade and tariff laws. On January 28, 1915, the Act to Create the Coast Guard combined the Revenue Cutter Service and the Life-Saving Service into the U.S. Coast Guard.

In 1939, the Lighthouse Service was also moved under the Coast Guard's control. This placed the operation of lighthouses under the authority of the Coast Guard. However, recent improvements in navigational technology, such as the satellite-based Global Positioning System (GPS), have made most U.S. lighthouses obsolete. Currently, there is only one lighthouse still in use, the light station in Boston Harbor.

Over the years, the duties of the Coast Guard have been expanded to include more law-enforcement responsibilities, as well as search-and-rescue tasks, with the merging of various other services under the Coast Guard. In 1946 the Bureau of Marine Inspection was eliminated and its duties—the safety of merchant vessels and merchant marine licensing—were also transferred to the Coast Guard. Additionally, the Coast Guard has been charged with charting the U.S. coastline and protecting the marine environment. The Coast Guard also responds to oil spills throughout the world, creating the National Strike Force for this purpose in 1973.

Due to the ever-changing international and domestic political environment, certain duties have received greater emphasis during different periods in the Coast Guard's history. During Prohibition, the Coast Guard found itself primarily focused on the prevention of smuggling. After World War II, navigation and safety became a much more important responsibility for the Coast Guard. The law-enforcement duties of the Coast Guard again rose to prominence during the 1960s, in response to increased emigration from Cuba in the wake of Fidel Castro's communist takeover of the island. Preventing drug smuggling became an increasing challenge to the Coast Guard starting in the 1970s.

The Coast Guard has for much of its history been under the control of the Treasury Department. However, in 1967 the Coast Guard was placed under the Department of Transportation. Later, in 2003, it was moved to its current placement under the Department of Homeland Security. During wartime, however, the Coast Guard comes under the supervision of the U.S. Navy. The Guard's smaller ships with shallower drafts often prove useful when supplementing the navy's fleet. Under the navy, Coast Guard ships have been sent to foreign waters and its personnel have participated in many military actions.

Soon after its founding, the Coast Guard began to make use of aircraft for its missions. As technology has improved over the years, airpower has increasingly been used to carry out many of the Coast Guard's duties. In 1941, the Coast Guard created the Office of Air Sea Rescue. During World War II, Coast Guard aircraft patrolled the seas for German U-boats. Aircraft are especially suited to the Coast Guard's search-and-rescue missions. Helicopters, originally developed for antisubmarine warfare, were found to be particularly effective in a search-and-rescue role.

There are currently two U.S. Coast Guard commands: the Atlantic and Pacific commands. The Coast Guard has approximately 1,400 boats and 211 aircraft under its authority. It is made up of civilian, active-duty, reserve, and auxiliary personnel. Throughout its more than 200-year history, the U.S. Coast Guard has performed a valuable service in both war and peacetime, and it continues to do so today.

See also Border and Transportation Security; Coast Guard, The, and National Security; U.S. Navy

Further Reading

Conner, Kit, and Caroline Conner. *Always Ready: Today's U.S. Coast Guard.* St. Paul, MN: Motorbooks, 2004.

USE OF FORCE, AUTHORIZATIONS OF
See WAR POWERS ACT (1973)

U.S.–JAPAN ALLIANCE

Military and diplomatic partnership between the world's two largest economies. Official diplomatic relations between the United States and Japan date to the Treaty of Peace and Amity at the Convention of Kanagawa in March 1854. Since 1951, with the signing of the U.S.-Japan Security Treaty, the U.S. has been allowed to maintain bases in Japan in exchange for which the Japanese have received security guarantees, including the protection of the U.S. nuclear umbrella, a situation that has enabled Japan to maintain security at minimal cost.

HISTORY

In 1853, Japan was a country that had been sealed in a self-imposed isolation from the outside world for some 200 years. That era of Japanese history vanished with the appearance of four U.S. Navy ships under the command of Commodore Matthew Perry at Shimoda on July 8, 1853. The Treaty of Peace and Amity, signed the following year in Yokohama, established diplomatic relations between Japan and the United States. Japan opened itself to commerce and diplomacy with foreign powers and embarked on a lightning-quick modernization of its economy, infrastructure, education system, and military. With its formal annexation of Korea in 1910, Japan was fast on its way to becoming a world power. It also embarked on a collision course with its powerful Pacific Rim ally, the United States.

Japan's militarism and expansionism culminated in its 1941 attack on the U.S. fleet in Pearl Harbor, an act that brought the United States into World War II. Four years later, the Japanese empire came to a tragic end with the U.S. atomic bombing of Hiroshima and Nagasaki and Japan's subsequent surrender. The war was followed by a seven-year American occupation, which saw the writing of a new Japanese constitution, the establishment of the National Police Reserve (the forerunner of Japan's Self-Defense Forces), the rebirth of the Japanese economy, and the signing of the U.S.-Japan Security Treaty that laid the foundation for the current alliance. The postoccupation 1950s also saw the establishment of the '55 system, through which the Liberal Democratic Party (LDP) has controlled the Diet (Japanese parliament) and Japanese politics alone or by coalition since 1955.

The 1960s were marked by several controversial developments in the U.S.-Japan alliance. In 1960, Japanese Prime Minister Kishi Nobusuke rammed through the Diet a revised U.S-Japan Security Treaty in advance of a scheduled visit by President Dwight Eisenhower. Although widespread public protests led to the resignation of Kishi and the cancellation of the Eisenhower visit, the revised treaty went into effect. Ideological tensions between the United States and Japan in the immediate post-occupation period were relieved by the economic-growth policies of Kishi's successors, Prime Ministers Ikeda and Sato.

The Vietnam War tested the strength of the U.S.–Japan alliance. Japanese university students protested the decision to allow U.S. planes to use the Japanese island of Okinawa as a base for bombing raids on North Vietnam. Tensions on university campuses in Japan mirrored those in the United States,

and Japanese gathered outside U.S. military facilities to protest the war. At the same time, Japan's increasing economic might gave it the necessary leverage to negotiate the recovery of land held by the United States since World War II. In 1968, the Ogasawara Islands were returned to Japan and an agreement was reached to return to Japanese control large U.S. industrial facilities in the Tokyo area.

Diplomatic tensions eased somewhat with the return of Okinawa to Japanese control in 1972 and the U.S. withdrawal of troops from Vietnam the following year. The early 1970s also witnessed diplomatic rapprochement with China on the part of both alliance partners. The late 1970s, however, brought strain to the alliance. A booming Japanese economy and trade surplus with America, combined with an economic slump in the United States, led to allegations of Japanese protectionism. Another object of dispute between the two allies has been the 1978 Host Nation Support agreement, through which Japan pays maintenance and utilities costs at U.S. military bases.

The 1980s witnessed several conflicting trends within the alliance. Increasing Japanese trade surpluses with the United States led to public outcry and calls for protection of the American market and American jobs. On the other hand, the U.S.-Japan alliance remained strong in the waning years of the Cold War, guided as it was by the strong interpersonal ties between President Ronald Reagan and Prime Minister Nakasone. It was Nakasone who coined the phrase "unsinkable aircraft carrier" to characterize Japan's security role in the enduring U.S.–Japan partnership.

The following decade brought with it Japanese financial support of U.S.-led efforts to defeat Iraqi forces in Operation Desert Storm. This effort often has been derided as checkbook diplomacy due to the fact that Japan sent money but was prohibited by its constitution from sending troops. Japanese public support for the security alliance was eroded in 1995 with the rape of an Okinawan schoolgirl by three U.S. Marines. Tensions between the U.S. military and the people of Okinawa had been simmering for years; the rape incident brought them to boiling. The fact that 75% of U.S. bases in Japan are located in Okinawa prefecture further complicated the issue of civilian–military relations.

In the wake of the September 11 terrorist attacks on New York and Washington, DC, Japanese Prime Minister Junichiro Koizumi emerged as a staunch U.S. ally. Koizumi stretched the limits of public and parliamentary support—as well as Japan's own constitution—in dispatching the Japanese Maritime Self-Defense Force (JMSDF) to the Indian Ocean to support U.S.-led operations in Afghanistan. Following the U.S. invasion of Iraq in March 2003, Koizumi sent Ground Self-Defense Forces to Iraq in early 2004 as a show of support for coalition efforts. This deployment of troops has served to strengthen the U.S.–Japan security relationship but is greatly unpopular with the Japanese public.

CURRENT ISSUES

As the alliance moves into the 21st century, the relationship between the two strongest Pacific Rim economies faces a great number of challenges to its continued popular support and shared goals. Will the United States move its military facilities from Okinawa? Will the Japanese public continue to tolerate the U.S. military presence? How long will they tolerate having Japanese Self-Defense Forces deployed into harm's way in support of the American presence in Afghanistan and Iraq? Will Japan and the United States continue to maintain a joint approach to North Korea's claimed development of nuclear weapons? Will both powers take the same approach to growing Chinese military might?

The U.S.–Japan alliance, based on 50 years of common security interests, has weathered wars in Korea and Vietnam, a Cold War, disputes over trade, public protest against U.S. bases, and the very security treaty that binds the two nations together. Prime Minister Koizumi has chosen to cast his nation's lot with the security interests of the United States. Whether Japanese and American security interests will continue to converge is a question key to understanding the future of this alliance between the world's two largest economies.

—*Daniel P. McDonald*

See also Burdensharing; Iraq War of 2003; Korea, North and South; Okinawa; Trade and Foreign Aid; World War II (1939–1945)

Further Reading

Cronin, Patrick M., and Michael J. Green. *Redefining the U.S.–Japan Alliance: Tokyo's National Defense Program.* Stockton, CA: University Press of the Pacific, 2004.
Vogel, Steven K. *U.S.–Japan Relations in a Changing World.* Washington, DC: Brookings Institution, 2002.

U.S. MARINE CORPS

Branch of the U.S. armed services specializing in amphibious and combined land–sea–air operations. Marines, historically defined as soldiers who are transported by sea but fight on land, have a long combat history. Ancient navies often carried significant land forces into battle. For example, in the second century BCE, the Romans conquered their longtime rival Carthage with a seaborne invasion. The Dark Ages following the fall of the Roman Empire was a time of little maritime activity in Europe, and marines disappeared as a significant military force for several hundred years. However, expanded naval activity during the Age of Exploration in the 16th and 17th centuries revived the marines as part of European military forces.

HISTORY OF THE U.S. MARINES

By the time of the American Revolution in the late 18th century, all of the world's major navies included marine detachments. The U.S. Marines trace their history to November 15, 1775, when the Continental Congress decided to create two battalions of marines to add to the colonies' existing military forces. These two battalions were never actually formed, due primarily to a shortage of manpower, but small bands of U.S. marines did see action in the Bahamas. By the end of the war, marines had seen action on both land and sea, but their numbers remained small and they were a relatively insignificant part of the U.S. armed forces.

In 1798, the U.S. Congress passed an act to attach a Marine Corps of 33 officers and 848 soldiers to the U.S. Navy. One of the notable early missions undertaken by the new U.S. Marine Corps was an engagement with Barbary Coast pirates who had been threatening U.S. shipping interests in the Mediterranean Sea. After landing on the coast of North Africa and crossing the Libyan Desert, the Marines captured the city of Derna in Tripoli. This, however, was one of the few significant military roles the marines played in early U.S. history.

Though originally the marines focused on hand-to-hand combat aboard ship, due to the changing nature of technology, by the second half of the 19th century the U.S. Marine Corps began to train in amphibious warfare. Marine Corps participation in U.S. military campaigns increased steadily throughout the late 19th and 20th centuries. During the Spanish-American War of 1898, the corps played a larger role than it had in previous conflicts, attacking both Manila Bay in the Philippines and Guantánamo Bay in Cuba. President Theodore Roosevelt also frequently used the U.S. Marines to project U.S. power in Latin America during the early 1900s.

Although the United States entered World War I quite late in the conflict, the marines played a part in the Allied victory over Germany. The most notable example of the marine contribution was their reinforcement of the French troops at the Bois de Belleau against a major German advance. It was reportedly during this engagement that Marine Corps captain Lloyd Williams uttered the famous line, "Retreat, hell! We just got here!"

During World War II, the corps, with its training in amphibious assaults, played a decisive role in the fighting in the Pacific against the Japanese. From 1942 to 1945, the marines fought a series of brutal and costly battles against Japanese island fortresses such as Guadalcanal, Wake, Iwo Jima, and Okinawa. In the battle for the small island of Iwo Jima off the coast of Japan, 23,000 out of the 60,000 marines who landed on the island were killed or wounded. Fighting against Japanese forces that refused to surrender even in the face of overwhelming odds, the marines proved victorious despite suffering extremely high casualties.

The aftermath of World War II brought several changes to the marines. The National Security Act of 1947 reorganized the U.S. military structure and gave the Marine Corps a measure of formal independence, although it still remained under the general authority of the navy. In the 1960s, the Marine Corps was called upon to play a major role in the Vietnam War. In fact, more marines fought in Vietnam than had fought during World War II. However, the Vietnam War severely depleted marine manpower and forced the Corps to lower standards to meet recruiting goals. The U.S. pullout from Vietnam reduced the demand for active-duty troops and eased recruiting pressures on the marines. As a result, the quality of marines and their training improved during the late 1970s and 1980s. In 1973, the Marine Corps was given a separate seat on the Joint Chiefs of Staff.

Recruitment for the Marine Corps today is highly selective; candidates must have a high school diploma as well as meet certain physical requirements, such as minimum height, weight, and physical fitness. An enlistee enters the marines as a private, the lowest enlisted rank. Corps officers either serve under a warrant from the service secretary or receive a commission from the president and are confirmed by the U.S. Senate. The Marine Corps officer generally begins at the rank of second lieutenant and can work his or her way up the ranks to achieve the highest rank of general. The ratio of officers to enlistees in the Corps is approximately 1 to 8.6, a ratio that is much lower than in the other service branches.

MARINE CORPS ORGANIZATION

As of 2004, there were about 172,000 active-duty marines, organized into three divisions. Each division consists of three infantry regiments of three battalions each. Three companies make up each battalion, and three platoons make up each company. A platoon contains three squads, each of which is composed of three fire teams. In addition to active-duty troops, the Marine Corps has reserves that can be called up in times of need. These reserves were used during both the Gulf War of 1991 and the Iraq War of 2003. The requirements for joining the reserves are slightly more relaxed than for the regular marines.

Marines can choose to serve in one of several fields, including infantry, supporting combat units, or aviation. Aviation is a particularly sought-after field. Marines are stationed on several of the Corps' bases located in various locations in the United States. The commandant of the Marine Corps is headquartered at the oldest U.S. Marine post, found in Washington, DC. Other marine bases are located at Quantico, Virginia; Camp LeJeune, North Carolina; and Camp Pendleton, near San Diego, California. The marines also have several training bases on Parris Island, South Carolina.

The U.S. Marine Corps has had a complex history and has at certain periods found itself on the verge of extinction. Over time, the marines have had to adapt to the changing military environment to find their role. With the current need for flexible specialized forces that can be deployed rapidly, it is likely that the marines will play a significant role in future conflicts.

—*Rebecca S. Perkins*

See also Amphibious Warfare; Marine Barracks, Beirut (1983); Spanish-American War (1898); World War II (1939–1945)

Further Reading

Krulak, Victor H. *First to Fight: An Inside View of the U.S. Marine Corps.* Annapolis, MD: Naval Institute Press, 1999.
Moskin, J. Robert. *The U.S. Marine Corps Story.* 3rd ed. New York: Konecky & Konecky, 2004.

U.S. MILITARY ACADEMY (WEST POINT)

Military academy established to educate and train commissioned officers for the United States Army. The mission of the academy is "to educate, train, and inspire the Corps of Cadets so that each graduate is a commissioned leader of character committed to the values of Duty, Honor, Country; professional growth throughout a career as an officer in the United States Army; and a lifetime of selfless service to the nation."

Located on the Hudson River in West Point, New York, the U.S. Military Academy has been an integral part of the American military since the Revolutionary War. At that time, West Point was the site of a key American fortress that the revolutionaries, including General George Washington, considered the most strategically important location in America. Legislation signed by President Thomas Jefferson in 1802 transformed West Point from a fortress to an educational establishment: the United States Military Academy. In its more than 200 years of existence, the United States Military Academy has produced many notable graduates, including Ulysses S. Grant, Robert E. Lee, William Tecumseh Sherman, Dwight D. Eisenhower, Thomas "Stonewall" Jackson, Douglas MacArthur, Omar Bradley, and George Patton.

Initially, the academy provided only engineering training to students. Throughout the ensuing two centuries, the curriculum was expanded to include a broader range of sciences and humanities. However, academics are only one part of the broader educational experience required by the academy. In addition to the academic program, cadets participate in a physical program, a military program, and moral-ethical development to produce a well-rounded graduate prepared to carry out the duties of a U.S. Army officer. There are approximately 4,000 graduates enrolled at the academy under the current legislative provisions.

The academy graduates approximately 900 cadets a year. Each graduate is awarded a bachelor of science and is commissioned as a second lieutenant in the United States Army. Following their commission, the graduates are obligated to provide at least five years of military service. These newly commissioned graduates account for approximately 25% of the army's annual need for new lieutenants. Despite their relatively small numbers in the overall force, academy graduates are considered an indispensable part of the modern U.S. Army.

See also U.S. Air Force Academy; U.S. Naval Academy

U.S. NAVAL ACADEMY (ANNAPOLIS)

Educational establishment responsible for training and educating officers for the United States Navy. The United States Naval Academy is charged with the mission of developing students (known as midshipmen) "morally, mentally, and physically," thereby by producing graduates who are effective marine and naval officers.

Prior to the founding of the United State Naval Academy, the navy oversaw the Philadelphia Naval Asylum and a few smaller naval schools in New York City, Norfolk, and Boston. In 1845, Secretary of the Navy George Bancroft moved the Naval School to Fort Severn in Annapolis, Maryland. The institution's name was changed to the United States Naval Academy in 1850 and a four-year study program was implemented. In 1933, Congress authorized the Naval Academy to award bachelor of science degrees. Among the Naval Academy's notable alumni are Senator John McCain, former president Jimmy Carter, former chief of naval operations Arleigh Burke, and Admirals Chester Nimitz and George Dewey.

Today, the academy's curriculum has been expanded beyond the core classes to include nearly 20 different majors encompassing the sciences and humanities. However, the education provided to students at the Naval Academy is not limited to academics. The academy also provides moral, physical, and professional education to produce future officers trained and equipped to carry out the duties of a naval or marine officer in the United States military.

See also U.S. Air Force Academy; U.S. Military Academy

U.S. NAVY

Branch of the United States armed forces responsible for naval operations. The navy is the oldest of the U.S.

armed services to be officially established by Congress. Throughout its long and colorful history. it has played a key role in defending U.S. interests, assisting U.S. allies, and projecting U.S. power.

REVOLUTIONARY WAR PERIOD (1775–89)

On October 13, 1775, the Continental Congress authorized the creation of the Continental Navy to intercept supplies and arms destined for the British soldiers occupying Boston. Others in the rebellious colonies had also seen the need for a naval fighting force. Even before Congress acted, George Washington had assumed command of several vessels and some colonial governors also had outfitted warships. The Continental Navy would prove to be an effective weapon against the British and would signal to the world that America was a mature nation.

Cadets at the United States Military Academy at West Point, New York, tossing their caps in the air at the conclusion of their graduation ceremony on May 29, 2004. Established in 1802, the United States Military Academy has been training future army officers for more than 200 years. In addition to teaching basic military skills and preparing cadets for leadership roles, West Point works to develop their intellect, physical abilities, and moral and ethical values.

Source: U.S. Army.

In March 1776, U.S. Naval Commander in Chief Esek Hopkins led a small American fleet against the city of Nassau in the Bahamas, where the British had been stockpiling gun power. On April 6, Hopkins's armada, joined by the USS *Fly,* engaged HMS *Glasgow* in America's first major sea battle. The successful engagement enabled Hopkins's forces to capture Nassau. Congress soon authorized the construction of 13 frigates to supplement the fleet of refitted merchant ships that were serving as naval vessels. The Continental Navy performed a variety of missions throughout the war, including raiding British supply lines, protecting American commercial vessels, and resupplying American troops.

The Navy's contribution to the American victory in the Revolution demonstrated its value to the new nation. When the United States Constitution was ratified in 1789, it charged Congress with maintaining the navy. In this capacity, Congress ordered the construction of six frigates to replace ships lost in the Revolution. It also called for construction of the *America,* a 76-gun ship given to France to compensate that country for the loss of its ship *Magnifique* during the war.

THE CONTINENTAL PERIOD (1790–1890)

In the years following the war, the cash-poor Congress was forced to sell most of the navy's ships to raise funds to run the new nation. Lacking an effective navy to protect them, American merchant vessels increasingly became the targets of pirates. The problem was particularly acute in the Mediterranean Sea, where North African Barbary pirates preyed on U.S. merchant ships. The British, not eager to assist their former colonies, refused to protect American ships. Although the United States lost relatively few ships to pirates, the insult of seeing their countrymen held for ransom or sold into slavery outraged many Americans.

Actor and comedian Robin Williams entertaining the crew of the USS *Enterprise* during a holiday special hosted by the United Service Organization (USO) in the Arabian Gulf in December 2003. The troops onboard the *Enterprise* were part of Operation Iraqi Freedom (the U.S.–Iraq War) and the continuing war on terrorism. Performers such as Williams have been entertaining U.S. troops abroad since World War II.

Source: U.S. Navy.

Public support for a strong navy grew; the cause was championed by Thomas Jefferson, among others. The need for a strong navy became even more apparent after British swept U.S. merchant ships from the sea and blockaded U.S. ports during the War of 1812.

The United States' clear vulnerability at sea convinced Congress to commit to the construction of a formidable navy in the early 19th century. Struggling to keep up with innovations in ship-building technology, the navy experimented with armor plating, improved weapons such as breechloaders and shell guns, steam-powered propulsion systems, and the telegraph. In 1845, Congress established the Naval Academy at Annapolis, Maryland, to educate and train officers for service in the U.S. Navy. The early curriculum focused almost solely on engineering, a reflection of the importance of technology in this era of naval development.

During both the Mexican War (1846–48) and the American Civil War (1860–65), the navy performed its most valuable service blockading enemy ports. During the Mexican War it also provided significant support for U.S. ground forces. When the Mexicans refused to negotiate with the United States, President James Polk authorized the navy to conduct a sea invasion at Veracruz that proved to be one of the decisive battles of the conflict.

During the Civil War, the U.S. Navy gave the Union a virtual monopoly on naval power. When the war began, the Confederate states had no oceangoing ships and most of the country's men-of-war were in northern ports. As the war progressed, the South managed to purchase several swift cruisers that combined steam and sail power. For a time these vessels took a serious toll on commercial shipping in the North. However, the Union's superior industrial and economic power enabled the U.S. Navy to maintain numerical and technological superiority over the Confederate Navy. The Union effected a blockade of key Southern ports that crippled Southern trade and forced the Confederates to keep tens of thousands of soldiers posted on the shore against possible sea invasions.

The Union flexed its naval might on inland waterways as well. Armor-clad gunboats accompanied Union ground operations south and protected important river supply routes. During critical battles along the Mississippi River, the Union's oceangoing and inland water forces combined in a classic campaign to cut the Confederacy in half.

Ship-building technology was changing the face of warfare. This change may be no more apparent than in the May 1862 clash between the Confederate ironclad *Virginia*—a captured Union vessel named *Merrimack* that the Confederates outfitted with iron plate and rechristened—and the Union ironclad *Monitor*. The *Monitor* was one of the most innovative vessels of all time. It was made entirely out of iron in nine sections that were assembled in less than 120 days. Its innovations included a rotating turret containing cannon—the first time such a device was ever used. The *Monitor* was also the first vessel fitted with a marine screw propeller, anticipating some elements of submarine design. All of the facilities of the ship except the pilot station and the turret were underwater.

THE OCEANIC PERIOD (1890–1945)

In the 1880s, the United States entered an era of change. With the wounds of the Civil War healing and the American frontier closed, the nation turned its sights outward. The United States was a growing industrial power that desired foreign markets for its goods. The advent of steam-powered vessels in this period put the Caribbean and Central and South America within easy reach of U.S. merchantmen. As the United States expanded its role as a maritime nation, the navy took on a greater role in U.S. national security.

During the late 19th and early 20th centuries, the navy became a tool of foreign policy. It was particularly useful for protecting American commercial interests and denying any significant European presence in the Western Hemisphere. The navy moved to the forefront of military operations when the Spanish-American War broke out in 1898. It moved quickly against the Spanish Pacific fleet, annihilating it in Manila Bay and trapping most of Spain's remaining ships in Cuba. By destroying a Spanish armada considered one of the world's leading navies, the U.S. Navy established dominance in the western Atlantic and ended Spain's colonial ambitions.

The United States launched a new ship-building campaign following the war. In 1907–1908, President Theodore Roosevelt sent the so-called Great White Fleet of 16 new battleships on a global cruise to demonstrate to the world the might of America's navy. The message was aimed particularly at Japan, a growing naval rival in the Pacific. The U.S. Navy had become America's first defenders, sentries on a line far from American shores.

When World War I broke out in 1914, the United States—although neutral in the conflict—faced a dual threat in the Atlantic. Germany had ordered submarine attacks against shipping to and from Great Britain, a move that endangered U.S. merchant vessels. Meanwhile Britain, concerned about the effects of submarine warfare exploitation of its economy, tried to use its naval power to force entry into American-dominated markets. In 1916, the United States embarked on another massive naval build-up. A year later, after

several German provocations, including the sinking of U.S. merchant ships, President Woodrow Wilson asked Congress to declare war on Germany. He dispatched the navy to deliver the troops of the American Expeditionary Force across the Atlantic. The entrance of fresh troops and American economic might against a war-weary Germany assured the Allied victory.

The lessons of World War I were not lost on naval policymakers. Although there were a couple of major naval surface battles during the war, none were decisive. The greatest naval threat of the war was the German U-boat, which wrought havoc on merchant shipping and came close to crippling the British economy. To counter the German U-boats, the navy needed smaller, faster ships such as destroyers. This need for smaller vessels went hand in hand with a wave of naval disarmament following the war.

For more than a decade after World War I, the navy struggled to maintain forces at levels permitted by postwar naval treaties. However, during this time the navy adopted new doctrines and technologies that would prove valuable in the next major war. The navy embraced air power by moving its resources away from battleships and toward building aircraft carriers. With the knowledge garnered from the German U-boat, the navy sought improved designs for submarines capable of coastal operations as well as fleet support in the vast Pacific. During the 1930s, the navy began to build a two-ocean force capable of meeting threats in both the Pacific and the Atlantic. At this time also, the Japanese imperial fleet emerged as the main rival of the U.S. Navy.

On December 7, 1941, the Japanese attacked and destroyed the U.S. Pacific Fleet in Pearl Harbor using carrier-based aircraft. Luckily for the United States, none of its aircraft carriers—the principal intended target of the attack—were in port at the time. Four days later, the Germans declared war on the United States and the nation faced a two-ocean war. The early phase of the war went poorly for the United States. In the Atlantic, U-boats torpedoed Allied tankers and freighters within sight of the East Coast. In the Pacific, the attack on Pearl Harbor bought Japan a window of uncontested naval superiority that it used to expand and secure its island empire.

By mid-1942, however, the tide had begun to turn in the Allies' favor. In June 1942, a U.S. task force built around two U.S. aircraft carriers dealt a severe blow to the Japanese fleet at the Battle of Midway. The much smaller U.S. force sank four Japanese carriers and several other large surface ships. The loss of ships and experienced aircrew was a setback from which the Japanese navy never recovered.

In the Atlantic, German U-boats remained a menace throughout the war. The struggle for control of the sea-lanes, known as the Battle of the Atlantic, was still in grave doubt throughout 1942. However, new anti-submarine technology—and U.S. industrial might, which continued to produce new ships—finally turned the course of the naval war in favor of the Allies by mid-1943. Once the sea-lanes were secure, the Allies were able to bring to bear all of their forces around the perimeter of Hitler's empire. The U.S. Navy supported amphibious assaults in North Africa, Italy, and France that allowed the Allies to liberate Europe from German control.

While the United States played a valuable supporting role in the Atlantic, it played the lead in the Pacific. Japan built a far-flung empire across the Pacific that the United States had to recapture step by step. The Americans fought their way across the Pacific in a series of large-scale amphibious operations, part of an island-hopping strategy supported by carrier-based aircraft. In 1944, decisive victories at the Battles of the Philippine Sea and the Leyte Gulf virtually ended the Japanese military threat. By the end of the war, U.S. submarines had devastated Japanese shipping, and amphibious marine landings denied Japan the resources from its captured territories. The U.S. victory in the Pacific demonstrated the mobility, sustainability, flexibility, and striking power of the U.S. Navy.

THE TRANSOCEANIC PERIOD (1945–PRESENT)

With the defeat of Germany and Japan, the navy needed to consider a new enemy—the Soviet Union. During the coming Cold War between the United States and the Soviet Union, the navy would play a very active and visible role. The Cold War marked a shift in thinking about U.S. national-security policy. Instead of passively waiting for Soviet aggression, the United States adopted a policy of active deterrence. Aircraft-carrier battle groups deployed on all the world's oceans became a symbol of U.S. might and America's commitment to its allies.

Carrier task forces gave the United States a quick strike capability anywhere in the world. In the case of war with the Soviet Union, these carriers could launch attacks on naval and air bases on the periphery of the USSR. Amphibious forces would then invade, reinforce, or retake strategic land positions. Submarines

also played a key role in the new naval strategy. Rather than attacking Soviet merchant ships, Allied submarines would try to bottle up their Russian counterparts attempting to leave base.

The decade of the 1950s brought revolutionary development in the navy. At the beginning of the decade, the navy still relied on World War II–era tactics. This force proved viable and even decisive during the Korean War, deploying and supporting troops in the amphibious invasion at Inchon in September 1950. Carrier-based aircraft also supported Allied ground forces in Korea. However, Korea marked the last major conflict for the steam-powered carrier and propeller-driven aircraft. The navy would soon enter both the jet age and the atomic age.

In 1955, the navy launched the world's first nuclear-powered naval vessel, the submarine USS *Nautilus.* The year before saw the construction of the world's first supercarrier, the USS *Forrestal,* designed specifically to handle jet-powered aircraft. Five years after the *Nautilus* was launched, the aircraft carrier USS *Enterprise* became the world's first nuclear-powered surface vessel. All U.S. carriers commissioned since that time have been powered by nuclear reactors. Advances in nuclear technology led to the development of smaller reactors, which by the 1960s powered many naval vessels other than carriers.

Nuclear power led to a revolution in submarine design. The old diesel-electric submarines could stay underwater for only relatively short periods before they had to surface to charge their batteries. Nuclear-powered submarines can stay underwater for months at a time, surfacing only when they need to take on food. New missile-guidance technology led to the development of mobile, stealthy submarines capable of launching intercontinental ballistic missiles (ICBMs). The United States considered submarine-based nuclear missiles perhaps its most valuable military asset during the Cold War because of their near invulnerability to detection and destruction by the USSR. They ensured a U.S. retaliatory strike in case of a Soviet nuclear attack on the United States.

The navy benefited from continuing technological evolution during the 1970s and 1980s. During the 1980s, President Ronald Reagan committed the United States to a military buildup to counter the threat of Soviet expansion. During this time, the navy was expanded and equipped with updated technology. Quieter submarines armed with improved Trident nuclear missiles patrolled the oceans as a nuclear deterrent. Carrier groups supported by ships carrying long-range cruise missiles and the latest antisubmarine warfare technology continued to patrol the north Atlantic, Mediterranean, and western Pacific.

The navy was not simply a strategic deterrence after the Korean War. Naval airpower played a major part in the Vietnam War, as carrier-based aircraft bombed North Vietnam and supported American ground assaults. Navy *swift boats* patrolled the Vietnamese coasts and rivers to locate and destroy North Vietnamese forces. During the 1980s, the Navy supported military action in Lebanon, Libya, Grenada, Panama, and the Persian Gulf.

Carriers in the Red Sea and Gulf of Oman played a crucial role during the Gulf War of 1991, guarding sea-lanes and protecting the huge troop buildup before the Allied invasion of Iraq. Twelve years later, the navy once again supported ground and air operations against Iraq, during the Iraq War of 2003. Because of the strategic importance of the Middle East, the navy retains a significant presence in the region.

Headed by the secretary of the navy, the U.S. Navy today has more than half a million men and women on active and reserve duty operating more than 300 ships and 4,000 aircraft. The navy continues to play its traditional role as defender of the nation's interests at sea, as well as its more modern role as a deterrent to aggression against the United States and its allies abroad.

—Will Hughes

See also Aircraft Carrier; Cruise Missile; Inchon Landing (1950); Leyte Gulf, Battle of (1944); Midway, Battle of (1944); Pearl Harbor; Sea-Launched Ballistic Missiles (SLBMs); Sealift; Secure Second Strike; Strategic Nuclear Triad; Submarine Warfare; Submarines; Washington Naval Treaty (1922); World War I (1914–1918); World War II (1939–1945)

Further Reading

Cutler, Thomas J. *A Sailor's History of the U.S. Navy.* Annapolis, MD: Naval Institute Press, 2004.
Hagan, Kenneth J. *This People's Navy: The Making of American Sea Power.* New York: Free Press, 1991.
Howarth, Stephen. *To Shining Sea: A History of the United States Navy, 1775–1991.* New York: Random House, 1991.

U.S. NORTHERN COMMAND (USNORTHCOM)

A regional headquarters responsible for planning and conducting U.S. military activity in the continental United States, Alaska, Canada, Mexico, Puerto Rico, and the U.S. Virgin Islands.

United States Northern Command (NORTHCOM) was established in 2002 in response to the September 11, 2001, terrorist attacks in New York City and Washington, DC. Located at Peterson Air Force Base in Colorado Springs, Colorado, NORTHCOM is one of the nine combatant commands established and operated by the United States Department of Defense. Northern Command centralizes the homeland defense activities being conducted by other Defense Department agencies, by putting them under a single command. Organizationally, it is under the same command as North American Aerospace Defense Command.

According to the Department of Defense, Northern Command's mission is homeland defense and civil support. It conducts operations to deter, prevent, and defeat threats and aggression aimed at the United States, its territories, and interests within the assigned area of responsibility. It also provides military assistance to civil authorities, as directed by the president or secretary of defense. Like the other combatant commands, NORTHCOM does not maintain its own standing forces; rather, the troops are tasked to the command as needed. NORTHCOM's permanent staff consists of approximately 500 civilian and uniformed personnel.

Northern Command's operations on domestic soil are regulated by the Posse Comitatus Act. The act limits the role of the military in domestic affairs, including the prohibition of the military from participating in the interdiction of vehicles, vessels, and aircraft; execution of surveillance, searches, pursuits, and seizures; or arresting individuals in lieu of civilian law-enforcement agencies. A congressional exception can allow the military to assist civilian law-enforcement agencies at the federal, state, and local levels on a case-specific basis.

See also September 11/WTC and Pentagon Attacks; U.S. Central Command; U.S. Pacific Command; U.S. Southern Command

U.S. PACIFIC COMMAND (USPACOM)

A regional headquarters responsible for planning and conducting U.S. military activity in the Asia-Pacific region. As a Unified Combatant Command, PACOM is composed of forces from the army, navy, air force, and marines and has a broad and ongoing mission.

The regional division of commands allows defense planning to be focused on a specific region.

USPACOM is one of nine Unified Combatant Commands that include U.S. Northern Command (NORTHCOM), U.S. European Command (EUCOM), U.S. Central Command (CENTCOM), U.S. Southern Command (SOUTHCOM), U.S. Joint Forces Command (JFCOM), U.S. Special Operations Command (SOCOM), U.S. Transportation Command (TRANSCOM), and U.S. Strategic Command (STRATCOM). PACOM is headquartered at Camp H. M. Smith in Oahu, Hawaii. As of October 2002, by direction of the secretary of defense, the title "Commander in Chief, U.S. Pacific Command" was changed to "Commander, U.S. Pacific Command" (CDRUSPACOM). The PACOM commander reports directly to the secretary of defense.

Component commands of PACOM from the four services consist of U.S. Army Pacific, U.S. Pacific Fleet, Marine Forces Pacific, and U.S. Pacific Air Forces. Unified commands subordinate to PACOM are U.S. Forces, Japan; U.S. Forces, Korea; Alaskan Command; and Special Operations Command, Pacific. PACOM forces are organized into three categories: forward deployed, forward based, and CONUS (Continental U.S.). Additional support units located in Hawaii and throughout PACOM's area of responsibility include the Asia-Pacific Center for Security Studies, the Information Systems Support Activity, Pacific Automated Server Site Japan, Cruise Missile Support Activity, Special Intelligence Communications, Joint Intelligence Center Pacific, Joint Intelligence Training Activity Pacific, Joint Interagency Task Force West, and Joint Task Force Full-Accounting.

PACOM was established in 1947 and is the oldest and largest of the Unified Combatant Commands. PACOM's area of responsibility covers 43 countries, 10 territories and possessions, and 10 U.S. territories. Some of the major countries in the PACOM area include China, India, Japan, Australia, New Zealand, South Korea, North Korea, Indonesia, and the Philippines. Antarctica was recently added to USPACOM's area of responsibility. Although Russia is included in the U.S. European Command (USEU-COM) area of responsibility, USPACOM, in coordination with USEUCOM, retains responsibility for force protection in the areas of the Russian Federation east of 100° east longitude, counterterrorism (CT) planning for U.S. diplomatic missions, and noncombatant evacuation operations (NEO). A Memorandum of Understanding signed between USEUCOM and USPACOM outlines Theater Security Cooperation responsibilities in eastern Russia.

The stated mission of PACOM is to enhance security and promote peace and stability in the Asia-Pacific region by deterring aggression, responding to crises, and winning quickly and decisively in the event of war. The U.S. military through PACOM also seeks to establish and maintain security relationships with countries in the region and deter future conflicts. PACOM is also responsible for providing support to the mutual defense treaties forged in the region, including the U.S.–Japan Treaty of Mutual Cooperation and Security (1960); South East Asia Collective Defense among the United States, France, Australia, New Zealand, Thailand, and the Philippines (1955); ANZUS (Australia, New Zealand, U.S., 1952); the U.S.–Republic of Korea Mutual Defense Treaty (1954); and the U.S.–Republic of the Philippines Mutual Defense Treaty (1952). PACOM has participated in more than 1,500 exercises and other engagement activities with foreign military forces. Disaster-relief operations are also conducted as needed in the region by PACOM.

The Asia-Pacific region is of strategic importance to the United States. A potentially hegemonic China with growing military and economic power, another China–Taiwan crisis, and the instability on the Korean peninsula remain primary concerns for U.S. national security. Economic interests are also central, because 35% of U.S. trade is within the region. After the September 11, 2001, terrorist attacks in the United States, PACOM has increased counterterrorism operations in the Philippines and Indonesia.

See also ANZUS Security Treaty; Counterterrorism; U.S. Central Command; U.S. Northern Command; U.S. Southern Command

U.S.–PHILIPPINE ALLIANCE

U.S. military agreement between the United States and the Philippines that guaranteed a U.S. military presence in the Philippines from 1901 until 1991. For almost a century, the U.S. military maintained two major bases in the Philippines: Clark Air Force Base and Subic Bay Naval Station. Subic Bay was designated a U.S. naval station after the 1901 U.S. invasion that ended Spanish rule in the Philippines. Prior to

World War I, Subic Bay was the largest training facility for U.S. Marines. In 1902, Fort Stotsenberg, renamed Clark Air Base in 1947, was opened in the Philippines' Pampanga province.

The United States controlled the Philippines until the end of World War II, when the islands finally gained independence. Then, in March 1947, the Philippines signed an agreement that allowed the United States to maintain military bases on the islands for 99 years. In addition to the U.S. military presence, the Central Intelligence Agency (CIA) maintained an active role in the Philippines. Throughout the Cold War and the Korean War, Subic Bay and Clark Air Base remained important logistical support bases for the United States. During the Vietnam War, air traffic at Clark Air Base reached as high as 40 transports per day bound for Vietnam.

In 1966, the duration of the U.S.–Philippine agreement was reduced to 25 years, with the expiration to occur in September 1991. The bases remained important to U.S. interests during the oil crises of the 1970s, and regular deployment of Subic Bay–based naval units to the Indian Ocean began at that time. Carrier forces from Subic Bay were also deployed to the Indian Ocean and Arabian Sea during the 1979 Iranian revolution and during the Soviet intervention in Afghanistan in 1979 and 1980.

In 1986, long-standing political opposition to dictator Ferdinand Marcos within the Philippines finally pressured the Philippine government into calling an election. The opposition, led by Corazon Aquino (the widow of Marcos's main political opponent, Benigno Aquino), campaigned on a demand for the withdrawal of U.S. forces from the bases. Aquino triumphed in the election, and her victory led to the drafting of a new Philippine constitution.

Under the new constitution, foreign bases, troops, and facilities would not be allowed in the country unless a new treaty was ratified by a two-thirds vote in the Senate. Although President Aquino went against her campaign promises and called for the extension of the bases treaty, the Philippine Senate voted 12–11 to reject it, as thousands of Filipinos marched in opposition. As a result, the U.S. bases were closed in 1992.

Since the closures of Clark and Subic Bay, the United States has been looking for ways to maintain its influence in the region. Following the September 11, 2001, terrorist attacks, the government has been even more concerned with the establishment of military bases near vital U.S. interests in Southeast Asia.

The United States became concerned that the Philippines could become a sanctuary for al-Qaeda operatives fleeing Afghanistan after the U.S. invasion there. Domestic terrorism in the Philippines, including the kidnapping of foreigners, perpetrated by the terrorist group Abu Sayyaf, made the Philippine government eager for an antiterrorist alliance, as well.

In 2001, President George W. Bush and Filipino president Gloria Macapagal-Arroyo came to an agreement following the September 11 attacks. They agreed to work together to combat terrorism and to revive the dormant alliance between the two nations. Since that time, the United States has provided the Philippine government with at least $100 million in military aid, as well as 660 U.S. troops to help Filipino authorities hunt down members of the Abu Sayyaf terrorist group. Meanwhile, the Subic Bay base has been reopened to the U.S. Navy for the maintenance of its warships, and in 2002 it was revealed that the U.S. military was in the process of building a new military base on the Philippine island of Basilan.

Besides the war on terrorism, a strong military presence in the Philippines remains important to U.S. interests for several other reasons. The ongoing thaw in relations between North and South Korea endangers the continued presence of U.S. bases and other U.S. assets in South Korea. A Philippine presence would allow the United States to keep a closer eye on China's growing military power and on its conflict with Taiwan. Finally, the control of key shipping lanes in the South China Sea remains an important issue, as well.

See also Imperialism; September 11/WTC and Pentagon
    Attacks; Terrorism, War on International; Terrorists, Islamic

U.S.–ROK ALLIANCE

Security pact based on the 1954 Mutual Defense Treaty between the United States and the Republic of Korea (ROK). Originally offered as enticement to then Korean president Syngman Rhee to accept the armistice ending the Korean War, the U.S.–Republic of Korea alliance has had a major impact on the Republic of Korea. Under this security umbrella, South Korea has become one of the most dynamic economies in the world and has developed a thriving democratic government. At present, some 37,000 U.S. military personnel are stationed there.

COLD WAR ALLIANCE

On June 25, 1950, the opening shots of the Korean War were fired when North Korean forces stormed across the 38th parallel, sweeping South Korean troops and hastily assembled U.S. reinforcements down the Korean peninsula to a perimeter around the city of Pusan. The tide of the communist offensive turned, however, following a daring amphibious landing at Inchon led by General Douglas MacArthur in September of the same year. Although truce talks between UN forces and opposing North Korean and Chinese forces began at Panmunjon in July 1951, war would rage for two more years. The signing of an armistice occurred two years later, but a formal peace treaty has yet to be signed. For the past 50 years, South Korea has enjoyed an uneasy peace guaranteed by the U.S.–ROK alliance.

The Korean War took place against the backdrop of the Cold War, which arrayed the United States and its allies against the Soviet Union and fellow communist nations. Under the security guarantee of the United States, South Korea experienced a dramatic political and economic transformation. From a backward agrarian economy under military dictatorship and later authoritarian rule, South Korea grew into a democracy with the third-largest economy in Asia exporting a wide variety of manufactured goods to the United States and other nations. During this period, Korea received large amounts of technical and financial support from the U.S. and its allies, most notably Japan. This aid was aimed at preventing the spread of communism in east Asia and strengthening South Korea as a key ally of the United States in the Cold War struggle.

The long-standing alliance was further strengthened by developments during the Vietnam War. South Korean economic growth was spurred by wartime U.S. defense contracts to Korean industrial conglomerates called *chaebol*. In addition, South Korea sent more than 300,000 troops to Vietnam over the course of the war. Cold War peace on the Korean peninsula was occasionally tested by confrontations such as the capture of the USS *Pueblo* by North Korea in 1968. In the 1976 Poplar Tree Incident, two U.S. Army officers were killed by axe-wielding North Korean troops, Despite these incidents, South Korea has prospered economically and, since 1988, has enjoyed democratic elections as a result of the stability created by the alliance.

The rise of democratic government has seen the emergence of an active, increasingly strong political left, exemplified by the 2002 election of human-rights lawyer Roh Moo-hyun as president of South Korea. Roh stated during his campaign that the South might remain neutral in the event of war between North Korea and the United States. His rise to the presidency is seen by many as a reflection of the political views of the *386* generation (in their 30s, went to college in the '80s, born in the '60s), who tend to be less trustful of the United States, more conciliatory toward North Korea, and more focused on ties with Korea's other Asian neighbors.

POST–COLD WAR DEVELOPMENTS

With the end of the Cold War and the collapse of the global communist threat, the U.S.–ROK alliance has been tested. Many observers have noted a refocusing of U.S. foreign policy away from strengthening relationships with traditional allies and toward fighting the global war on terror following the attacks of September 11, 2001. The alliance has been plagued by lack of awareness of U.S.–Korea relations among the American public. Growing anti-American sentiment from a generation of Koreans eager for a country free of American troops and geopolitical influence has also put strains on the alliance.

Furthermore, the administration of President George W. Bush entered office in 2001 with a policy of mistrust and confrontation toward North Korea over the issue of development of nuclear weapons. This position, along with the labeling of the North Korean regime as a member of the "axis of evil" in January 2002, was at odds with the Sunshine Policy of engagement with the North adopted by then South Korean President Kim Dae Jung. This has led many left-wing, younger Koreans to question whether the U.S.–ROK alliance actually represents the security interests of South Korea.

The alliance has also been strained by the U.S. military itself, whose stabilizing presence has contributed so much to prosperity in the South. In June 2002, massive anti-American demonstrations followed the accidental killing of two schoolgirls by a U.S. military vehicle in the village of Donggucheon. The location of headquarters for U.S. forces in Korea in downtown Seoul is yet another issue dividing the partners. The existence of the headquarters will continue to impede further development of Seoul until the projected relocation of the base to an undecided location in the southern part of the country in 2006. Critics also claim that lack of sufficient language and cultural training for U.S. military personnel hinders public support for the alliance. A 2003 survey suggests that roughly 70% of South Koreans desire the withdrawal of U.S. forces from the peninsula.

Over considerable protest and controversy, in May 2003 the South Korean government dispatched troops to Iraq in support of Operation Iraqi Freedom. This deployment indicates that the U.S.-ROK alliance remains strong despite the changing political environment in South Korea. Both nations continue to face the threat of a reclusive, nuclear-armed North Korea some 50 years after the beginning of the alliance and have rushed to each other's aid in times of conflict. The United States and South Korea enjoy strong ties in the cultural arena, as well, evidenced by the immigration of more than 2 million Koreans to the United States and the large number of U.S.-educated university professors in Korea. The two nations have also established a robust economic partnership. South Korea is the seventh-largest trading partner of the U.S., with $58 billion in goods and services exchanged in 2002.

The deterrence of North Korean aggression, the establishment of a democratic government in the Republic of Korea, and the transformation from an economic backwater to the 12th-largest economy in the world are certainly cause for celebration. At the beginning of the 21st century, however, questions remain regarding the future of the U.S.–ROK alliance. The terror attacks of September 11, 2001, have shifted U.S. national-security concerns, and the ascendance to political leadership in Korea of a generation born after the Korean War has led to a reassessment of Korean security ties to its powerful ally. A changing geopolitical environment will test and may ultimately transform the nature of one of the longest-standing U.S. security agreements.

—*Daniel P. McDonald*

See also Axis of Evil; Bush, George W., and National Policy; Cold War; Inchon Landing (1950); Korea, North and South; Korean War; Pueblo Incident; Vietnam War (1954–1975)

Further Reading

Carpenter, Ted G., and Doug Bandow. *The Korean Conundrum: America's Troubled Relations with North and South Korea.* New York: Palgrave Macmillan, 2004.

Kim, Tae-Hyo, and Brad Glosserman. *The Future of U.S.–Korea–Japan Relations: Balancing Values and Interests.* Washington, DC: Center for Strategic and International Studies, 2004.

USS *COLE* BOMBING

Attack on a U.S. naval vessel carried out by the international terrorist group al-Qaeda. The attack on the USS *Cole* was one in a series of terror attacks on U.S. overseas interests by al-Qaeda during the second term of President Bill Clinton. The attack on the *Cole* confirmed al-Qaeda as a significant threat to the United States, although at the time the perpetrators remained unknown.

On October 12, 2000, the destroyer USS *Cole* stopped in the port of Aden, Yemen, for a routine refueling. A small boat later pulled alongside the destroyer and detonated a bomb close to the *Cole*. The suicide bombing left a hole approximately 40 feet square in the side of the *Cole*. Seventeen sailors were killed and an additional 39 were injured in the blast. In response to the attack, then President Bill Clinton said, "If, as it now appears, this was an act of terrorism, it was a despicable and cowardly act. We will find out who was responsible and hold them accountable."

Despite this threat, a legal debate emerged surrounding the bombing of the USS *Cole* because the perpetrators had attacked a military target. Under U.S. law at the time, attacks on military targets did not fall under the definition of terrorism. No overt military responses were initiated in response to the attack. After the September 11, 2001, terrorist attacks on New York and Washington, the United States learned that al-Qaeda was behind the bombing of the *Cole*.

See also Al-Qaeda; Terrorism, War on International; Terrorists, Islamic

U.S. SOUTHERN COMMAND (USSOUTHCOM)

Regional headquarters responsible for planning and conducting U.S. military activity in the Latin American region. As a Unified Combatant Command, SOUTHCOM is composed of forces from the army,

United States Navy and Marine Corps security personnel patrolling past the damaged U.S. Navy destroyer USS *Cole* following the terrorist attack on the ship off the coast of Yemen on October 12, 2000. The security personnel established checkpoints and searched incoming vessels for contraband and explosives while the *Cole* was prepared for its trip back to the United States. The ship rejoined the Atlantic Fleet in April 2002 after undergoing 14 months of repairs at a shipyard in Pascagoula, Mississippi.

Source: Getty Images.

navy, air force, and marines and has a broad and ongoing mission. The regional division of commands allows defense planning to be focused on a specific region.

SOUTHCOM is one of nine Unified Combatant Commands, along with U.S. Northern Command (NORTHCOM), U.S. European Command (EUCOM), U.S. Pacific Command (PACOM), U.S. Central Command (CENTCOM), the U.S. Joint Forces Command (JFCOM), U.S. Special Operations Command (SOCOM), U.S. Transportation Command (TRANSCOM), and U.S. Strategic Command (STRATCOM). SOUTHCOM is headquartered in Miami, Florida. The SOUTHCOM commander reports directly to the secretary of defense.

SOUTHCOM is responsible for all U.S. military activity on the land mass of Latin America south of Mexico; the waters adjacent to Central and South America; the Caribbean Sea, its 13 island nations, and the European and U.S. territories there; the Gulf of Mexico; and a portion of the Atlantic Ocean. Southern Command's area of responsibility covers 32 countries (19 in Central and South America and 13 in the Caribbean).

Component commands of SOUTHCOM from the four services consist of U.S. Army South (USARSO), U.S. Naval Forces Southern Command (COMNAVSO), U.S. Marine Corps Forces South (MARFORSO), U.S. Southern Command Air Forces, Special Operations Command South, Joint Interagency Task Force South, Joint Task Force Bravo, and Joint Task Force Guantánamo.

SOUTHCOM's 26 Security Assistance Organizations (SAO) form an important component of the command and work in support of U.S. interests in the region. The SAOs manage U.S. security assistance programs and special activities in Central and South America and the Caribbean. SOUTHCOM also has responsibility for security assistance in Cuba, Mexico, and the Bahamas even though these countries are outside the command's area of responsibility.

Training programs and joint exercises between the United States and regional militaries are a major aspect of SOUTHCOM's activities in the region. Military Groups (MILGPs) exist in Argentina, Bolivia, Chile, Colombia, Ecuador, and Venezuela. MILGP commanders serve as liaisons to the regional militaries and oversee most U.S. military activities in their respective countries. Military Liaison Offices (MLOs) are located in Belize, Mexico, Brazil, Haiti, Jamaica, Barbados, Trinidad and Tobago, Bahamas, and Nicaragua. Offices of Defense Cooperation (ODCs) can be found in Costa Rica, Paraguay, Uruguay, and Panama. Military Assistance Advisory Groups (MAAGs) are in the Dominican Republic, El Salvador, Honduras, Guatemala, and Peru, and Defense Assistance Offices (DAOs) exist in Suriname and Barbados. SOUTHCOM also includes liaison officers and representatives from the Department of State, Drug Enforcement Administration (DEA), Coast Guard, U.S. Customs Service, and other U.S.

government agencies. Foreign military interaction in the form of military-to-military contact programs has historically been an important component of U.S.–Latin American relations and has sometimes resulted in U.S. support for dictatorial regimes and military governments in the region.

SOUTHCOM's stated mission is to conduct military operations and promote security cooperation to achieve U.S. national-security objectives. In support of the U.S. interest of ensuring hemispheric security, SOUTHCOM is responsible for building regional partnerships that strengthen democratic principles and that can collectively deter, dissuade, and defeat transnational threats to the stability of the region.

Forces assigned to USSOUTHCOM also support local law-enforcement agencies in antinarcotics operations, perform joint and bilateral/multilateral exercises, engage in engineering and medical exercises, and conduct search-and-rescue operations, disaster-relief operations, and humanitarian and civic-assistance operations. After the September 11, 2001, terrorist attacks in the United States, SOUTHCOM has increased its counterterrorism efforts in the Tri-Border Area of South America between Brazil, Argentina, and Paraguay.

See also Latin America and U.S. Policy; U.S. Central Command; U.S. Northern Command; U.S. Pacific Command

U.S.–THAILAND ALLIANCE

Alliance formed as part of the Southeast Asia Treaty Organization (SEATO) in which the United States helped Thailand suppress its communist rebels in exchange for support during the Vietnam War.

At the Geneva Convention in April 1954, the French government agreed to withdraw its forces from Indochina in an effort to quiet the rebellions that had erupted across the region at the conclusion of World War II. Although France's concession was widely welcomed, it still troubled the United States. Communist parties were highly active in most of the Southeast Asian nations. With the Cold War unfolding, the United States feared that Southeast Asia would become a fertile ground for communist uprisings. Therefore, the United States quickly assembled the Southeast Asia Treaty Organization (SEATO). Consisting of the nations of Australia, New Zealand, the

Philippines, and Thailand, the organization pledged to halt the spread of communism.

Because of Thailand's crucial central location in the region, the United States heavily supported the smaller nation. The two nations signed bilateral security pacts, the United States established military bases throughout Thailand, and enormous levels of financial aid were used to bolster the Thai economy. From 1954 to 1958, the United States sent nearly $30 million per year in aid to Thailand. As other area nations, such as Cambodia, Laos, and especially South Vietnam, became increasingly unstable, the United States relied upon Thailand to promote U.S. interests in the region.

Neither the United States nor Thailand, however, was completely pleased with the alliance. When SEATO was formed, Phibun Songgram was Thailand's premier. A former general, Phibun had seized power during a military coup in 1947. Although Phibun was, in effect, a dictator, he was a generous leader and commonly upheld the Thai constitution. However, in 1957, Phibun's government was overthrown during another military coup. The new Thai leader, Sarit Thanarat, suspended the constitution, declared martial law, and outlawed all political parties. The United States strongly objected to these policies, and many government officials felt uneasy aligning the United States with such an overtly undemocratic regime. However, the situation in South Vietnam was rapidly worsening, and the United States desperately needed to maintain a firm presence in Southeast Asia. Therefore, the alliance continued.

The Thai government had at first enthusiastically welcomed the alliance. In 1951, a communist group named Free Thai launched an insurgency in northern Thailand with the assistance of China. United States military aid helped to suppress the rebellious party. However, by the 1960s, the alliance had an adverse effect on Thailand's stability. Because of its close relationship with the United States, Thailand was increasingly drawn into the Vietnam War. As the South Vietnamese government collapsed and communists gained control of the Laotian government, Thailand faced new communist uprisings both in the north and along its southern border with Malaysia.

Consequently, Thailand was relieved in 1969 when the United States began to withdraw from Vietnam. Although the loss of aid from the United States temporarily depressed the economy, Thailand was able to revise its relations with its neighbors. Increased trade with China soon replaced the lost assistance from the

United States. In 1972, a new constitution was adopted, and in 1976 the first free elections in nearly three decades were held.

Thailand's alliance with the United States, however, did not completely dissolve. Thailand remained the one solidly noncommunist nation in Southeast Asia and therefore occupied a position in the United States' interests. Thailand also frequently backed the United States in SEATO policy making. In 2003, Thailand reaffirmed the importance of the alliance by sending troops to aid in the occupation of Iraq.

See also Alliances; Geneva Conventions; Southeast Asia Treaty Organization; Vietnam War (1954–1975)

U2 SPY PLANE INCIDENT (1960)

One of the biggest international crises of the Cold War period, sparked by the downing of an American spy plane over the territory of the Soviet Union. The illicit spy mission that the U2 plane was undertaking at the time of its destruction infuriated the Soviet Union, which accused the United States of gravely damaging the relationship between the two superpowers by resorting to aggressive measures. The entire episode was heavily publicized around the world, as the Soviet Union released footage of the trial of the captured U2 pilot. An embarrassment to the United States, the incident temporarily brought to light the large-scale spying operations that characterized so much of the Cold War period.

On May 1, 1960, CIA-employed pilot Francis Gary Powers took off from Pakistan in a superlight U2 spy plane. His mission required him to fly over 3,000 miles of USSR territory, in an attempt to photograph an entire range of Soviet secret factories and military installations. U2 spy planes had been used by the United States for more than four years with tremendous success: The groundbreaking technology of the U2s permitted them to fly high enough to be out of the reach of the Soviet air defenses. The intelligence acquired by these planes constituted the most valuable USSR-related information to date. Powers's flight, however, put an end to that stream of information.

Using an innovative ground-to-air missile, the Soviets were able to reach the U2 and shoot it down. The plane had been flying at an altitude 68,000 feet, some 1,200 miles inside USSR territory. Powers bailed out of the stricken plane and parachuted to safety, but he was subsequently captured with all of his equipment. He was brought to Moscow and interrogated by the KGB on the specifics of his mission.

In August 1960, Powers was publicly tried for espionage in a Soviet military court. He pleaded guilty and was sentenced to 10 years in solitary confinement but stayed imprisoned for only two of those years. In 1962, Powers was traded for a Soviet spy who had been apprehended by the Americans in the late 1950s while attempting to establish a spy network in New York. It was to be the first in a series of such exchanges between the two superpowers.

Although Powers came out of the incident relatively unharmed, the already tenuous relationship between the United States and the Soviet Union had been seriously affected. At the time of the U2 incident, the two countries had been engaged in a negotiation process aimed at relaxing the arms race. Soviet leader Nikita Khrushchev and U.S. President Dwight Eisenhower were planning to continue these negotiations at the upcoming summit in Paris, but the spy plane incident put an end to the conference before it began.

See also Cold War; Espionage; Intelligence and Counterintelligence

V

VERIFICATION

The process of ensuring compliance with an agreement usually involving some system or means of observation. In arms control and reduction, verification is considered a critical element because it provides a warning to noncompliance with treaty elements. It also provides a measure of confidence in the process itself because it proves that all parties are doing what they agreed to do.

Means of verification include both intrusive and nonintrusive means. *Intrusive* means can involve the imposition of teams of personnel on the ground in a country, as well as counting and checking the numbers and types of weapons platforms. Both the United States and the former Soviet Union had these kinds of teams on the ground in the 1980s and 1990s.

Nonintrusive means of verification include overhead surveillance, including spy planes and satellites. An example of this type occurred in the Cuban Missile Crisis of 1962, when American spy planes discovered the emplacement of Soviet missiles. As later demonstrated by U.S. actions prior to the Iraq War, however, this system is not comprehensive, nor is it foolproof, and it cannot be applied to all types of weapons systems. Biological and chemical weapons can be easily dispersed and hidden, making verification difficult, if not impossible. Other forms of warfare, such as information warfare, are also difficult to control or even monitor. Nonetheless, verification remains a critical concern for any form of arms control and reduction.

VETERANS ADMINISTRATION

The organization responsible for taking care of the veterans of the nation's military services. The Veterans Administration provides a number of programs, services, and benefits to veterans and their families—including medical and health care, psychological care, educational and rehabilitative services, housing, transitional assistance to the civilian sector, and burial services.

In the United States, the Department of Veterans Affairs (VA) is responsible for providing federal benefits to veterans and their families. The department was established on March 15, 1989, succeeding the previous Veterans Administration. The VA, headed by the secretary of veterans' affairs, is the second largest of the 15 Cabinet departments and operates nationwide programs for health care, financial assistance, and burial benefits.

There are approximately 26 million living U.S. veterans, of which nearly three-quarters served during a war or an official period of conflict. Approximately one-quarter of the nation's population, approximately 70 million people, are potentially eligible for VA benefits and services because they are veterans, family members, or survivors of veterans.

The nation's responsibility to care for its veterans, spouses, survivors, and dependents can last a long time. As noted in the literature of the VA, the last dependent of a Revolutionary War veteran died in 1911. Six children of Civil War veterans still draw VA benefits. Approximately 440 children and widows of Spanish-American War veterans still receive VA compensation or pensions.

Benefits for veterans include disability compensation and pensions, education and training, medical care, research, vocational rehabilitation, home loan assistance, insurance, and VA national cemeteries. For example, disability compensation is a monetary benefit paid to veterans who are disabled by injury or disease incurred or aggravated during active military service. As of 2003, approximately 2.8 million veterans received disability compensation or pensions from the VA. Also receiving VA benefits were 568,146 spouses, children, and parents of deceased veterans. Among them are 147,291 survivors of Vietnam-era veterans and 272,883 survivors of World War II veterans.

Likewise, education and training is also a benefit for veterans. The most well-known program is the GI Bill. Created in 1944, the GI Bill was the first veteran's training and education program, allowing veterans to go to school, providing tuition and fees for the costs of school, and providing a living allowance during the time the veteran attended school. Since its inception, more than 21 million veterans, service members, and family members have received $77 billion in GI Bill benefits for education and training. The number of GI Bill recipients includes 7.8 million veterans from World War II, 2.4 million from the Korean War, and 8.2 million post-Korean and Vietnam-era veterans (in addition to active-duty personnel). Since the dependents program was enacted in 1956, the VA also has assisted in the education of more than 750,000 dependents of veterans whose deaths or total disabilities were service-connected.

VIETNAM WAR (1954–1975)

Conflict in Southeast Asia that became the longest war in U.S. history, which took the lives of 58,000 Americans and ended with the unification of Vietnam in 1975. The Vietnam War grew out of a long conflict with France over its colonial rule of Vietnam and Cold War tensions following the Korean War (1951–1953).

BACKGROUND

After the Vietnamese nationalist guerillas known as the Vietminh defeated French colonial forces at Diem Bien Phu in 1954, the French sued for peace. The Geneva Peace Accord, signed by Vietnam and France in the summer of 1954, temporarily divided the Southeast Asian nation of Vietnam in half at the 17th parallel.

The Democratic Republic of Vietnam (North Vietnam) was led by Ho Chi Minh, whose forces had defeated the French. Ngo Dinh Diem was the president of the Republic of South Vietnam.

The Geneva Accord provided that elections be held in 1956 for the unification of the country. However, Diem canceled the elections when it became apparent that the communists would win. In so doing, Diem ensured the continued division of the country. However, approximately 10,000 communist troops remained in hiding in the South. These insurgents, called the Vietcong, became masters of guerilla warfare, which escalated after the cancellation of the elections. By 1960, despite U.S. aid and advisers sent by the Central Intelligence Agency (CIA), the Vietcong had established a political organization in the South called the National Liberation Front.

In 1961, concerned about South Vietnam falling under a communist regime and still stinging from the Korean War, the United States signed a military and economic aid agreement with Diem's government. The first U.S. support troops landed in South Vietnam later that year, and the U.S. Military Assistance Command was established in 1962.

Meanwhile, Diem faced stiff opposition in the South. He used the CIA to identify his enemies and he arrested thousands of people. Diem convinced the United States to support his counterrevolutionary government by claiming that the North Vietnamese communists wanted to invade the South. In 1959, Diem passed *Law 10/59*, which made it legal to hold suspected communists in jail without bringing charges. Students, intellectuals, Buddhists, and others opposed Diem's repressive policies and joined the National Liberation Front. Diem represented his government to be a peace-loving democracy, whereas the communists sought to reunite the country through elections.

In November 1963, following years of growing dissatisfaction with his corrupt and ineffectual government, Diem was executed following a successful coup by elements of the South Vietnamese military led by Duong Van Minh. The leadership of South Vietnam remained in flux for the next few years as U.S. aid increased.

THE GULF OF TONKIN RESOLUTION

Early in 1964, U.S. President Lyndon B. Johnson and his military advisers developed a detailed plan to launch major attacks on North Vietnam, which supported and supplied the Vietcong insurgents in the South.

Johnson and his advisers feared they lacked public support for expanding the war and were concerned about provoking North Vietnam's communist allies, the Soviet Union and China.

On August 2, 1964, after South Vietnamese gunboats carried out a raid on the coast of North Vietnam, the USS *Maddox* (which was conducting electronic espionage in the area) was fired on by North Korean torpedo boats. Two days later, the *Maddox* and another destroyer reported that they were under attack—reports that later proved inaccurate.

Responding to these reports, Johnson authorized air strikes against North Vietnam in retaliation and assembled the heads of Congress to accuse North Vietnam of open aggression on the high seas. Congress acted quickly—although without a complete set of facts—and authorized the Tonkin Gulf Resolution, which rapidly escalated U.S. involvement in the war.

Six years later, in the wake of public outrage at President Richard Nixon's authorization of raids on Cambodia, the Tonkin resolution was terminated by Congress. Yet, the war was sustained by continued military appropriations. Although Johnson cited the resolution as congressional support for the war, critics used it as a symbol of the escalation they opposed, and later of the dishonesty of the top levels of government about the prosecution of the war.

THE WAR ESCALATES

The first American combat troops arrived in Vietnam in March 1965. Following an attack on two U.S. bases in South Vietnam by the National Liberation Front, President Johnson ordered sustained bombing raids on the North—an action known as Operation Rolling Thunder. The introduction of U.S. combat forces, coupled with the air strikes, forced the North Vietnamese communists to reassess their strategy.

Originally, the North Vietnamese thought they could easily defeat the South militarily and reunite the country. The U.S. presence forced a change in strategy, as suddenly the South's hand was greatly strengthened. Beginning in 1965, the communists moved to a protracted war strategy, hoping to bog the U.S. military down into a long conflict it could not win.

The North Vietnamese reasoned that the United States had no clearly defined strategy and would tire of incessant guerrilla attacks. Ultimately, a political settlement to the war could be negotiated. Ironically, the Johnson administration wanted to pursue a similar tack, using precision strikes against the North with little disruption to the everyday lives of Americans.

THE WAR IN AMERICA

Television grew exponentially since the end of the end of World War II, and advances in miniaturized cameras and satellite technology facilitated unprecedented coverage of the Vietnam War. The war in Vietnam became the living room war; each night, television footage from the battlefield brought the death, destruction, and horror of the war into the homes of hundreds of millions of Americans.

The Vietnam War became a disruption in American society. College campuses and major cities exploded with protests after the draft was reimposed. Meanwhile, the North Vietnamese and the National Liberation Front launched massive coordinated attacks on major cities in South Vietnam in January 1968, in an attempt to drive the Johnson administration to the negotiating table.

Every corner of the United States felt the war's impact, and in March 1968, Johnson announced he would not run for reelection. At the Democratic National Convention in Chicago in 1968, armed police clashed with antiwar demonstrators. Meanwhile, Johnson began secret negotiations with the North Vietnamese.

THE NIXON YEARS

Despite progress with the North Vietnamese in the Paris negotiations throughout 1968, the Democrats could not keep the White House, and Republican candidate Richard Nixon was elected president.

Nixon advocated a policy of *Vietnamization*, in which massive air strikes would cover a gradual withdrawal of American troops. At the same time, Nixon expanded the war into Cambodia and Laos in an attempt to cut communist supply routes and destroy troops operating on both sides of the borders with Vietnam. The stepped-up bombing raids with concomitant civilian casualties, as well as news of the secret wars in Laos and Cambodia, triggered a second wave of protests on college campuses throughout the United States.

In late April 1970, Ohio National Guard troops were called to Kent State University to preserve order following a series of anti-Nixon protests on the campus. After the protesters set the Reserve Officers' Training Corps (ROTC) building ablaze, the guard opened fire, killing four students and wounding nine

Visitors to the Vietnam Veterans Memorial in Washington, DC, reading the names of the American men and women who lost their lives during the Vietnam War. Designed by Chinese American Maya Lin and completed in 1982, the wall contains more than 58,000 names of Americans killed or missing in action. The memorial grew out of a need to heal the nation's wounds over the very divisive Vietnam War.

Source: U.S. Navy.

others. Following a similar protest at Jackson State University in Mississippi, police fired into a dormitory and killed two more students. These incidents turned even more Americans against the Vietnam War as the violence spread at home.

Nixon's expanded air war did not deter the North Vietnamese communists, who continued to press their demands at the Paris peace negotiations. Although the withdrawal of troops appeased some domestic critics, the destructive air war and the deaths of the students energized the antiwar movement at home.

By the fall of 1972, Secretary of State Henry Kissinger, the U.S. chief negotiator at the Paris talks, and North Vietnamese representatives Xuan Thuy and Le Duc Tho reached a preliminary peace proposal. But the new leadership in Saigon, President Nguyen Van Thieu and Vice President Nguyen Cao Ky, rejected the peace plan and refused to make any concessions to the North Vietnamese communists.

Nixon hoped to force peace by unleashing deadly bombing raids against North Vietnam's largest cities: Hanoi and Haiphong. The so-called Christmas Raids backfired as the United States was condemned by the international community, forcing the Nixon administration to press the negotiations.

In January 1973, the White House convinced the South Vietnamese that America would stand by the regime if they signed the peace accord. At the same time, Hanoi convinced the National Liberation Front that political prisoners would be released after the accord was signed. Open hostilities between the United States and North Vietnam ended on January 23, 1973, but the war continued. From March 1973 to April 1975, the Thieu-Ky administration continued to battle the communist forces. Saigon finally fell on April 30, 1975, when the presidential palace was captured by North Vietnamese tanks.

—*Will Hughes*

See also Cold War; Johnson, Lyndon B., and National Policy; Kennedy, John F., and National Policy; Nixon, Richard, and National Policy; Vietnam War Protests

Further Reading

Diem, B. *In the Jaws of History*. Bloomington: University of Indiana Press, 1987.

Halberstam, David. *The Best and the Brightest*. New York: Ballantine Books, 1972.

Hareue, George C, ed. *The Pentagon Papers*. New York: McGraw-Hill, 2003.

Karnouw, Stanley. *Vietnam: A History*. New York: Penguin, 2003.

McNamara, Robert S. *Argument without End: In Search of Answers to the Vietnam Tragedy*. New York: David McKay, 1999.

VIETNAM WAR PROTESTS

The collective antiwar sentiment in America, expressed through demonstrations and marches during the 1960s and 1970s by individuals and groups opposed to the U.S. military presence in Vietnam. The Vietnam conflict, whose origins and relevance many did not understand, left an entire nation questioning the policies of a government it had always trusted. The country had not been so divided since the American Civil War. Every American family was affected, more than 50,000 Americans were killed, and many of those who returned suffered (and continued to suffer) deep physical and emotional scars.

ORIGINS OF THE ANTIWAR MOVEMENT

The origins and growth of the protests and adversary culture before and during the Vietnam era stemmed from the monumental social changes taking place at the time. The so-called baby boomers witnessed unprecedented economic expansion, hypnotic effects of television, and insecurity induced by the development of the nuclear bomb and the ongoing Cold War with Soviet Russia. They saw the exponential growth of suburbia and the birth of the consumer society—two phenomena that many believe contributed to the breakdown of both the extended and nuclear family, and the religious bonds that typically went with them. The nature of music also changed from the acoustic rhythms of blues and boogie-woogie in the mid-1950s to the electric rumble of rock and roll, whose lyrics became increasingly politicized.

In sum, most members of the Vietnam generation grew up with a sense of moral engagement, unlimited social prospects, and social hopefulness. Racism and social injustice, made more glaring by the power of television, threatened to burst the bubble of optimism and invincibility, and the civil rights struggle became the most important catalyst of the antiwar movement. Predisposed to protest, this generation was enticed by counterculture.

NATURE AND EVOLUTION

The antiwar movement passed through three broad phases. In the first phase (before 1966), opposition to expanding the war in Vietnam was primarily liberal in inspiration. In the second phase (between 1966 and 1969), the movement's center of gravity shifted to being increasingly radical as the war's unpopularity was growing in the country at large. In the third phase (from 1969 to the fall of Saigon in 1975), the more liberally centered movement again took over, which

some argue helped to limit U.S. military activity in Vietnam.

For the liberals, the idealism engendered in a new generation inspired by the youngest president in the nation's history established the foundations of the early movement. Before 1965, public demonstrations against the war were small, rare, and went largely unnoticed by the administration and the press. Very few demonstrations were sponsored by the liberal organizations, with the exception of the National Committee for A Sane Nuclear Policy (SANE), which in 1963 called publicly for a U.S. disengagement from Vietnam.

Small-scale radical actions continued. In August 1963, a march commemorating the destruction of Hiroshima and Nagasaki was organized by a group of demonstrators called the Student Peace Union (SPU). At the same time in New York, the Catholic Worker Movement marched in front of Vietnam's permanent observer mission to the United Nations. In the same month, 250,000 people participated in the March on Washington and listened to Dr. Martin Luther King, Jr. deliver his *I Have a Dream* speech.

Meanwhile, in 1963 and 1964, the effort by what soon became known as the right wing of the antiwar movement tried to restrain U.S. involvement in Southeast Asia through well-connected private conversations, newspaper articles, and advertisements by the social networks of the ruling liberal elite. The New Pacifists were also involved.

The psychological turning point for the antiwar movement, and for most Americans, came on November 22, 1963, when President John F. Kennedy—the American symbol of hope, youth, vitality, and idealism—was assassinated. The incident left the entire nation stunned, shaken, and angry. The war was not yet fully Americanized until the end of 1964; at the year's end, there were only 23,300 U.S. military personnel in Vietnam. The administration, however, was Americanized in the immediate post-Diem epoch mainly because of a North Vietnamese–driven escalation of the war.

By late 1964, there was televised coverage of American soldiers coming home in body bags. The most notable event that triggered an escalation of the war was a November 1, 1964, Vietcong attack on a U.S. air base at Bien Hoa, during which five American soldiers were killed and six B-57 bombers were destroyed. However, it was not until President Lyndon B. Johnson decided on a massive bombing campaign against North Vietnam in 1965 that the antiwar movement really took hold.

ESCALATION AND CAMPUS PROTESTS

In 1965, the Vietnam War became an American war. It was the year that the air bombardment campaign known as Rolling Thunder began in earnest, and the American contingent in Vietnam grew from 23,000 to 184,000 soldiers. It was also the year when dissent in the Democratic Party began to be expressed, albeit privately. Liberals, leftists, radicals, and pacifists all found fresh causes in which to participate and become part of the movement.

Over the next two years, the antiwar movement snowballed. Demonstrations became national in nature. The Free Speech movement started at Berkeley, and kindred movements joined in and bolstered antiwar activism. The country's youth, many dying in the line of fire, began demanding reasons for America's presence in Vietnam. They wanted to know why peace talks were organized and continually failed. They wanted to know what they were fighting for.

After the instatement of the draft, young people on college and university campuses around the country began to organize protests against the war. The teach-in movement developed, attracting thousands of students, and soon spread to almost every campus. Student organizations held rallies and marches, the first of which occurred in Washington, in April 1965. More than 25,000 students gathered under the sponsorship of an organization called the SDS, Students for a Democratic Society.

Extensive media coverage brought the violent and bloody guerrilla war home each night to every American living room. People realized that the glowing reviews of the war effort released by the government were manipulated and far from the truth. Even congressional senators began questioning Vietnam policies. Through it all, the bombings continued and more American GIs came home in body bags.

Activists, celebrities, and musicians—including Abbie Hoffmann, Timothy Leary, Allen Ginsberg, Jane Fonda, Jimi Hendrix, Jefferson Airplane, and countless others—took up the antiwar cause. Their speeches and their music reflected the anger and hopelessness that Americans felt over the Vietnam War. Even the GIs stationed overseas began supporting the antiwar movement, from wearing peace symbols to refusing to obey orders.

CIVIL UNREST, WOODSTOCK, AND KENT STATE

By 1967, America was also mired in its own urban problems. As the bombings and body count in Vietnam continued to escalate, so did civil unrest. One hundred thousand antiwar protesters gathered in New York, and thousands more gathered in San Francisco. There were urban riots in Detroit. Johnson's support was falling drastically on all fronts. Antiwar rallies, speeches, demonstrations, and concerts continued being organized all over the country. There was a backlash against all that was military. Soldiers returning home from the war were no longer regarded as heroes but as "baby killers." Young men sought to evade the draft by being conscientious objectors or leaving for Canada.

In 1968, a North Vietnamese general led a surprise attack against American and South Vietnamese forces. Known as the Tet Offensive, the attack resulted in horrendous casualties on both sides and further eroded the situation at home. The assassinations of Martin Luther King, Jr. and Robert Kennedy also sparked racial tension and unrest. Wisely, Lyndon Johnson did not seek reelection.

The new president, Richard Nixon, had made a campaign promise to Americans that he would end the war with Vietnamization, or systematic troop withdrawals. Yet the American presence in Vietnam remained high while the casualties and costs of war mounted. In 1969, as the miasma of Vietnam worsened, legions of the young made their way to Woodstock for a music festival billed by its promoters as "three days of peace and love." A concert brought 500,000 young people from all across America to a nonviolent protest against the war.

Meanwhile, Nixon announced his plans to attack communist supply locations, a strategy that failed and set off another round of protests. May 4, 1970, the day after Nixon's announcement, marked the tragic culmination of a weekend of antiwar protests at Kent State University in Ohio. Four students were killed during a protest on the school grounds, following a face off with the Ohio National Guard. Students across the country became enraged, and campuses all over the United States came to a virtual standstill in the following days.

MY LAI MASSACRE AND TROOP PULLOUT

As 1970 ended, Nixon's plans to end the Vietnam War were not realized, and American citizens demanded to know why their country was still involved in a war in which a resolution seemed impossible. In 1971, the My Lai massacre came to light, an atrocity committed by American soldiers that shocked the world and gained huge media attention. An intended search-and-destroy mission led by Lieutenant William Calley in the village of My Lai, Vietnam, soon degenerated into the massacre of more than 300 apparently unarmed civilians, including women, children, and the elderly. As the gruesome details of the massacre reached the American public, serious questions arose concerning the conduct of American soldiers in Vietnam. Another round of peace talks was organized on the heels of this controversy, but again all attempts to end the fighting in Vietnam failed.

Finally, after some failed attempts and more bombing, peace talks resumed in Paris; by the end of January 1973, a pact was signed by the United States, South Vietnam, North Vietnam, and the Vietcong. By March, all American troops were pulled out of the country and a systematic release of prisoners of war on both sides was initiated. However, when the Watergate scandal came to light and destroyed Nixon's presidency at the close of 1974, communist forces had overrun Saigon. Within a few months, most of Indochina fell into communist hands, and the antiwar movement's mantra of "what are we fighting for" seemed eerily prophetic.

Today, many agree that the antiwar movement had significant impact on the length and perhaps even the outcome of the Vietnam War. Others disagree, saying that the massive protests were part of an eroding and troubled society. What is certain, however, is that the antiwar movement left an everlasting mark on an entire generation and its country.

—Divya Gupta

See also Johnson, Lyndon B., and National Policy; Nixon, Richard, and National Policy; Tet Offensive; Vietnam War (1954–1975)

Further Reading

Buzzanco, Robert. *Masters of War: Military Dissent and Politics in the Vietnam Era.* New York: Cambridge University Press, 1996.

Garfinkle, Adam M. *Telltale Hearts: The Origins and Impact of the Vietnam Anti-war Movement.* New York: St. Martin's, 1998.

Hixson, Walter L., ed. *The Vietnam Anti-War Movement.* New York: Garland Publishers, 2000.

Hunt, Andrew. E. *The Turning: A History of Vietnam Veterans Against the War.* New York: New York University Press, 1999.

Woods, Randall. B., ed. *Vietnam and the American Political Tradition: The Politics of Dissent.* New York: Cambridge University Press, 2003.

REFLECTIONS

Kent State Killings: A Sad Legacy

The day after Richard Nixon's announcement to send U.S. troops into Cambodia, an estimated 500 students gathered in the school commons at Kent State University for a student rally. Protesting Nixon's decision to send troops into Cambodia without Congress' approval, students spilled into the city. Broken windows and other damage to a number of downtown businesses prompted fear, rumors, and eventually a call by the city's mayor to the governor for assistance.

The Ohio National Guard arrived, and on the same night of their arrival, some students set fire to the campus headquarters of the Army Reserve Officers Training Corps (ROTC). The next morning, the governor came to Kent, and in a press conference, he said that the university would remain open.

After a Sunday of relative calm, an antiwar rally at noon on Monday brought 2,000 to 3,000 people to the University Commons. When the Guard gave the order to disperse, some in the crowd responded with verbal epithets and stones. The Guard answered with tear gas, and, attempting to enforce the Ohio Riot Act with raised bayonets, forced demonstrators to retreat. The Guard then changed formation and as they approached a hill, some seconds away from safety, some Guardsmen turned to face the parking lot and started to fire their rifles at random. Between 61 and 67 shots were fired. Four students were killed, and nine were wounded. It was the only time federal troops shot U.S. students. That afternoon, the university president ordered the Kent State University closed. Through scholarships in their name, the university continues to remember the four students who died on May 4, 1970: Allison Krause, Jeffrey Miller, Sandra Scheuer, and William Schroeder.

Some people, from today's students to yesterday's protesters to historians, believe the Kent State shootings helped turn the tide against the Vietnam War more than any other single event, and that the shift in attitude helped save lives. Many of the Kent State victims and their family members see that as an important legacy.

—Gary Tuchman "Kent State Forever," May 4, 2000 (CNN Interactive)

VOICE OF AMERICA

The official U.S. government broadcasting service and a primary component of America's public diplomacy abroad. Created to counter enemy propaganda in World War II, the Voice of America (VOA) now oversees a network of radio, television, and Internet media that spans the globe.

The VOA Charter describes three basic functions: to accurately and objectively report the news, to clarify American philosophy and political institutions to international listeners, and to explain American foreign policies. The VOA Charter stresses the need for objectivity. To become a credible source, VOA strives to make sure that the news it presents is accurate, objective, and comprehensive. The Charter for the service mandates "responsible discussions and opinion" of U.S. policies to avoid the perception that it is simply a source of propaganda.

From the start, VOA officials emphasized the importance of objectivity. In 1941, President Franklin D. Roosevelt authorized the creation of the Foreign Information Service (FIS) and appointed playwright Robert Sherwood as its director. The first broadcast to Germany began with the phrase, "Here speaks a voice from America." FIS thus became known as the Voice of America, and soon it was transmitting in more than two dozen languages. The VOA's commitment to truth telling was tested immediately because it had to report a string of German and Japanese victories in the early stages of the war.

With the end of World War II, the VOA lost its original purpose, and a variety of domestic critics sought to disband the outfit. Some congressmen complained that the VOA needlessly competed with American businesses, arguing that news reporting should be a private enterprise. To make things worse, the Associated Press and United Press International stopped working with the VOA because they felt that associating too closely with the government would threaten their own reputations.

The VOA was initially part of the Office of War Information (OWI). However, President Harry S. Truman liquidated the office in August 1945 and moved the VOA into the U.S. State Department. This nearly proved disastrous, however, because the VOA became a target for Senator Joseph McCarthy's anti-communist crusade, along with other sections of the State Department. The VOA survived the McCarthy witch hunts, however, when it moved from the State Department to the independent U.S. Information Agency in 1953. At around that time, the war of ideas with the Soviet Union gave new purpose to the VOA and permitted its resurgence during the administration of President Dwight D. Eisenhower.

During the Cold War, some critics denounced the VOA as a propaganda vehicle for the U.S. government. Despite the high-sounding purpose in its charter, they argued that the VOA was nothing more than a mouthpiece for U.S. policy. VOA representatives rejected these claims, taking pains to demonstrate the organization's objectivity.

Nevertheless, American diplomats admitted that foreign leaders often doubt that the VOA, as a government-sponsored institution, can be truly independent. The tension of explaining government policy while remaining independent from government influence is built into the structure of the VOA. This dilemma probably explains why VOA doctrine places such a strong emphasis on impartiality.

Today, the VOA believes that public diplomacy plays a pivotal role in the ongoing war on terrorism. If this is the case, the VOA might indeed be an important part of U.S. national security. On the other hand, lingering doubts remain that the VOA will be perceived as credible by important audiences in the Middle East and elsewhere.

See also Media and National Security; Propaganda; Radio Free Europe

Further Reading

Heil, Alan L., Jr. *Voice of America: A History.* New York: Columbia University Press, 2003.

Krugler, David F. *The Voice of America and the Domestic Propaganda Battles, 1945–1953.* Columbia: University of Missouri Press, 2000.

Tuch, Hans N. *Communicating with the World: U. S. Public Diplomacy Overseas.* New York: St. Martin's Press, 1990.

VON BRAUN, WERNER (1912–1977)

German-American rocket scientist and advocate of manned space travel. Von Braun was born in Germany in 1912. In 1930, he began to assist German scientist Hermann Oberth in early experiments with small liquid fuel rockets. Von Braun received his bachelor's degree in 1932 from the Berlin Technical Institute and his Ph.D. from the University of Berlin in 1934.

Von Braun was a research professor and the technical director of the German rocket research center at Peenemunde from 1937 to 1945. In 1943, he gave up his professorship to pursue the development of the V-2 rocket and other liquid fuel rocket weapons for the German government. (When von Braun died, the U.S. government declassified many documents that revealed that he had been a supporter and active member of the Nazi party during the 1930s and the early 1940s).

After World War II, von Braun was brought to the United States and became a technical adviser at the White Sands Proving Grounds (from 1945 to 1950). He was also a project director at Fort Bliss and became the chief of the guided missile development division at the Redstone Arsenal in Huntsville, Alabama, in 1950.

One year after becoming a U.S. citizen in 1956, von Braun was appointed director of the development operations division of the Army Ballistic Missile Agency (now the Marshall Space Flight Center). He was instrumental in designing rockets used to launch manned deep space flights, most notably the Apollo moon missions.

Von Braun became deputy associate administrator of the National Aeronautics and Space Administration (NASA) in 1970 and was a well-known spokesperson for space exploration and rocket development. He is the author of several books, including *Across the Space Frontier* (1952), *The Exploration of Mars* (with Willy Ley, 1956), and *First Men to the Moon.*

VON CLAUSEWITZ, KARL
(1780–1831)

Prussian soldier and thinker, author of *On War*, one of the most influential books on military strategy. The book introduced to the field of military theory concepts such as friction, fog of war, and center of gravity, which became common currency in military strategy as well as in other military fields. In the United States, von Clausewitz became particularly prominent after the Vietnam War. *On War* was adopted as a key text at the Naval War College (NWC) in 1976, the Air War College in 1978, and the Army War College (AWC) in 1981.

LIFE

Karl Philipp Gottlieb von Clausewitz was born on June 1, 1780, near Magdeburg, Germany, part of the former Prussian empire. Coming from middle-class origins, the von Clausewitz family reached nobility in 1827, thanks to Karl's achievements. At age 12, von Clausewitz entered the Prussian army and spent five years in garrison duties while broadening his education beyond military topics. He studied art, science, and education and entered the Institute for Young Officers in Berlin in 1801.

Prussia declared war on France in 1806, and von Clausewitz was eager to fight. Prussians were defeated in battles at Jena and Auerstadt, and von Clausewitz was captured and detained until 1808. In the peace settlement at the end of the war, Prussia lost half of its population and territory and became a French satellite. Writing in the 1820s, von Clausewitz offered a strong critique of 1806 Prussia called *Observations on Prussia in its Great Catastrophe.*

When Prussia provided an army corps to Napoleon's France to assist in the 1812 invasion of Russia, von Clausewitz, along with many other Prussian officers, resigned from the Prussian army. He then accepted a commission in the Russian army, fought in the battle of Borodino, and witnessed the disastrous French retreat from Moscow.

After Prussia changed sides in the French-Russian struggle, von Clausewitz was reintegrated in the Prussian army as a colonel. Between 1813 and 1814, he participated in many battles of the War of Liberation. At Lützen, he led several cavalry charges and was wounded. In 1818, von Clausewitz was promoted to general and became administrative head of the General War College in Berlin. During those years, he began to draft some theoretical work that eventually became *On War.*

Von Clausewitz returned to active duty with the army in 1830, when he was appointed commander of a group of artillery brigades stationed in eastern Prussia. He was later sent to the Polish border. Before leaving, he sealed his unfinished manuscripts. Back from Poland in 1831, he fell ill with cholera and died on November 16, at the age of 51, leaving a number of manuscripts unfinished.

ON WAR

In the first pages of *On War*, von Clausewitz introduced the term absolute war, a concept that does not exist in the real world. It means war in a pure form— unlimited by frictional effects of time, space, and human behavior—that takes place in one instantaneous maximum effort by both warring parties. In the rest of the book, von Clausewitz dealt with real war—war as it exists in the real world. Real war is constrained by social and political context, by human nature, and by the restrictions imposed by time and space.

"War is merely the continuation of policy by other means," is perhaps the most-quoted line from *On War*. With this quote, von Clausewitz did not mean that a state should routinely resort to war to achieve its goals. Rather, he wanted to reject the idea that war is an irrational act. He suggested that war is a purely rational act of state policy and a legitimate means to achieve a state's interests. He defined war as an act of force to compel our enemies to do our will. If war is an extension of policy, military leaders must be subordinated to the political leadership. However, political leaders must understand the nature and limitations of war. Politicians must avoid waging war to achieve goals for which it is unsuited.

After laying out the argument that war is a rational act, von Clausewitz introduced concepts that make war real. These concepts include the *fog of war* (a lack of knowledge that occurs during a war) and *friction* (caused by incidents, difficulties, and chance—such as weather).

Another von Clausewitz concept that became important in American doctrine is *center of gravity*—the hub of all power and movement upon which everything depends. It represents a point from which the enemy derives its physical strength or will to fight. The center of gravity can be a physical object, a skill, the will to fight, or public opinion.

Also particularly interesting is von Clausewitz's analysis of strategic aspects of defense. Offense inevitably weakens as it advances from its starting point. The need to defend and maintain the lines of supply and communications dilute the aggressor's might. Every offensive has a culminating point of attack. Beyond that point, the scale turns, and the reaction follows with a force that is usually much stronger than that of the original attack. Also, victory has a culminating point, at which the success provokes sufficient counteraction to be reversed.

On War represents the most significant attempt in western military doctrine to understand war, both in its internal dynamics and as an instrument of policy. It has been read throughout the world and has inspired generations of militarists, statesmen, and scholars.

See also Military Doctrine

Further Reading

Angstrom, Jan, and Isabelle Duyvesteyn, eds. *The Nature of Modern War: Clausewitz and His Critics Revisited*. Stockholm: Swedish National Defence College, 2003.

Clausewitz, Karl von. *On War*. Edited and Translated by Michael Howard and Peter Paret. Princeton, NJ: Princeton University Press, 1976.

Handel, Michael I. *Masters of War*. London: Frank Class Publishers, 2002.

Howard, Michael. *Clausewitz: A Very Short Introduction*. New York: Oxford University Press, 2002.

V-22A OSPREY

Multimission aircraft with vertical takeoff and landing capability (VTOL). The V-22A Osprey is a tilt-rotor aircraft with a 38-foot rotor system and engine/transmission unit (nacelle) mounted on each wing tip. The unique design enables the Osprey to operate like a helicopter when taking off and landing vertically. Once airborne, the nacelles rotate forward 90 degrees to facilitate high-speed, fuel-efficient horizontal flight as a turboprop airplane. The wing rotates for compact storage enabling the Osprey to operate from ships or expeditionary airfields.

The U.S. Marines are the lead service in the development of the Osprey, which will be utilized as a joint service, multimission aircraft. The Marines and Army will use the Osprey (MV-22A) as an assault transport for troops, equipment, and supplies. The Navy version (HV-22A) will provide combat search and rescue, delivery, retrieval of special warfare teams, and fleet logistical support. The Air Force Osprey (CV-22A) will conduct long-range, special-operations missions.

With an operating ceiling of 25,000 feet, the Osprey can cruise at 257 knots. The aircraft was first flown in March 1989, and were grounded briefly in August 2000 after pilots encountered a problem with one of the driveshaft assemblies. The aircraft was returned to service in September 2000 following an investigation. Bell-Boeing, which manufacturers the V-22A Osprey, will provide the Marines with 360 aircraft, the Navy with 48, and the Air Force with 50. The aircraft have provisions for two .50-caliber machine guns.

See also Air Warfare

WAR COLLEGES

Six U.S. institutions of higher education that offer professional military education to senior officers, defense department civilians, and foreign military officials. Four of the institutions—the Army War College (AWC) at Carlisle Barracks, Pennsylvania; the Naval War College (NWC) at Newport, Rhode Island; the Air War College at Maxwell Air Force Base in Alabama; and the Marine Corps War College (MCWAR) at Quantico in Virginia—are linked to their respective service branches.

The concept of joint military leadership training grew from concern about the difficulties of coordinating land, sea, and air attacks during World War II. Although their student bodies vary according to their missions, the colleges share similar goals: improving the professional education of the highest levels of military leadership and applying lessons learned during war.

NATIONAL DEFENSE UNIVERSITY (NDU)

The National Defense University (NDU), established in 1976 and headquartered at Fort McNair in Washington, DC, includes the National War College and the Industrial War College, which were created after World War II to provide leadership education for members of different service branches. The NDU also includes the Joint Forces Staff College and the Information Resources Management College.

The NDU serves as the primary research and policy development institution for the Department of Defense as well as providing a joint educational program for senior military leadership. NDU centers provide outreach to the leadership of countries on every continent. In 1994, the NDU began granting a master of science degree in National Resource Strategy to graduates of the Industrial War College and a master of science in National Security Strategy to graduates of the National War College.

NAVAL WAR COLLEGE (NWC)

The oldest military institution in the United States is the NWC, which was established in 1884 on Coasters Harbor Island, Newport, Rhode Island, to offer an advanced course of professional study for naval officers. The founding president, Commodore Stephen B. Luce, viewed the college as a place for senior officers to study strategy, tactics, and operations based on the examination of history. He expanded a one-month course for junior officers into a full-year program integral to a naval officer's career pattern.

The school gained international notoriety when Luce's successor, Alfred Thayer Mahan, published *The Influence of Seapower Upon History* in 1890. Mahan's writings and lectures greatly influenced Theodore Roosevelt, Henry Cabot Lodge, and other world leaders, including Kaiser Wilhelm II, shaping global policy based on sea power at the beginning of the 20th century.

In 1887, the NWC introduced an elaborate program of war-gaming. The college soon emerged as an internationally recognized laboratory for war planning and military operations. Tactical, operational, and even technical problems were routinely submitted to the college for solution.

World War I interrupted studies at the NWC, and when the college reopened in 1919, its program focused on four major subjects: command, strategy, tactics, and policy. Since 1949, the NWC has published a journal currently titled *Naval War College Review* and hosted the annual Current Strategy Forum.

ARMY WAR COLLEGE (AWC)

The AWC, established in 1903, traces its roots to the aftermath of the Spanish-American War. Although the United States easily defeated the Spanish, the American military was criticized in the media and political arenas.

Henry Ball's history of the AWC, *Of Responsible Command*, identified three distinct incarnations. The first AWC sought to improve the professional preparation of the Army's general staff. The AWC was closed during World War I.

The second AWC emerged in response to the lessons of the nation's first Industrial Age conflict when the college reopened following World War I. The curriculum was expanded to include history and analysis of the political, economic, and social factors that influenced the conduct of World War I.

The third AWC appeared after World War II and was shaped by the Cold War and unilateral conflicts such as Korea and Vietnam. During the post–World War II era, the need for joint command led to the establishment of the NWC and Industrial War College. To better prepare senior Army officers, the third AWC expanded its scope to include global strategy, national military strategy, and international security. It continued to train its graduates for high-level staff and command positions.

The fourth AWC emerged in the 1980s in response to the end of the Cold War and the appearance of new threats such as international terrorism, regional conflicts, and drug lords.

AIR UNIVERSITY

The Air University, established in 1946 near Montgomery, Alabama, is a major component of the Air Force system of education. Several specialized schools, including the Air War College, were brought together to form the university. The Montgomery area has a long history associated with flight. The Wright Brothers established the first civilian air school there in 1910. In the 1930s, the Army Air Corps Tactical School moved to the area.

The Air War College is the senior school in the Air Force's professional military education system. Its mission is to educate planners and leaders in air and space power for the Air Force, other branches of the armed forces, federal government civilians, and many international organizations.

MARINE CORPS WAR COLLEGE (MCWAR)

The MCWAR in Quantico, Virginia, is the smallest of the war colleges. Established in 1990, MCWAR has been offering a certificate in Art of War Studies since 1994. MCWAR's mission is to educate select senior officers for decision making during war and military operations. The typical class at MCWAR includes seven USMC officers; two Navy, Army, and Air Force officers; a Coast Guard officer; and a civilian military official.

Further Reading

Ball, Harry. *Of Responsible Command: A History of the U.S. Army War College.* Carlisle Barracks, PA: Alumni Association, U.S. Army War College, 1994.

Chilcoat, Richard. "The Fourth Army War College: Preparing Strategic Leaders for the Next Century," *Parameters* 25 (Winter 1995–96): 3–17.

History of the National Defense University, http://www.ndu.edu/info/history.cfm

Newland, Samuel J. "A Centennial History of the U.S. Army War College," *Parameters* 31, no. 3 (Autumn 2001): 34–47.

Stiehm, Judith Hicks. "Civil-Military Relations in War College Curricula," *Armed Forces & Society: An Interdisciplinary Journal* 27, no. 2 (Winter 2001): 273–299.

WAR CRIMES

Committed in the context of international armed conflicts, criminal acts that violate international norms regarding the conduct of war. The doctrine of *jus militaire* (a just war) and the rise of humanism in the Middle Ages and the Renaissance, respectively, started forming an ethic that limited the means and conduct of war.

Further efforts in the 19th century, such as the first Geneva Convention and the Lieber Code (which regulated the U.S. Army laws of war), helped to humanize conflict. The Hague Peace Conferences, held near the turn of the 20th century, also helped to diminish the evils of war and began to regulate the new and frightening technology that was created in the last half of the 19th century—technology that permitted total war. The conventions, ideas, and norms that came from these sources helped constitute an idea of war crimes.

VARYING DEFINITIONS OF WAR CRIMES

Definitions of war crimes vary. A common definition, however, and that used by the International Criminal Court, is based on the idea that war crimes are intentional acts that violate the rules for the conduct of war, or the Geneva Accords of 1949. These accords protect noncombatants in belligerent countries in times of war—both civilians and soldiers who have been removed from combat (because of illness, injury, capture, and so on). Many past definitions of war crimes (and the Geneva Accords themselves) focused on international armed conflicts, but because many modern wars are interethnic, intrastate wars, these definitions are changing.

Not all illegal or immoral acts committed in time of war are war crimes. To fit into that category, acts must meet certain criteria. They must be acts that violate the Geneva Accords' provisions in the context of an armed conflict. The perpetrator must know that the victim has protected status in the conflict. The crime must be committed as part of the war effort, with the perpetrator acting on the part of a belligerent party, with the consent or agreement of an individual who is acting in an official capacity.

AN INTENTION TO HARM

War crimes require an intention to harm, but can be committed directly or indirectly. Many statutes regarding war crimes agree that those who order (or persons of authority who tacitly support) such crimes are as guilty as those who actually carry out the prohibited acts. Thus, military personnel as well as civilians—members of government, judges, prosecutors, doctors and nurses, executioners, and businessmen—can be equally guilty of crimes under the appropriate circumstances.

War crimes include deliberate killing, torture, and inhuman treatment caused by omission or commission of certain acts. They also include using improper weapons, violating norms about conducting warfare, and committing postwar crimes against civilians (such as armed robbery or looting). Deliberate killing includes murder, massacre, and direct killings of criminal suspects without trial. Courts have also recognized indirect methods of causing death—withholding adequate food or medical treatment from prisoners of war, and forced marches—as war crimes.

Torture is defined as a belligerent act, deliberately inflicting significant mental or physical pain on a noncombatant. Activity legally categorized as torture would have been perpetrated to extract information or confessions; to punish, humiliate, coerce, or intimidate a victim, or for reasons based on discrimination. Specific activities that have been recognized by international conventions as physical torture include beatings during questioning, rape and sexual aggression, burns, electric shock, sleep deprivation, prolonged denial of food, and denial of appropriate medical treatment. Mental torture includes threats of execution of the victim or the victim's relatives, threats of exposure to others' torture, isolation, sensory deprivation, and simulated executions and burials.

Inhuman treatment resembles torture; in some conventions, it is a difference in the degree of suffering inflicted; in others, the reason for the torture makes the difference. They may occur simultaneously. Inhuman treatment includes "outrages upon personal dignity," murder, and torture, and may also include detainees being subject to biological experiments, being mutilated, being deprived of their livelihoods, being put on display to the public, having inadequate food or medical care, or being used as human shields.

Related to both inhuman treatment and torture is the crime of *willfully causing great suffering, or serious injury to body or health*. This crime does not require that the act have the same purposes as torture, but the two categories may overlap. Offenses of this nature might include enslavement, deportation, detention of people in ghettos, and detention in concentration camps.

USE OF WEAPONS AND OTHER CRIMES

The use of certain weapons or tactics may also constitute war crimes. Using biological or chemical weapons against a civil population would be regarded as a war crime; flamethrowers are likewise taboo. Tactics such as disguising combat personnel as medical staff, declaring that no prisoners will be taken, or firing on military or civilian medical facilities are considered crimes. Other condemned tactics include making improper use of flags of truce, military insignias, or uniforms that cause death or injury. Deliberately targeting civilians or relief workers, or civilian targets such as schools—anything that is not a specific military objective—is also regarded as a war crime. Such attacks may involve concerted efforts or the use of indiscriminate weapons.

Other crimes include specific misdoing in the conduct of war, such as using children in combat, taking hostages, unlawful detentions, compelling captured combatants to serve in their captors' forces, and denying fair trials to captives. Other war crimes include deliberate shifts in population (occupation or deportation), acts against civilians after the fighting is over (such as looting), and the use of military personnel for nonmilitary objectives such as terrorizing and intimidating a local population for political reasons.

The prosecution of war crimes has been occurring since late 1945, when senior Nazi officials were tried at Nuremberg. It continued on an ad hoc basis into the 1990s. During that decade, the international community established two war crimes tribunals: the International Criminal Tribunal for the Former Yugoslavia (ICTY), for atrocities committed in the former Yugoslavia; and the International Criminal Tribunal for Rwanda (ICTR), for perpetrators of the Rwandan genocide. The International Criminal Court was designed with the intention of creating a more permanent seat for trying war crimes. Each court has had successes and failures, but each is part of continuing international security efforts to create accountability for some of history's worst crimes and, by creating accountability, to prevent recurrences.

See also Geneva Conventions

WAR GAMES

Simulations meant to replicate real war scenarios. War games vary in design from simple board games like chess to modern computer simulations. Also included under this term are mock scenarios or exercises engaging real equipment with actual soldiers.

War games, no matter how simple or complex, have a common basic structure: A player or players respond to an opposing side's action. The reactions of the players during the scenarios tend to be similar to real reactions. War games are often based on the Lanchester equations, which use two variables to predict warfare: size of the forces involved and quality of these forces. As these equations have limited predictive ability when tested against real war situations, more variables have been added to the original ones to attempt to fix the problem.

War games hold the promise of enabling military officers to predict outcomes of strategies and tactics without the loss of human life. War games also help to prepare soldiers and officers for the real thing. The type of war game commonly used in military colleges evolved from the Prussian war game *Kriegspiel*. The basic elements, such as the colors blue and red for the opposing teams, have remained the same although the game has been continuously improved upon. Historically, the U.S. Navy has been one of the most frequent users of war games. Civilian military leaders are increasingly using war games themselves, generally focusing on political-military games. The *Strategic Analysis Simulation* (SAS), created in 1980, is a prime example of this type of political-military game. Before the Gulf War the game *Operation Internal Look*, which used computer technology, was able to predict what the war would look like and its duration, although there was some variation.

Although some war games are focused on the decision-making process of war, others provide the soldiers with battle practice. SIMNET (*Simulation Network*), a war game developed in the late 1980s and early 1990s and heavily reliant on computer technology, became an extremely useful tool for preparing soldiers for combat. Today, war games, specifically computer war games, are used commercially as well as militarily.

War games are useful tools of analysis, but critics contend that an overreliance on their predictions can be dangerous. A great deal of trust has been placed on the outcomes of war games based on mathematical calculations despite the criticism that the games oversimplify war situations. Another significant problem is the human factor. Humans who use these games often do not want to take into account certain negative factors that might occur in real-world situations, such as miscommunication. The search continues for the ideal war game that will remove the unpredictability involved in waging war.

WAR PLANNING

Planning for a military campaign or campaigns, either offensive or defensive in orientation. War planning potentially allows a country to be prepared for various future military scenarios that it may face. However, there has been controversy over the years regarding the effectiveness of war planning.

War planning concentrates on developing an effective plan for winning a conflict. To plan for war, models such as war games are often used. Additionally, lessons learned from previous conflicts serve as important sources of information for military planning.

War planning can take place during times of peace or in the midst of a conflict. War plans are often generated during times of peace in preparation for future conflict. During peacetime, plans are made for likely scenarios and some unlikely ones. A primary historical example of preconflict war planning often cited is the period before the outbreak of World War I. Before World War I, the great powers were all engaged in extensive offensive prewar planning.

Criticisms have been made against the practice of prewar planning, however, suggesting that planning for war, specifically offensive war, increases the likelihood of going to war. Some scholars argue that wars have been started by accident because of extensive offensive war planning, which encourages or even compels a nation into war. World War I, with the lead-up to the conflict consisting of heavy offensive war planning, is a commonly cited example of this phenomenon.

Arguably, the rigidity of the war plans and lack of exit strategies may have led these countries into a world war before they realized it. The situation in this case is unlike an ideal situation, in which a politician decides on a course of action and then looks for war plans to achieve the objectives. The war plans became the focus, and the politicians found themselves in a war without a political objective.

However, other scholars have argued that the war plans that were made did not necessarily propel the great powers into war, and that furthermore the assumptions that were made in this case, such as the rigidity of the war plans, were inaccurate. What is clear is that the war planning affected how the war was carried out.

War planning has potential benefits, however. For instance, plans can affect the decision-making apparatus during a crisis because those who can cite specific plans are more likely to have their positions carry more weight. There have also been many past examples of the usefulness of war planning. For example, in World War II, creative war planning helped the Germans achieve much of their battlefield success, although obviously not in the long term.

In practice, there are two types of U.S. planning: that executed as a situation occurs and planning conceived during peacetime. Plans are made on several levels, from the operational level to the strategic level, and occur up and down the military hierarchy. The planning timeline ranges from the beginning stage of a conflict through the potential subsequent stages of the campaign.

War planning, both defensive and offensive, allows a nation to be prepared for potential future scenarios. Due to the impact of chance and the inability of war planners to predict accurately the shape of future conflict, war plans have to be adaptable if they are expected to work. As long as there exists an awareness of the potential limitations of the plan, strategists maintain that war planning is of great benefit to both the military and civilian leadership of a country.

See also War Games

WAR POWERS ACT (1973)

Law addressing the balance of power between the president and Congress in declaring war. The War Powers Act clarifies the mechanism by which the president may use U.S. armed forces. It spells out the situations under which he can deploy the forces with and without a congressional declaration of war. The resolution that created the War Powers Act was passed over the veto of President Richard Nixon on November 7, 1973.

Supporters viewed the War Powers Act as a reaction to Presidents Nixon and Lyndon B. Johnson, who acted without congressional approval or a declaration of war during the Vietnam War. During the Korean and Vietnam wars, the United States found itself involved for many years in undeclared wars. As a result, many members of Congress became concerned with the erosion of congressional authority. Opponents saw the law as an unconstitutional effort to restrict the commander in chief.

The War Powers Act indicates the necessary and proper clause of the Constitution as the basis for legislation on the war powers. It states that the president's powers as commander in chief to introduce U.S. forces into hostilities or imminent hostilities are exercised only following (1) a declaration of war; (2) specific statutory authorization; or (3) a national emergency created by an attack on the United States or its forces.

The law requires the president to consult with Congress before using armed forces, unless there has been a declaration of war or other specific congressional authorization. Consultation in this case means that a decision is pending and the president is asking members of Congress for advice and opinions. It also requires the president to report to Congress any introduction of forces into hostilities or imminent hostilities, as well as any introduction or substantive enlargement of combat forces into foreign countries. After a report is submitted, Congress must authorize the use of forces within 60 to 90 days or the forces must be withdrawn.

In the absence of a declaration of war or congressional authorization, the president has to report within 48 hours the introduction of U.S. armed forces into hostilities. Hostilities refer to a situation in which fighting actually has begun or where there is a clear and present danger of armed conflict.

The War Powers Act seeks to clarify interpretations of the president's authority. For example, Section 8 of the Act states that authority to introduce armed forces is not to be assumed from any provision of law or treaty unless it is specifically mentioned. This section aimed to avoid the use of a broad resolution, such as the Tonkin Gulf resolution, to justify hostilities abroad. That resolution stated that the United States was prepared to take "all necessary steps, including use of armed force," to assist certain nations, and it was cited by presidents and many members of the Congress as congressional authorization for the Vietnam War.

The War Powers Act also makes clear that it does not prevent U.S. forces from participating in joint military exercises with allied or friendly organizations or countries, such as the North Atlantic Treaty Organization (NATO) and the United Nations. Another important specification appears in Section 8(c) of the Act, which defines the introduction of armed forces to include the assignment of armed forces to accompany regular or irregular military forces of other countries when engaged, or potentially engaged, in hostilities. The purpose of this provision was to prevent secret or unauthorized military support to foreign countries. The deployment of U.S. ground troops in Vietnam began with the assignment of advisers to South Vietnamese forces.

Since the beginning, the War Powers Act has been controversial. The war powers are not assigned by the Constitution in a definitive way between the president and Congress. By the early 1970s, the congressional majority thought that the constitutional balance of war powers had swung too far toward the president.

In his veto message, President Nixon said the War Powers Act would impose restrictions upon the authority of the president that would be dangerous to the safety of the nation. President Nixon challenged the constitutionality of the proposal. In particular, every president since Nixon has maintained the position against the provision requiring withdrawal of troops after 60 to 90 days unless Congress authorizes the deployment. U.S. presidents claim that it is unconstitutional because it checks presidential powers without affirmative congressional action.

The Congressional view has always been that the Constitution gave Congress alone the power to declare war. Most members of Congress agree that the president, as commander in chief, has power to lead the U.S. forces once the decision to wage war has been made. However, most members of Congress believe that the president does not have the power to commit armed forces to war. The executive branch replies to that view, arguing that the president has broader authority to use forces. For example, the president can use forces to rescue American citizens abroad, protect U.S. embassies, enforce a cease-fire involving the United States, or carry out the terms of security commitments contained in treaties.

See also Nixon, Richard, and National Policy; Tonkin Gulf Resolution

WARSAW PACT

A central symbol of the Cold War, an organization (also known as the Warsaw Treaty Organization) that bound together the Soviet bloc countries of central and Eastern Europe in a military alliance pitted against the North Atlantic Treaty Organization (NATO). Soviet leader Nikita Khrushchev drafted the founding document of the Warsaw Pact in 1955, and the member nations signed the Treaty on Friendship, Cooperation, and Mutual Assistance later that year (on May 14) in Warsaw.

Although NATO was established in 1949, the Warsaw Pact's agreement stated that recent events—particularly a remilitarized West Germany's integration into NATO—had created a new ominous atmosphere. Faced with the threat of another war and a "menace to the national security of peaceloving states," the pact's signatories decided to establish an alliance that would supersede the existing bilateral agreements that the countries had concluded since communist regimes took over central and Eastern Europe after World War II. The pact agreement bound member states to defend one another if attacked and set the pact's duration at 20 years with an automatic 10-year extension. The Warsaw Pact was renewed once, in 1985.

The signatories of the Warsaw Pact included the Soviet Union, Albania, Bulgaria, Romania, East Germany, Hungary, Poland, and Czechoslovakia; China was given observer status. Yugoslavia, which sought to chart its own socialist course and broke with the Soviet Union in 1948, was never a member. Albania ceased cooperating with the pact in 1961, after its Stalinist regime fell out with the Soviets and became more closely allied with Communist China.

Although the countries were all nominally equal members in the pact, in reality Moscow dictated all the alliance's moves and effectively ran it through the Soviet Ministry of Defense and General Staff, without a NATO-like independent structure. Top Warsaw Pact soldiers were trained in the Soviet Union. In its early history, the pact held few joint exercises, and the Soviet Union made no real attempt to integrate the members' armies into a multinational pact force.

That changed after Khrushchev and the Soviet elite saw de-Stalinization and attempts to permit the satellite states more autonomy spin out of control in the 1950s, first with Polish workers' riots in October 1956 and the Hungarian revolution that soon followed. During the Hungarian revolution, Budapest unilaterally announced plans to withdraw from the Warsaw Pact, a key reason behind Moscow's decision to use its troops to defeat the uprising, which left 25,000 Hungarians dead.

Faced with such defiance, the Soviets decided to transform the Warsaw Pact armies into more of an integrated multinational force that could suppress similar uprisings and, as a byproduct, limit the ability of any national forces to act independently of the Soviet Union. As part of that trend, many more joint military exercises between Soviet forces and the allied national armies began taking place in the 1960s.

The most notorious use of Warsaw Pact troops occurred during the so-called Prague Spring of 1968, when Czechoslovak Prime Minister Alexander Dubcek and his allies introduced liberalizing reforms aimed at creating what they called "socialism with a human face." In contrast with the Hungarians, however, the Czechoslovaks did not seek to leave the Warsaw Pact, but to restructure and reform it.

Nevertheless, Warsaw Pact armies invaded Czechoslovakia. Dozens of people were killed, and hard-line forces were brought in to end all reforms. Already pursuing a comparatively independent foreign policy line, Romania condemned the invasion and refused to participate. Also in response, Albania formally left the pact (although cooperation had already ended in the early 1960s), claiming that the invasion had transformed a defense pact against imperialist aggression into an aggressive pact against the socialist countries themselves.

Attempting to justify the invasion, the Soviet leadership formulated the so-called Brezhnev Doctrine. This doctrine, named after Soviet leader Leonid Brezhnev, stated that "When forces that are hostile to socialism try to turn the development of some socialist country towards capitalism, it becomes not only a problem of the country concerned, but a common problem and concern of all socialist countries."

The Brezhnev Doctrine, which for all practical purposes had already been in effect for many years, began to lose its validity only with the rise of the reform-minded Mikhail Gorbachev in the mid-1980s. In a series of speeches, as well as behind the scenes, the new Soviet leader began to make clear that Moscow would not intervene militarily in central and Eastern Europe. (This position came to be known colloquially as the Sinatra Doctrine after the famous Frank Sinatra song "My Way"—the socialist states could now do it their way). At a Warsaw Pact meeting in Bucharest, Romania, in July 1989, Gorbachev went a step further, suggesting that the organization transform into a mainly political grouping.

After the changes that swept the region following the 1989 fall of the Berlin Wall and the end of communism, some initial attempts were made at reforming the Warsaw Pact. Most of the new national leaders, however, quickly concluded that the security of their states would be better served by dissolving the alliance as soon as possible and individually applying to enter NATO. The last meeting of the political committee of the Warsaw Pact took place in Moscow on June 7, 1990, with central European leaders pushing for the group's dissolution rather than democratization as originally planned. Gorbachev agreed, and in Prague on July 1, 1991, the member states officially ended the Warsaw Pact.

The true symbolic death of the Warsaw Pact and everything it had represented perhaps occurred when the old member states entered NATO, beginning with the Czech Republic, Poland, and Hungary in 1999, followed by Bulgaria and Romania in 2004.

See also Alliances; Cold War; Eastern Bloc; North Atlantic Treaty Organization (NATO)

Further Reading

Henderson, Karen, and Neil Robinson. *Post-Communist Politics*. New York: Prentice Hall, 1997.
Rothschild, Joseph. *Return to Diversity: A Political History of East Central Europe Since World War II*. Oxford, UK: Oxford University Press, 1993.

WASHINGTON NAVAL TREATY (1922)

Conference that attempted to resolve the naval arms race among the United States, Great Britain, and Japan, and to resolve disagreements in the Pacific. The Washington Naval Treaty of February 6, 1922, had five signatories: the United States, Great Britain, Japan, France, and Italy. The United States ratified the agreement in 1923.

Under the treaty, with specified exceptions for current or under-construction vessels, the navies of the United States and Great Britain were limited to 525,000 tons. The Japanese were limited to 315,000 tons, while the French and Italians could keep 175,000 tons apiece. The maximum size of an individual ship was 35,000 tons, and the maximum gun size was 16 inches.

The Washington Naval Treaty included aircraft carriers—the United States and Britain were limited to 135,000 tons, France and Italy to 60,000 tons apiece, and Japan to 81,000 tons. Each nation could support two carriers over 27,000 tons, but they could not exceed 33,000 tons each. The aircraft carrier section limited the number of large guns on a carrier and specified that a battleship with an airplane on it was not called a carrier.

The treaty led the United States to convert from battleships to carriers because it was over the battleship limits at ratification and had to decommission older ships to get under the limit. It was well under on carriers, however, having only the USS *Langley* (11,500 tons), a converted collier. The *Langley* was experimental and not charged against the total, so the Navy had the whole tonnage to work with.

The United States converted the over-the-limit battle cruisers *Lexington* (41,000 tons) and *Saratoga* (33,000 tons) to carriers, even though the Navy did not really care for naval aviation. By 1931, still under the limit, the United States finally had a true carrier—the USS *Ranger* (14,500 tons)—primarily because it was at the limits in the other classes. With the *Yorktown* and *Enterprise* (19,800 tons each) authorized in 1933, the U.S. carrier fleet was at 128,100 tons, where it remained until termination of the treaty in 1936. Experience with the carriers led the Navy to appreciate their benefits. In 1936, the keel of the *Wasp* (14,700 tons) was laid.

The Washington Naval Treaty also encouraged new techniques for making guns more efficient and armor lighter because of the desire to get more bang for the pound.

The status quo prevailed with respect to naval bases and fortifications in the Pacific. There would be no new construction or improvements on certain specific areas, usually small islands. For instance, the United States could build on Hawaii and Alaska, but not on the Aleutians. Britain could not build on Hong Kong, but it could on New Zealand and Australia. Japan could build on its home islands, but Formosa was off-limits. The British and Americans would find at the onset of World War II in the Pacific that their unimproved possessions—Hong Kong, the Philippines, and others—would be easy conquests for the Japanese military.

As the United States turned toward normalcy and disarmament, the impulse to get agreements on the cheap meant that there were no enforcement provisions, and the United States gave Japan unwarranted advantage in the Pacific. In return, it retained the Open Door in China. The treaty remained in effect until 1936, although Japan announced its intent to terminate as early as December 1934.

See also U.S. Navy

Further Reading

Goldstein, Erik, et al. *The Washington Conference, 1921–22: Naval Rivalry, East Asian Stability and the Road to Pearl Harbor.* London, UK: Frank Cass Publishers, 1994.

Lepore, Herbert P. *The Politics and Failure of Naval Disarmament, 1919–1939: The Phantom Peace.* Lewiston, NY: Edwin Mellen Press, 2003.

WEAPONS OF MASS DESTRUCTION (WMD)

A relatively new term, initially used in civilian policy talk, but passing to the military terminology in the 1990s, that refers to a class of weapons able to destroy a large number of people and cause other damage of catastrophic size, out of proportion to their limited size and cost. The use of delivery systems to place these weapons on or near targets usually does not form part of the term or its discussion.

Despite significant success in the use of international accords to reduce the danger of the employment or export of weapons of mass destruction (WMD) and their component materials and technologies, increased attention to terrorism in recent years has caused considerable apprehension and debate over the real and perceived threats that these weapons pose.

ORIGINS OF WMD

The U.S. military establishment defines WMD as weapons capable of a high order of destruction and/or of being used in such a way that can destroy large numbers of people. WMD can be high explosives or nuclear, biological, chemical, and radiological weapons, but the term generally excludes the means of transporting or propelling the weapon where such means is a separable and divisible part of the weapon.

The origins of the term WMD in current usage probably relates to a perception that the public remained insensitive to the dangers of chemical and biological warfare. Decades of living under Cold War conditions had raised awareness of nuclear weapons, and the public certainly recognized the need to control and dissuade their use at nearly any cost. However, the same public awareness was not apparent for chemical or biological weapons.

The armed forces, for an equally long time, had used the term *nuclear-biological-chemical* (NBC) in its basic training and in the organization and training of damage control and monitoring teams. In European parlance, the term was *chemical, biological, and radiological* (CBR). However, the expertise for each type of warfare resided in separate branches of the services.

Ultimately, the terminology of WMD probably came into being to bring the dangers of chemical and biological attack home to the public and to highlight the importance of impending treaty negotiations on chemical and biological warfare. WMD as a term is close enough to MAD, or mutually assured destruction, a nuclear doctrine of the early Cold War era, to attract appropriate attention.

ASSESSING THE PROBLEM

Apart from the origins of the term WMD, its usage remains fraught with ambiguities and potential error. In support of its usage, authorities have cited endless studies illustrating how a small amount of anthrax spores (a potential biological weapon) could kill 600,000 people in New York City, or how a few milliliters of nerve agent (a potential chemical weapon) could kill more than 100,000 persons. Such laboratory specifications can never be matched in the field, however, because of the problems of dispersal, weather conditions, and the random protection level of the target population.

The 1995 attack on the Tokyo subway by the Japanese Aum Shinrikyo terrorist group demonstrated very limited lethality for such an ideal target. Moreover, the nonhuman damage of the chemical-biological branch of WMD seldom registers any grave danger. There is a contamination problem, to be sure, but buildings, vehicles, and other infrastructure can be decontaminated and renovated, and damaged crops and animal herds can be disposed of, by using techniques and procedures that are well-known and available.

However, the detonation of a strategic nuclear device over a major city would likely level most of the buildings, kill most of the population, and cause considerable loss of life and ancillary damage for tens of miles outside the city. The resulting radiation levels would likely render large sections of the ruined city unrestorable and uninhabitable for a significant period.

By comparison, a surprise attack on a city with a lethal nerve agent might cause the deaths of several hundreds, or thousands, or tens of thousands of inhabitants and tax sorely needed emergency and government services. However, the survivors would find all structures intact, and the city would be usable after a short period of decontamination (or longer, without decontamination).

An attack by airborne anthrax spores or the placing of a botulinum virus in a city water supply would cause thousands of deaths, depending upon random probabilities of time of discovery or warning; ambient conditions of temperature, humidity, wind, and sunlight; and the relative alertness of civil utility, health, and emergency services. Once again, the physical surroundings would be returned to normalcy following a decontamination process using technology and procedures already available.

Without downplaying the impact of chemical and biological attacks on a population, or their cost to government, one can see the extreme differences between the nuclear and the chemical-biological wings of the supposed WMD triad. One might just as easily classify knives, pistols, and 155mm howitzers as weapons of personal destruction. However, the uses, effects, and dangers associated with each weapon remain totally disparate.

Recent statements by the U.S. executive branch seem to recognize the disparity. Because of the failure to find nuclear weapons or evidence of an active weapons program in Iraq after the 2003 U.S. invasion of that country, authorities now are referring to the Iraqi history of manufacturing weapons of mass murder as justification for the preemptive attack. That characterization simply confirms the lesser magnitude of the chemical-biological branch of WMD.

RESTRAINTS TO USE

Historian John L. Gaddis noted in his study of the end of the Cold War that nuclear weapons had altered the continuing growth of warfare and the automatic application of technology to killing and destruction. Despite massive production of all kinds of nuclear weapons of all sizes and applications during the Cold War, a peace reigned for 50 years. Although the weapons remained aimed at one country or another during that period, not a single device was ever used, nor could any reason be found to consider such use. Indeed the unlikelihood of using WMD has proven most difficult for experts and critics to understand.

Thus, it can no longer be assumed that every innovation in military technology will provoke its use at the next opportunity. Even in the minds of some irrational people, the use of weapons of such massive lethality and destructiveness seems counterproductive. To a far more limited extent, the use of chemical and biological weapons might follow this same logic, with important exceptions.

The 20th century illustrated the soldiers' dislike of chemical weapons, despite their ready availability in most armies after 1920. Developments in bioweaponry proved equally lacking in practical demonstration. The chemical warfare escalation of the Iraq-Iran War of 1980–88, under threat of absolute conquest, proved an exception, but only because each side proved totally inept in conventional military operations.

In addition to new forms of chemical weapons, military forces have or will develop prototype-directed energy weapons, blinding devices, and frangible (fragile or breakable) ammunition, all capable of inflicting high casualties. Yet nations have also turned to nonlethal weapons and banned antipersonnel land mines in an attempt to limit suffering.

Gaddis may err to the extent that he apparently assumes that the hawks on both sides of the Cold War remained under sufficient restraint. Events since the end of the Cold War suggest that not all states exercise such restraint. In 2002, some Pakistani officers suggested that a nuclear exchange with India would be a boon, for it would settle some accounts with India, raise Pakistani prestige, and kill a portion of the population of both countries, populations that remain in desperate straits with no hope from impoverished governments. Similar musings came from India. One hopes that these hawks experienced the same restraints imposed on officers in the United States and the Soviet Union.

The development and employment of WMD remains no easy task, despite the availability of designs and formulas. The required special handling, storage, and employment techniques have dogged the most sophisticated armed forces for decades. One does not simply pour several gallons of botulinum into a crop-dusting airplane and launch a WMD attack. Unfortunately, the weaknesses of popularly based governments in the face of any risk has fed new fears that a vulnerability exists and that massive preparations to prevent, endure, and recover from WMD attacks must be undertaken, perhaps returning us to the duck and cover days of life in the 1950s under the shadow of Cold War nuclear exchanges. Perhaps we will eventually come to downgrade constructs like WMD in the same way we have emerged from that earlier Cold War era.

—Kenneth W. Estes

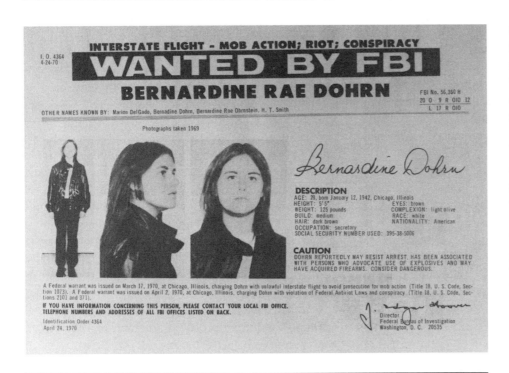

A Federal Bureau of Investigation (FBI) wanted poster from 1970 listed Bernardine Rae Dohrn as one of its most wanted fugitives. Dohrn, a self-proclaimed communist revolutionary, was the reputed underground leader of the violence-oriented Weathermen faction of the Students for a Democratic Society (SDS). By the 1980s, the Weathermen, then known as the Weather Underground, were essentially history, although several of the fugitives remained successfully hidden for decades, emerging only in recent years to answer for their crimes.

Source: Corbis.

See also Anthrax; Arms Control; Asymmetric Warfare; Atomic Bomb; Aum Shinrikyo; Biodefense/Biosecurity; Biological Weapons Convention; Bioterrorism; Chemical Weapons Convention; Cold War; Dirty Bomb; Germ Warfare; Loose Nukes; Neutron Bomb; Nuclear Weapons; Terrorism, U. S. (Domestic)

Further Reading

Gaddis, John L. *We Now Know.* New York: Oxford University Press, 1997.

Laqueur, Walter. *The New Terrorism: Fanaticism and the Arms of Mass Destruction.* Oxford, UK: Oxford University Press, 2000.

van Creveld, Martin. *The Transformation of War.* New York: Free Press, 1991.

WEATHERMEN, THE

Radical organization cofounded in 1969 by Bill Ayers, John Jacobs, Bernardine Dohrn, Kathy Boudin, and others as an offshoot of the Students for a Democratic Society (SDS), which was dedicated to the violent overthrow of American imperialism.

The Weathermen, or Weather Underground, emerged following a meeting in Flint, Michigan, at which cofounder John Jacobs said, "We are against everything that is good and decent in honky America. We will burn and loot and destroy." Following a trip to Havana to plot strategy with representatives of other members of the global communist movement's terrorist fifth column, the Weather Underground turned radical thought into action.

In 1969, the Weather Underground organized Days of Rage in Chicago with other militant left-wing groups. During Days of Rage, hundreds of people stormed the city's downtown areas, smashing hotel and store windows to protest the Vietnam War. Dozens of people were injured in the melee, including a current Chicago judge who was crippled for life.

Between 1970 and 1972, the Weather Underground carried out bombings against targets that included the headquarters of the New York City Police Department, the U.S. Capitol, the Pentagon, Reserve Officer Training Corps (ROTC) buildings, draft offices, corporate headquarters, and even statues of "oppressors." In March, 1970, three members of the group died in a Greenwich Village townhouse when a bomb they were working on exploded prematurely. The bomb was intended for a dance at nearby Fort Dix, New Jersey.

Kathy Boudin, who survived the Greenwich Village bombing, went on to join the Black Liberation Army, an ultraviolent wing associated with the Black Panther Party. She was on the Federal Bureau of Investigation (FBI) most wanted list for nearly a decade. Boudin was involved in the 1981 New York Brinks robbery that left two guards dead. The proceeds of the robbery were to fund the "republic of New Afrika" in the southwestern United States. When Boudin was arrested, she possessed bomb-making materials and plans for a bombing campaign against New York City police stations. She was sentenced to 20 years to life and was paroled in 2003.

Ayers and Dohrn were fugitives before surrendering in December 1980. Charges against them were dropped because of improper surveillance. Ayers, a professor at the University of Illinois-Chicago, has written a book about his experiences in the Weather Underground. Dohrn, now a law professor at Northwestern University, has been denied admittance to the bar because of her association with the Weather Underground.

See also Terrorism, U.S. (Domestic)

Further Reading

Ayers, B. *Fugitive Days*. New York: Penguin, 2003.
Braudy, S. *Family Circle: The Boudins and the Aristocracy of the Left*. New York: Knopf, 2003.

WESTMORELAND, WILLIAM
(1914–2005)

Commander of the U.S. forces in Vietnam from 1964 to 1968. General William Westmoreland was a key architect of the U.S. military strategy in Vietnam and a consistent advocate for a greater commitment from Washington. He oversaw the buildup of U.S. ground troops in Vietnam beginning in 1965.

Son of a textile plant manager in South Carolina, Westmoreland graduated from West Point in 1936, winning the coveted John J. Pershing sword for leadership and military proficiency. During World War II, he commanded artillery battalions in Sicily and North Africa. During 10 months of front-line combat, he suffered from malaria, and a land mine blew a truck out from under him (and fortunately left him almost unhurt).

Westmoreland volunteered for the Korean War in 1952, in which he was in command of the 187th Regimental Combat Team. In 1960, after becoming the Army's youngest major general at age 42, he was named superintendent of the U.S. Military Academy at West Point, where he expanded the facilities and increased enrollment from 2,500 to 4,000. In 1964, he was sent to Saigon, South Vietnam as deputy to General Paul Harkins. By midyear, when Harkins returned to the United States, Westmoreland became head of the Military Assistance Command (MACV) and received a fourth star.

Westmoreland was the top U.S. adviser to South Vietnamese armed forces and the commander of about 6,000 U.S. advisers attached to the Vietnamese units. He commanded U.S. forces in Vietnam as they gradually expanded from a few thousand to more than half a million. Westmoreland continuously requested more ground troops for Vietnam. In 1968, President Lyndon Johnson refused to send more troops and finally recalled Westmoreland after he successfully stopped the North Vietnamese Tet Offensive. Westmoreland was replaced by General Creighton W. Abrams.

Back in Washington, Westmoreland served as U.S. Army chief of staff. His biggest challenge was to withdraw the troops from Vietnam and redeploy them for duty in other regions of the world. General Westmoreland retired in 1972.

See also Vietnam War (1954–1975)

WEST POINT
See U.S. MILITARY ACADEMY (WEST POINT)

WORLD BANK

A multilateral development institution for poverty reduction and promotion of sustainable economic development worldwide, also known as the International Bank for Reconstruction and Development. Ironically, the development aspect of the World Bank, which is now its main mandate, was possibly an afterthought, emphasized only later by the developing country delegations present at a conference in Bretton Woods, New Hampshire, in 1944. It was from there that the bank was created—along with its sister organization, the International Monetary Fund (IMF) and the third pillar of the newly proposed multilateral Bretton Woods system, the General Agreement on Tariffs and Trade (GATT). The World Bank finally came into official existence in 1946 when the United Nations was established.

HISTORICAL CONTEXT

The creation of the World Bank was a result of the geostrategic and global economic conditions present in Europe and America just before World War II. In 1942, both the American and British governments were planning innovations that would prevent the international economy from sinking back into the economic disasters of the 1930s after World War II was over. In Britain, noted economist John Maynard Keynes and his associates were advocating full employment policies, emphasizing the need for government action to redress the shortfalls of the market and building new multilateral institutions to manage an increasingly interdependent global economy and provide a counterbalance for any single rising force in Europe.

In America, Harry Dexter White of the U.S. Treasury, along with Keynes, was also concerned with forming an institution or international bank to supplement financing a depression, the war-shocked private financial markets, reconstruction of the economies of Europe, and finally to advance the economies of less-developed countries.

ORGANIZATIONAL STRUCTURE AND POLICIES

Since its birth in 1946, the World Bank has expanded into a large organization employing nearly 10,000 people. It comprises an amalgam of five organizations—collectively called the World Bank Group—that operate under a common governing board but with different functions. These include the International Bank for Reconstruction and Development (IBRD), the International Development Agency (IDA), the International Finance Corporation (IFC), the Multinational Investment Guarantee Agency (MIGA), and the International Center for Settlement of Investment Disputes (ICSID).

The World Bank is headed by a president, appointed for a five-year term by the United States, the institution's single largest shareholder and financier. An executive board, composed of representatives from various member countries, oversees and approves the day-to-day operational and lending activities of the World Bank.

Over time, the World Bank has had to adapt its role to changing economic challenges and the perceptions of the contribution that a multilateral public sector institution can make to development. Postwar reconstruction dominated the first 15 years of the institution's life. As this role became redundant over time, there was a widening of the bank's mandate, emphasized in shifts through its different decades of existence. This broader mandate included poverty reduction, economic growth, debt restructuring, developmental research, structural adjustment policies, and other program-based lending forms to the bank's clients: mainly poor and developing countries of Asia, Africa, and Latin America.

There has been extensive and complex analysis of the World Bank's past five decades of existence in terms of its projects, lending policies, and overall developmental impact. There have been both successes and failures, and the lessons learned from them provide critical feedback for yet another role the institution has recently adopted—that of a knowledge bank, or the repository of best practice in developmental assistance. How this relatively recent role shapes the bank's future direction, policies, and indeed its effectiveness remains to be seen.

See also Bretton Woods Conference; International Monetary Fund (IMF); United Nations

WORLD CUSTOMS ORGANIZATION (WCO)

An independent intergovernmental body aiming to enhance the effectiveness of customs agencies. Seventeen European countries founded the Customs Cooperation Council, now known as the World Customs Organization (WCO), in 1952. Since then, membership in the WCO has grown to 162 states, stretching around the globe. WCO members are responsible for processing more than 95% of international trade.

Headquartered in Brussels, Belgium, the WCO promotes technical and legal improvements to help participating countries cope with the rise in international trade. The WCO strives for the standardization and uniform application of simplified customs procedures. It also enables members to share best practices and to cooperate more effectively.

The WCO's network of international partnerships encourages efficient customs administration at the national level. It contributes to a more transparent and predictable customs environment, which facilitates world trade. The WCO also promotes mutual assistance among customs agencies to combat arms trafficking, the illegal movement of chemical, biological, and nuclear materials. In addition, the organization helps detect activities that finance terrorism, such as drug trafficking and money laundering.

In July 2004, the WCO urged its member states to implement stringent cargo-security standards similar to the ones adopted by the United States after the September 11, 2001, terrorist attacks. Such measures include the requirement that sea carriers provide advance cargo information to customs officials at destination ports. U.S. customs requires sea carriers to present data on United States-bound cargo 24 hours before it is loaded at a foreign port. By harmonizing national cargo-security regulations, the WCO hopes to safeguard the supply chain and to reduce the cost of compliance for shipping companies. The WCO insists that stricter security measures should not hinder the flow of legitimate trade.

In addition, since 1998, the WCO prepares and circulates a code of conduct for customs officials and holds training courses to promote professional integrity. The WCO also offers regional seminars to provide a forum for sharing best practices and for identifying strategies to prevent corruption among customs officials. In 2003, the WCO helped open a regional education center outside Baku, Azerbaijan, to improve the professional skills of local customs officers. The United States, Japan, and Germany contribute nearly half of the WCO's annual budget. As of 2005, the organization's secretary-general was Michel Danet, formerly a French customs official.

See also Trade and Foreign Aid; World Trade Organization (WTO)

WORLD TRADE CENTER ATTACK (2001)
See SEPTEMBER 11/WTC AND PENTAGON ATTACKS

WORLD TRADE ORGANIZATION (WTO)

A multilateral organization established in 1995 at the conclusion of the Uruguay Round of negotiations of the General Agreement on Tariffs and Trade (GATT), the World Trade Organization (WTO) succeeds the GATT as the world's preeminent international trade organization.

The WTO administers trade agreements, provides a forum for trade negotiations, handles trade disputes, monitors national trade policies, offers technical assistance and training for developing countries, and cooperates with other international organizations. Nearly 150 nations are members of the WTO, and 30 others were negotiating membership as of 2004. The current members of the WTO account for 97% of all international trade.

The WTO is governed principally by ministerial conferences that are required to take place at least every two years under the terms of the WTO agreement. At this level, decisions are made not by voting but by consensus building among member nations (although there are provisions for voting to take place under special circumstances). During the last ministerial conference, held in Cancun, Mexico, in 2003, WTO members failed to reach a consensus.

The day-to-day government of the organization is found in its general council. Representatives from member nations (typically ambassadors) meet regularly and have the authority to make decisions on behalf of the ministerial conferences. The administrative agency of the organization, known as the WTO secretariat, consists of nearly 600 Geneva-based policy and legal specialists.

Proponents of trade liberalization and the mission of the WTO note that the volume of world trade is 22 times greater today than it was when the GATT was formed in 1947. The WTO is said to promote peace, handle disputes constructively, reduce the cost of living in member nations, enhance consumer choices, raise national incomes, stimulate economic growth, shield governments from lobbying efforts, and encourage efficient government. Moreover, given that rules are applied equally to all WTO members and that decisions are made by consensus (rather than simple majority), smaller nations enjoy more leverage with the WTO than without it; developing nations are afforded lengthier periods to adjust to WTO provisions.

Since its founding, the WTO has triggered fierce opposition, perhaps most graphically illustrated by the enormous protests and riots surrounding the 1999 ministerial conference in Seattle. Critics of the organization claim that the WTO (not sovereign governments) drives international policy making, places commercial interests above those of development, destroys the global environment, generates poverty, destroys jobs, and threatens safety. Notions of free trade at any cost and their subsequent calls for rapid trade liberalization have widened trade deficits in developing countries. Such nations are obligated to open up their domestic markets (and allow in more imports), but have little control over export flows. During the 1990s, the average trade deficit (as a percentage of national income) for developing countries was 3% higher than in the 1970s, just as the average rate of economic growth was 2% lower.

See also General Agreement on Tariffs and Trade (GATT); Multilateralism; Trade and Foreign Aid

Further Reading

Bhagwati, Jagdish. *In Defense of Globalization.* Oxford, UK: Oxford University Press, 2004.
Jawara, Fatoumata, and Aileen Kwa. *Behind the Scenes of the WTO: The Real World of International Trade Negotiations.* London: Zed Books, 2003.

REFLECTIONS

Opportunities Offered by the Global Economy

For over two decades, Mauritius has grown by nearly 6% per year. At independence in 1968, Mauritius had a per capita income of about US $260. Today, it is about US $3,800. Improvements in human development indicators have been equally impressive. Life expectancy at birth has increased from 61 years in 1965 to 71 years in 2001. The infant mortality rate has gone down dramatically—from 64 per 1,000 in 1970 to 19 per 1,000 in 2001. Virtually all households now have access to sanitation and water, and more children are being enrolled at school than ever before. The fact that economists today are able to quibble over the causes of the Mauritian miracle is proof of the astounding progress that has been achieved.

These achievements are due, in no small measure, to your determination, your creativity, and your confidence to take advantage of all the opportunities offered by the global economy. However, this was not the end of the story. One can quite reasonably ask why did a small island developing country heavily dependent on a single commodity, vulnerable to terms of trade shocks, situated at a considerable distance from world markets and faced with a rapidly growing population succeed where other better-endowed countries have failed.

The answer will come as no surprise to you. The key ingredients to your success have been political and macroeconomic stability, the rule of law, human capital, a coherent economic development strategy, judicious use of preferential access to key markets, a staunch belief in free enterprise, and most importantly the ability to adjust and turn adverse conditions into economic assets. Mauritius successfully turned the disadvantage of rapid population growth into the blessing of a dynamic and plentiful workforce. You used your ethnic diversity, which could so easily have led instead to social fragmentation, to gain advantageous business links throughout the world. And you invested heavily in educating your people and in building the institutions needed to support development.

—WTO Director-General Supachai Panitchpakdi
Speech at Mauritius National
Day Celebration, 2004

WORLD WAR I (1914–1918)

The first major conflict of the 20th century, which resulted in the deaths of more than 16 million people and launched a new era of total war. Issues of national and international security would become commonplace during the 20th century.

The assassination of the Austrian Archduke Franz Ferdinand in Sarajevo on June 28, 1914, is typically cited as the starting point of the conflict that would transform not only the map of Europe but also the concept of war itself. World War I led to the demise of three empires, as well as to the idea that conflicts between modern European societies could be quick, decisive, or inexpensive.

An alliance system constructed for more than half a century split Europe into opposing antagonistic camps, each of which formulated war plans and maintained large standing armies. Meanwhile, the Industrial Revolution had resulted in the development of tremendous resources that, once mobilized, could not be stopped. Add to this the tensions of nascent nationalism, and the outcome was a conflict that ultimately claimed the lives of more than eight million combatants and nearly the same number of civilians. Of further significance was a reorientation of power and influence, as the Russian, Ottoman, and Austro-Hungarian empires disappeared from the map of Europe to be replaced by a number of smaller states and the new role of the United States as a global power.

Members of the American expeditionary forces wearing gas masks in the trenches at Lorraine in France during World War I. The use of poison gas by both sides was one of the most horrifying dangers of trench warfare during the war. Beginning in the spring of 1915, the Germans released thousands of cylinders of deadly chlorine gas, and the gas attacks left gaping holes in Allied defenses as soldiers fled choking and gasping from the fumes. The use of gas masks, which became vital equipment in the trenches, eventually lessened the threat.

Source: Corbis.

STALEMATE AND TRENCH WARFARE

The Battle of the Marne in early September 1914 ended all hope of the Germans for a quick victory, although their successful retreat also ended all hope for a short war on either side. In the meantime, the Russian defeat at the battle of Tannenberg in August 1914 was so devastating that the Russian general committed suicide, and in Britain, all news of what happened was kept from the public.

Trench warfare immediately became a feature of World War I as the Germans began digging trenches in September 1914 to protect them from advancing French and British forces. The trenches soon came to symbolize the apparent intractability of the conflict, and the conditions of trench life—rats, flooding, cold, and the constant vulnerability to shelling and poisoned gas—forever undermined romantic associations of war with cavalry charges or heroic combat. The oft-repeated promise that the troops would be home by Christmas soon came to sound more like mockery.

The worst day in the history of the British military was the first day of the Battle of the Somme—July 1,

1916. The futile advance of British troops in parade ground formation across the so-called No Man's Land of barbed wire and shrapnel between enemy trenches lasted less than a half hour. By the end of the day, there were about 58,000 British casualties. The battle continued for five more months, and the Somme Campaign did not end until November 1919, with 600,000 casualties exchanged for an advance of less than 10 miles.

Technological innovation in the forms of poison gas, aircraft, tanks, and machine guns played an important role in shaping the conflict. Poison gas was first used by the French, who fired tear gas grenades at Germans advancing through Belgium during the first month of the war. The French attack was more irritating than lethal, however. The gas used by the Germans against the French at Ypres in April 1915 had a more devastating impact, which surprised even the Germans themselves. Using poison or toxic gas required perfection, as the British found when the wind blew their own gas back upon them in an attack on September 25, 1915. Gas masks were continually perfected as standard equipment, and by 1916, gas shells were being produced for use with heavy artillery to increase the range of attacks and protect the troops when weather conditions for launching a gas attack were not ideal.

The first zeppelin attack took place on the east coast of England in January 1915, and the first air raid on London took place that May. The zeppelins were successful at conducting long-range bombing missions, but they were vulnerable to attack and bad weather. The airplane played a more vital role, and by 1917, the Germans had stopped using zeppelins for bombing raids.

The motivation for tank design was to find a way of combating the machine gun, which was responsible for the deaths of thousands of infantry advancing toward enemy trenches. The first use of tanks was by the British army during the battle of the Somme in July 1916 (although most of the tanks broke down). The first effective use of tanks was at the Battle of Cambrai in 1917, but the soon-to-be-obsolete horse cavalry, assigned the task of following up on the breakthrough, were not successful.

THE UNITED STATES ENTERS THE WAR

Two incidents played an important role in bringing the United States into World War I on the side of the Allied Powers: the sinking of the *Lusitania* and the Zimmerman telegram. In February 1915, the German government announced a policy of unrestricted warfare at sea, indicating that any ship delivering goods to an Allied country was in danger of being attacked. Although this policy broke with international agreements concerning nonmilitary vessels and the endangerment of civilian passengers, it was motivated by awareness that imports from the United States were an important source of supplies for Britain and France.

The British ship *Lusitania* left New York Harbor for Liverpool on May 1, 1915. A few days before, a statement was issued by the German embassy, reminding transatlantic travelers that a state of war existed between Great Britain and Germany. Thus, passengers on vessels flying the flag of Great Britain entered the war zone, including waters adjacent to the British Isles, at their own risk. Six days later a German submarine spotted the *Lusitania* and sank it with a torpedo. The Germans later apologized, but also claimed that the ship was carrying a cargo of heavy munitions. The American public was outraged.

U.S. President Woodrow Wilson ran for reelection in 1916 using the slogan "He Kept Us Out of War." However, Germany's announcement of a new submarine offensive in January 1917, half a year after the sinking of the *Lusitania*, caused Wilson to break off diplomatic relations. That same month, German Foreign Secretary Arthur Zimmerman sent a coded telegram to the German minister in Mexico City, instructing him to propose an alliance with Mexico if war broke out between Germany and the United States. As compensation, the Germans promised that they, along with Japan, would help Mexico regain the territories it lost to the United States in 1848 (Texas, New Mexico, and Arizona).

The so-called Zimmerman telegram was intercepted by the British government, shown to President Wilson in February, and by April, Wilson was asking Congress for permission to go to war. Isolationist tendencies still existing in the conduct of American foreign policy were evidenced by the fact that war was declared only against the German government, not German citizens, and war was not declared on Austria-Hungary until December 1917.

THE BOLSHEVIK REVOLUTION AND THE END OF THE WAR

Despite possessing the largest army in Europe, Russia entered World War I with tremendous liabilities. The country lagged far behind Germany in industrial output, and its literacy rate was the level of Great Britain's in 1750. Both of these factors were exacerbated by an indiscriminate draft policy that called up skilled industrial workers along with illiterate peasants. Russian morale was also burdened by recent defeats in the Crimean and Russo-Japanese wars, not to mention the humiliating peace imposed upon them by Europe after the Russian defeat in the Russo-Turkish war. After a series of early defeats, the czar personally took over as commander of the Russian military.

The Russian army was further hobbled by class stratification, with peasant soldiers, whose local identities superseded nationalist sentiment, commanded by an aristocratic officer class, rumored to be rife with German sympathy. This led to riots in the rear against recruitment and the continued spread of disgust with the war among soldiers at the front. After the Russian Revolution in 1917, the Bolshevik's primary foreign policy interest was to remove Russia from the war.

Meanwhile, the Allies were deeply suspicious of the Bolshevik regime led by Vladimir Lenin, which many considered the outcome of a German plot. The Russians concluded a separate armistice with the Central Powers in December 1917 and a peace treaty at Brest-Litovsk in March 1918, eight months before the general armistice signed between the remaining Allies and the Central Powers in November 1918. With the entry of the United States into the war, the defeat of the Central Powers was only a matter of time. By July of 1918, there were more than a million U.S. troops in France. Although more than two million troops would eventually reach Europe, a large number arrived too late to see any action.

The Treaty of Versailles, signed on June 28, 1919, was unsatisfactory to all sides and is often cited by historians as one of the causes of World War II. The U.S. Congress refused to ratify the treaty, Germany bitterly resented what they considered unnecessarily harsh reparations, and Britain and France were upset that there was no trial of the kaiser or other wartime German leaders. One significant outcome, however, was the creation of the League of Nations, proposed by Woodrow Wilson in his famous Fourteen Points. Although the League itself eventually proved a failure, it provided a model for the creation of the United Nations after World War II.

—Will Hughes

See also Air Warfare; Tanks; World War II (1939–1945)

Further Reading

Fussell, Paul. *The Great War and Modern Memory*. Oxford, UK: Oxford University Press, 2000.

Howard, Michael. *The First World War*. Oxford, UK: Oxford University Press, 2004.

Joll, James. *Origins of the First World War*. New York: Longman, 2000.

WORLD WAR II (1939–1945)

Global conflict that resulted in the deaths of 50 million civilians and combatants. World War II pitted the Allies, which included the United States, the Soviet Union, Great Britain, and France, against the fascist forces of Germany, Italy, and Japan. The most widespread conflict in history, the war was waged on battlefronts from Europe to North Africa to the Pacific and prompted new debates over national security.

BACKGROUND AND ORIGINS

The Treaty of Versailles, signed in 1919 at the conclusion of World War I, forced Germany to admit responsibility for the Great War, cede territory to its neighbors, reduce its military to a fraction of its former strength, and pay heavy reparations. The German people, who suffered greatly after the war, blamed the humiliation and severe economic consequences of the treaty on the new Weimar government.

The rising leader of the National Socialist German Workers' (Nazi) party, a man named Adolf Hitler, attributed German defeat in World War I to a stab in the back. Hitler won much popular support by vowing to amend the outrage committed at Versailles. Named Chancellor of the Reich in January 1933, Hitler helped suspend substantial elements of the Weimar constitution. He also directed German rearmament in violation of the peace agreements from 1935 onward, and that same year he reclaimed the Saar region, which had been ceded to France after World War I.

Germany's future allies, Japan and Italy, were likewise attempting to consolidate power and land holdings. Japan took over the Chinese region of Manchuria (Manchukuo) in 1931 to gain access to its resources and to south Asia. Italy invaded Ethiopia to try to establish an empire in Africa. In both cases, the League of Nations, the Western European powers, and the United States failed to take significant action—the former for fiscal reasons; the latter because of a retreat into isolationism.

In 1936, Germany, Japan, and Italy signed the anti-Comintern pact, which provided a basis for the Axis alliance. Facing little opposition, each country pursued particular strategies of expansionist rule, including Hitler's *anschluss* (union) with Austria to fulfill his dream of reuniting German-speaking peoples under one Reich. In September 1938, Hitler negotiated with representatives from Great Britain and France and gained control of the Sudetenland from Czechoslovakia. The western powers hoped that Hitler would be appeased by these concessions. Instead, he effectively took over the rest of Czechoslovakia in early 1939. A nonaggression pact between Germany and the Soviet Union completed Hitler's preparations.

THE OPENING PHASES, 1939–1942

War was declared officially on September 1, 1939, when Hitler launched a devastating *blitzkrieg* (lightning war) against Poland. The attack combined tactics of speed, surprise, and divide-and-conquer maneuvers using the most up-to-date technology, stunning the world with its force.

Poland was invaded again by the Soviet Union on September 17 and surrendered on September 27. The Soviets next launched an attack against Finland in November and dictated a settlement in which Finland ceded some of its territory by March of 1940. Meanwhile, Germany took over Denmark in one day in April and then invaded Norway, creating a puppet state there by June to secure food and other supplies.

Response to these actions from the French and British was limited—described as a phony war—until

Germany turned westward and invaded Belgium, the Netherlands, and Luxembourg in May 1940. The Germans likewise broke through France's Maginot line on May 13, and France fell on June 22. Marshall Pétain, the beloved French World War I hero, was made the puppet ruler in the German-controlled Vichy government.

Under its fascist leader, Benito Mussolini, Italy entered the war in June, launching an attack against and occupation of British Somaliland in August and beginning a series of North Africa campaigns. Numerous battles took place between Italian and British forces from Egypt to Libya, but neither side could gain more than a temporary advantage.

Back in Europe, Germany began the Battle of Britain in August, an all-out air offensive in preparation for a planned amphibious invasion of the British Isles. The use of radar and coordinated British resistance helped repel the German advance. Meanwhile, Hungary, Romania, and Bulgaria joined forces with the Germans in late 1940.

On April 6, 1941, Germany attacked Yugoslavia and Greece, followed by Crete in May, and quickly prevailed in those areas. Hitler then launched Operation Barbarossa, invading the Soviet Union on June 22 in blatant violation of their nonaggression pact. The advancing German army, aided by Finland and other German-allied east European nations, swept through much of the Soviet Union west of the Caucasus Mountains with land forces and air attacks. Bitter weather, however, forced a halt to the advance and created a war of attrition rather than a quick victory. Stung by German treachery in violating the nonaggression pact, the Soviet Union joined forces with the Allies against Germany.

U.S. president Franklin Roosevelt met with British prime minister Winston Churchill at sea in August 1941 and created the Atlantic Charter. This document established principles of democracy, self-determination, and nonaggression, which helped form a basis for further cooperation after the war. The United States entered the war on the side of the Allies after December 7, 1941, when the Japanese bombed the American fleet in a surprise attack at Pearl Harbor. The United States declared war the following day.

TURNING OF THE TIDE: 1942–1945

In the early part of 1942, the Allies had their first major victories with successes against Japan at the battles of Coral Sea and Midway. These were followed by a U.S. success on the Japanese-held island of Guadalcanal (which was finally captured early in 1943). Nevertheless, at the same time, German forces under General Erwin Rommel replaced Italian troops in North Africa and gained an advantage there. Germany and its allies also launched an intense attack against the Soviet city of Stalingrad. With the help of American aid fueled through a lend-lease program, the Soviets managed to keep the enemy at bay. By October, the British forces in Africa received reinforcements from Australia and the United States and pushed Rommel back, turning the tide of the war.

In January 1943, the Allied leaders—Churchill, Roosevelt, Charles de Gaulle (leader of the Free French), and Henri Giraud (leader of the French forces in North Africa)—attended the Casablanca Conference, where they pledged to seek unconditional surrender of the Axis powers. The German army surrendered at Stalingrad in February, after which the Russians marched westward uninterrupted.

The Allies finally defeated Rommel and prevailed in North Africa in May 1943. That summer saw the Allied conquest of Sicily, and invasion and success in Italy, which finally surrendered to the Allies on September 8, 1943. Germany reoccupied the country briefly, but the Allies reclaimed it in June of 1944. Meanwhile, in the Pacific, the Allies won victories in the Solomon Islands late in the year.

The Allies also began bombing Germany in the spring of 1944 to weaken her capabilities to continue to conduct the war. Moreover, they designed a plan to liberate occupied Europe. The Allies launched Operation Overlord (known as the D-Day invasion) on June 6, 1944, landing at Normandy to regain control of occupied France. They neutralized principal German defenses by late August and controlled most of France and Belgium by October.

At the same time, Soviet forces moved through eastern and central Europe, pushing back German and Axis forces as they progressed, eventually reaching as far as Germany in early 1945. After battles in New Guinea, the Allies grew progressively stronger in the Pacific and reclaimed the island groups bit by bit from the Japanese, fighting in the Philippines, Bougainville, New Guinea, the Mariana Islands, Okinawa, Iwo Jima, and Manila.

The Nazis launched one final major offensive at the Battle of the Bulge in Belgium, which began on December 16, 1944. Early successes in that protracted battle gave way to Allied victory by January 25, 1945. In February 1945, Roosevelt, Churchill, and Stalin met at the Yalta Conference, at which they began designing final strategies for the Pacific, including Soviet entry into the war there.

At Yalta, the Allied leaders also laid plans for the postwar order, including the temporary partition of Germany, the resolution of Japanese/Chinese/Soviet territorial disputes, the management of east European nations, and the design of the future United Nations. After the conclusion of the conference, the German forces went into retreat, and the Allied forces pushed into Germany. The Nazi defenses finally collapsed at Torgau on April 25. Hitler committed suicide five days later, and surrender of the German forces was finalized on May 8, 1945.

The war in the Pacific came to a rapid close soon after. In early 1945, the United States bombed the Japanese home islands to cut it off from its empire and prepare the way for a later land invasion. The United States also convinced the Soviet Union to enter the Pacific war by August 1945. Meanwhile, U.S. scientists were secretly developing nuclear weaponry as part of the Manhattan Project. Following a successful July test of an atomic bomb in New Mexico, President Harry S. Truman ordered the *Little Boy* bomb dropped on the Japanese city of Hiroshima on August 6. When the Japanese still did not surrender, the United States dropped a second bomb, nicknamed *Fat Man*, on the city of Nagasaki. Japan surrendered unconditionally on August 14, 1945.

THE HIDDEN WARS

After Hitler came to power in Germany, concentration camps created by Nazi storm troopers (the SA) proliferated. Prisoners, including political dissidents and criminals, were put into the camps to remove them from society and break their spirits. By 1938, the list of potential detainees was expanded to include antisocials of all types—tramps, beggars, gypsies, pimps, and some already imprisoned male Jews. They were detained usually without having committed any crime, usually without trial, and usually without hope of release. The mentally ill and insane were likewise sent to the death camps, usually being killed upon arrival.

With the outbreak of war, the concentration camps were mobilized in Germany and occupied territories to eliminate all undesirables from the Reich, including homosexuals, Jehovah's Witnesses, and other persons deemed to be antisocial. Slavs became targets as well, but the primary population the Nazis wanted to eliminate was the Jews. The Office for Jewish Emigration under Adolf Eichmann became an agency that organized Jewish deportation to the concentration camps, which served as detention centers, work camps, and sites of extermination. Jews were taken from their homes throughout German-occupied territories and sent to camps such as Dachau and Auschwitz to do hard labor, for the Nazis were desperately short of laborers.

The prisoners lacked food, clothing, and medical care; families were divided. They were sometimes used for horrendous medical experiments. As the war progressed, the Nazis arrived at their Final Solution to the Jewish Question—extermination. Those who did not die of exhaustion, starvation, or cold were sent to their deaths by firing squads or gas chambers. Approximately six million Jews were killed, and an estimated five million others died at the hands of the Nazis.

See also Atlantic Alliance; D-Day; Hiroshima; Manhattan Project (1942–1945); Midway, Battle of (1942); Nagasaki; Roosevelt, Franklin D., and National Policy; Truman, Harry S., and National Policy; World War I (1914–1918); Yalta Conference (1945)

SECRETS REVEALED

Japanese Internment

The Nazis were not alone in establishing camps to detain suspected opponents. In the United States, President Franklin Roosevelt signed Executive Order 9066, stating that Japanese Americans should be detained in internment camps in the American west out of "military necessity."

Racial prejudice, wartime paranoia, and economic pressures contributed to the signing of the order. Japanese Americans were suspected of sabotage or collaboration, despite the fact that no proof existed that they had ever been engaged in such activities.

More than 120,000 people—more than half of them children—were crowded into the camps. Some died because of inadequate medical care, and some were killed by guards. President Roosevelt gave the order to close the camps in 1944; the last of them was finally closed in 1945. In 1988, the U.S. government issued a formal apology and paid reparations to many of the Japanese Americans who were detained in the camps.

WORLD WAR II AND ESPIONAGE

Covert intelligence activities during World War II. The combined intelligence operations of the United States and its allies were crucial to the course of World War II military campaigns and were responsible for hastening victories in both the European and Pacific theaters.

After the Japanese attack on Pearl Harbor in December 1941, President Franklin D. Roosevelt fully recognized the importance of intelligence to the war effort and was instrumental in making intelligence gathering a vital component of the U.S. government. During the war, U.S. intelligence analysts studied and reported on information gathered from spies, double agents, encrypted radio communications, aerial reconnaissance photos, and prisoner and deserter interviews, as well as from analyses of open radio communications, books, magazines, pamphlets, newspapers, and other archival data.

U.S. ESPIONAGE PRIOR TO A DECLARATION OF WAR

In 1939, at the beginning of World War II in Europe, the United States had no official, separate intelligence organization. In the 1920s, the United States had been a world leader in cryptanalysis, or codebreaking. However, President Herbert Hoover's secretary of state, Henry Stimson, had a great distaste for the deceptive, ungentlemanly nature of intelligence work, and as a result, U.S. intelligence fell into a period of neglect in the 1930s. In 1939, the intelligence available to U.S. leaders was inferior to the intelligence that most European leaders took for granted.

As war loomed large, President Roosevelt took steps to remedy the deficiency. Deeply concerned about U.S. national security, Roosevelt explored a number of intelligence options in the early 1940s. In 1940 and 1941, he privately and informally enlisted his distant cousin, the wealthy philanthropist Vincent Astor, and columnist John Franklin Carter to each develop a small, private network of spies to engage in espionage. Astor and Carter reported only to Roosevelt and were hired largely because the president distrusted intelligence from other sources, including U.S. military intelligence.

Realizing Astor and Carter's limitations, Roosevelt was open to a proposal by former assistant attorney general William J. Donovan that the United States cooperate with Britain's superior intelligence organizations. Donovan also advocated a centralized U.S. intelligence service. In July 1941, Roosevelt established the first U.S. intelligence organization, the Office of the Coordinator of Intelligence (COI), with Donovan as its director.

The COI functions were not to overlap or impinge on the work of other U.S. intelligence groups, including the Office of Naval Intelligence (ONI), the Military Intelligence Division (MID), the Federal Bureau of Investigation (FBI), and the State Department. Although not the centralized organ that he had proposed to Roosevelt, Donovan immediately set to work, hiring distinguished academic experts for the COI's research and analysis group. He also collaborated with British intelligence officials, searched for accomplished espionage agents, and created a group dedicated to training spies.

PEARL HARBOR

Touted as the grossest intelligence failure of World War II, the Japanese attack on Pearl Harbor on December 7, 1941, shocked Americans, including Roosevelt and U.S. military and intelligence leaders. Although they knew weeks before December 7 that a Japanese attack on U.S. forces was imminent, they did not know where the enemy would strike. The intelligence available suggested that Southeast Asia was the most likely target.

Months before Pearl Harbor was attacked, U.S. cryptographers decoded the cipher used by Japanese diplomats, nicknamed Purple. The coded messages, called MAGIC by U.S. analysts, did not in and of themselves indicate an upcoming attack on Hawaii. Although an analysis of decoded messages from all sources available at the time point to the conclusion that Pearl Harbor was to be attacked, there was no person or office in charge of this coordinated function who could have alerted the government.

THE OFFICE OF STRATEGIC SERVICES (OSS)

After Pearl Harbor and the U.S. declarations of war on Japan, Germany, and Italy, President Roosevelt was determined to expand U.S. intelligence capabilities. On June 13, 1942, he issued a military order establishing an expanded COI, to be renamed the U.S.

Office of Strategic Services (OSS). Donovan was to remain the director.

The OSS was still under the jurisdiction of the Joint Chiefs of Staff and continued to be locked in competition with the ONI, MID, FBI, and the State Department. In fact, the latter four organizations colluded to prevent the OSS from intruding on their traditional domains. The military insisted that the OSS not be involved in cryptography; the FBI declared that the OSS must not work in the Western Hemisphere, including the Caribbean and Latin America; and General Douglas MacArthur ordered that the Pacific Theater must remain off-limits (although the OSS was permitted to conduct espionage on the mainland of Asia).

Despite its limited jurisdiction, the OSS capitalized on its original mandate, focusing much of its work on the war in Europe. OSS agents engaged in sabotage, subterfuge, counterespionage, fifth-column (individuals within the country aiding the enemy), guerrilla, and commando operations. The research and analysis group of the OSS produced a tremendous volume of information about the geography, culture, history, economics, industry, demographics, and architecture of Europe, all necessary to military commanders as they planned their campaigns.

Although the OSS was never the equal of British intelligence, it was highly successful in the work of its spies on the ground in Germany, in operations that the British dismissed as being too risky in terms of the amount and quality of the intelligence likely to be collected. The OSS proved them wrong. OSS agents sent to Germany excelled in roaming the country undercover, gathering critical tactical information that was then communicated to U.S. military commanders on the ground in Europe.

Historians concluded that the work of the OSS had less of an impact on battle outcomes than the British and U.S. signals operations (codebreaking). Nevertheless, U.S. commanders, including General Dwight D. Eisenhower, commander of all Allied forces in Europe, attested to the importance of the OSS in its contribution to the Allied victory in Europe.

FEARS OF FOREIGN ESPIONAGE IN THE UNITED STATES

Donovan, Carter, and FBI director J. Edgar Hoover, reporting to Roosevelt in the weeks and months after the attack on Pearl Harbor, independently concluded that there was no evidence that Japanese aliens or

Japanese Americans presented any threat to U.S. national security. Despite this intelligence, Roosevelt, citing the Alien Enemies Act of 1798, issued an executive order in February 1942 that called for the internment of Japanese citizens and Americans of Japanese descent.

Public fear, distrust, and racial prejudice toward the Japanese in the United States, especially rife among Americans living on the west coast where the vast majority of Japanese Americans lived, pressured the president politically. Heeding the public's call for action, and responding to his own deeply seated fear of enemy infiltration, Roosevelt acted and ordered the internment of thousands of Japanese in America. Similarly, though to a far lesser extent than the Japanese, 11,000 Germans and 11,600 Italians were also interned.

Roosevelt's concern about fifth-column sabotage contributed to his reluctance to permit Jews from Nazi-occupied Europe to immigrate to the United States. As early as 1938, FBI director Hoover informed Roosevelt that Nazi leaders ordered some of their espionage agents to pose as Jewish refugees. In 1942, the capture of eight Nazi saboteurs (two of them U.S. citizens) on the east coast reconfirmed Roosevelt's suspicion that enemy infiltration in the United States was a definite threat to national security. He insisted that the eight men be tried by a military tribunal rather than a civilian court. The tribunal found the eight saboteurs guilty, and they were sentenced to death. Roosevelt upheld the sentence for six of the saboteurs, sparing the lives of the two Nazis who had turned in the rest of the group.

CODEBREAKING

The cryptanalysis of the Army's Signal Intelligence Service (renamed the Signal Service Agency in 1943) and U.S. Navy codebreakers was of paramount importance to U.S. naval commanders in the war in the Pacific. Because the United States had been able to crack the Japanese Purple code and decode its MAGIC messages, U.S. naval forces were decisive in the Battle of the Coral Sea and the Battle of Midway in 1942, a turning point in the naval war against Japan.

Purple was also important to U.S. commanders in Europe because it decoded the diplomatic messages of Japan's ambassador to Germany, Hiroshi Oshima. Oshima met frequently with Adolf Hitler and his aides, who kept their ally's ambassador informed about German military campaigns, industry, and Hitler's projections about the future course of his military campaigns. The United States and its allies profited from this window into Hitler's top secret plans.

As much as General Eisenhower commended the contributions of the OSS and the decoding of MAGIC to the war effort, he depended most heavily on British intelligence to remain informed about German troop movements and numbers, the positions of German U-boats in the Atlantic and the North Sea, and data about the struggles of the French Resistance. Ultra, the messages decoded by Britain's German Enigma code machine (acquired from the Poles), was also vital to the execution of Operation Overlord, the code name for the Allies' D-day invasion on the Normandy coast of northern France in June 1944.

COUNTERESPIONAGE
AND THE D-DAY INVASION

Counterespionage, important to all World War II intelligence operations, was critical to the success of the D-day invasion. Through an operation known as *Fortitude*, the Allies collaborated to persuade the Germans that the landing would occur both at Pas de Calais in France, north of the Normandy coast, and in Norway. The Allies went to enormous expense to pull off this elaborate, unprecedented ruse. Eisenhower ordered General George Patton, the best U.S. field commander, to move his army to Kent on the south coast of Britain, within striking distance of Pas de Calais, to deceive the Germans into believing that he would lead the invasion across the English Channel.

Weeks and weeks of false and misleading radio communications were broadcast. Fake jeeps, tanks, and planes fooled German interpreters of aerial reconnaissance. The United States even put pseudogas tanks in place. The grand intelligence stratagem of Overlord, known as the Double-Cross System, also involved the British military's use of German double agents, who were convinced (when threatened with death for noncompliance) to pass on false information to persuade the Germans to believe that invasions at Pas de Calais and on the Norwegian coast were imminent.

Eisenhower also directed security for Overlord, ensuring that the time, location, and strength of the invading Allied armies would not be revealed to the Germans. He convinced British Prime Minister Churchill to evacuate all British civilians from the invasion launch area and to prohibit all open diplomatic communication. Due to the painstaking planning, most of the German defensive forces were concentrated at Pas de Calais when the Allies landed in Normandy, enabling Overlord to be a success.

THE MANHATTAN PROJECT

Throughout the war years, the Manhattan Project—the U.S. operation to build an atomic bomb—was shrouded in secrecy that was unprecedented in U.S. history. General Leslie Groves, director of the project, supervised the procedures that enabled the Manhattan Project's goal to be unknown, even to most of the tens of thousands of workers involved. The bomb laboratory, located at Los Alamos, on an isolated mesa in the mountains of New Mexico, allowed the physicists and engineers (including the few who knew that the gadget, as it was nicknamed, was an atomic bomb) to openly discuss the weapon they were producing. Yet, despite the intense efforts at secrecy, the Soviet Union and Germany knew that the United States was working on an atomic bomb.

As adept as U.S. cryptographers were at decoding enemy radio communications, the United States was ineffective in monitoring the heavy flow of Soviet information. (The United States gathered intelligence from all its allies.) Had the United States successfully decoded all Soviet messages, U.S. leaders would have known how deeply the Soviets had penetrated the Manhattan Project, a fact that would have enormous influence on the Soviet Union's development of its own atomic bomb in 1949.

Much later, long after the war, U.S. leaders learned how severely security was breached at Los Alamos. A German-born communist, Klaus Fuchs, a former resident of Britain and a specialist in the separation of uranium-235 (essential to nuclear fission), became a Los Alamos scientist and passed information about bomb production to the Soviets. Nineteen-year-old American Theodore Hall, a physics prodigy and expert in quantum mechanics at Los Alamos, also informed the Soviets about the implosion method of atomic bomb detonation because he believed that the United States should not have a monopoly on atomic weapons. Soviet sympathizers and spies infiltrated other parts of the Manhattan Project and even the White House, though to a less serious extent.

Throughout most of the war, President Roosevelt was extremely concerned that the Nazis were developing an atomic weapon. In 1944, as the Allies were liberating Paris, a U.S. army intelligence agent named Boris T. Pash discovered that the Germans, despite their years of extensive research in nuclear physics, had not produced and would not be producing an atomic bomb. Despite the good news, Roosevelt demanded that all security remain at the highest levels.

In September, 1945, one month after World War II ended, President Harry S. Truman disbanded the OSS. Truman distrusted the organization and disliked Donovan. He was also concerned that the British had infiltrated the OSS. Truman recognized the need for a centralized intelligence organization, however, so he established the Central Intelligence Group in January 1946. In December 1947, due to a provision of the National Security Act, the Central Intelligence Agency (CIA) was created.

See also Covert Action; Covert Operations; Cryptology; Espionage; Federal Bureau of Investigation (FBI); Japanese Internment; Los Alamos; Manhattan Project (1942–1945); Office of Strategic Services (OSS); Roosevelt, Franklin D., and National Policy; World War II (1939–1945)

Further Reading

Ambrose, Stephen E. "Eisenhower and the Intelligence Community in World War II." *Journal of Contemporary History* 16, no. 1 (January 1981): 153–166.

O'Donnell, Patrick K. *Operatives, Spies, and Saboteurs: The Unknown Story of the Men and Women of WWII's OSS.* New York: Free Press, 2004.

Persico, Joseph E. *Roosevelt's Secret War: FDR and World War II Espionage.* New York: Random House, 2001.

Richelson, Jeffrey T. *A Century of Spies: Intelligence in the Twentieth Century.* New York: Oxford University Press, 1995.

Zegart, Amy. *Flawed by Design: The Evolution of the CIA, JCS, and NSC.* Stanford, CA: Stanford University Press, 1999.

PUBLIC PORTRAITS

"Wild Bill" Donovan, Director of the Office of Strategic Services (OSS)

William J. Donovan was born to first-generation Irish American parents in Buffalo, New York, on January 1, 1883. He received a law degree from Columbia University and returned to Buffalo to practice. In World War I, he enlisted in the U.S. Army and commanded a battalion on the front lines in France. Nicknamed "Wild Bill" for his fearless pursuit of the enemy, he was awarded four medals for his courageous exploits, including the Congressional Medal of Honor.

After the war, Donovan served as district attorney general for western New York State from 1922 to 1924. From 1924 to 1929, he was assistant attorney general in the U.S. Justice Department in Washington, DC. In 1940, President Franklin Roosevelt asked Donovan, a Republican, to embark on a secret mission to Great Britain and the Mediterranean to report on the strength of British forces and their ability to withstand a war with Germany.

As a director of the Office of Coordinator of Intelligence (COI) and the U.S. Office of Strategic Services (OSS) during World War II, Donovan created an intelligence organization that was the precursor to the postwar Central Intelligence Agency (CIA). His leadership of the OSS in Europe demonstrated how effective covert operations could be in infiltrating the enemy's occupied territory and homeland. Although his critics attacked him for his deficiencies as an administrator and organizer, Donovan's vigor and ingenuity in creating an organization dedicated to exploiting every means of covert action will remain his legacy.

After supervising the dismantling of the OSS in late 1945, Donovan returned to the practice of law. In 1946, he served for a brief time as an assistant to Robert Jackson, the chief U.S. prosecutor at the Nuremburg War Crimes Tribunal in Germany. During the administration of President Dwight D. Eisenhower, Donovan was ambassador to Thailand from 1953 to 1954. He died in Buffalo in 1959 at age 76.

See also Office of Strategic Services (OSS)

Y

YALTA CONFERENCE (1945)

Meeting held near the end of World War II and attended by the leaders of the United States (President Franklin Roosevelt), the United Kingdom (Prime Minister Winston Churchill), and the Soviet Union (Premier Joseph Stalin). The purpose of the conference was to discuss Europe's postwar reconstruction and organization. Often referred to as the beginning of the Cold War, the Yalta Conference was instrumental in the secret division of the continent (as well as other regions of the world) into competing spheres of influence—the Western bloc, led by the United States, and the Eastern bloc, led by the Soviet Union.

The Yalta Conference took place in February 1945 in a former czarist palace in the Soviet province of Crimea (part of present-day Ukraine). The negotiations lasted for one week, during which the "Big Three" (as the attending leaders became known) resolved a variety of issues from the establishment of the United Nations to the fate of the Soviet-liberated central and Eastern Europe.

At the time of the meeting, Hitler's army was on the brink of final defeat. The Soviet army, having entered Germany from the east, was awaiting word from its supreme commander to advance on Berlin. Given the imminent takeover of the German capital by the Soviet army, Europe's largest, Joseph Stalin bargained from a position of strength. He was able to extract a series of concessions from his British and American allies—concessions that later became the object of widespread criticism.

THE PROVISIONS

The first issue that the world leaders dealt with at Yalta was the forthcoming occupation of Germany. With Hitler's armies almost entirely defeated, the Allies divided Germany into four occupation zones, one for each of the powers represented at the conference, plus France. France's interests were ardently backed by Winston Churchill, despite Stalin's disdain for a country that had been defeated by the Nazis.

Next, the Big Three discussed the case of Poland, which had been successively occupied by Nazi Germany and then by the Soviet Union. Fearing that an already Stalin-dominated Poland would become a mere satellite of Russia, Churchill and Roosevelt convinced Stalin to agree to the formation of a broad coalition government there, which would be joined by Western-supported Polish émigrés as well as procommunist leaders. As a principle, the Yalta participants declared the right of all European countries that had been conquered by Hitler to hold free and fair popular elections. In effect, many of these countries—particularly those of Eastern Europe—were to be placed under the indirect control of the three great powers.

With respect to the Asian front, where fierce battles were still raging in the Pacific, the Soviet Union agreed to join in the battle against Japan a few months after Germany had been defeated in Europe. In exchange, Stalin was guaranteed a series of territorial rights in the Far East.

A GOOD DEAL?

Most historians agree that the 1945 Yalta Conference was an event of immense historical significance. The

Yalta agreements spelled the defeat of both Germany and Japan, set up the United Nations, and, most important, created a genuinely new world order in Europe.

It is that last accomplishment, however, that gave rise to countless questions and interpretations. Was the political partition of Europe inevitable, or could the subsequent Cold War have been avoided had the Western powers not conceded so much to Stalin? Critics of Roosevelt and Churchill argued that the Yalta protocols, though written in a cautious diplomatic language, practically awarded Stalin all of Eastern Europe on a silver platter. During the next few years after the war, the Soviet Union was able to install puppet regimes in most of the countries in the region, creating a communist bloc that became increasingly hostile to America and its allies.

Critics argued that because Roosevelt and Churchill were unable to keep Stalin's demands in check, the stage for the Cold War was set even before Germany and Japan were completely defeated. Eastern European historians and politicians, in particular, speak of the Yalta agreements as a sellout to the Soviets, who were given a green light to lord over all of Eastern Europe.

From another point of view, however, the concessions given to Stalin by the West were inevitable. Because the immense Soviet Red Army was already firmly in charge of half of Europe, Churchill and Roosevelt secured the best deal possible, giving up control over some European countries in exchange for the Soviets' precious military aid on the Japanese front. Whichever perspective one takes, the Yalta Conference remains a high-profile example of the pragmatic nature of international politics.

See also Cold War; Eastern Bloc; Iron Curtain; Soviet Union, Former (Russia), and U.S. Policy; World War II (1939–1945)

Further Reading

Tucker, Spencer. *The Second World War*. New York: Palgrave Macmillan, 2003.
Tyler, William R. *Yalta: Yesterday, Today, Tomorrow.* New York: Harper & Row, 1988.

PUBLIC PORTRAITS

Winston Churchill

A gifted politician, orator, and military strategist, Winston Churchill led Great Britain during World War II from the brink of defeat to victory over the Nazi aggressors. Throughout his lengthy political career (almost 60 years of active service in various representative bodies), Churchill was both highly admired and utterly disliked by his colleagues and compatriots.

Churchill first appeared on the British political stage in 1900 as a Conservative member of Parliament, but he subsequently twice changed his party affiliation. He was known as an accomplished public speaker and somewhat of an eccentric who was rarely seen without a large Cuban cigar in his mouth. Churchill became prime minister of Great Britain in 1940, when the country was already in its ninth month of war with Nazi Germany. His subsequent performance as commander in chief of the British forces won him renown as one of the most remarkable leaders of all times.

YELTSIN, BORIS (1931–)

Soviet and Russian politician and president of Russia from 1991 to 1999, who struggled to lead his country through the troubled years that followed the collapse of the Soviet Union in 1991. Boris Yeltsin was born in 1931 in Yekaterinburg, a city several hundred miles east of Moscow near the Ural Mountains. Yeltsin began his career as a construction worker and did not join the Communist Party until 1961. In 1985, Soviet premier Mikhail Gorbachev chose him as Moscow party boss, and in 1986, Yeltsin was inducted into the Communist Party's ruling Politburo.

In October 1987, Yeltsin's career took the first of several fateful turns. After opposing party conservatives and criticizing Gorbachev's perestroika and glasnost reforms as inadequate, he was removed from his Moscow post. His stance against the ruling elite cast him as a populist advocate of radical reform and attracted a large constituency of followers.

When a group of conservative plotters attempted a coup d'état and struck out against Gorbachev in August 1991, Yeltsin led the opposition against the plot. His successful opposition shifted power from the party elite to the reformers and individual Soviet republics. Soon after, Yeltsin renounced the Communist Party and helped to found the Commonwealth of Independent States, a loose federation of Soviet republics. Yeltsin's political savvy and personal resolve during this crisis helped to end attempts by conservative Communists to preserve the Soviet Union. His leadership and example carried him into office as Russia's first popularly elected president later that same year.

After the fall of the Soviet Union, Yeltsin moved to end state control of the economy and to privatize most enterprises. However, his presidency eventually came under assault as economic difficulties and political opposition mounted. When the legislature, the Supreme Soviet, resorted to open conflict, Yeltsin used the army to crush the revolt. Although Yeltsin continued to advocate human rights, a free press, and the guarantee of private property, many of his opponents later returned to office through the support of a population that was dissatisfied with the conditions of a struggling economy and longed for the security and glory of the old days.

In foreign affairs, Yeltsin enjoyed marginally greater success. He significantly improved relations with the West and signed the Strategic Arms Reduction Treaty with the United States in 1993. Yet his attempts to secure more than a restricted amount of economic aid from multilateral institutions and other industrialized countries fell short. In 1994, he dispatched forces to the Russian region of Chechnya, where a separatist revolt had erupted. Suppression of this separatist rebellion continued to be an unpopular and unyielding struggle that lasted beyond Yeltsin's tenure as leader of Russia.

During his second term as president, Boris Yeltsin's hold on power appeared to fade away. The Russian economy lumbered along spasmodically, and Yeltsin's judgment, and even his health, fell into question. After repeated cabinet reshuffling, Yeltsin settled on the little-known Vladimir Putin as prime minister in August 1999. That December, Yeltsin resigned abruptly. He named Putin as his successor and quietly departed from public life after a career marked by crises, challenges, and monumental historical events.

See also Commonwealth of Independent States (CIS); Soviet Union, Former (Russia), and U.S. Policy

Z

ZERO SUM GAME

A game theory term that refers to situations in which one party's gain is contingent upon a second party's loss. For example, if there is a situation in which one person receiving 1 million dollars means another person losing 1 million dollars, the wins and losses add up to zero. Another example is an employment situation in which one person's receiving a job means a second person is unemployed, or in a budgeting situation in which one department's funding comes at the expense of another department's. Zero sum situations typically arise in the context of distributive bargaining, where there is a set amount to be divided.

In contrast to the zero sum game are the positive sum game and the negative sum game. The term *positive sum game* refers to situations in which the total of the wins and losses adds up to more than zero, even if one side may still get more than another. The term *negative sum game* refers to situations in which gains and losses taken together add up to less than zero. In such a situation, the only way for one party to maintain its current position is to take something from another party. It is in the context of negative sum games that the most serious competition tends to occur.

List of National Security Acronyms

ARMS CONTROL AGREEMENTS

Bilateral Agreements between U.S. and Soviet Union/Russia

Efforts to control weapons have led to a number of treaties, conventions, and protocols over the years, some of which are shown in the following list.

Antiballistic Missile Treaty (ABM Treaty)
May 26, 1972

United States and Soviet Union agree to have only two ABM deployment areas, restricted and located so they cannot provide a nationwide ABM defense or become the basis for developing one.

Intermediate-Range Nuclear Forces Treaty (INF Treaty)
December 8, 1987

Eliminated all nuclear-armed, ground-launched ballistic and cruise missiles with ranges between 500 and 5,500 kilometers, and their infrastructure; was the first nuclear arms control agreement to actually reduce nuclear arms rather than establish ceilings that could not be exceeded

Strategic Arms Limitation Talks (SALT I)
November 1969–May 1972

Ended with the signing of the ABM Treaty on May 26, 1972
Agreement freezes existing levels of the number of strategic ballistic missile launchers and permits an increase in SLBM launchers up to an agreed-on level

Strategic Arms Limitation Talks (SALT II)
November 1972–June 1979

Ended with SALT II agreement on June 18, 1979
Established a long-term comprehensive treaty providing broad limits on strategic offensive weapons systems

Strategic Arms Reduction Treaty (START I)
July 31, 1991

Reduced aggregate levels of strategic offensive arms, carried out in three phases over seven years representing a 30% to 45% reduction in the number of total deployed strategic warheads permitted under START II

Strategic Arms Reduction Treaty (START II)
January 3, 1993

Eliminates heavy intercontinental ballistic missiles and all other multiple warhead ICBMs; also reduces by two-thirds below existing levels the total number of strategic nuclear weapons deployed by the United States and Russia

Strategic Arms Reduction Treaty (START III)
Negotiations of details pending

To establish a ceiling of 2,000–2,500 strategic nuclear weapons for each of the signatories to the treaty, representing a 30–45 percent reduction in the number of total deployed strategic warheads permitted under START II.

Strategic Offensive Reduction Treaty (SORT)
May 24, 2002

United States and Russia agree to reduce strategic nuclear warheads to a level of 1,700–2,200 by December 31, 2012.

Multilateral Agreements

Biological Weapons Convention (BWC)
Opened for signature on April 10, 1972

Prohibits signatories from developing, producing, stockpiling, or acquiring biological agents or toxins in quantities that have no justification for protective and other peaceful purposes

Chemical Weapons Convention (CWC)
April 29, 1997

Bans the production, acquisition, stockpiling, transfer, and use of chemical weapons; signatories agree to destroy chemical weapons and any chemical weapons production facilities

Comprehensive Test Ban Treaty (CTBT)

A number of nations signed the treaty as of September 26, 1996; U.S. Congress still has not ratified the treaty; prohibits any nuclear explosions, whether for weapons or peaceful purposes

Limited Test Ban Treaty (LTBT)
Opened for signature on July 25, 1963

Prohibits nuclear weapons tests or any other nuclear explosion in the atmosphere, in outer space, or under water

Nuclear Non-Proliferation Treaty (NPT)
Opened for signature on July 1, 1968

Obligates signatories not to transfer nuclear weapons, other nuclear explosive devices, or their technology to any nonnuclear weapon states

Open Skies Treaty
March 24, 1992

Establishes a regime for the conduct of observation flights over the territories of the signatory nations and regulates the technicalities of the flights

Conventional Forces in Europe Treaty
November 17, 1990

Complex treaty that provided ceilings for major weapons and equipment systems, providing national limits for each signatory

CURRENT UN PEACEKEEPING OPERATIONS, BY COUNTRY

As of 2005, the United Nations was engaged in peacekeeping operations around the globe. This chart shows the current, ongoing UN operations as of that year.

AFRICA

Acronym	Name of Mission	Purpose	Headquarters	Duration	Head of Mission	Strength as of February 2005
UNMIS	UN Mission in the Sudan	Provide humanitarian assistance and promote human rights	Khartoum, Sudan	March 2005 to present	Jan Pronk (Netherlands)	Up to 10,000 military personnel, 715 civilian police, 1,018 international civilian staff, 2,623 national staff, 214 UN volunteers
MINURSO	UN Mission for the Referendum in Western Sahara	Monitor cease-fire between government and rebel groups; organize and conduct a referendum on future status of Western Sahara	Laayoune, Western Sahara	April 1991 to present	Alvara de Soto (Peru)	237 uniformed personnel, 125 international civilian personnel, 113 local civilian staff
UNAMSIL	UN Mission in Sierra Leone	Assist in implementation of disarmament, demobilization, and reinte-gration of the government	Freetown, Sierra Leone	October 1999 to present	Daudi Ngelautwa Mwakawago (Tanzania)	3,622 uniformed personnel, 134 military observers, 79 civilian police, 243 international civilian personnel, 517 local civilian staff
UNMEE	UN Mission in Ethiopia and Eritrea	Establish a mechanism for verifying cease-fire between Ethiopia and neighboring Eritrea	Asmara, Eritrea; and Addis Ababa, Ethiopia	July 2000 to present	Legwaila Joseph Legwaila (Botswana)	3,335 military personnel, 214 military observers, 212 international civilian personnel, 251 local civilian staff
MONUC	UN Mission in the Democratic Republic of the Congo	Help maintain cease-fire among five regional states	Kinshasa, Democratic Republic of the Congo	November 1999 to present	William Lacy Swing (United States)	16,270 uniformed personnel, 563 military observers, 734 international civilian personnel, 1,154 local civilian staff
UNMIL	UN Mission in Liberia	To help implement cease-fire	Monrovia, Liberia	September 2005 to present	Jacques Paul Klein (United States)	16,017 uniformed personnel, 1,074 civilian police, 486

(Continued)

(Continued)

						international civilian personnel, 668 local civilian staff
UNOCI	UN Operation in Cote d'Ivoire	Help implement peace agreement between warring factions	Abidjan, Cote d'Ivoire	April 2004 to present	Pierre Schori (Sweden)	6,237 uniformed personnel, 218 civilian police, 266 international civilian personnel, 225 local civilian staff
ONUB	UN Operation in Burundi	Help implement and restore lasting peace between warring factions and bring about national reconciliation	Bujumbura, Burundi	June 2004 to present	Carolyn McAskie (Canada)	5,445 uniformed personnel, 313 international civilian personnel, 217 local civilian staff

AMERICAS

Acronym	Name of Mission	Purpose	Headquarters	Duration	Head of Mission	Strength as of February 2005
MINUSTAH	UN Stabilization Mission in Haiti	Help stabilize situation between warring factions	Port-au-Prince, Haiti	June 2004 to present	Juan Gabriel Valdes (Chile)	7,413 uniformed personnel, 359 international civilian personnel, 800 local civilian staff

ASIA

Acronym	Name of Mission	Purpose	Headquarters	Duration	Head of Mission	Strength as of February 2005
UNMISET	UN Mission of Support in East Timor	Provide assistance in establishing independence for East Timor	Dili, East Timor	May 2002 to present	Sukehiro Hasegawa (Japan)	608 uniformed personnel, 268 international civilian personnel, 539 local civilian staff
UNMOGIP	UN Military Observer Group in India and Pakistan	Supervise cease-fire agreement between India and Pakistan over the State of Jammu and Kashmir	Rawalpindi, Pakistan; and Srinagar, India	January 1949 to present	Major-General Guido Palmieri (Italy)	44 military observers, 23 international civilian personnel, 47 local civilian staff

EUROPE

Acronym	Name of Mission	Purpose	Headquarters	Duration	Head of Mission	Strength as of February 2005
UNFICYP	UN Peacekeeping Force in Cyprus	Supervise cease-fire lines between Greek and Turkish Cypriots; maintain a buffer zone; undertake humanitarian activities	Nicosia, Cyprus	March 1964 to present	Zbigniew Wlosowicz (Poland)	937 uniformed personnel, 42 international civilian personnel, 110 local civilian staff
UNOMIG	UN Observer Mission in Georgia	Verify compliance with cease-fire agreement between government of Georgia and opposition factions	Sukhumi, Georgia	August 1993 to present	Heidi Tagliavini (Switzerland)	130 uniformed personnel, 101 international civilian personnel, 181 local civilian staff
UNMIK	UN Mission in Kosovo	Promote establishment of autonomy and self-government; coordinate humanitarian relief; support reconstruction of infrastructure; maintain civil law and order; promote human rights; assure safe and unimpeded return of all refugees and displaced persons	Priština, Kosovo	June 1999 to present	Soren Jessen-Petersen (Denmark)	19,000 uniformed personnel, 910 international civilian personnel; 2,900 local civilian staff

(Continued)

MIDDLE EAST

Acronym	Name of Mission	Purpose	Headquarters	Duration	Head of Mission	Strength as of February 2005
UNDOF	UN Disengagement Observer Force	Supervise the implementation of the disengagement of Israeli and Syrian forces on the Golan Heights and maintain a cease-fire	Camp Faouar, Golan Heights, Syria	May 1974 to present	Major-General Bala Nanda Sharma (Nepal)	1,030 uniformed personnel, 35 international civilian personnel, 108 local civilian staff
UNIFIL	UN Interim Force in Lebanon	Confirm Israeli withdrawal from Lebanon; restore international peace and security; help Lebanese government restore effective authority	En Naqoura, Lebanon	March 1978 to present	Major-General Alain Pellegrini (France)	1,994 uniformed personnel, 103 international civilian personnel, 296 local civilian staff
UNTSO	UN Truce Supervision Organization	Monitor cease-fires; supervise armistice agreements; prevent isolated incidents from escalating; assist other UN peacekeeping operations in the region	Jerusalem, Israel	May 1948 to present	Brigadier General Clive Lilley (New Zealand)	165 military observers, 96 international civilian personnel, 121 local civilian staff

COMMON U.S. NATIONAL SECURITY ACRONYMS

2MTW	two-major-theater war
ABM	antiballistic missile
ACDA	Arms Control and Disarmament Agency
ANZUS	Australia, New Zealand, United States Security Treaty
APEC	Asia-Pacific Economic Cooperation Forum
ARPA	Advanced Research Projects Agency
ASEAN	Association of Southeast Asian Nations
ASW	antisubmarine warfare
ATF	Bureau of Alcohol, Tobacco and Firearms (past); Bureau of Alcohol, Tobacco, Firearms and Explosives (present name of the bureau; uses same acronym)
ATGM	antitank guided missile
AWACS	Airborne Warning and Control System
AWC	Army War College
BTS	Bureau of Transportation Security
BWC	Biological Weapons Convention
CAP	Civil Air Patrol
CENTCOM	U.S. Central Command
CERT	computer emergency response team
CFE	Conventional Armed Forces in Europe Treaty
CFR	Council on Foreign Relations
CFSP	Common Foreign and Security Policy
CIA	Central Intelligence Agency
CIG	Central Intelligence Group
CIS	Commonwealth of Independent States
COMINT	communications intelligence
CPI	Committee on Public Information
CTR	cooperative threat reduction
CSCE	Conference on Security and Cooperation in Europe
CTBT	Comprehensive Nuclear Test Ban Treaty
CWC	Chemical Weapons Convention
DARPA	Defense Advanced Research Projects Agency
DCA	Defense Communications Agency
DEA	Drug Enforcement Agency
DEW	Distant Early Warning
DHS	Department of Homeland Security
DIA	Defense Intelligence Agency
DISA	Defense Information Systems Agency
DMZ	demilitarized zone
DoD	Department of Defense
DOE	Department of Energy
DPKO	Department of Peacekeeping Operations
DPRK	Democratic People's Republic of Korea
ECOSOC	Economic and Social Council
ECOWAS	Economic Community of West African States
ECSC	European Coal and Steel Community
EDC	European Defense Community
EEC	European Economic Community
ELINT	electronic intelligence
EPCA	Energy Policy and Conservation Act
ERP	European Recovery Program
ESDI	European Security and Defense Identity
EU	European Union
EUCOM	European Command
FAA	Federal Aviation Agency
FAO	Food and Agriculture Organization
FBI	Federal Bureau of Investigation
FEMA	Federal Emergency Management Agency
FFRDC	Federally Funded Research and Development Center
FOIA	Freedom of Information Act
FTAA	Free Trade Area of the Americas
GATT	General Agreement of Tariffs and Trade
GPS	Global Positioning System
HUAC	House Un-American Activities Committee
HUMINT	human intelligence
IAEA	International Atomic Energy Agency
IBIS	Interagency Border Inspection Service
ICBM	intercontinental ballistic missile
ICC	International Criminal Court
ICJ	International Court of Justice
IMF	International Monetary Fund
IMINT	image intelligence
INF	intermediate-range nuclear forces
INS	Immigration and Naturalization Service
Interpol	International Crime Police Organization
IRA	Irish Republican Army
IRBM	intermediate-range ballistic missile
ITO	International Trade Organization

JAST	Joint Advanced Strike Technology	OMB	Office of Management and Budget
JCS	Joint Chiefs of Staff	ONA	Office of Net Assessment
JFCOM	Joint Forces Command	ONR	Office of Naval Research
JSS	Joint Surveillance System	OOTW	operations other than war
JSTPS	Joint Strategic Target Planning Staff	OPCW	Organization for the Prohibition of Chemical Weapons
MAD	mutually assured destruction		
MCWAR	Marine Corps War College	OPEC	Organization of Petroleum Exporting Countries
Mercosur	Mercado Commun del Sur (Southern Common Market)		
		OSCE	Organization for Security and Cooperation in Europe
MFN	most-favored nation		
MIA	missing in action	OSI	Office of Special Investigations
MIRV	multiple independently targeted reentry vehicle	OSS	Office of Strategic Services
		OWI	Office of War Information
MLRS	multiple launch rocket system	PACOM	U.S. Pacific Command
MRBM	medium-range ballistic missile	PCIJ	Permanent Court of International Justice
MRC	major regional conflict		
MSC	Military Sealift Command	PDD	Presidential Decision Directive
NAFTA	North American Free Trade Agreement	PLO	Palestine Liberation Organization
		POW	prisoner of war
NATO	North Atlantic Treaty Organization	PRC	People's Republic of China
NDEA	National Defense Education Act	PSYOPS	psychological operations
NDU	National Defense University	QDR	Quadrennial Defense Review
NGA	National Geospatial-Intelligence Agency	RDD	radiological dispersion devices
		RFE/RL	Radio Free Europe/Radio Liberty
NGO	nongovernmental organization	RICO	Racketeer Influenced and Corrupt Organizations Act
NID	national intelligence		
NIST	National Institute of Standards and Technology	ROTC	Reserve Officer Training Corps
		SAC	Strategic Air Command
NORAD	North American Aerospace Defense Command	SALT	Strategic Arms Limitation Talks
		SAM	surface-to-air missile
NORTHCOM	U.S. Northern Command	SDI	Strategic Defense Initiative
NPT	Treaty on the Non-Proliferation of Nuclear Weapons; *also* Non-Proliferation Treaty	SEATO	Southeast Asia Treaty Organization
		SIGINT	signals intelligence
		SIOP	Single Integrated Operational Plan
NRO	National Reconnaissance Office	SLBM	sea-launched ballistic missile
NSA	National Security Agency	SOCOM	U.S. Special Operations Command
NSABB	National Science Advisory Board for Biosecurity	SORT	Strategic Offensive Reduction Treaty
		SOUTHCOM	U.S. Southern Command
NSAM	National Security Action Memoranda	SPR	Strategic Petroleum Reserve
		SRBM	short-range ballistic missile
NSC	National Security Council	SSC	small-scale contingencies
NSDD	National Security Decision Directive	START	Strategic Arms Reduction Treaty
NSPD	National Security Presidential Directive	STRATCOM	U.S. Strategic Command
		TRANSCOM	U.S. Transportation Command
NUT	nuclear utilization theory	TSA	Transportation Security Administration
NWC	Naval War College		
NWFC	Nuclear Weapons Freeze Campaign	UAV	unmanned aerial vehicle
OAS	Organization of American States	UCMJ	Uniform Code of Military Justice
OAU	Organization of African Unity	UCP	Unified Command Plan
ODP	Office of Domestic Preparedness	UN	United Nations

UNCTAD	United Nations Conference on Trade and Development	USAID	United States Agency for International Development
UNEP	United Nations Environmental Programme	USCNS	U.S. Commission on National Security
UNESCO	United Nations Educational, Scientific, and Cultural Organization	USIA	United States Information Agency
UNHCR	United Nations High Commission for Refugees	USSR	Union of Soviet Socialist Republics
		VA	Veterans Administration
UNICEF	United Nations Children's Fund	VOA	Voice of America
UNMOVIC	United Nations Monitoring, Verification and Inspection Commission	WCO	World Customs Organization
		WEU	Western European Union
		WHO	World Health Organization
		WMD	weapons of mass destruction
UNSCOM	United Nations Special Commission	WTO	World Trade Organization

Selected Bibliography

Abadinsky, Howard. *Organized Crime.* 7th ed. Belmont, CA: Wadsworth, 2003.

Abbott, G. F. *Thucydides: A Study in Historical Reality.* New York: Russell & Russell, 1970.

Abbot, John. *Politics and Poverty: A Critique of the Food and Agriculture Organization of the United Nations.* New York: Routledge, 1992.

Abele, Robert P. *A User's Guide to the USA PATRIOT Act and Beyond.* Lanham, MD: University Press of America, 2004.

Abuza, Zachary. *Militant Islam in Southeast Asia: Crucible of Terror.* Boulder, CO: Lynne Rienner, 2003.

Acronym Institute for Disarmament Diplomacy. Conventional Forces in Europe (CFE) Treaty Flank Document: Congressional Testimony. *Disarmament Diplomacy* 14 (April 1997). www.acronym.org.uk/dd/dd14/14flank.htm.

Adamy, David L. *Introduction to Electronic Warfare: Modeling and Simulation.* Norwood, MA: Artech House, 2003.

Ahmad, Hisham H. *From Religious Salvation to Political Transformation: The Rise of Hamas in Palestinian Society.* Jerusalem: Palestinian Academic Society for the Study of International Affairs, 1994.

Alexander, Ann, and Mark S. Roberts, eds. *High Culture: Reflections on Addiction and Modernity.* Albany: State University of New York Press, 2003.

Alexander, Brian, and Alexander Millar, eds. *Tactical Nuclear Weapons: Emergent Threats in an Evolving Security Environment.* Washington, DC: Brassey's, 2003.

Alexander, Yonah, and Michael S. Swetnam. *Usama bin Laden's al-Qaida: Profile of a Terrorist Network.* Ardsley, NY: Transnational Publishers, 2001.

Algar, Hamid. *Wahhabism: A Critical Essay.* Oneonta, NY: Islamic Publications International, 2002.

Alger, John I. *Definitions and Doctrine of the Military Art: Past and Present.* West Point Military History Series. New York: Avery, 1985.

Alibek, Ken, with Stephen Handelman. *Biohazard: The Chilling True Story of the Largest Covert Weapons Program in the World—Told From the Inside by the Man Who Ran It.* New York: Random House, 1998.

Allen, Patrick. *Rapid Reaction Forces.* Shrewsbury, UK: Airlife Publishing, 2002.

Allison, Graham. *The Essence of Decision.* New York: Longman, 1999.

Allison, Graham T., ed. *Avoiding Nuclear Anarchy: Containing the Threat of Loose Russian Nuclear Weapons and Fissile Material.* Cambridge, MA: MIT Press, 1998.

Ambrose, Stephen E. "Eisenhower and the Intelligence Community in World War II." *Journal of Contemporary History* 16, no. 1 (1981): 153–166.

Amnesty International. *Unmatched Power, Unmet Principles: The Human Rights Dimensions of U.S. Training of Foreign Military and Police Forces.* New York: Amnesty International, 2002.

Anderson, C. V., ed. *The Federal Emergency Management Agency.* Hauppauge, NY: Nova Science, 2002.

Andrianopoulos, Gerry. *Kissinger and Brzezinski.* New York: St. Martin's, 1991.

Angstrom, Jan, and Isabelle Duyvesteyn, eds. *The Nature of Modern War: Clausewitz and His Critics Revisited.* Stockholm: Swedish National Defence College, 2003.

Arkin, William M., Darnian Durrant, and Marianne Cherni. *On Impact: Modern Warfare and the Environment—A Case Study of the Gulf War.* Washington, DC: Greenpeace, 1991.

Armistead, Leigh. *AWACS and Hawkeyes: The Complete History of Airborne Early Warning Aircraft.* St. Paul, MN: Motorbooks, 2002.

Arquilla, John, and David Ronfeldt. "Cyberwar Is Coming!" *Comparative Strategy* 12, no. 2 (Spring 1993): 141–165.

Art, Robert J., and Kenneth N. Waltz, eds. *The Use of Force: Military Power and International Politics.* Lanham, MD: University Press of America, 1993.

Asprey, Robert B. *War in the Shadows: The Guerrilla in History.* New York: William Morrow, 1994.

Assersohn, Roy. *The Biggest Deal.* London: Methuen, 1982.

Atkinson, Rick. *Crusade: The Unknown Story of the Persian Gulf War.* Boston: Houghton Mifflin, 1999.

Axell, Albert, and Hideaki Kase. *Kamikaze: Japan's Suicide Gods.* London: Pearson Education Limited, 2002.

Axlerod, Robert. *The Evolution of Cooperation.* New York: Basic Books, 1984.

Ayers, B. *Fugitive Days.* New York: Penguin, 2003.

Bacevich, Andrew J., and Eliot A. Cohen, eds. *War Over Kosovo: Politics and Strategy in a Global Age.* New York: Columbia University Press, 2001.

Bacon, Edwin, and Mark Sandle. *Brezhnev Reconsidered.* New York: Palgrave Macmillan, 2002.

Bagby, Wesley M. *America's International Relations Since World War I.* New York: Oxford University Press, 1999.

Bailey, Dennis. *The Open Society Paradox: Why The Twenty-First Century Calls for More Openness—Not Less.* Dulles, VA: Potomac Press, 2004.

Bailey, Kathleen C., and Robert Rudney. *Proliferation and Export Controls.* London: Rowman & Littlefield, 1992.

Baker, Richard W. *The ANZUS States and Their Region: Regional Policies of Australia, New Zealand, and the United States.* New York: Praeger, 1994.

Baldwin, David A. *Economic Statecraft.* Princeton, NJ: Princeton University Press, 1985.

Ball, Harry. *Of Responsible Command: A History of the U.S. Army War College.* Carlisle Barracks, PA: Alumni Association of the U.S. Army War College, 1994.

Bandow, Doug. *Fixing What Ain't Broke: The Renewed Call for Conscription.* Washington, DC: Cato Institute, 1999.

Banks, William C., and Peter Raven-Hansen. *National Security Law and the Power of the Purse.* New York: Oxford University Press, 1994.

Barnaby, Frank, ed. *Plutonium and Security: The Military Aspects of the Plutonium Economy.* London: Palgrave Macmillan, 1992.

Barnet, R. J., and R. A. Falk, eds. *Security in Disarmament.* Princeton, NJ: Princeton University Press, 1965.

Barnett, Frank R., and Carnes Lord, eds. *Political Warfare and Psychological Operations: Rethinking the U.S. Approach.* Washington, DC: National Defense University Press, 1989.

Baum, Dan. *Smoke and Mirrors: The War on Drugs and the Politics of Failure.* Boston: Back Bay Books, 1997.

Beard, Tom. *The Coast Guard.* Westport, CT: Hugh Lauter Levin, 2004.

Beck, Robert. *The Grenada Invasion: Politics, Law, and Foreign Policy Decision-Making.* New York: Westview Press, 1993.

Beck, Sara, and Malcolm Downing. *The Battle for Iraq: BBC News Correspondents on the War Against Saddam.* Baltimore: Johns Hopkins University Press, 2003.

Beestermöller, Gerhard, and David Little, eds. *Iraq: Threat and Response.* New Brunswick, NJ: Transaction Publishers, 2003.

Belkin, Aaron, and Geoffrey Bateman. *Don't Ask, Don't Tell: Debating the Gay Ban in the Military.* Boulder, CO: Lynne Rienner, 2003.

Bellamy, Alex J., Paul Williams, and Stuart Griffin. *Understanding Peacekeeping.* Cambridge, UK: Polity, 2004.

Bennhold-Thomsen, Veronika, Nicholas G. Faraclas, and Claudia von Werlhof. *There Is an Alternative: Subsistence and Worldwide Resistance to Corporate Globalization.* New York: Palgrave, 2001.

Benton, Jeffrey C. *Air Force Officer's Guide.* Mechanicsburg, PA: Stackpole Books, 2002.

Benvenisti, Meron. *Intimate Enemies: Jews and Arabs in a Shared Land.* Berkeley: University of California Press, 1995.

Bercovitch, Jacob. *ANZUS in Crisis: Alliance Management in International Affairs.* London: Palgrave Macmillan, 1988.

Berger, Suzanne. *How We Compete.* New York: Doubleday, 2005.

Berkowitz, Bruce. *The New Face of War: How War Will Be Fought in the 21st Century.* New York: Free Press, 2003.

Bernard, Lewis. *From Babel to Dragomans: Interpreting the Middle East.* New York: Oxford University Press, 2004.

Bernays, Edward. *Propaganda.* New York: Ig Publishing, 2004.

Betts, Raymond F. *Decolonization: The Making of the Contemporary World.* New York: Routledge, 1998.

Betts, Richard K. *Nuclear Blackmail and Nuclear Balance.* Washington, DC: Brookings Institution, 1987.

Betts, Richard K. "Striking First: A History of Thankfully Lost Opportunities." *Ethics and International Affairs* 17, no. 1 (2003): 22–26.

Bhagwati, Jagdish. *In Defense of Globalization.* Oxford, UK: Oxford University Press, 2004.

Biddle, Stephen D. *Military Power: Explaining Victory and Defeat in Modern Battle.* Princeton, NJ: Princeton University Press, 2004.

Black, Conrad. *Franklin Delano Roosevelt: Champion of Freedom.* New York: Public Affairs, 2003.

Blacker, Coit D., and Gloria Duffy. *International Arms Control: Issues and Agreements.* Palo Alto, CA: Stanford University Press, 1984.

Blair, Bruce G. *The Logic of Accidental Nuclear War.* Washington, DC: Brookings Institution, 1993.

Blair, John D., Myron Fottler, and Albert C. Zapanta. *Bioterrorism Preparedness: Attack and Response: Advances in Health Care Management.* New York: Elsevier Science, 2004.

Blanchard, James J. *Behind the Embassy Door: Canada, Clinton, and Quebec.* Toronto: Sleeping Bear Press, 1998.

Blechman, Barry M. *The Politics of National Security: Congress and U.S. Defense Policy.* New York: Oxford University Press, 1990.

Blumenthal, Sidney. *The Clinton Wars.* New York: Farrar, Straus and Giroux, 2003.

Bly, Robert. *Iron John.* New York: Vintage, 1990.

Bock, Alan W. *Ambush at Ruby Ridge: How the Government Set Randy Weaver Up and Took His Family Down.* New York: Berkley, 1995.

Bodansky, Yossef. *Bin Laden: The Man Who Declared War on America.* Rocklin, CA: Forum, 1999.

Bolz, Frank, Kenneth J. Dudonis, and David P. Schulz. *The Counter-Terrorism Handbook: Tactics, Procedures, and Techniques.* Boca Raton, FL: CRC Press, 2001.

Bornet, Vaugn Davis. *The Presidency of Lyndon B. Johnson.* American Presidency Series. Lawrence: University Press of Kansas, 1984.

Bose, Meena. *Shaping and Signaling Presidential Policy: The National Security Decision Making of Eisenhower and Kennedy.* College Station: Texas A&M University Press, 1998.

Bose, Sumantra. *Kashmir: Roots of Conflict, Paths to Peace.* Cambridge, MA: Harvard University Press, 2003.

Bottome, Edgar M. *The Missile Gap: A Study of the Formulation of Military and Political Policy.* Rutherford, NJ: Fairleigh Dickinson University Press, 1971.

Bourne, Peter G. *Jimmy Carter: A Comprehensive Biography from Plains to Post-Presidency.* New York: Scribner, 1997.

Boutros-Ghali, Boutros. *Egypt's Road to Jerusalem: A Diplomat's Story of the Struggle for Peace in the Middle East.* New York: Random House, 1997.

Bovard, James. *Terrorism and Tyranny: Trampling Freedom, Justice, and Peace to Rid the World of Evil.* New York: Palgrave Macmillan, 2003.

Bowden, Mark. *Black Hawk Down: A Story of Modern War.* New York: Atlantic Monthly Press, 1999.

Bowie, Robert R., and Richard H. Immerman. *Waging Peace: How Eisenhower Shaped an Enduring Cold War Strategy.* New York: Oxford University Press, 1998.

Boyne, Walter J. *The Influence of Air Power on History.* New York: Pelican, 2003.

Boyne, Walter J. *The Yom Kippur War and the Airlift Strike That Saved Israel.* New York: St. Martin's Griffin, 2003.

Bradford, James C., ed. *Crucible of Empire: The Spanish-American War and Its Aftermath.* Annapolis, MD: Naval Institute Press, 1993.

Brandt, Willy. *My Road to Berlin.* Garden City, NY: Doubleday, 1960.

Braudy, S. *Family Circle: The Boudins and the Aristocracy of the Left.* New York: Alfred A. Knopf, 2003.

Bregman, Ahron. *A History of Israel.* New York: Palgrave Macmillan, 2003.

Brill, Steven. *After: The Rebuilding and Defending of America in the September 12 Era.* New York: Simon & Schuster, 2003.

Brock, Peter, and Nigel Young. *Pacifism in the Twentieth Century.* Syracuse, NY: Syracuse University Press, 1999.

Broderick, Jim. "Berlin and Cuba: Cold War Hotspots." *History Today* 48, no. 12 (1998): 23.

Buchan, Glenn. *Future Roles of U.S. Nuclear Forces: Implications for U.S. Strategy.* Santa Monica, CA: RAND, 2004.

Buckley, William F. *The Fall of the Berlin Wall.* Hoboken, NJ: John Wiley, 2004.

Buhite, Russell D. *Calls to Arms: Presidential Speeches, Messages, and Declarations of War.* Wilmington, DE: Scholarly Resources, 2003.

Buira, Ariel, ed. *Challenges to the World Bank and IMF: Developing Country Perspectives.* London: Wimbledon, 2003.

Buncombe, Andrew, and Anne Penketh. "Rumsfeld Told Officers to Take Gloves Off with Lindh." *The Independent,* June 10, 2004.

Burgess, Guy M., and Burgess, Heidi. "Definition of Zero-Sum, Negative Sum, Positive Sum." In *Encyclopedia of Conflict Resolution.* Santa Barbara; CA: ABC-CLIO, 1997.

Burgleman, Robert, Clayton M. Christensen, and Steven C. Wheelwright. *Strategic Management of Technology and Innovation.* New York: McGraw-Hill, 2003.

Burke, Jason. *Al-Qaeda: Casting a Shadow of Terror.* London: I. B. Tauris, 2004.

Butler, Richard. *Saddam Defiant: The Threat of Weapons of Mass Destruction and the Crisis of Global Security.* London: Ekeus, 2000.

Buzo, Adrian. *The Making of Modern Korea.* London: Routledge, 2001.

Buzzanco, Robert. *Masters of War: Military Dissent and Politics in the Vietnam Era.* New York: Cambridge University Press, 1996.

Cameron, Fraser. *U.S. Foreign Policy After the Cold War.* London: Routledge, 2002.

Cameron, Gavin. *Nuclear Terrorism: A Threat Assessment for the 21st Century.* New York: St. Martin's, 1999.

Campbell, Geoffrey A. *Vulnerable America: An Overview of National Security.* San Diego, CA: Lucent Books, 2003.

Cannon, James. *Time and Chance: Gerald Ford's Appointment with History.* New York: HarperCollins, 1993.

Caplan, Richard, and John Feffer, eds. *State of the Union, 1994: The Clinton Administration and the Nation in Profile.* Boulder, CO: Westview Press, 1994.

Carothers, Thomas. "Promoting Democracy and Fighting Terror." *Foreign Affairs* 82, no. 1 (2003): 84–98.

Carpenter, Ted G., and Doug Bandow. *The Korean Conundrum: America's Troubled Relations With North and South Korea.* New York: Palgrave Macmillan, 2004.

Carter, Ashton B., and William J. Perry. *Preventive Defense: A New Security Strategy for America.* Washington, DC: Brookings Institution, 1999.

Carter, John J. *Covert Operations and the Rise of the Modern American Presidency, 1920–1960.* Lewiston, NY: Edwin Mellen Press, 2002.

Casper, Lawrence E. *Falcon Brigade: Combat and Command in Somalia and Haiti.* Boulder, CO: Lynne Rienner, 2001.

Casserly, John J. *The Ford White House: Diary of a Speechwriter.* Boulder, CO: Colorado Associated University Press, 1977.

Cassidy, Robert M. *Peacekeeping in the Abyss: British and American Peacekeeping Doctrine and Practice After the Cold War.* New York: Praeger, 2004.

Causewell, Erin V. *National Missile Defense: Issues and Developments.* Hauppauge, NY: Nova Publishers, 2002.

Charles, J. Daryl. *Between Pacifism and Jihad: Just War and Christian Tradition.* Nottingham, UK: InterVarsity Press, 2005.

Cherry, Andrew, Mary E. Dillon, and Douglas Rugh. *Substance Abuse: A Global View.* Westport, CT: Greenwood, 2002.

Chilcoat, Richard. "The Fourth Army War College: Preparing Strategic Leaders for the Next Century." *Parameters* 25 (Winter 1995/96): 3–17.

Cigar, Norman. *Genocide in Bosnia.* College Station: Texas A&M University Press, 1995.

Cimbala, Stephen J., ed. *Deterrence and Nuclear Proliferation in the Twenty-First Century.* New York: Praeger, 2000.

Cimbala, Stephen J. *First Strike Stability: Deterrence After Containment.* Westport, CT: Greenwood, 1990.

Clark, Anthony Arend. "International Law and the Preemptive Use of Military Force." *Washington Quarterly* 26, no. 2 (2004): 89–103.

Clarke, Richard A. *Against All Enemies: Inside America's War on Terror.* New York: Free Press, 2004.

Clarke, Walter, and Jeffrey Herbst, eds. *Learning From Somalia: The Lessons of Armed Humanitarian Interventions.* Boulder, CO: Westview Press, 1997.

Clausewitz, Karl von. *On War.* Edited and translated by Michael Howard and Peter Paret. Princeton, NJ: Princeton University Press, 1976.

Cleveland, William L. *A History of the Modern Middle East.* Boulder, CO: Westview Press, 1999.

Coggins, Edward V. *Wings That Stay On: The Role of Fighter Aircraft in War.* Nashville, TN: Turner Publishing, 2000.

Cohen, David B., and John W. Wells, eds. *American National Security and Civil Liberties in an Era of Terrorism.* New York: Palgrave Macmillan, 2004.

Cohen, Eliot A. *Supreme Command: Soldiers, Statesmen, and Leadership in Wartime.* New York: Free Press, 2002.

Cohen, Frederick B. *A Short Course on Computer Viruses.* New York: John Wiley, 1994.

Cohen, Stephen Philip. "The United States, India, and Pakistan: Retrospect and Prospect." In *India and Pakistan: The First Fifty Years,* edited by Selig S. Harrison, Paul H. Kreisberg, and Dennis Kux, 189–205. Cambridge, MA: Woodrow Wilson Center Press, 1999.

Cohn-Sherbok, Daniel, and Dawoud Sudqi El-Alami. *The Palestine-Israeli Conflict.* Oxford, UK: Oneworld, 2001.

Cole, David. *Enemy Aliens.* New York: New Press, 2003.

Cole, David, James X. Dempsey, and Carole Goldberg. *Terrorism and the Constitution: Sacrificing Civil Liberties in the Name of National Security.* New York: New Press, 2002.

Coll, Steve. *Ghost Wars: The Secret History of the CIA, Afghanistan, and Bin Laden, From the Soviet Invasion to September 10, 2001.* New York: Penguin, 2004.

Collins, Martin J. *Space Race: The U.S.–USSR Competition to Reach the Moon.* Petaluma, CA: Pomegranate Communications, 1999.

Committee on Assuring the Health of the Public in the Twenty-First Century, and the Institute of Medicine. *The Future of the Public's Health in the Twenty-First Century.* Washington, DC: National Academies Press, 2003.

Conner, Kit, and Caroline Conner. *Always Ready: Today's U.S. Coast Guard.* St. Paul, MN: Motorbooks, 2004.

Connor, Mary E. *The Koreas: A Global Studies Handbook.* Santa Barbara, CA: ABC-CLIO, 2002.

Cook, Thomas I., and Malcolm Moos. *Power Through Purpose: The Realism of Idealism as a Basis for Foreign Policy.* Baltimore: Johns Hopkins University Press, 1954.

Cooper, Phillip J. *By Order of the President: The Use and Abuse of Executive Direct Action.* Lawrence: University Press of Kansas, 2002.

Copeland, Dale. "Economic Interdependence and War: A Theory of Trade Expectations." *International Security* 20, no. 4 (1996): 5–41.

Corbin, Jane. *The Base: In Search of Al-Qaeda—The Terror Network That Shook the World.* New York: Simon & Schuster, 2003.

Cordesman, Anthony H. *Strategic Threats and National Missile Defenses: Defending the U.S. Homeland.* Westport, CT: Praeger, 2001.

Cordesman, Anthony H. *The Lessons of Afghanistan: War Fighting, Intelligence, and Force Transformation.* Washington, DC: Center for Strategic and International Studies Press, 2002.

Cordesman, Anthony H., with Justin G. Cordesman. *Cyberthreats, Information Warfare, and Critical Infrastructure Protection: Defending the U.S. Homeland.* London: Praeger, 2002.

Cornbise, Alfred. *War as Advertised: The Four Minute Men and America's Crusade, 1917–1918.* Philadelphia: American Philosophical Society, 1984.

Cortwright, David. *Economic Sanctions: Panacea or Peacebuilding in a Post–Cold War World?* Boulder, CO: Westview Press, 1995.

Cortwright, David. *Smart Sanctions: Targeting Economic Statecraft.* Lanham, MD: Rowman & Littlefield, 2002.

Corum, James S. *The Roots of Blitzkrieg: Hans van Seeckt and German Military Reform.* Lawrence: University Press of Kansas, 1994.

Costigan, Sean, and Ann Markusen. *Arming the Future: A Defense Industry for the Twenty-First Century.* New York: Council on Foreign Relations Press, 1999.

Cousens, Elizabeth M., and Charles K. Carter. *Toward Peace in Bosnia: Implementing the Dayton Accords.* Boulder, CO: Lynne Rienner, 2001.

Crabb, Cecil V, Jr. *Nations in a Multipolar World.* New York: Harper & Row, 1968.

Crawford, Steve. *Twenty-First Century Military Helicopters.* St. Paul, MN: Motorbooks, 2003.

Crockett, Richard. *The Fifty Years' War: The United States and the Soviet Union in World Politics, 1941–1991.* New York: Routledge, 1995.

Croddy, Eric. *Chemical and Biological Warfare: A Comprehensive Survey for the Concerned Citizen.* New York: Copernicus Books, 2002.

Cronin, Patrick M., and Michael J. Green. *Redefining the U.S.–Japan Alliance: Tokyo's National Defense Program.* Stockton, CA: University Press of the Pacific, 2004.

Cull, Nicholas John. *Selling War: The British Propaganda Campaign Against American "Neutrality" in World War II.* New York: Oxford University Press, 1995.

Cumings, Bruce. *North Korea: Another Country.* New York: New Press, 2004.

Cutler, Thomas J. *A Sailor's History of the U.S. Navy.* Annapolis, MD: Naval Institute Press, 2004.

Cyr, Arthur I. *After the Cold War.* New York: New York University Press, 1997.

Daalder, Ivo H., and James M. Lindsay, eds. *America Unbound: The Bush Revolution in Foreign Policy.* Washington, DC: Brookings Institution, 2003.

Dallek, Robert. *Lyndon B. Johnson: Portrait of a President.* New York: Oxford University Press, 2003.

Daniels, Robert V. *The End of the Communist Revolution.* London: Routledge, 1993.

Darmer, M. Katherine, Robert M. Baird, and Stuart E. Rosenbaum. *Civil Liberties vs. National Security: In a Post-9/11 World.* Loughton, UK: Prometheus Books, 2004.

Davidson, Lawrence. *Islamic Fundamentalism: An Introduction.* Westport, CT: Greenwood, 2003.

Davis, Brian L. *Qaddafi, Terrorism, and the Origins of the U.S. Attack on Libya.* New York: Praeger, 1990.

Davis, Jim A., and Barry R. Schneider, eds. *The Gathering Biological Warfare Storm.* Westport, CT: Praeger, 2004.

Davis, John. "Defining the Analytic Mission: Facts, Findings, Forecasts, and Fortunetelling." In *Intelligence and the National Security Strategist: Enduring Issues and Challenges,* edited by Roger Z. George and Robert Kline. Washington, DC: National Defense University, 2004.

Deering, Christopher J. "Decision Making in the Armed Services Committees." In *Congress Resurgent: Foreign and Defense Policy on Capitol Hill,* edited by Randall B. Ripley and James M. Lindsay. Ann Arbor: University of Michigan Press, 1993.

Deffeyes, Kenneth S. *Hubbert's Peak: The Impending World Oil Shortage.* Princeton, NJ: Princeton University Press, 2003.

Deighton, Len, and Walther K. Nehring. *Blitzkrieg: From the Rise of Hitler to the Fall of Denmark.* New York: Book Sales, 2000.

Dershowitz, Alan. *Shouting Fire: Civil Liberties in a Turbulent Age.* Boston: Little, Brown, 2002.

DeSalle, Rob. *Epidemic! The World of Infectious Disease.* New York: Norton, 1999.

Deutsch, Morton, and Peter T. Coleman, eds. *Handbook of Conflict Resolution: Theory and Practice.* San Francisco, CA: Jossey-Bass, 2000.

Dicken, Peter. *Global Shift.* New York: Guilford, 1998.

Diehl, Paul. *International Peacekeeping.* Baltimore: Johns Hopkins University Press, 1994.

Diem, B. *In the Jaws of History.* Bloomington: Indiana University Press, 1987.

Dinges, John L. *The Condor Years.* New York: New Press, 2004.

DiPrizio, Robert C. *Armed Humanitarians: U.S. Interventions from Northern Iraq to Kosovo.* Baltimore: Johns Hopkins University Press, 2002.

Divine, Robert A. *Eisenhower and the Cold War.* New York: Oxford University Press, 1981.

Dixit, J. N. *India-Pakistan in War and Peace.* London: Routledge, 2002.

Dobriansky, Paula. "Democracy Promotion." *Foreign Affairs* 82, no. 3 (2003): 102–105.

Dockrill, Michael, and Barrie Paskins. *The Ethics of War.* Minneapolis: University of Minnesota Press, 1979.

Dodds, Klaus, and David Atkinson, eds. *Geopolitical Traditions: A Century of Geopolitical Thought.* New York: Routledge, 2000.

Donnelly, Jack. *Realism and International Relations.* Cambridge, UK: Cambridge University Press, 2000.

Donovan, Robert J. *The Second Victory: The Marshall Plan and the Postwar Revival of Europe.* Lanham, MD: Madison Books, 1988.

Dorr, Robert F. *Chopper: A History of American Military Helicopter Operators from WWII to the War on Terror.* New York: Berkley, 2005.

Drew, Elizabeth. *On the Edge—The Clinton Presidency.* New York: Simon & Schuster, 1994.

Duiker, William J. *Ho Chi Minh.* New York: Hyperion, 2000.

Dumbrell, John. *The Carter Presidency: A Re-evaluation.* Manchester, UK: Manchester University Press, 1995.

Dunn, Lewis A. *Controlling the Bomb.* New Haven, CT: Yale University Press, 1982.

Dycus, Stephen, Arthur L. Berney, William C. Banks, and Peter Raven-Hansen. *National Security Law.* 3rd ed. Gaithersburg, NY: Aspen, 2002.

Echevarria, Antulio Joseph. *Clausewitz's Center of Gravity: Changing Our Warfighting Doctrine—Again!* Carlisle, PA: Strategic Studies Institute of the U.S. Army War College, 2002.

Ellis, Jason D. *Defense by Other Means.* Westport, CT: Praeger, 2001.

Ellsberg, Daniel. *Secrets: A Memoir of Vietnam and the Pentagon Papers.* New York: Viking, 2000.

Elshtain, Jean B. *Just War Against Terror: The Burden of American Power in a Violent World.* New York: Basic Books, 2003.

Ely, John Hart. *War and Responsibility: Constitutional Lessons of Vietnam and Its Aftermath.* Princeton, NJ: Princeton University Press, 1993.

Etcheson, Craig. *Arms Race Theory: Strategy and Structures of Behavior.* Westport, CT: Greenwood, 1989.

Etzione, Amitai. *How Patriotic Is the Patriot Act? Freedom Versus Security in the Age of Terrorism.* London: Routledge, 2004.

Evan, William H., and Stephen Hilgartner, eds. *The Arms Race and Nuclear War.* Englewood Cliffs, NJ: Prentice Hall, 1987.

Evans, Nicholas D. *Military Gadgets: How Advanced Technology Is Transforming Today's Battlefield—and Tomorrow's.* Englewood Cliffs, NJ: Prentice Hall, 2004.

Evans, Rowland. *Lyndon B. Johnson: The Exercise of Power—A Political Biography.* St. Leonards, Australia: Allen and Unwin, 1967.

Ewing, Alphonse B. *The USA PATRIOT Act.* New York: Novinka Books, 2002.

Ewing, James. "The 1972 U.S.–Soviet ABM Treaty: Cornerstone of Stability or Relic of the Cold War?" *William and Mary Law Review* 43, no. 2 (2001): 787–805.

Fairbank, John King. *The United States and China.* 4th ed. Cambridge, MA: Harvard University Press, 1976.

Falkenrath, Robert A., Robert D. Newman, and Bradley A. Thayer. *America's Achilles' Hell: Nuclear, Biological, and Chemical Terrorism and Covert Attack.* Cambridge, MA: MIT Press, 1999.

Fallows, James. *Breaking the News: How the Media Undermine American Democracy.* New York: Vintage, 1996.

Faringdon, Hugh. *Confrontation: The Strategic Geography of NATO and the Warsaw Pact.* London: Routledge/Kegan Paul, 1986.

Fawaz, Leila Tarazi, and C. A. Bayly. *Modernity and Culture: From the Mediterranean to the Indian Ocean.* New York: Columbia University Press, 2002.

Featherstone, K. "Jean Monnet and the 'Democratic Deficit' in the European Union." *Journal of Common Market Studies* 32, no. 2 (1994): 147–170.

Feaver, Peter D., and Richard H. Kohn, eds. *Soldiers and Civilians: The Civil-Military Gap and American National Security.* Cambridge, MA: MIT Press, 2001.

Feldman, David Lewis. *The Energy Crisis: Unresolved Issues and Enduring Legacies.* Baltimore: Johns Hopkins University Press, 1996.

Ferguson, Charles D., Tahseen Kazi, and Judith Perera. *Commercial Radioactive Sources: Surveying the Security Risks.* Monterey, CA: Monterey Institute of International Studies, Center for Nonproliferation Studies, 2003.

Ferguson, Niall. *Colossus: The Price of America's Empire.* New York: Penguin, 2003.

Ferris, John R., et al. *World History of Warfare.* Lincoln: University of Nebraska Press, 2002.

Fiakla, John J. *War by Other Means: Economic Espionage in America.* New York: Norton, 1999.

Fiala, Andrew G. *Practical Pacifism.* New York: Algora Publishing, 2004.

Fieldhouse, D. K. *The West and the Third World: Trade, Colonialism, Dependence, and Development.* Oxford, UK: Basil Blackwell, 1999.

Fink, Steven. *Sticky Fingers: Managing the Global Risk of Economic Espionage.* Chicago: Dearborn Trade Publishing, 2002.

Fischer, Julie Elizabeth. *Dual-Use Technologies: Inexorable Progress, Inseparable Peril.* Washington, DC: Center for Strategic and International Studies, 2005.

Fisher, Ernst F. *Guardians of the Republic: A History of the Noncommissioned Officer Corps of the U.S. Army.* New York: Fawcett Books, 1994.

Flynn, George Q. *Conscription and Democracy: The Draft in France, Great Britain, and the United States.* Berkshire, UK: Greenwood, 2001

Flynn, Stephen. *America the Vulnerable.* New York: HarperCollins, 2004.

Fogel, Steven K. *U.S.–Japan Relations in a Changing World.* Washington, DC: Brookings Institution, 2002.

Ford, Gerald R. *A Time to Heal: The Autobiography of Gerald R. Ford.* New York: Harper & Row, 1979.

Forsberg, Randall, Rob Leavitt, and Steve Lily-Weber. "Conventional Forces Treaty Buries Cold War." *Bulletin of the Atomic Scientists* 47, no. 1 (1991).

Fouda, Yosri, and Nick Fielding. *Masterminds of Terror: The Truth Behind the Most Devastating Attack the World Has Ever Seen.* Edinburgh, UK: Mainstream Publishing, 2003.

Frankel, Max. *High Noon in the Cold War: Kennedy, Khrushchev, and the Cuban Missile Crisis.* New York: Presidio Press, 2004.

Franks, Norman. *Aircraft Versus Aircraft: The Illustrated Story of Fighter Pilot Combat Since 1914 to the Present Day.* London: Grub Street Publishing, 1999.

Freedman, Lawrence. *Deterrence.* Themes for the Twenty-First Century. Cambridge, UK: Polity, 2004.

Freedman, Lawrence. *The Evolution of Nuclear Strategy.* New York: St. Martin's, 1982.

Freedman, Lawrence. *The Evolution of Nuclear Strategy.* New York: Palgrave Macmillan, 2003.

Freedman, Robert O., ed. *The Intifada: Its Impact on Israel, the Arab World, and the Superpowers.* Miami, FL: International University Press, 1991.

Freidel, Frank B. *The Splendid Little War.* Springfield, NJ: Burford Books, 1958.

Friedman, Ellen G., and Jennifer D. Marshall. *Issues of Gender.* Longman Topics. New York: Longman, 2003.

Friedman, George. *America's Secret War: Inside the Hidden Worldwide Struggle Between America and Its Enemies.* New York: Doubleday, 2004.

Friedman, George, and Meredith Friedman. *The Future of War: Power, Technology, and American World Dominance in the Twenty-First Century.* New York: St. Martin's, 1998.

Friedman, Norman. *Desert Victory: The War for Kuwait.* Annapolis, MD: Naval Institute Press, 1991.

Friedman, Norman. *The Fifty-Year War: Conflict and Strategy in the Cold War.* Annapolis, MD: Naval Institute Press, 1999.

Friedman, Norman. *Submarine Design and Development.* Annapolis, MD: Naval Institute Press, 1984.

Freidman, Norman. *U.S. Submarines Since 1945.* Annapolis, MD: Naval Institute Press, 1994.

Fullinwider, Robert. *Conscripts and Volunteers: Military Requirements, Social Justice, and the All-Volunteer Force.* Maryland Studies in Public Philosophy. Lanham, MD: Rowman & Littlefield, 1983.

Fussell, Paul. *The Great War and Modern Memory.* Oxford, UK: Oxford University Press, 2000.

Gabriel, Mark A. *Islam and Terrorism: What the Quran Really Teaches About Christianity, Violence, and the Goals of the Islamic Jihad.* Lake Mary, FL: Charisma House, 2002.

Gaddis, John L. "Bush's Security Strategy." *Foreign Policy* 133 (November/December 2002): 50–57.

Gaddis, John L. *Strategies of Containment. A Critical Appraisal of Postwar American National Security Policy.* New York: Oxford University Press, 1982.

Gaddis, John L. *Surprise, Security, and the American Experience.* Cambridge, MA: Harvard University Press, 2004.

Gaddis, John L. *The United States and the Origins of the Cold War, 1941–1947.* New York: Columbia University Press, 1972.

Gaddis, John L. *We Now Know.* New York: Oxford University Press, 1997.

Gaffney, Timothy. *Secret Spy Satellites: America's Eyes in Space.* Berkeley Heights, NJ: Enslow Publishers, 2000.

Galbraith, John K. *Ambassador's Journal: A Personal Account of the Kennedy Years.* Boston: Houghton Mifflin, 1969.

Gallagher, Nancy W., ed. *Arms Control: New Approaches to Theory and Policy.* Portland, OR: Frank Cass, 1998.

Gansler, Jacques S. *Affording Defense.* Cambridge, MA: MIT Press, 1989.

Garfinkle, Adam M. *Telltale Hearts: The Origins and Impact of the Vietnam Anti-War Movement.* New York: St. Martin's, 1998.

Garrett, Laurie. *The Coming Plague: Newly Emerging Diseases in a World out of Balance.* New York: Penguin, 1994.

Gayston, Lynch L. *Decision for Disaster: Betrayal at the Bay of Pigs.* Dulles, VA: Brassey's, 2000.

Genovese, Michael A. *The Nixon Presidency; Power and Politics in Turbulent Times.* Westport, CT: Greenwood, 1990.

Gentile, Gian P. *How Effective Is Strategic Bombing? Lessons Learned From World War II to Kosovo.* New York: New York University Press, 2000.

Gentry, Curt. *J. Edgar Hoover: The Man and the Secrets.* New York: Norton, 2001.

George, Alexander L. *Inadvertent War in Europe: Crisis Simulation.* Washington, DC: Center for International Security and Cooperation, 1985.

Gerner, Deborah J., and Jillian Schwedler. *Understanding the Contemporary Middle East.* Boulder, CO: Lynne Rienner, 2004.

Gerolymatos, Andre. *The Balkan Wars: Conquest, Revolution, and Retribution from the Ottoman Era to the Twentieth Century and Beyond.* New York: Basic Books, 2003.

Gill, Graeme. *The Dynamics of Democratization.* New York: St. Martin's, 2000.

Gilligan, Carol. *In a Different Voice: Psychological Theory and Women's Development.* Cambridge, MA: Harvard University Press, 1993.

Gilpin, Robert. *Global Political Economy.* Princeton, NJ, Princeton University Press, 2001.

Gilroy, Curtis L., Roger D. Little, and Eric J. Fredland. *Professionals on the Front Line: Two Decades of the All-Volunteer Force.* Dulles, VA: Brassey's, 1996.

Giordano, Geraldine. *The Oklahoma City Bombing.* New York: Rosen, 2003.

Girard, Joylon P. *America and the World.* Westport, CT: Greenwood, 2001.

Golay, Michael. *The Tide of Empire: America's March to the Pacific.* Hoboken, NJ: John Wiley, 2003.

Goldberg, Alfred. *The Pentagon: The First Fifty Years.* Washington, DC: Historical Office of the Secretary of Defense, 1992.

Goldblat, Jozef. *Arms Control: The New Guide to Negotiations and Agreements.* Thousand Oaks, CA: Sage, 2002.

Goldstein, Erik, et al. *The Washington Conference, 1921–22: Naval Rivalry, East Asian Stability, and the Road to Pearl Harbor.* London: Frank Cass, 1994.

Goodstein, David. *Out of Gas: The End of the Age of Oil.* New York: Norton, 2004.

Gorst, Anthony, and Lewis Johnman. *The Suez Crisis.* London: Routledge, 1997.

Gottfried, Ted. *Homeland Security vs. Constitutional Rights.* New York: Twenty-First Century Books, 2003.

Graham, Thomas, and Damien J. LaVera. *Cornerstones of Security: Arms Control Treaties in the Nuclear Era.* Seattle: University of Washington Press, 2003.

Green, William, and Gordon Swanborough. *An Illustrated Anatomy of the World's Fighters: The Inside Story of Over 100 Classics in the Evolution of Fighter Aircraft.* St. Paul, MN: Motorbooks, 2002.

Greene, John Robert. *The Limits of Power: The Nixon and Ford Administrations.* Bloomington: Indiana University Press, 1992.

Grewal, Mohinder, and Lawrence Weill. *Global Positioning Systems, Inertial Navigation and Integration.* New York: Wiley Interscience, 2000.

Griffin, Clifford E. "Democracy and Political Economy in the Caribbean." In *The Political Economy of Drugs in the Caribbean,* edited by Ivelaw L. Griffith. New York: St. Martin's, 2000.

Griffith, Robert K. *The U.S. Army's Transition to the All-Volunteer Force, 1968–1974.* Collingdale, PA: Diane Publishing, 1999.

Grimes, Roger A. *Malicious Mobile Code: Virus Protection for Windows.* New York: O'Reilly, 2001.

Grondahl, Paul. *I Rose Like a Rocket: The Political Education of Theodore Roosevelt.* New York: Free Press, 2004.

Gross, Charles J. *American Military Aviation.* College Station: Texas A&M University Press, 2002.

Grossberg, Lawrence, Ellen Wartella, and D. Charles Whitney. *MediaMaking: Mass Media in a Popular Culture.* Thousand Oaks, CA: Sage, 1998.

Gruber, Ben. "50 Years Later, Nuclear Blast Felt on Bikini Atoll." *Washington Post,* March 1, 2004.

Gunaratna, Rohan. *Inside Al Qaeda: Global Network of Terror.* New York: Berkley, 2003.

Gutman, Roy. *Banana Diplomacy: The Making of American Policy in Nicaragua, 1981–1987.* New York: Simon & Schuster, 1988.

Hack, Richard. *Puppetmaster: The Secret Life of J. Edgar Hoover.* Cambridge, MA: New Millennium, 2004.

Haddow, George, and Jane Bullock. *Introduction to Homeland Security.* Burlington, MA: Butterworth-Heinemann, 2004.

Hagan, Kenneth J. *This People's Navy: The Making of American Sea Power.* New York: Free Press, 1991.

Hahn, Walter F., ed. *Central America and the Reagan Doctrine.* Lanham, MD: University Press of America, 1987.

Halberstam, David. *The Best and the Brightest.* New York: Ballantine, 1972.

Halberstam, David. *War in a Time of Peace.* New York: Scribner, 2001.

Hall, Harold V., ed. *Terrorism: Strategies for Intervention.* New York: Haworth, 2003.

Hamm, Mark S. *Apocalypse in Oklahoma: Waco and Ruby Ridge Revenged.* Boston: Northeastern University Press, 1997.

Hammel, Eric. *Six Days in June: How Israel Won the 1967 Arab-Israeli War.* Pacifica, CA: Pacifica Press, 2001.

Hammond, James W., Jr. *Poison Gas: The Myths Versus Reality.* Westport, CT: Greenwood, 1999.

Handel, Michael I. *Masters of War: Classical Strategic Thought.* London: Frank Cass, 2002.

Handelman, Philip. *Combat in the Sky: The Art of Air Warfare.* St. Paul, MN: Motorbooks, 2003.

Hanley, Charles J. "Exiled Bikinians Sing of Promises But Face Exodus Without End." *Associated Press,* April 4, 2004.

Hanson, Philip. *The Rise and Fall of the Soviet Economy: An Economic History of the USSR, 1945–1991.* New York: Longman, 2003.

Harclerode, Peter. *Fighting Dirty: The Inside Story of Covert Operations From Ho Chi Minh to Osama bin Laden.* London: Cassell, 2003.

Harding, James, and Richard Wolff. "We Worry a Good Deal More . . . September 11 Clarified the Threats You Face in the Post-Cold-War Era." Interview with Condoleezza Rice. *Financial Times,* September 23, 2002, 13.

Hareue, George C, ed. *The Pentagon Papers.* New York: McGraw-Hill, 2003.

Harvey, David. *The New Imperialism.* New York: Oxford University Press, 2005.

Haulman, Daniel L. *The United States Air Force and Humanitarian Airlift Operations, 1947–1994.* Washington, DC: Air Force History and Museum Program, 1998.

Hauter, Brad D. *Counter Terrorism.* Skyland, NC: Kivaki Press, 2004.

Heidler, David, and Jeanne T. Heidler. *Manifest Destiny.* Westport, CT: Greenwood, 2003.

Heil, Alan L., Jr. *Voice of America: A History.* New York: Columbia University Press, 2003.

Henderson, Donald A., Thomas V. Inglesby, and Tara O'Toole. *Bioterrorism: Guidelines for Medical and Public Health Management.* Chicago: American Medical Association, 2002.

Henderson, Jeannie. *Reassessing ASEAN.* New York: International Institute for Strategic Studies, 1999.

Henderson, Karen, and Neil Robinson. *Post-Communist Politics.* New York: Prentice Hall, 1997.

Henderson, W. Darryl. *The Hollow Army.* Westport, CT: Greenwood, 1990.

Henkin, Louis. *Foreign Affairs and the Constitution.* Mineola, NY: Foundation Press, 1972.

Henkin, Louis, Gerald L. Neuman, Daniel F. Orentlicher, and David W. Leebron. *Human Rights.* Mineola, NY: Foundation Press, 1999.

Hentoff, Nat. *The War on the Bill of Rights and the Gathering Resistance.* New York: Seven Stories Press, 2003.

Herring, George C. *America's Longest War: The United States and Vietnam, 1950–1975.* Boston: McGraw-Hill, 2002.

Hersh, Burton. *The Old Boys: The American Elite and the Origins of the CIA.* St. Petersburg, FL: Tree Farm Books, 2001.

Hershey, John. *Hiroshima.* New York: Vintage Books, 1946.

Herz, John H. *Political Realism and Political Idealism.* Chicago: University of Chicago Press, 1951.

Heuser, Beatrice. *Reading Clausewitz.* London: Pimlico, 2002.

Higgins, Trumbull. *The Perfect Failure: Kennedy, Eisenhower, and the CIA at the Bay of Pigs.* New York: Norton, 1989.

Hixson, Walter L., ed. *The Vietnam Anti-War Movement.* New York: Garland, 2000.

Hixson, Walter L. *The Anti-War Movement.* Vol. 5, *The Vietnam War.* London: Taylor and Francis, 2000.

Hoff, Joan. *Nixon Reconsidered.* New York: Basic Books, 1994.

Hogan, Michael J. *A Cross of Iron: Harry S. Truman and the Origins of the National Security State, 1945–1954.* New York: Cambridge University Press, 2000.

Holbrooke, Richard. *To End a War.* New York: Random House, 1998.

Holzgrefe, J. L., and Robert O. Keohane. *Humanitarian Intervention: Ethical, Legal, and Political Dilemmas.* New York: Cambridge University Press, 2003.

Hook, Steven W. *U.S. Foreign Policy: The Paradox of World Power.* Washington, DC: CQ Press, 2004.

Hosmer, Stephen T. *Operations Against Enemy Leaders.* Santa Monica, CA: RAND, 2001.

Howard, Michael. *Clausewitz: A Very Short Introduction.* New York: Oxford University Press, 2002.

Howard, Michael. *The First World War.* Oxford, UK: Oxford University Press, 2004.

Howarth, Stephen. *To Shining Sea: A History of the U.S. Navy, 1775–1991.* New York: Random House, 1991.

Howell, William, G. *Power Without Persuasion: The Politics of Direct Presidential Action.* Princeton, NJ: Princeton University Press, 2003.

Hoyt, Edwin Palmer. *The Kamikazes.* Springfield, NJ: Burford Books, 1999.

Hroub, Khaled. *Hamas: Political Thought and Practice.* Washington, DC: Institute for Palestine Studies, 2000.

Hughes, Jeff. *The Manhattan Project: Big Science and the Atom Bomb.* New York: Columbia University Press, 2002.

Human Rights Watch. *Erased in a Moment: Suicide Bombing Attacks Against Israeli Civilians.* New York: Human Rights Watch, 2002.

Hunt, Andrew. E. *The Turning: A History of Vietnam Veterans Against the War.* New York: New York University Press, 1999.

Hunter, Robert E. *The European Security and Defense Policy: NATO's Companion or Competitor?* Santa Monica, CA: RAND, 2002.

Huth, Paul. *Extended Deterrence and the Prevention of War.* New Haven, CT: Yale University Press, 1988.

Hy-Sang Lee. *North Korea: A Strange Socialist Fortress.* Westport, CT: Praeger, 2001.

Inada, Lawson Fusao, ed. *Only What We Could Carry: The Japanese Internment Experience.* Berkeley, CA: Heyday Books, 2000.

Independent Task Force on Public Diplomacy. *Finding America's Voice: A Strategy for Reinvigorating U.S. Public Diplomacy.* New York: Council on Foreign Relations, 2003.

Inderfurth, Karl F., and Johnson, Loch K. *Fateful Decisions: Inside the National Security Council.* New York: Oxford University Press, 2004.

Ippolito, Dennis S. *Blunting the Sword: Budget Policy and the Future of Defense.* Washington, DC: National Defense University Press, 1994.

Irii Locher, James R., and Sam Nunn. *Victory on the Potomac: The Goldwater-Nichols Act Unifies the Pentagon.* College Station: Texas A&M University Press, 2002.

Iriye, Akira. *Pearl Harbor and the Coming of the Pacific War: A Brief History With Documents and Essays.* New York: Bedford/St. Martin's, 1999.

Janis, Mark W. *An Introduction to International Law.* New York: Aspen, 2003.

Jansen, Johannes J. G. *The Dual Nature of Islamic Fundamentalism.* Ithaca, NY: Cornell University Press, 1997.

Jawara, Fatoumata, and Aileen Kwa. *Behind the Scenes of the WTO: The Real World of International Trade Negotiations.* London: Zed Books, 2003.

Jentleson, Bruce. "Tough Love Multilateralism." *Washington Quarterly* 1 (2003): 7–24.

Jervis, Robert. *The Illogic of American Nuclear Strategy.* Ithaca, NY: Cornell University Press, 1984.

Jervis, Robert. "Understanding the Bush Doctrine." *Political Science Quarterly* 118, no. 3 (2003): 365–388.

Johnson, Robert Erwin. *Guardians of the Sea: History of the United States Coast Guard, 1915 to the Present.* Annapolis, MD: Naval Institute Press, 1987.

Joll, James. *Origins of the First World War.* New York: Longman, 2000.

Jones, Robert A. *The Politics and Economics of the European Union.* Northampton, MA: Edward Elgar, 2001.

Jordan, Amos A., William J. Taylor, and Michael J. Mazarr. *American National Security.* Baltimore: Johns Hopkins University Press, 1998.

Judge, John F. "Strategic Missile Warning Systems Being Upgraded." *Defense Electronics* 17 (May 1985): 86.

Kagan, Robert. "Multilateralism, American Style." *Washington Post,* September 13, 2002.

Kaplan, Lawrence S. *The Long Entanglement: NATO's First Fifty Years.* Westport, CT: Praeger, 1999.

Karnouw, Stanley. *Vietnam: A History.* New York: Penguin, 2003.

Katz, Milton S. *Ban the Bomb: A History of SANE, the Committee for a Sane Nuclear Policy.* New York: Praeger, 1987.

Katz, Samuel M. *Jihad: Islamic Fundamentalist Terrorism.* Minneapolis, MN: Lerner Publishing, 2003.

Keane, Michael. *Dictionary of Modern Strategy and Tactics.* Annapolis, MD: Naval Institute Press, 2005.

Keay, John. *India: A History.* New York: Atlantic Monthly Press, 2000.

Keegan, John. *A History of Warfare.* New York: Vintage, 1994.

Keegan, John. *Intelligence in War: Knowledge of the Enemy From Napoleon to Al-Qaeda.* New York: Knopf, 2003.

Kelly, Michael. "Highway to Hell." *New Republic,* April 1991, 12.

Kennan, George F., and John Lukacs. *George F. Kennan and the Origin of Containment, 1944–1946: The Kennan-Lukacs Correspondence.* Columbia: University of Missouri Press, 1997.

Kennedy, Paul, Dirk Messner, and Franz Nuscheler, eds. *Global Trends and Global Governance.* London: Pluto Press, 2002.

Kenney, Dennis J., and James O. Finckenauer. *Organized Crime in America.* Belmont, CA: Wadsworth, 1995.

Keohane, Robert O., and Joseph S. Nye. *Power and Interdependence.* Boston: Little, Brown, 1989.

Keohane, Robert O., and Joseph S. Nye, Jr. "Power and Interdependence in the Information Age." *Foreign Affairs* 77, no. 5 (1998), 81–94.

Kessler, Ronald. *The Bureau: The Secret History of the FBI.* New York: St. Martin's, 2003.

Kessler, Ronald. *The CIA at War: Inside the Secret Campaign Against Terror.* New York: St. Martin's, 2004.

Kessler, Ronald. *FBI: Inside the World's Most Powerful Law Enforcement Agency.* New York: Pocket Books, 1994.

Khrushchev, Sergei. *Nikita Khrushchev and the Creation of a Superpower.* University Park: Pennsylvania State University Press, 2000.

Kim, Tae-Hyo, and Brad Glosserman. *The Future of U.S.–Korea–Japan Relations: Balancing Values and Interests.* Washington, DC: Center for Strategic and International Studies, 2004.

Kirk, Philip. *Smart Bombs.* Dorchester, UK: Dorchester Publishing, 1979.

Kirwin, Donald, Harry Brandon, Vincent Cannistraro, and Angela Kelley. *Immigration Policy, Law Enforcement, and National Security.* New York: Center for Migration Studies, 2002.

Kisala, Robert J., and Mark R. Mullins, eds. *Religion and Social Crisis in Japan: Understanding Japanese Society Through the Aum Affair.* New York: Palgrave, 2001.

Kitfield, James. *Prodigal Soldiers.* New York: Simon & Schuster, 1995.

Klare, Michael T. *Resource Wars: The New Landscape of Global Conflict.* New York: Henry Holt, 2002.

Kleidman, Robert. *Organizing for Peace: Neutrality, the Test Ban, and the Freeze.* Syracuse, NY: Syracuse University Press, 1993.

Klun, Ernest V. *Declarations of War.* Hauppauge, NY: Novinka Books, 2002.

Knell, Hermann. *To Destroy a City: Strategic Bombing and Its Human Consequences in World War II.* Cambridge, MA: Da Capo Press, 2003.

Koenig, Louis W., James C. Hsiung, and King-yuh Chang, eds. *Congress, the Presidency, and the Taiwan Relations Act.* New York: Praeger, 1985.

Kornbluh, Peter, and Malcolm Byrne, eds. *The Iran-Contra Scandal: The Declassified History.* New York: New Press, 1993.

Krauss, Ellis S., and T. J. Pempel. *Beyond Bilateralism: U.S.–Japan Relations in the New East Asia.* Stanford, CA: Stanford University Press, 2003.

Kreisberg, Paul H., ed. *American Hostages in Iran.* New Haven, CT: Yale University Press, 1985.

Krieg, Joann P., ed. *Dwight D. Eisenhower: Soldier, President, Statesman.* Westport, CT: Greenwood, 1987.

Kriesberg, Louis. "Basics of Zero Sum." In *Constructive Conflicts: From Escalation to Resolution,* by Louis Kriesberg. New York: Rowman & Littlefield, 2002.

Krietemeyer, George E. *The Coastguardsman's Manual.* Annapolis, MD: Naval Institute Press, 2000.

Krugler, David F. *The Voice of America and the Domestic Propaganda Battles, 1945–1953.* Columbia: University of Missouri Press, 2000.

Kupchan, Charles. *End of the American Era: U.S. Foreign Policy and the Geopolitics of the Twenty-First Century.* New York: Alfred A. Knopf, 2003.

LaFeber, Walter. *America, Russia, and the Cold War, 1945–1992*. New York: McGraw-Hill, 1993.

LaFeber, Walter. *America, Russia, and the Cold War, 1945–1996*. New York: McGraw-Hill, 1997.

Lamb, Karl A. *Reasonable Disagreement: Two U.S. Senators and the Choices They Make*. New York: Garland, 1998.

Lancaster, Carol. *Transforming Foreign Aid: United States Assistance in the 21st Century*. New York: Institute for International Economics, 2000.

Langguth, A. J. *Our Vietnam: The War 1954–1975*. New York: Simon & Schuster, 2000.

Laqueur, Walter. *Europe in Our Time—A History: 1945–1992*. New York: Viking, 1992.

Laqueur, Walter. *Guerrilla: A Historical and Critical Study*. Boston: Little, Brown, 1976.

Laqueur, Walter. *A History of Terrorism*. New Brunswick, NJ: Transaction Publishers, 2001.

Laqueur, Walter. *The New Terrorism: Fanaticism and the Arms of Mass Destruction*. New York: Oxford University Press, 2000.

Larrabee, Eric. *Commander in Chief: Franklin Delano Roosevelt, His Lieutenants, and Their War*. Annapolis, MD: Naval Institute Press, 2004.

Larsen, Jeffrey A. *Arms Control: Cooperative Security in a Changing Environment*. Boulder, CO: Lynne Rienner, 2002.

Larsen, Jeffrey A., and Gregory J. Rattray. *Arms Control Toward the 21st Century*. Boulder, CO: Lynne Rienner, 1996.

Latham, Robert. *Bombs and Bandwidth: The Emerging Relationship Between Information Technology and Security*. New York: New Press, 2003.

Laurance, Edward J. *The International Arms Trade*. New York: Macmillan, 1992.

Leach, Garry M. *Killing Peace: Colombia's Conflict and the Failure of U.S. Intervention*. New York: Information Network of the Americas (INOTA), 2002.

Lee, David Tawei. *The Making of the Taiwan Relations Act: Twenty Years in Retrospect*. Oxford, UK: Oxford University Press, 2000.

Lennon, Alexander T. J. *Contemporary Nuclear Debates: Missile Defenses, Arms Control, and Arms Races in the Twenty-First Century*. Cambridge, MA: MIT Press, 2002.

Lennon, Alexander T. J., ed. *The Battle for Hearts and Minds: Using Soft Power to Undermine Terrorist Networks*. Cambridge, MA: MIT Press, 2003.

Leone, Richard C., and Gregory Anrig. *The War on Our Freedoms*. New York: Perseus Publishing, 2003.

Lepore, Herbert P. *The Politics and Failure of Naval Disarmament, 1919–1939: The Phantom Peace*. Ceredigion, UK: Edwin Mellen Press, 2003.

Lesch, David W. *Syria and the United States: Eisenhower's Cold War in the Middle East*. Boulder, CO: Westview Press, 1992.

Levering, Ralph B. *The Cold War: A Post–Cold War History*. Arlington Heights, IL: Harlan Davidson, 1994.

Levy, L. *The Emergence of a Free Press*. New York: Ivan R. Dean, 2004.

Libicki, Martin C. *What Is Information Warfare?* Washington, DC: Center for Advanced Command Concepts and Technology, 1995.

Lichterman, Andrew, and Jacqueline Cabasso. "The End of Disarmament and the Arms Races to Come." *Social Justice* 29, no. 3 (2002): 73–81.

Lifton, Robert Jay. *Destroying the World to Save It: Aum Shinrikyo, Apocalyptic Violence, and the New Global Terrorism*. New York: Metropolitan Books, 1999.

Litwak, Robert S. *Détente and the Nixon Doctrine: American Foreign Policy and the Pursuit of Stability, 1969–1976*. New York: Cambridge University Press, 1984.

Lockman, Zachary, and Joel Beinin, eds. *Intifada: The Palestinian Uprising Against Israeli Occupation*. Boston: South End Press, 1989.

Lorelli, John A. *To Foreign Shores: American Amphibious Operations in World War II*. Annapolis, MD: Naval Institute Press, 1995.

Louis, William Roger, and Roger Owen, eds. *Suez 1956: The Crisis and Its Consequences*. Oxford, UK: Clarendon Press, 1989.

Lowenthal, Mark M. *Intelligence: From Secrets to Policy*. Washington, DC: CQ Press, 2003.

Lugar, Richard G. *Letters to the Next President*. New York: Simon & Schuster, 1988.

Lumbard, Joseph E. B. *Islam, Fundamentalism, and the Betrayal of Tradition: Essays by Western Muslim Scholars*. Bloomington, IN: World Wisdom, 2004.

Lundestad, Geir. *East, West, North, South: Major Developments in International Politics 1945–1996*. Oslo, Norway: Scandinavian University Press, 1997.

Lundestad, Geir. *The United States and Western Europe Since 1945: From "Empire" by Invitation to Transatlantic Drift*. New York: Oxford University Press, 2003.

Machiavelli, Niccolò. *The Prince*. New York: Penguin, 1975.

MacKenzie, David, and Michael W. Curran. *Russia and the USSR in the Twentieth Century*. Belmont, CA: Wadsworth, 2001.

MacKenzie, Lewis. *The Road to Sarajevo*. Toronto: HarperCollins, 1994.

MacQueen, Norrie. *Peacekeeping and the International System*. London: Routledge, 2005.

Mahle, Melissa Boyle. *Denial and Deception: An Insider's View of the CIA from Iran-Contra to 9/11*. New York: Nation's Books, 2005.

Maley, William. *The Afghanistan Wars*. New York: Palgrave Macmillan, 2002.

Malkasian, Carter. *Charting the Pathway to OMFTS: A Historical Assessment of Amphibious Operations from 1941 to the Present*. Washington, DC: CNA Corporation, 2002.

Malone, David, ed. *The UN Security Council: From the Cold War to the Twenty-First Century*. Boulder, CO: Lynne Rienner, 2004.

Mandel, Robert. *Deadly Transfers and the Global Playground: Transnational Security Threats in a Disorderly World*. New York: Praeger, 1999.

Mangold, Tom, and Jeff Goldberg. *Plague Wars: The Terrifying Reality of Biological Warfare.* New York: St. Martin's, 2001.

Manheim, Jarol. *Strategic Public Diplomacy and American Foreign Policy: The Evolution of Influence.* New York: Oxford University Press, 1994.

Mann, James, and Howard Zinn. *Peace Signs: The Anti-War Movement Illustrated.* Zurich, Switzerland: Edition Olms, 2004.

Marchisio, Sergio, and Antonietta Di Blase. *The Food and Agriculture Organization. International Organization and the Evolution of World Society* 1. Amsterdam, The Netherlands: Martinus Nijhoff, 1991.

Marcovitz, Hal. *The Oklahoma City Bombing.* Northborough, MA: Chelsea House, 2002.

Mares, David R. *Security, Democracy, and Development in U.S.–Latin American Relations.* Lars Schoultz, William C. Smith, and Augusto Varas, eds. Coral Gables, FL: University of Miami Press, 1994.

Markusen, Ann R., and Sean S. Costigan, eds. *Arming the Future: A Defense Industry for the 21st Century.* New York: Council on Foreign Relations Press, 1999.

Marquis, Susan L. *Unconventional Warfare: Rebuilding U.S. Special Operations Forces.* Washington, DC: Brookings Institution, 1997.

Martin, Laurence. *The Changing Face of Nuclear Warfare.* New York: Harper & Row, 1987.

Martin, Stephen. *The Economics of Offsets: Defense Procurement and Countertrade.* Amsterdam, The Netherlands: Harwood Academic Publishers, 1996.

Marx, Karl, and Friedrich Engels. *The Communist Manifesto.* London: Verso, 1998.

Matsumura, John, et al. *Lightning Over Water: Sharpening America's Light Forces for Rapid Missions.* Santa Monica, CA: RAND, 2001.

Mauroni, Al. *Chemical and Biological Warfare: A Reference Handbook.* Santa Barbara, CA: ABC-CLIO, 2003.

May, Ernest R. *Imperial Democracy: The Emergence of America As a Great Power.* New York: Imprint Publications, 1961.

May, Ernest R. *American Cold War Strategy: Interpreting NSC-68.* New York: St. Martin's, 1993.

May, Ernest R., and Philip Zelikow, eds. *The Kennedy Tapes: Inside the White House During the Cuban Missile Crisis.* Cambridge, MA: Belknap Press, 1998.

McCarthy, James P. *The Air Force.* Westport, CT: Hugh Lauter Levin, 2002.

McMahon, K. Scott. *Pursuit of the Shield.* Lanham, MD: Rowman & Littlefield, 1987.

McMahon, Robert J., ed. *Major Problems in the History of the Vietnam War: Documents and Essays.* Lexington, MA: DC Heath, 1995.

McManus, Doyle. *Free at Last!* New York: New American Library, 1981.

McMaster, H. R. *Dereliction of Duty: Lyndon Johnson, Robert McNamara, the Joint Chiefs of Staff, and the Lies That Led to Vietnam.* New York: HarperCollins, 1997.

McNamara, Robert S. *Argument without End: In Search of Answers to the Vietnam Tragedy.* New York: David McKay, 1999.

McNamara, Robert S. *In Retrospect: The Tragedy and Lessons of Vietnam.* New York: Times Books, 1995.

McNeil, William H. *Plagues and Peoples.* New York: Doubleday, 1977.

McPherson, Cameron. *Life in the Navy Reserves.* Victoria, BC: Trafford Publishing, 2003.

McRaven, William H. *Spec Ops: Case Studies in Special Operations Warfare: Theory and Practice.* Novato, CA: Presidio Press, 1995.

Mearsheimer, John J. *The Tragedy of Great Power Politics.* New York: Norton, 2001.

Medvedev, R. A., and Z. A. Medvedev. *Khrushchev Remembers: The Last Testament.* New York: HarperCollins, 1974.

Meiser, Stanley. *United Nations: The First Fifty Years.* New York: Atlantic Monthly Press, 1997.

Melanson, Richard, and Kai P. Schoenhals. *Revolution and Intervention in Grenada: The New Jewel Movement, the United States, and the Caribbean.* Boulder, CO: Westview Press, 1985.

Mendel, William W., and Graham H. Turbiville, Jr. *The CINC's Strategies: The Combatant Command Process.* Carlisle Barracks, PA: Strategic Studies Institute of the U.S. Army War College, 1998.

Metz, Steven, ed. *Revising the Two MTW Force Shaping Paradigm.* Carlisle, PA: Strategic Studies Institute of the U.S. Army War College, 2001.

Mickelson, Sig. *America's Other Voices: The Story of Radio Free Europe and Radio Liberty.* New York: Praeger, 1983.

Milkis, Sidney M., and Michael Nelson. *The American Presidency: Origins and Development, 1776–2002.* Washington, DC: CQ Press, 2003.

Millard, Mark. *Jihad in Paradise: Islam and Politics in Southeast Asia.* Armonk, NY: M. E. Sharpe, 2004.

Miller, Charles E. *Airlift Doctrine.* Maxwell Air Force Base, AL: Air University Press, 1988.

Miller, Judith, Stephen Engelberg, and William Broad. *Germs: Biological Weapons and America's Secret War.* New York: Simon & Schuster, 2001.

Milton-Edwards, Beverley, and Peter Hinchcliffe. *Conflicts in the Middle East Since 1945: The Making of the Contemporary World.* New York: Routledge, 2001.

Milward, Alan S. *The European Rescue of the Nation-State.* London: Routledge, 1992.

Minh, Ho Chi. *Selected Writings.* Hanoi, Vietnam: Foreign Languages Publishing House, 1973.

Misra, Amalendu. *Afghanistan.* Malden, MA: Polity, 2004.

Mitchell, Carl. *Marching to an Angry Drum: Gays in the Military.* New York: Writer's Club Press, 2002.

Mitchell, George J., Bruce L. Brager, and James I. Matray. *The Iron Curtain: The Cold War in Europe.* Northborough, MA: Chelsea House, 2004.

Mittelman, James. *The Globalization Syndrome: Transformation and Resistance.* Princeton, NJ: Princeton University Press, 2000.

Moody, Walton S. *Building a Strategic Air Force.* Washington, DC: Government Reprints Press, 2001.

Moody, Walton S., and Warren A. Trest. "Containing Communism." In *Winged Shield, Winged Sword: A History of the United States Air Force,* edited by Bernard C. Nalty. Washington, DC: Air Force History and Museum Program, 1997.

Morgenthau, Hans J. *Politics Among Nations: The Struggle for Power and Peace.* Boston: McGraw-Hill, 1993.

Moseley, Alexander, and Richard Norman, eds. *Human Rights and Military Intervention.* Burlington, VT: Ashgate, 2002.

Mosher, David E. *Rethinking the Trident Force.* Washington, DC: Congressional Budget Office, 1993.

Mosher, David E., et al. *Beyond the Nuclear Shadow: A Phased Approach for Improving Nuclear Safety and U.S.–Russian Relations.* Santa Monica, CA: RAND, 2003.

Moskos, Charles C., ed. *The Postmodern Military: Armed Forces After the Cold War.* New York: Oxford University Press, 1999.

Muldoon, James. P., Jr. *Multilateral Diplomacy and the United Nations Today.* 2nd ed. Boulder, CO: Westview Press, 2005.

Müller, Harald, David Fischer, and Wolfgang Kötter. *Nuclear Non-Proliferation and Global Order.* Oxford and New York: Oxford University Press, 1994.

Murray, Williamson, and Robert H. Scales Jr. *The Iraq War: A Military History.* Cambridge, MA: Harvard University Press, 2003.

Myers, Lawrence. *Smart Bombs: Improvised Sensory Detonation Techniques and Advanced Weapons Systems.* Boulder, CO: Paladin Press, 1990.

Myers, Robert J. *Korea in the Cross Currents: A Century of Struggle and the Crisis of Reunification.* New York: Palgrave, 2001.

Mylroie, Laurie. "The World Trade Center Bomb: Who Is Ramzi Yousef? And Why It Matters." *The National Interest* 42 (Winter 1995/1996): 3–15.

Naimark, Norman. *Fires of Hatred: Ethnic Cleansing in Twentieth-Century Europe.* Cambridge, MA: Harvard University Press, 2001.

Narine, Shaun. *Explaining ASEAN.* Boulder, CO: Lynne Rienner, 2002.

Nasheri, Hidieh, Alfred Blumstein, and David Farrington, eds. *Economic Espionage and Industrial Spying.* Cambridge, UK: Cambridge University Press, 2004.

Nassar, Jamal R. *The Palestine Liberation Organization: From Armed Struggle to the Declaration of Independence.* New York: Praeger, 1991.

Nathan, Andrew J., and Robert Ross. *The Great Wall and the Empty Fortress: China's Search for Security.* New York: Norton, 1997.

Nation, Craig R. *Black Earth, Red Star: A History of Soviet Security Policy, 1917–1991.* Ithaca, NY: Cornell University Press, 1992.

National Academy of Sciences. *Nuclear Arms Control: Background and Issues.* Washington, DC: National Academy Press, 1985.

National Commission on Terrorist Attacks. *The 9/11 Commission Report: Final Report of the National Commission on Terrorist Attacks Upon the United States.* New York: Norton, 2004.

Naylor, R. T. *Economic Warfare: Sanctions, Embargo Busting, and Their Human Cost.* Boston: Northeastern University Press, 2001.

Nelson, Keith L. *The Making of Detente: Soviet-American Relations in the Shadow of Vietnam.* Baltimore: Johns Hopkins University Press, 1995.

Neuman, Stephanie G., and Robert E. Harkavy. *Arms Transfers in the Modern World.* New York: Praeger, 1980.

Newland, Samuel J. "A Centennial History of the U.S. Army War College." *Parameters* 31, no. 3 (2001): 34–47.

Ng, Wendy L. *Japanese American Internment During World War II: A History and Reference Guide.* Westport, CT: Greenwood, 2002.

Nicholas, Kenneth D. *The Road to Trinity.* New York: Morrow, 1987.

Nieves, Evelyn. "A U.S. Convert's Path From Suburbia to a Gory Jail for Taliban." *New York Times,* December 4, 2001.

Noel-Baker, P. *Disarmament.* New York: Garland, 1972.

Nordeen, Lon O., and Walter J. Boyne. *Air Warfare in the Missile Age.* Washington, DC: Smithsonian Books, 2002.

Norman, Richard. *Ethics, Killing, and War.* New York: Cambridge University Press, 1995.

Norton, Augustus R., and Martin H. Greenberg. *The International Relations of the Palestine Liberation Organization.* Carbondale: Southern Illinois University Press, 1989.

Novick, Lloyd F., ed. *Public Health Issues Disaster Preparedness: Focus on Bioterrorism.* Bedfordshire, UK: Aspen, 2003.

Nüsse, Andrea. *Muslim Palestine: The Ideology of Hamas.* Amsterdam, The Netherlands: Overseas Publishers Association, 1998.

Nye, Joseph. *Bound to Lead.* New York: Basic Books, 1988.

Nye, Joseph S. *Soft Power: The Means to Success in World Politics.* New York: Public Affairs, 2004.

Oberdorfer, Dan. *The Two Koreas.* Reading, MA: Addison-Wesley, 1997.

O'Brien, Michael T. *Guardians of the Eighth Sea: A History of the U.S. Coast Guard on the Great Lakes.* Stockton, CA: University Press of the Pacific, 2001.

O'Donnell, Patrick K. *Operatives, Spies, and Saboteurs: The Unknown Story of the Men and Women of WWII's OSS.* New York: Free Press, 2004.

Office of the Department of Defense Inspector General. *The Tailhook Report: The Official Inquiry Into the Events of Tailhook '91.* New York: St. Martin's, 1993.

Offner, Arnold A. *Another Such Victory: President Truman and the Cold War, 1945–1953.* Stanford, CA: Stanford University Press, 2002.

O'Hanlon, Michael. *Beyond the Desert Storm Framework: Defense Planning for the Late 1990s.* Washington, DC: Brookings Institution, 1995.

Oren, Michael B. *Six Days of War: June 1967 and the Making of the Modern Middle East.* New York: Ballantine, 2002.

Østerud, Øyvind. "The Uses and Abuses of Geopolitics." *Journal of Peace Research* 25, no. 2 (1988): 191–199.

Paddock, Alfred H., Jr. *U.S. Army Special Warfare: Its Origins.* Lawrence: University Press of Kansas, 2002.

Painter, David S. *Cold War: An Interdisciplinary History.* New York: Routledge, 1999.

Pape, Robert A. *Bombing to Win: Air Power and Coercion in War.* Ithaca, NY: Cornell University Press, 1996.

Parker, Geoffrey. *Geopolitics: Past, Present and Future.* Washington, DC: Pinter, 1998.

Parrish, Thomas. *Berlin in the Balance, 1945–1949.* Reading, MA: Addison-Wesley, 1998.

Parrish, Thomas. *The Submarine: A History.* New York: Viking, 2004.

Paterson, Thomas G. *Meeting the Communist Threat: Truman to Reagan.* New York: Oxford University Press, 1988.

Patterson, Richard North. *Balance of Power.* New York: Ballantine, 2004.

Paul, T. V., James J. Wirtz, and Michael Fortman. *Balance Of Power: Theory and Practice in the Twenty-First Century.* Stanford, CA: Stanford University Press, 2004.

Peretz, Don. *Intifada: The Palestinian Uprising.* Boulder, CO: Westview Press, 1990.

Perloff, Harvey S. *Alliance for Progress: A Social Invention in the Making.* Baltimore: Johns Hopkins University Press, 1969.

Persico, Joseph E. *Roosevelt's Secret War: FDR and World War II Espionage.* New York: Random House, 2001.

Peterson, V. Spike. *Global Gender Issues.* Dilemmas in World Politics. Boulder, CO: Westview Press, 1999.

Pfiffner, James P. *The Modern Presidency.* Belmont, CA: Wadsworth, 2005.

Pierre, Andrew J., ed. *Cascade of Arms: Managing Conventional Weapons Proliferation.* Washington, DC: Brookings Institution, 1997.

Pika, Joseph A., and John Anthony Maltese. *The Politics of the Presidency.* Washington, DC: CQ Press, 2004.

Pike, John. "The Paradox of Space Weapons." In *Stockholm International Peace Research Institute Yearbook 2003.* Oxford, UK: Oxford University Press, 2003.

Plischke, Elmer. *U.S. Department of State: A Reference History.* Westport, CT: Greenwood, 1999.

Pollis, Adamantia, and Peter Schwab. *Human Rights: New Perspectives, New Realities.* Boulder, CO: Lynne Rienner, 2000.

Pose, Barry R. *Sources of Military Doctrine: France, Britain and Germany Between the World Wars.* Ithaca, NY: Cornell University Press, 1986.

Poundstone, William. *Prisoner's Dilemma.* New York: Doubleday, 1992.

Powaski, Ronald E. *Return to Armageddon: The United States and the Nuclear Arms Race, 1981–1999.* New York: Oxford University Press. 2000.

Powell, Colin L., with Joseph E. Persico. *My American Journey.* New York: Random House, 1995.

Powers, Thomas. *Intelligence Wars: American Secret History from Hitler to Al-Qaeda.* New York: New York Review of Books, 2004.

Prados, John. *Keepers of the Keys: A History of the National Security Council from Truman to Bush.* New York: William Morrow, 1991.

Prados, John. *Presidents' Secret Wars: CIA and Pentagon Covert Operations from World War II Through the Persian Gulf.* Chicago: Ivan R. Dee, 1996.

Prange, Gordon W., Donald M. Goldstein, and Katherine Dillon. *Pearl Harbor: The Verdict of History.* New York: McGraw-Hill, 1986.

Prange, Gordon W., Donald M. Goldstein, and Katherine Dillon. *December 7, 1941: The Day the Japanese Attacked Pearl Harbor.* New York: McGraw-Hill, 1988.

Pratkinis, Anthony, and Elliot Aronson. *Age of Propaganda: The Everyday Use and Abuse of Persuasion.* New York: Freeman, 2001.

Prebeck, Steven R. *Preventive Attack in the 1990s?* Maxwell Air Force Base, AL: Air University Press, 1993.

Preston, Bob, Dana J. Johnson, Sean Edwards, Michael Miller, and Calvin Shipbaugh. *Space Weapons Earth Wars.* Santa Monica, CA: RAND, 2002.

Price, Richard M., and Zacher, Mark W., eds. *The United Nations and Global Security.* London: Palgrave Macmillan, 2004.

Proctor, Dennis. *The Experience of Thucydides.* Warminster, UK: Aris & Phillips, 1980.

Puddington, Arch. *Broadcasting Freedom: The Cold War Triumph of Radio Free Europe and Radio Liberty.* Lexington: University Press of Kentucky, 2000.

Quinn-Judge, Sophie. *Ho Chi Minh: The Missing Years, 1919–1941.* Berkeley: University of California Press, 2003.

Rabie, Mohamed. *U.S.–PLO Dialogue: Secret Diplomacy and Conflict Resolution.* Gainesville: University Press of Florida, 1995.

Rabinovich, Abraham. *The Yom Kippur War: The Epic Encounter That Transformed the Middle East.* New York: Schocken Books, 2004.

Ravinder, Pal Singh, ed. *Arms Procurement Decision Making.* New York: Oxford University Press, 1998.

Ray, Ronald. *Gays: In or Out? The U.S. Military & Homosexuals—A Source Book.* New York: Brassey's, 1993.

Read, Anthony, and David Fisher. *Berlin: The Biography of a City.* London: Hutchinson, 1984.

Reader, Ian. *Religious Violence in Contemporary Japan: The Case of Aum Shinrikyo.* Honolulu: University of Hawaii Press, 2000.

Record, Jeffrey. "The Bush Doctrine and the War in Iraq." *Parameters* 33 (Spring 2003): 4–21.

Reeve, Simon. *The New Jackals: Ramzi Yousef, Osama bin Laden and the Future of Terrorism.* London: André Deutsch, 1999.

Ressa, Maria A. *Seeds of Terror: An Eyewitness Account of al-Qaeda's Newest Center of Operations in Southeast Asia.* New York: Free Press, 2003.

Reuter, Christoph. *My Life as a Weapon: A Modern History of Suicide Bombing.* Princeton, NJ: Princeton University Press, 2002.

Rhodes, Benjamin D. *United States Foreign Policy in the Interwar Period, 1918–1941.* Westport, CT: Praeger, 2001.

Rhodes, Edward. *Power and Madness: The Logic of Nuclear Coercion.* New York: Columbia University Press, 1989.

Rhodes, Richard. *The Making of the Atomic Bomb.* New York: Simon & Schuster, 1986.

Richelson, Jeffrey T. *A Century of Spies: Intelligence in the Twentieth Century.* New York: Oxford University Press, 1995.

Riconda, Harry P. *Prisoners of War in American Conflicts.* Lanham, MD: Scarecrow Press, 2003.

Ringholz, Raye C. *Uranium Frenzy: Saga of the Nuclear West.* Logan: Utah State University Press, 2002.

Ripley, Tim. *Jane's Pocket Guide: Modern Military Helicopters.* New York: HarperResource, 1999.

Robertson, A. H., and J. G. Merrills. *Human Rights in the World: An Introduction to the Study of the International Protection of Human Rights.* Oxford, UK: Manchester University Press, 1996.

Roderick, Hilliard. *Avoiding Inadvertent War: Crisis Management.* Austin: University of Texas, 1983.

Rodrik, Dani. *Has Globalization Gone Too Far?* Washington, DC: Institute for International Economics, 1997.

Rogel, Carole. *The Breakup of Yugoslavia and Its Aftermath.* Westport, CT: Greenwood, 2004.

Roland, Alex. *Military Industrial Complex.* Washington, DC: American Historical Association, 2002.

Roman, Peter J. *Eisenhower and the Missile Gap.* Ithaca, NY: Cornell University Press, 1995.

Rose, John P. *The Evolution of U.S. Army Nuclear Doctrine, 1945–1980.* Boulder, CO: Westview Press, 1980.

Rosenau, James, N. *Distant Proximities: Dynamics Beyond Globalization.* Princeton, NJ: Princeton University Press, 2003.

Rothchild, Joseph. *Return to Diversity: A Political History of East Central Europe Since World War II.* Oxford, UK: Oxford University Press, 1993.

Rourke, John T. *International Politics on the World Stage.* Guilford, CT: Dushkin/McGraw-Hill, 1989.

Rubin, Barry. *Paved with Good Intentions: The American Experience and Iran.* New York: Oxford University Press, 1980.

Rudenstine, David. *The Day the Presses Stopped: A History of the Pentagon Papers Case.* Berkeley: University of California Press, 1996.

Ryan, Patrick J., and George E. Rush, eds. *Understanding Organized Crime in Global Perspective: A Reader.* Thousand Oaks, CA: Sage, 1997.

Sagan, Scott, and Kenneth N. Waltz. *The Spread of Nuclear Weapons: A Debate.* New York: Norton, 1995.

Said, Edward. *Culture and Imperialism.* New York: Vintage, 1994.

Sandoz, Yves. *The Geneva Conventions: Protecting People in Times of War.* United Nations Chronicle 36. New York: United Nations, 1999.

Sanger, David E. "Beating Them to the Prewar." *New York Times,* September 28, 2002.

Schain, Martin A. *The Marshall Plan: Fifty Years After.* New York: Palgrave Macmillan, 2001.

Schell, Jonathan. *Fate of the Earth and the Abolition.* Palo Alto, CA: Stanford University Press, 1999.

Schellenberg, James A. *Conflict Resolution: Theory, Research, and Practice.* Albany: State University of New York Press, 1996.

Schelling, Thomas C. *Arms and Influence.* New Haven, CT: Yale University Press, 1966.

Schelling, Thomas C. *Strategy and Arms Control.* New York: Twentieth Century Fund, 1961.

Scheuer, Michael. *Imperial Hubris.* Dulles, VA: Brassey's, 2004.

Scheuer, Michael. *Through Our Enemies' Eyes: Osama bin Laden, Radical Islam, and the Future of America.* Washington, DC: Brassey's, 2002.

Schier, Steven E., ed. *The Postmodern Presidency: Bill Clinton's Legacy in U.S. Politics.* Pittsburgh, PA: University of Pittsburgh Press, 2000.

Schleher, Curtis D. *Introduction to Electronic Warfare.* Norwood, MA: Artech House, 1986.

Schnabel, James F. *History of the Joint Chiefs of Staff: The Joint Chiefs of Staff and National Policy.* Washington, DC: Scholarly Resources, 1996.

Scott, David, and Aleksei Leonov. *Two Sides of the Moon: Our Story of the Cold War Space Race.* New York: Thomas Dunne Books, 2004.

Scott, James M. *Deciding to Intervene: The Reagan Doctrine and American Foreign Policy.* Durham, NC: Duke University Press, 1996.

Scott, Peter Dale, and Jonathon Marshall. *Cocaine Politics: Drugs, Armies and the CIA in Central America.* Berkeley: University of California Press, 1998.

Sen, Amartya. *Development as Freedom.* New York: Knopf, 1999.

Shanty, Frank, Raymond Picquet, and John Lalla, eds. *Encyclopedia of World Terrorism.* Armonk, NY: M. E. Sharpe, 2003.

Shapley, Deborah. *The Life and Times of Robert S. McNamara.* New York: Little, Brown, 1993.

Shaw, Malcolm M. *International Law.* Cambridge, UK: Cambridge University Press, 2003.

Shetreet, Shimon. *Free Speech and National Security.* Boston: Brill Academic Publishers, 1996.

Shields, John M., and William C. Potter, eds. *Dismantling the Cold War.* Cambridge, MA: MIT Press, 1997.

Shilts, Randy. *Conduct Unbecoming: Gays and Lesbians in the U.S. Military.* New York: St. Martin's, 1993.

Shimko, Keith. *Images and Arms Control: Perceptions of the Soviet Union in the Reagan Administration.* Ann Arbor: University of Michigan Press, 1991.

Short, Philip. *Mao: A Life.* New York: Henry Holt, 2000.

Shroyer, Jo Ann. *Secret Mesa: Inside Los Alamos National Laboratory.* New York: John Wiley, 1998.

Sicker, Martin. *The Geopolitics of Security in the Americas: Hemispheric Denial from Monroe to Clinton.* Westport, CT: Praeger, 2002.

Simpson, Christopher. *National Security Directives of the Reagan and Bush Administrations: The Declassified History of U.S. Political and Military Policy, 1981–1991.* Boulder, CO: Perseus Books, 1995.

Simpson, Christopher. *Science of Coercion: Communication Research and Psychological Warfare, 1945–1960.* New York: Oxford University Press, 1994.

Sinclair, Andrew. *An Anatomy of Terror: A History of Terrorism.* London: Macmillan, 2003.

Skolnikoff, Eugene B. *The Elusive Transformation: Science, Technology, and the Evolution of International Politics.* Princeton, NJ: Princeton University Press, 1994.

Slusser, Robert M. "The Berlin Crises of 1958–59 and 1961." In *Force Without War: U.S. Armed Forces as a Political Instrument,* edited by Barry M. Blechman, 356–396. Washington, DC: Brookings Institution, 1978.

Small, Melvin. *Covering Dissent: The Media and the Anti-Vietnam War Movement.* Perspective on the Sixties. Rutgers, NJ: Rutgers University Press, 1994.

Smith, Gaddis. *The Last Years of the Monroe Doctrine, 1945–1993.* New York: Hill and Wang, 1994.

Smith, Jennifer. *The Antinuclear Movement.* San Diego, CA: Greenhaven Press, 2004.

Smith, John E. *Biotechnology.* Cambridge, UK: Cambridge University Press, 2004.

Smith, John T. *Rolling Thunder: The Strategic Bombing Campaign, North Vietnam 1965–1968.* London: Crecy Publishing Limited, 1995.

Smith, Perry M. *Assignment: Pentagon, The Insider's Guide to the Potomac Puzzle Palace.* New York: International Defense Publishers, 1989.

Sobol, Robert. *The Life and Times of Dillon Reed.* New York: Dutton, 1991.

Solidum, Estrella D. *The Politics of ASEAN.* Singapore: Eastern Universities Press, 2003.

Southworth, Samuel A., and Stephen Tanner. *U.S. Special Forces: A Guide to America's Special Operations Units, The World's Most Elite Fighting Force.* Cambridge, MA: Da Capo Press, 2002.

Spaeth, H. J., and E. C. Smith. "The Right to Privacy." In *The Constitution of the United States,* New York: HarperCollins, 1991.

Speller, Ian, and Christopher Tuck. *Amphibious Warfare: Strategy and Tactics; The Theory and Practice of Amphibious Operations in the Twentieth Century.* London: Spellmount, 2001.

Spender, Percy Claude. *Exercise in Diplomacy: The ANZUS Treaty and the Colombo Plan.* New York: New York University Press, 1970.

Spero, Joan Edelman. *The Politics of International Economic Relations.* New York: St. Martin's, 1990.

Spiers, Edward M. *Chemical and Biological Weapons: A Study of Proliferation.* London: Macmillan, 1994.

Spinardi, Graham, with Steve Smith, Thomas Biersteker, Chris Brown, Phil Cerny, and A. J. R. Groom, eds. *From Polaris to Trident: The Development of U.S. Fleet Ballistic Missile Technology.* Cambridge, UK: Cambridge University Press, 1994.

Springhall, John. *Decolonization Since 1945: The Collapse of European Overseas Empires.* Studies in Contemporary History. New York: Palgrave, 2001.

Sray, John S. *U.S. Policy and the Bosnian Civil War: A Time for Reevaluation.* Washington, DC: Foreign Military Studies Office, 1995.

Stares, Paul B. *The Militarization of Space.* Ithaca, NY: Cornell University Press, 1985.

Stepan, Alfred C. *Rethinking Military Politics: Brazil and the Southern Cone.* Princeton, NJ: Princeton University Press, 1988.

Stern, Jessica. *The Ultimate Terrorists.* Cambridge, MA: Harvard University Press, 1999.

Stern, Sheldon M. *The Week the World Stood Still: Inside the Secret Cuban Missile Crisis.* Stanford, CA: Stanford University Press, 2005.

Stiehm, Judith Hicks. "Civil-Military Relations in War College Curricula." *Armed Forces and Society: An Interdisciplinary Journal* 27, no. 2 (2001): 273–299.

Stiglitz, Joseph E. *Globalization and Its Discontents.* New York: Norton, 2003.

Stine, Harry G. *ICBM: The Making of the Weapon That Changed the World.* New York: Orion, 1991.

Strong, Robert A. *Working in the World: Jimmy Carter and the Making of American Foreign Policy.* Baton Rouge: Louisiana State University Press, 2000.

Sun Tzu. *Art of War.* Translated by Ralph D. Sawyer. Boulder, CO: Westview Press, 1994.

Suny, Ronald Grigor. *The Soviet Experiment: Russia, the USSR, and the Successor States.* New York: Oxford University Press, 1997.

Suri, Jeremy. *Power and Protest: Global Revolution and the Rise of Détente.* Cambridge, MA: Harvard University Press, 2005.

Syed, M. H. *Islamic Terrorism.* Delhi, India: Kalpaz Publications, 2003.

Takeyh, Ray. *The Origins of the Eisenhower Doctrine: The U.S., Britain, and Nasser's Egypt, 1953–1957.* New York: Macmillan, 2000.

Tanner, Stephen. *Afghanistan: A Military History from Alexander the Great to the Fall of the Taliban.* New York: Da Capo Press, 2002.

Tardy, Thierry. *Peace Operations After 11 September 2001.* London: Frank Cass, 2005.

Taubman, William. *Khrushchev: The Man and His Era.* New York: Norton, 2003.

Terrill, Ross. *Mao: A Biography.* Stanford, CA: Stanford University Press, 1999.

Thakur, Ramesh, and Albrecht Schnabel, eds. *United Nations Peacekeeping Operations: Ad Hoc Mission, Permanent Engagement.* Tokyo: UN University Press, 2001.

Theoharis, Athan G., ed. *A Culture of Secrecy: The Government Versus the People's Right to Know.* Lawrence: University of Kansas Press, 1998.

Theoharis, Athan G., Tony G. Poveda, Susan Rosenfeld, and Richard G. Powers, eds. *The FBI: A Comprehensive Reference Guide.* New York: Checkmark Books, 2000.

Thomas, Caroline. "Global Governance and Human Security." In *Global Governance: Critical Perspectives*, edited by Rorden Wilkinson and Steve Hughes. New York: Routledge, 2002.

Thomas, Ward. *The Ethics of Destruction: Norms and Force in International Relations*. Ithaca, NY: Cornell University Press, 2001.

Thompson, David B. *A Guide to the Nuclear Arms Control Treaties*. Los Alamos, NM: Alamos Historical Society, 2001.

Thompson, E. P., and Mary Kaldor. *Mad Dogs: The U.S. Raid on Libya*. London: Pluto Press, 1986.

Thornborough, Anthony. *Modern Fighter Aircraft Technology and Tactics: Into Combat With Today's Fighter Pilots*. Cambridge, UK: Patrick Stephens, 1995.

Thurow, Lester C. *The Future of Capitalism: How Today's Economic Forces Shape Tomorrow's World*. New York: William Morrow, 1996.

Tierney, Kathleen J. *Facing the Unexpected: Disaster Preparedness and Response in the United States*. Washington, DC: National Academies Press, 2001.

Tisch, Sarah J., and Michael B. Wallace. *Dilemmas of Development Assistance: The What, Why, and Who of Foreign Aid*. Boulder, CO: Westview Press, 1994.

Trask, David. *The War with Spain in 1898*. Lincoln: University of Nebraska Press, 1997.

Trask, Roger R., and Alfred Goldberg. *The Department of Defense, 1947–1997: Organization and Leaders*. Washington, DC: Historical Office, Office of the Secretary of Defense, 1997.

Trento, Joseph J. *The Secret History of the CIA*. Roseville, CA: Prima Publishing, 2001.

Treverton, Gregory F. *Making the Alliance Work: The United States and Western Europe*. London: Macmillan, 1985.

Trewhitt, Henry L. *McNamara*. New York: Harper & Row, 1971.

Triay, Victor Andres. *The Bay of Pigs*. Gainesville: University Press of Florida, 2001.

Tuch, Hans N. *Communicating With the World: U.S. Public Diplomacy Overseas*. New York: St. Martin's, 1990.

Tucker, Spencer. *The Second World War*. New York: Palgrave Macmillan, 2003.

Tunner, William H. *Over the Hump*. New York: Duell, Sloan and Pierce, 1964.

Turner, James T., and Michael G. Gelles. *Threat Assessment: A Risk Management Approach*. Binghamton, NY: Haworth, 2003.

Tyler, William R. *Yalta: Yesterday, Today, Tomorrow*. New York: Harper & Row, 1988.

Urban, George R. *Radio Free Europe and the Pursuit of Democracy: My War Within the Cold War*. New Haven, CT: Yale University Press, 1998.

U.S. Congress, Office of Technology Assessment. *Global Arms Trade: Commerce in Advanced Military Technology and Weapons*. Washington, DC: Government Printing Office, 1991.

U.S. Department of Defense. *21st Century U.S. Army Law of Land Warfare Manual: Rules, Principles, Hostilities, Prisoners of War, Wounded and Sick, Civilians, Occupation, War Crimes, Geneva Conventions*. Dulles, VA: Progressive Management, 2003.

U.S. Department of Homeland Security. *Securing Our Homeland*. Washington, DC: Government Printing Office, 2004.

U.S. Department of State. *Diplomacy: The State Department at Work*. Washington, DC: U.S. Department of State, Bureau of Public Affairs, 1996.

U.S. Department of State. *Fact Sheet: Conventional Armed Forces in Europe (CFE) Treaty*. Washington, DC: Bureau of Arms Control, 2002.

U.S. General Accounting Office. *Investigations of Major Drug Trafficking Organizations: Report to the Honorable Joseph R. Biden, Jr., United States Senate*. Washington, DC: General Accounting Office, 1984.

U.S. Government. *Arms Control and Disarmament Agreements: Texts and Histories of the Negotiations*. Washington, DC: Government Printing Office, 1996.

U.S. Government. *21st Century Complete Guide to Bioterrorism, Biological and Chemical Weapons, Germs and Germ Warfare, Nuclear and Radiation Terrorism*. Dulles, VA: Progressive Management, 2001.

U.S. Government. *21st Century Complete Guide to Congressional Armed Services Committees: House and Senate Armed Services Committees: Military Readiness, Missile Defense, National Security, Testimony, Reports, Reviews*. Dulles, VA: Progressive Management, 2003.

Van Allen, James A., Matt Bille, and Erika Lishock. *The First Space Race: Launching the World's First Satellites*. College Station: Texas A&M University Press, 2004.

Van Belle, Douglas A. *Press Freedom and Global Politics*. New York: Praeger, 2000.

Vance, Jonathan F., ed. *Encyclopedia of Prisoners of War and Internment*. Santa Barbara, CA: ABC-CLIO, 2000.

Van Cleave, William R., and S. T. Cohen. *Tactical Nuclear Weapons: An Examination of the Issues*. New York: Crane, Russak, 1978.

Vandemark, Brian. *Pandora's Keepers: Nine Men and the Atomic Bomb*. Boston: Little, Brown, 2003.

Van Riper, A. Bowdoin. *Rockets and Missiles: The Life Story of a Technology*. Westport, CT: Greenwood, 2004.

Varg, Paul A. *America, from Client State to World Power*. Norman: University of Oklahoma Press, 1990.

Victor, Barbara. *Army of Roses: Inside the World of Palestinian Women Suicide Bombers*. Emmaus, PA: Rodale Press, 2003.

Viotti, Paul R., and Mark V. Kauppi. *International Relations Theory: Realism, Pluralism, Globalism, and Beyond*. Boston: Allyn & Bacon, 1999.

Vistica, Gregory L. *Fall From Glory: The Men Who Sank the U.S. Navy*. New York: Simon & Schuster, 1995.

Wainhouse, David W. *Arms Control Agreements: Designs for Verification and Organization*. Baltimore: Johns Hopkins University Press, 1992.

Walker, Martin. *The Cold War: A History.* New York: Owl Books, 1995.

Walsh, Lawrence E. *Iran-Contra: The Final Report.* New York: Random House, 1994.

Walter, Barbara. *Committing to Peace.* Princeton, NJ: Princeton University Press, 2002.

Walter, J. *Ruby Ridge: The Truth and Tragedy of Randy Weaver.* New York: HarperCollins, 2001.

Waltz, Edward. *Information Warfare: Principles and Operations.* Boston: Artech House, 1998.

Waltz, Kenneth N. *Theory of International Politics.* New York: Random House, 1979.

Walzer, Michael. *Just and Unjust Wars: A Moral Argument with Historical Illustrations.* New York: Basic Books, 1977.

Weber, Rachel Nicole. *Swords Into Dow Shares: Governing the Decline of the Military-Industrial Complex.* Boulder, CO: Westview Press, 2001.

Weeks, William Earl. *Building the Continental Empire.* Chicago: Ivan R. Dee, 1996.

Weigley, Russell F. *The American Way of War: A History of United States Military Strategy and Policy.* Bloomington: Indiana University Press, 1973.

Weiss, Thomas G. *United Nations and Changing World Politics.* Boulder, CO: Westview Press, 2004.

Wells, Tom. *Wild Man: The Life and Times of Daniel Ellsberg.* New York: Palgrave, 2001.

Welsh, Jennifer M., ed. *Humanitarian Intervention and International Relations.* New York: Oxford University Press, 2004.

Werrell, Kenneth P. *Chasing the Silver Bullet: U.S. Air Force Weapons Development from Vietnam to Desert Storm.* Washington, DC: Smithsonian Books, 2003.

Werrell, Kenneth P. *The Evolution of the Cruise Missile.* Maxwell Air Force Base, AL: Air University Press, 1985.

Wetta, Frank J., and Stephen J. Curley. *Celluloid Wars: Guide to Film and the American Experience.* New York: Greenwood, 1997.

Wexler, Imanuel. *The Marshall Plan Revisited: The European Recovery Program Economic Perspective.* Westport, CT: Greenwood, 1983.

Wheeler, Nicholas J. *Saving Strangers: Humanitarian Intervention in International Society.* New York: Oxford University Press, 2001.

Whitcomb, Roger S. *The American Approach to Foreign Affairs.* Westport, CT: Praeger, 1998.

White, Jonathan R. *Defending the Homeland: Domestic Intelligence, Law Enforcement, and Security.* Belmont, CA: Wadsworth, 2003.

Whitehead, Laurence. *Democratization: Theory and Experience.* New York: Oxford University Press, 2002.

White House Office of Homeland Security. *National Strategy for Homeland Security.* Washington, DC: Pavilion Press, 2004.

Wiarda, Howard J. *Comparative Democracy and Democratization.* Belmont, CA: Wadsworth, 2001.

Wiberg, Hakan, Ib Damgaard Petersen, and Paul Smoker. *Inadvertent Nuclear War.* New York: Pergamon, 1994.

Wiecek, William M. *Nuclear America: Military and Civilian Nuclear Power in the United States, 1940–1980.* New York: Harper & Row, 1984.

Wiest, Andrew, and M. K. Barbier. *Strategy and Tactics: Infantry Warfare.* St. Paul, MN: Motorbooks, 2002.

Wilkinson, Rorden, and Steve Hughes, eds. *Global Governance: Critical Perspectives.* New York: Routledge, 2002.

Williams, Phil, ed. *Russian Organized Crime: The New Threat.* Transnational Organized Crime. London: Frank Cass, 1997.

Wilson, David A., ed. *Universities and the Military.* Newbury Park, CA: Sage, 1989.

Windass, Stan, ed. *Just War and Genocide: A Symposium.* London: Macmillan, 2001.

Winkler, John D. *Future Leader Development of Army Noncommissioned Officers: Workshop Results.* Arlington, VA: RAND, 1998.

Wirtz, James J., and Jeffrey A. Larsen, eds. *Rockets' Red Glare: Missile Defenses and the Future of World Politics.* Boulder, CO: Westview Press, 2001.

Wittner, Lawrence. *Resisting the Bomb: A History of the World Nuclear Disarmament Movement, 1954–1970.* Stanford, CA: Stanford University Press, 1997.

Woods, Randall. B., ed. *Vietnam and the American Political Tradition: The Politics of Dissent.* New York: Cambridge University Press, 2003.

Woodward, Bob. *Bush at War.* New York: Simon & Schuster, 2002.

Woodward, Bob. *Plan of Attack.* New York: Simon & Schuster, 2004.

Woolf, Amy F. *U.S. Nuclear Weapons: Changes in Policy and Force Structure.* New York: Novinka Books, 2005.

Wyden, Peter. *Wall: The Inside Story of Divided Berlin.* New York: Simon & Schuster, 1989.

Yarbrough, Steve. *Prisoners of War.* New York: Knopf, 2004.

Yergin, David. *The Prize: The Epic Quest for Oil, Money, and Power.* New York: Free Press, 1992.

Young, Nancy Beck, ed. *Franklin D. Roosevelt and the Shaping of American Political Culture.* Armonk, NY: M. E. Sharpe, 2001.

Zimmerman, Jean. *Tailspin: Women at War in the Wake of Tailhook.* New York: Doubleday, 1995.

Zimmerman, P. D., and C. Loeb. *Dirty Bombs: The Threat Revisited.* Washington, DC: National Defense University, 2004.

Zimmerman, Warren. *First Great Triumph: How Five Americans Made Their Country a World Power.* New York: Farrar, Straus and Giroux, 2004.

Zubok, Vladislav, and Constantine Pleshakov. *Inside the Kremlin's Cold War: From Stalin to Khrushchev.* Cambridge, MA: Harvard University Press, 1996.

Index

Timeline

Timeline of Major Events, National Policies, and Establishment of Government Agencies Involved in U.S. National Security

1790—August 4	U.S. Coast Guard founded as part of Department of the Treasury
1791—December 15	Adoption of the U.S. Bill of Rights
1815—September 26	Holy Alliance established among Holy Roman Empire, Prussia, and Russia
1819—February 22	Spain cedes Florida to United States in Transcontinental Treaty
1848—February	Treaty of Guadalupe Hidalgo
1863	First Geneva Convention
1886—May 4	Haymarket Bombing, one of the worst domestic terrorist attacks in U.S. history
1898—April–August	Spanish-American War
1899	First Hague Convention
1904—May	Theodore Roosevelt articulates his Roosevelt Corollary to the Monroe Doctrine
1906	Second Geneva Convention
1906—June–August	Second Hague Peace Conference
1909—December 4–February 26	First London Naval Conference
1914—June 28	Assassination of Austrian Archduke Franz Ferdinand is the spark that ignites World War I
1917—April 6	United States enters World War I
1917—May 18	President Woodrow Wilson signs draft law to enlist soldiers for World War I
1917—November 2	Balfour Declaration
1918—October	Native American codetalkers first employed during World War I
1920—January 10	League of Nations convenes for first time
1920—September 16	Terrorist bombing of Wall Street in New York City
1922—February 6	Washington Naval Treaty signed by the United States, Great Britain, Japan, France, and Italy
1923	Interpol founded

1925—June 17	Gas Protocol signed by many nations
1928—August 27	Kellogg-Briand Pact signed in Paris
1929	Third Geneva Convention
1930—January 21–April 22	Second London Naval Conference
1938—May 26	Creation of House Un-American Activities Committee (HUAC)
1939—August 23	Soviet Union and Nazi Germany sign nonaggression pact
1939—September 1	Nazi forces launch blitzkrieg against Poland, marking the official start of World War II
1939—November 4	Neutrality Act
1940—June 22	France falls to Nazi Germany
1940—September 16	First peacetime draft takes place in the United States
1941—March 11	U.S. Congress passes Lend-Lease Act
1941—July	Creation of the Foreign Information Service (FIS) by President Franklin D. Roosevelt
1941—August 9	Atlantic Charter signed by Winston Churchill and Franklin D. Roosevelt
1941—October	Manhattan Project launched to produce atomic bomb
1941—December 1	Civil Air Patrol founded by Mayor Fiorello La Guardia of New York
1941—December 7	Japanese attack Pearl Harbor, bringing the United States into World War II
1942—February 19	Executive order allowing for internment of Japanese Americans in the United States
1944—June 1–22	Bretton Woods Conference held in New Hampshire
1944—June 6	Allied forces launch the D-Day invasion of France
1944—December	Battle of the Bulge, World War II
1945—February 3	Allies begin bombing Dresden, Germany
1945—February 4–11	Yalta Conference of the Big Three—Franklin Roosevelt, Winston Churchill, and Joseph Stalin
1945—May 8	German forces officially surrender, ending the European phase of World War II
1945—June 26	Formation of the United Nations
1945—July 16	Successful atomic bomb test at Trinity test site in New Mexico
1945—August 6	United States drops atomic bomb on Japanese city of Hiroshima
1945—August 9	United States drops atomic bomb on Japanese city of Nagasaki
1945—August 14	Japan surrenders unconditionally to the United States, ending World War II
1945—October 24	Ratification of the United Nations Charter
1946—March 5	Winston Churchill gives "Iron Curtain" speech
1947—January 2	National Security Committee established as part of Legislative Reorganization Act
1947—June 5	Announcement of the European Recovery Program, better known as the Marshall Plan

1947—July 26	◆ National Security Act
1947—August 15	◆ United States and 19 Latin American countries sign the Rio Pact
1947—October 30	◆ Creation of General Agreement of Tariffs and Trade (GATT)
1948—April 3	◆ President Harry S. Truman signs the Marshall Plan into law
1948—June 28	◆ Start of Berlin airlift
1948—December 9	◆ UN General Assembly adopts Convention on the Prevention and Punishment of the Crime of Genocide
1949—March 26	◆ Camp David Accords signed by Israel and Palestinians
1949—April 4	◆ North Atlantic Treaty establishes the North Atlantic Treaty Organization (NATO)
1949—April–August	◆ Fourth Geneva Convention
1949—May 12	◆ Soviet Union ends blockade of Berlin
1949—October 1	◆ Formation of the communist People's Republic of China
1949—October	◆ Chinese Communist Party takes control in China
1950—June 25	◆ North Korean troops attack South Korea, beginning the Korean War
1950—July 4	◆ Radio Free Europe begins broadcasting to Eastern Europe
1951—September 1	◆ Australia, New Zealand, United States Security Treaty (ANZUS) established
1953—July 27	◆ Cease-fire in Korea
1953—July	◆ Demilitarized zone (DMZ) established in Korea along the 38th parallel
1953—October 1	◆ Mutual Defense Treaty signed between United States and Republic of Korea
1953—December 8	◆ Dwight D. Eisenhower presents Atoms for Peace speech at the United Nations
1954—March 1	◆ United States detonates hydrogen bomb on Bikini atoll in the Pacific
1954—April 7	◆ Dwight D. Eisenhower first articulates the domino theory
1954—July 21	◆ Vietnam and France sign the Geneva Peace Accord
1954—September 8	◆ Formation of the Southeast Asian Treaty Organization (SEATO)
1955—May 14	◆ Formation of the Warsaw Pact in Eastern Europe
1956—July 26	◆ Egypt nationalizes the Suez Canal
1956—October	◆ Revolt in Hungary
1956—October 29	◆ Great Britain and Israel attack Egypt, initiating the Suez War
1956—November 6	◆ Cease-fire in the Suez War
1957—January 5	◆ Dwight D. Eisenhower proposes Eisenhower Doctrine
1957—March	◆ Establishment of the European Economic Community (EEC)
1957—July 29	◆ International Atomic Energy Agency (IAEA) founded
1957—October 4	◆ Soviet Union launches *Sputnik 1*, the first satellite to reach outer space

1957—November	Gaither Report presents proposals to narrow the missile gap between the United States and Soviet Union
1958—January 31	First U.S. satellite, *Explorer I*, sent into orbit around the earth
1958—August 6	U.S. Congress passes Defense Reorganization Act
1958—September 2	National Defense Education Act (NDEA)
1959	Formation of the Organization of Petroleum Exporting Countries (OPEC)
1960—May 1	U.S. spy plane piloted by Francis Gary Powers shot down by Soviets over Soviet territory
1961—March	John F. Kennedy launches Alliance for Progress program
1961—April 17	Cuban exiles begin so-called Bay of Pigs invasion
1961—August 13	East German government begins building a wall between East and West Berlin
1961—September 4	Creation of the U.S. Agency for International Development (USAID)
1962—October	Cuban Missile Crisis
1963—July	Limited Test Ban Treaty signed in Moscow
1964—August	U.S. Congress passes the Gulf of Tonkin Resolution
1966	Great Proletarian Cultural Revolution begins in China
1967—June 5	Israel attacks Egypt, precipitating the Six-Day War
1967—August 8	Association of Southeast Asian Nations (ASEAN) established
1968—January 23	North Korea seizes U.S. intelligence ship, the *Pueblo*
1968—January 31	Tet Offensive launched by North Vietnamese against South Vietnam
1969—July 20	U.S. places first humans on the moon with the *Apollo 11* flight
1970	Racketeer Influenced and Corruption Organized Act (RICO)
1970—March 5	Nuclear Non-Proliferation Treaty entered into force
1970—May 4	Shootings of students at Kent State University by Ohio National Guard troops
1971—January 2	Congress repeals Tonkin Gulf Resolution
1971—June 13	*New York Times* begins to publish the Pentagon Papers
1972—February 27	Richard Nixon and Zhou Enlai sign U.S.-China joint communiqué
1972—April 10	Biological Weapons Convention goes into effect
1972—May	Moscow Summit between United States and Soviet Union
1972—May 26	United States and Soviet Union sign the Antiballistic Missile (ABM) Treaty
1973—January 23	North Vietnam and South Vietnam sign peace agreement ending the war
1973—July 1	Conscription (the draft) ends in the United States
1973—October	OPEC nations impose production restraints and an embargo on the United States
1973—October 6	Egypt and Syria launch surprise attack on Israel, beginning the Yom Kippur War

1973—November 7	Congress passes the War Powers Act
1975—May 15	Cambodian gunboats seize the *Mayaquez*, a U.S. merchant vessel
1976	National Defense University formed from the National War College and the Industrial College of the Armed Forces
1977—June	U.S. Congress establishes Department of Energy
1978—May 26	First attack of the Unabomber, Theodore Kaczynski
1979—April 10	President Jimmy Carter signs the Taiwan Relations Act
1979—June 18	United States and Soviet Union sign the SALT II Treaty
1979—November 4	Iranian hostage crisis begins with seizure of U.S. embassy in Tehran
1980—April 11	Operation Desert One, attempt to free U.S. hostages in Iran
1981—January 20	End of Iranian hostage crisis, with release of the hostages
1983—March 23	President Ronald Reagan announces his Strategic Defense Initiative
1983—October 25	U.S. forces invade Caribbean island of Grenada
1986—April 15	United States launches bombing raid against Libyan cities of Tripoli and Benghazi
1986—October	Summit meeting in Reykjavik, Iceland, between the United States and Soviet Union
1986—October 1	Goldwater-Nichols Department of Defense Reorganization Act
1986—December 20	United States invades Panama and captures Manuel Noriega
1987—May–August	Televised hearings on the Iran-Contra affair
1987—December	Founding of radical Islamic organization Hamas
1987—December 8	Intermediate-Range Nuclear Forces (INF) Treaty signed by Reagan and Gorbachev
1990—August 2	Iraq invades and seizes neighboring nation of Kuwait
1990—October 3	People of East and West Germany vote to reunite their countries
1990—November 5	Defense Closure and Realignment Act
1990—November 19	Conventional Forces in Europe Treaty signed by NATO and Warsaw Pact members
1990—November 21	Charter of Paris for a New Europe signed by various European nations
1990—November 29	United Nations authorizes use of force against Iraq after Iraqi invasion of Kuwait
1991—January 9	U.S. Congress authorizes use of force against Iraq
1991—January 17	Beginning of Operation Desert Storm, offensive against Iraq in first Gulf War
1991—February 24	Beginning of Operation Desert Sabre, the ground invasion of Kuwait
1991—March	Founding of Mercosur, the so-called Southern Common Market
1991—July	Break up of the former Warsaw Pact
1991—August 18	Attempted coup by communist hardliners against Mikhail Gorbachev and Soviet government
1991—September 25	Collapse of the Soviet Union

1991—December	◆	National Security Education Act passed by Congress
1991—December 12	◆	Maastricht Treaty establishes the European Union (EU)
1991—December 31	◆	Soviet Union is officially dissolved and broken up into separate republics
1992—March 24	◆	United States and Russia sign the Open Skies Treaty
1992—May	◆	United Nations authorizes sending of humanitarian aid to Bosnia
1992—August	◆	FBI siege of white separatists at Ruby Ridge, Idaho
1993—January 3	◆	United States and Russia sign the Strategic Arms Reduction Treaty (START II)
1993—February 26	◆	Terrorist bombing of the World Trade Center in New York City
1993—February 28	◆	Bureau of Alcohol, Tobacco and Firearms launches Operation Trojan Horse against Branch Davidians in Waco, Texas
1993—September 13	◆	Israel and the PLO sign the Oslo Accords
1993—October 3	◆	Start of the Battle of Mogadishu in Somalia
1994—January 1	◆	North American Free Trade Agreement (NAFTA) takes effect
1994—October 21	◆	Agreed Framework signed by United States and North Korea
1995—January	◆	Creation of World Trade Organization (WTO)
1995—March 20	◆	Japanese cult, Aum Shinrikyo, releases deadly sarin gas in Tokyo subway
1995—April 19	◆	Oklahoma City bombing of the Murrah Federal Building
1995—November 21	◆	Signing of Dayton Accords by Serbia, Bosnia, and Croatia
1996—June 25	◆	Terrorist attack on Al-Khobar complex housing U.S. forces in Dhahran
1996—September	◆	Taliban seizes power in Afghanistan
1996—September 24	◆	Signing of the Comprehensive Test Ban Treaty
1997—April	◆	Chemical Weapons Convention entered into force
1998—July 17	◆	Rome Statute creates the International Criminal Court
1998—August	◆	Terrorist bombings of U.S. embassies in Kenya and Tanzania
1998—October 1	◆	Defense Threat Reduction Agency established
1999—March 1	◆	Ottawa Treaty outlaws land mines
1999—December 17	◆	Establishment of the UN Monitoring, Verification and Inspection Commission (UNMOVIC)
2000—October 12	◆	Terrorist bombing of USS *Cole* at the port of Aden, Yemen
2000—November 30	◆	Congress passes the Freedom of Information Act (FOIA)
2001—September 11	◆	Terrorist attacks against World Trade Center and the Pentagon
2001—October 7	◆	United States begins bombing campaign against the Taliban in Afghanistan
2001—October 8	◆	Homeland Security Council established by executive order
2001—October 26	◆	George W. Bush signs USA PATRIOT Act into law

2002—January	◆	George W. Bush refers to "axis of evil" in state of the union address
2002—March	◆	Adoption of Homeland Security Advisory System
2002—May 24	◆	Strategic Offensive Reductions Treaty (SORT) signed by United States and Russia
2002—October 12	◆	Terrorist bomb explodes on island of Bali
2002—November 25	◆	U.S. Congress passes Homeland Security Act
2003—January	◆	U.S. Department of Homeland Security begins operation
2003—March 20	◆	United States begins air strikes against Iraq in Iraq War of 2003
2003—May 1	◆	George W. Bush proclaims end to major combat operations in Iraq